ON THE SCALES OF RIGHTEOUSNESS

Program in Judaic Studies
Brown University
Box 1826
Providence, RI 02912

BROWN JUDAIC STUDIES

Edited by

David C. Jacobson
Ross S. Kraemer
Saul M. Olyan
Michael L. Satlow

Number 348

ON THE SCALES OF RIGHTEOUSNESS
Neo-Babylonian Trial Law and
the Book of Job

by
F. Rachel Magdalene

# ON THE SCALES
# OF RIGHTEOUSNESS

## NEO-BABYLONIAN TRIAL LAW
## AND THE BOOK OF JOB

F. Rachel Magdalene

Brown Judaic Studies
Providence, Rhode Island

© 2007 Brown University. All rights reserved.

No part of this work may be reproduced or transmitted in any form or by any means, electronic or mechanical, including photocopying and recording, or by means of any information storage or retrieval system, except as may be expressly permitted by the 1976 Copyright Act or in writing from the publisher. Requests for permission should be addressed in writing to the Rights and Permissions Office, Program in Judaic Studies, Brown University, Box 1826, Providence, RI 02912, USA.

*Library of Congress Cataloging-in-Publication Data*

Magdalene, F. Rachel.
   On the scales of righteousness : neo-Babylonian trial law and the book of Job / by F. Rachel Magdalene.
      p. cm. — (Brown Judaic studies ; no. 348)
   Includes bibliographical references and index.
   ISBN 978-1-930675-44-5 (cloth binding : alk. paper)
   ISBN 978-1-930675-82-7 (paper binding : alk. paper)
   1. Bible. O.T. Job—Criticism, interpretation, etc. 2. Criminal procedure—Iraq—Babylonia—History—To 1500. I. Title. II. Series.

BS1415.52.M34 2007
223'.1067—dc22

2007024748

Printed on acid-free recycled paper
conforming to ANSI/NISO Z39.48-1992 (R1997) and ISO 9706:1994
standards for paper permanence.

With love to those who sacrificed for my success,
especially Ben and Anna

and

לכבד אלהים
for the glory of God!

*Let him weigh me on the scales of righteousness
and let God know my integrity.*
                                          Job 31:6

# Contents

*Preface* .......................................................... xi

1 • Introduction ................................................ 1
2 • Disease, Disability, and Disaster as Law .................... 13
3 • Reading Law in Job's Story ................................. 27
4 • Trial Procedure in the Neo-Babylonian Courts ............... 55
5 • The Satan's Accusation and Investigation ................... 95
6 • Job's Counteraccusation .................................. 127
7 • Job's Defense and Demand ................................. 177
8 • The Friends as God's Witnesses ........................... 199
9 • Elihu as God's Second Accuser-Prosecutor ................. 225
10 • God's Defense and Settlement of Claims ................... 247
11 • Conclusions .............................................. 263

*Appendix A: List of Neo-Babylonian Trial and*
*Trial-Related Documents in Sample* ............................ 267

*Abbreviations* ................................................ 271

*Bibliography* ................................................. 279

*Index of Citations* ........................................... 339

*Index of Authors* ............................................. 353

*Index of Subjects* ............................................ 359

# Preface

This monograph is a revision of my dissertation, which I completed at the University of Denver and Iliff School of Theology Joint Ph.D. Program in March 2003. The research is, in the simplest terms, a comparative historical study of the legal metaphors in the book of Job in relation to Neo-Babylonian trial procedure. Its origins lie in 1995, now more than a decade ago. Because I was, at the time, an attorney and a legal historian, as well as a budding biblical scholar, I was seeking to do a dissertation in biblical law. I also have great interest in theology and theodicy, which I had pursued during my masters and doctoral programs. Consequently, Dr. Raymond Westbrook, of The Johns Hopkins University, proposed in September 1995 that I study some aspect of the law in the book of Job, a project that would integrate all my interests. I thought, at the time, that this was an outstanding idea. Later, I became a bit more conflicted about it.

My original plan was to examine the legal metaphors in the book of Job in light of published trial documents from ancient Near Eastern history from the first and second millennia because no comprehensive study of Neo-Babylonian texts existed. I intended to rely heavily on the secondary Assyriological literature. As I investigated the secondary literature on ancient Near Eastern litigation and began to examine a few Neo-Babylonian texts, however, I felt that a study of Job against litigation in other periods would be less fruitful. I therefore determined to begin to fill the legal-historical and Assyriological lacuna with my own study of the Neo-Babylonian documents. Since that time, much more work has been done on the Neo-Babylonian litigation corpus, which I have attempted to incorporate into my work as it has become available.

I thought, in my naivety, that I might be dealing with approximately one hundred texts. In the end, I collected over six hundred and realized that hundreds to thousands more might exist. Three things became obvious to me along the way. First, as a person with disabilities and a student with time restrictions on the project, I required assistance in collecting all the tablets. Second, I needed a computer database to manage this much material. Third, my Assyriological skills were in their infancy. Thus, I recruited Dr. Bruce Wells to the project. He ultimately joined me in collecting, organizing, and analyzing the Neo-Babylonian litigation documents related to this study. He offered me unending assistance and support in this project and beyond. He became my partner-in-crime—Neo-Babylonian crime, that is. While the legal-historical insights of this study are mine, except where otherwise attributed to Dr. Wells, I could not have produced the level of work in chapter 4 without his superior Assyriological and information technology skills, many flashes of legal genius, and patience in reviewing each draft. I am indebted to him. Of course, the blame for any and all remaining errors should be laid at my door alone.

I had worked through about 340 of the 600 texts when I observed that I had not found anything new from a legal historical perspective in quite a while. At that point, I decided to write up my tentative findings. I am keenly aware that potentially many other texts exist in the published and unpublished record and that they may prove these findings to be in error. I am also keenly aware that there are Assryiological Neo-Babylonian specialists whose work puts mine to shame. All projects, however, must come to an end—especially dissertations—and there is value in making inroads into a fairly unexplored topic of study even if one cannot fully chart the area. Thus, I offer this study only as a springboard for further work, mine and others. My goal can be to attempt to offer neither the definitive study of Neo-Babylonian trial procedure nor one on the legal metaphors of the book of Job. Rather, I offer only a new method for the study of the book of Job—one that involves the methods of legal history and the law-as-literature movement. I hope that I will inspire much new work on the Neo-Babylonian litigation documents and the book of Job. If any of my findings should withstand the test of time, it will be a delightful bonus.

I must also acknowledge that, in looking at the text through a methodological lens designed to bring the legal materials into sharper focus, other aspects of the text necessarily recede into the blurry background. Consequently, the goals of this book also do not include advocacy of the superiority of my approach to other approaches by engaging in detailed comparisons of it with other studies. Joban studies are legion; time and space make such an undertaking prohibitive; and such chauvinism belittles the intricacy of the book. The task of assessing carefully the merits, rewards, disadvantages, and/or failings of the various approaches to the book must lie with its reader.

Moreover, although I speak in terms that may seem assured throughout the book, I must confess that this reading is tentative, as all readings of Job must be. D. Patrick is correct when he says there is more in the book of Job than one mind can process quickly. Moreover, one cannot begin to control all the literature produced on the book over the millennia; my substantial bibliography is but a fraction of the relevant materials. The masters who have studied and interpreted this book further humble me; I cannot count myself among them. As a result, my thinking is still evolving. There is, however, a problem even more fundamental than these. The book of Job is a book that continues to work on those who study it. It just has a way with its readers. The fact that many of the greats, such as D. J. A. Clines, E. Good, and N. C. Habel, to name just a few, have offered more than one major study, with sometimes profound changes between them, testifies to this experience. Consequently, I am cognizant that this study represents only the first leg in what has already been a long, sometimes wonderful, sometimes terrible journey with both the Neo-Babylonian trial records and the book of Job.

Notwithstanding the stated caveats, I believe that this research will reveal that the legal metaphors in the book are more prevalent and organized than scholars have generally recognized heretofore. This new approach to its legal material will allow scholars to explain more of the book's legal data than have previous approaches. Moreover, this study will produce fewer legal anomalies than have previous approaches. By examining the legal materials of the book against the framework of the structure of litigation in the ancient Near East during the time in which it most likely was written, we will obtain a useful key to unraveling several of the book's enigmas.

In regard to that sometimes wonderful, sometimes terrible journey with Job, I must say that this project took on a life of its own. Finishing both the dissertation and this revision felt at times like a quest of mythic proportions. D. J. A. Clines has aptly remarked that those who work on the book of Job start to live it. This was certainly true for me. Completing the dissertation and this revision became nothing short of an adventure as I suffered my own version of the trials of Job. Some would say that they included learning Akkadian and Assyriology—or, at least, learning just enough to be dangerous. They certainly included dealing with a traumatic brain injury, surgery and another medical emergency, the death of someone close to me, my son's extended service in the war in Iraq, the witnessing of two terrible murders on the streets of Baltimore, the flooding of my apartment building by a major hurricane, then the accidental burning of it by a neighbor, the theft of my car on three separate occasions in spite of antitheft devices, eight moves in eight years, endless job hunting, demanding teaching loads, and still more of equal magnitude. At one point, I even contracted a skin disease! Through these ordeals, Job and I became intimate friends, and I have appreciated very much our conversation over the years. I have never tired of returning to him. I did begin to wonder, however, just why I had elected to study *this* subject. If what Dr. Clines says about Job should hold true generally, I would have preferred to have worked with one of the great love stories of the Bible, such as that of Jacob and Rachel or the Song of Songs! Nonetheless, Job it was, and strive mightily I had to do.

Job, unfortunately, had difficult and unsympathetic friends and colleagues when he labored through his trials. I, on the other hand, had countless wonderful people, who saw me through mine. The miracle represented by the completion of the dissertation and this book in the face of such obstacles was worked out by God, one person, one gift, at a time. Herein, I would like to acknowledge and thank several of those who helped.

Charting the course of such an adventure is no mean feat, and I am deeply indebted to Dr. Frederick E. Greenspahn, my dissertation chair. His constant encouragement, guidance, and patience helped me to stay the course. He was and remains mentor, coach, problem solver, editor, and rabbi to me. I will always remember with gratitude our first conversation about the burning of my home. He was warm, concerned, and inspiring. That conversation represents best the understanding, kindness, and determination with which he handled every situation.

My readers, Dr. Ved Nanda, Dr. Gene M. Tucker, and Dr. Raymond Westbrook, also contributed to my success by their enthusiasm for the project and many valuable insights regarding it. Dr. Westbrook, in particular, consistently went beyond the call of duty, reading every draft of every chapter and often offering comments as detailed as those of Dr. Greenspahn. Moreover, he contributed his expertise to the reading of a number of particularly difficult Neo-Babylonian texts. I remain very appreciative of his long companionship on my journey into the earliest records of the law. It has now spanned fifteen years and survived many challenges.

Additionally, Dr. Westbrook offered me several independent studies with him in Akkadian and comparative law and made it possible for me to spend a year in the Department of Near Eastern Studies of The Johns Hopkins University. There I took supplemental classes in Hebrew Bible, Assyriology, and comparative law and began the comparative work of this project. There I met Dr. Wells, then a student colleague. I give thanks to the faculty, students, and staff of Hopkins, who provided me access to their extensive resources and who taught me much during the time I was in residence. I am chiefly obliged to Dr. Westbrook, of course. Dr. P. Kyle McCarter also provided me with much assistance. Dr. Thomas Izbicki and Mr. Zackery Jaffe of the Milton S. Eisenhower Library were always ready to lend a hand, even long after my formal tenure at Hopkins had passed. Dr. Yekaterina Barbash translated works in Russian for me.

Beyond my committee, many faculty members assisted me over the years. First, I owe Dr. Kent Harold Richards more thanks than words allow for his mentoring during the early years of my biblical studies. It was not my intention to study Bible when we first met. His passion for the subject and his commitment to persons with disabilities enticed me into a Hebrew class and the rest, as they say, is history. For half a decade, we met almost every week for several hours. I grew up as a scholar in his office. Dr. Tamara C. Eskenazi and Dr. Gregory A. Robbins also stood ready in times of need. My former colleagues of the Towson University College of Liberal Arts Writers' Response Group, including Dr. Karen Cicmanec, Dr. Fil Dowling, Dr. Karl G. Larew, Dr. Cecilia Rio, and Dr. Linda Sweeting, read diligently most of my dissertation, offering invaluable comments. Moreover, my colleagues in the Biblical Law Section of the Society of Biblical Literature, especially Dr. Cheryl B. Anderson, Dr. Richard E. Averbeck, Dr. Samuel Greengus, Dr. Bernard M. Levinson, Dr. Victor H. Matthews, Dr. William S. Morrow, Dr. Eckart Otto, Dr. Carolyn Pressler, Dr. Martha T. Roth, Dr. Raymond Westbrook, and Dr. John W. Welch, have been unstinting in their support of me since I first appeared at an annual meeting in 1991.

I am also most grateful to Dr. Athalya Brenner and Dr. Saul Olyan of the Brown Judaic Studies series, who brought this work to publication. Dr. Brenner's support of my scholarship has now extended over more than a decade. Dr. Olyan did the hard work of guiding the manuscript from dissertation to monograph. He had to exercise great patience while waiting for this manuscript far beyond my deadline. Fortunately, he had more patience than Job.

Further, the financial assistance of many made possible my time in Baltimore and the production of this book. They include: Dean Jeff Abernathy of Augustana College (Rock Island), who provided $1,000 for indexing this volume; the American Association of University Women Educational Foundation, which named me one of its American Dissertation Fellows for the 1999–2000 year; the faculty of the Iliff School of Theology, who awarded me the Elizabeth Iliff Warren Prize in support of further studies at Hopkins during the 1998–99 year; and the Franciscan Sisters of Baltimore and all those who lived at Francis House from 1998 to 1999, whose ministry of hospitality gave this stranger in their midst a home and a place to work. Numerous individuals, some anonymous, also made unsolicited donations, great and small, to the cause: many checks and dollar bills appeared in the mail, were slipped under my door, or were tucked into my pockets. They kept me going long after the fellowships ended. With gratitude I received each gift.

Still others aided me. Ms. Katie Fisher of the Ira J. Taylor Library at the Iliff School of Theology worked diligently to keep up with my intense demand for books. Ms. Audrey Cutler, Mr. Philip Frank, Dr. Mitchell Gabhart, Dr. Paul Kobelski, Dr. Saul Olyan, Dr. David M. Valeta, and Dr. Bruce Wells all assisted in the copyediting of this work at one time or another, although any remaining errors are again mine.

I thank additionally the two publishers who gave permission to publish here the materials that I had previously published in their journals. Much of the material of chs. 4, 8, and 9 first appeared in "Who Is Job's Redeemer: Job 19:25 in Light of Neo-Babylonian Law," *ZABR* 10 (2004): 292–316. All of ch. 2 appeared originally in "The ANE Legal Origins of Impairment as Theological Disability and the Book of Job," *PRSt* 4 (2007): 23–60.

Finally, I would be remiss not to give thanks to the many other colleagues and counselors, family and friends, who have helped in incalculable ways. While there is not space to name them all, they are in my heart with the deepest of appreciation, especially my family, SSgt. Benjamin P. Varlese, Ms. Anna K. Varlese, the Rev. Rebekah E. Simon-Peter, and Ms. Judith R. Heller.

To all who assisted go innumerable thanks. ברכת יהוה אליכם. May the blessing of the Lord be upon you.

F. Rachel Magdalene<br>Rock Island, Illinois<br>January 2006

# 1

# Introduction

The study of literature is always the study of metaphor. As D. Robertson explains: "Everything in a work of literature, whether actions, dramatic personae, thoughts, or objects, is essentially metaphoric."[1] Hence, any study of the book of Job is necessarily a study of its metaphors. This book investigates the use of law in the design of Job's metaphorical world.

In his 1928 master's thesis, "The Legal Background of Hebrew Thought and Literature," C. H. Gordon was one of the first to recognize that the book of Job contains much litigation metaphor.[2] In her 1975 study, "Lawsuit Drama in the Book of Job," S. H. Scholnick suggested that early investigators tended to see Job's legal vocabulary as part of his characterization as an elder, who served a judicial role at the gate (27:7–8, 16).[3] She demonstrated convincingly, however, that, through its use of legal metaphor, the book sets

---

1. D. Robertson, *The Old Testament and the Literary Critic* (Guides to Biblical Scholarship; Philadelphia: Fortress, 1977), 5.
2. C. H. Gordon, "The Legal Background of Hebrew Thought and Literature" (M.A. thesis, University of Pennsylvania, 1928). Others followed suit; see, e.g., B. Gemser, "The *rîb*—or Controversy-Pattern in Hebrew Mentality," in *Wisdom in Israel and in the Ancient Near East Presented to Professor Harold Henry Rowley* (ed. M. Noth and D. W. Thomas; VTSup 3; Leiden: Brill, 1955), 135; L. H. Köhler, "Justice in the Gate," in *Hebrew Man: Lectures Delivered at the Invitation of the University of Tübingen, December 1–16, 1952* (trans. P. R. Ackroyd; London: SCM, 1956), 136; M. H. Pope, *Job* (3rd ed.; AB 15; Garden City, N.Y.: Doubleday, 1979); and J. J. Stamm, "Die Theodizee in Babylon und Israel," *JEOL* 9 (1944): 99–107. Additionally, J. J. M. Roberts addressed Job's legal material, although his article tended to undercut forensic meanings of seemingly legal vocabulary in favor of theological meanings ("Job's Summons to Yahweh: The Exploitation of a Legal Metaphor," *ResQ* 16 [1973]: 159–65).
3. S. H. Scholnick, "Lawsuit Drama in the Book of Job" (Ph.D. diss., Brandeis University, 1975, vi). See also eadem, "The Meaning of *Mišpat* in the Book of Job," in *Sitting with Job: Selected Studies on the Book of Job* (ed. R. B. Zuck; Grand Rapids: Baker, 1992), 349–58; repr. from *JBL* 101 (1982): 521–29; and eadem, "Poetry in the Courtroom: Job 38–41," in *Directions in Hebrew Poetry* (ed. E. Follis; JSOTSup 40; Sheffield: Sheffield Academic, 1987), 185–204. In other words, the characterization of Job as a judge demands that Job's conversations on the topic of justice reflect his legal knowledge. Such scholars did not go much deeper in their analysis.

out a legal altercation between God and Job.⁴ Commentators have now almost uniformly accepted this idea.⁵ In fact, many scholars maintain that litigation metaphors structure the book's articulation of theological ideas.⁶

---

4. Although a number of researchers were taking the legal content of Job more seriously, Scholnick finally persuaded most scholars of the great importance of law in the book. H. Richter made the strongest argument before Scholnick, stating that 444 verses were related to legal genres while only 346 were related to wisdom genres (*Studien zu Hiob: Der Aufbau des Hiobbuches dargestellt an den Gattungen des Rechtslebens* [ThArb 11; Berlin: Evangelische Verlagsanstalt, 1959], 131; cf. idem, "Erwägungen zum Hiobproblem," *EvT* 18 [1958]: 302–11). See also, e.g., C. Westermann, *The Structure of the Book of Job: A Form-Critical Analysis* (Philadelphia: Fortress, 1981), 4–5. For further discussion of the pre-1975 views regarding the legal materials in the book of Job, see Scholnick, "Lawsuit Drama," vi–xii.

5. M. B. Dick assumed this idea when he brought ancient Near Eastern legal and wisdom material to bear in a form-critical and comparative study of Job 31, although his focus was on the wisdom materials ("Job 31: A Form-Critical Study" [Ph.D. diss., The Johns Hopkins University, 1977]; see also idem, "The Legal Metaphor in Job 31," *CBQ* 41 [1979]: 37–41; and idem, "Job 31, The Oath of Innocence, and the Sage," *ZAW* 95 [1983]: 31–53). In 1985, N. C. Habel, following Scholnick in significant measure, produced a major narrative reading of the book of Job that concentrates on the legal materials (*The Book of Job: A Commentary* [OTL; Philadelphia: Westminster, 1985]; his agreement with Scholnick is especially evident on pp. 54, 184–86, 192–200). Studies that give serious attention to the law in the book of Job are now growing quickly and are discussed in nn. 14–30 below.

6. Although I agree that the legal metaphors structure the book, I maintain the traditional genre classification of the book of Job, that of didactic wisdom (see, e.g., S. R. Driver and G. B. Gray, *A Critical and Exegetical Commentary on the Book of Job* [ICC; Edinburgh: T&T Clark, 1921], xxi–xxii; R. Gordis, *The Book of God and Man: A Study of Job* [Chicago: University of Chicago Press, 1965; repr., 1978], 41–45; and L. J. Sheldon, "The Book of Job as Hebrew Theodicy: An Ancient Near Eastern Intertextual Dispute Between Cosmology and Law" [Ph.D. diss., University of California Berkeley and Graduate Theological Union Joint Degree Program in Near Eastern Religion, 2002], 38–41). In making this decision, I note the book's many points of contact with other ancient Near Eastern wisdom theodicies, including (1) the Egyptian pieces "The Protest of an Eloquent Peasant" (also known as "The Tale of an Eloquent Peasant"), "The Dispute between a Man and his *Ba*" (also known as "A Dispute over Suicide" and "The Man Who Was Tired of Life"), and the "Admonitions of Ipuwer"; (2) the Sumerian "Man and His God"; (3) the Babylonian works "The Babylonian Theodicy," "*Ludlul bēl nēmeqi*" (also known variously as "I Will Praise the Lord of Wisdom," "The Poem of the Righteous Sufferer," "The Pious Sufferer," and the "Babylonian Job"), and "A Dialogue of Pessimism" (also known as "A Dialogue Between a Master and His Slave"); (4) the Ugaritic "The Just Sufferer" (RS 25.460); and (5) the Canaanite poem *Kirta*. Cf. the Hittite "Appu and His Two Sons." For the most significant general discussions of this body of literature and its relationship to the book of Job, see R. G. Albertson, "Job and Ancient Near Eastern Wisdom Literature," in *Scripture in Context II: More Essays on the Comparative Method* (ed. W. W. Hallo, J. C. Moyer, and L. G. Perdue; Winona Lake, Ind.: Eisenbrauns, 1983), 215–30; J. Gray, "The Book of Job in the Context of Near Eastern Literature," *ZAW* 82 (1970): 251–69; H.-P. Müller, *Das Hiobproblem: Seine Stellung und Entstehung in Alten Orient und im Alten Testament* (Darmstadt: Wissenschaftliche Buchgesellschaft, 1978), 67–69; idem, "Keilschriftliche Parallelen zum Biblischen Hiobbuch: Möglichkeit und Grenze des Vergleichs," *Or* n.s. 47 (1978): 360–75; C. Newsom, "The Book of Job," *NIB* 4:328–34; Sheldon, "Job as Hebrew Theodicy"; Stamm, "Theodizee," 99–107; and M. Weinfeld, "Job and Its Mesopotamian Parallels—A Typological Analysis," in *Texts and Context: Old Testament and Semitic Studies for F. C. Fensham* (ed. W.

A careful study of these metaphors is, therefore, vital in extracting meaning from the book. The exploration of these metaphors is, however, only in its infancy.

One of the most significant gaps in Joban scholarship arises from the lack of any comprehensive comparative historical study of the litigation records of the ancient Near East and the book of Job. Examination of these records is a crucial undertaking in order to understand the litigation metaphors employed by the author of Job. This is because in creating a textual world for the reader to enter, an author must draw images from his or her social world. The author must construct a place that, though illusory, feels so real that the reader cannot help but suspend his or her knowledge that this world is a fictitious one. J. Miles discusses this phenomenon in the context of character development:

> [T]he biographical effect—the artistic suggestion of a life—is inseparable from the dramatic or literary effect itself. Unless the viewer of *Hamlet* can believe that Hamlet was born and will die, unless the viewer's imagination is carried offstage into the life for which there is no direct evidence onstage, the play dies with its protagonist. A character understood to have no life offstage can have no life onstage.[7]

So, too, must the world of the characters live offstage in the mind of the reader if it is to live onstage. The only way to accomplish this sense of authenticity is to employ common images and ideas from a shared cultural context. Consequently, to comprehend the world of the text, one must comprehend something of the world behind the text.[8] It is, therefore, essential to explore Job's litigation metaphors in the context of their time.

A growing number of scholars have recognized this. Mostly they have compared Job's legal metaphors with other legal vocabulary contained within the Hebrew Bible.[9] Their view is that the specific trial law of ancient

---

Claassen; JSOTSup 48; Sheffield: Sheffield Academic, 1988), 217–26. Many alternative genre proposals have been offered (see F. R. Magdalene, "On the Scales of Righteousness: Law and Story in the Book of Job" [Ph.D. diss., Iliff School of Theology and University of Denver (Colorado Seminary), 2003], 3–4 n. 6). I suggest that no one interpretive model for the book can lay claim to solving every conundrum and tying every loose end of the book. Nevertheless, this study maintains that didactic wisdom is the best fit among the choices of genre. All forms are subservient to this genre.

7. J. Miles, *God: A Biography* (New York: Knopf, 1995), 10.

8. The converse is also true. The metaphors can tell us something of the reality behind the text, as L. J. Sheldon clarifies in the context of Job: "To a large extent, creative poetic endeavors of the ancient (and modern) world are inevitably marked by the use of metaphors. In the book of Job, these units of speech comprise far more than a brief analogous picture of reality; rather they both formulate a reality of their own and create a window on the reality that gave rise to them in the first place" ("Job as Hebrew Theodicy," 7).

9. See esp. C. Chin, "Job and the Injustice of God: Implicit Arguments in Job 13.17–

4   On the Scales of Righteousness

Israel is the optimal source of comparative data. Sadly, only a few legal documents of practice from ancient Palestine have survived.[10] Investigators, therefore, turn to the Bible, which is the richest fund of information about Israelite trial law. Disappointingly, biblical trial accounts are also limited in number.[11] Even considered collectively, such reports are insufficient to furnish a complete picture of Israelite trial law in any period of its history. One must supplement that information with other ancient Near Eastern legal materials. This study maintains that the great corpus of Neo-Babylonian litigation records of the late seventh to fifth centuries, B.C.E.,[12]

---

14.12," *JSOT* 64 (1994): 91–101; E. L. Greenstein, "A Forensic Understanding of the Speech from the Whirlwind," in *Texts, Temples, and Traditions: A Tribute to Menahem Haran* (ed. M. V. Fox et al.; Winona Lake, Ind.: Eisenbrauns, 1996), 241–58; Habel, *Book of Job: Commentary*; G. Many, "Der Rechtsstreit mit Gott [rîb] im Hiobbuch" (Ph.D. diss., Katholisch-theologische Fakultät der Ludwig-Maximilian Universität, 1970); and Scholnick, "Lawsuit Drama."

10. M. Greenberg, "Crimes and Punishments," *IDB* 1:736. One important exception is the Hebrew Meṣad Ḥashavyahu Ostracon, which is an extrajudicial petition of the late seventh century B.C.E. (*IEJ* 10 [1960]: 130). See most importantly F. W. Dobbs-Allsopp, "The Genre of the Meṣad Ḥashavyahu Ostracon," *BASOR* 295 (1994): 49–55; P. K. McCarter, *Ancient Inscriptions: Voices from the Biblical World* (Washington, D.C.: Biblical Archaeology Society, 1996), 116; J. Naveh, "A Hebrew Letter from the Seventh Century B.C.," *IEJ* 10 (1960): 129–39; and R. Westbrook, *Studies in Biblical and Cuneiform Law* (Paris: Gabalda, 1988), 35 n. 128. Three Neo-Assyrian legal documents from ancient Palestine also exist (Gezer 3, Gezer 4, and Samaria 2). See W. Horowitz, T. Oshima, and S. Sanders, "A Bibliographical List of Cuneiform Inscriptions from Canaan, Palestine/Philistia, and the Land of Israel," *JAOS* 122 (2002): 753-66. Unfortunately, these texts are somewhat obscure and unhelpful for our purposes. An Old Babylonian lawsuit tablet from Hazor, ca. the eighteenth to the sixteenth centuries B.C.E., has also been found (see W. W. Hallo and H. Tadmor, "A Lawsuit from Hazor," *IEJ* 27 [1977]: 1–11, esp. 3). Another Hebrew legal document from this area might also have been discovered. The Widow's Plea Ostracon, published by P. Bordreuil, F. Israel, and D. Pardee, purports to be a plea, from the late eighth or seventh century B.C.E., to the local governor to reconsider a prior decision regarding a certain parcel of land ("Deux ostraca Paléo-Hébreux de la collection Sh. Moussaïeff," *Sem* 46 [1996]: 61). Its authenticity is, however, under dispute at the time of this writing. See I. Eph'al and J. Naveh, "Remarks on the Recently Published Moussaieff Ostraca," *IEJ* 48 (1998): 269–73; C. A. Rollston, "Non-Provenanced Epigraphs I: Pillaged Antiquities, Northwest Semitic Forgeries, and Protocols for Laboratory Tests," *Maarav* 10 (2003): 135-93, esp. 158-73. Because I find the arguments of the contestants significant, I will not discuss the Widow's Plea Ostracon further herein.

11. Gen 29:25–28; 31:25–55; Lev 24:10–23; Num 15:32–36; Josh 7:19–26; 1 Sam 22:6–23; 1 Kgs 3:16–28; 21:1–16; and Jer 26:1–24 [two trials]. See also Sus 1–64. 2 Sam 14:4–11 contains an extrajudicial plea. Additionally, other references to trial procedure exist outside the main trial accounts throughout the Hebrew Bible. See, e.g., Gen 39:17–19; 42:7–17; Num 5:11–31; and Neh 5:1–13. P. Bovati has completed a comprehensive study of litigation terminology in the Hebrew Bible (*Re-Establishing Justice: Legal Terms, Concepts and Procedures in the Hebrew Bible* (trans. M. J. Smith; JSOTSup 105; Sheffield: Sheffield Academic, 1994). Although, from an attorney's and a legal historian's perspective, I do not always agree with Bovati's assessments, this volume is an excellent starting point and should be consulted for all biblical references to trial procedure.

12. The Neo-Babylonian dialect of Akkadian was in use from the end of the second mil-

are particularly helpful in that task for three reasons. First, they are representative of a tradition of ancient Near Eastern legal procedure in which Israelite trial law shared. Second, the corpus is quite large, thereby giving us a fuller picture of ancient Near Eastern litigation procedure. Third, the majority of scholars place the book of Job's composition in this time period.[13] Consequently, I suggest that, by examining the rules of legal pro-

---

lennium into the Hellenistic period. I include in my sample texts some that are characterized as Late Babylonian. See D. S. Vanderhooft, *The Neo-Babylonian Empire and Babylon in the Latter Prophets* (HSM 59; Atlanta: Scholars Press, 1999), 9 n. 1; and A. Kuhrt, "Non Royal Women in the Late Babylonian Period," in *Women's Earliest Records from Ancient Egypt and Western Asia* (ed. B. Lesko; BJS 116; Atlanta: Scholars Press, 1989), 216. My focus is on those documents from the time of the Neo-Babylonian and Persian Empires. In thus using the term "Neo-Babylonian period" for the seventh to fifth centuries B.C.E., I embrace it in its linguistic and cultural senses rather than in its political or historical senses (see F. Joannès, "Les textes judiciaires néo-babyloniens," in *Rendre la justice en Mésopotamie: Archives judiciaires du Proche-Orient ancien [III$^e$–I$^{er}$ millénaires avant J.-C.* [ed. F. Joannès; Saint-Denis: Presses Universitaires de Vincennes, 2000], 201–2). A few documents outside of the stated language, time period, and/or geographic locale are used, however, where such documents can shed light on a particular aspect of Neo-Babylonian litigation in general, or on the book of Job in particular.

13. While dating of biblical books must always be tentative, the best argument allows for a fifth-century B.C.E. date for the book of Job. For various explications of this position, see, e.g., E. Dhorme, *A Commentary on the Book of Job* (trans. H. Knight; Nashville: Thomas Nelson, 1984), clxix–clxxi; Driver and Gray, *Book of Job*, lxviii–lxix; G. Fohrer, *Das Buch Hiob* (KAT 16; Gütersloh: Gerd Mohn, 1963), 31; J. J. M. Roberts, "Job and the Israelite Religious Tradition," *ZAW* 89 (1977): 107–14; and H. H. Rowley, "The Book of Job and Its Meaning," in *From Moses to Qumran: Studies in the Old Testament* (London: Lutterworth, 1963), 173. Among all of the arguments in support of this position, the intertextuality in the book of Job is the most persuasive to me. It appears that the author of Job was familiar with a vast amount of the literature of the Hebrew Bible and that he may have been engaged in a number of intertextual plays on such literature, although this study acknowledges that the purported fact and direction of any asserted textual dependency in the Bible are rarely certain (E. J. Kissane, *The Book of Job* [Dublin: Browne & Nolan, 1939], xlix). Nevertheless, the author of the book of Job seems to be engaged in discourse that has some relationship to materials in the Primeval History, most especially its Priestly materials; a number of the legal provisions of Exodus, Leviticus, Numbers, and Deuteronomy, including the Decalogue; several stories in 1 Samuel through 2 Kings; the hymnic passages of both Deutero-Isaiah and Amos; the laments of Jeremiah and Lamentations; the important reference to Job in Ezek 14:14, 20; the prophetic lawsuits; Malachi; quite a few of the Psalms; and many proverbs. For further discussion, see M. Fishbane, "The Book of Job and Inner-Biblical Discourse," in *The Voice from the Whirlwind: Interpreting the Book of Job* (ed. L. G. Perdue and W. C. Gilpin; Nashville: Abingdon, 1992), 86–98, 240; and T. N. D. Mettinger, "Intertextuality: Allusion and Vertical Context Systems in Some Job Passages," in *Of Prophets' Visions and Wisdom of Sages: Essays in Honour of R. Norman Whybray on His Seventieth Birthday* (ed. H. A. McKay and D. J. A. Clines; JSOTSup 162; Sheffield: Sheffield Academic, 1993), 257–80. If true, this would make a strong case for dating the book of Job in the postexilic period: not only must all these documents have been written prior to the composition of Job, but they must have been in an advanced stage of collection. Moreover, while the presence of Aramaisms in the language of the book cannot be determinative of its date, as N. H. Snaith has well demonstrated (*The Book of Job: Its Origin and Purpose* [SBT 2/11; London: SCM, 1968], 104–12), I do feel that their presence increases the likelihood of a post-

cedure throughout the Neo-Babylonian period, one can more easily identify the legal metaphors in the book of Job. This, in turn, might allow us to solve several of the book's enigmas, legal, literary, and theological.

Forensic studies of Job have left many puzzles. For instance, what is the exact nature of the altercation? Is it a mere wager or test that uses legal language in its description of events?[14] Or does it give rise immediately or eventually to a formal legal action? If the latter, is the action a trial,[15] an appeal,[16] or an independent collateral attack on a prior judgment in the

---

exilic date when combined with other factors. See A. Hurvitz, "The Date of the Prose Tale of Job Linguistically Reconsidered," *HTR* 67 (1974): 17–34; Kissane, *Book of Job*, xlviii–xlix; and H. H. Rowley, *Job* (Century Bible; London: Thomas Nelson, 1970), 22; cf. 23. I argue for the fifth century B.C.E., rather than the fourth, based on the congruity of the Hebrew and the Aramaic versions of the book of Job found at Qumran (11QtgJob and 4QtgJob). (While 11QtgJob follows the Hebrew *Vorlage* closely, there are a few significant differences, including a *terminus* at 42:11; the substitution of 40:5 for 42:3; a different ordering of the lines from 37:16 to 37:18; and a reference in 11QtgJob 25:7 [= Job 34:31]. The Targum also maintained the LXX reading of 13:15.) For additional discussion, see J. L. Crenshaw, "Job, Book of," *ABD* 3:867; and E. Tov, *Textual Criticism of the Hebrew Bible* (Minneapolis: Fortress, 1992), 149. Furthermore, in my view, Job's understanding of death is very much in line with the prophets and the Psalms and does not seem to reflect Zoroastrian apocalyptic thinking, which began to influence Judaism in the very late Persian and Hellenistic periods.

14. This is the predominant position, particularly in the earlier scholarship. For later examples, see, e.g., F. I. Andersen, *Job: An Introduction and Commentary* (TOTC; Downers Grove, Ill.: InterVarsity, 1976); G. Gutiérrez, *On Job: God-Talk and the Suffering of the Innocent* (trans. M. J. O'Connell; Maryknoll, N.Y.: Orbis, 1987); R. E. Murphy, *Wisdom Literature: Job, Proverbs, Ruth, Canticles, Ecclesiastes, and Esther* (FOTL 13; Grand Rapids: Eerdmans, 1981); and R. N. Whybray, *Job* (Sheffield: Sheffield Academic, 1998). Cf. S. Bakon, "God and Man on Trial," *JBQ* 21 (1993): 226–235.

15. Among forensic commentators, this is the favored view. See, e.g., Chin, "Job and Injustice," 95; Gemser, "*Rîb*-Pattern," 135; Greenstein, "Forensic Understanding," 241–42; M. Laserson, "Power and Justice," *Judaism* 2 (1953): 54; Many, "Der Rechtsstreit mit Gott"; and D. Patrick, *Arguing with God: The Angry Prayers of Job* (St. Louis: Bethany, 1977), 65, 67. L. Alonso Schökel and J. L. Ojeda believe that the Satan initiates a wager, but that Job demands a trial (*Job* [Los Libros Sagrados 16; Madrid: Ediciones Cristiandad, 1971], 11; see also L. Alonso Schökel, "Toward a Dramatic Reading of Job," *Semeia* 7 [1977]: 52). S. Bakon argues that Job 1–2 sets out two trials of Job and that Job's speeches establish another trial, one against God ("God and Man on Trial," 227–31). R. Sutherland maintains that the book of Job contains "a number of overlapping and interlocking trials" (*Putting God on Trial: The Biblical Book of Job* [Victoria, B.C.: Trafford, 2004], 12.

16. See, e.g., E. F. Beach, "More Righteous than God? A Legal Formula (*zedek min*) and Theological Conundrum in Job" (paper presented at the annual meeting of the Chicago Society for Biblical Research, Chicago, Ill., April 19, 1997); Gordon, "Legal Background," 30; and J. A. Wharton, *Job* (Westminster Bible Companion; Louisville: Westminster John Knox, 1999), 49. Scholnick, although not specific about the nature of Job's lawsuit, does indicate that Job has suffered verdict and punishment ("Lawsuit Drama," viii, ix). Thus, her view of the lawsuit drama is that the legal altercation must be either an appeal or collateral action. I believe her language best suits the view that it is an appeal.

nature of a writ of habeas corpus?[17] Who brings the action: the Satan,[18] God,[19] Job,[20] or does it remain unclear?[21] When does the action start: in chapter 1, chapter 13, or chapter 31?[22] Who is its judge: God,[23] Job,[24] the friends,[25] Elihu,[26] or readers external to the story?[27] Did Job ultimately curse

---

17. Dick, "Job 31: Form-Critical Study," 38–40; and B. Zuckerman, *Job the Silent: A Study in Historical Counterpoint* (New York: Oxford University Press, 1991), 107. For more on collateral attacks on judgments and the writ of habeas corpus, see "Collateral Attack," *BLD*, 261; "Habeas Corpus," *BLD*, 709; and "Habeas Corpus ad Subjiciendum," *BLD*, 709–10.

18. See, e.g., P. L. Day, *An Adversary in Heaven: śāṭān in the Hebrew Bible* (HSM 43; Atlanta: Scholars Press, 1988), 76 n. 18, 80–81 (suggesting that the Satan actually puts God on trial); Bakon, "God and Man on Trial," 226–27; cf. E. M. Good, *In Turns of the Tempest: A Reading of Job* (Stanford: Stanford University Press, 1990), 195, 223–34.

19. See, e.g., Dick, "Job 31: Form-Critical Study," 40 (but Job is the plaintiff in the collateral action); J. B. Frye, "The Use of Māšāl in the Book of Job," *Semitics* 5 (1977): 63–64; and E. M. Good, *Irony in the Old Testament* (2nd ed.; Bible and Literature Series 3; Philadelphia: Westminster, 1982), 238. Sutherland argues that God starts the several trials of the book, but that numerous other plaintiffs exist as trial compounds upon trial, including Satan, Job's friends, and Job (*Putting God on Trial*).

20. See, e.g., Chin, "Job and Injustice," 94; Gemser, "*Rîb*-Pattern," 135; Greenstein, "Forensic Understanding," 242–43; Laserson, "Power and Justice," 54; Many, "Der Rechtsstreit mit Gott," 196; Patrick, *Arguing with God*, 65, 67; Richter, *Studien zu Hiob*, 71; Scholnick, "Lawsuit Drama," 106–8; Stamm, "Theodizee," 104; F. Stier, *Das Buch Ijjob, hebräisch und deutsch* (Munich: Kösel, 1954), 217; and Wharton, *Job*, 55–56. D. Robertson argues that events in chapter 3 shift matters from a test of Job's loyalty to a trial of God ("The Book of Job: A Literary Study," *Sound* 56 [1973]: 451). Bakon, while acknowledging that the Satan brings charges against Job, also understands that Job has put God on trial ("God and Man on Trial," 229–30).

21. W. L. Holladay noted some perplexity, but most accurately: "It is not always clear in the Book of Job who is the plaintiff and who is the defendant. Sometimes Job seems to be the plaintiff, taking the initiative to establish his innocence.... Sometimes Job seems to be the defendant in a monstrously unfair suit brought by God.... But the language of the lawcourts is constant..." ("Jeremiah's Lawsuit with God," *Int* 17 [1963]: 280–87).

22. For those who suggest chapter 1, see, e.g., Bakon, "God and Man on Trial," 226–27; Day, *Adversary in Heaven*, 76 n. 18, 80–81; and Frye, "Use of Mašal," 63. For those who suggest chapter 13, see, e.g., Chin, "Job and Injustice," 91–101; Greenstein, "Forensic Understanding," 243-44; Habel, *Book of Job: Commentary*, 224, 228, 230-31; Laserson, "Power and Justice," 53; and Scholnick, "Lawsuit Drama," 136–77. For an argument in favor of chapter 31, see, e.g., Dick, "Legal Metaphor," 45–49 (for Job's writ of habeas corpus/appeal).

23. The vast majority of interpreters take this position. See, e.g., Frye, "Use of Mašal," 63; Dick, "Job 31: Form-Critical Study," 119–20; idem, "Legal Metaphor," 50; and Patrick, *Arguing with God*, 68; cf. Chin, "Job and Injustice," 96.

24. Many, "Der Rechtsstreit mit Gott," 198–99.

25. See, e.g., Scholnick, "Lawsuit Drama," ii; Gemser, "*Rîb*-Pattern," 135 (although Gemser says that God is the ultimate judge); and Stamm, "Theodizee," 104.

26. See, e.g., Habel, *Book of Job: Commentary*, 32–33, 36; and idem, "'Only the Jackal Is My Friend': On Friends and Redeemers in Job," *Int* 31 (1977): 227–36 (or, at least, Habel maintains that Elihu thinks he is the judge of the case).

27. D. Cox, "The Book of Job as Bi-Polar Mašal: Structure and Interpretation," *Anton* 62 (1987): 12–25; and S. Lasine, "Job and His Friends in the Modern World: Kafka's *The Trial*," in

God[28] or not?[29] No scholarly consensus exists on these important issues. So perplexing are the legal metaphors that a single commentator may take unacknowledged multiple positions in answer to these questions.[30]

The thesis of this book is that a comparison of Neo-Babylonian litigation procedure, which will be gleaned from approximately 340 Neo-Babylonian litigation records, with the book of Job reveals that the legal metaphors track a very complicated and procedurally complete trial.[31] On the one side is God, whose private prosecutor, the Satan, has charged that

---

*The Voice from the Whirlwind: Interpreting the Book of Job* (ed. L. G. Perdue and W. C. Gilpin; Nashville: Abingdon, 1992), 144–55, 247–51; cf. E. M. Good, "Job and the Literary Task: A Response [to David Robertson]," *Sound* 56 (1973): 472–73.

28. See, e.g., J. T. Wilcox, *The Bitterness of Job: A Philosophical Reading* (Ann Arbor: University of Michigan Press, 1989), 51–83; cf. the work of J. B. Burns, who says: "[H]e [Job] will come perilously close" ("Cursing the Day of Birth," *PEGLMBS* 8 [1993]: 17).

29. All but a very few commentators take this view.

30. For example, Habel says that the altercation is fundamentally a test (*Book of Job: Commentary*, 52) or a wager (ibid., 95). Nonetheless, he argues that the Satan is a "professional accuser," who accuses Job, although Job identifies God as the accuser (ibid., 54). Perplexingly, however, Habel maintains on the very next page that Job brings suit (ibid., 55), one that God acknowledges (ibid., 56). Later, on that same page, Habel seems to reject Job as plaintiff by stating that it is Job who is on trial. P. Bovati falls into this same trap, alternating between believing that God brings the formal suit and that Job brings it (*Re-Establishing Justice*, 114–17, 120). For example, he states, just five pages after claiming that Job begins the trial, that Job "earnestly desires that the *rîb* against him should come to an end" (ibid., 120). Scholnick asserts that Job may become either a defendant or a plaintiff: "Knowing nothing he has done to warrant such a severe sentence, Job demands litigation with God as plaintiff to charge him formally with specific offenses or as defendant to answer the charge of unlawful seizure of Job's property" ("Meaning of *Mišpāṭ*," 350). Dick also perceives this duality. He says: "But on the other hand, Job's defense against the judgment implies an indictment of Eloah. In virtue of his defense he becomes a plaintiff!" ("Job 31: Form-Critical Study," 125). Holladay also struggles with Job's apparent movement between plaintiff and defendant, although his discussion of the problem is clearer than are those of the above commentators (see n. 21 above). In a confusion of a different sort, Scholnick speaks of the trial of Job throughout her work ("Lawsuit Drama"). Nevertheless, she sees the case as one contesting a final verdict with attendant post-trial punishment (ibid., viii, ix). If this should be the case, then the trial is really an appeal or a collateral action. I believe she means to suggest that this is an appeal. Dick, while arguing that the action is in the nature of a writ of habeas corpus, also indicates that the legal altercation is a "defendant's appeal for a civil trial after pre-trial arbitration has failed" ("Legal Metaphor," 41–45; cf. idem, "Job 31, Oath of Innocence," 31, relying upon J. G. Lautner's false distinction between hearings that were mere arbitrations and those with legal effect in the Old-Babylonian period [*Die richterliche Entscheidung und die Streitbeendigung im altbabylonischen Prozessrechte* (Leipziger rechtswissenschaftliche Studien 3; Leipzig: Theodor Weicher, 1922)]; for greater explication and debunking of this idea, see ch. 4, n. 29 below). From a legal standpoint, this is a profoundly different legal action from a writ of habeas corpus. The legal confusion among researchers is understandable because its cause lies within the book. I hope, however, to offer a clearer explanation of why Job appears to be both defendant and plaintiff.

31. For a complete list of documents, see the Index of Citations and Documents below.

Job has the guilty mind of a blasphemer, which, I maintain, is a legally sufficient charge in the Divine Council. The Satan alleges that, when the carefully constructed hedge of divine protection is removed, Job will commit what we humans think of as the guilty act of the crime: he will blaspheme with his mouth against God. While the guilty act is not a required element of the crime that must be proven in order to get a conviction according to the legal standards of the Divine Council, it will serve as the best evidence of Job's guilty mind in a case before it. Job, on the other hand, does not stand still for what seem, from his perspective, to be false accusations, malicious prosecution, and overly severe pretrial punishment perpetrated against him by God. He, therefore, threatens to counteraccuse God on the charge of abuse of authority. I propose that the suit/countersuit structure of the litigation is why so many commentators have wrestled with the question of precisely who is plaintiff and who is defendant in the trial. A lengthy settlement negotiation, in which the various characters offers accounts of their expected testimony in the trial, results from the accusations. I further argue that Elihu intends to serve as the critical second accuser on the charge of blasphemy, a role essential to trial success under Neo-Babylonian law. Unfortunately, Job, for all his rhetoric, is unable to convince a single person to stand with him in his accusation against God in the course of these negotiations. As a result, Job must surrender the case, even though he has offered an oath of innocence and continues to believe that he is in the right. In spite of Job's concession, God, knowing that Job is an upright man of deep integrity, ultimately settles the dispute in Job's favor, as could happen under Neo-Babylonian law. Consequently, I maintain that a comparison of the book with a large sample of Neo-Babylonian litigation records discloses that the legal events in the book of Job move from an initial accusation to an early settlement of both the claim and a potential counterclaim. Interestingly, the book reflects the full scope of ancient Near Eastern litigation procedure notwithstanding the midtrial settlement.

I also believe that my analysis may solve some of the textual disruptions and oddities of the book.[32] The study maintains that, despite the

---

32. For extensive summaries of earlier positions on the book's compositional history, see R. H. Pfeiffer, *Introduction to the Old Testament* (New York: Harper & Brothers, 1948), 670–72; and Rowley, "Book of Job," 162–64. For later bibliography on the point, see J. E. Hartley, *The Book of Job* (NICOT; Grand Rapids: Eerdmans, 1988), 24–25, esp. p. 24 n. 17. While I attempt to read the bulk of the text synchronically, I believe that theologically driven dislocations and corruptions due to lost material exist from chapter 21 to chapter 28. I also suggest that 31:35-37 originally followed 31:38-40b. I tentatively propose the following rearrangement of the third cycle based on thematic and stylistic considerations: Job 21:1–34; Eliphaz 22:1–20; 25:2–6; 27:8–12; Job 23:1–24:12; Bildad 25:1; 24:13–25; 26:5–14; Job 26:1–4; 27:1–7; and Zophar 22:21–30; 27:13–23. My stance is not shared by any other commentator. My primary disagreement with most other positions is their assignment of all of chapter 22 to Eliphaz and 25:2–6 to Bil-

book's literary breaks and quirks, it is a more cohesive unit than previously allowed by most scholars.[33] Not all interpretive problems can be resolved,

---

dad. My view that 22:21–30 is part of Zophar's speech is based on (1) the similarity between 11:15 and 22:26; (2) the use of בר in both 11:4 and 22:30; (3) the removal of unrighteousness in 22:23; and (4) the overall sense of Zophar's position in chapters 11 and 20. I would replace the lost material in Eliphaz's speech with 25:2–6, based on (1) the commonalities of 27:8–12 and 4:17–19; 15:14–16; and 25:4–6. This is due, in part, to the idea of calling or summoning God expressed in both 5:1 and 27:10. Pope (*Job*, xxvii) and D. J. A. Clines (*Job 1–20* [WBC 17: Dallas: Word, 1989], lix) note that the wisdom poem of chapter 28 seems odd coming from Job's mouth (see Pfeiffer, *Introduction to the Old Testament*, 672). Both Bildad and Zophar have taken up some of its themes previously. Pope (ibid.) and Habel (*Book of Job: Commentary*, 392) observe the similarities between certain metaphors in the wisdom poem and those in the divine speeches. Nevertheless, chapter 28 does not fit precisely within these speeches either. Thus, the wisdom poem remains a perplexity and probably is an interpolation.

33. The most important issue in the discussion of the book's coherence is the textual break between the narrative prose prologue and epilogue that surround the poetic dialogues. The majority of scholars believe that the author of Job used a preexisting folktale or epic when he composed the book. His poetic section split the folk piece into the book's prologue and epilogue. One of the main supports of this view is the fact that the Satan disappears from the story after the prologue. For more on the prologue and epilogue as the remnants of a folktale or epic, see, most importantly, N. M. Sarna, "Epic Substratum in the Prose of Job," *JBL* 76 (1957): 13–25; W. B. Stevenson, *The Poem of Job: A Literary Study with a New Translation* (Schweich Lectures of the British Academy 1943; London: British Academy [Oxford University Press], 1947), 76–78; and J. Wellhausen, review of A. Dillmann, ed., *Kurzgefaßtes exegetisches Handbuch zum Alten Testament. Zweite Lieferung: Hiob, JDT* 16 (1871): 555. While this might be the case, we note that other ancient Near Eastern wisdom texts have narrative prose prologues to, or frames around, their poetic material, including: the "Protest of the Eloquent Peasant," "The Dispute Between a Man and His *Ba*," the "Aramaic Proverbs of Ahiqar," and "The Prophecies of Neferti." A similar phenomenon exists in the so-called law codes of the ancient Near East, specifically, the Laws of Ur-Namma, the Laws of Lipit-Ishtar, and the Code of Hammurabi (although there has also been much discussion of whether these texts reflect redactional activity; see, e.g., V. A. Hurowitz, *Inu Anum ṣīrum: Literary Structures in the Non-Juridical Sections of Codex Hammurabi* [Occasional Publications of the Samuel Noah Kramer Fund 15; Philadelphia: University Museum, 1994]; M. T. Roth, "Mesopotamian Legal Traditions and the Laws of Hammurabi," *CKLR* 71 [1995]: 13–39; R. Westbrook, "Biblical and Cuneiform Law Codes," *RB* 92 [1985]: 247–65; and idem, "Cuneiform Law Codes and the Origins of Legislation," *ZA* 79 [1990]: 201–22). Still more scholars believe that Elihu's speeches are not original to the work. Elihu's absence from both the prologue and the epilogue is part of the evidence given for the position that this section is an interpolation. See, e.g., A. Bentzen, *Introduction to the Old Testament* (2 vols.; 2nd ed.; Copenhagen: Gad, 1952), 175–77; Habel, *Book of Job: Commentary*, 35–40; and J. G. Janzen, *Job* (IBC; Atlanta: John Knox, 1985), 22–24. E. M. Good, arguing for the literary merit of the book in our possession, has an excellent discussion of the problems with diachronic analyses of Job (*In Turns of Tempest*, 9; cf. Day, *Adversary in Heaven*, 71). All the same, Good accepts the view that the Elihu speeches are a later addition (*In Turns of Tempest*, 8, 182–85). In accord is Newsom, "Book of Job," 320–25. N. H. Snaith and R. Gordis argue that the same author wrote the narrative frame and the poetic section of the book, including Elihu's speeches, but that he wrote the book in several stages, with Elihu coming later (Snaith, *Book of Job*, 8; and Gordis, *Book of God*, 100–103, 110–12, 209–15). J. E. Hartley maintains that the narrative and poetic sections of the book had diverse origins, but he believes that the poet also wrote the Elihu speeches (*Book of Job*, 21–32). The congruity

of course, through this analysis. The book of Job is a complex document, full of textual difficulties and unusual Hebrew terms and grammatical constructions. Moreover, its author drew metaphors and literary forms from a broad sweep of life and literature.[34] I must also acknowledge that the law in Job's world deviates somewhat from the actual legal system of its time. Because the book is literature that exploits the law in furtherance of its literary and theological ends, its law need not follow the Neo-Babylonian system perfectly, especially given the fact that the book's concern is a divine trial. The examination of the book's law against the Neo-Babylonian litigation documents, therefore, reveals not only the book's dependence on the legal norms of its time but also its occasional departure from those norms. It additionally discloses the author's apparent desire to maintain some level of legal and theological ambiguity.[35] Although its narratives mimic to a large degree the narratological features of ancient trial records and its metaphors correspond to the legal procedural components of a complete trial, there are aspects of the book that undermine any sense of certainty with regard to the book's trial. Furthermore, the work contains other well-studied ambiguities, creating a greater level of interpretive openness than is found in many works. I believe that this is intentional on the author's part and has contributed to the great diversity of opinion among the book's readers. Consequently, no approach, no grand theory can explain every nuance of the book. D. Patrick states this idea helpfully:

---

between the Hebrew text and the *Targum of Job* (11QtgJob) might suggest, however, the originality of the current book or, possibly, its reorganization at a relatively early date (Crenshaw, "Job," 867; and Tov, *Textual Criticism*, 149).

34. As A. S. Peake states: "The poet is a master of metaphors, taken from many spheres of life" (*Job* [NCB; London: T. C. & E. C. Jack, 1904], 41). Beyond the ancient Near Eastern theodicies, scholars have speculated that other documents in the ancient Near East, both within and outside of wisdom literature, may have contributed either directly to the book of Job or to the cultural milieu from which it arose. For exemplars of such studies and a few relevant translations, see A. E. Cowley, "The Aramaic Proverbs of Ahiqar," *ANET*, 427–30; P. E. Dion, "Formulaic Language in the Book of Job: International Background and Ironical Distortions," *SR* 16 (1987): 187–93; Gordis, *Book of God*, 55–56; H. A. Hoffner, "Some Contributions of Hittology to Old Testament Study," *TynBul* 20 (1969): 27–55; and G. von Rad, "Hiob xxxviii und die altägyptische Weisheit," in *Wisdom in Israel and in the Ancient Near East: Presented to Professor Harold Henry Rowley in Celebraion of His Sixty-Fifth Birthday* (ed. M. Noth and D. W. Thomas; VTSup 3; Leiden: Brill, 1955), 293–301; translated as "Job XXXVIII and Ancient Egyptian Wisdom," in *The Problem of the Hexateuch and Other Essays* (New York: McGraw Hill, 1966), 281–91; and in *Studies in Ancient Israelite Wisdom* (ed. J. L. Crenshaw; New York: Ktav, 1976), 267–77 (contra M. V. Fox, "Egyptian Onomastica and Biblical Wisdom," *VT* 36 [1986]: 302–10).

35. D. W. Cotter calls ambiguity one of the "dominating factors" in Job and has an excellent, if brief, discussion of the point (*A Study of Job 4–5 in Light of Contemporary Literary Theory* [SBLDS 124; Atlanta: Scholars Press, 1992], 109–15, quote at 109). See also A. Berlin's important discussion of point of view and ambiguity in the Hebrew Bible (*Poetics and Interpretation of Biblical Narrative* [Winona Lake, Ind.: Eisenbrauns, 1994], 43–50).

"A work like Job is too fertile for one mind. Indeed, its greatness lies in the fact that it is as complex and many sided as life itself."[36] I must admit, then, that my conclusion proposes the trial pattern that I believe best fits the data, but room for disagreement will certainly remain.

This book contains ten chapters beyond the introduction. Chapter 2 will address the important relationship between suffering and law in the ancient world, which is the foundation of the book of Job. The chapter seeks to explain why legal metaphors appear in the book at all and will assist us in determining the appropriate methodology for the study. Chapter 3 will discuss in detail my methods, which are drawn from the disciplines of Assyriology, biblical studies, and law. Chapter 4 will set forth the study's understanding of Neo-Babylonian courts and their legal procedure. Chapters 5 through 10 will address the litigation metaphors in the book of Job. Chapter 11 will conclude the study with a brief summary of my results and discuss a few possible implications of the findings.

---

36. Patrick, *Arguing with God*, 63.

# 2

# Disease, Disability, and Disaster as Law

Before investigating the individual legal metaphors in the book of Job and what they amount to collectively, and even before examining what methodological tools are appropriate to such an inquiry, a preliminary set of questions should be asked.[1] They are: Why does the book contain legal metaphor at all? How does legal language relate to Job's incidents of disease, disability, and disaster? What are the connections between human suffering, divine action, and law that give the legal metaphors meaning in the context of this theodicy? Only after answering these questions can we determine the best methodology for the study.

I posit that an important link between human suffering and divine trial law existed in the worldview of the ancient Near East. This link is reflected in a number of Mesopotamia's ritual incantation texts, prayers, psalms, and theodicies. This link inspired both the author's use of litigation language in the book of Job and his shaping of the book's structure. Because human suffering and divine trial law are so intimately connected in the ancient Near East, a trial structure, with its attendant language, was the author's best means through which to question whether retributive justice actually functions in the world.

## Suffering as Law in the Ancient Near East

W. G. Lambert argues that the emergence of law gave rise to wisdom being cast in terms of law: "If, in the microcosm, a matter could be taken to law and redress secured, why, in the macrocosm, should one not take up a matter with the gods?"[2] A plethora of ancient Near Eastern texts indicate that suffering could be attributed to natural causes, witchcraft, or demons or

---

1. This chapter is also the basis of my findings in F. Rachel Magdalene, "The ANE Legal Origins of Impairment as Theological Disability and the Book of Job," *PRSt* (2007): forthcoming.
2. *BWL*, 10; cited in Albertson, "Job and Ancient Near Eastern Wisdom Literature," 224.

other supernatural causes and that the sufferer would approach the gods for assistance in bringing the affliction to an end.³ The gods served as the court of last resort over the cosmos and could rectify all wrongs. BMS 19, one of the Assyrian "Prayers of the Lifting of the Hand" (*nīš qāti* or ŠU.IL.LA), states this well. In this prayer, the petitioner is praying for protection after an eclipse, which portended evil. The petitioner acknowledges the gods as his final judge in his supplication. He addresses Marduk as: "O Lord! Lord! Lord! Father of the great [gods!] The Lord of the fates, [the god?] of decrees! Ruler of heaven and earth, the lord of lands! The one who renders the final verdict, whose utterance cannot be changed, determiner of the fates!" (lines 4–9).⁴ In BMS 6, the petitioner addresses Šamaš as "O judge of the gods," when he requests that a difficult dream portend good not evil (line 11).

Lambert also notices, however, another connection between law and suffering in early Mesopotamian history; that is, suffering could result from the commission of sin. He first observes this in a common Akkadian name from the Third Dynasty of Ur, Mina-arni, meaning "What-is-my-guilt?"⁵ Lambert argues that the name "implies the line of reasoning: I have

---

3. The literature on ancient Near Eastern medicine is growing rapidly. On the supernatural causes of illness, see most importantly J. Scurlock and B. R. Andersen, *Diagnoses in Assyrian and Babylonian Medicine: Ancient Sources, Translations, and Modern Medical Analyses* (Urbana: University of Illinois Press, 2005), 429–528. See also, e.g., I. Tzvi Abusch, *Babylonian Witchcraft Literature: Case Studies* (BJS 132; Atlanta: Scholars Press, 1987); H. Avalos, *Illness and Health Care in the Ancient Near East: The Role of the Temple in Greece, Mesopotamia, and Israel* (HSM 54; Atlanta: Scholars Press, 1995), 129–42, 185–92; G. Cunningham, *"Deliver Me from Evil": Mesopotamian Incantations 2500–1500 BC* (Studia Pohl Series Maior 17; Rome: Pontifical Biblical Institute, 1997); I. L. Finkel, "A Study in Scarlet: Incantations against Samana," in *Fs. Borger*, 71–106; M. J. Geller, "An Incantation against Curses," in *Fs. Borger*, 127–40; idem, "A New Piece of Witchcraft," in *Fs. Sjöberg*, 193–205; idem, *Forerunners to Udug-Hul: Sumerian Exorcistic Incantations* (Stuttgart: Franz Steiner, 1983); Gemser, "*Rîb*-Pattern," 127 n. 1; N. P. Heeßel, "Diagnosis, Divination and Disease: Towards an Understanding of the Rationale Behind the Babylonian *Diagnostic Handbook*," in *Magic and Rationality in Ancient Near Eastern and Graeco-Roman Medicine* (ed. H. F. J. Hortmanshoff and M. Stol; Studies in Ancient Medicine 27; Leiden: Brill, 2004), 97–116; J. V. Kinnier Wilson, "Medicine in the Land and Times of the Old Testament," in *Studies in the Period of David and Solomon* (ed. T. Ishida; Winona Lake, Ind.: Eisenbrauns, 1982), 337–75, esp. 349; *BMS*, xxvii–xxix, nos. 19, 22, 50; R. Labat, *Traité akkadien de diagnostics et pronostics médicaux* (Leiden: Brill, 1951); R. C. Thompson, *The Devils and Evil Spirits of Babylonia*, vol. 1 (London: Luzac, 1903); and K. van der Toorn, *Sin and Sanction in Israel and Mesopotamia* (Assen/Maastricht: Van Gorcum, 1985). T. J. Collins has demonstrated, however, that a number of Babylonian medical incantations do not appear to state or assume any particular cause for the illness in question ("Natural Illness in Babylonian Medical Incantations" [2 vols.; Ph.D. diss., University of Chicago, 1999]).

4. Translation by J. N. Lawson, "The Concept of Fate in Ancient Mesopotamia of the First Millennium: Toward an Understanding of 'Simtu' (First Millennium B.C.E., Namburi Ritual)" (Ph.D. diss., Hebrew Union College-Jewish Institute of Religion [Cincinnati], 1992), 85.

5. *BWL*, 10.

suffered: I must have done wrong: What can it be? Suffering necessarily implies guilt."[6] He maintains that ancient peoples believed that their gods, as the ultimate judges of humanity, could inflict suffering as a punishment for wrongs that humans committed. In other words, those suffering some adverse condition, such as illness, death of a loved one, crop failure, drought, or political disaster, might interpret the event or condition as punishment pursuant to a guilty verdict in a divine trial for a sin committed. N. P. Heeβel also states this well:

> [F]or the Babylonians the aetiology of disease and sickness was situated in the realm of the gods. Falling ill was seen as a sign that the patient had lost the equilibrium he ideally lived in. Either some god had turned against him and through physical contact had placed the sickness directly inside the human body, or the personal protective god had left the person open to attacks by demons or ill-wishing human beings. . . . The reconciliation of the patient with the god is, therefore, essential for healing the patient. . . . The divine sender of a disease, however, was not regarded as the ultimate cause of the patient falling sick. The reasons for being taken ill were understood to lie on the human side: known or unknown breaking of taboos, committing crimes or violations of moral standards by the sick himself or the machinations of an often unknown adversary—a witch or a sorcerer, for example—were thought to result in illness, and also in other forms of misfortune such as financial loss or bad reputation.[7]

If this were the case, one would expect to find prayers, hymns, and ritual incantations wherein the sufferer or a mediator diviner sought judicial relief from the gods' punishments in the records of the ancient Near East. Indeed, such documents do exist. For instance, one Babylonian psalm states:

> O my Lord, my wrongdoings are many, great are my sins.
> God in the rage of his heart has confronted me;
> The Goddess has become angry with me and made me ill. (*RawlCu* 4, line 10)[8]

Here, the petitioner confesses that his sin has resulted in the god's and goddess's anger, which has brought about his punishing illness. Another example lies in the Old Babylonian text "Prayer to Anūna," where the petitioner has suffered illness, headaches, and insomnia.[9] He has also been rejected by

---

6. Ibid.
7. Heeβel, "Diagnosis, Divination and Disease," 99.
8. Text translated by Dick, "Legal Metaphor in Job 31," 39. See also S. Langdon, *Babylonian Penitential Psalms* (OCuT 6; Paris: Librairie Orientaliste Paul Geuthner, 1927), 41.
9. PBS 1/1, 2. See further W. G. Lambert, "A Babylonian Prayer to Anūna," in *Fs. Sjöberg*, 321-29. All quotations from this text are taken from Lambert.

his family and abandoned by his gods. The petitioner states through his priestly intercessor: "The weeper has been negligent, have pity on him! He has bowed down and has groaned when confronted with [his] guilt, He cries [to you] for sin committed. . . . 'I have committed a [. . . ] sin. . . . Inninna prosecuted me for my guilt, that I had not stood in awe of her praise'" (lines 78–80, 85, 89).[10] The "Prayers of the Lifting of the Hand" are similar. Each incantation typically has three parts: (1) an introduction in which the deity, his or her powers, and his or her special functions are named and/or praised; (2) a recitation of the sufferer's distress and a petition for assistance and for pardon or other relief; and (3) a brief doxology of praise.[11] These incantations frequently refer to the anger of a particular god or goddess, which needs appeasing.[12]

In each of the above cases, the sufferer apparently knew of the wrongdoings that led to his illness. We can imagine that he or she had already been experiencing guilt over some indiscretion and had, therefore, connected the indiscretion to the punishment.[13] The sufferer would then simply request that a priest perform an expiation ritual in order to appease the anger of the gods and/or goddesses and to ask for a pardon, or reversal, of the divine conviction.[14] The religio-legal crime and punishment demanded a ritual-legal request for relief.[15] The Mesopotamian ritual incantation texts and many other hymns and prayers were used as part of expiation rituals that sought to release a sufferer from the harm imposed.[16]

---

10. Occasionally the petitioner saw the problem as stemming from the sin of a parent instead of him- or herself (see, e.g., W. G. Lambert, "DINGIR.ŠÀ.DIB.BA Incantations," *JNES* 33 [1974]: 270, no. 1, lines 115-18; and E. Reiner, *Šurpu—A Collection of Sumerian and Akkadian Incantations* [AfO Beiheft 11; Graz: Weidner, 1958], tablet 3, lines 176-83).

11. *BMS*, xxii-xxiii.

12. See, e.g., *BMS* 1.

13. See, e.g., Cunningham, *Deliver Me*, 37.

14. Such rites also made offerings of various sorts. For example, in the "Prayers of the Lifting of the Hand," the incantations contain instructions as to how to perform the ritual. Typically, the priest was to burn incense when reciting the incantation. Additional offerings of some sort of drink or libation, water, oil, honey, or butter might be a part of the ritual. Sometimes foodstuffs, parts of plants, and jewels were also offered. Rituals involving the casting of a seed in oil or the untying of a knot sometimes also accompanied the incantation. For fuller a discussion of "Prayers of the Lifting of the Hand" and these rituals, see *BMS*, xxvii–xxix; and Lambert, "DINGIR.ŠÀ.DIB.BA," 270. The Šurpu Incantations also are accompanied by ritual instructions on tablet 1.

15. We see a similar connection between the doing of ill, suffering, and the use of legal metaphor in the Mesopotamian incantations against witchcraft (see, e.g., *Fs. Sjöberg*, 204-5) and demons (see, e.g., *Fs. Borger*, 156-58).

16. For other discussions of the ritual incantation texts, see most importantly Cunningham, *Deliver Me*; M. J. Geller, "The Šurpu Incantations and Lev. V.1–5," *JSS* 25 (1980): 181–85; *BMS*, xxvii-xxix; Lambert, "DINGIR.ŠÀ.DIB.BA," 270; E. Reiner, "Lipšur Litanies," *JNES* 15 (1956): 129–49; and idem, *Šurpu*.

These texts also indicate that the people of the ancient Near East supposed that the gods typically convicted the guilty person during a summary hearing, in which the accused neither appeared nor testified. As a result, many of the accused had no inkling that they stood accused until the postconviction punishment fell, at which point the guilty one would seek relief from the summary judgment and punishment. Consequently, if the sufferer did not have an immediate awareness of his or her sin, then he or she had to attempt to discover the sin or crime committed in order to remedy it.

In fact, many ritual texts and the Babylonian *Diagnostic Handbook* reveal that the sufferer often did not know precisely what he or she had done to bring on the judgment.[17] As a result, the bewildered person would approach a priest for clarity regarding the sin. In a number of cases, a priest could diagnose the illness and its cause by the sufferer's symptoms.[18] J. Scurlock and B. R. Andersen point out, for example, that Šamaš as the god of justice could mete out illness for failing to pay one's tithe.[19] One's personal gods could bring illness upon one who had pondered untruths in one's heart.[20] Blasphemous conduct could also bring on some alteration of mental functioning: " 'Hand' of a god (is when) he curses the gods, speaks blasphemy, (and) strikes whatever he sees."[21] Sometimes that type of diagnostic course was insufficient to determine the cause of the difficulty. The Šurpu Incantations indicate that, in such a case, the priest would inquire through divination as to the charges underlying the conviction and its attendant punishment.[22] Usually the priest would ask the gods for a sign either identifying the sin and/or confirming the petitioner's guilt.[23] As part

---

17. The Babylonian *Diagnostic Handbook* has been edited by N. P. Heeßel, *Babylonisch-assyrische Diagnostik* (AOAT 43; Münster: Ugarit Verlag, 2000); see also M. Stol, *Epilepsy in Babylonia* (Cuneiform Monographs 2; Groningen: Styx, 1993), 55–90. See further Heeßel, "Diagnosis, Divination and Disease," 97–116; Labat, *Traité akkadien de diagnostics*; and Scurlock and Andersen, *Diagnoses in Assyrian and Babylonian Medicine*. With regard to effort in the ritual incantation texts to uncover the cause of the harm, see Geller, "Šurpu Incantations," 182; Reiner, *Šurpu*, 2–3; B. Wells, *The Law of Testimony in the Pentateuchal Codes* (BZABR 4; Wiesbaden: Harrassowitz, 2004), 91; and Westbrook, *Studies*, 27.

18. Heeßel, "Diagnosis, Divination and Disease," 97–116; Labat, *Traité akkadien de diagnostics*.Labat, *Traité akkadien de diagnostics*; Scurlock and Andersen, *Diagnoses in Assyrian and Babylonian Medicine*.

19. Scurlock and Andersen, *Diagnoses in Assyrian and Babylonian Medicine*, 431.

20. Ibid., 439.

21. Ibid.

22. Geller, "Šurpu Incantations," 182; and Reiner, *Šurpu*, 2–3.

23. It should also be noted that law and divination are associated in other contexts as well. For example, numerous scholars have observed the connection between the omen texts and the so-called law codes of the ancient Near East. See, e.g., J. Bottéro, "The 'Code' of Hammurabi," in *Mesopotamia: Writing, Reasoning, and the Gods* (trans. Z. Bahrani and M. Van de Mieroop; Chicago: University of Chicago Press, 1992), 156–84; F. R. Kraus, "Ein zentrales

of the process, the priest would recite a lengthy list of possible offenses with the hope that he would have included the committed offense. Once the sufferer knew the source of his problem, the sufferer could make confession and expiation, receive his or her pardon, and, one would hope, be healed. That an illness is connected to sin, in some circumstances, is suggested by tablets 5–6, lines 60–72, which state: "Like this onion he (the priest) peels and throws into the fire, . . . (so) invocation, oath, retaliation, questioning, the pain of my hardship, sin, transgression, crime, error, the sickness that is in my body, my flesh, my veins, may be peeled off like this onion, may the fire consume it entirely today . . . ."[24] Matting is used similarly in lines 83–92: "As this matting is unraveled and thrown into the fire, . . . (so) invocation, oath, retaliation, questioning, the pain of my hardship, sin, transgression, crime, error, the sickness that [is] in my body, my flesh, my veins, [may] be [un]raveled like this matting, may [the fire] consu[me] it entirely today. . . ." Tablets 5–6, lines 195–99 of the Šurpu Incantations make the point explicit. The petitioner states there: "[T]oday may the angry heart of my god and goddess be pacified, and the oath removed from my body. Because you are the judge, I stand before you, and (because) you are beneficent, I turn constantly to you. Judge my cau[se], decide my [deci]sion!"[25] It is important to note that petitioners in Mesopotamian human lawsuits often asked the court *to judge my cause* and *to decide my decision*. In Dalley *Edinburgh* 69, the plaintiff asks for judgment with the words *dīn dīnu* and *purussâ parāsu*, as are used in the ritual texts. In *RA* 12,

---

Problem des altmesopotamischen Rechts: Was ist der Codex Hammu-rabi?" *Geneva* 8 (1960): 283–96; and R. Westbrook, "What is the Covenant Code?" in *Theory and Method in Biblical and Cuneiform Law: Revision, Interpolation, and Development* (ed. B. M. Levinson; JSOTSup 181; Sheffield: Sheffield Academic, 1994), 15–36. Lawson has discussed in some detail the legal metaphors found in the omen texts. He argues that the implications of the presence of such metaphors are of utmost importance and that "the formal and grammatical resemblances between law code and omen series is not merely coincidental but rather intentional" ("Concept of Fate," 121). Although I disagree with him when he asserts that the law codes established norms (being, in my view, more in the nature of law treatises than in the nature of statutory law), I agree that the people of the ancient Near East comprehended the omen as a prognosticator of the gods' judgments for good and ill (ibid., 115–21; see also Gemser, "*Rîb*-Pattern," 127). Similarly, legal language is used in the political omens of kings (see further, e.g., W. G. Lambert, "Questions Addressed to the Babylonian Oracle: The Tamītu Texts," in *Oracles et prophéties dans l'antiquité: Actes du Colloque de Strasbourg, 15-17 Juin 1995* [ed. J.-G. Heintz; Paris: Boccard, 1997], 86; and F. M. Fales, "The Impact of Oracular Material on the Political Utterances and Political Action of the Sargonic Dynasty," in *Oracles et prophéties dans l'antiquité*, 104, 106). The relationship between human and deity is often cast in legal terms.

24. All translations of the Šurpu Incantations are by Reiner, *Šurpu*.
25. The legal language is most prominent on tablet 2, lines 129–33, 186–92; tablet 3, lines 176–83; tablet 4, lines 11–17, 37–44, 67–108; tablets 5–6, lines 60–143, 195–99; and tablet 8, lines 41–47, 79–82.

6–7, the plaintiff uses *dīn epēšu* to convey this same idea. A number of legal texts use the expression *purussâ šakānu* to the same purpose.[26]

The same or quite similar language can be found in other ritual incantations, prayers, and hymns. For example, B. Gemser quotes a passage from *KAR* 184: "In the (legal) cause of the illness which has seized me, I am lying on my knees for judgment. Judge my cause, give a decision for me."[27] In *BMS* 4, the petitioner demands of the goddess Damkina: "Give judgment! Make a decision! Compensate my damage! I have turned to you. I have sought you. I have grasped the fringe of your garment like the fringes of my (patron) god and goddess. Give me my judgment! Make my decision!" (lines 28–30).[28] *BMS* 6 states: "I have sought you [Bau], I have turned to you, like the *ulinnu* of my god and of my goddess your *ulinnu*, I have grasped[,] because to give judgment, to make a decision, to raise to life, and to give prosperity rests with you" (lines 73–75). In *BMS* 12, the sufferer declares: "My powers and my soul are bewitched, and there is no righteous decision! O lord, at this time stand beside me and hearken to my cries, give my judgment, make my decision! The sickness ... do you destroy, and take away the disease of my body! O my god (and) goddess, you judge humanity and possess me!" (lines 58–61). *BMS* 30 follows suit. The petitioner pleads: "You are the judge of my cause.... You are the director of my path.... May my god who is angry with me turn! Sorrow, the grave, and the bonds may he ...! May he remove the sickness of my body...."

Other language of the human law court is also employed in these petitions. *BMS* 2 is a particularly interesting example. The incantation states: "In Íkur, the house of decision, exalted are your heads, and Bîl, your father has granted you that your hand should hold the law of all the gods! You judge the judgment of humanity! ... From him whom sin possesses, the sin you do remove! ... My sighing remove and accept my supplication! Let my cry find acceptance before you!" (lines 16–19). The *house of decision* (*bīt tašilāti*) is similar to Neo-Babylonian references to a law court found in litigation documents. Several such documents record that there was a *house of judgment* (*bīt dīni*) in Babylon.[29] Similarly, evidence also exists for a *house of judges* (*bīt dayyāni*).[30]

---

26. See, e.g., AnOr 8, 56; *AfO* 44, 78 no. 6; 44, 88 no. 19; TCL 13, 222, and 13, 219 (= *Nbn* 720).

27. Gemser, "*Rîb*-Pattern," 127 n. 1. A. Falkenstein and W. Von Soden noted earlier that the petition is asking Šamaš to reconsider a prior judgment that had resulted in the sufferer's illness (*Sumerische und akkadische Hymnen und Gebete* [Zurich: Artemis, 1953], 323–25).

28. See also *BMS* 30, line 11.

29. See, e.g., *AfO* 44, 81 no. 9; *CT* 22, 105; TCL 13, 222; YOS 3, 35; and YOS 7, 31. See further *CAD* B, 156.

30. See, e.g., UrET 4, 186.

The DINGIR.ŠÀ.DIB.BA Incantations, also known as the "Incantations for Appeasing an Angry God," are a group of texts found in Late Assyrian and Late Babylonian libraries.[31] They also reflect situations where the sufferer believes that he or she is subject to a divine judgment but is quite bewildered as to his or her crime. The first of these texts, which has three sections, reflects the sufferer's multipronged approach to the problem. First, by specifically listing many possible iniquities and then making several general confessions of sin, the sufferer hopes to include the possible sin he, she, or a family relation has committed in order to ask pardon for it.[32] This strategy is quite similar to the one used in the Šurpu Incantations. His or her second tack is to attempt to coax the deities to reveal the source of the problem to him or her so that he or she can ask for a pardon. This, too, is reminiscent of the Šurpu Incantations. His or her third strategy is, however, unknown in the Šurpu Incantations. The petitioner in the DINGIR.ŠÀ.DIB.BA Incantations asserts that he or she has acted in some righteous ways by listing a series of good deeds (tablet 1, lines 80–84). In so doing, he or she hopes to convince the petitioned god and goddess that he or she is a good man who has done many good acts and, therefore, deserves pardon for any possible indiscretion that he or she may have committed.

The close connection between illness, divine wrath, and divine trial law is also manifested in many rituals against witchcraft. The theological basis of this connection lies in the understanding that, owing to the sufferer's sins, the gods used various demons or witchcraft to bring the suffering to bear on the sufferer.[33] In *SBUT* II 110, no. 22, tablet 2, lines 8-16, a man is suffering persecution, rejection, and dejection because of sorcery and divine wrath. The petitioner states:

> If a man acquired an enemy (*bēl lemutti*) (and) his accuser (*bēl dabābi*) surrounded him with hatred, unjustice [sic], murder, aphasia, works of evil—he is rejected by king, patrician and prince. He is constantly brought into fear, he feels bad day and night, he suffers constant (financial losses), they calumniate him, his words being changed, his profits stop, he is not welcome in the palace, his dreams are confused . . . , he sees in his dreams dead people, an evil finger is pointing at him behind him, and evil eye chases him all the time, he fears verdict because (?) the extispicy expert and dream interpreter do not provide him a verdict or decision.[34]

---

31. Lambert, "DINGIR," 267.
32. Possible iniquities are listed on tablet 1, lines 23–25, 124-27, and 136–47. General confessions of sin are listed on tablet 1, lines 114–17, 121–23, 135, 148, 154–56; tablet 2, line 7.
33. See further M. Stol, "Psychosomatic Suffering in Ancient Mesopotamia," in *Mesopotamian Magic: Textual, Historical, and Interpretive Perspectives* (ed. T. Abusch and K. van der Toorn; Groningen: Styx, 1999), 57–68; and T. Abusch, "Witchcraft and the Anger of the Personal God," in *Mesopotamian Magic*, 83–121.
34. Translation from Stol, "Psychosomatic Suffering," 60–61.

Here, prior divination has failed to reveal the crime on which the petitioner's suffering is based. This ritual promises, however, that the individual will be "reconciled with god, king, and patrician" and he will "be made to stand above his accuser," who in this case is a sorcerer.[35] T. Abusch argues convincingly, after studying many texts either related to or variations of this text, that "a composition that originally made no mention of witchcraft and regarded the anger of the personal gods as the primary cause of the misfortune has been revised and adapted first to include witchcraft and then to present witchcraft as the primary diagnosis and cause."[36] First, sorcerers became human instruments of divine justice. Later, the language of divine anger and litigation was softened by shifting the blame to witches. Divine trials for misdeeds are the origins of many of these texts.

On some occasions, the petitioner pleaded only to be able to understand the cause of the distress and not for relief. In *LKA* 139, an individual was apparently unsuccessful in gleaning the cause of his suffering from the priest whom he had consulted. As a result, he demanded an exceptional type of help from Šamaš:

> [Wh]y have you imposed upon me such unpleasant anxiety? Let them (my ancestral ghosts) reveal it to me in a dream, and let them speak to me. Let them reveal my [s]in, whether it was conscious or inadvertent, and I will live with my punishment. Šamaš, speak to my ancestral ghosts, that they may show me, and interpret for me the oracle of human misfortunes which I have been made to endure.[37]

This sufferer had apparently given up seeking relief; rather, he wanted only to comprehend his error.

The petitioner's reference to both conscious and unwitting sin is important. Sufferers ignorant of their crime often believed that their crime may have been committed inadvertently; otherwise, they would have recognized it immediately. We note this again in a prayer that reads: "A terrible disease has weakened my entire body; a terrible illness is afflicting me. For a known and unknown sin—because I was disrespectful, because I sinned, was careless, committed misdeeds—I became fearful and afraid and I brought my life before your great divinity. . . ."[38] The DINGIR.ŠÀ.DIB.BA Incantations are similar. They even make reference to possible sins of the parent.[39] In such a case, the petitioner often has no knowledge of any such

---

35. Abusch, "Witchcraft and Anger," 100-101; and Stol, "Psychosomatic Suffering," 61.
36. Abusch, "Witchcraft and Anger," 110.
37. Translation by Avalos, *Illness and Health Care*, 138.
38. E. Ebeling, *Die Akkadische Gebetsserie "Handerhebung"* (Deutsche Akademie der Wissenschaften zu Berlin Institut für Orientforschung 20; Berlin: Akademie-Verlag, 1953), 8:7–12; text translated by Dick, "Legal Metaphor in Job 31," 39.
39. See n. 10 above.

crime, let alone active participation in the crime coupled with an evil intent. The Šurpu Incantations also seek relief from any possible sins of the sufferer's parents, descendants, other relatives, as well as "the sin he knows and (the sin) he does not know."[40] Unintentional sins are clearly covered by such incantations.

The language of litigation is also employed in *namburi* rituals meant to forestall negative omens. In these situations, a diviner would bring a message of judgment and impending doom to an individual who had not yet suffered any calamity. In order to avoid such harm befalling the individual, he or she would bring the diviner before the divine court and plead innocence in the case. This was, in effect, a rehearing of an issue that was decided on summary judgment in light of the testimony of the now present defendant.[41]

Ancient Near Eastern wisdom literature reflects thinking identical to that of the ritual texts. Lambert notes that line 13 of "A Man and His God," a theodicy much compared with the book of Job, uses legal language to discuss the cause of the protagonist's suffering. In that piece, the sufferer begs his god to relieve some unnamed suffering, which he believes has been caused by some unintentional sin he has committed: "The crime which I did, I know not."[42] In "The Just Sufferer" from Ugarit, the sufferer is frustrated because various oracular procedures have not resolved his illness nor disclosed how long he must continue to suffer: "My liver oracles remain obscure; they become like [. . .]. The haruspex cannot resolve my case; the judge does not give any sign . . . . The scholars who deliberate on tablets concerning my case do not tell me the time limit of my sickness."[43] The petitioner in this case cannot get the attention of his divine judge by the normal means of divination in order to determine what he did to deserve his illness and resolve the difficulty. In the Babylonian "*Ludlul bēl nēmeqi*," the sufferer states in his list of complaints: "I sought the favor of the *zaqīqu*-spirit, but he did not enlighten me; [a]nd the incantation priest with his ritual did not appease divine wrath against me" (tablet 2, lines 8–9).[44] Ancient Near Eastern wisdom literature demonstrates unmistakably that it can

---

40. Reiner, *Šurpu*, tablet 3, lines 176–83.
41. S. M. Maul, "How the Babylonians Protected Themselves against Calamities Announced by Omens," in *Mesopotamian Magic: Textual, Historical, and Interpretive Perspectives* (ed. T. Abusch and K. van der Toorn; Groningen: Styx, 1999), 123–29.
42. *BWL*, 10. See also Lambert, "A Further Attempt at the Babylonian 'Man and His God,'" in *Language, Literature and History: Philological and Historical Studies Presented to Erica Reiner* (ed. F. Rochberg-Halton; AOS 67; New Haven: American Oriental Society, 1987), 191, where he translates this phrase, "I do not know what sin I have committed."
43. *Ugaritica* 5, 162; text translated by Martti Nissinen, with contributions by C. L. Seow and Robert K. Ritner, *Prophets and Prophecy in the Ancient Near East* (ed. P. Machinist; SBLWAW 12; Atlanta: Society of Biblical Literature, 2003), 184.
44. Translation from *BWL*, 39.

share with the ritual incantation texts the conception that some suffering arises because the gods have convicted one for an unknown sin in a divine trial.[45]

A few of the ritual incantation texts specify that the sufferer believed that he or she could not get relief from his or her patron god, who had executed punishment upon him or her. Thus, he or she needed to appeal to a god higher in status within the pantheon for resolution of his or her case. In other words, the petitioner comprehended his or her request for relief as an appeal of an adverse decision in the court of lower deities. We observe this in some of the texts in the "Prayers of the Lifting of the Hand," where the petitioner listed his or her patron deities, rather than the petitioned deity, as those whom he or she had angered. The sufferer then indicated that these deities had not given him or her relief. Consequently, the petitioner required the help of superior deities to act as mediators or judges between the sufferer and his patron gods in the dispute.[46]

Thus, a number of variations exist on the essential view in the ancient Near East that suffering is often the result of a legal conviction by the gods for a sin committed, whether or not that sin was known to the sufferer. It is, therefore, the gods who must bring solution. Human suffering and divine law are deeply connected in the theodicy of the ancient world.[47] Disease, disability, and disaster are important aspects of divine law.

Similar thinking can be seen within the Hebrew Bible. For instance, H. Avalos argues that Deut 28:15, 22 make clear that "Yahweh used illnesses to enforce covenants made with humans. Such covenants promised health and longevity to those who followed Yahweh's stipulations, but illness and death to those who did not."[48] He further asserts that repeatedly "Yahweh employs illnesses to ... punish evildoers in DtrH and in the Chronicler, and to test Job."[49] J. Wilkinson extends this

---

45. See also, e.g., "The Protest of an Eloquent Peasant" and *"Ludlul bēl nēmeqi."*
46. *BMS*, xxiii, no. 4.
47. This study is by no means the first to acknowledge such relationship existed. Dick states it plainly: "[T]here are ... Mesopotamian texts which describe in the language of the court man's suffering as a legal judgment of guilt" ("Legal Metaphor in Job 31," 39). L. J. Sheldon elaborates on the development of this idea: "Belief in the causal nexus between sin and illness or guilt and affliction can be found in the relatively early stages of intellectual history during the first part of the second millennium B.C.E. ... The concept emerged more fully during the Kassite Period (1400–1200 B.C.E.). ... [I]n judicial language a man's suffering rendered him legally judged as guilty" ("Job as Hebrew Theodicy," 84). See also Avalos, *Illness and Health Care*, 128–39; Gemser, "*Rîb*-Pattern," 127 n. 1; Hasel, "Health and Healing," 198; H. Vorländer, *Mein Gott: Die Vorstellungen vom persönlichen Gott im Alten Orient und im Alten Testament* (AOAT 23; Neukirchen-Vluyn: Neukirchener Verlag, 1975), 99; and van der Toorn, *Sin and Sanction*, 72–80. Cf. Geller, "An Incantation against Curses," 127–40.
48. Avalos, *Illness and Health Care*, 242.
49. Ibid., 244.

idea to include passages from Exodus, Leviticus, Psalms, Jeremiah, Ezekiel, and Hosea.[50] Avalos also addresses the remedy of such illness in ancient Israel:

> One of the effects was that patients assumed that transgressions or a poor relationship with Yahweh was the cause of their illness. Under this conceptual system, searching for reconciliation with Yahweh became part of the therapeutic process itself. The petitions and thanksgiving rituals related to illness were permeated by the patient's search for reconciliation with the deity. The search also included a concern for "hidden" sins that might have caused the illness.[51]

The fact, and reversibility, of Yahweh's judgments are indisputable where illness is concerned.[52]

Avalos's and Wilkinson's evidence is not the only evidence of linkage between the ritual incantation texts and passages of the Hebrew Bible. Both M. J. Geller and B. Wells observe it in Leviticus 4–5.[53] W. G. E. Watson notes the relationship between the incantation texts and the metaphors of the book of Hosea.[54] K. J. Cathcart notices it in regard to Micah 5.[55] Thus, other texts of the Hebrew Bible seem to reflect thinking similar to that of the Mesopotamian ritual incantation texts.

This is true also of the book of Job. M. B. Dick, B. Gemser, L. J. Sheldon, D. T. Stewart, and R. Westbrook all maintain that the author of Job incorporated the worldview reflected in the Mesopotamian ritual incantations, hymns, prayers, and theodicies in shaping his book.[56] I agree and will return to this point repeatedly throughout this study. It is no accident that

---

50. "While the Old Testament is quite clear that all healing comes from God, it is equally clear that God may send disease, inflicting injury on his people for their disobedience.... Obedience to God's law is the best form of preventative medicine" (J. Wilkinson, *The Bible and Healing: A Medical and Theological Commentary* [Grand Rapids: Eerdmans, 1998], 14–15; citing Exod 15:26; 23:20–26; Lev 26:14–16, 23–26; Ps 38:3–8; Prov 3:7–8; among others also discussed by Avalos.

51. Avalos, *Illness and Health Care*, 244–45.

52. See Bovati, *Re-Establishing Justice*, 123–43, 155–61.

53. Geller, "Šurpu Incantations," 181–92; Wells, *Law of Testimony*, 68–69. Their analyses of precisely how the Šurpu Incantations inform the Leviticus passages differ. I am more closely aligned with Wells's analysis.

54. W. G. E. Watson, "Reflexes of Akkadian Incantations in Hosea," *VT* 34 (1984): 242–47.

55. K. J. Cathcart, "Micah 5, 4–5 and Semitic Incantations," *Bib* 59 (1978): 38–48.

56. Dick, "Legal Metaphor in Job 31," 39; Gemser, "Rîb-Pattern," 127 n. 1; Sheldon, "Job as Hebrew Theodicy," 84; D. T. Stewart, "A Comparison of the Legal Tradition of Job's Oath of Clearance and Ancient Near Eastern Legal Codes" (paper presented at the annual meeting of the Society of Biblical Literature, San Francisco, Calif., 23 November 1992), 2; and R. Westbrook, "Lex Talionis and Exodus, 21, 22–25," *RB* 93 (1986): 59 n. 33.

the book of Job is replete with legal metaphors. Job and his friends embrace wholeheartedly the outlook of the ritual texts and wisdom literature in the ancient Near East in connecting trial law to theodicy. Job's sufferings—his diseases, disabilities, and disasters—are manifestations of God's law. Consequently, the legal metaphors are a crucial element of Job's theodicy. This cognition drives this study in both its fundamental questions—Is there a divine trial in the book of Job and, if so, what does it look like?—and the methods used to answer these questions.

In conclusion, some of the names, ritual texts, and wisdom texts of the ancient Near East indicate that suffering could be attributed to a conviction of sin in a divine trial held by a god or group of gods. The defendant was typically tried *in absentia* and the conviction was often summary. The crime may have been unwitting or the punishment vicarious, that is, suffered because of the sins of one's relatives. Because of these factors and the mercy of the gods, the sufferer could petition the court for a postpenalty accounting of the crime, offer proof of innocence or confession, and request pardon in the case where confession was appropriate. It was believed that such acts would bring both legal and physical relief to the sufferer. The book of Job is an ancient Near Eastern theodicy that contains much legal language. Consequently, this investigation wishes to explore further the legal language in the book of Job in order to discover whether it, in fact, stands in line with other ancient Near Eastern literature and exhibits characteristics of a divine trial. I use Neo-Babylonian trial law as my template for the investigation. I use legal methods in addition to those from Assyriology and biblical studies in pursuit of this end. I turn now to methodology.

# 3

# Reading Law in Job's Story

The methods of this study arise from the supposition that the legal metaphors in the book of Job are of great consequence. The cause of Job's suffering may be a divine lawsuit much like that which was supposed by the sufferers who used the ritual texts delineated in chapter 2 of this study. If this should be the case, the interaction in the Divine Council between God and the Satan may have both legal and theological import for Job. This study will use Neo-Babylonian trial procedure as a framework for investigating whether the book of Job contains a divine trial and, if so, what the trial's exact parameters might be. In this regard, the study uses the Neo-Babylonian information heuristically, as a guide to comprehending the metaphors.[1] Because authors typically draw their literary metaphors from their social world, I suggest that Job's author probably drew his legal metaphors from the legal world of his time. The fundamental methodological assumption of the research here is that the many legal documents of practice from ancient Mesopotamia should reveal the workings of the author's legal world. This knowledge should, in turn, disclose much about the legal metaphors in the book of Job and should assist us in understanding the nature of any possible legal altercation of the book.

The study, therefore, proceeds by a two-step process: the first is Assyriological; the second is biblical. I report the findings from my initial analysis of approximately 340 Neo-Babylonian litigation and related documents,[2] which I studied in order to determine the nature of the court system and trial procedure in the period from the mid-seventh to the fifth

---

1. I do not seek to make numerous definitive historical claims regarding ancient Israelite trial law.
2. Not every case in my data set is discussed or noted in this report of findings. A list of cases in the sample can be found in Appendix A. For more on the sources of trial law in the Neo-Babylonian period, see J. Oelsner, B. Wells, and C. Wunsch, "Neo-Babylonian Period," in *A History of Ancient Near Eastern Law* (ed. R. Westbrook; 2 vols.; Handbook of Oriental Studies 72; Leiden: Brill, 2003), 2:911–14.

century B.C.E.[3] After presenting my tentative view of the Neo-Babylonian trial system, I will use those findings as a conceptual framework by which to investigate the juridical language of the book of Job. My method, therefore, involves legal comparative historical analysis. The use of this method in the project raises several important questions on both the biblical and Assyriological sides of the comparison. This chapter explicates my comparative historical method and addresses those questions.

Moreover, the author's use of legal metaphor in his story raises issues concerning not only the relationship between law and suffering but also the relationship between law and narrative. To discern whether a legal trial is embedded in the narrative of the book, we must ask how the narrative evokes a sense that a trial exists. If the story should reflect the legal procedural rules of the ancient world, then certainly the story provides one important index that it contains a literary trial. Yet that is only one indicator. As I will soon discuss, legal trials also have narratological features. We must, therefore, in our search for a literary trial, also inquire whether the narrativity of the story is in any manner consistent with the narrativity of trial law. Hence, this chapter will additionally address the method I use in exploring the relationship between Neo-Babylonian trial narratives and the narratives of the book of Job. Such method derives from the study of law and literature.

## Biblical Comparative Historical Considerations

The primary question to address with regard to the study's comparative historical method is whether the Neo-Babylonian legal world is at all relevant to the author's legal world. I believe it is highly relevant. This is based on two considerations. First, this particular Mesopotamian legal system was deeply connected to a tradition of litigation procedure that existed throughout the ancient Near East for almost three millennia. While the Neo-Babylonian system demonstrates certain levels of legal innovation and streamlines particular ancient procedures, as demonstrated in chapter 4, the existence of many critical points of contact with prior legal systems can be validated. Thus, the detail gained from the vast data contained in the Neo-Babylonian trial documents provides a helpful window into litigation throughout the ancient Near East. Second, the Neo-Babylonian and/or Persian empires had colonial control over Israel in the period in which the book of Job was most likely composed. It is quite plausible to suggest, then, that the legal system in use by these empires had direct influence on that

---

3. Only my initial and quite tentative findings are reported here. My detailed analysis of Neo-Babylonian trial procedure, using a far larger data set, with selected text editions, is in process toward publication.

of Israel during the period when the author of Job created this work. I will take up these issues one at a time.

As noted in chapter 1, the fund of Israelite trial law is limited. Scholars often supplement their study of aspects of Israelite law with other ancient Near Eastern sources. The large size of the Neo-Babylonian litigation corpus makes it attractive as a means to enhance our knowledge of ancient Near Eastern trial law.[4] Size cannot, however, be the determining factor in the validity of its use. The connection between the comparative sample and the system under study is the critical concern. The degree and quality of the connection that is necessary for suitable use have provoked much discussion in comparative historical circles, both within and beyond the biblical academy. The conversation among scholars of the ancient Near East regarding the appropriateness of the comparative method and the various ways in which it might be applied to scholarly problems of the region is, at this point, quite lengthy and complex.[5] This same debate is also occurring within the subfield of ancient Near Eastern legal history.[6]

Historically, there have been two competing positions. The first argues that some universal principles operated across the ancient Near East as a result of certain shared cultural attributes, such as language structures, scientific reasoning, technological advances, and educational processes. One can, therefore, make fruitful comparisons across the ancient Near East's vast geographic and chronological expanses.[7] Scholars who employ this method often start with the assumption of sameness between cultures and see difference as unusual. The phrase *the comparative approach on the grand scale* is now frequently used to describe this approach, because it has fallen out of favor.[8]

---

4. While this research analyzes carefully approximately 340 Neo-Babylonian litigation records, which I believe is a representative sample, hundreds of other documents are available for study. B. Wells and I in collaboration, have collected over three hundred additional trial records in the Neo-Babylonian dialect. Furthermore, many more documents remain uncollected from the corpus, both published and unpublished. As a result, this study does not claim to be comprehensive nor conclusive in its analysis of Neo-Babylonian trial transcripts and related records, only representative and provisional.

5. The bibliography is now extensive. For selected bibliography, see my, "On the Scales of Righteousness: Law and Story in the Book of Job" (Ph.D. diss., Iliff School of Theology and University of Denver [Colorado Seminary], 2003), 22 n. 6.

6. See, e.g., G. Cardascia, "Droits cunéiformes et droit biblique," in *Proceedings of the 6th World Congress of Jewish Studies* (ed. A. Shinan; Jerusalem: World Union of Jewish Studies, 1977), 1:63–70; H. J. Boecker, *Law and the Administration of Justice in the Old Testament and Ancient East* (trans. J. Moiser; Minneapolis: Augsburg, 1980), 15–19; and the essays in B. M. Levinson, ed., *Theory and Method in Biblical and Cuneiform Law: Revision, Interpolation, and Development* (JSOTSup 181; Sheffield: Sheffield Academic, 1994).

7. M. Malul, *The Comparative Method in Ancient Near Eastern and Biblical Legal Studies* (AOAT 227; Neukirchen-Vluyn: Neukirchener Verlag, 1990), 14–16.

8. This term was first coined by M. Bloch ("Two Strategies of Comparison," in *Comparative Perspectives: Theories and Methods* [ed. A. Etzioni and F. L. Dubow; Boston: Little, Brown,

The second position contends that ancient Near Eastern cultures are most specific in regard to their social artifacts and, thus, cross-cultural comparisons are not easily made. This position accepts E. Durkheim's observation that "[s]ocial facts are functions of the social system of which they are a part; therefore they cannot be understood when they are detached. For this reason, two facts which come from two different societies, cannot be fruitfully compared merely because they seem to resemble one another."[9] Comparisons, then, should be undertaken only when it is determined that there is a clear historical or genetic connection between the cultures and the societal features in comparison.[10] In order to undertake comparisons, according to this approach, one must demonstrate that the cultures and artifacts under study lie in the same "historic stream."[11] Scholars who apply this method often begin with an assumption of difference between cultures and see sameness as atypical. This is known as the contrastive approach and is much in vogue.[12]

The contextual approach is a new position that lies between these two older schools of thought. Scholars using this approach attempt to examine both similarities and differences between cultures.[13] These researchers accept the view that some, but not all, cultural attributes were shared across the ancient Near East. They acknowledge, however, that, even where the societies in comparison shared some fundamental aspects of culture, exactly how those aspects were expressed could have differed. Investiga-

---

1970], 41; cf. S. Talmon, "The 'Comparative Method' in Biblical Interpretation—Principles and Problems," in *Congress Volume: Göttingen, 1977* [VTSup 29; Leiden: Brill, 1977], 320–56; repr. in *Essential Papers on Israel and the Ancient Near East* [ed. F. E. Greenspahn; Essential Papers on Jewish Studies; New York: New York University Press, 1991], 381–419).

9. Cited by Talmon, "'Comparative Method,'" 384; referencing only A. J. F. Kübben, "Comparativists and Non-Comparativists in Anthropology," in *A Handbook of Method in Cultural Anthropology* (ed. R. Naroll and R. Cohen; New York: Columbia University Press, 1970), 582.

10. Malul, *Comparative Method*, 14–16.

11. According to Malul (*Comparative Method*, 13 n. 1), M. J. Herskovits coined this phrase. Talmon also uses the phrase in "Comparative Method," 386, relying on S. C. Thrupp, "Editorial," *Comparative Studies in Society and History* 1 (1958/59): 3; cf. Bloch, "Two Strategies of Comparison," 41.

12. W. W. Hallo, "New Moons and Sabbaths: A Case-Study in the Contrastive Approach," *HUCA* 43 (1977): 1–13.

13. This approach is discussed by W. W. Hallo, "Biblical History in its Near Eastern Setting: The Contextual Approach," in *Scripture in Context: Essays on the Comparative Method* (ed. C. D. Evans, W. W. Hallo, and J. B. White; Pittsburgh: Pickwick, 1980), 2; and idem, "Compare and Contrast: The Contextual Approach to Biblical Literature," in *The Bible in the Light of Cuneiform Literature: Scripture in Context III* (ed. W. W. Hallo, B. W. Jones, and G. L. Mattingly; ANETAS 8; Lewiston, N.Y.: Edwin Mellen, 1990), 1–7. Hallo attributes the term to a 1971 article by P. D. Hanson ("Jewish Apocalyptic Against Its Near Eastern Environment," *RB* 78 [1971]: 33). See Hallo, "Compare and Contrast," 3.

tors using this method often prefer source materials lodged in the most obvious historic stream; they may in some cases, however, view the historic stream more broadly than would a contrastive methodologist. Whatever sources they ultimately select for study are examined for evidence of both similarity and difference. I believe that the contextual approach is the best comparative method when dealing with the legal materials of the ancient Near East.

Within the study of ancient Near Eastern law, contextual comparisons are most critical. It is my view that such law should be examined comparatively on two different levels: the cross-cultural (macro) level and the societal (micro) level. Genetically, legal systems have often been related across cultures. For example, there is substantial philosophical and procedural accord among the common law systems of the world, which are of British origin. So too, we find significant commonalities in the basic philosophy and structures of the Continental legal systems, which are of Roman origin. One cannot fully understand these legal systems without some understanding of their shared legal assumptions.[14] Similarly, there is a legal meta-tradition that is operating across vast time periods and geographic expanses of the ancient Near East.[15] In order to understand any of its legal systems, one must see that system within this broader legal meta-tradition.[16] This is especially important given the gaps in our legal sources from the ancient world and the highly cryptic nature of the legal materials that we possess. Reading across legal systems of similar philosophy and structures will assist us in filling in those lacunae.

---

14. R. Westbrook argues this point particularly well with regard to the common attributes of the legal systems of the ancient Near East. See most importantly *Studies*, 1–8, 133–35; "Covenant Code?" 15–36; and "Cuneiform Law Codes," 210–22.

15. I thank B. Wells for his coining of the term "meta-tradition" to describe those common legal attributes across the ancient Near East.

16. There is much discussion concerning whether or not a meta-tradition exists. For the most important pieces in this discourse since 1990, see the collection of articles in Levinson, *Theory and Method*; B. S. Jackson, "Modeling Biblical Law: The Covenant Code," *CKLR* 70 (1995): 1745–1827; and Roth, "Mesopotamian Legal Traditions," 13–39. I agree with those who argue that the stability and conservatism of law drive the existence of a common legal philosophy and abundant shared attributes in the legal systems of the ancient Near East (see esp. J. J. Finkelstein, *The Ox that Gored* [Transactions of the American Philosophical Society 71.2; Philadelphia: American Philosophical Society, 1981]; S. M. Paul, *Studies in the Book of the Covenant in the Light of Cuneiform and Biblical Law* [VTSup 18; Leiden: Brill, 1970], 4–10; and Westbrook, "Covenant Code," 15–36). Ancient legal systems are not modern legal systems that can adjust and refine to the degree that we find in the West since the late nineteenth century. Nor are we dealing with cultures that use law as a means of social engineering, as began to occur in the West in the early twentieth century. The foundational legal principles of stability and conservatism have ruled the history of law with an iron grip until very recently. For more on this point, see my, "On the Scales of Righteousness," 25-26 n. 17.

32   On the Scales of Righteousness

Comparative work cannot stop there, however, because cultures with shared legal attributes have, historically, adapted those attributes to meet their unique needs and values. Consequently, on the societal level, important divergences can exist in the law of specific cultures, just as one finds in the variations in detail and application of contract law among common law jurisdictions, or even within the different state jurisdictions of the United States. Thus, specific ancient Near Eastern cultures did, in fact, make necessary adjustments to the common legal structures and principles operating across the region in order to reflect their particular needs and values. Comparisons must consider such differences. As a result, this study takes the general view that the more attenuated the connection between cultures or sources being compared, the less valuable that information might potentially be on the societal level and the more careful a researcher must be in employing it.

With respect to litigation, extensive research reveals that cultures across the ancient Near East, excepting in some regards Egypt, did indeed share their elemental procedural structures as we might predict.[17] The many commonalities in legal procedure across the Asian ancient Near East before, during, and after the Neo-Babylonian period are so substantial that it is reasonable to use the Neo-Babylonian litigation documents in comparative studies of litigation in the Hebrew Bible generally, and in Job specifically, whatever the possible date of such works. Furthermore, these commonalities allow us to supplement our knowledge of litigation procedure with documents outside of the Neo-Babylonian corpus in the rare instances where gaps exist in that corpus.

At the same time, not every procedure remained the same in detail and application over time and geography. For example, the fourth chapter of this study will reveal, as previously mentioned, two important changes in

---

17. Documents from Sumer to Hellenistic Uruk contributed to this comparative view. All the major litigation studies were employed (see nn. 38–40 below), as well a large number of more minor studies. Unfortunately, the list is far too cumbersome to cite in its entirety here. See, e.g., L. T. Doty, "Cuneiform Archives from Hellenistic Uruk" (Ph.D. diss., Yale University, 1977); J. D. Fortner, "Adjudicating Entities and Levels of Legal Authority in Lawsuit Records of the Old Babylonian Era" (Ph.D. diss., Hebrew Union College-Jewish Institute of Religion, 1996); R. T. Fuller, "Cuneiform Texts XLVIII: A Transliteration and Translation with Philological Notes, Commentary, and Indices" (Ph.D. diss., Hebrew Union College-Jewish Institute of Religion, 1992); O. R. Gurney, *Middle Babylonian Legal and Economic Texts from Ur* (London: British School of Archaeology in Iraq, 1983); A. G. McDowell, *Jurisdiction in the Workmen's Community of Deir-el-Medina* (Leiden: Nederlands Instituut voor het Nabije Oosten, 1990); M. Schorr, *Urkunde des altbabylonischen Zivil- und Prozessrechts* (Vorderasiatische Bibliothek 5; Leipzig: Hinrichs, 1913); A. Walther, *Das altbabylonischen Gerichtswesen* (Leipziger semitische Studien 6/4–6; Leipzig: Hinrichs, 1917). See also the many litigation studies in R. Westbrook, ed., *A History of Ancient Near Eastern Law* (2 vols.; Handbook of Oriental Studies 72; Leiden: Brill 2003).

ancient Near Eastern law. First, it appears that, during the Neo-Babylonian period, a move away from the use of suprarational evidence occurred in Mesopotamia. This represents an important shift in a Mesopotamian legal tradition that had been relatively stable for almost three millennia—although the seeds of this shift can be noticed long before the Neo-Babylonian period. Second, certain other formalities associated with particular legal procedures in earlier Mesopotamian systems also dropped away in this period. The Neo-Babylonian system is, therefore, not absolutely representative of all legal systems in the ancient Near East over the millennia. We see some differentiation and must, therefore, be wary when making comparisons to systems of greater antiquity with regard to these aspects of litigation. This is not a factor, however, in comparisons of ancient Near Eastern legal systems contemporaneous with the Neo-Babylonian legal system.

Yet, even in comparing systems contemporaneous with the Neo-Babylonian systems, some care must be taken because individual societies adapt aspects of legal systems that are virtually identical at the philosophical and structural levels. If we are to maintain that the Neo-Babylonian and Judean legal systems are very similar during the exilic and postexilic periods, we must attempt to show some nexus between the two systems. I believe that the conquest of Judah by Babylon in 586 B.C.E. created a historical linkage between the two legal systems.

Colonial powers may impose their legal systems, in whole or in part, on conquered regions in order to achieve stability and consistency across their empire. Even where the indigenous legal system of a colonized nation is allowed to remain in place, specific accommodations to the legal system of the colonizer may be made. This is true in both modern and ancient settings.[18] It is, unfortunately, difficult to assess fully the impact of the Neo-Babylonian legal system on the land of Judah during the exilic period. Scholars disagree on the extent of Babylon's decimation of Judah and the level of Babylonian involvement in the region after the temple was destroyed.[19] Even the extent of the destruction of the temple and whether any traditional worship could continue within its walls is under dispute.[20]

---

18. For example, there is clear evidence that Assyria imposed its administrative and legal system in the periphery during the Neo-Assyrian period (Vanderhooft, *Neo-Babylonian Empire*, 82–83, 90; cf. 40).

19. See, e.g., H. M. Barstad, *The Myth of the Empty Land: A Study in the History and Archaeology of Judah during the "Exilic" Period* (SOFS 28; Oslo: Scandinavia University Press, 1996); J. L. Berquist, *Judaism in Persia's Shadow: A Social and Historical Approach* (Minneapolis: Fortress, 1995), 14–15; J. N. Graham, "'Vinedressers and Plowmen': 2 Kings 25:12 and Jeremiah 52:16," *BA* 47 (1984): 55–58; P. Machinist, "Palestine, Administration of (Assyrio-Babylonian)," *ABD* 5:76–80; and Vanderhooft, *Neo-Babylonian Empire*.

20. See esp. Machinist, "Palestine, Administration of," 79.

My opinion is that Judah suffered significant destabilization and was stripped of a fair portion of its governmental structures and personnel during the exilic period. The best evidence for this is that the capital city was moved from Jerusalem to Mizpah. It is, therefore, unlikely that preexilic law could have remained in place without modification when the basic structures that supported it were seriously damaged and the fundamental goals of the area's administration had changed. For this reason, I aver that it is highly probable that Judah felt the impact of the Neo-Babylonian legal system to a substantial degree.

Moreover, Neo-Babylonian influence did not end with the demise of the Neo-Babylonian Empire. It is long established that no changes of consequence to legal procedure occurred after the Persian conquest of the Babylonian Empire until the legal reforms instituted toward the end of the reign of Darius I.[21] This continuity manifested itself not only procedurally, but also substantively,[22] and resulted from the decision of the Persian Empire to use the administrative and legal structures already in place within conquered regions wherever possible.[23] These structures were of

---

21. For example, courts in the reign of Cyrus enforced legal obligations undertaken during the reign of Nabonidus (see, e.g., *Cyr* 332; cf. YOS 7, 91) and prosecuted crimes committed in the prior reign (see, e.g., YOS 7, 7 and 10). M. A. Dandamaev and V. G. Lukonin assert: "[A]t the end of Darius I's reign, reforms in the economic structure and state administration also entailed some changes in the field of private law. . . . Nevertheless, the Achaemenid administration utilized the local law during contact with the Babylonians, and the Persians, who had begun to take an active part in the business life of the country, were guided by Babylonian laws" (*The Culture and Social Institutions of Ancient Iran* [ed. and trans. P. L. Kohl; Cambridge: Cambridge University Press, 1989], 121). See also M. A. Dandamaev, *Slavery in Babylonia: From Nabopolassar to Alexander the Great (626–331 B.C.)* (ed. M. A. Powell and D. B. Weisberg; trans. V. A. Powell; DeKalb, Ill.: Northern Illinois University Press, 1984), 46; P. Koschaker, *Babylonisch-assyrisches Bürgschaftsrecht: Ein Beitrag zur Lehre von Schuld und Haftung* (Leipzig: Teubner, 1911), 150; M. San Nicolò, *Beiträge zur Rechtsgeschichte im Bereiche der keilschriftlichen Rechstquellen* (Cambridge, Mass.: Harvard University Press, 1931), 84; and I. Spar, "Studies in Neo-Babylonian Economic and Legal Texts" (Ph.D. diss., University of Minnesota, 1972), 7.

22. Substantive law is the fundamental law of rights and duties related to particular areas of law, such as, in the modern period, criminal law, tort law, contract law, property law, family law, estates and trusts, and so forth. Such law is to be contrasted with procedural law, which is the mechanism of enforcing or making otherwise effective the rights and duties of those in the society that are established by substantive law. See "Procedural law," *BLD*, 1203; and "Substantive law," *BLD*, 1428.

23. Scholars disagree on the extent of Darius I's reforms, whether there was, in fact, any codification of the law, what any such codification of law might have looked like, and the scope of local authority within the Persian Empire. The bibliography on these questions is substantial. For a diversity of opinion, see, e.g., J. M. Cook, *The Persian Empire* (London: Dent, 1983), 71; M. A. Dandamaev, "Politische und wirtschaftliche Geschichte," in *Beiträge zur Achämenidengeschichte* (ed. G. Walser; Historia 18; Wiesbaden: Franz Steiner, 1972), 27; P. Frei, "Zentralgewalt und Lokalautonomie im Achämenidenreich," in *Reichsidee und Reichsorganisation im Perserreich* (ed. P. Frei and K. Koch; 2nd ed.; OBO 55; Göttingen: Vandenhoeck

Neo-Babylonian origin or under Neo-Babylonian influence across a great swath of land. Additionally, Babylon and the land Beyond the River, which included Judah, were part of one satrapy until at least the early years of Xerxes, if not later,[24] though the different provinces of the satrapy may have been administered distinctly.[25] Even after the period of reform, the litigation documents reflect no major procedural changes. Darius's reforms appear to have been directed at setting local law to writing and unifying the law across the empire to whatever extent possible.[26] The reforms were not meant, however, to be so radical as to disrupt the systems already in place. Rather, they were meant to provide a smooth transition to a more unified system that would permit better management of the empire, while placating any local unrest.[27] L. S. Fried notes that so-called codifications of law within the ancient Near East often served a propagandistic function, that is, to assure the population that the king would establish justice in the land; the work of Darius I was no exception.[28] Thus, the codification was

---

& Ruprecht, 1996), 14–17; A. T. Olmstead, "Darius as Lawgiver," *AJSL* 51 (1934/1935): 247–49; the collection of articles in J. W. Watts, ed., *Persia and Torah: The Theory of Imperial Authorization of the Pentateuch* (SBLSymS 17; Atlanta: Society of Biblical Literature, 2001); and J. Wiesehöfer, "'Reichsgesetz' oder 'Einzelfallgerechtigkeit'? Bemerkungen zu P. Freis These von der Achämenidischen 'Reichs-autorisation,'" *ZABR* 1 (1995): 38–41. I take the view that Darius I did initiate reforms.

24. Following M. W. Stolper, "The Governor of Babylon and Across-the-River in 486 B.C.," *JNES* 4 (1989): 283–305. For a survey of the different positions held regarding the timing of the division of the satrapy, see ibid., 292–93 nn. 9–12.

25. H. G. M. Williamson, "Palestine, Administration of (Persian)," *ABD* 5:82–84.

26. As Dandamaev and Lukonin report: "Intensive work on the codification of the laws of the conquered peoples was carried out during the reign of Darius I, while ancient laws, particularly the Code of Hammurapi, were also studied.... The laws existing in various countries were made uniform within the limits of a given country, while where necessary they were also changed according to the policy of the king" (*Culture and Social Institutions*, 117; cf. 125).

27. J. Blenkinsopp points out that there was a "tensive relationship between centralism and local autonomy, between coercive power projected from the center and provincial self-regulation" ("Was the Pentateuch the Civic and Religious Constitution of the Jewish Ethnos in the Persian Period?" in *Persia and Torah: The Theory of Imperial Authorization of the Pentateuch* [ed. J. W. Watts; SBLSymS 17; Atlanta: Society of Biblical Literature, 2001], 46). He later states: "Darius's action [the codification of Egyptian law recorded with the Demotic Chronicle] was part of a pacification program following on the crisis of 520–519, a crisis that was not confined to Egypt" (ibid., 50). C. Tuplin summarizes: "In short, it was the Persian way to use existing institutions and seek to harness the energies and interests of native dominant classes to their own ends" ("The Administration of the Achaemenid Empire," in *Coinage and Administration in the Athenian and Persian Empires: The Ninth Oxford Symposium on Coinage and Monetary History* [ed. I. Carradice; BAR International Series 343; Oxford: B.A.R., 1987], 112).

28. L. S. Fried, "'You Shall Appoint Judges': Ezra's Mission and the Rescript of Artaxerxes," in *Persia and Torah: The Theory of Imperial Authorization of the Pentateuch* (ed. J. W. Watts; SBLSymS 17; Atlanta: Society of Biblical Literature, 2001), 79–81; cf. J. J. Finkelstein, "Ammiṣaduqa's Edict and the Babylonian 'Law Codes,'" *JCS* 15 (1961): 91–104; and Roth, "Mesopotamian Legal Traditions," 13.

meant to demonstrate that Darius I was bringing justice to all regions of the empire, which would tend to appease the disquieted.

There is rigorous debate regarding the impact of the legal reforms of Darius I on Persian Judah (Yehud).[29] The question is whether Ezra's mandate from Artaxerxes to create a new legal system based on the "law of God" (Ezra 7:11–26) followed the protocol set by Darius I and is, therefore, historical.[30] On this answer turns another salient question: What was the actual extent of Judah's self-rule under the Persian kings? Most scholars have accepted that Ezra's mandate is largely historically accurate and that Judah enjoyed tremendous independence.[31] If the biblical account of Ezra's mandate is based in historical realities, the mandate would lend support to the position that the Neo-Babylonian legal system controlled Judah during the exilic and early postexilic periods. Otherwise there would have been no need for Ezra to establish a new legal system in Judah based on the Law of Moses, as one would have already been in place.[32] A growing number of voices, however, oppose the position that the Persian government authorized Ezra to establish a new legal system based on the religious law of ancient Israel.[33] For example, Fried contends: "There was no self-rule in Judah, as there was none in any province in the Empire."[34] She contends

---

29. For a small sampling of the extensive literature on these questions, see my, "On the Scales of Righteousness," 33 n. 34.

30. One of the problems in the historical analysis is that we do not know to which Artaxerxes (Longimanus, I, or Mnemon) the book of Ezra refers.

31. Noted by L. L. Grabbe, "Reconstructing History from the Book of Ezra," in *Second Temple Studies I. Persian Period* (ed. P. R. Davies; JSOTSup 117; Sheffield: Sheffield Academic, 1991), 98, 105. See, e.g., J. Blenkinsopp, *Ezra-Nehemiah* (OTL; Philadelphia: Westminster, 1988), 144–57; D. J. A. Clines, *Ezra, Nehemiah, Esther* (NBC; Grand Rapids: Eerdmans, 1984), 101–6; G. N. Knoppers, "An Achaemenid Imperial Authorization of Torah in Yehud," in *Persia and Torah: The Theory of Imperial Authorization of the Pentateuch* (ed. J. W. Watts; SBLSymS 17; Atlanta: Society of Biblical Literature, 2001), 115–34; and R. C. Steiner, "The *mbqr* at Qumran, the *episkopos* in the Athenian Empire, and the Meaning of *lbqrʾ* in Ezra 7:14: On the Relation of Ezra's Mission to the Persian Legal Project," *JBL* 120 (2001): 623–46.

32. Cf. G. W. Ahlström, *The History of Ancient Palestine from the Palaeolithic Period to Alexander's Conquest* (ed. D. Edelman, with a contribution by G. O. Rollefson; JSOTSup 146; Sheffield: Sheffield Academic, 1993), 884.

33. See, e.g., L. L. Grabbe, "What was Ezra's Mission?" in *Second Temple Studies 2. Temple Community in the Persian Period* (ed. T. C. Eskenazi and K. H. Richards; JSOTSup 175; Sheffield: Sheffield Academic, 1994), 286–99; and idem, "The Law of Moses in the Ezra Tradition: More Virtual Than Real," in *Persia and Torah: The Theory of Imperial Authorization of the Pentateuch* (ed. J. W. Watts; SBLSymS 17; Atlanta: Society of Biblical Literature, 2001), 91–114; D. Janzen, "The 'Mission' of Ezra and the Persian-Period Temple Community," *JBL* 119 (2000): 621–23; H. Niehr, "Religio-Historical Aspects of the 'Early Post-Exilic' Period," in *The Crisis of Israelite Religion: Transformation of Religious Tradition in Exilic and Post-Exilic Times* (ed. B. Becking and M. C. A. Korpel; OTS 42; Leiden: Brill, 1999), 243; and R. North, "Civil Authority in Ezra," in *Studi in onore di Edoardo Volterra*, vol. 6 (Università di Roma Facoltà di giurisprudenza 45; Milan: Giuffré, 1971), 404.

34. Fried, "You Shall Appoint Judges," 89.

that Ezra's commission was to appoint Persian judges who would judge "according to Persian concepts—not Jewish."[35] G. W. Ahlström argues that Ezra's authority was limited to matters of sacral law and that Persian administration and law ruled the area.[36] Such self-rule was probably less than is traditionally supposed. The preponderance of the evidence seems to establish that the Persians, in an unusual colonial move, did, in principle, allow preexisting or traditional legal systems to remain in place, although that would have been, in many cases, a legal system under the influence of Neo-Babylonian law. In practice, however, the policy was not completely hands-off. All significant administrative and legal operations had to be consistent with the goals of the empire. Total self-rule in Judah, based exclusively on the Hebrew law of God, without any Neo-Babylonian or Persian sway, is, therefore, historically unlikely.

In terms of Mesopotamian influence over the law of Judah in the Persian period, an additional factor was operating. A great deal of Judah's intelligentsia had been exiled to Babylon for a minimum of fifty years and, in many cases, far longer. The immersion of these exiles and their descendants in the legal system of their colonizer would have been complete.[37] When they returned to Judah, they might well have understood and interpreted their law from a Babylonian perspective. It is, therefore, plausible to suggest that Neo-Babylonian law made its influence felt in the judicial system of this land before and during the Persian conquest through direct

---

35. Ibid., 88. Although I agree with much of Fried's work, I take exception to her assertion that all (or nearly all—she seems to contradict herself) of the judges across the Persian Empire were Persian (ibid., 65–67). The Neo-Babylonian prosopographic evidence under the Persian kings indicates otherwise. See, e.g., Baʾu-eriš, the judge named in *A* 32117 (edited in M. T. Roth, "A Case of Contested Status," in *Fs. Sjöberg*, 481–89) and YOS 7, 137; Rimut, the judge mentioned in YOS 7, 137 (royal judge), YOS 7, 151 (judge), YOS 7, 159 (judge of the king); and YOS 7, 161 (judge); and Ṣur- . . . , the *sartennu* (chief judge), Nabu-apla-iddin (judge), Nabu-balsassu-iqbi (judge), Kabti-Marduk (judge), Nabu-ušallim (judge), Rimut-Bel (judge), and Nabu-ašared-ili (judge), all named in *Cyr* 312. Furthermore, the local assemblies, some of which were of specific ethnic composition, probably had far more power than Fried allows. See, e.g., *Camb* 85, where elders of the Egyptians of Babylon constituted the judicial assembly that heard the case (discussed in M. A. Dandamaev, "The Neo-Babylonian Elders," in *Societies and Languages of the Ancient Near East: Studies in Honour of I. M. Diakonoff* [ed. M. A. Dandamaev et al.; Warminster: Aris and Phillips, 1982], 38).

36. Ahlström, *History of Ancient Palestine*, 830. See also K. Koch, "Ezra and the Origins of Judaism," *JSS* 19 (1974): 185; and North, "Civil Authority in Ezra," 404.

37. See generally S. Daiches, *The Jews in Babylonia in the Time of Ezra and Nehemiah according to Babylonian Inscriptions* (London: Publication of Jews' College of London, 1910); and R. Zadok, *The Jews in Babylonia during the Chaldean and Achaemenian Periods according to the Babylonian Sources* (Haifa: Haifa University, 1979); and idem, "The Representation of Foreigners in Neo- and Late-Babylonian Legal Documents (Eighth through Second Centuries B.C.E.)," in *Judah and the Judeans in the Neo-Babylonian Period* (ed. O. Lipschits and J. Blenkinsopp; Winona Lake, Ind.: Eisenbrauns, 2003), 471–589; cf. idem, *On West Semites in Babylonia during the Chaldean and Achaemenian Periods: An Onomastic Study* (Jerusalem: Wanaarta, 1977).

application of its law in colonial areas and through the influence of its legal system on the legal worldview of Judahites once held in Babylonian captivity. The author of Job might even have been one of those individuals. Consequently, employing the Neo-Babylonian legal system in a comparative study of the exilic or postexilic Judean legal system on both the cross-cultural (macro) and societal (micro) levels is highly useful. This, in turn, makes a knowledge of Neo-Babylonian law relevant for understanding legal aspects of the Joban author's social world.

## Assyriological Considerations

The Assyriological work of this project also presents some methodological assumptions and difficulties. The greatest obstacle to Joban forensic investigators has been the limit of our knowledge of litigation in the ancient Near East generally. It is impossible to do comparative work where there is no comparative data. Current scholarship regarding ancient Near Eastern legal procedure is quite restricted. Few large studies existed before the 1990s.[38] While scholars have recently offered further insight into legal procedure during a number of earlier periods of Mesopotamian history,[39] no more comprehensive study of litigation during the Neo-Babylonian period has been published to date.[40] Additionally, most of the larger studies of

---

38. See primarily E. Cuq, "Essai sur l'organisation judiciaire de la Chaldée à l'époque de la première dynastie babylonienne," *RA* 7 (1910): 65–101; A. Falkenstein, *Die neusumerischen Gerichtsurkunde* (3 vols.; ABAW 39, 40, 44; Munich: Bayerischen Akademie der Wissenschaften, 1956–1957); Lautner, *Altbabylonischen Prozessrechte*; R. E. Hayden, "Court Procedure at Nuzi" (Ph.D. diss., Brandeis University, 1962); and R. A. Veenker, "The Old Babylonian Judiciary and Legal Procedure" (Ph.D. diss., Hebrew Union College-Jewish Institute of Religion, 1967).

39. See, e.g., E. Dombradi, *Die Darstellung des Rechtsaustrags in den Altbabylonischen Prozessurkunden* (2 vols.; Freiburger Altorientalische Studien 20; Stuttgart: Franz Steiner, 1996); and R. M. Jas, *Neo-Assyrian Judicial Procedures* (SAAS 5; Helsinki: Neo-Assyrian Text Corpus Project-University of Helsinki, 1996).

40. There are, however, numerous smaller studies of litigation in the Neo-Babylonian period. M. San Nicolò, who had a great interest in the legal history of this era, wrote numerous books and articles, many of which offered insights into litigation. Some of the most important for purposes of this study are: "Parerga Babylonica VII: Der §8 des Gesetzbuches Ḫammurapis in den neubabylonischen Urkunden," *ArOr* 4 (1932): 327–48; "Parerga Babylonica IX: Der Monstreprozeß des Gimillu, eines širku von Eanna," *ArOr* 5 (1933): 61–77; "Parerga Babylonica XI: Die *maš'altu*-Urkunden im neubabylonischen Strafverfahren," *ArOr* 5 (1933): 287–302; "Eine Kleine Gefängnismeuterei in Eanna zur Zeit des Kambyses," in *Festschrift für Leopold Wenger: Zu seinem 70. Geburtstag dargebracht von Freunden, Fachgenossen und Schülern* (2 vols.; Münchener Beiträge zur Papyrusforschung und antiken Rechtsgeschichte 34–35; Munich: Beck, 1945), 2:1–10. F. Joannès is currently involved in studying litigation in this period. His works include, "La pratique du serment à l'époque néo-

Reading Law in Job's Story   39

ancient Near Eastern litigation have a philological focus rather than a legal-historical one.[41] These two factors have resulted in a substantial gap in ancient Near Eastern legal-historical scholarship. This gap has brought the added misfortune of hampering comparative studies of the legal materials in the book of Job. One of the goals of this study is to begin to fill this legal-historical lacuna by uncovering the machinery of justice in the Neo-Babylonian period—that is, those formal steps that gave shape to a legal action and were used to enforce the culture's substantive legal rights and duties.[42] Although need in the Joban project was the mother of this inven-

---

babylonienne," in *Jurer et maudire: pratiques politiques et usages juridiques du serment dans le Proche-Orient ancien* (ed. S. Lafont; Paris: L'Harmattan, 1997), 163–74; and "Textes judiciaries néo-babyloniens," 201–39. C. Wunsch is also examining litigation in the Neo-Babylonian period and has published "Und die Richter berieten . . . : Streitfälle in Babylon aus der Zeit Neriglissars und Nabonids," *AfO* 44–45 (1997–1998): 59–100; "Eine Richterurkunde aus der Zeit Neriglissars," in *Arbor Scientiae: Estudios del Proximo Oriente Antiguo dedicados a Gregorio del Olmo Lete con ocasión de su 65 aniversario* (ed. J. Sanmartín et al.), *Aula Orientalis* 17–18 (1999–2000): 241–54; *Das Egibi-Archiv I: Die Felder und Gärten* (2 vols.; Cuneiform Monographs 20A-B; Groningen: STYX, 2000); "Neubabylonische Geschäftsleute und ihre Beziehungen zu Palast- und Tempelverwaltungen: Das Beispiel der Familie Egibi," in *Interdependency of Institutions and Private Entrepreneurs: Proceedings of the Second MOS Symposium (Leiden: 1998)* (ed. A. C. V. M. Bongenaar; Istanbul: Nederlands Historisch-Archaeologisch Instituut, 2000), 95–118; and "Die Richter des Nabonid." in *Fs. Oelsner*, 557–98. The most recent study is Oelsner et al, "Neo-Babylonian Period," 911–74. The above-mentioned pieces are but a few items of a large bibliography.

41. See, e.g., Jas, *Neo-Assyrian Judicial Procedures*; and Veenker, "Old Babylonian Judiciary." E. Dombradi's study of Old Babylonian civil suits is predominantly philological, but the second half of the study does organize itself around legal administration and procedure (*Die Darstellung des Rechtsaustrags*). K. Radner's work on Neo-Assyrian private legal documents is also similarly organized, although litigation-related documents are not central to the work (*Die neuassyrischen Privatrechtsurkunden als Quelle für Mensch und Umwelt* [SAAS 6; Helsinki: Neo-Assyrian Text Corpus Project, 1997]).

42. Although philological study is essential, we can, at times, lose sight of the legal-historical forest for our study of the philological trees. Different verbal signifiers can be used to indicate the same signified concept within ancient legal systems. For example, many variants are used in the Neo-Babylonian period to articulate that a judge has rendered his judgment or decided the case. *RA* 12, 6–7 is an excellent illustration of this point because the scribal narrator uses three different expressions to convey the deciding of the case: (1) *dīn dīnu*; (2) *dīn dabābu*; and (3) *dīn bâru*. In the same case, the plaintiff asks for judgment with the words *dīn epēšu*. Furthermore, *dīn dīnu* may be coupled with *purussâ parāsu* to convey this same idea (see, e.g., Dalley *Edinburgh* 69). We also find the expression *purussâ šakānu* used to the same purpose in other texts (see, e.g., AnOr 8, 56; *AfO* 44, 78 no. 6; *AfO* 44, 88 no. 19, TCL 13, 222, and TCL 13, 219 [= *Nbn* 720]). R. Westbrook acknowledges that different words or expressions can convey the same legal idea ("Recensiones: Eva Dombradi, *Darstellung des Rechtsaustrags in den Altbabylonischen Prozessurkunden*," *Orientalia* n.s. 68 [1999]: 123.) He points out, however, that, in some instances, it can be difficult to determine whether there are substantive legal differences represented in the use of particular words or whether they function as simple synonyms. In discussing the court's use of the words *burrum*, *kinnum*, and *nasāḫum* to describe the actions of both witnesses and judges with regard to facts at issue in a case, West-

tion, the result has scholarly integrity apart from its benefits to Joban scholarship.

This contribution to a better understanding of ancient Near Eastern litigation from a legal-historical perspective begins with a report of my examination of approximately 340 Neo-Babylonian litigation records and related documents, such as letters and sale documents that refer to some actual or intended litigation, from the seventh to fifth centuries B.C.E.[43] Even though

---

brook asks: "In modern systems, . . . witnesses *prove* facts but only judges can *establish* facts. Is there a different concept of the court's role at issue here, or merely an ambiguity of language, which did not disturb the pragmatic [Old] Babylonian mind?" (ibid.). My position is that the intense formality often found in earlier periods of ancient Near Eastern legal history was loosening, and, therefore, we have many instances where there is simply more than one way for the court to communicate the same legal action, idea, or consequence. As a result, a methodological focus on the mechanism of justice, rather than word studies, may reveal some connections that might be otherwise overlooked.

43. Letters, sale documents, and even literary texts can give us insight into litigation and court procedure in this period. Letters often reveal pretrial procedures that are not typically recorded, such as the demand, searches for missing parties, arrest procedures, prison conditions, jurisdictional questions, and certain late-stage trial procedures, including settlements and executions of judgment (see, e.g., BIN 1, 49; CT 22, 105; 22, 210; 22, 202; 22, 234; UrET 4, 191, and YOS 3, 182; cf. Lindenberger 14, 31, 32, 40, and 47 [all Aramaic], and OIP 114, 5; 114, 19; 114, 21; and 114, 109). Moreover, in some circumstances, sale documents offer up information about prior lawsuits. For example, *AfO* 17, 2 is a sale document that discusses an underlying lawsuit that resulted in a forfeiture of property and its sale. For further discussion of this text, see E. Weidner, "Hochverat gegen Nebukadnezar II: Ein Grosswürdenträger vor dem Königsgericht," *AfO* 17 (1954–56): 1–9; and Dandamaev, *Slavery in Babylonia*, 106. Literary compositions can also reveal information about certain legal procedures (R. Westbrook, "The Trial Scene in the Iliad," *HSCP* 94 [1991]: 70). For example, CT 46, 45 is a literary composition that contains a very detailed description of the river ordeal. Regarding this text, see primarily B. F. Foster, *Before the Muses: An Anthology of Akkadian Literature* (2 vols.; 2nd ed.; Bethesda, Md.: CDL, 1996), 748–52 no. 6.13; T. Frymer-Kensky, "The Judicial Ordeal in the Ancient Near East" (2 vols.; Ph.D. diss., Yale University, 1977), 462–73; and W. G. Lambert, "Nebuchadnezzar King of Justice," *Iraq* 27 (1965): 1–11. The text is discussed also in P.-A. Beaulieu, "A Note on the River Ordeal in the Literary Text 'Nebuchadnezzar King of Justice,'" *NABU* (1992–93): 58–60; J. Bottéro, "L'ordalie en Mésopotamie ancienne," *Annali della Scuola Normale Superiore di Pisa* 11 (1981): 1005–67; and Dandamaev, *Slavery in Babylonia*, 24. Nevertheless, S. Greengus rightly warns us that, while "literary sources may faithfully mirror the activities of life, . . . they may also contain invention and fantasy" ("The Old Babylonian Marriage Contract," *JAOS* 89 [1969]: 517). Greengus maintains that we should accept such evidence only to the extent that it "can be correlated with practices revealed in documents from daily life" (ibid.). Unfortunately, that is not always possible. Literary compositions do manipulate law and legal scenarios to accomplish their literary purposes, and such compositions may use law from periods different from the one in which the document is set. At the same time, there must be sufficient points of contact between the social realities of the text and those behind the text for the text to make sense in the mind of the reader. Thus, literary compositions can be a useful source of historical information, even if they are not the best source of such information and must be used with care. See the discussion in chapter 4 for further development of this idea.

these are not all the records from the period, this is a representative sample both of the surviving documents and of litigation in the period.[44] This latter conclusion is not obvious, however, since most records did not survive. The bulk of the litigation records in this sample are cuneiform records from the archives of the Eanna Temple at Uruk and the Ebabbar Temple from Sippar, as well as from a few private archives of economically important families in southern Mesopotamia.[45] This creates two potential problems regarding the integrity of our source data.

The first relates to the fact that, as the Neo-Babylonian period progressed into the Persian period, the *lingua franca* of the ancient Near East shifted from Akkadian to Aramaic.[46] Consequently, we would expect an increasing number of legal documents to have been written in Aramaic, particularly those issuing forth from the center of the Persian Empire.[47] Such legal documents would have generally been written on perishable materials, and in fact, few have survived. The question this leaves is whether the Aramaic materials might have demonstrated legal procedures different from those in the cuneiform record, which originated in a peripheral region of the Persian Empire and which, therefore, was under some level of local control. There is simply no way to know. What we do have, however, is a sizable surviving remnant from an important area of the Persian Empire that had once controlled a considerable portion of the empire's land, including Judah. Those records document the existence of a very sophisticated and comprehensive court system that does not appear to have particular quirks. With rare exception, the documents reflect the continuation of an ancient legal tradition. Where apparent breaks from the tradition did occur, the seeds of that change can be found in older systems.

---

44. See n. 4 above.

45. Collection of the study's sample was accomplished through careful search of the known collections of Neo-Babylonian document copies and journals dealing with ancient Near Eastern studies. I did not collate any tablets for purposes of this study. Copies that seemed especially problematic were dropped from the sample or used only to represent points that seemed clear on the face of the copy. Documents cited herein are typically noted by reference to the cuneiform copy in my possession, whether found in one of the large collections of copies or in an article that also includes a transliteration and/or a translation of the cuneiform copy.

46. Cf. Dandamaev and Lukonin, *Culture and Social Institutions*, 112–16.

47. D. S. Vanderhooft asserts, however, with regard to a similar quandary in the Neo-Babylonian archival evidence related to imperial administration: "The thesis that much of the documentation may have been written in Phoenician or Aramaic and upon perishable materials is probable, but hard to prove" (*Neo-Babylonian Empire*, 62 n. 3). Moreover, Dandamaev and Lukonin state that, in spite of the widespread use of Aramaic, certain areas of the empire used their native tongue for legal documents, citing Demotic legal texts in Egypt and Akkadian texts in Babylon (*Culture and Social Institutions*, 115). Nevertheless, based on the gaps in the substantive law of the trial documents, it is reasonable to suggest that there are many lost documents in both the cuneiform and Aramaic script.

Additionally, much of what we find in the southern Mesopotamian legal records is confirmed by the biblical record, which demonstrates a connection between systems with different language bases. Consequently, it is doubtful that there were substantial differences between the Persian system at the heart of the empire and what is manifested in the cuneiform record from southern Mesopotamia.

Second, the limitations of our archaeological finds might also restrict our ability to answer precisely the question concerning whether significant differences in legal procedure existed between the temple and secular courts. Because the lion's share of the records come from the temple courts, it is currently impossible to do a comprehensive analysis of the issue.[48] While M. San Nicolò felt that he could speculate as to certain procedural differences, the particular differences about which he opines are clearly not established based on the collection amassed here.[49] As is more fully discussed in chapter 4, it appears that the two courts had identical procedures available to them and functioned in quite similar ways. Owing to their similarity at the trial court level, this study includes tablets from both courts in its sample.[50]

With regard to the nature of the records, the sample includes records of trials that the modern legal mind might consider both civil and criminal in nature because I accept as valid J. Renger's view that the modern distinction between civil and criminal law is unhelpful when studying ancient Near Eastern law and the procedures that govern its enforcement.[51] The differences between the various types of harms and their compensation are more graduated than sharply stepped in the ancient world. Hence, their distinction is not as great as it is in the modern world. Nor does any civil/criminal distinction manifest itself procedurally, as the evidence collected here bears out. Even litigation based in breach of contract or other economic disputes does not demonstrate considerable variation in basic form from that found in the injury records, although certain procedures are more commonly used therein while others recede into the background. Consequently, this study does not distinguish between civil and criminal procedure and employs all litigation records in determining its views.

---

48. See, however, the important study of the Babylonian secular courts by C. Wunsch ("Richter Berieten," 59–100).

49. San Nicolò, "Eine Kleine Gefängnismeuterei," 8–10.

50. A more thorough study should be undertaken, however, in order to resolve this issue with better accuracy.

51. J. Renger, "Wrongdoing and Its Sanctions: On 'Criminal' and 'Civil' Law in the Old Babylonian Period," *The Treatment of Criminals in the Ancient Near East* (ed. J. Sasson; *JESHO* 20; Leiden: Brill, 1977), 71–72; see also Westbrook, *Studies*, 8; and idem, "Punishments and Crimes," *ABD* 5:548; disagreeing with A. Phillips, *Ancient Israel's Criminal Law: A New Approach to the Decalogue* (Oxford: Blackwell, 1970).

This study examines a generous number of records because most ancient trial accounts were partial and quite brief. Writing was a cumbersome process in the ancient world, and only what was most essential is reflected in the records.[52] Because of the need for brevity, what records we do have are often very cryptic and almost impossible to decipher without consideration of their larger context.[53] They typically do not demonstrate any similarity to modern trial pleadings, transcripts, or judicial opinions at either our trial or appellate court levels. Indeed, in the Neo-Babylonian period, we have no document that records all the litigation procedures that are available to a court.[54] An ancient litigation record will often address just one aspect or phase of a trial.[55] Verdict records typically do not contain their justification or reasoning.[56] The courts' criteria for deciding which pre-verdict matters needed to be recorded and how they might have used such records in deciding the case are not completely clear from the records.[57]

Additionally, ancient courts sometimes conducted investigations and

---

52. Certain of these documents are memoranda and are particularly short. Such records are signified by the presence of the word *taḫsistu* at the end of the document (see, e.g., *BIN 1*, 142; *TCL 13*, 212; and *VAS 6*, 38). The largest trial transcript that we have is YOS 7, 7, now known as the "Monster Trial" (San Nicolò, "Monstreprozeß," 61–77). In it, one Gimillu, an incorrigibly corrupt temple official, is tried on twelve counts of theft of temple property. It contains 148 lines of text, including a list of the trial's many witnesses. Gimillu was involved not only in this case; he was also involved in fifteen other cases of which I am aware. They date from 539 to 521 B.C.E. For more about the criminal exploits of Gimillu, see Dandamaev, *Slavery in Babylonia*, 533–37. CT 2, 2 is also is a very lengthy transcript. It records, however, a complex pre-trial investigation in which the suspect was cleared, rather than a trial.

53. See, e.g., GCCI 2, 350 and YOS 6, 60.

54. It is therefore doubtful that every procedure available to the court was used in each case.

55. For instance, a single record might speak only to an accusation (see, e.g., AnOr 8, 21; TCL 13, 134; and VAS 6, 82), a summons (see, e.g., *BIN 1*, 142 and *Nbn* 343), a confession (see, e.g., YOS 6, 79 [= YOS 6, 80]), a witness statement (see, e.g., Sack 78; TCL 13, 124; YOS 6, 57, 80, 186; and YOS 7, 102), the verdict (see, e.g., TCL 13, 147 and YOS 7, 56), a list of witnesses at trial (see, e.g., TCL 13, 212; cf. YOS 17, 320), the execution of the judgment (see, e.g., NBDM 28), post-trial release of liability (see, e.g., TCL 12, 26 and 115), or other single facet of what was most likely an involved trial process.

56. See, e.g., AnOr 8, 74, 79; BE 8/1, 42, *Camb* 321, *Iraq* 13 (1951) 96–97, and TCL 12, 86; cf. O 3714 of the Royal Museum of Brussels, which is an Aramaic verdict document (translation given in E. Lipiński, "Textes juridiques et économiques araméens," *AAASH* 22 [1974]: 373–79). We find, however, two remarkable exceptions to this rule in Dalley *Edinburgh* 69 and *RA* 12, 6–7.

57. It seems likely that one reason for taking down certain witness statements and other pre- and mid-trial matters is that witnesses might not be available at a later time, either because they are moving or the trial is moving. TCL 1, 35 and VAS 16, 181 demonstrate that, in the Old Babylonian period, tablets were transported to be used as evidence in other locations. Unfortunately, we have no direct evidence of the movement of tablets in this research's sample.

trials in stages over an extended period, just as in the modern world.[58] This means that different aspects of the trial might well be found on discrete tablets. We even have two documents from one case that record what appears to be the original setting of a hearing date in the case and then an order of continuance of the matter, which delayed the hearing by several weeks.[59] To complicate matters further, different phases of the arrest and trial of an individual might be held in different geographic locations; a case might require that witnesses or evidence be transported across jurisdictions for trial elsewhere; the venue (location) of a case might be moved midstream; or the case might be moved from one court to another.[60] Fur-

---

58. See, e.g., AnOr 8, 56 and YOS 7, 96; cf. TCL 13, 219 [= *Nbn* 720] and YOS 6, 144. We also have an example of a very early Neo-Babylonian trial record, wherein the court acknowledged that the recording of various phases of the case was, or would be, set forth on different tablets (*BaghM* 5, 15). After the verdict, which is broken in part, the court states: "A tablet of not returning and suing Nabu-damiq (the plaintiff) against Nabu-ušallim (the defendant) [made out/established]." (H. Hunger reconstructed the broken verb in the preterite, but it might have been in the durative ["Das Archiv des Nabû-Ušallim," *BaghM* 5 (1970): 222]). Other verdict documents often contain a court order that the plaintiff not return and sue (see, e.g., *ROM* 2, 38); thus, *BaghM* 5, 15 reflects a two-stage verdict process. Further evidence that in this period some cases occurred in stages is found in OIP 114, 110, which records that a judge had taken testimony in a dispute earlier, but had not yet decided the case. The letter writer implores the judge to send the parties to the river ordeal to test their words. Moreover, the conditional verdict tablets of the Neo-Babylonian period indicate that the court had the power to allow additional testimony to be taken at a later hearing. These documents are discussed at length by B. Wells in *The Law of Testimony in the Pentateuchal Codes*, 108-26 and in chapter 4 of this study. For further investigation concerning the possibility that a trial could consist of a number of separate hearings, see generally San Nicolò, "Die *maš'altu*-Urkunden," 301–2; idem, "Eine kleine Gefängnismeuterei," 8–9; and I. Spar, "Three Neo-Babylonian Trial Depositions from Uruk," in *Studies in Honor of Tom B. Jones* (ed. M. A. Powell and R. H. Sack; AOAT 203; Neukirchen-Vluyn: Neukirchener Verlag, 1979), 157–72.

59. TCL 12, 96 and YOS 6, 153 reflect a dispute over the repayment of a debt that transpired in stages (fortuitously, we have two debt guarantee documents related to the case that were executed two years prior [*JCS* 9, 26 and YOS 6, 119]; we also have the original debt document of a secondary case to which the court refers in the course of this litigation [YOS 6, 105]). In TCL 12, 96, the court ordered a man to deliver his brother to the court for repayment of one-half of a debt, upon which they were both liable, within eleven days. In the second document, YOS 6, 153, which was executed two days later, the court gave him three months to bring in his brother. Consequently, TCL 12, 96 appears to be a hearing setting and YOS 6, 153, an order of continuance in the case. (It should be noted that J. W. Snyder's discussion of these tablets is imprecise ["Babylonian Suretyship Litigation: A Case History," *JCS* 9 (1955): 25–28]. He misreads the two original guarantee documents as litigation-related. While *JCS* 9, 26 has some unusual features for a debt guarantee contract, it does contain the standard guarantee language before adding a provision that the guarantor will have no rights against the creditor, but only against the debtor. Thus, the litigation itself did not extend over two years, as Snyder claims. Furthermore, his focus on the small differences in the two litigation tablets, rather than on their broader commonalities, causes him to miss that the second document is an order of continuance of the case.)

60. See, e.g., *CT* 22, 210, 228, 229, 234, 235; *IMT* 105 (joined to *EE* 109); *Durand Textes*

ther, only by collecting a large number of documents can we locate the trial records of co-defendants, co-conspirators, aiders and abettors, and similarly connected persons, whose cases might be found on different tablets.[61] Related and collateral matters might also be found on discrete tablets.[62] Thus, we can comprehend the legal procedural system only by pasting together a number of disjointed images into a more unified whole.

Finally, I will clarify the use of some more modern legal vocabulary and concepts in the my exploration of ancient Near Eastern law. I do not mean to suggest by such use that ancient Babylonians—or Israelites—thought in modern legal categories. They did not. H. J. Boecker warns strongly against identifying modern ideas with ancient facts in an uncritical manner.[63] He further advises that the correspondence between modern and ancient legal terms, practices, and categories must always be demonstrated, not presumed. In spite of the fact that the ancients did not think in modern legal terms, we do, and, thus, modern legal categories are, at a minimum, a useful way for us to enter into a more refined discourse concerning law in the ancient Near East. Just as we have brought the modern scholarly vocabularies, principles, and techniques of history, literature, comparative studies,

---

*babyloniens* 6; TCL 13, 222; VAS 6, 99; YOS 7, 137 and 189; cf. YOS 7, 177. YOS 7, 137 seems the clearest exemplar of an extradition order that we have. YOS 7, 115 is either a writ of appeal or an extradition order. The former is the better understanding of the text, in accord with San Nicolò, "Gesetzbuches Ḫammurapis," 338–39. Questions related to venue and trial removal are issues also in need of additional study.

61. One set of related cases is documented in YOS 6, 191, 214, and 235. They were all written on the same day during the twelfth year of Nabonidus in the Eanna Temple at Uruk, and all three involved a theft or embezzlement by a certain Itti-Šamaš-balaṭu. In YOS 6, 235, Itti-Šamaš-balaṭu is charged with theft or embezzlement of temple precious metals. YOS 6, 191 and 214 address who received the stolen goods from him and another thief, Kalba-Ba'u, his possible co-defendant. YOS 6, 175 may be a related case as well because it chronicles another search for the fence of Kalba-Ba'u by this same court just five days earlier. According to Joannès, AnOr 8, 21; GCCI 2, 350; and *JCS* 28, 45 no. 39, all appear to be documents that are related to the conviction of those involved in another theft ring ("Textes judiciaries néo-babyloniens," 212, 215–17). There are, however, some discrepancies among and oddities in the documents that might cause one to believe that they are not connected to the same case, as Joannès proposes. The most logical explanation for the texts, in my opinion, is that the ring, led by one Isinnaya (who apparently confessed the names of most, but not all, of his gang in AnOr 8, 21), has been accused of multiple counts of theft, and the court must sort out all of their criminal activity over some period of time. How proximate these particular tablets are in time is uncertain, however, because GCCI 2, 350 and *JCS* 28, 45 no. 39 are missing dates.

62. See, e.g., *Cyr* 311 and 312, which are tablets recorded within five days of each other, and related to a marriage contract dispute involving one groom and two brides, one of whom was jilted. See additionally the documents published and discussed in M. T. Roth, "ᶠTašamētu-damqat and Daughters," in *Fs. Oelsner*, 387–400. Other series of documents are discussed in chapter 4 below.

63. Boecker, *Administration of Justice*, 16-18. When I refer to modern law, I mean the common and civil law systems, which include most of the world's legal systems today.

sociology, and anthropology to bear on biblical texts and, in so doing, have discovered more of the profound complexity of ancient life, it is equally important to bring modern legal concepts to bear in our discussions of ancient Near Eastern law. If our prior experience with new methodologies has any meaning, then to avoid this conversation for fear of misunderstanding our cultural forebearers is to assure that we will only partially understand them. Although we must remain cognizant of the difficulties that can arise when we apply overbroadly or irresponsibly the methods, data, and theories of modern social-scientific approaches, including a legal approach, to refuse to explore what a legal method might reveal during the discourse concerning biblical law would be most unfortunate. The field is slowly beginning to recognize this and bring modern legal concepts to bear on the conversation.[64]

This study seeks to offer a legal-historical analysis of Neo-Babylonian records. Describing such findings demands the use of modern legal terms as employed by legal historians. Consequently, I will utilize the vocabulary of modern legal-historical analysis in order to better explicate some basic principles of ancient Near Eastern law, while attempting to be faithful to ancient Near Eastern legal philosophy.

## Genre and Narratological Considerations

I have concentrated thus far on the biblical and Assyriological historical presuppositions and methods that undergird my research. Nonetheless, this study is fundamentally literary in nature because it is a study of legal metaphors. Literary issues, therefore, must not be ignored. I now address the literary presuppositions and methods of the investigation.

In this study I seek to determine whether the author of Job used legal metaphors to embed a legal trial within his narrative. In order to draw a conclusion, one must probe how one recognizes a trial and a trial record. What constitutes a trial? What are its forms and features? How does one discern the trial record genre? This inquiry is certainly important in the Assyriological work itself, because many litigation texts have missed scholars' notice. It becomes still more critical in the Joban work, because we are inquiring whether a trial is embedded in a story narrative, which makes the investigation still more difficult. Certainly if known legal vocabulary should appear in the text, this will assist us in the matter. Identification of trial records also demands that one look for litigation concepts, categories,

---

64. See, e.g., R. Westbrook, *Property and the Family in Biblical Law* (JSOTSup 113; Sheffield: JSOT Press, 1991) 24-35; and G. P. Miller, "Contracts of Genesis," *Journal of Legal Studies* 22 (1993): 15-45.

and features, such as an accusation, testimony markers, a defendant statement and so forth, because, as discussed previously, not all writings that have legal effect manifest the same identifiable vocabulary.[65] Finally, one must explore the narratological traits of trial records because legal narratives have special narrative features. Only after one determines what constitutes a trial genre can one ask whether the book of Job replicates these features within its pages.

It may seem odd, at first glace, to investigate the literary structure of trial records, because we typically do not think of trials as narratives. Yet all trials are narratives and contain narratives because all trials involve stories. Parties and witnesses tell stories at trial.[66] Such stories have literary features. Thus, exploring the narrativity of trial records is both possible and essential. Until we know what constitutes trial narratives and what constitutes a trial record in the ancient world, it will be difficult to ascertain whether the book of Job contains something in the nature of a trial or a trial record.

Legal narratives have much in common with other types of narrative. We can usually recognize a story when we hear one in whatever setting it arises. Nonetheless, some differences exist between legal and nonlegal stories owing to the nature of a trial and how much is at stake. Consequently, legal stories have five special attributes.[67] First, a trial has multiple strands of narrative because the parties and witnesses tell different stories during the course of a trial. Second, those narrative strands are in conflict. Witnesses typically represent a position; they take one side in a lawsuit. Their stories arise from their distinct points of view, and they disagree.[68] Third, these stories are in competition before an adjudicator, who will resolve the conflict. Thus, the parties and witnesses seek to persuade through their narratives.[69] Fourth, trial stories are often fractured. They are not necessarily presented in a smooth, uninterrupted manner. For example, in America each witness tells his or her story through a series of question-and-answer periods. He or she may not be able to present the facts in either a logical or chronological order.[70] Fifth, legal narratives are regulated not just by cus-

---

65. See n. 42 above.
66. P. Gewirtz observes: "As a descriptive matter, we all know that trials involve the telling of stories" ("Narrative and Rhetoric in the Law," in *Law's Stories: Narrative and Rhetoric in the Law* [ed. P. Brooks and P. Gewirtz; New Haven: Yale University Press, 1996], 7).
67. Ibid., 2-22.
68. Gewirtz continues: "[W]itnesses are sponsored storytellers ... ," limited only by the "ritual oaths" they are required to take (ibid., 7).
69. "[O]ne side's narrative is constantly being met by the other side's counternarrative (or sidestepping narrative), so that 'reality' is always disassembled into multiple, conflicting, and partly overlapping versions, each version presented as true, each fighting to be declared 'what really happened' — with very high stakes riding on that ultimate declaration" (ibid., 8).
70. "[O]ne side does not get to tell its story, then the other side. Instead, the main part

tomary narratological rules but also by the rules of legal procedure and evidence.⁷¹ Gewirtz notes that the rules of procedure and evidence arose, in fact, because the law's stories are so fundamental to the law. These rules, which developed over an extended historical period, constitute a system of regulation that governs what stories may be told, by whom, and in what manner within the legal setting.⁷² Legal procedure, therefore, sets the bounds of legal storytelling. Indeed, legal procedure is the most important mechanism controlling the law's literary production.⁷³

---

of each side's story must be presented through evidence, not by a single person in a continuous narrative. Each side has to present its story by calling witnesses to offer elements of the story piecemeal.... Witnesses, moreover, do not usually tell their stories as uninterrupted narratives. All stories must be elicited by a series of questions and answers, and the form of the questioning and answering is governed by an elaborate system of rules. In addition, because a witness's knowledge of the case is usually selective, that person's story is rarely a narrative with beginning, middle, and end (rarely, at least, do its beginning, middle, and end correspond to those of the plaintiff's or defendant's narrative). Rather, a witness's story usually furnishes discrete pieces in a mosaic whose overall shape emerges only as the trial progresses. Neither side is allowed to keep its perspective uninterruptedly before the decisionmaker until its overall story can be fully presented. Instead, immediately after one side elicits a witness's story, the opposing side cross-examines, thereby introducing the opposing side's perspective even as the first side's story is unfolding" (ibid., 7-8). B. S. Jackson rightly points out, however, that the law's stories are substantially less fractured under inquisitorial systems of adjudication, as we have in the ancient Near East, than they are the adversarial model with which common law jurisdictions are most familiar ("Narrative Models in Legal Proof," *Narrative and the Legal Discourse: A Reader in Storytelling and the Law* [ed. D. R. Papke; Liverpool: Deborah Charles, 1991], 161-62). This results from inquisitorial systems' cooperative approach to conflict resolution, which is not the basis of adversarial systems. The trials of inquisitorial systems, therefore, do not show the heightened level of conflict or story fracturing that one finds in the trials of adversarial systems.

71. Gewirtz explains: "It is the fragmentation and contending multiplicities of narrative, regulated by special rules of narrative form and shaping, that marks the central distinctiveness of narratives at trial—along with, obviously, the high stakes in how the narrative combat is resolved" ("Narrative and Rhetoric," 8). These high stakes are another critical, if nonliterary, factor in the distinction between legal narratives and literary narratives. In the context of the interpretation of the constitutional narratives from the United States Supreme Court, R. Cover says of this phenomenon: "The practice of constitutional interpretation is so inextricably bound up with the real threat or practice of violent deeds that it is—and should be—essentially a different discipline from 'interpretation' in literature and the humanities. ... For legal interpretation occurs on a battlefield—it is part of a battle—which entails the instruments of both war and of poetry. Indeed, constitutional law is, I would argue, more fundamentally connected to war than it is to poetry" ("The Bonds of Constitutional Interpretation: Of the Word, the Deed, and the Role," *Georgia Law Review* 20 [1986]: 816-17).

72. Gewirtz, "Narrative and Rhetoric," 9. What we must then acknowledge is not only what stories have been told but also which stories or facets of stories have remained untold. For further explication of this point, see R. A. Ferguson, "Untold Stories in the Law," in *Law's Stories: Narrative and Rhetoric in the Law* (ed. P. Brooks and P. Gewirtz; New Haven: Yale University Press, 1996), 84-98.

73. Gewirtz, therefore, calls procedural law the "law of narrative" ("Narrative and Rhetoric," 9).

Although these five attributes of trial narrative are fundamental to the law's stories, they are also subservient to the overarching (meta) narrative created by the trial's adjudication. In adjudication, the trier of fact, whether it be judge, jury, or ancient assembly, mediates the legal stories set before it. Adjudication is, therefore, an interpretation of the multiple stories before the adjudicator.[74] The adjudicator decides who is credible, what really happened, and who is responsible. In so doing, the adjudicator also produces a meta-narrative of the case.[75] Any verdict that issues forth is based on that meta-narrative, whether or not the court states it explicitly. Paradoxically then, adjudication involves the interpretation of storytelling through storytelling.

To understand the law's stories, one must, therefore, keep both regular and legal storytelling conventions in mind. One must additionally remain aware that the law's stories exist on multiple levels. To do less is to fall short in comprehending trial law.

Such awareness is especially important when reading ancient litigation records because they are so brief and cryptic. Their primary purpose was to serve as a later mnemonic device. The terse prose omits many of the details of the stories behind the text. This leaves later readers testing various scenarios to see which might best fill in the text's lacunae. The terseness of the text, however, often provokes the reader into a state of unconsciousness concerning the process of reading. The legal documents of practice often contain so little text that, at times, it is impossible to tell whether the document is, in fact, trial related.[76] It is also quite easy to lose sight of their narrativity. Authors who embed a trial within a story are, on the other hand, most cognizant of the literary character of trials. They employ quite intentionally that trial's narrativity to drive the main story

---

74. With regard to appellate adjudication, O. Fiss states: "Adjudication is interpretation: Adjudication is the process by which a judge comes to understand and express the meaning of an authoritative legal text and the values embodied in that text" ("Objectivity and Interpretation," *Stanford Law Review* 34 [1982]: 739). See also R. M. Dworkin, "How Is Law like Literature," in *A Matter of Principle* (Cambridge, Mass.: Harvard University Press, 1985), 146-66. See contra, R. L. West, "Adjudication Is Not Interpretation: Some Reservations about the Law-As-Literature Movement," *Tennessee Law Review* 54 (1987): 203-78.

75. Cf. Gewirtz, "Narrative and Rhetoric," 8.

76. Approximately one hundred documents that I have read to date contain materials that cannot be clearly attributed to litigation, either because they have characteristics that may pertain to either litigation or nonlitigation records (see, e.g., *BIN* 1, 106; YOS 6, 131, 186, and 200) or because, in the final analysis, they are not sufficiently complete to reveal their nature to us (see, e.g., GCCI 1, 15; 1, 260; YOS 6, 165, 200; and YOS 7, 25; cf. YOS 6, 152). Others were ultimately rejected as administrative rather than litigation related. To determine whether a record was litigation related, I examined each tablet for evidence of known legal terminology, the five special attributes of legal narrative, evidence of the typical legal concepts of litigation, and the presence of known judicial officials.

toward its literary goals. The intersection of the trial narrative with the greater narrative is of great import.

If the book of Job should contain a legal altercation, we would expect to find several key attributes in the text. First, we would expect to find legal vocabulary in use. Second, we would expect to see the five special narratological features of trial stories in the text. Third, we would expect the record of that trial to be somewhat brief and cryptic in the fashion of trial documents in the ancient Near East. Fourth, we would expect the use of these literary characteristics to be salient in the overall literary goals of the Joban project.

My research will bear this out. The presence of legal terms in the book of Job is long noted. I will attempt to demonstrate that the book additionally sets forth multiple narrative strands in the dialogue between the characters. The characters have different points of view on the nature of the legal altercation before the court, the reason for Job's suffering, his innocence or guilt, and what Job ought to do about his suffering.[77] The stories arising out of these different points of view make truth claims that struggle to win the day.[78] Thus, the stories are in conflict, are in competition, and seek to persuade. The stories are fractured by the text's seeming literary breaks and its dialogue format. They do not always proceed in a logical or chronological fashion. One has to sort through the material, sometimes reading in a nonsequential manner, to uncover the full story of each character and its legal import. This characteristic of Job's legal stories, in fact, requires a nonsequential reading of the legal metaphors, which one would not typically do in a nonlegal literary analysis. Furthermore, as closer examination will reveal, the multiple, conflicting, fractured stories of the book are regulated by legal procedural metaphors. If this latter characteristic is, indeed, present, then all five features of legal narrative are present. Finally, I hope to prove that the gaps and perplexities of the text make the book feel very much like a trial transcript, even though the literature's purpose is not mnemonic. These disruptions require the reader to test various scenarios to determine the story behind the story as one must do with Neo-

---

77. I employ S. Chapman's understanding of literary point of view. He maintains that point of view can be applied along three senses, or dimensions: (1) the perceptual point of view, which is the angle through which the character perceives the story's events; (2) the conceptual point of view, which is a construct of the character's conceptions, attitudes, values, and worldview; and (3) the interest point of view, which is the result of the character's perceptions of what will advantage or disadvantage him or her (*Story and Discourse* [Ithaca: Cornell University Press, 1978], 151-53). A. Berlin argues that this schema can be applied in the study of both biblical narrative and poetry (*Poetics and Interpretation of Biblical Narrative*, 43-50).

78. J. M. Lotman proclaims: "[p]oint of view introduces a dynamic element into a text: every one of the points of view in a text makes claims to truth and struggles to assert itself in the conflict with opposing ones" ("Point of View in a Text," *New Literary History* 6 [1975]: 352).

Babylonian trial documents. All these attributes of the book of Job encourage the reader to engage in the act of interpreting the text, to seek its metanarrative, just as the adjudicating individual or body will do with the stories in a court of law. The author of Job used both the worldview of the ancient Near Eastern ritual incantation texts and ancient Near Eastern legal storytelling techniques to invite the reader into theological reflection. The legal narratives of the book serve the fundamental literary and theological purposes of the book. The book's law and theology are inseparable.

If this is the case, the author is still inviting readers into the act of literary-forensic interpretation and theological discourse. We modern readers are invited to answer several interpretive questions along the way, for example: What is the nature of the altercation in the book? Who started it? What is its basis? Who is judging it? Which characters speak the truth? Is Job innocent or guilty? Is God fair or unfair? What is the correct theodicy to hold? In answering these questions, the reader becomes the final arbiter of the text's dispute. Readers answer the questions quite differently. This array of reader responses explains the wide range of existing interpretations of the book.[79]

The above discussion has focused on the similarities between the legal stories of the book of Job and Neo-Babylonian trial records. Yet one should be aware of a critical difference. Authors who embed a trial in a work of literature are free to play with the law because the law is in service to literary goals, not legal ones. Hence, not every nuance of the law related to the story may find its way into the literary work. Some aspects of the law in the text may stray from reality. The overall manner in which the literature uses the law may leave an impression of the legal system that is not entirely accurate.[80] As a result, in analyzing the law in literature, one must be pre-

---

79. In this understanding of reader response, I follow the work of W. Iser, particularly *The Implied Reader: Patterns of Communication in Prose Fiction from Bunyan to Beckett* (Baltimore: Johns Hopkins University Press, 1974); *The Act of Reading: A Theory of Aesthetic Response* (Baltimore: Johns Hopkins University Press, 1978); and "Talk Like Whales: A Reply to Stanley Fish," *Diacritics* 11 (1981): 82-87. Two other interpreters have noticed that the book of Job is written in such a way that readers become the final judge of the text's legal stories: D. Cox ("Bi-Polar Mašal,"12-25) and S. Lasine ("Job and His Friends," 144-55, 247-52).

80. The twentieth-century *Perry Mason* novels, written by E. S. Gardner, are a case in point. Every novel in this series has a trial or pre-trial hearing as a central part of the book, and Gardner, as an attorney, made few errors in describing the substantive law, legal procedure, and forensic science of his time. Nevertheless, these trials are fiction. Gardner used scenes and metaphors based on legal reality to draw the reader into the story's mystery and its solution. In furtherance of those ends, Gardner created characters who were far different from their human counterparts. For example, actual criminal lawyers, unlike Perry Mason, rarely represent only the innocent, rarely find the true culprit when their client is innocent, never have unlimited resources for investigative work, in only a few relatively short periods devote every second of their lives to their jobs, rarely have staff that will do the same, and

pared for deviations from the norm consistent with the narratological goals of the work.

This phenomenon occurs in the book of Job as well. My comparative analysis will reveal that, even though the book's law has extensive points of contact with the actual law of the time in order to impel the reader into the act of interpretation, the correspondence is not perfect.[81] There are points where actual law does not control the text. These deviations may, paradoxically, additionally move the reader outside clear interpretive boundaries and allow for a still larger range of interpretation and theological reflection. This solution to some of the puzzles of Job ironically undermines our certitude in regard to any solution. The very structure of the book produces a puzzle that may be solved in numerous ways. My literary-forensic reading of the book may diverge from other literary-forensic readings. My conclusions can only reflect my interpretation of the book of Job, but others are possible. That is the beauty of Job.

## Conclusion

The methods of this investigation arise from several fields. I use the methods of Assyriology, legal history, and the law-as-literature movement of modern law to identify and analyze a large number of Neo-Babylonian trial transcripts. My goal is to achieve a broad picture of the trial procedure and learn something of the nature of the trial documents of this time. With this framework established, I will use a biblical historical comparative method as a hermeneutical tool to understand whether the book of Job contains the typical features and content of ancient Near Eastern trial documents. My biblical method stands within the contextual approach of ancient Near Eastern comparative analysis and is sensitive to both the macro- and micro-levels in its comparative work. The law-as-literature methods will also help us to determine whether the author of Job embedded a trial in the narrative. Additionally, if we should find a trial, these methods will help us to uncover exactly how this trial is embedded and how the author used law in furtherance of his theological ends.

These many methods, when applied to the text sample, will reveal that

---

rarely eschew taking a fee. There are, as S. Greengus puts it, elements of legal "invention and fantasy" in the text (see n. 43 above).

81. As R. E. Murphy states, in discussing the *Sitz im Leben* of the legal material of the book of Job: "[A] reconstruction of a detailed setting, such as a given element in a legal process, is exceedingly hypothetical. It seems better to recognize that within the speeches there are *imitations* of judicial processes, but the evidence will not bring us beyond that" (*Wisdom Literature*, 20).

a sophisticated litigation system existed in the Neo-Babylonian period. Further, literary-forensic analysis of the book of Job will demonstrate that the litigation metaphors in the book follow in great measure this system of litigation. The author appears to have drawn upon the legal system of his social world in constructing the social world of the text. The analysis will also divulge that a number of the literary structures in the trial narratives of the documents of practice are similar to the trial narratives in Job. The book of Job, therefore, might very well have left ancient readers with the sense that a trial was before them, one that they were invited to adjudicate. This resulted in theological deliberation on the part of the ancient reader. Although modern readers may not be as cognizant that the book reads, to some degree, like an ancient trial transcript, the content, conflicts, and literary conundrums of Job nevertheless invite us into this same theological deliberation. As a result, a wide variety of readings exists. The balance of this study will discuss in detail the analyses and findings that brought me to these conclusions.

# 4

# Trial Procedure in the Neo-Babylonian Courts

This chapter is an initial and tentative report of my study of Neo-Babylonian trial procedure based on nearly 340 Neo-Babylonian litigation and related documents from approximately 650 to 400 B.C.E. The findings to date disclose a highly complex, sophisticated judicial system that involved a number of courts. Before examining the specific procedures that these documents record, we will take a brief look at the constitution of the courts in southern Babylonia in the seventh to fifth centuries B.C.E. We examine the courts because the book of Job also involves questions relating to the composition of divine and human courts.

## The Courts

No word for *court* exists in either Sumerian or Akkadian;[1] this exclusion reflects the fluidity of the ancient Near Eastern court systems. While the courts exercised important power, the judiciary did not have the same structure that we find in many modern court systems. The constitution of the court is not always immediately apparent in a Neo-Babylonian litigation document.[2] Another aspect of the fluidity of the court systems is demonstrated by the failure of the records to expose with certainty whether

---

1. S. Lafont, "Considérations sur la pratique judiciaire en Mésopotamie," in *Rendre la justice en Mésopotamie: Archives judiciaires du Proche-Orient ancien (III$^e$–I$^{er}$ millénaires avant J.-C.)* (ed. F. Joannès; Saint-Denis: Presses Universitaires de Vincennes, 2000), 19.
2. Sometimes the full court is named at the beginning of the document. See, e.g., Dalley *Edinburgh* 69; *Nbn* 1128; YOS 7, 7; and YOS 17, 320. At other times, the document identifies in stages those trying the case. See, e.g., A 32117 (edited in M. T. Roth, "Case of Contested Status," 482–83); AnOr 8, 56; and TCL 13, 181. In yet other instances, the judges are disclosed at the end of the document proper or in the document's witness list. See, e.g., AnOr 8, 27 and 39, and YNER 1, 2.

any of the courts sat regularly or had a fixed location. The secular courts of Babylon and the temple court at Uruk may have been more fixed, while the others convened as needed, but the current data are inconclusive.[3] Fortunately, some aspects of the court are discernible. The records that disclose the general constitution and power of the courts are sufficient to allow us to begin to draw a picture of this complex court system.

The Neo-Babylonian corpus divulges that legal administration was in the hands of several classes of persons, including the king, judges (*dayyānu*), diverse state officials, temple officials, and various temple and lay assemblies.[4] A court typically comprised a panel or group; one judge

---

3. The exact frequency is difficult to determine because of the vagaries of archaeology. Moreover, exactly where a court convened is open to interpretation, which also indicates that the courts were not, for the most part, regularly sitting bodies. "Les tribunaux siègent dans les lieux les plus divers, aucun bâtiment réservé exclusivement à la justice n'ayant été identifié au Proche-Orient ancien" (Lafont, "Considérations," 19). Several documents record that there was a "house of judgment" (*bīt dīni*) in Babylon, but we know little about it. See, e.g., *AfO* 44, 81 no. 9; *CT* 22, 105; TCL 13, 222; YOS 3, 35; and YOS 7, 31 (see further *CAD* B, 156). The literary text *CT* 46, 45 also has a reference to the "house of judgment." Oelsner et al. assert that all types of courts could meet in the house of judgment ("Neo-Babylonian Period," 918). Similarly, evidence also exists for a "house of judges" (*bīt dayyāni*). See, e.g., UrET 4, 186. The court apparently met most commonly at the gate of the temple, an administrative building, or a city. The gate was typically an open space where the public could gather (Lafont, "Considérations," 19). See additionally V. H. Matthews, "Entrance Ways and Threshing Floors: Legally Significant Sites in the Ancient Near East," *Fides et Historia* 19 (1987): 25–40; cf. P. N. Scafa, " '*ana pani abulli šaṭir*': Gates in the Texts of the City of Nuzi," in *Studies on the Civilization and Culture of Nuzi and the Hurrians* (ed. D. Owen and G. Wilhelm; Bethesda, Md.: CDL, 1988), 9:139–62. For example, the assembly in Uruk often conducted its affairs at the Great Gate of Eanna (see, e.g., TCL 12, 117). A nonlitigation document makes a specific reference to the existence of the "gate of justice" (*abulli dīnu*) during the reign of Nabopolassar (GCCI 2, 65). VAS 6, 128 lists a "judge of the palace" gate as a witness to the determination of monthly rations. Other locations were possibly used, such as a storehouse (YOS 7, 198) and the gate of the house of a royal officer (*Nbk* 183).

4. Among others are named a *sartennu* (see, e.g., *CT* 22, 234; *Nbn* 1128; VAS 4, 87; VAS 6, 99; YOS 6, 60; and YOS 7, 159); the *puḫru* (see, e.g., AnOr 8, 21; *BIN* 1, 113; *Camb* 329; Spar 3; YOS 6, 224; and UrET 4, 201); the *mār banî* (see further *CAD* M/1, 256–57; M. A. Dandamaev, "The Neo-Babylonian Citizens," *Klio* 63 [1981]: 45–49); *šibûti* (see, e.g., *Camb* 85 and 412; *Cyr* 281 and 332; and Dalley *Edinburgh* 69); and *mukinnu* (see, e.g., VAS 6, 82; YOS 6, 57; and YOS 17, 320). All of these individuals and groups performed other political and administrative functions simultaneously: "À toutes les époques, les officiers administratifs reçoivent des attributions judiciaires venant compléter leurs fonctions principales: le gouverneur d'une province par exemple est saisi des litiges importants survenant dans son ressort géographique, qu'il transmet à la capitale ou qu'il juge en collaboration avec d'autres dignitaires ou notables locaux" (Lafont, "Considérations," 17). R. Westbrook observes: "The ancient legal systems did not strictly separate administrative and judicial powers" ("Social Justice in the Ancient Near East," in *Social Justice in the Ancient World* [ed. K. Irani and M. Silver; Westport, Conn.: Greenwood, 1995], 152). One of the most important examples of this in the Neo-Babylonian period involves the temple administrators, Nabu-mukin-apli and Nabu-aḫ-iddin, whose joint tenure spanned both Neo-Babylonian and Persian kings. They presided

rarely served alone.⁵ Such panels might be drawn from one class of individuals or might be a mixed assortment. A single temple or royal official could, apparently, have heard an accusation, taken a witness statement, or issued a conditional verdict document.⁶ Nonetheless, a number of other individuals usually witnessed the document in such cases.

However a court might be constituted, all legal authority ultimately derived from the king, who was both the source and defender of justice.⁷ Many Neo-Babylonian documents refer to this role.⁸ The king's supervisory power over the legal system in this period is further demonstrated by

---

over a great number of cases, but also played other critical roles in temple administration. We can see this in a comparison of a few texts wherein they served in a judicial capacity (*Iraq* 13, 96–97; YOS 7, 96 and 152), and others wherein they served in an administrative capacity (AnOr 8, 61; *BIN* 2, 108; and YOS 3, 145). This multiplicity of roles should not be seen, however, as a diluting of any group's judicial power, as some have argued. For example, S. Lafont, in discussing the judicial authority of the assembly, states: "Certaines tablettes de procès mentionnent l'assemblée, instance représentant la ville et regroupant les citoyens et les anciens, compétente pour trancher des affaires civiles, pénales mais aussi politiques ou administratives. Il ne s'agit donc pas d'un tribunal au sens étroit, mais d'un organe de gouvernement local possédant des attributions judiciaires" ("Considérations," 19). The fact that those who judged also participated in other government services does not make the court any less of a court when it did convene to decide legal disputes, no matter who its particular judges were and what else the body might have done. The idea of a separate professional judiciary is a fairly new development in the history of the law.

5. See Oelsner et al., "Neo-Babylonian Period," 919.
6. See, e.g., *Dar* 128.
7. See Oelsner et al., "Neo-Babylonian Period," 915; E. Otto, "Neue Aspekte zum keilschriftlichen Prozeßrecht in Babylonien und Assyrien," *ZABR* 4 (1998): 268; M. T. Roth, *Law Collections from Mesopotamia and Asia Minor* (2nd ed.; SBLWAW 6; Atlanta: Scholars Press, 1997), 2–3; and M. Weinfeld, "Judge and Officer in Ancient Israel and in the Ancient Near East," *IOS* 7 (1977): 73. Westbrook points out: "[t]he king upholds *kittum*, which is justice achieved by ensuring that the correct procedures are followed . . . and *mīšarum*, which is justice achieved by correcting distortions in the economic or legal system. . . . M. Weinfeld has shown that when the two terms are used together, they form a hendiadys meaning 'social justice'" (*Studies*, 11 n. 6, citing M. Weinfeld, *Justice and Righteousness in Israel and the Nations: Equality and Freedom in Ancient Israel in Light of Social Justice in the Ancient Near East* [Jerusalem: Magnes, 1985], 12–18 [in Hebrew]; Weinfeld's discussion can be found in English in "'Justice and Righteousness' in Israel against the Background of 'Social Reforms' in the Ancient Near East," in *Mesopotamien und seine Nachbarn: Politische und kulturelle Wechselbeziehungen im Alten Vorderasien vom 4. bis 1. Jahrtausend v. Chr.* [ed. H.-J. Nissen and J. Renger; 2 vols.; Rencontre Assyriologique Internationale Berlin 25; Berlin: Dietrich Reimer, 1982], 2:491–92). Westbrook also notes that the king not only stood at the head of the court system like a modern court of appeal, but "[h]e also had discretionary authority to act entirely outside the system when it failed to do justice" (*Studies*, 134). The prose materials of the Laws of Ur-Nammu, the Laws of Lipit-Ishtar, and the Laws of Hammurabi disclose the ancient Near Eastern understanding of the king's role in establishing and maintaining justice.

8. See also, e.g., VAS 4, 66 (Nabopolassar); *AfO* 17, 2 and VAS 4, 192 (Nebuchadrezzar); VAS 4, 252 (Nabonidus); and *RawlCu* 5, 5 (Cyrus). See further *CAD* K, 470–71; and *CAD* M/2, 116–19.

CT 22, 231. In that letter, the author (whose identity is broken, but who is probably the royal judges in Babylon) informs the temple administrator of Sippar that the king has issued a rule involving trial procedure. Regrettably, the text is too broken to reveal the content of the rule.[9] In earlier historical periods, the king played a more prominent role in adjudication than he apparently did in the Neo-Babylonian period.[10] In fact, the Neo-Babylonian litigation corpus indicates that the king's *direct* involvement in trials was virtually nonexistent outside of matters of treason against the king—*AfO* 17, 2, which involves King Nebuchadnezzar, is the only case that we currently have.[11] Further, only very few letters note the king's judicial participation. Even in the case of letters, however, one has to read the king's participation carefully. For instance, in CT 22, 160, the king's involvement in a claim of abuse of authority may underlie the correspondence, but this is not certain.[12] Because of the paucity of records involving the king during the Neo-Babylonian and Persian Empires, we believe that the kings

---

9. See further A. C. Bongenaar, *The Neo-Babylonian Ebabbar Temple at Sippar: Its Administration and its Prosopography* (Uitgaven van Het Nederlands Historisch-Archaeologisch Instituut te Istanbul 80; Istanbul: Nederlands Historisch-Archaeologisch Instituut te Istanbul, 1997), 23 n. 49; and E. Ebeling, *Neubabylonische Briefe* (ABAW Philosophisch-historische Klasse n.F. 30; Munich: Bayerische Akademie der Wissenschaften, 1949), 124 no. 231.

10. We have many instances of the king's participation in the Old Babylonian period (see further, e.g., J. M. Sasson "Treatment of Criminals at Mari: A Survey," in *The Treatment of Criminals in the Ancient Near East* (ed. J. Sasson; *JESHO* 20; Leiden: Brill, 1977), 99–101; and J. J. Finkelstein, "Some New *Misharum* Material and its Implications," in *Studies in Honour of Benno Landsberger on His Seventy-Fifth Birthday* [ed. H. G. Güterbock and T. Jacobsen; AS 16; Chicago: University of Chicago Press, 1965], 233–51). We have significantly fewer records of the king's engagement in judicial affairs during the Neo-Assyrian period. R. M. Jas states that no trial records document the king serving in a judicial capacity; there are, however, numerous letters and petitions requesting the king to involve himself in judicial matters (*Neo-Assyrian Judicial Procedures*, 4). See, e.g., ABL 928; CT 54, 170, 463, 510; and OIP 114, 20. See further S. Parpola, *Letters from Assyrian and Babylonian Scholars* (SAA 10; Helsinki: Helsinki University Press, 1993), 96, 124–26, 128, 142; J. N. Postgate, "Royal Exercise of Justice under the Assyrian Empire," in *Le palais et la royauté et civilisation: compte rendu* (ed. P. Garelli; CRRA 19; Paris: Geuthner, 1974), 417–26; and S. W. Cole, *Nippur IV: Early Neo-Babylonian Governor's Archive from Nippur* (OIP 114; Chicago: University of Chicago Press, 1996), 76–77. See additionally a report of an incident in which King Assurbanipal ripped out the tongues of two men who spoke blasphemy against Assur and then skinned them alive (E. Weidner, "Assyrische Beschreibungen der Kriegs-Reliefs Aššurbanipals," *AfO* 8 [1932–34]: 184 no. 28).

11. I note here that a number of documents from the Neo-Babylonian period contain a line that states: "he shall bear a sin of the king." This is not a reference to the king's participation in the legal system, as many have suggested. Instead it is a finding of guilt on a breach of an administrative duty.

12. Moreover, in CT 22, 247, an unknown letter writer who is a military commander and noble complains to the king that he did not receive the king's justice in two matters after the king was informed of the situations. This latter document is probably not, however, a formal petition for justice, as the letter writer mentions the problem in the midst of numerous other matters.

of these empires probably delegated most of their authority.[13] Thus, courts other than the one presided over by the king himself handled the vast majority of legal disputes.

Now we turn to the jurisdiction of the various courts.[14] Jurisdiction is the "power of the court to decide a matter in controversy and presupposes the existence of a duly constituted court with control over the subject matter and the parties."[15] In modern legal parlance, such authority actually encompasses three types of jurisdiction: *subject matter jurisdiction, jurisdiction in personam,* and *jurisdiction in rem*. Subject matter jurisdiction is the

> power of a particular court to hear the type of case that is before it. . . . The term refers to the jurisdiction of the court over the class of cases to which a particular case belongs. . . . [It is j]urisdiction over the nature of the cause of action and relief sought. . . . A court is without authority to adjudicate a matter over which it has no jurisdiction even though the court possesses jurisdiction over the parties to the litigation.[16]

Jurisdiction *in personam* is the "power which a court has over the defendant's person and which is required before a court can enter a personal or in personam judgment."[17] This means that the court can affect the defendant's personal rights or duties. Jurisdiction *in rem* is the "power of the court over a thing so that its judgment is valid as against the rights [and duties] of every person in [relation to] the thing."[18] In contemporary times, courts must typically have simultaneously two types of jurisdiction to hear a case. First, the court must have subject matter jurisdiction over the matter in dispute. For example, each U.S. Federal District Court has very strict, limiting rules concerning what type of state matters it can try. If a case does not fall within its subject matter limitations, it cannot hear the case. Second, the court must have either jurisdiction *in personam* over the defendant in the case, where the defendant's rights and duties are under dispute, or jurisdiction *in rem* over the property of the case, where the status of the property of the dispute is being litigated. Although we do not believe that ancient courts thought in exactly these terms or used such vocabulary, the corpus discloses that similar concepts controlled which panels heard the various types of cases in the Neo-Babylonian period. Exactly how such jurisdiction operated, however, is different from current American law.

---

13. Lafont summarizes this phenomenon by observing that, even though royal inscriptions seem to indicate the king's substantial involvement in adjudication throughout ancient Near Eastern history (see, e.g., *BBSt.* 9, *BBSt.* 10, and *CT* 46, 45), in practice, it was small ("Considérations," 18).
14. The jurisdictional section of this analysis was performed in tandem with B. Wells.
15. *BLD*, 853.
16. Ibid., 854.
17. Ibid.
18. Ibid.

When we examine the courts that are composed of a single class of individuals—such as only temple officials or only royal judges—it appears that subject matter jurisdiction is a significant determiner of the court's power. Temple personnel typically handled cases involving temple matters, and non-temple personnel typically handled non-temple or secular matters. Let us examine this more closely.

The judges (*dayyānu*) of the day were always judges of the king (royal judges). We have no evidence at this time of such judges apart from the royal judges of Babylon.[19] Such judges were secular, rather than temple, officials and were important players in judicial affairs. They usually served on panels composed entirely of judges. Often supervisory officials, such as the *sartennu* and the *sukkallu*, led the judges of Babylon.[20] Most of the cases we have studied thus far reveal that a court composed exclusively of royal judges routinely handled matters regarding non-temple personnel and secular subject matters.[21]

In a few instances, state officials, such as provincial governors, heard matters related to litigation.[22] Again, their power seems to have followed subject matter jurisdiction. That is, they handled non-temple affairs.

Temple officials also appear to have served in a judicial capacity. In fact, the available corpus of Neo-Babylonian litigation documents comes in great measure from the archives of the Eanna Temple at Uruk and the Ebabbar Temple at Sippar. Temple officials heard testimony, rendered verdicts, imposed punishments, and enforced their rulings.[23] Such panels even had the judicial power to order royal officials to cooperate with them in their resolution of temple matters, as Durand *Textes babyloniens* 6 indicates. Other texts mention collections of temple personnel serving as judges with temple officials. These include elders of the god Šamaš (e.g., *Nbk* 104); the *puḫru* ("assembly") of a temple (e.g., Durand *Textes babyloniens* 6); priests (*ērib bīti*; e.g., *Cyr* 281 and 332);[24] and temple scribes (e.g., YOS 7, 66).[25] Thus,

---

19. See, e.g., *AfO* 44, 78 no. 6; AnOr 8, 74; *Cyr* 312; *Nbn* 13 and 1128; *RA* 12, 6–7; TCL 12, 86 and 122; and TCL 13, 219 [= *Nbn* 720].

20. See also, e.g., CT 22, 234; VAS 4, 87; VAS 6, 99; YOS 6, 60; and YOS 7, 159. See further *CAD* S, 185–86.

21. See, e.g., *AfO* 44, 83 no. 13; TCL 12, 122; and *Nbn* 1128.

22. See, e.g., AnOr 8, 38; CT 22, 160; *Cyr* 312; *Nbk* 183; YOS 6, 224; and YOS 7, 198.

23. See, e.g., AnOr 8, 27; *BIN* 1, 113; and YOS 7, 192.

24. See, e.g., *Camb* 412 and *Spar* 3.

25. See, e.g., *Cyr* 281; Durand *Textes babyloniens* 6; and YOS 7, 146. See further Bongenaar, *Neo-Babylonian Ebabbar Temple*, 19; *CAD* E, 290–92; Dandamaev, "Neo-Babylonian Elders," 38–39; H. M. Kümmel, *Familie, Beruf und Amt im spätbabylonischen Uruk* (Berlin: Gebr. Mann, 1979), 162–64; J. Renger, "Notes on the Goldsmiths, Jewelers and Carpenters of Neo-Babylonian Eanna," *JAOS* 91 (1971): 497–98; and Spar, "Three Neo-Babylonian Trial Depositions from Uruk," 168 n. 13. Moreover, a few texts mention the presence of the temple assembly (*kiništu*), which may have served along side temple officials. See, e.g., Durand *Textes babyloniens* 6 and

our texts disclose that a fully constituted temple court, without involved non-temple personnel, could investigate and adjudicate matters of concern to the temple.[26] Thus, there is ample evidence to conclude that Neo-Babylonian temple officials had full judicial authority over temple subject matters.

The local assembly also held tremendous power in the period.[27] They typically handled secular matters, as disclosed by *Fs. Walker* 356, PBS 2/1,

---

Spar 3; cf. *CT* 2, 2 and YOS 6, 71 [= YOS 6, 72]. See further J. Bloom, "Ancient Near Eastern Temple Assemblies" (Ph.D. diss., Annenberg Research Institute, 1992); *CAD* K, 386–87; R. P. Dougherty, *Nabonidus and Belshazzar: A Study in the Closing Events of the Neo-Babylonian Empire* (YOSR 15; New Haven: Yale University Press, 1929), 126 n. 411.

26. See, e.g., AnOr 8, 27 and 39; Sack 80; Durand *Textes babyloniens* 6; and YOS 7, 15.

27. While much has been made of the supposed lessening of the power of the local assembly in favor of the royal courts, this hypothesis is not borne out by the Neo-Babylonian corpus. For example, Dandamaev asserts: "The centuries-old rivalry between the royal court and the popular assembly had already under the Chaldean kings ended in the defeat of the assembly, and only property disputes and private offences of a local nature [including family, property, and criminal law] were now subject to its jurisdiction" ("Neo-Babylonian Elders," 40; cf. idem, "The Neo-Babylonian Popular Assembly," in *Šulmu: Papers on the Ancient Near East Presented at International Conference of Socialist Countries, Prague, 30 September to 3 October, 1986* (ed. P. Vabroušek and V. Souček; Prague: Univerzita Karlova, 1998), 68–69; and San Nicolò, *Babylonische Rechtsurkunden*, 146–47). Repeatedly in the history of the scholarship on litigation in the ancient Near East, the power of the local assembly has been misunderstood and underestimated. For example, a number of German scholars argued that the local courts of the Old Babylonian period could offer only advisory opinions and had no enforcement powers (see, e.g., J. Kohler and A. Ungnad, *Hammurabi's Gesetz* (6 vols.; Leipzig: Pfeiffer, 1909), 4:98–99; Lautner, *Altbabylonischen Prozessrechte*, 1–4; Schorr, *Urkunde des altbabylonischen Zivil- und Prozessrechts*, 351; and Walther, *Altbabylonischen Gerichtswesen*, 227–28; for additional bibliography and discussion, see Veenker, "Old Babylonian Judiciary," 5–6). Later scholars demonstrated, however, that this conception is false. For example, L. Evans argued that the ancient assembly of Uruk was divided into an advisory board of elders and the full assembly; only the full assembly had substantial powers ("Early Mesopotamian Assemblies," *JAOS* 78 [1958]: 1–11; see also Veenker, "Old Babylonian Judiciary"). E. Dombradi's 1996 study of Old Babylonian litigation laid all doubts aside as to the powers of the Old Babylonian assembly (*Die Darstellung des Rechtsaustrags*). Lafont subtly hints that the power of the assembly was constrained throughout the ancient Near East (see n. 4 above). Others have maintained that the assembly had once held substantial legal authority, but that it grew weaker in later periods. For example, with regard to the Israelite assembly, B. Levinson contends that the two-witness rule of Deut 17:2–7 is an innovation meant to undermine the power of the assembly and to centralize legal process in Jerusalem (*Deuteronomy and the Hermeneutics of Legal Innovation* [New York: Oxford University Press, 1997], 117–33). I believe, however, that the two-witness rule served a purpose related to the weakening of the evidentiary oath. See the materials at nn. 123–47 below. H. J. Boecker has an excellent discussion of the continuing power of the Israelite assembly (*Administration of Justice*, 46–49), although he agrees with Lautner and others on the power of the most ancient assemblies of Mesopotamia (ibid., 24). For others who believe that ancient Near Eastern assemblies had more advisory roles, see also A. Malamat, "Kingship and Council in Israel and Sumer," *JNES* 22 (1963): 252–53; and T. M. Willis, *The Elders of the City: A Study of the Elders-Laws in Deuteronomy* (SBLMS 55; Atlanta: Society of Biblical Literature, 2001), 61–82.

140, and *ROM* 38. With regard to the Neo-Babylonian period, the evidence supports the idea that the assembly maintained broad authority.[28] Acting alone or in tandem with various officials, the assembly witnessed demands (e.g., *Camb* 329 and YOS 7, 198); witnessed bail guarantees (e.g., *Cyr* 281); heard accusations (e.g., VAS 6, 82);[29] conducted investigations and interrogations (e.g., Spar 3);[30] took or heard witness statements (e.g., TCL 13, 133);[31] heard oaths (e.g., TCL 13, 170);[32] sealed physical and documentary evidence in cases (e.g., TCL 12, 117 and YOS 7, 102);[33] heard trials (e.g., YOS 7, 7, which is the infamous Gimillu's "monster trial" where twelve counts of impropriety were before the court);[34] witnessed and/or issued conditional verdicts (e.g., *Nbk* 104);[35] pronounced final verdicts (e.g., *Iraq* 13, 96–97);[36] approved settlements (e.g., *BE* 9, 69 and Stolper 399–400);[37] and witnessed the satisfaction of verdicts (e.g., *Camb* 321). Moreover, not all of the matters considered by the assembly were of a local nature, as some scholars assert.[38] Additionally, there were disputes that apparently crossed local jurisdictions and were handled by assemblies comprising individuals from two cities (e.g., AnOr 8, 38).

When we examine mixed court panels, it appears that subject matter jurisdiction still follows in a large percentage of these cases. In other words, if secular matters are under dispute, the court will consist only of secular adjudicators, such as the royal judges, state officials, and/or lay judicial assemblies.[39] Temple officials do not handle secular matters. Where temple matters are under adjudication, however, one or more temple officials must be involved.[40] My data sample also strongly suggests that the presence of temple personnel on mixed panels can be explained by the fact that some matter of temple business or one or more temple personnel are involved, either directly or indirectly. At least one temple official must weigh in on such decisions.

---

28. See also, e.g., *AfO* 17, 2; AnOr 8, 38; *BIN* 1, 113; *Camb* 85; Spar 2, UrET 4, 201; and YOS 7, 189. See further *AHw* 876–77; and San Nicolò, *Babylonische Rechtsurkunden*, 146–47. For general background on the assembly in Neo-Babylonian times, see Dandamaev, "Neo-Babylonian Popular Assembly," 63–71.
29. See also, e.g., AnOr 8, 38; Spar 2; and YOS 7, 10.
30. See also, e.g., YOS 6, 77; YOS 7, 42 and 146.
31. See also, e.g., YOS 6, 57.
32. See also, e.g., TCL 13, 181 and YOS 6, 169 [= YOS 6, 231].
33. Cf. AnOr 8, 38.
34. See also, e.g., Dalley *Edinburgh* 69; *Cyr* 332; YOS 6, 208 and 224; and YOS 7, 97.
35. See also, e.g., YOS 6, 208.
36. Disagreeing with H. H. Figulla's assessment of the constitution of the court ("Lawsuit Concerning a Sacrilegious Theft at Erech," *Iraq* 13 [1951]: 100). See, e.g., YOS 6, 169 (= YOS 6, 231) and YOS 7, 7.
37. Cf. *IMT* 105 (joined to *EE* 109).
38. Dandamaev, "Neo-Babylonian Popular Assembly," 63–71.
39. See, e.g., *Cyr* 312 and *Fs. Walker* 356.
40. See, e.g., AnOr 8, 38; *CT* 2, 2; *Iraq* 13, 96-97; and YOS 7, 196.

What is peculiar is the presence of non-temple personnel, such as royal judges, provincial governors, or a lay assembly, working with temple officials in the resolution of temple matters, as in AnOr 8, 74. We simply cannot discern at this point why the temple may have called in such people, or why the legal system allowed, and possibly encouraged, such people to be present. In other cases, temple officials clearly had complete authority to decide matters without the participation of outsiders. No conclusion can be drawn at this point.

We do know that subject matter jurisdiction was not the sole factor in determining the constitution of the court. Cases point to the import of concepts equivalent to jurisdiction *in personam* and jurisdiction *in rem* in Neo-Babylonian times. These include cases in which only *non-temple* personnel judged trials related to *temple* matters, thereby violating the general rule of subject matter jurisdiction. In YOS 7, 189, for instance, a temple herdsman testifies that he was assaulted and some of his herd stolen by two slaves owned by a private individual who had no apparent connection to the temple. The court that heard the testimony was a lay assembly. This is a perplexity, because the subject matter is theft of temple property, a matter normally within the purview of temple officials. Moreover, in AnOr 8, 74, a father marked his daughter with the star of Ištar of Uruk. He then later sold her to a foreigner. The temple sued for possession of the daughter. The document discloses that the *sartennu* and the governor of Uruk ordered the daughter to be given to the temple. Again, no temple officials are on the court. The explanation of these two cases is that in these situations jurisdiction *in personam*—jurisdiction over a defendant in a case—appeared to have taken precedence over subject matter jurisdiction. The defendants in these cases were not temple personnel; thus, the temple did not have jurisdiction over the defendant. These cases, then, suggest that the temple court needed to possess both jurisdiction *in personam* over the defendant and subject matter jurisdiction in order to hear the case. If the temple court did not have both types of jurisdiction, secular personnel had to be in charge of the matter.

Yet another type of jurisdiction, jurisdiction *in rem*, also appears to operate in certain instances. In YOS 7, 56, a female temple slave was seen keeping company with an inappropriate man.[41] The man, who does not appear to have been related to the temple, was forbidden to see her anymore: a restraining order was issued against him. Here the temple did not

---

41. The exact nature of the problem is in dispute. Dandamaev asserts that the woman was a temple prostitute (*Slavery in Babylonia*, 135-36 n. 74). Because the man was a foreigner and might skip out on his bill, the woman could not service him. R. P. Dougherty, on the other hand, believes that the man was making "unseemly advances" toward the temple slave (*The Shirkûtu of Babylonian Deities* [YOSR 5/2; New Haven: Yale University Press, 1923], 66). For numerous reasons, I believe that Dougherty's scenario is the more probable.

have jurisdiction *in personam* over the defendant. What the temple court does seem to have is jurisdiction *in rem* over the property under dispute, the female slave and her sexual resources. If this were the case, the temple court then had the power to determine the rights of any person with respect to the property at hand, whether or not it had jurisdiction *in personam*, thus allowing the restraining order to be issued against the man. I believe that, in this case, jurisdiction *in rem* attached, making the need for jurisdiction *in personam* over the defendant irrelevant. An important question arises from this, however. Why should the temple court have had jurisdiction *in rem* in this case (YOS 7, 56) over a temple slave so that it might determine whom she could see, but not have jurisdiction *in rem* in the previous case (AnOr 8, 74) over a person whose very status as a temple slave was at stake in the case? I suggest that the answer rests in the fact that jurisdiction *in rem* attached to temple slaves only once it was determined that they were, in fact, temple slaves. Making that determination fell under the jurisdiction of a non-temple court.

This leads to one more question: Why did the temple court have jurisdiction *in rem* over its slave in YOS 7, 56 but not apparently its other temple property in YOS 7, 189 (the case of theft of temple property by a non-temple person)? My response to that question is that the temple court indeed had jurisdiction *in rem* over its property, but the rights of the defendant with respect to the property were not at issue in the case: everyone knew the property was temple property and did not belong to the defendant. The issue was whether that particular defendant stole the property. That determination required jurisdiction *in personam* over the defendant. I believe that jurisdiction *in rem* was required in only in the rarest of cases. Nonetheless, it cannot be ignored in understanding how the Neo-Babylonian courts operated.

Consequently, I maintain that the temple court had power to determine a case only when it had (1) subject matter jurisdiction; and (2) either jurisdiction *in personam* over the defendant in matters relating to the defendant, or jurisdiction *in rem* over temple property when a determination of the rights of individuals with respect to the property was involved. In cases where the temple possessed the two necessary types of jurisdiction, it appears that at least one temple official generally had to have been on the court. Where the temple lacked such jurisdiction, temple personnel were not involved in the adjudication of the case.

Finally, one last class of cases must be addressed. These are cases in which the judges of Babylon handled temple personnel, property, or affairs without a temple official on the adjudicating panel. These tablets include AnOr 8, 45, 46, and 50; YOS 6, 224; YOS 7, 31; and YOS 7, 115. What distinguishes these cases is that the temple was, or may have been, the defendant in the case. I believe that the temple was the defendant on appeal, or the appellee, in a case that had been taken to a higher court. I propose that the above documents are all related to an appeal in the royal courts of a temple court decision. These will be discussed later in this chapter under appeals.

In conclusion, for the temple courts, jurisdiction required both subject matter and either jurisdiction *in personam* or jurisdiction *in rem*. We do not fully understand why secular officials were involved in lower temple court decisions, but we do know they could be so involved. The secular courts had broad powers to hear cases. Generally, they heard all cases that the temple courts did not hear. Typically, they had subject matter and either jurisdiction *in personam* or jurisdiction *in rem*, like the temple courts. One important difference does emerge. The Babylonian royal courts also had appellate jurisdiction over temple court decisions. This may have been a check on possible abuse of temple court decisions that went in their favor, because the temple served as both judge and party in those cases.

In sum, the royal courts of Babylon seem to have had more power than either the temple court or the judicial assembly, but both of these courts were critical components of a court system that was growing in complexity. All participants shared in the administration of the legal system. Each played an important role. Thus, the jurisdictional power of any of the Neo-Babylonian courts should not be minimized. With our overview of the Neo-Babylonian courts complete, we turn to trial procedure.

## Neo-Babylonian Trial Procedure

The Neo-Babylonian legal system was an inquisitorial system of adjudication, as opposed to the adversarial systems found today in such countries as the United States, Canada, and Great Britain. Inquisitorial systems, as are found today in continental Europe and were found in the ancient Near East, are marked by two characteristics: (1) a higher degree of cooperation between the parties than in adversarial systems; and (2) a judge who is more likely to be involved in developing the evidence at trial.[42] The Neo-

---

42. Adversarial systems assume that the truth is best served through the competition of the parties, although the dispute is never an unrestrained affair. The imposition of certain duties, the existence of certain rights, and procedural and evidentiary rules all limit the competition in some very important ways. Inquisitorial systems are fundamentally based, however, on the notion of cooperation. They expect all parties to participate in finding the truth. While there are, of course, duties, rights, and procedural and evidentiary rules that regulate inquisitorial trials, they are conceived somewhat differently than in adversarial systems. For example, in inquisitorial trials, the presiding official (in most modern systems, the judge) is much more likely to direct her or his own questions to the parties and witnesses or demand the production of documentary evidence. The presider is not only a referee but also an addi-

Babylonian legal system had highly sophisticated, but quite flexible, rules of procedure and evidence. Trial procedure was somewhat fluid in the period: one cannot always clearly delineate pre-trial, trial, and post-trial phases of litigation. Furthermore, it appears that not every procedure available to the court was employed in every case (although one might postulate that every step did occur, but often some of the procedures or phases were not recorded for various reasons). Consequently, one can only discuss what generally happened at trial.

The basic phases of litigation include, in their typical order of occurrence:

1. the accusation
2. the demand
3. the investigation[43]
4. the summons
5. the defendant's declaration or oath
6. a possible second accusation or the testimony of a corroborating witness
7. the taking of additional evidence[44]
8. the verdict
9. an appeal, if taken
10. the execution of the verdict

Settlement of the claim, which might be sanctioned by either the court or the public assembly, was possible at any stage of the proceedings. We will look at these steps in sequence.

*Accusations and demands.* Litigation began with some form of accusation. Typically, an individual or group would have stated that another individual or group had breached an obligation or caused an injury.[45] Occasionally, however, the accusation was recorded later in the trial transcript in order

---

tional elicitor of facts. For evidence of this in the Neo-Babylonian period, see, e.g., *Nbn* 1128; *RA* 12, 6–7; *RA* 67, 148–49; TCL 12, 86; and TCL 13, 219 (= *Nbn* 720). Numerous texts record the actual words of the judges' questioning (see, e.g., *RA* 67, 148–49; TCL 13, 181; YOS 6, 225; and YOS 7, 96). They could also order evidence to be brought into court on their own initiative (Oelsner et al., "Neo-Babylonian Period," 922; see, e.g., CT 2, 2). Because the trials of inquisitorial systems are based on a model of cooperative truth-finding, they do not show the heightened level of conflict that one finds in adversarial systems and do not afford the same protections against self-incrimination.

43. This may have included the taking of witness statements, which I handle under nos. 6 and 7 of this list.

44. This includes a wide variety of evidence including third-party witness statements, documentary evidence, circumstantial evidence, and more.

45. See, e.g., *BE* 10, 9; *BIN* 1, 113; *Fs. Walker* 356; YOS 7, 97; Dalley *Edinburgh* 69; *IMT* 105 (joined to *EE* 109); *RA* 67, 148–49; Spar 2; YOS 6, 208; and YOS 7, 189.

to rebut the testimony of the defendant or to raise new matters beyond the scope of the defendant's statement.⁴⁶ Accusations may also have been lodged during pre-trial investigations or interrogations.⁴⁷ In earlier periods of Mesopotamian history, there was a complaint-and-answer process⁴⁸ in which the parties pronounced, out of court, a formal accusation and reply, with or without the presence of a court official.⁴⁹ Only after this exchange could one or both of the parties bring the dispute to court by *seizing* (*ṣabātu*) the adverse party.⁵⁰ The complaint and answer were then read

---

46. See, e.g., YOS 6, 235, in which a certain Itti-Šamaš-balaṭu was charged with theft or embezzlement of temple precious metals. His statement preceded the accusation because he denied liability. The testimony of the accuser was used to rebut the denial to a significant degree. On this basis, the court held the defendant liable. In YOS 7, 152, the defendant made an oath in which he denied that he took bribes in the form of money and other goods from runaway slaves and then released them (reading against Dandamaev [Slavery in Babylonia, 477] and Dougherty [*Shirkûtu*, 58], both of whom misread the oath as an oath of confession because they seem to misunderstand the function of the *kî* in the protasis of the typical Neo-Babylonian oath formula, in which the apodosis that brings the curse upon the speaker is unstated. This difficulty occurs frequently, and examples can be found in translations of *Dar* 53; TCL 13, 170; and YOS 6, 224). This oath of denial is followed in the text, however, by a declaration of accusation, which establishes that the defendant did indeed do as charged. The verdict was not recorded. (By way of aside, the two accusers in YOS 7, 152, Itti-Nana-iniya and Suqa, were themselves runaway slaves who also came to testify against yet another criminal in YOS 7, 137, a case of treason). Furthermore, YOS 7, 42 contains a defendant confession that does not end the proceedings but instead provokes another accusation. Here the tablet records in order (1) an interrogation; (2) a confession as to the theft of two items from one person; (3) a second confession regarding a theft of silver from another person; (4) an accusation by the second victim, which indicates that other items were stolen in addition to the items to which the defendant confessed; and (5) another statement by the defendant, in which he confesses that he took the named items but in an amount less than he is accused of taking. Finally, his house is searched and the amount of the goods to which he confessed to having taken in his third confession is brought into court as evidence. We see here that the accusatory material can come after a defendant's confession in order to raise new matters beyond the scope of the confession. In AnOr 8, 38, the accusation follows the taking of third-party testimony. Sometimes we have a record in which only the accusation is recorded; thus, it affords us no information regarding when it occurred in the process. See, e.g., TCL 13, 125 and 134, and VAS 6, 82.

47. See, e.g., CT 2, 2 and TCL 13, 170; cf. BE 9, 69.

48. In using modern legal vocabulary and categories to describe ancient legal phenomena, I am not suggesting that those in the ancient Near East thought precisely as we moderns think about law. Ancient legal thinking is different from our own. See Bottéro, "'Code' of Ḥammurabi," 156–84; Kraus, "Ein zentrales Problem des altmesopotamischen Rechts," 283–96; and Westbrook, "What Is the Covenant Code?" 15–36. I am using modern vocabulary and categories here simply as tools to help us conceptualize a foreign system.

49. See, e.g., CT 6, 34b and YOS 12, 325. See also Dombradi, *Die Darstellung des Rechtsaustrags*, 1:295–96.

50. "Seizure" did not always entail an arrest; it was in many cases merely a summons. Although either party might seize the other, and cases of mutual seizure exist, the defendant was the party typically seized (ibid.).

in court so that they would have evidentiary effect. This procedure seems to have dropped away by the Neo-Babylonian period in favor of a more expedited practice. In this period, accusations were presented directly to the investigative or adjudicating officials.[51]

Still, a pre-trial demand to rectify a wrong was not uncommon in the Neo-Babylonian period. Such demands were usually private and are typically attested in letters.[52] Litigation records demonstrate, however, that a demand for redress might be quite formal, presented in public before an assembly of free persons or temple personnel.[53] The individual might be seized upon accusation and brought into court to receive the demand.[54]

Judicial accusations could be made by simple accusatory declarations, posed as interrogatives,[55] or offered as sworn statements.[56] In the latter case,

---

51. The judges, officials, and/or assembly who were to hear the trial itself might well conduct the preliminary investigation (see, e.g., TCL 13, 170 and YOS 6, 223). We also have evidence, however, that one who was not to serve later in trying the case might conduct the investigation (see, e.g., YOS 6, 144).

52. Cf. CT 22, 202. NBDM 49, a pre-litigation settlement agreement concerning a dispute over the title to a parcel of real estate, also documents the existence of a pre-trial demand. Among the early Neo-Babylonian documents, see OIP 114, 109; cf. OIP 114, 65, in which the letter writer complains to the recipient that the recipient has wrongfully taken silver that does not belong to the letter writer and, as a result, the letter writer is being sued. This demand could give rise to the letter writer's ability to join the recipient of the letter to the legal action by impleader (see further the material in nn. 65–66 below). In addition, see BIN 1, 28, which seems to be dealing with a situation that may develop into litigation.

53. In *Camb* 329, the agent of a creditor had the debtor's son-in-law seized and brought into the assembly to receive the demand for payment. The son-in-law had to explain why the creditor could not be paid immediately. We are left to assume that trial proceedings against the debtor would follow. YOS 7, 198 also appears to be in the nature of a formal demand. In this case, Gimillu, the notorious temple con artist and thief, was brought before temple officials and the assembly to account for missing temple livestock and birds, which he was supposed to have sent to the desert. A temple official demanded of him: "Go, and the remainder, concerning which you were given instructions, confine and restore to the Eanna," at which point Gimillu bolted from the court in a brazen escape attempt. Unfortunately for Gimillu, he was seized at the gate of the place of the proceedings.

54. See, e.g., *Camb* 329, discussed in the preceding note.

55. See, e.g., YOS 6, 208; TCL 13, 170 and 181; and YOS 7, 96.

56. TCL 13, 179 contains what is most likely an oath in support of a prior accusation. It appears that the negation in the oath is broken. If this should not be the case, however, the oath would have to be an oath of confession. Because such oaths do not appear elsewhere in the corpus, I think reading the oath as an oath of confession is the less likely reading. Consequently, I suggest that this text contains a broken oath of accusation. In PBS 2/1, 140, the accuser swears to his position, but only after the defendant offered an oath of his own (for more on this text, see n. 128 below). Many interpreters, including Joannès ("Pratique du serment," 170), J. Kohler and F. E. Peiser (*Aus dem babylonischen Rechtsleben* [4 vols.; Leipzig: Pfeiffer, 1890–98], 3:51), Spar (*Studies*, 10), Dandamaev (*Slavery in Babylonia*, 223), and R. Westbrook ("Slave and Master in Ancient Near Eastern Law," *CKLR* 70 [1995]: 1664), believe that *Dar* 53 also represents an accuser's oath. I believe, however, that the translation that supports such an understanding of the text is in error. See n. 46 above. It is actually a defendant oath. A more detailed discussion of this text will, unfortunately, have to wait until a later time.

the full oath formula normally read: "If he has [or you have] not done X [the content of the accusation], then may I be cursed by DN." Sometimes, however, an abbreviated oath formula was used: "If he has [or you have] not done X [the content of the accusation] ... ," with a negative protasis and an unstated cursing apodosis to be supplied by the listener or reader.[57] In the Neo-Babylonian corpus, only the abbreviated oath formula is represented. Obviously, accusatory oaths were nondispository, meaning that they did not settle the matter. We will take up this point more fully later in the chapter.

Accusations could address a large variety of situations. For instance, accusations could contain multiple counts, wherein an individual was either charged with a number of occurrences of the same substantive crime or with occurrences of more than one type of crime, which arose out of the same or similar circumstances.[58] Accusations could be issued against a single person or against multiple persons.[59] One could issue an accusation against one's co-defendant or co-defendants.[60] Counterclaims could also be lodged. The evidence for the counterclaim in ancient Mesopotamia generally, and the Neo-Babylonian period specifically, is far more subtle and indirect than we might expect. H. J. Boecker correctly states: "quite often the defendant turned the tables and himself became the accuser. When we are dealing with a legal case in the ancient east, we cannot always say with total certainty who the plaintiff was and who the accused."[61] This uncertainty stems from the fact that the tablets were often

---

57. The apodosis was often deleted when convention or context could furnish the imprecation (Dobbs-Allsopp, "Genre," 295, citing J. Lyons, *Semantics* 2 [Cambridge: Cambridge University Press, 1977], 589; cf. G. Ries, "Zur Strafbarkeit des Meineids im Recht des Alten Orients," in *Festschrift für Dieter Medicus zum 70. Geburtstag* [ed. V. Beuthien et al.; Cologne: Heymanns, 1999], 464). See, e.g., TCL 13, 179 (where the negation is probably broken; see further the preceding note) and PBS 2/1, 140. See further B. Conklin, "The Means of Marking Oath Content in Hebrew and Akkadian" (paper presented at the annual meeting of the Society of Biblical Literature, San Antonio, Texas, November 23, 2004). On the translation errors that often accompany such oaths, see n. 46 above.

58. Even though we do not have all the accusations set forth as clearly as we might like in YOS 7, 7, the great trial of the infamous Gimillu, the text does exhibit the trial of a twelve-count accusation. One of the best examples of a multicount indictment is the "Turin Indictment Papyrus," which comes from Elephantine ca. 1150 B.C.E. This accusation contains thirty counts against a number of different individuals and covers a plethora of crimes, including, among others, violations of cultic prescriptions, adultery, embezzlement, theft, receiving stolen goods, arson, assault, aborting a fetus, and murder. For a recent translation and the publication history of this text, see B. Porten, *The Elephantine Papyri in English: Three Millennia of Cross-Cultural Continuity and Change* (Idocumenta et Monumenta Orientis Antiqui Studies in Near Eastern Archaeology and Civilization 22; Leiden: Brill, 1996), 45.

59. For accusations coming against multiple persons, see, e.g., AnOr 8, 21; *BE* 9, 69; and YOS 7, 97.

60. See, e.g., AnOr 8, 21; *Iraq* 13, 96–97; YOS 6, 137 and 144.

61. Boecker, *Administration of Justice*, 23.

written with the victor's need for evidence of the outcome in mind.[62] As a result, there are only a few clear indications of these types of suits in any period of Mesopotamia legal history.[63] The Neo-Babylonian evidence is

---

62. On the fact that the victor's need for evidence drove the drafting process, see Westbrook, "Recensiones: Dombradi," 123; C. Locher, *Die Ehre Einer Frau in Israel: Exegetische und rechtsvergleichende Studien zu Deuteronomium 22,13–21* [OBO 70; Göttingen: Vandenhoeck & Ruprecht, 1986], 96–98, 379; and idem, "Deuteronomium 22, 13–21: Vom Prozeßprotokoll zum kasuistischen Gesetz," in *Das Deuteronomium* (ed. N. Lohfink; Leuven: University Press, 1985], 302–3). Moreover, some trial records in the period close with the statement, "the judges wrote out a document, sealed it with their seals and gave it to PN [the victor]" or very similar language. See, e.g., *AfO* 44, 76 no. 5; 44, 78 no. 6; *Nbn* 668; and *RA* 12, 6–7; cf. Dalley *Edinburgh* 69 and *Nbn* 1128. Hence, it is possible that, no matter who originally instituted the action, the winner was often the notated plaintiff. The fact that we have so few cases that chronicle the release of a suspect (see *CT* 2, 2) or a win by the defendant (see *Cyr* 332; *Nbn* 13 and 1113; TCL 12, 122; and YOS 6, 156; cf. YOS 6, 225) argues for this possibility. Additionally, we should observe that in both *Cyr* 332 and *Nbn* 13 a false-suit penalty was, or might have been, involved. (For a full discussion of the false-suit penalty, see n. 180 below.) While the tablets in these two cases seem to reveal that the court instigated the assessment of the false-suit penalty, it is more likely that the defendant counterclaimed with an accusation of false suit at the start of the litigation or raised the claim immediately after the conclusion of the plaintiff's evidence. Then, given the need for brevity, the scribe simply reduced the complexities down to its most essential elements. Consequently, the probability that counterclaims were permissible is quite high even though we do not have them well documented in the Neo-Babylonian corpus.

63. The best example originates in Nuzi. In AASOR 16, 73, the plaintiff sued the defendant for unlawful distraint of his son. The defendant countersued, claiming that the plaintiff owed him money and the distraint, therefore, was justified. The court chastised the defendant for bringing the counterclaim and awarded the plaintiff judgment. See further T. S. Frymer-Kensky, "Suprarational Legal Procedures in Elam and Nuzi," in *Studies on the Civilization and Culture of Nuzi and the Hurrians in Honor of Ernest R. Lacheman on his Seventy-Fifth Birthday, April 29, 1981* (ed. M. Morrison and D. Owen; Winona Lake, Ind.: Eisenbrauns, 1981), 124–25. The other texts are less forthright. E. Dombradi asserts that, in the Old Babylonian period, either or both of the parties to the dispute might bring the lawsuit: "Der Belangte wird nicht mehr mit Gewalt von Gericht geführt, er hat vielmehr die Möglichkeit, sich selbst mit einer Klage an die Richter zu wenden. Wie bereits erwähnt, kommt es zudem vor, daß die Streitteile sich gegenseitig 'packen' (ṣabatu/tiṣbutu) und dann gemeinsam den Klageweg betreten" (*Die Darstellung des Rechtsaustrags*, 1:298; see also Westbrook's discussion of this point in "Recensiones: Dombradi," 123). For example, in *CT* 2, 43, both parties, who were temple personnel, "seized" (ṣabātum) each other over a disputed contribution to Ištar and "approached the governor of Sippar and the judges," which means that they entered into the legal dispute by either the ritual, symbolic formalities of suit initiation or other, possibly less formal, means before the court. In spite of her above-mentioned assertion, Dombradi expresses some concern over whether *CT* 2, 43 can actually reflect the more typical formal situation because of its reference to a mutual seizure; she speculates that this text might rather chronicle some sort of quarrel or dispute (*Die Darstellung des Rechtsaustrags*, 2:228 n. 1785a). I contend, however, that this seeming oddity can be resolved by understanding that the text refers to a claim/counterclaim situation and is not at all improbable. *Alalakh* 7 is a case of a contested estate in which a certain Abban brought a lawsuit against his sister, Bittatti. Abban claimed that Bittatti had been cut out of their mother's estate. Bittatti claimed, on the other hand, that she was included, stating: "[W]h[y] should you take an extra share?" This appears to be a coun-

particularly subtle.⁶⁴ Consequently, we must take care in assessing the documents. Lastly, other parties might have been joined to the suit by an impleader (or joinder) accusation, whereby the defendant asserted that a third party was actually responsible to the plaintiff on the claim rather than the defendant.⁶⁵ In the Neo-Babylonian period, defendants often accused others who were not yet involved in the case of true responsibility. Indications that the court permitted joinder in such suits exist: several documents indicate that such an accused third-party individual was brought before the court.⁶⁶

---

teraccusation in interrogatory form. The text continues: "The case was brought to court." The estate was ultimately divided between the two. BM 78156 [= BM 40717] contains a Neo-Assyrian post-trial settlement of a claim/counterclaim suit (edited by E. Leichty, "A Legal Text from the Reign of Tiglath-Pileser III," in *Language, Literature, and History: Philological and Historical Studies Presented to Erica Reiner* [ed. F. Rochberg-Halton; AOS 67; New Haven: American Oriental Society, 1987], 227–29). The tablet reads in relevant part: "Šulaja and his brothers sued each other and they went before the judges and pleaded the case. Afterward, they returned from before the judges and they agreed among themselves (concerning) two shares . . ." (ibid., 228). H. Z. Szubin and B. Porten argue convincingly that Kraeling 1, an Aramaic document from fifth-century Elephantine, is a settlement contract of what was probably a claim/counterclaim suit over an abandoned piece of property, although that is not entirely evident on the face of the document ("Litigation Concerning Abandoned Property at Elephantine," *JNES* 42 [1983]: 279–84, esp. pp. 282–83). Cf. *TAD* B2.8.

64. The best indication of the phenomenon in our corpus is *ROM* 2, 38, an execution-of-judgment document that chronicles: "Ubar sued Nabu-iqiša and in the assembly of . . . they litigated [their] cases, and their case was distinguished (as right from wrong), and they decided 1/3 shekel of silver against Nabu-iqiša. Nabu-iqiša weighed out 1/3 shekel of silver and gave it to Ubar. To return and litigate between them, [they will] not [do]. Their case is settled. Nabu-iqiša has paid the silver. He is free." While the first clause indicates that there is an originating plaintiff and defendant, the rest of the document seems to hold the parties on an equal footing, treating them as if they sued one another. Contrast TCL 12, 24 and *BaghM* 5, 15, wherein the language "their case was distinguished (as right from wrong)" is missing, and only one of the parties was prohibited by the court from instituting further suit; cf. TCL 12, 4, which is a similar Neo-Assyrian text.

65. For example, in American law, the impleader procedure allows the defendant to bring into the lawsuit a third party who is, or may be, liable to the defendant for all or part of the plaintiff's claim against the defendant ("Implead," *BLD*, 754; "Third-party practice," ibid., 1480; and Federal Rules of Civil Procedure §14). Either party might join to the suit any additional party who is necessary to settling the matter ("Joinder: Compulsory joinder," *BLD*, 836; Federal Rules of Civil Procedure §19(a); cf. "Joinder: Joinder of parties," *BLD*, 837; Federal Rules of Civil Procedure §§19–20).

66. In TCL 12, 77, a certain Nabu-naṣir was required to hand his shepherd over to court or pay a thirtyfold theft penalty, because, when Nabu-naṣir was accused of this theft, he denied responsibility and implicated his shepherd. In YOS 7, 96, an individual was suspected of the theft of temple livestock. He denied the allegations, saying that he had legitimately disposed of some of the livestock through sale and that the infamous Gimillu had stolen the rest. He had to guarantee the appearance and testimony of Gimillu and the others who were involved with the sales. Cf. TCL 13, 181, YOS 6, 152, and YOS 6, 175, where the impleader procedure was probably involved in the case but is not completely clear on the face of the text.

Either the victim[67] or a third party for the benefit of the victim[68] could have lodged an accusation. The parties referred to each other as an "adversary at law" (*bēl dīni*[69] or *bēl dabābi*[70]), although this term referred most often to the accusing party. Third-party accusers could be either public officials or private individuals. In the Old Babylonian and Neo-Assyrian periods, we have evidence that a certain official (a *qabba'um* officer, in the Old Babylonian period;[71] a *bātiqu*, in the Neo-Assyrian period[72]) served in the capacity of a public accuser. This individual should not be confused with what we moderns think of as a public prosecutor. He was not interested in simple criminal cases involving the public but was part of the king's internal

---

In spite of the existence of this apparent right, it was not always utilized. Sometimes further lawsuits were required to clear matters. See, e.g., the related documents *Nbn* 314; *AfO* 44, 83 no. 13, and *TCL* 12, 122 (discussed further in n. 191 below). In the complex situation disclosed by those texts, the guarantor was sued by a creditor for payment of a debt incurred by a couple who were by then deceased. The guarantor brought a separate action against the heirs rather than joining them to the original suit. It appears, at the current state of the research, that joinder was used more frequently in injury cases than in those involving some sort of economic harm.

67. See, e.g., *BE* 9, 24, *Dar* 128, and *YOS* 7, 42.
68. See, e.g., *YOS* 6, 208 and *YOS* 7, 137.
69. See, e.g., *CT* 22, 231, *CT* 22, 234; cf. *OIP* 114, 20 and *VAS* 1, 36. See also *CAD* D, 156.
70. See, e.g., *CT* 22, 105. This title might also, however, refer to any enemy (see, e.g., *CT* 22, 144 and *YOS* 3, 6) or be a term of abuse (cf. *ABL* 326). See further *CAD* D, 3–4.
71. Lafont, "Considérations," 20. See further *CAD* Q, 2, whose examples are of some, but not strong, supporting value to Lafont. B. Landsberger argued that the *munaggirum* was a public prosecutor in the Old Babylonian period ("Remarks on the Archive of the Soldier Ubarum," *JCS* 9 [1955]: 123–24). The few available texts do not bear out that interpretation. See *CAD* M/2, 198–99; A. L. Oppenheim, "The Eyes of the Lord," *JAOS* 88 (1968): 177; cf. *munaggirūtu* in *CAD* M/2, 199; and *nugguru* in *CAD* N/2, 313. Landsberger also suggested that the term *ākil karṣi* was used to signify a public prosecutor through the Middle Babylonian period ("Remarks," 123–24). He supported his argument with vocabulary lists rather than any litigation or related documents. Landsberger's position has not gained acceptance. Oppenheim suggests that *ākil karṣi* refers to an "occasional informant" ("Eyes of the Lord," 177). *CAD* defines the term as "false denouncer" or "maligner" (*CAD* A/1, 266). I believe, however, that it can refer to reliable accusers as well. See Day, *Adversary in Heaven*, 41; P. K. McCarter, "Rib-Adda's Appeal to Aziru (EA 162, 1–21)," *OrAnt* 12 (1973): 15–18; cf. S. Greengus, *Old Babylonian Tablets from Ishchali and Vicinity* (Uitgaven van het Nederlands Historisch-Archaeologisch Instituut te Istanbul 44; Istanbul: Dutch Historical-Archaeological Institute, 1979), no. 23; and B. Halpern and J. Huehnergard, "El Amarna Letter 252," *Or* 51 (1982): 228–29. W. von Soden asserts that *BE* 9, 24 is evidence that *karṣi* stands for a true accusation in the Neo-Babylonian period (*AHw* 450), but I do not believe that *karṣi* is represented in *BE* 9, 24, reading the cuneiform signs with *CAD* (B, 166) and G. Cardascia (*Les Archives des Murašû: Une famille d'hommes d'affaires Babyloniens à l'époque perse [455–403 av. J.-C.]* [Paris: Imprimerie Nationale, 1951], 184) against von Soden.
72. Jas, "Neo-Assyrian Judicial Procedures," 50. See further the text copied and discussed in L. Kataja, "A Neo-Assyrian Document on Two Cases of River Ordeal," *SAAB* 1 (1987): 66–68.

affairs apparatus and handled major acts against the king, his property, or his government, particularly those crimes committed by the king's officers.[73] No direct evidence exists regarding this internal affairs officer during the Neo-Babylonian period. A. L. Oppenheim suggests that a *muraššû* was an official temple prosecutor in the period.[74] This term does not, however, appear in any of the litigation records sampled here but rather in lexical lists and temple economic texts.

Across the ancient Near East most third-party accusers were private prosecutors, that is, individuals who, upon becoming aware that a crime had been committed, brought the crime and the suspect to the attention of public officials for investigation and trial. Anyone, whether public official or layperson, whether free person or slave, had the right, nay the duty, to press charges when he or she had knowledge of an actionable offense.[75] Such persons fulfilled an important function in bringing the accusation before the court. In earlier periods of ancient Near Eastern history the term *ākil karṣī* signified an accuser, whether he or she was a reliable one or a false one.[76] In those situations where the term referred to a reliable accuser, it would have included a third-party private prosecutor. We do not see this term used in the sense of a reliable accuser in the Neo-Babylonian period. One case in the Neo-Assyrian period uses the term *bātiqu* to describe such an individual.[77] In the Neo-Babylonian period, the term *bātiqu* is used in conjunction with the term *mukinnu* in the conditional verdict documents[78] to refer to those persons who must appear if the party is to win his or her day in court. In these instances, the term *bātiqu* means an accuser (a second accuser in these contexts) and is distinguished from a regular third-party witness (*mukinnu*).[79] From these records, it appears that the *bātiqu* could be

---

73. Lafont, "Considérations," 20.

74. Oppenheim, "Eyes of the Lord," 178. *CAD* disagrees, defining this as a "slanderer" (*CAD* M/2, 218, citing only ZA 43, 92).

75. This is seen best in the Sumerian "Nippur Homicide Trial," where a wife who did not report her husband's killers was found guilty of the crime and executed. For discussions of this text, see most importantly T. Jacobsen, "An Ancient Mesopotamian Trial for Homicide," in *Studia Biblica et Orientalia*, vol. 3, *Oriens Antiquus* (AnBib 12; Rome: Biblical Institute Press, 1959), 130–50; rprt. in *Toward the Image of Tammuz and Other Essays on Mesopotamian History and Culture* (ed. W. L. Moran; HSS 21; Cambridge, Mass.: Harvard University Press, 1970), 193–214; and M. T. Roth, "Gender and Law: A Case Study from Ancient Mesopotamia," in *Gender and Law in the Hebrew Bible and the Ancient Near East* (ed. V. H. Matthews, B. M. Levinson, and T. Frymer-Kensky; JSOTSup 262; Sheffield: Sheffield Academic, 1998), 173–84. See also LH §109. For a clear example of a third-party accusation in the Neo-Babylonian period that serves to inform the victim of the crime, see, e.g., VAS 6, 82.

76. See n. 71 above.

77. See, e.g., RA 24, 112 (= Jas 31). See also *ABL* 307; cf. *ABL* 314 [= SAA 15, 73], in which an accusation (*batiqtu*) is made, although the text is too broken to give us much detail.

78. See the materials at nn. 114-51 below.

79. San Nicolò, "Gesetzbuches Ḫammurapis," 328 n. 2.

either a public or private person, depending on the matter before the court. I suggest, in light of these facts, that a *bātiqu*, from the Neo-Assyrian period onward, was any person who brought a claim for the benefit of another or served as a second accuser for another.

The accusing party often approached (*maḫāru/kašādu*) the judges.[80] Then he or she typically spoke only once during the investigation or trial, unless he or she[81] reappeared in order to testify concerning some collateral matter.[82] The statement or oath of a second accuser might also appear later in the record. A full explication of this individual's role and import must wait, however, until a few other matters are discussed. Certain trial records report that, at the close of the accusation, the plaintiff might have demanded a judgment against his or her adversary from the court. Such a

---

80. See, e.g., *Nbn* 495; TCL 12, 120; VAS 6, 127 (*kašādu*); and *RA* 12, 6–7 (*maḫāru*).

81. While female participation in the legal system is not as frequent, we do find examples. Females could make accusations and sue, as evidenced by *AfO* 44, 76 no. 5; 44, 78 no. 6; Dalley *Edinburgh* 69; *Nbn* 13; and TCL 12, 122. Indications of female criminal activity in the period are sparse but do exist. See, e.g., Sack 79. More records reflect the importance of female aiders and abettors to male criminals. See, e.g., *RA* 14, 158 no. 152; YOS 7, 97; and YOS 19, 98. A female might be the defendant, or the subject matter, of civil suits. See, e.g., *Cyr* 307, 312; and *RA* 67, 148–49. Female witnesses at trial are more common still. See, e.g., *Nbn* 343 and YOS 6, 224.

82. See, e.g., TCL 13, 170 and YOS 6, 225, wherein the accusers speak a second time in order to clear themselves of possible charges that arise as the case progresses. In TCL 13, 170, a supply room official accused a man of stealing goods from the storeroom over a ten-year period. Temple officials quickly turned the tables on him, inquiring as to why he did not report this sooner. He was clearly under suspicion of participating in the crime as either a co-conspirator or as an aider and abettor. They then demanded that the accuser reclaim any goods that he had given to the accused and produce them before the court. The accuser said that the accused had no such goods remaining in his possession, presumably because he had immediately disposed of them. At that point, the court brought in a number of other people from the storeroom to question them as to whether the thief had also taken goods from them. These individuals swore an oath that the accused had not taken any goods from them. After this, the accuser swore that he had tried to stop the accused but that his words were not heeded and that he had not shared in the stolen grain (reading against E. W. Moore [*Neo-Babylonian Business and Administrative Documents* (Ann Arbor: University of Michigan Press, 1935), 168–71], who mistranslates the oath; see n. 46 above). This latter oath was probably proffered to clear the accuser of the charge that he was aiding and abetting the thief by ignoring the situation or by actively participating in the crime as a co-conspirator. Unfortunately, the end of the tablet is broken, so that we do not know the outcome of the investigation. In YOS 6, 225, the plaintiffs, who were brothers, made an accusation against an individual for failure to tender certain goods to the temple as instructed. The court interrogated the defendant, and he explained his legitimate reasons for failing to make the delivery. Although the text is broken or obscure in various sections, it is clear that the plaintiffs spoke again in order to offer an oath that they had not sued maliciously. I presume that they were accused of bringing a false suit and were defending on those grounds, but the text is too unclear to enable us to make this assertion with any certainty. For clear cases in which the false-suit penalty was assessed, see the material at n. 180 below.

demand might have been expressed by the words "make a judgment" (*dīn epēšu*)⁸³ or "establish/render a decision" (*purussâ šakānu*).⁸⁴ This is an early form of prosecutorial language, although a victim-plaintiff most commonly expressed it in this period. Ancient Near Eastern records of prosecutorial argument for the benefit of another are extremely rare.⁸⁵

*Investigations.* If there were no formal demand or if the demand were not satisfied, some form of investigation was then conducted. Most often, this occurred in the midst of the trial, but a number of Neo-Babylonian records document what appear to be distinct pre-trial investigations.⁸⁶ In inquisitorial legal systems, the investigatory process drives the trial process.⁸⁷ Fact-finding is highly cooperative and progresses from the pre-trial phase through the trial phase in a more fluid manner than in common law adversarial systems. The Neo-Babylonian documents disclose that this facet of inquisitorial systems was enhanced in this period;⁸⁸ hence, it is not always readily apparent whether a document contains a pre-trial or a mid-trial investigation. Investigations might have been conducted by the adjudicator (whether a judge, an official, or the assembly) who was to hear the trial itself⁸⁹ or by an independent investigator.⁹⁰

---

83. See, e.g., A 32117 (edited in M. T. Roth, "Case of Contested Status," 481–89) and *RA* 12, 6–7.

84. See e.g., *AfO* 44, 78 no. 6; *CT* 22, 229; and *TCL* 13, 219 [= *Nbn* 720]. Outside the Neo-Babylonian period, "judge him a judgment" or "convict him" (*dīnšu dīn*) is also employed (*CAD* D, 102–3).

85. The "Nippur Homicide Trial" (discussed in n. 75, *supra*) has patent prosecutorial language exhibited by a third party. The trial record reports the discussions in the assembly regarding the guilt or innocence of the wife. Several individuals who desire the wife's conviction state: "Those three males and that woman shall be killed before the chair of Lu-Inanna . . ." (translation by Roth, "Gender and Law," 177). See also Jer 26:10–11. These are the only two examples of prosecutorial language in ancient Near Eastern literature known to me.

86. For investigations and interrogations in the course of a trial, see, e.g., *AfO* 44, 76 no. 5, and *Cyr* 312; cf. *TAD* B7.1 and *TAD* B7.2, which are Aramaic oath documents from Elephantine that record mid-trial interrogations. For investigations that do not appear, on the face of the document, to be held in the midst of trial, see, e.g., *CT* 2, 2; Spar 3; *TCL* 13, 170; *YOS* 6, 137, 144, 223; and *YOS* 7, 42.

87. See n. 42 above.

88. See, e.g., *AnOr* 8, 56, where the court takes some evidence in an investigatory manner, issues temporary orders, and then promises to conduct a further investigation and come to a final decision. For more on this case, see n. 164 below.

89. See, e.g., *RA* 12, 6–7; *RA* 67, 148–49; *TCL* 13, 170, 219 (= *Nbn* 720); *YOS* 6, 223; and *YOS* 7, 42; cf. *YOS* 7, 96. The court might also demand that one of the parties produce documentary evidence. See, e.g., *AfO* 44, 76 no. 5; 44, 78 no. 6; *Nbn* 13; and *Nbn* 1128.

90. See, e.g., Spar 3 and *YOS* 6, 144. G. J. P. McEwan argues that the witness list of a sale document for slaves refers to the job title "court-interrogator" (*mitiprazu*) (*ROM* 2, 36; see his discussion of this in *The Late Babylonian Tablets in the Royal Ontario Museum* [Royal Ontario Museum Cuneiform Texts 2; Toronto: Royal Ontario Museum, 1982], 49 n. 6).

76   On the Scales of Righteousness

Such investigations, whether they occurred at the pre- or mid-trial stage, were often quite involved and most unpleasant affairs.[91] Persons could have been immediately arrested (*ṣabātu*) and imprisoned,[92] although a temporary[93] or permanent release[94] of the incarcerated could have been arranged if someone were willing to guarantee the prisoner's appropriate behavior. Such investigations could also be quite brutal. These interrogations might have involved torture.[95] Property that was the subject of the

---

91. *CT* 2, 2 is an unusually lengthy and involved investigation. There we find recorded an accusation, an ordered and executed search and seizure, the testimony of third parties, and a defendant denial. (It is also unusual in that it is one of the rare documented injury cases where the suspect is cleared of the charges.) See also TCL 13, 170, discussed in n. 82 above.

92. Imprisonment was typically used to detain the suspect while awaiting trial or for political reasons. Whether imprisonment was also used as a means of punishment remains uncertain (see San Nicolò, "Kleine Gefängnismeuterei in Eanna," 1; Oelsner et al., "Neo-Babylonian Period," 967; and Westbrook, "Punishments and Crimes," 555). The practice of pre-trial seizing of persons is made apparent in YOS 6, 144; cf. OIP 114, 20. TCL 13, 215 gives details of an order to arrest (cf. YOS 7, 137, which notes that an arrest was made pursuant to written orders). See also CTMMA 3, 83. Going to prison (*ina kīli*), or the prison, itself (*bīt kīli*), is mentioned in several Neo-Babylonian texts (see, e.g., *CT* 22, 174, 230; TCL 13, 151; YOS 7, 97 and 137). A storehouse might also serve as a prison in some instances (see, e.g., *Cyr* 281). See further M. San Nicolò, *Zur Nachbürgschaft in den Keilschrifturkunden und in dem gräko-ägyptischen Papyri* (SBAW 6; Munich: Bayerischen Akademie der Wissenschaften, 1937), 26 n. 1.

93. Prisoners were permitted temporary leaves under certain conditions. In such a situation, someone usually stood guarantee that the prisoner would return to the court or prison by a specific date. See, e.g., YOS 7, 144; TCL 13, 151 and 154 display that the court simply expected the return of the incarcerated when it summoned him.

94. YOS 7, 77 records that a certain temple slave, Šamaš-bel-kullati, was put into irons and later released to his brother, who guaranteed that the prisoner would not be seen in the wine cellar again, presumably because he was a wine thief (following the translation of Dandamaev [*Slavery in Babylonia*, 498] against Joannès ["Texts judiciaries néo-babyloniens," 209–10] and Dougherty [*Shirkûtu*, 66–67]). *Cyr* 281 records an imprisonment wherein a slave was held in iron chains in a storehouse. In that case, however, we are not told why the slave was imprisoned, only that another slave vouched for him and he was, therefore, released—apparently permanently. The penalty to the surety should the individual flee is that he will have to do the work of the runaway as well as his own.

95. Six documents, *CT* 55, 110; YOS 6, 77, 137, 144, 223; and YOS 7, 42, all indicate, by use of the word *maš'altu*, that an interrogation is taking place. For example, in YOS 6, 137, two thieves are caught in the act of stealing four sheep by a shepherd in the employ of the owner of the sheep. The shepherd also accuses them of slaughtering one of the sheep. He seizes them and immediately hauls them into court for interrogation. They confess to the crime and implicate an accomplice. See further Dandamaev, *Slavery in Babylonia*, 539; San Nicolò, "Die *maš'altu*-Urkunden," 289–91; and idem, "Der Monstreprozeß," 72. See additionally F. Joannès, "Une chronique judiciaire d'époque hellénistique et le châtiment des sacrileges à Babylone," in *Fs. Oelsner*, 206. Such interrogations may have been effectuated by a "ladder of interrogation" (*simmiltu ša maš'alti*) (M. Jursa, "Akkad, das Eulmaš und Gubāru," *WZKM* 86 [1996]: 199, 210). On the other hand, several documents say that testimony was given without interrogation (*ša lā maša'ltu*). In AnOr 8, 27, an individual confessed that he and a cohort burgled a house and stole temple property that was in the dwelling. YOS 7, 10

lawsuit or that constituted a piece of critical evidence might also have been seized.[96] Additionally, the court might have seized all the property of the accused by way of criminal forfeiture.[97]

*Summonses.* In the Neo-Babylonian period, once the basic accusation had been asserted and any separate investigation completed, what we might think of as the trial phase generally began. If the defendant had not already been arrested or contacted, he or she was typically summoned before the court.[98] The accusation itself might contain a summons to appear.[99] Trial transcripts also display the issuance of immediate postaccusation summonses of the accused.[100] The court might have also issued summonses to both the plaintiff and the defendant for further proceedings after the accusation was lodged.[101] Other summonses of accusers tended to be a call to reappear at a later hearing in the trial process.[102] Many records document a summons to recall the defendant for a later proceeding of the trial, as well.[103] A party's failure to appear pursuant to a summons could result in a default judgment.[104] Third-party witnesses were also subject to the sum-

---

records that a slave testified without interrogation. Furthermore, YOS 7, 78 indicates that a man who appears to be a free citizen testified without interrogation. In these last two cases, however, the testimony amounts to an accusation.

96. See, e.g., *CT* 2, 2 and YOS 6, 137. AnOr 8, 27, 38; and YOS 7, 42 document other pre- and mid-trial seizures of property that were the object of the crime.

97. *AfO* 17, 2 is a sale document that records the disposal of property that was the subject of a criminal forfeiture. In this situation, the defendant was executed for treason against the king. Apparently, his property was forfeited and sold rather than being subject to any inheritance rights. For further discussion of this last document, see Weidner, "Hochverat gegen Nebukadnezar," 1–9; and Dandamaev, *Slavery in Babylonia*, 106. Durand *Textes babyloniens* 6 documents both a pre-trial seizing of stolen goods and the criminal forfeiture of other property belonging to the defendant. *CT* 22, 230 reflects a seizure and sale of stolen property. The proceeds of the sale in this case were to go to the injured party. Cf. *Alalakh* 17.

98. R. P. Dougherty notes that the idiom "to lift up his head" (*rêša našû*) conveys the idea of summoning ("Suretyship," 98 n. 1). This idiom is used throughout the Neo-Babylonian period. See, e.g., *BIN* 1, 113; *TCL* 13, 151 and 154; YOS 6, 191 and 214; and YOS 7, 144.

99. See, e.g., YOS 7, 189, wherein the assembly of Uruk instructed the owner of two accused slaves to produce them before the royal judges in Uruk for trial.

100. In A 32117 (edited in Roth, "Case of Contested Status," 482–83); *Nbn* 13; *RA* 12, 6–7; and *RA* 67, 148–49, we find an accusation and the defendant summons noted in a verdict document.

101. YOS 6, 225, which records both a verdict and the execution of judgment, tells of two brothers who accused the defendant of theft before temple administrators. Temple officials then summoned both plaintiffs and the defendant to appear before them and the assembly for further proceedings. For more on this text, see n. 82 above. Cf. *TCL* 13, 132, wherein the court summoned both the accuser and the defendant in a matter regarding temple livestock. It appears that the temple might have been the first accuser in this case.

102. See, e.g., *Nbk* 52, 183, 365; and YOS 7, 15.

103. See, e.g., *BIN* 1, 113; *Fs. Walker* 356; YOS 6, 191 and 214.

104. In YOS 7, 189, the default judgment is recorded as a conditional verdict. In a case

mons power of the court.[105] It was extremely common for another individual to stand surety for the appearance of a summoned person.[106] If the witness did not appear, the guarantor either had to pay a penalty to the court or, if he or she were a party, lose the case.

*Defendant declarations and oaths.* Once the accusation was lodged in a Neo-Babylonian lawsuit, evidence was taken. Most importantly, the defendant testified.[107] The defendant's statement is an essential part of the process in any inquisitorial legal system. Usually no, or limited, protection against self-incrimination exists.[108] This was also true of Neo-Babylonian trial procedure. The defendant's statement may have been either a denial of liability or culpability,[109] or a confession.[110] The defendant's testimony might

---

where the defendant had apparently disappeared, YOS 7, 15, the court issued a summons for the accuser to reappear once the defendant surfaced. No conditional verdict was issued in that situation; the accuser had to reaccuse the defendant at a later date. It may be that, where the court knew that the defendant was available for service of the summons, a conditional default judgment was issued, as in YOS 7, 189, and that, where the court had been informed that the defendant was unavailable, the court would afford the parties another opportunity to try the matter, as in YOS 7, 15.

105. *BIN* 1, 142 is a memorandum of a summons, which was presumably issued by the court, to twenty-one third-party witnesses to testify for one of the parties of a case. The end of the tablet is broken; thus, there is some question as to who issued the summons. Both YOS 6, 169 (= YOS 6, 231) and YOS 6, 224 record that a witness was summoned to court after the defendant named the individual as a possible witness.

106. Some of these cases involve an individual's guarantee of the appearance of the defendant or reappearance of the defendant before the court in later proceedings (see, e.g., YOS 6, 191, 193, 203, and 214). We also see instances where a defendant has impleaded an individual in the course of his defense and must then guarantee the testimony of the impleaded party or pay the penalty (see, e.g., TCL 12, 77). The surety guaranteed the appearance of third-party witnesses in several instances (see, e.g., YOS 6, 175 and 208; and YOS 7, 96). Once *Cyr* 311 is read in conjunction with *Cyr* 312, a companion tablet, it is clear that third-party witnesses to a dispute guaranteed the testimony of yet another person who could verify their testimony at trial. In a number of records, we see this same type of summons and guarantee but do not know why the court or administrator is summoning the individual; in other words, either litigation or some administrative matter might have been before the court (see, e.g., YOS 6, 165, 213, and 230; and YOS 7, 3). In these cases, the individual may need to return by a specific day (see, e.g., YOS 6, 230) or whenever the court should call (see, e.g., YOS 7, 3).

107. See, e.g., *BIN* 1, 113; Dalley *Edinburgh* 69; *Fs. Walker* 356; *RA* 12, 6–7; *RA* 67, 148–49; YOS 6, 191, 208, 214, 224, 235; YOS 7, 42 and 152. As indicated previously, the defendant's statement typically follows the accusation. See, e.g., *BIN* 1, 113; Dalley *Edinburgh* 69; *RA* 12, 6–7; *RA* 67, 148–49; YOS 6, 208 and 224. There are instances, however, when the defendant's testimony is recorded as coming before the accusation, as in YOS 6, 235; YOS 7, 42; and YOS 7, 152. For further discussion, see the materials at n. 46 above.

108. See n. 42 above.

109. See, e.g., Dalley *Edinburgh* 69; *RA* 67, 148–49; YOS 6, 169 (= YOS 6, 231); YOS 6, 208; and YOS 6, 225. We also have statements that are denials in part and confessions in part. See, e.g., YOS 7, 7 (tenth count).

110. See, e.g., *Iraq* 13, 96–97; *RA* 12, 6–7; YOS 6, 137 and 144; and YOS 7, 7 (wherein the

have been given by means of either a simple or a sworn statement.[111] Usually, the defendant offered one brief statement in his or her defense. Cases exist, however, where the defendant made a lengthy statement[112] or multiple statements.[113]

Three types of oaths were used in ancient Near Eastern litigation. The first is a promissory oath, which usually accompanied a contractual or administrative obligation. One or both of the parties might have offered such an oath to assure that they would abide by the terms of the verdict or settlement agreement.[114] The other two oaths are evidentiary in nature and, therefore, are important aspects of trial procedure. We now turn to them.

The court-ordered assertory oath, which is closely related to the ordeal, was typically taken at the end of a suit by one of the parties and disposed of the case in favor of the party who took the oath.[115] Such suprarational

---

defendant confesses to seven of twelve counts and also denies in part and confesses in part to another one of the counts). In TCL 13, 219 (= *Nbn* 720), the co-defendants offer two confessions in an attempted fraud case. They had attempted to use a forged debt tablet to extract money from the son of the buyer of their land. A payment of a certain amount of silver would have prevented the supposed execution of the pledge against the land. In the first confession, they said that the debt had been paid and that no funds were owed. After the court called for the production of the holder of the debt, they admitted that the document was entirely false. For further discussion of this text, see Joannès, "Textes judiciaire néo-babyloniens," 227–29. In a very interesting case, *Nbn* 1113, the plaintiff confesses to having had no basis on which to sue.

111. Innumerable examples exist of simple defendant statements in the Neo-Babylonian period. See, e.g., BE 9, 24; TCL 13, 219 (= *Nbn* 720); YOS 6, 169 (= YOS 6, 231); YOS 6, 235; and YOS 7, 96.

112. TCL 12, 122 reflects a very lengthy defendant statement. There the defendant must discuss prior related legal proceedings in order to explain his position to the court. Helpfully, we have record of one of these prior cases in *AfO* 44, 83 no. 13. For further discussion of these texts, see n. 191 below.

113. In TCL 13, 181, during an investigation, the defendant maintains that he is innocent of failing to surrender temple debt records. The court resumes questioning him in regard to some specific debt tablets, and he denies culpability by assigning responsibility to his brother (reading with Joannès ["Textes judiciaire néo-babyloniens," 225–27] and against E. W. Moore [*Neo-Babylonian Business Documents*, 184–87], who mistranslates the oath; see n. 46 above). Similarly, in YOS 7, 42, another investigation file, the defendant made three separate statements confessing to the charges facing him. The second confession immediately followed the first, but the third was interrupted by an accusation. For more on this text, see n. 46 above. YOS 7, 96 contains two statements by the defendant. In the first, he summarizes his denial. In the second, he offers specifics to support his claim of innocence and implicates another individual in the crime. These two statements are not separated, however, by intervening accusations, testimony, or significant scribal narration. See also TCL 13, 170 (discussed in n. 82 above) and TCL 13, 219 (= *Nbn* 720) (discussed in n. 110 below).

114. See, e.g., BE 10, 9; IMT 105 (joined to EE 109); Stolper 399–400; and VAS 6, 38. While most of these oaths are postverdict oaths, VAS 6, 38 is a promise on the part of both parties to abide by the decision of the court before it renders its verdict.

115. There is much literature on the dispository nature of most oaths and ordeals in the ancient Near East. For a few items of the bibliography, see ch. 3 n. 43 above; S. H. Blank, "The

evidence was often introduced where the available rational evidence was insufficient to determine the case.[116] This oath was a very formal affair. The court commanded the oath from the party of its choosing; in the Old Babylonian period, that was typically the defendant.[117] The court then moved to the site of the oath, most commonly the temple, or the temple gate, where the actual oath was performed, although on rare occasions a symbol of the god was moved to the site of the dispute.[118] The relevant documents give us only limited information about the oath process. We do know, however, that the ritual usually involved stating the oath before some divine statue or emblem.[119]

The Old Babylonian court often issued a *ṭuppi burtim*, in which the court set forth its decision, along with any specified action that was required in order for a final verdict to issue.[120] In some cases, the court required the swearing of the formal oath before the court would give the verdict final effect. Such tablets are known in the scholarly literature as *Beweisurteil* documents.[121] In the words of R. A. Veenker, these *Beweisurteil* documents were "a 'conditional' verdict, which was to become effective after the swearing ...."[122] The formal oath predominated in the Old Babylonian period and retained importance through the Neo-Assyrian period, as evidenced by numerous conditional and final verdict documents.

In the Old Babylonian period, a weakened form of the oath also existed. It might have been taken by any party or witness, and it added more weight to the evidence he or she offered.[123] Such oaths did not necessarily resolve the case; but they did increase the efficiency of the witness's

---

Curse, the Blasphemy, the Spell, the Oath," *HUCA* 23 (1950–51): 73–95; G. R. Driver and J. C. Miles, "Ordeal by Oath at Nuzi," *Iraq* 7 (1940): 132–38; S. E. Loewenstamm, "The Cumulative Oath of Witnesses and Parties in Mesopotamian Law," in *Comparative Studies in Biblical and Ancient Near Oriental Literatures* (AOAT 204; Neukirchen-Vluyn: Neukirchener Verlag, 1980), 341–45; S. Lafont, "La procédure par serment au Proche-Orient ancien," in *Jurer et maudire: pratiques politiques et usages juridiques du serment dans le Proche-Orient ancien* (ed. Sophie Lafont; Paris: L'Harmattan, 1997), 197–98; and A. I. Lieberman, "Studies in the Trial by River Ordeal in the Ancient Near East during the Second Millennium B.C.E." (Ph.D. diss., Brandeis University, 1969).

116. Jas, *Neo-Assyrian Judicial Procedures*, 73.
117. Dombradi, *Die Darstellung des Rechtsaustrags*, 1:330.
118. J. N. Postgate, *Early Mesopotamia: Society and Economy at the Dawn of History* (London: Routledge, 1992), 280.
119. Dombradi, *Die Darstellung des Rechtsaustrags*, 1:330.
120. See further *CAD* B, 339.
121. Postgate, *Early Mesopotamia*, 281; and G. Ries, "Altbabylonische Beweisurteile," *ZSS* 106 (1989): 56–80.
122. Veenker, "Old Babylonian Judiciary," 45–53, quote on 47.
123. Dombradi calls this "hardening" the evidence (*Die Darstellung des Rechtsaustrags*, 1:330–31). We see the weakened oath in Nuzi, as well. See further Frymer-Kensky, "Suprarational Legal Procedures," 115–31.

testimony in meeting the party's burden of proof. This oath might not necessarily be court-ordered,[124] and it did not typically comply with all the formalities of the significantly more common formal oath. For example, in the Old Babylonian period, the declarant did not usually swear the weakened form of the oath by the gods.[125]

While it is possible that this two-tiered evidentiary oath system may have remained in place in the Neo-Babylonian period, little evidence of the formal oath exists in the available corpus.[126] Instead, the weakened form of

---

124. Dombradi asserts that it is very difficult to tell in which situations the Old Babylonian courts might seek the weakened oaths from parties or witnesses (*Die Darstellung des Rechtsaustrags*, 1:331). It is possible that parties and witnesses offered them primarily on their own initiative. That appears to be the typical scenario in the Neo-Babylonian period. See further the material at nn. 127, 128, and 130 below.

125. Dombradi, *Die Darstellung des Rechtsaustrags*, 1:331.

126. One letter, UrET 4, 186, makes reference to what might be a formal evidentiary oath, but it is outside a litigation setting (my reading follows *CAD* D, 33; and B. Wells, "The Law of Testimony in the Pentateuchal Codes" [Ph.D. diss., The Johns Hopkins University, 2002], 178 n. 148, against Ebeling, *Neubabylonische Briefe*, 175 no. 321). Westbrook suggests that NBL §1 may also contain a reference to a formal oath (private communication February 7, 2002). It is, however, extremely fragmentary, and nothing can be determined with certainty. C. Wunsch seems to suggest that BM 77425 contains a formal dispository oath (Oelsner et al., "Neo-Babylonian Period," 924). In that case, however, it was third-party witnesses who swore at the court's insistence to the contents of a missing adoption document, to which they had been the recording witnesses and which was the subject of the current dispute. See similarly CM 20, 166. M. Stolper reconstructs Durand *Textes babyloniens* 6, line 18, as stating that an individual swore an oath by an iron dagger ("Late Achaemenid Texts from Dilbat," *Iraq* 54 [1992]: 123–24; cf. Oelsner et al., "Neo-Babylonian Period," 925), but the reconstruction is speculative. UrET 4, 171 appears to record an oath that was sworn before a *kudurru*, which typically had a divine symbol on it. The oath involves a dispute, but whether the oath was offered or ordered in the context of litigation is uncertain on the face of the text. See further W. von Soden, review of H. H. Figulla, *Ur Excavations, Texts IV: Business Documents of the New Babylonian Period*, *JAOS* 71 (1951): 267–68. Outside of Mesopotamia, in Elephantine, evidence of the formal oath exists in this period (see, e.g., *TAD* B7.1, B7.2, and B7.3. *TAD* B7.4 also refers to an oath but is too damaged to give us its specifics). It appears that, in a pattern quite opposite to that of Mesopotamia, the oath gained in importance in Egypt over time. Early Egyptian oaths did not always resolve the case, while, later in Egyptian history, they apparently became dispositive. See S. Allam, *Hieratische Ostraka und Papyri aus der Ramessidenzeit* (Urkunden zum Rechtsleben im alten Ägypten 1; Tübingen: Mohr, 1973), 214–15; M. Malinine, "Deux documents égyptiens relatifs au dépot," *MDAIK* 16 (1958): 221–22; and E. Seidl, *Einführung in die ägyptische Rechtsgeschichte bis zum Ende des Neuen Reiches* (Ägyptologische Forschungen 10; Glückstadt: Augustin, 1951), esp. 64 no. 49. The law in Elephantine appears to be under Egyptian influence much more than under Neo-Babylonian influence in this instance. Cf. R. Yaron, who states that, in its Mesopotamian aspects, the law of Elephantine resembles Neo-Assyrian and earlier law rather than Neo-Babylonian law (*Introduction to the Law of the Aramaic Papyri* [Oxford: Clarendon, 1961], 119–20, rejecting the assertion of E. G. Kraeling that it is under Neo-Babylonian influence (*The Brooklyn Museum Aramaic Papyri: New Documents of the Fifth Century B.C. from the Jewish Colony at Elephantine* [New Haven: Yale University Press, 1953], 49–50). This, too, would account for the presence of formal oaths at Elephantine.

the oath strongly predominates.[127] In this period, even where the document explicitly mentions that the oaths were sworn before one or more gods, they remained nondispositive as to the litigation before the court.[128] Two instances of court-ordered oaths exist in the Neo-Babylonian corpus, but they still do not have dispositive effect.[129] While, in instances of the formal oath, the testimony of only one party was sworn, cases exist in the Neo-Babylonian record where both parties offered sworn testimony.[130] Rational evidence seemed to have greater evidentiary import than the oath.[131] It should also be noted here that no known cases of defendant oaths of confession exist; all defendant oaths were oaths of denial. A simple confession was sufficient for a finding of guilt. Third-party witnesses might also offer sworn testimony, but that, too, was the weakened form of the oath.[132] Thus, it appears that use of the formal oath was diminishing considerably in this period.

Consistent with the seeming reluctance to employ the oath as a means to resolve close cases, the Neo-Babylonian evidence of the use of the river ordeal is also quite limited.[133] S. Lafont and F. Joannès rightly observe that the sole Neo-Babylonian evidence of the ordeal is a description in a literary

---

127. We find an example of a weakened oath from an accuser in TCL 13, 179 (for more on this text, see n. 56 above) and examples of weakened oaths from defendants in *Dar* 53; TCL 13, 181; YNER 1, 2; and YOS 7, 152. Cf. TCL 13, 170 and YOS 6, 225, which are plaintiff oaths, but which address the plaintiff's own possible culpability in the matter (see n. 82 above). TCL 13, 170 and YOS 6, 169 (= YOS 6, 231) contain exculpatory oaths of third parties whom the court suspected of involvement in the matter under investigation.

128. See, e.g., PBS 2/1, 140; TCL 13, 181; and YNER 1, 2. Both *Dar* 53 and YOS 6, 225 contain oaths sworn before the gods; but, because the texts are so broken and obscure, it is difficult to assess with certainty what results the oaths bring.

129. Spar 1 and YOS 6, 156. Spar 1 indicates that the court asked an individual to swear to his testimony, but not that the individual did, in fact, swear to his testimony. Instead, the scribe only notes that the individual stated his position. Furthermore, the reported testimony is not stated in the common oath formula. Regrettably, this text is most obscure on a number of points. See Spar, "Three Neo-Babylonian Trial Depositions," 157–61. In YOS 6, 156, the accuser charged the defendant with causing to be butchered one more temple sheep than was required by the temple. The court questioned two others in the matter and ordered them to swear that they had not killed temple livestock on the same day. Presumably, they were being questioned as possible additional responsible parties. They took the exculpatory oath, using the common oath formula. The oath seems to have ended matters with respect to them (see similarly TCL 13, 170). The case continues, however, with regard to the defendant.

130. See, e.g., PBS 2/1, 140, wherein the plaintiff accused the defendant of carrying off the harvest of certain fields over a three-year period. The defendant answered by swearing an oath in the assembly that he did not do so. Then the plaintiff replied by oath that the defendant had done as charged. Both oaths were sworn before the gods. Apparently, either the court found for the plaintiff or the defendant conceded the case; the text is not clear which.

131. See, e.g., YOS 6, 169. See also Oelsner et al., "Neo-Babylonian Period," 923–24.

132. See, e.g., TCL 12, 70; YOS 6, 169 (= YOS 6, 231); and YOS 6, 224.

133. Lafont, "Considérations," 30; and Joannès, "Pratique du serment," 172.

document.¹³⁴ The latest legal references to such suprarational evidence are from the Neo-Assyrian period, some of which are in the Neo-Babylonian dialect.¹³⁵ L. Kataja makes the point: "There are quite a few references to the legal institution [of the river ordeal] in Mesopotamian texts of all periods, including the Neo-Assyrian one. Most of the references are however literary and actually executed ordeals are rarely reported."¹³⁶ She notes that only Nuzi documented a large number of river ordeals.¹³⁷ Thus, the literary reference cannot be considered reliable evidence that the ordeal was in use during the Neo-Babylonian period. Consequently, I infer that the ordeal probably disappeared in the late Neo-Assyrian or early Neo-Babylonian period.

We must be suspicious, however, of what appear to be extreme shifts in legal philosophy and practice in the ancient Near East.¹³⁸ Reforms in ancient law tended not to sweep away older practices. The law is an extremely conservative institution, and radical breaks from prior tradition are rare. Reforms, therefore, tended to coexist with older traditions and to replace them only gradually—but changes did occur.¹³⁹ Our Neo-Babylonian data are, of course, limited by our archival finds, and, therefore, we cannot assert anything with absolute certainty. The maxim "absence of evidence is not evidence of absence" could hold true in this instance.¹⁴⁰ At the same time, we cannot help but notice that the frequency of occurrence of suprarational evidence drops off steeply between the published Neo-Assyrian litigation corpus and the published Neo-Babylonian litigation corpus. Furthermore, the Neo-Babylonian evidence derives in large measure from temple archives. This is significant because we might expect suprarational evidence to be regarded more favorably in the temple courts

---

134. *CT* 46, 45. Cf. Ebeling, *Neubabylonische Briefe*, 60–61 no. 105, who speculates that *CT* 22, 105 contains a reference to the river ordeal.

135. *BIN* 2, 132, a very early Neo-Babylonian text from the reign of Esarhaddon, also documents the use of the river ordeal in a trial of temple slaves. See also three early Neo-Babylonian letters, *ABL* 965; *OIP* 114, 38 and 110, that testify to the use of the river ordeal to resolve cases in the Neo-Assyrian period.

136. Kataja, "Neo-Assyrian Document," 66.

137. Ibid., 66 n. 6.

138. Even while acknowledging the seeming discontinuation of the ordeal in the Neo-Babylonian period, Joannès expresses surprise concerning that discontinuation ("Pratique du serment," 172).

139. For instance, Westbrook observes that Israelite legal materials from the Neo-Assyrian and Neo-Babylonian period "share something of the intellectual ferment of contemporary Greek sources and thus some taste also of their new legal conceptions" ("Covenant Code," 28; see also idem, "Legalistic 'Glosses' in Biblical Narratives," *Israel Law Review* 33 [1999]: 796–97).

140. See A. Millard, "The Last Tablets of Ugarit," in *Actes du colloque: Le pays d'Ougarit autour de 1200 av. J.-C.* (Ras Shamra-Ougarit 11; Paris: ERC, 1995), 123.

than in the secular courts because the temple was often involved in administering formal oaths. Even the promissory oath seemed to have lost a great deal of its power in this period.[141] Consequently, it appears that suprarational evidence and procedures, which were regarded so highly in prior periods, were strongly disfavored in this period.[142] This is the most important Neo-Babylonian shift from the ancient Near Eastern meta-tradition regarding legal procedure.

*Second accusations, corroborating witness statements, and other additional evidence.* This growing rejection of the oath raised an important new problem, that is, how to resolve close cases. In prior periods, where the evidence hung in the balance, the court typically demanded that one of the parties take the oath; refusal was construed as an admission of culpability. A conditional verdict, where issued, hung quite often upon one of the parties taking the formal oath. In the Neo-Babylonian period, this resolution was highly disfavored; thus, the legal system had to devise an alternative method of resolution. According to B. Wells, the party on whom the burden of proof fell now had to produce additional rational evidence in order to win the case.[143] That additional evidence might be the statement of a second accuser or other corroborating witness or some other piece of evidence.

Numerous cases document the presence of a second accuser[144] or plain-

---

141. Westbrook notes the lessening importance of the promissory oath in the ancient Near East: "Documents recording the standard contractual forms may also record a promissory oath, by one or both parties. For the most part, the oath relates to ancillary matters: either special terms not usually found in that type of contract, or (most frequently) a promise not to deny, contest, or alter the terms of the completed contract in the future. In the third millennium, oaths are sometimes recorded for central obligations of the contract, e.g. repayment of a loan. This type of oath disappears in the second millennium, where only ancillary oaths are recorded. By the first millennium, it is rare to find any mention of an oath in the records of standard contracts" ("The Character of Ancient Near Eastern Law," in *A History of Ancient Near Eastern Law* [ed. R. Westbrook; 2 vols.; Handbook of Oriental Studies 72; Leiden: Brill 2003], 1:66).

142. In accord, Joannès, who maintains that, in the Neo-Babylonian period, the probative value of the oath was less than that of the available rational evidence, unlike the rule of priority in earlier periods of ancient Near Eastern history ("Pratique du serment," 169–70, citing YNER 1, 2 and YOS 6, 169 [= YOS 6, 231]). E. Otto observes that there is a "Säkularisierungstendenz" in the courts from the second to the first millennium ("Neue Aspekte zum keilschriftlichen Prozeßrecht," 282). I suspect that the shift began to accelerate during the Neo-Assyrian period, as evidenced by the existence of a few conditional verdict documents in that period (see, e.g., Jas 53 [= ADD 101]) and the declining number of river ordeals. See further Wells, *Law of Testimony*, 108–30, esp. 128–29.

143. Wells, *Law of Testimony*, 108–30, esp. 128–29. My discussion of the need for a second accuser or witness and the conditional verdict documents through the balance of this study relies on Wells's work.

144. For example, during Gimillu's great trial, YOS 7, 7, the record documents that two accusers appeared to testify as to the fifth count, after which Gimillu confessed. Addition-

tiff's witness.¹⁴⁵ The best evidence that a second accuser or witness was needed is, however, a new form of the conditional-verdict document.¹⁴⁶ Wells has located a substantial number of cases in the Neo-Babylonian

---

ally, with regard to the sixth count, four accusers appeared to convict Gimillu, although neither their specific words nor any confession is recorded as in count 5. Additionally, YOS 7, 10 records a case in which two accusations were put forward without the benefit of any statement on the part of the defendant. In YOS 7, 137, four persons joined in a statement of accusation before temple officials. The result was a court order that the defendant be transported to Babylon for trial. In YOS 7, 88, three persons joined in a statement of accusation, which led to the conviction of the criminal. See also YOS 7, 152, discussed in n. 46 above.

145. As to the tenth count of YOS 7, 7, Gimillu denied the charge in part and confessed to the charge in part after hearing the accusation. A corroborating witness came forward to testify as to the denied matters. Gimillu was convicted on all matters of this count. YOS 6, 169 (= YOS 6, 231) records a suit in which a third-party witness swore an oath. In YOS 6, 224, the temple accused an individual of being a temple slave. During the defendant's testimony, he neither denied nor confessed to his status as a slave. Instead, he said only that another individual had better knowledge than he had regarding his status. This individual was then called forward to testify. She swore an oath that she did indeed see a slave mark on the hand of the defendant's grandmother (disagreeing with the translations of Dandamaev [*Slavery in Babylonia*, 477] and Dougherty [*Shirkûtu*, 36–37], both of whom read the oath formula to say that she did not see a slave mark on the grandmother's hand. This reading would make the woman the defendant's witness and misunderstands the function of the *kî* in the protasis [see n. 46 above]). Consequently, the woman serves as another witness for the temple. One would think it odd that the defendant points to a witness whose testimony will demonstrate that he is a temple slave. There are, however, two possible explanations for this. First, the defendant may not be free, which one might presume, but rather already be a slave in the possession of someone else and be living under conditions that are more unfavorable than those in the temple. If this should be true, the temple and the defendant are probably in collusion against an unnamed third party who is in unlawful possession of the defendant. In the alternative, the defendant might be currently free and an unwilling participant in the trial, who had been forced, under interrogation, to reveal the names of anyone who might have information concerning his status. YOS 7, 97 was an investigation of a prisoner rebellion and escape attempt, in which another prisoner was assaulted. The prison chief accused two co-defendants of the charges. They confessed and implicated two other individuals. A pair of iron shears, which were to be used by the defendants, presumably, to cut their way out or to stab the guards, was then introduced into evidence. Another witness came forward at that point to testify that she supplied the weapon to one of the defendants. She was, apparently, an aider and abettor to the crime and confessed her role in the course of her testimony but was not on trial here. Proceedings related to her might have been recorded elsewhere, or she might have been under compulsion to bring the weapon to the defendants because she was the slave of one of their fathers and, therefore, free from any criminal accountability. Lastly, in *RA* 67, 148–49, an individual accused the defendant of owning a slave with a temple mark on her hand. The defendant denied the charge, stating that he had bought the slave but that she had run away and put the mark on her own hand. The slave woman then came forward to testify that she was dedicated to the temple by her previous master. The judges of the case brought in a scribe to interpret the inscription in the slave's mark. The scribe testified that the mark was older than the defendant's story would allow. Thus, the court found for the temple. I observe here that not only did a second accuser come forward in the case, but an expert third-party witness was also called upon to supply his testimony.

146. Wells, *Law of Testimony*, 108–30.

period in which the offered evidence was insufficient for the court to resolve the case.[147] This situation might have occurred even in cases where sworn testimony had been offered to the court.[148] In such cases, the court would allow the party on whom the burden of proof rested to bring additional evidence later. A verdict conditional upon the offer of that proof was then issued—to take effect at the time when the additional evidence was offered to the court. That may or may not have been a date specifically delineated by the court. The copious use of this type of conditional verdict in the Neo-Babylonian period, coupled with a complete absence in the published corpus of the older form of conditional-verdict documents, also seems to lay bare the courts' hesitation to use the formal oath and the preferred use of an alternative means of dispute resolution in close cases. The Neo-Babylonian courts would rather wait for rational evidence than dispose of the case immediately through suprarational means.

Although the need for two witnesses is sometimes evident prior to the Neo-Babylonian period,[149] it was in this period that the need for a second accuser, a corroborating witness, or some other rational evidence became significantly more important. A superficial reading of the court records might seem to indicate that the court did not always demand evidence beyond the word of the first accuser. Wells observes, however, that, in lawsuits involving temple property or affairs that were tried before the temple court, the temple was, in fact, the implied first accuser.[150] Those documents that seem to record only one accusation may, therefore, be recording the second accusation without referring back to the first.[151] The temple might also have been the unstated second accuser in cases in which the first accuser was a private prosecutor who brought the crime to the attention of temple personnel. Non-temple cases that do not record the presence of a second accuser might be most easily explained by the need for brevity in the tablets. Still, it is possible that what was demanded in theory was not always put into practice. In spite of the imperfections in the records, it can

---

147. The conditional-verdict documents where the burden of proof was assigned to the accuser are AnOr 8, 39; BE 9, 24; GCCI 1, 380; Nbk 52, 104, 183, 365, 419; RA 14, 158 no. 52; Sack 79; TCL 12, 50, 60, 70, 106; UCP 9/1, 2 37; YNER 1, 2; YOS 6, 122, 134, 148, 179, 191, 193, 203, 214; YOS 7, 24, 26, 141, 192; YOS 17, 32; YOS 19, 97 and 98. The conditional-verdict documents where the burden of proof was assigned to the defendant are *Iraq* 41, 138 no. 49; Nbk 361, 363, 366; Sack 80; TCL 12, 77; YOS 6, 153, 175, and 208.

148. See, e.g., YNER 1, 2.

149. M. A. Losier, "Witness in Israel of the Hebrew Scriptures in the Context of the Ancient Near East" (Ph.D. diss., University of Notre Dame, 1973), 108–12.

150. Wells, *Law of Testimony*, 112, 125.

151. One excellent illustration of this is YOS 7, 152, wherein two accusers appear together to rebut the defendant after he has offered an oath of denial. It is possible that they appear second in the record because they rebut the denial (see the material at n. 46 above). It is also possible, however, that they are actually the second accusers in the case.

be said with certainty that a second accuser or corroborating witness was required for conviction in a substantial number of cases during the Neo-Babylonian period.

Two difficult questions remain. First, must there be a second accuser or will any corroborating witness do? Second, how might we distinguish a third-party second accusation from a third-party witness statement? In the conditional-verdict records, the Neo-Babylonian courts differentiate *accusers* (*bātiqu*)[152] from other *witnesses* (*mukinnu*).[153] Although the exact distinction between the two is not clear on the face of the documents, accusations seem to have had a discrete quality and status in the legal culture, even if the difference remains elusive to us.

Beyond accusations and corroborating witness statements, other evidence might have been introduced. The full contingent of supplemental evidence that a court might have admitted into the record included additional third-party testimony,[154] including expert witness testimony,[155] documentary evidence,[156] physical evidence,[157] and circumstantial evidence.[158] Hearsay evidence was acceptable.[159] Crime-scene views or inspections may also have been permitted. The direct evidence for this is lacking in this period, although it exists for the Old Babylonian period.[160] In the Neo-Babylonian period, the closest that one can find is a case in which the

---

152. See, e.g., AnOr 8, 39; *BE* 9, 24; GCCI 1, 380; *RA* 14, 158 no. 152; TCL 12, 106; YOS 6, 122, 148, 191, 203, 214; and YOS 19, 98.

153. See, e.g., the cases cited in the preceding note and *Iraq* 41, 138; *Nbk* 104, 183; Sack 79; TCL 12, 50; YNER 1, 2; YOS 6, 134; YOS 17, 32; and YOS 19, 97.

154. See, e.g., *CT* 2, 2, in which exculpatory third-party evidence was introduced.

155. See the discussion of *RA* 67, 148–49 in n. 145 above.

156. See, e.g., A 32117 (edited in Roth, "Case of Contested Status," 482–83); *AfO* 44, 83 no. 13 (which is broken at the significant place, but which is recounted as history in the suit documented in TCL 12, 122); *Cyr* 332; Dalley *Edinburgh* 69; *Nbn* 13, 1113, 1128; TCL 12, 119; YOS 6, 116, 208; and YOS 7, 7; cf. YOS 7, 91. We have the actual document that was before the court in a number of cases, including *Nbn* 314 (before the court in *AfO* 44, 83 no. 13, as recounted in TCL 12, 122), *Ner* 23 (before the court in *Nbn* 13); and *JCS* 9, 26; YOS 6, 105 and 119 (before the court in TCL 12, 96 and YOS 6, 153). In TCL 12, 119, the documentary evidence is center stage in the trial. In YOS 6, 169 (= YOS 6, 231), the court, in issuing its verdict, maintained that the defendant did not produce sufficient documentary evidence to support his claim.

157. See, e.g., AnOr 8, 38; YOS 6, 137; YOS 7, 7, 42, 66, 88, 97; and *Iraq* 13, 96–97 (suggesting that Figulla's copying and transliteration of line 14, reading *maḫ(?)-ra-nu* rather than *pag-ra-nu*, is erroneous; I thank R. Westbrook for his assistance with this reading). In YOS 6, 208, the accuser seized the cow in question, but we do not know whether it was brought into court, as is often the case in such seizures.

158. See, e.g., TCL 12, 77 and YOS 6, 175.

159. See, e.g., *JCS* 28, 45 no. 39.

160. In the Old Babylonian period, LE §§36–37 requires that the house of a bailee be inspected for signs of break-in where the bailee claims that he was victimized by a burglary and the bailed goods were pilfered.

assembly inspected a house that was the subject of an ownership dispute.[161] Indirect Neo-Babylonian evidence for the procedure also exists in the period's records of mid-trial searches and seizures of property.[162] In those situations, the court might have ordered its agents to enter the defendant's home during the course of the trial, in order to search for and seize any property subject to the lawsuit.[163] Consequently, it is not farfetched to imagine the court moving to the scene of the crime. It might also be noted here that the testimony of any parties to the dispute or of third-party witnesses need not have been offered in person. Written statements similar to the modern deposition and affidavit might also have been offered into evidence in the party's absence.[164] In some circumstances, a person stood surety for the testimony of a third-party witness before the court.[165]

*Verdicts and execution of judgment.* Upon conclusion of the presentation of evidence, the court rendered its verdict. As I have already noted, where the evidence was insufficient to issue a final judgment, the court might have issued a conditional verdict. It could also issue temporary orders in the case, pending further proceedings.[166] Where the evidence was sufficient for a finding, the court ordered sanctions against the losing party. Before issuing their verdict in the case, the judges of Babylon often acknowledged that they had heard either the plaintiff's statement or the case in its entirety[167] and then decided the case.[168] Moreover, records from the judges

---

161. YOS 7, 28.

162. See, e.g., YOS 7, 42. Many commentators suggest that *Dar* 53 involves a mid-trial search and seizure, where the court ordered a search of the possible location of a runaway slave whose ownership is in dispute (see n. 56 above). The proffered translation of this section of the text is somewhat conjectural owing to a significant break at this point and is dependent on the commentators' particular reading of the oath in the case. Unfortunately, the oath has been consistently mistranslated (see n. 46 above). Hence, it is unlikely that this case discloses a mid-trial search and seizure.

163. Oelsner et al., "Neo-Babylonian Period," 922. Cf. *CT* 2, 2.

164. In *CT* 22, 210, an individual who may well be one of the judges of Babylon wrote to the temple court administrator in Sippar, wanting the temple court to take the opponent's testimony and then to ship the case to Babylon for decision. This procedure would reflect something more in the nature of a deposition. In AnOr 8, 56, the court was involved in an investigation and hearing for temporary orders in a matter involving the ownership of a slave. One of the parties submitted his testimony via a letter. There is no evidence that the written document was sworn, as is the case in a modern affidavit, but as previously discussed, testimony was not required to be sworn in ancient Mesopotamian courts in order to be given effect. Based on the letter, the court ordered the slave to be transferred from the defendant to the plaintiff pending further investigation and decision.

165. See n. 106 above.

166. See, e.g., AnOr 8, 56, discussed in n. 164 above.

167. See, e.g., *AfO* 44, 76 no. 5; 44, 78 no. 6; *Nbn* 13, 1113; and TCL 12, 86.

168. See, e.g., *AfO* 44, 76 no. 5; 44, 78 no. 6; Dalley *Edinburgh* 69; *Nbn* 13, 1113, 1128; *RA*

of Babylon commonly closed with the statement: "The judges wrote out a document, sealed it with their seals and gave it to PN [the victor] (*dayyānū ṭuppi išṭurū ina kunukkīšunu ibrumūma ana PN iddinū*)."[169] Permanent relief to plaintiffs in the Neo-Babylonian period included compensation in silver or goods,[170] specific performance,[171] orders of eviction,[172] and injunctions,[173] depending on the nature of the harm, the level of culpability, and the specifics of the matter at hand.[174] Defendants were subject to capital punishment in egregious cases.[175] Criminal forfeiture of defendants' property was also possible.[176] Evidence of various forms of corporal punishment exists, as well as of payments in lieu of corporal punishment.[177] One Neo-Babylonian trial record apparently refers to a payment in lieu of blood revenge.[178] In the case of compensation to the victim, we find damage mul-

---

12, 6–7; TCL 12, 86 and 122. The tablets also often indicate that the judges "deliberated" (Gt *malāku*) before reaching their verdict. See, e.g., *Cyr* 332; *Nbn* 13 and 1128.

169. See n. 62 above.

170. See, e.g., *BE* 9, 24; *BIN* 1, 113; *Iraq* 13, 96–97; NBL §7; Sack 79; TCL 13, 219; and YOS 6, 208.

171. See, e.g., AnOr 8, 74 and *Nbk* 419.

172. See, e.g., *BE* 8/1, 42.

173. See, e.g., *Cyr* 307, 312; and YOS 7, 66.

174. Some scholars claim that another penalty existed in the Neo-Babylonian period. In numerous administrative and judicial texts originating in Uruk, the court or administrator indicates that, on violation of its order, the party will "bear a sin of the king" (see, e.g., AnOr 8, 67; YOS 6, 108; YOS 7, 50, 137, and 187; cf. YOS 7, 116 (a sin of Cambyses); YOS 7, 25 (a sin of Cyrus); TCL 13, 137 and YOS 7, 69 (sin of god and king); *Iraq* 59, 155 no. 9 and TCL 12, 80 (a sin of the gods and the king); and *BIN* 1, 169 and GCCI 2, 103 (a sin of Gobryas). This language has provoked much speculation, with the vast majority of scholars asserting that it is a general penalty in either judicial, administrative, or contractual settings. See P.-A. Beaulieu, "New Light on Secret Knowledge in Late Babylonian Culture," ZA 82 (1992): 105–6; Joannès, "Textes judiciaire néo-babyloniens," 202–3, 205, 208–9; idem, "Pratique du serment," 169; H. Petschow, *Neubabylonisches Pfandrecht* (Abhandlungen der Sächsischen Akademie der Wissenschaften zu Leipzig, Philologisch-historische Klasse 48/1; Berlin: Akademie Verlag, 1956), 29–30; T. G. Pinches, "Two Late Tablets of Historical Interest," *PSBA* 38 (1916): 26–28; Renger, "Notes on the Goldsmiths," 497; Ries, "Strafbarkeit des Meineids," 457–68; San Nicolò, "Gesetzbuches Ḫammurapis," 336; and D. B. Weisberg, *Guild Structure and Political Allegiance in Early Achaemenid Mesopotamia* (YNER 1; New Haven: Yale University Press, 1967), 18–19. Compare Dougherty, *Shirkûtu*, 52. I suggest that this phrase arises out of ancient administrative law and signifies a finding of guilt for breach of an administrative duty and is not a form of relief.

175. See, e.g., *AfO* 17, 2.

176. See n. 97 above.

177. Cf. *EE* 91 and *ZA* 3, 224 no. 2. In situations where a woman violated a court's injunction against seeing a given man, she might be branded with the slave mark (see, e.g., *Cyr* 307 and 312; see also Oelsner et al., "Neo-Babylonian Period," 966–67).

178. *Fs. Walker* 356.

tiples of one, two, three, ten, and thirty.[179] The thirtyfold penalty is clearly used only in the case of theft of, or damage to, temple property. The specific justification for selecting one of the other multiples remains obscure. In addition, on rare occasion, the court found for the defendant and assessed penalty for false suit against the plaintiff.[180] Sometimes verdict documents included a court-ordered prohibition upon one or both of the parties not to sue on the claim again.[181] Such court-ordered releases and prohibitions on suits were sometimes executed as separate documents.[182] In this period, we also find documents that reflect the execution of the court's order.[183] Releases of liability and prohibitions of further suit are observed in execution documents as well.[184]

---

179. For various examples of the multiples of damages that might be assessed, see, e.g., BE 9, 24 and Nbk 419 (onefold); Sack 79 (twofold); NBL §7 (threefold); TCL 13, 219 (tenfold); and Iraq 13, 96–97 and YOS 6, 208 (thirtyfold). Twelvefold was also apparently awarded in the Neo-Assyrian period (see, e.g., BaghM 5, 1 and 5, 7; cf. Fs. Sjöberg 39, in which a contractual liquidated penalty provision contains a twelvefold penalty).

180. See, e.g., Cyr 332 and Nbn 13. In TCL 12, 122, the court found for the defendant but did not assess a false-suit penalty. In that case, the slave was suing for her freedom from the guarantor of her former owner, based on a legitimate manumission tablet that she held. She was not granted her freedom from the guarantor, however, because the court found that her manumission was superseded by the fact that she had been previously pledged as security on a debt of her owners and transferred to the guarantor as a result of their default (for more on this text, see n. 191 below). I suspect that the false-suit penalty was not assessed because she had entered into the suit in good faith based on the legitimate tablet.

181. See, e.g., Dalley Edinburgh 69 and ROM 2, 38.

182. See, e.g., TCL 12, 24 and 115. In BaghM 5, 15, a very early Neo-Babylonian verdict document, the record reflects the occasional bifurcation of the verdict document from the release and prohibition document: "A tablet of not returning and suing Nabu-damiq (the plaintiff) against Nabu-ušallim (the defendant) [made out/established]." H. Hunger reconstructed the broken verb in the preterite, but it might be in the durative ("Das Archiv des Nabû-ušallim," 222).

183. See, e.g., AfO 17, 2; 8, 74; Camb 321; NBDM 28; and ROM 2, 38. It might also be noted that the existence of independent execution documents in this period would cast some doubt on E. Dombradi's assertion that, for the Old Babylonian period, execution of judgments always took place immediately before the court (Die Darstellung des Rechtsaustrags, 1:357–58; cf. 1:365). Westbrook criticizes Dombradi's position ("Recensiones: Dombradi," 123–24). Jas finds the same type of documents in the Neo-Assyrian period but notes: "When the judge imposes a fine, the payment of that fine is often already recorded in the same text, even if it cannot possibly have taken place during the trial" (Neo-Assyrian Judicial Procedures, 6). It is highly unlikely that all executions of judgments could be accomplished immediately before the court. In such records, it is more likely that the drafting of the final verdict document was delayed until execution was complete in many cases, allowing the accounts of the verdict and execution phases to be collapsed into one document. In other cases, however, it seems possible that the verdict was recorded immediately and execution accomplished later, with or without record. The Neo-Babylonian litigation corpus supports this view.

184. See, e.g., ROM 2, 38.

*Appeals.* We have little information about the appellate process. We do know, however, that an appeal of a decision was possible in at least some cases, because we have records that appear to be attached to an appellate process.[185] These tablets are always one of two types. First, they may be writs of appeal that may have notified the appellant that his appeal to the higher court had been granted, summoned him to the court of review, given him the scheduled time of his appearance, established any guarantors of his appearance, and/or indicated the consequences of a failure to appear—he would lose to the temple.[186] Most of the tablets fall into this group, and they address several or all of these matters.[187] Second, the tablets may be part of the actual appeal proceedings. One example of this is YOS 6, 224. This document contains a case in which two temple officials claim that a particular man belongs to them as an oblate. An assembly of freemen (*mār banî*) hear, in Uruk, testimony of a witness who can deter-

---

185. Again, B. Wells contributed significantly to the thinking in this section of the work.

186. AnOr 8, 50 is an excellent illustration. It records that a certain Ardiya was ordered to appear in Uruk before the royal judges of the king in nineteen days in order to "protest with (*itti*) Nidintu-Bel . . . and Nabu-aḫ-iddin the judgment regarding the slave of Šakin-šumi . . . , which Ardiya received from the hands of Ṣilim-Bel..., who owes arrears to the Lady of Uruk." Nidintu-Bel and Nabu-aḫ-iddin were high-ranking temple officials, with extensive judicial powers. The court stated: "If he [Ardiya] does not come, he will pay, from the day that the slave was in his possession, a slave and quitrent to the Lady of Uruk." Ardiya was an appellant who was protesting a decision of the temple court that had given the pledged slave to the temple as a result of default on a debt. Ardiya had no guarantors of his appearance in Babylon. Consequently, if he should not have appeared, he would have defaulted in the appeal and would have had to pay for his improper use of the slave, consistent with the decision of the lower court.

187. In AnOr 8, 46, a text dated less than one year after AnOr 8, 50, one Nadinu is ordered to go to Babylon and appear before Gobryas in a very short period of time. The text says that he will appear with (*itti*) Nidinti-Bel and Nabu-aḫ-iddin. I believe again that the word *itti* means that Nadinu is appearing in court against the two temple officials in an appeal of a prior judgment that the officials made against Nadinu. AnOr 8, 45 is yet another relevant case. It is virtually identical to AnOr 8, 46 and was decided within one day of AnOr 8, 46. Here, one Balaṭu is the appellant. He is also appealing a decision of Nidintu-Bel and Nabu-aḫ-iddin; and he has to appear in the same time frame as Nadinu from AnOr 8, 46. Balaṭu has two guarantors of his appearance. YOS 7, 31 is quite similar. With respect to YOS 7, 115, two individuals had to guarantee that the defendant would accompany two important temple officials from the temple of Uruk to Babylon. If the defendant did not appear, he would be liable for whatever the witness could prove against the defendant. San Nicolò argues well that this document is probably a writ of appeal from the temple courts to the Babylonian secular courts even though it is not as complete as the other texts ("Gesetzbuches Ḥammurapis," 338–39). If it were not a writ, however, then it would seem to be more in the nature of an extradition order. These documents always contain a summons to appear, with failure bringing upon the appellant the institution of the prior judgment.

mine the slave's status. I believe that the assembly is taking a deposition for the judges of Babylon for the case on appeal.

*Settlements.* It is clear that litigants took advantage of opportunities to settle a claim, whether in the pre-trial,[188] mid-trial,[189] or post-trial stage.[190] A series of documents related to a single case includes records of two trials and the post-trial settlement of one of the lawsuits.[191] Settlement documents typically contain release-of-liability and covenant-not-to-sue provisions.[192] Interestingly, one record documents the settlement of a substantial claim of trespass and looting where the defendant explicitly denied having any lia-

---

188. See, e.g., *BE* 9, 69; 10, 9; and *NBDM* 49.
189. See, e.g., PBS 2/1, 140; TCL 12, 115; and Stolper 399–400. *IMT* 105 (joined to *EE* 109) appears to be a mid-trial, court-approved settlement, but certainty eludes us because the text is broken in key places.
190. See, e.g., *JCS* 28, 198–99 and *Nbn* 668. Some settlement documents give no indication of the point of settlement, including TCL 12, 26.
191. This series of documents addresses the disposition of the estate of a husband and wife. For a complete discussion of these texts, see Wunsch, "Richter Berieten," 68–70. The case involves three lawsuits that deal principally with the disposition of one debt and one slave of the couple. The first document, *Nbk* 359, seems to mention the original inheritance tablet. The second document, *Nbn* 314, shows a debt of the couple for which they pledged their property and slaves. The third document, *Nbn* 626, executed immediately before the wife's death, manumitted one of the pledged slaves. Then the wife died, probably having survived her husband. Within two months of the wife's death, the creditor sued the guarantor for payment of the debt. He won his suit. This text is, unfortunately, lost to us. We do have, however, the transcript of a second lawsuit, *AfO* 44, 83 no. 13, in which the guarantor sued the heirs for repayment of the debt that he was compelled to pay. This second suit gave the property and slaves of the heirs to the guarantor. We do not learn this, however, from *AfO* 44, 83 no. 13 itself, because it is broken at the relevant place. Rather, the fifth document, TCL 12, 122, which recounts all this history, gives us this critical piece of information. It seems that in the midst of this debt dispute, one of the slaves who was transferred to the guarantor under the decision of *AfO* 44, 83 no. 13, sued the guarantor for her freedom. Her claim was based on a manumission document that she held from her late mistress. The manumission document that we have, *Nbn* 626, is actually not that of this particular slave but rather is a similar one, probably executed at or about the same time (Wunsch, "Richter Berieten," 69–70). The slave introduced her manumission document into evidence, but the court did not free her. Instead, it invalidated her manumission because she was a subject of the pledge, and ordered that she and the other pledged slaves remain in the custody of the guarantor, pursuant to *AfO* 44, 83 no. 13. *Nbn* 665 indicates that the guarantor sold her about three weeks later. One month after the suit by the slave and two weeks after her transfer to the guarantor, our seventh document, *Nbn* 668, was executed. This document appears to be a postverdict, court-approved settlement agreement of the dispute between the heirs and the guarantor recorded in *AfO* 44, 83 no. 13. The terms of the settlement were that the guarantor would receive the slaves only. I should mention here that there are two more documents, *Nbn* 679 and 682, that may be related to this series of events. They both refer to a slave by the same name as the slave who brought the third lawsuit. By this time, however, she belonged to yet a different owner.
192. See, e.g., *BE* 9, 69; *BE* 10, 9; *JCS* 28, 198–99; *Nbn* 668; and Stolper 399–400.

bility.¹⁹³ Documents also expose that the court or assembly often approved settlements.¹⁹⁴ Sometimes the court had to enforce a settlement.¹⁹⁵ Apparently, settlements might also be modified later.¹⁹⁶

Finally, the power of the parties to settle disputes at any stage in the litigation process and the need of the court to authorize those settlements in certain situations have given rise to the idea that ancient Near Eastern courts served more as arbiters or counselors than judges.¹⁹⁷ This view is misguided. The authority to impose sanctions on the parties is the driving force behind any legal system.¹⁹⁸ Sanctions are the reason that litigants seek

---

193. See *BE* 10, 9, wherein a group of Nippurians apparently invaded and looted the town of Rabiya. One Baga'data accused a certain Bel-nadin-šuma, an individual of the economically important house of Murašu, and his servants of trespassing on and looting his property during the raid. Bel-nadin-šumu denied liability. In spite of his denial, Bel-nadin-šumu paid a large amount, including 20 oxen, 200 female sheep, 350 gur of barley, 200 gur of dates, 50 gur of wheat, one gur of spelt, 50 jars of old wine with bottles, 50 jars of new wine with bottles, and five talents of wool, a healthy sum, in consideration for dropping the suit.

194. See, e.g., *IMT* 105 (joined to *EE* 109); *Nbn* 668; and Stolper 399–400. In *Nbn* 668, the court had pronounced a verdict and written out a tablet for the winner. Later the defendant wanted to settle for property of a lesser value. The court approved this postverdict settlement and oversaw the execution of the settlement. The winner got yet another tablet documenting his lawful title to the new property. See additionally Wunsch, "Richter Berieten," 67–68.

195. See, e.g., *Nbk* 365, which contains a court proceeding in which one of the parties was attempting to enforce a pre-trial settlement.

196. See, e.g., *BIN* 1, 141, which shows the modification of a prior settlement of a claim concerning the illegal use of a runaway slave. See further Dandamaev, *Slavery in Babylonia*, 119, 222–23.

197. Jas articulates this best in *Neo-Assyrian Judicial Procedures*, 97. But see also Boecker, *Administration of Justice*, 24; Kohler and Ungnad, *Hammurabi's Gesetz*, 98–99; Lautner, *Richterliche Entscheidung*, 1–4; Malamat, "Kingship and Council," 252–53; Otto, "Neue Aspekte zum keilschriftlichen Prozeßrecht," 282–83; Schorr, *Urkunde des Altbabylonischen Zivil- und Prozessrechts*, 351; Willis, *Elders of the City*, 61–82; and Walther, *Das Altbabylonischen Gerichtswesen*, 227–28. For additional bibliography and discussion, see Veenker, *Old Babylonian Judiciary*, 5–6.

198. All legal systems seek the resolution of disputes with as little controversy as possible. All seek to reconcile the parties. For example, today only a very small number (somewhere around 5 percent) of all filed lawsuits actually go to trial in the American adversarial system. The rest are dismissed or settled. Few people, however, would suggest that the vast majority of legal opinions of our system are advisory; nor would they suggest that they are advisory in modern inquisitorial systems that are still more cooperative in outlook. What makes a legal system effective is its ability to coerce compliance with its resolution of the dispute by the imposition of some form of sanction. This coercive power helps to bring the parties to settlement. As A. Sarat and T. R. Kearns state: "[V]iolence, as a fact and a metaphor, is integral to the constitution of modern law, and that law is a creature of both literal violence, and of imaginings and threats of force, disorder, and pain. . . . [I]n the absence of such imaginings and threats there is no law . . . . [M]odern law is built on representations of aggression and disruption. Law is in this sense, an extended meditation on a metaphor" (*Law's Violence* [Ann Arbor: University of Michigan Press, 1992], 1). Ancient Near Eastern legal systems were no different in this regard. The evidence is overwhelming that they had the power to enforce

to use the system at all. The court not only typically offers an impartial view of the dispute but also puts teeth behind its view. The coercive powers of courts place additional pressure on the parties to resolve the matter themselves. Settlements are the mechanism through which parties are able to avoid many of those sanctions. The Neo-Babylonian legal system's active encouragement of, and participation in, settlement additionally displays its fundamental coercive power.

In conclusion, although each trial document of the Neo-Babylonian period offers only a limited amount of data as a whole, these records when considered together provide sufficient information to enable us to piece together the workings of the litigation system. They disclose a fluid but intricate, sophisticated, and powerful structure that could respond to a variety of needs. This system was also innovative, streamlining procedures of earlier periods and favoring rational evidence over suprarational evidence. Thus, the Neo-Babylonian litigation documents disclose a versatile scheme of legal procedure that sought to satisfy the demands of a complex society. Such a system was in effect during the life of the author of the book of Job and may have either been the same as or strongly influenced the trial system of the author's society. We will now explore whether a trial with such characteristics can be unearthed within the pages of the book of Job.

---

their decisions. This power motivated parties to comply with the culture's established legal standards. For more on the law's coercive power as the heart of its effectiveness, see N. Bobbio, "Law and Force," *Monist* 49 (1965): 321; R. Cover, "The Supreme Court, 1982 Term—Forward: Nomos and Narrative," *Harvard Law Review* 97 (1983): 1–63; idem, "Bonds of Constitutional Interpretation," 815–33; idem, "Violence and Word," *Yale Law Journal* 95 (1986): 1601–29; J. Derrida "Force of Law: 'The Mystical Foundation of Authority,' " *Cardozo Law Review* 11 (1990): 925; and the series of articles in Sarat and Kearns, *Law's Violence*.

# 5

# The Satan's Accusation and Investigation

Now that we are familiar with some important facets of the Neo-Babylonian courts, their legal procedure, and their trial record structure, we will use this knowledge as a hermeneutical tool with which to explore whether the narratives of the Book of Job have any or all of the characteristics of Neo-Babylonian legal narratives. We will proceed with the book of Job in the same manner as we did when attempting to determine which of the many hundreds of Neo-Babylonian texts examined were, in fact, litigation-related records and what aspects of the litigation process the tablet reflected. These queries include: Are there identifiable parties and witnesses who tell different stories? If such characters exist and produce multiple strands of narrative, do such stories reflect different points of view that conflict, make competing truth claims, or seek to persuade? If these narratives are in any way persuasive, whom do the parties seek to persuade: each other alone or some third person or entity? In other words, does an identifiable independent court exist? If we can discover a court, what is its constitution? Do the stories interrupt each other and, therefore, fragment the linearity of each story? Is the text's overall narrative complete and straightforward, or does it move at times in nonsequential order, have the gaps that are common to legal records, and possess in places the perplexing order of ancient trial documents? Does the book seem to contain any marks of traditional trial procedure when compared with Neo-Babylonian practice, and does the book contain the vocabulary of the trial court? For instance, does the book contain any statement, question, or oath that may constitute a legally sufficient accusation? If so, with which substantive crime does the accusation charge the defendant? Does the book contain demand language? Are any of the parties or witnesses summoned to appear? Is an investigation conducted by the court? Does the defendant offer a statement or oath? Do witnesses testify? Is other evidence presented? Is there any movement toward settlement? And so forth. The judgment whether or not the book of Job contains a formal legal trial rests on the answers to these queries.

This manner of investigation establishes that we use a literary-forensic analysis, grounded in the book's probable legal-historical context. This has one important ramification for our reading. I diverge from a purely sequential reading of the book, which one would normally expect in a literary analysis, in order to search for evidence of each characteristic of the legal narrative, all relevant legal vocabulary, and each legal procedure in the Joban text.[1] Interestingly, should any relevant legal materials or information be scattered throughout the text, the fact of such scattering would be additional evidence of the fragmented nature of the text and would lend support to the idea that the text seeks to embed a trial process. With these initial matters settled, we turn to the analysis of the book of Job. This chapter will examine the book's prologue and the events in the Divine Council.

## An Introduction to Job the Man

As the book of Job opens, the narrator introduces its protagonist, Job. He is a foreigner from Uz, a land associated with wisdom.[2] He is a man of "integrity (תם) and uprightness (ישר)" (1:1aα).[3] He fears God (ירא אלהים) and shuns evil (סר מרע) (1:1aβ). These characteristics indicate a man who, following the path of wisdom, is completely devoted to Yahweh.[4] This is confirmed by Job's acts of worship in 1:20. Job's avoidance of evil is also made evident by the fact he does not sin (חטא) in word or deed in the face

---

1. Although we will not be reading in a perfectly sequential manner, I believe that the text has a gross literary structure to it. I follow the structure of E. B. Smick: (a) the prologue in chs. 1–2; (b) Job's opening lament in ch. 3; (c) the three cycles of dialogues in chs. 4–27; (d) the interlude on wisdom in ch. 28; (c') the three monologues of Job, Elihu, and God in chs. 29–41; (b') Job's closing remarks in 40:3–5; 42:1–6; and (a') 42:7–17 ("Architectonics, Structural Poems, and Rhetorical Devices in the Book of Job," in *A Tribute to Gleason Archer* [ed. W. C. Kaiser and R. F. Youngblood; Chicago: Moody Press, 1986], 87–88. This structure is imperfect in that part of b' (Job's closing remarks in 40:3–5) is imbedded in part of c' (God's monologue in chs. 38–41). In this, we see again that the book of Job rarely follows Hebrew literary conventions perfectly.

2. M. Weiss, *The Story of Job's Beginning: Job 1–2, A Literary Analysis* (Jerusalem: Magnes, 1983), 21–24.

3. All biblical translations are my own unless otherwise indicated. Where my text-critical or translation decision follows one of the more commonly known scholarly positions, the translation is generally not discussed. Innovative translations and some of the more difficult translation decisions are, however, taken up. The commentaries of D. J. A. Clines (*Job 1–20*) and H. H. Rowley (*Job*) are particularly helpful for illuminating the scholarly conversation about the textual and translation difficulties in the book of Job. I follow the lead of the NRSV in making my translations gender inclusive. Translations include the significant Hebrew in parentheses. For verbs, typically the root alone is given; the lexical form is usually given in the case of nouns; and other parts of speech are generally recorded as in *BHS*, except in rare instances.

4. See, e.g., Job 28:28; Ps 111:10; Prov 1:7; 2:5–8; 3:7; 9:10; 15:33; 16:6.

of the Satan's challenge (1:22; 2:10).[5] Moreover, 2 Chr 19:8–9 reveals that one who fears Yahweh is the kind of man who can be trusted to uphold Yahweh's justice.[6] Later we learn that Job is, indeed, involved in adjudicating disputes (29:7, 16b–17, 25)[7] and is concerned about issues of social justice (29:12–16a). Fear of Yahweh may also bring wealth (Prov 22:4).[8] Job's life is rich. He has seven sons, three daughters, 7000 sheep, 3000 camels, 500 yoked pairs of oxen, 500 female donkeys, and many servants (1:2–3a). The narrator relates that Job was the greatest man in the East.[9] He was so good and God-fearing, in fact, that he regularly presented burnt offerings just

---

5. The title השׂטן is variously rendered in English translations as haśśāṭān, the Satan, Satan, the Adversary, the Accuser, the Prosecutor, the Advocate, a certain adversary, or a certain accuser. P. L. Day makes the case well that the best English translation is either "the adversary" or "the accuser" (*Adversary in Heaven*, 1–43). In my opinion, all the renderings except "Satan," the "Prosecutor," and the "Advocate" are acceptable. I prefer "the Satan," the anglicized version of haśśāṭān. This rendering recognizes the term as a title or role that is used instead of the Satan's actual name, much in the way that Helen Keller called Annie Sullivan "Teacher" or one might address a district attorney as "Mr. Prosecutor." For the best discussion of the literature regarding the origins of השׂטן, the role he plays in the Hebrew Bible, and the translation alternatives for the title, see ibid. I would add to Day's extensive bibliography on the subject, N. Forsyth, *The Old Enemy: Satan and the Combat Myth* (Princeton: Princeton University Press, 1987); J. G. Gammie, "The Angelology and Demonology in the Septuagint of the Book of Job," *HUCA* 56 (1985): 1–19; V. P. Hamilton, "Satan," *ABD* 5:985–89; D. Kinet, "The Ambiguity of the Concepts of God and Satan in the Book of Job," in *Job and the Silence of God* (ed. C. Duquoc and C. Foristan; New York: Seabury, 1983), 30–35; H. Kruse, "Das Reich Satans," *Bib* 58 (1977): 29–62; P. J. Nel, "The Conception of Evil and Satan in Jewish Traditions in the Pre-Christian Period," in *Like a Roaring Lion: Essays on the Bible, Church, and Demonic Powers* (ed. P. G. R. de Villiers; Pretoria: University of South Africa, 1987), 1–21; and A. Pinker, "Satanic Verses: Satan in the Hebrew Bible," *JBQ* 25 (1997): 90–100.

6. 2 Chr 19:8–9: "Jehoshaphat also appointed in Jerusalem some Levites and priests and heads of the clans of Israelites for rendering judgment in matters of Yahweh, and for disputes. Then they returned to Jerusalem. He charged them, 'This is how you shall act: in fear of Yahweh, with fidelity, and with whole heart.'" Cf. Ps 19:10.

7. Like most ancient Near Eastern courts, the Israelite courts typically met at the gates of the city and the temple to decide cases and to carry out execution of their sentences. For references to the gate in a judicial context, see Deut 17:5; 21:19; 22:15, 24; 25:7; Josh 8:29; 20:4; 2 Kgs 10:8; Isa 29:21; Jer 26:10; 38:7; Amos 5:10, 12, 15; Zech 8:16; cf. Ruth 4:1, 10–11; 2 Sam 15:2; Prov 31:23. For further discussion, see, among others, Boecker, *Administration of Justice*, 31–32; L. H. Köhler, "Justice in the Gate," 149–75; Matthews, "Entrance Ways and Threshing Floors," 25–40; D. McKenzie, Judicial Procedure at the Town Gate," *VT* 14 (1964): 100–104; and R. Westbrook, "Biblical Law," in *An Introduction to the History and Sources of Jewish Law* (ed. N. S. Hecht et al.; Oxford: Clarendon, 1996), 2, 8.

8. "The reward for humility, the fear of Yahweh, is wealth and honor and life."

9. While most interpreters relate this greatness to Job's wealth, Weiss suggests that it refers to the greatness of his wisdom (*Job's Beginning*, 26–27). I believe it carries both meanings. Habel acknowledges this possibility: "This summative statement refers to Job's renowned wisdom, wealth, piety, and integrity" (*Book of Job: Commentary*, 87). The book of Job's language is full of double entendres. This is especially true in the legal-theological area, but it is also true of other phrases.

in case his children "sinned and blasphemed (ברך) God in their hearts (לבב)" (1:5).¹⁰ Thus, we learn that Job, in his piety, has a profound awareness of the problem of blasphemy. He watches his children for this and attempts to safeguard them against it. He scolds his wife for any possible signs of such (2:10). He apparently guards his own words (1:22; 2:10). Moreover, he performs other appropriate religious rituals when necessary, such as those of grief (1:20; 2:9).

The narrator is not the only one to inform us about Job's character. Yahweh (1:8; 2:3), Job's wife (2:9), and Eliphaz (4:6) all testify to Job's integrity. Yahweh (2:3) and Job's wife (2:9) report that he can hold fast (חזק) to it in a crisis. Yahweh confirms Job's uprightness (1:8; 2:3). Yahweh (1:8), the Satan (1:9), and Eliphaz (4:6), all agree that Job fears God. Yahweh also imparts that Job shuns evil (1:8; 2:3) and calls Job "my servant" (עבדי), which is an honorific title (1:8; 2:3).¹¹ Job's brief words in the first two chapters of the book also say something about his basic character. His acceptance of his status as a human in relationship to Yahweh as expressed in 1:21 and 2:10 and his blessing of Yahweh in 1:21 further demonstrate his devotion. He also maintains traditional social hierarchies, which is evident in his chastisement of his wife (2:10).¹² Over the course of the book, we learn addi-

---

10. For more on 1:5 and the expiatory nature of the burnt offering in this instance, see Milgrom, *Leviticus: A New Translation with Introduction and Commentary* (3 vols.; AB 3, 3A, 3B; New York: Doubleday, 1991–2001), 1:153–54, 174–76. The use of ברך for "curse" or "blasphemy" has traditionally been taken as a *tiqqûn sōpĕrîm* (see, e.g., Dhorme, *Commentary on the Book of Job*, 4–5). S. H. Blank argues, in the alternative, that the euphemism is attributable to the author, not a later scribe ("The Curse, the Blasphemy, the Spell, the Oath," 83–85; see also Gordis, *Book of Job*, 13; and Habel, *Book of Job: Commentary*, 88). It is also possible, however, that ברך contains both the meanings "curse" and "blessing" in its semantic range (see, e.g., Andersen, *Job*, 81; M. Buttenwieser, *The Book of Job* (Chicago: University of Chicago Press, 1922), 155–56; and Weiss, *Job's Beginning*, 30). I follow M. Cheney, whose discussion is the most nuanced and who suggests that ברך has *blasphemy* (as opposed to the more general *curse*) specifically within its semantic range (*Dust, Wind, and Agony: Character, Speech and Genre in Job* [ConBOT 36; Stockholm: Almqvist & Wiksell, 1994], 62–67). Cf. T. Linafelt, "The Undecidability of ברך in the Prologue to Job and Beyond," *BibInt* 4 (1996): 154–72.

11. The title "my servant," places Job among such important and divinely favored men as Abraham (Gen 26:23; cf. Exod 32:13; Deut 9:27), Moses (see, e.g., Num 12:7–8; Josh 1:2, 7), Caleb (Num 14:24), David (see, e.g., 2 Sam 3:18; 7:5, 8), Isaiah (see, e.g., Isa 20:3; 49:3), Eliakim (Isa 22:20), and Zerubbabel (Hag 2:23); cf. Isaac (Gen 24:14; Exod 32:13; Deut 9:27), Jacob (Exod 32:13; Deut 9:27), Ahijah (1 Kgs 14:8; 15:29), Elijah (2 Kgs 9:36; 10:10), Jonah (2 Kgs 14:25), and Hezekiah (2 Chr 32:16). Israel-Jacob is also God's servant (see, e.g., Isa 41:8–9; 44:1–2, 21; 45:4), as is King Nebuchadrezzar of Babylon (see, e.g., Jer 25:9; 27:6). Finally, the Suffering Servant Songs of Isaiah 40–55 also contain references to "my servant" (see, e.g., 52:13). See generally Andersen, *Job*, 83; Habel, *Book of Job: Commentary*, 90; and Wharton, *Job*, 9–11.

12. I will not dwell on Job's wife during this study. She is an extremely important character, because she offers Job an alternative strategy, that is, to martyr himself in the cause against God rather than remain a passive recipient of God's oppressive justice. Martyrdom is always an alternative to one who is subject to state-sponsored torture, and it is an important

tionally that Job is a teacher (4:3) and a counselor-leader (4:4; 29:21–25; cf. 11:19b). He holds the respect of many (29:7–11, 21–25). Yahweh substantiates Job's greatness by stating: "there is no one like him on the earth" (1:8; 2:3). This is a rare accolade.[13]

Job is a good man, devoted to Yahweh, scrupulous in his religious practice, involved in community leadership and service, and held in Yahweh's highest regard. There is much accord on these points. How surprising it is, then, to learn, when the narrator moves us to the heavenly realm, that not everyone agrees that all is right with Job.

## The Satan's Accusation

The scene shifts to a meeting of the Divine Council.[14] The narrator relates that the sons of God (בני האלהים) have come to present themselves (להתיצב)

---

means through which to challenge oppressive legal systems (Cover, "Violence and the Word," 1601–29; idem, "Bonds of Constitutional Interpretation," 815–33; idem, "Supreme Court, 1982 Term," 4–68; and M. M. Tillie "Ascetic Body and the (Un)Making of the World of the Martyr," *JAAR* 59 [1991]: 467–79). Martyrdom was known to the ancient Israelites and to the Jews of the Hellenistic period and was used to challenge abusive or foreign authority (see, e.g., Judg 16:26–31; Dan 3:17–18; 2 Macc 7:1–42; see also S. M. Paul, "Daniel 3:29 — A Case of 'Neglected' Blasphemy," *JNES* 42 [1983]: 291; J. D. Tabor "Martyr, Martyrdom," *ABD* 4:575–78; and A. J. Droge and J. D. Tabor, *A Noble Death: Suicide and Martyrdom Among Greeks and Romans, Jews and Christians in the Ancient World* [San Francisco: HarperSanFrancisco, 1992]). After his wife challenges him, Job changes from a quiet and passive recipient of God's abuse to contemplating the counterclaim in ch. 3. The alternative his wife presents motivates him to challenge God (E. van Wolde, "The Development of Job: Mrs. Job as Catalyst," in *Feminist Companion to Wisdom Literature* [ed. A. Brenner; FCB 9; Sheffield: Sheffield Academic, 1995], 203–4). For more on the reversal of Job's thinking between ch. 2 and ch. 3, see R. D. Moore, "The Integrity of Job," *CBQ* 45 (1983): 17–31. Consequently, Job's wife is hardly, in my view, the Satan's handmaiden, as many have pronounced over the years (see, e.g., Habel, *Book of Job: Commentary*, 96; Wharton, *Job*, 22; and Whybray, *Job*, 34). Rather, I believe that Job continues to hold the martyrdom card that his wife handed him up his sleeve throughout his speeches, thereby keeping the pressure on God to settle the case (cf. Bovati, *Re-Establishing Truth*, 120; and I. Pardes, *Countertraditions in the Bible: A Feminist Approach* [Cambridge, Mass.: Harvard University Press, 1992], 150). Unfortunately, fully delineating this idea would take considerable space, and both the study's thesis and my view of Job's wife would be diminished for the effort. The role of Job's wife was best discussed separately; see my "Job's Wife as Hero: A Feminist-Forensic Reading of the Book of Job," *BibInt* 14 [2006]: 374–423). Thus, my relative silence about Job's wife in this study should not be taken to mean that I think she is extraneous to the book or even to my argument. She is a critical player in the challenge of God and part of the book's schema to confront God's oppressive government.

13. In 1 Sam 10:24, Samuel says of Saul on his appointment as king: "There is none like him among all the people." In addition, in 2 Kgs 18:5, the narrator informs us: "There was none like him [Hezekiah] among all the kings of Judah...."

14. The council has various names, including: "council" (סוד; Jer 23:22); "council of Eloah" (Job 15:8, although this verse is ambiguous and may well mean "counsel of Eloah");

before Yahweh and that the Satan (השטן) has joined them (1:6). In this group, they constitute the Divine Council, with Yahweh at its head.

It appears that conflict exists between Yahweh and the Satan regarding whether Job is truly just. The Satan acknowledges that Job has a fear of God. Yet, to his mind, such fear does not stem from Job's inherent character, as God asserts, but, rather, from the many blessings that God has bestowed on Job: "Does Job fear God without cause (חנם)? Have you, yourself, not put a hedge (שוך) about him, his household, and all his possessions? You have blessed (ברך) the work of his hands so that his possessions have burst out over the land" (1:9–10).[15] The Satan maintains that this level of blessing is the cause of Job's devotion to God, and thus the Satan denounces Job as capable of committing blasphemy: "Oh, but stretch out your hand and strike all that is his! If he does not blaspheme (ברך) you to your face...!" (1:11).[16] Later, he expands his denunciation: "Skin for skin! All that a man has he will give up for his life. Oh, but stretch out your hand and strike his bones and his flesh! If he does not blaspheme (ברך) you to your face...!" (2:4–5). By these words, he invites Yahweh to remove his hedge of blessings from Job and let Job's true nature reveal itself.

Not every dispute between people involves legal principles or legal process. Some disputes are in the nature of a friendly disagreement; some might beg a wager. Others are more serious and may lead to a breach of the relationship. Still others are such that they are subject to regulation and resolution by the community or state. Moreover, not all conflicts that might be brought to law are, in fact, brought to law. Thus, the disagreement between God and the Satan could well be a friendly wager, as numerous commentators claim. It might be that the Satan is acting in a fiduciary

---

"the council of the holy ones" (Ps 89:8); "the council of Yahweh" (Jer 23:18; cf. v. 22); "assembly" (מועד; Isa 14:13); "the assembly (עדה) of El" (Ps 82:1); and the "assembly (קהל) of the holy ones" (Ps 89:6); cf. 1 Kgs 22:19; Isa 6:1; Zech 3:1–5; and Dan 7:9–10, where the council meets but remains unnamed. For more on the concept of the Divine Council and the many functions it served in the ancient Near East, see J. Ackerman, "An Exegetical Study of Psalm 82" (Th.D. diss., Harvard University, 1966); F. M. Cross, "The Council of Yahweh in Second Isaiah," *JNES* 12 (1953): 274–77; P. D. Miller, Jr., "Divine Council and the Prophetic Call to War," *VT* 18 (1968): 100–107; idem, "Cosmology and the World Order in the Old Testament: The Divine Council as Cosmic-Political Symbol," *HBT* 9 (1987): 58–78; E. T. Mullen, *The Divine Council in Canaanite and Early Hebrew Literature* (HSM 24; Chico, Calif.: Scholars Press, 1980); M. E. Polley, "Hebrew Prophecy Within the Council of Yahweh, Examined in Its Ancient Near Eastern Setting: The Contextual Approach," in *Scripture in Context: Essays on the Comparative Method* (ed. C. D. Evans, W. W. Hallo, and J. B. White; Pittsburgh: Pickwick, 1980), 141–56; H. W. Robinson, "The Council of Yahweh," *JTS* 45 (1944): 151–57; C. R. Seitz, "The Divine Council: Temporal Transition and New Prophecy in the Book of Isaiah," *JBL* 109 (1990): 229–47; and G. E. Wright, *The Old Testament Against its Environment* (SBT 2; London: SCM, 1950), 30–41.

15. Job eventually concurs that Yahweh once blessed him greatly (29:2–5).
16. I note the ironic use of ברך by the Satan.

capacity and is trying to warn God that he is mistaken about Job. If this is the nature of the altercation, the law would not be involved. How do we know whether this conflict is one of law? In order to formulate an answer, we must consider several factors: the relationship between the parties, the extent of the conflict; the nature of the conflict, whether the vocabulary and formulae of a legal accusation are used by one or both of the parties, and whether an adjudicating body is present.

We examine first the parties' relationship to each other. The initial conversation between Yahweh and the Satan indicates that the Satan may serve in a capacity similar to the Eye of the King, the *qabba'um* officer, or the *bātiqu* of earlier periods of the ancient Near East. As we discovered in chapter 4 above, such individuals were functionaries of the internal affairs division of the royal court.[17] They might denounce the unjust and formally accuse individuals of any misconduct of which they became aware. They were not, however, a type of public prosecutor in the modern sense because that role did not exist in the ancient Near East. Anyone with knowledge of a criminal matter might have investigated the matter and brought charges.[18] Such officials were no different. In the book of Job, the Satan's role is to search out the just and the unjust.[19] Some would argue that the Satan's sim-

---

17. Whether the Satan is a heavenly equivalent to an earthly Eye of the King is under debate. See, e.g., Blenkinsopp, "Civic and Religious Constitution?" 45–46 n. 13; Dandamaev and Lukonin, *Culture and Social Institutions*, 111; H. Haag, *Teufelsglaube* (Tübingen: Katzman, 1971), 199; A. Lods, "Les origins de la figure de satan, ses functions à la cour céleste," in *Mélanges Syriens offerts à Monsieur René Dussaud* (2 vols.; Paris: Geuthner, 1939), 2:656–60; Oppenheim, "Eyes of the Lord," 173–77; N. H. Tur-Sinai (Torczyner), "How Satan Came into the World," *ExpTim* 48 (1936–37): 563; and idem, *The Book of Job: A New Commentary* (2nd ed.; Jerusalem: Kiryath-Sepher, 1967), 42. I believe that Oppenheim makes an extremely good case that the figure of the Satan has important points of contact with such an office in the ancient Near East ("Eyes of the Lord," 173–77). For more on the Persian office of Eye of the King, see Tuplin, "Administration of the Achaemenid Empire," 120.

18. See, e.g., Deut 17:2–4; cf. 1 Kgs 2:9–13.

19. Yahweh inquires of the Satan where he has been (1:7a). The Satan answers that he has been roving the earth (1:7b). The root שוט, "to rove," includes the sense of searching for the just and the unjust. In Jer 5:1, God instructs his people to rove the streets of Jerusalem in search of one person who is just and whom he may pardon. Cf. 2 Chr 16:9a: "the eyes of Yahweh rove over the entire earth to strengthen those whose hearts are true to him"; and Zech 4:10b: "Those seven are the eyes of Yahweh, roving over the whole earth." While there is much discussion in the literature about just how extensive the connections between שטן and שוט are, I believe that they represent no more than a wordplay. Day argues that there is some semantic correspondences between the two roots, but the etymological connections between them, as was suggested by S. D. Luzzato (*Erläuterungen über einen Teil der Propheten und Hagiographen* [Lemberg, 1876], 197 [not available to this author]) and Tur-Sinai ("How Satan Came into the World," 564; *Book of Job*, 38–45) are not demonstrable (Day, *Adversary in Heaven*, 19–22; see also R. S. Kluger, *Satan in the Old Testament* [Evanston, Ill: Northwestern University Press, 1967], 25–34). Yet a significant wordplay exists between the two words: part of the Satan's role is to search out the unjust (Weiss, *Job's Beginning*, 44; cf. Kluger, *Satan*, 31).

ilarity to the Eye of the King restricts him to the role of spy, secret agent, or paid informant, and, thus, prevents him from bringing formal judical accusations.[20] The Eye of the King, however, as one who was much involved in investigative work, would be more likely to have knowledge of criminal activity. Being appointed the Eye of the King would not diminish the duty placed upon every person to notify the proper authorities of the commission of a crime. Rather, his superior knowledge and special relationship to the king would *require* that he bring such cases before judicial officials. If the Satan, indeed, fulfills such a role, he would be expected to bring cases before the court. The fact that the Satan is a heavenly figure makes him no less of an appropriate accuser. The Akkadian terms for a human adversary at law, *bēl dīni* and *bēl dabābi*, could also refer to divine adversaries in various legal and religious texts.[21] The Satan clearly has the power to accuse humanity within the Divine Council. The issue is whether this discussion is friendly or less than friendly. Is the Satan acting in Yahweh's best interests, or does he have an independent and not so benign purpose? Hence, we examine the conflict and its setting.

The text reports that Yahweh and the Satan are not alone; the whole Divine Council has assembled when the sons of God came להתיצב על־יהוה (1:6; 2:1). The verb יצב in the *hithpael* can signify "to present oneself before" another ready for service. That is how the verse is traditionally taken.[22] If this is the best reading of the Hebrew, then the Divine Council has assembled to some purpose or to receive some instruction. The council has many functions: one of the most important is judicial.[23] J. Ackerman explains correctly that, much like its ancient Near Eastern counterparts, the Divine Council of the Hebrew Bible has the power to try both humans and divine beings.[24] Both Yahweh alone and the council as a whole have authority to serve as a court, but they do not always serve as a court. We must, there-

---

20. See especially Lods, "Les origins," 656–60.
21. For instances of a divine *bēl dīni* in the Neo-Assyrian period, see, e.g., *ADD* 780; cf. Jas 11. For instances of a divine *bēl dabābi* in the Neo-Assyrian period, see T. Abusch, "Studies in the History of Interpretation of Some Akkadian Incantations and Prayers" (Ph.D. diss., Harvard University, 1972), 152–67. Moreover, the term *ākil karṣī*, which could signify a private prosecutor in earlier periods of ancient Near Eastern history, additionally applied to a celestial accuser (Day, *Adversary in Heaven*, 41; and F. Thureau-Dangin, *Rituels accadiens* [1921; Innsbruck: Zeller, 1975], 135, line 258).
22. See, e.g., BDB, 426; and *HALOT* 2:427.
23. See the bibliography in n. 14 above.
24. Ackerman, "Exegetical Study of Psalm 82," 176–272, 299–306; and Y. Zakovitch, "Psalm 82 and Biblical Exegesis," in *Sefer Moshe: The Moshe Weinfeld Jubilee Volume* (ed. C. Cohen, A. Hurvitz, and S. M. Paul; Winona Lake, Ind.: Eisenbrauns, 2004), 215–17. For example, Dan 7:9–10 manifests the council's judicial administration over the earth, and Psalm 82 demonstrates its judicial administration over heaven. Cf. Zechariah 3 for the Divine Council's judicial involvement in human affairs (Ackerman, "Exegetical Study of Psalm 82," 207).

fore, inquire why they are present in this case. Are they there to hear a case as a panel of judges? Are they just hapless witnesses to the conversation between Yahweh and the Satan? Or do they have some other intention? The author does not make this explicit. Instead, the author leaves some ambiguity in the text.

The phrase להתיצב על may not be as innocent or as neutral as readers often assume. Although the root יצב can mean to stand in readiness for service, as it is typically interpreted in 1:6 and 2:1, it can also mean "to answer a charge" or "to present a case" (see, e.g., Job 13:18; 23:4; 33:5; Ps 94:16), or "to hold one's ground, maintain one's position, or resist" (see, e.g., Job 41:22; 2 Chr 11:13).[25] The fact that the legal connotation of the verb יצב and the hostile use of the preposition על can be found in other places in the book of Job suggests that the entire discussion in the Divine Council is heavy with conflict.[26] The Satan does not appear to be fully on God's side or within God's control. Thus, I disagree with those commentators who suggest that the Satan can act only under the authority of God.[27] Nor do I believe that the Satan is acting in God's best interests. Further, this is no friendly wager or contest; there is tension in the room. The very name *the Satan* implies that this one is in an adversarial position. The idea that fervent conflict exists is further supported by the author's use of מעם/מאת פני יהוה when the Satan takes his leave of Yahweh in 1:12 and 2:7. One has the sense that this departing breaks some level of fellowship with God.[28] M. H. Pope notices the strain with regard to Yahweh's comments as well: "There is something of a taunt and provocation in Yahweh's query" in 1:8.[29] I agree. This comment appears to come out of some prior discussion of the matter that was not amicable.

The Hebrew Bible records conflict between members of the Divine Council. For example, the sons of God are in conflict with God in Gen 6:2, 4. In Psalm 82, God brings the sons of the Most High up on charges of failing to maintain social justice.[30] It is also important to remember that the Satan does not come before God alone; he comes among the sons of God (בתוכם) (1:6). In 2:1, the author states specifically that the Satan comes גם . . . בתכם להתיצב. The Satan is not isolated from the sons of God.[31] This

---

25. BDB, 426; and *HALOT* 2:427.
26. For the legal meaning of יצב, see, e.g., 33:5; 41:21. For the hostile use of על, see 6:4, 9, 10, 13; 19:12; 21:27; 30:12; cf. Deut 19:11.
27. See, e.g., Andersen, *Job*, 83; and T. H. Gaster, "Satan," *IBD* 4:224–25.
28. Cf. Job 28:4; BDB, 768–69; and *HALOT* 2:840.
29. Pope, *Job*, 4.
30. Ackerman, "Exegetical Reading of Psalm 82." Cf. the work of E. T. Mullen on the conflict in the Divine Council reflected in Ugaritic texts (*Divine Council*, 45–84).
31. I agree with D. J. A. Clines that the Satan should be included among the sons of God (*Job 1–20*, 19; contra S. Terrien and P. Scherer, "The Book of Job: Introduction and Exegesis," *IB* 3:912; and Andersen, *Job*, 82).

leads me to believe that the sons of God share the Satan's view of Job. The Satan serves only as a representative voice. The council is preparing for a fight, and at this moment it appears to be over Job. The magnitude of the conflict steers us to the view that the law may be involved.

Moreover, the text has demonstrated a few of the special attributes of legal narrative. First, multiple, conflicting strands of narrative have already appeared as a result of the disagreement between God and the Satan. Second, this conflict arises from different points of view regarding Job's character. Third, both narratives contain a truth claim regarding his character. Fourth, both narratives seek to persuade. At this point, we do not know for certain whom they seek to persuade—simply each other or the whole council in its judicial capacity. Before we can address this issue, we need to understand the precise nature of the conflict.

The conflict involves blasphemy.[32] The Satan has asserted that Job will curse God to his face if the divine hedge of blessings is removed. This cannot be ignored. One would expect a charge involving blasphemy to be taken with utmost seriousness. Blasphemy was a heinous crime in the ancient Near East.[33] It is one of the public offenses that carry high moral cul-

---

32. From a literary perspective, it is not particularly surprising that the charge involves blasphemy when we consider other ancient Near Eastern theodicies, some of which share a concern with blasphemy. For example, the friend of the sufferer in the "Babylonian Theodicy" twice accuses the protagonist of having blasphemed against his god: "You have forsaken right and blaspheme against your god's designs" and "in your anguish you blaspheme the god" (lines 79 and 255; translation from *BWL*, 77, 87. Although the signs are broken and the translation speculative, W. G. Lambert suggests that the protagonist of the Old Babylonian "A Man and His God" states: "I have not forgotten . . . all the kindness you have done to me, and all the blasphemy(?) I have spoken against you" ("A Further Attempt at the Babylonian 'Man and His God,'" 191, line 26). Hence, the attention that blasphemy receives in the book of Job is in no way unusual.

33. The Hebrew Bible primarily uses six Hebrew terms, some of which are euphemisms, to signify the act (see D. L. Bock, *Blasphemy and Exultation in Judaism: The Charge against Jesus in Mark 14:53–65* [Grand Rapids: Baker, 1998], 30; and J. E. Hartley, *Leviticus* [WBC 4; Dallas: Word, 1992], 408). The terms employed include ברך (1 Kgs 21:10, 13; Ps 10:3; Job 1:5, 11; 2:5, 9); גדף (2 Kgs 19:6, 22 [= Isa 37:6, 23]); חרף (2 Kgs 19:4, 16, 22, 23 [= Isa 37:4, 17, 23, 24]; Ps 74:10, 18; and 2 Chr 32:17); נבל (Isa 9:16; 32:6; Pss 14:1 [= Ps 53:2]; 74:18, 22; Job 2:10; 42:8); נקב (Lev 24:11, 16); and קלל (Exod 22:27; Lev 24:11, 14, 23; 1 Sam 3:13; Isa 8:21). Moreover, נאץ is often used in the general sense of *despising* God and probably includes blasphemy (Num 14:11, 23; 16:30; Jer 23:17; Pss 10:3, 13 [in parallel with ברך]; 74:10, 18; Neh 9:18, 26), as well as apostasy (Deut 31:20; Isa 5:24). Both BDB (p. 514) and *TWOT* (1:480) suggest that, in certain instances, לעג may carry the force of blasphemy. See, e.g., Job 11:3; 34:7; and 36:18. Finally, an Aramaic term, שלה, is also used to indicate blasphemy (Dan 3:29, discussed by Paul, "Daniel 3:29," 219–94). Paul discusses three ancient Near Eastern examples of blasphemy: (1) the Poem of Erra; (2) MAL A §2, wherein a woman who speaks blasphemy "shall bear her punishment; they shall not touch her husband, children, or daughters"; and (3) a report of an incident in which King Assurbanipal ripped out the tongues of two men who spoke blasphemy against Assur and then skinned them alive. For the Poem of Erra, see L. Cagni, *The Poem of Erra* (SANE 1; Mal-

pability.³⁴ Such acts offend Yahweh and pollute not only the offender but also the whole society. Accordingly, Yahweh might bring divine retribution upon the community at large, by way of famine, disease, or military defeat, in addition to any individual consequences that Yahweh might bring upon the perpetrator.³⁵ The gravity of the offense demanded that the culture remove this pollution through the perpetrator's death.³⁶ The penalty also could include forfeiture of the perpetrator's property to the king³⁷ and the possible destruction of his line.³⁸ According to 1 Sam 3:14, the blasphemy of the sons of Eli is not subject to expiation. This is an inexcusable capital offense that, if ignored, puts the entire Israelite community at risk. It is difficult to believe, then, that such a thing could be the subject of a wager. The law simply must be involved. God's law must be involved.

---

ibu: Undena, 1977), 42. For the Assurbanipal inscription, see Weidner, "Assyrische Beschreibungen der Kriegs-Reliefs Aššurbanipals," 184 no. 28. See also *SAAB* 1, 66–68, which reports two instances of blasphemy against the king. For additional ancient Near Eastern references, see "*miqtu (miqit pî)*," *CAD* M/2, 105; and "*šillatu*," *CAD* Š/2, 445–46. Cf. YOS 7, 137, where four inmates declare in court that a fifth man "spoke evil in the prison concerning the king" ([*ana mu*]*ḫḫi šarri lā ṭābātu ina bīt kīli* [*iq*]*tabi*).

34. Westbrook, "Punishments and Crimes," 548. Other crimes in this category are apostasy, misappropriation of taboo sacred property (חרם), sorcery, violation of the sabbath, and a number of sexual crimes (ibid., 548–50; cf. Greenberg, "Crimes and Punishments," 734). False prophecy, false swearing in the name of God, and certain types of errors of worship might also be included in this category (Lev 17:4; Deut 18:20; Jer 29:21–23; cf. Isa 65:7). There are such deep connections between these offenses that the same vocabulary is often used to express several different acts within this class of crimes. For example, the root גדף is used to describe sins against the sabbath and other similar high-handed acts against God (Num 15:30, 32–36) and apostasy (Ezek 20:27). The root חרף can mean a general affront to God through acting in unkind ways to one's neighbor (Prov 17:5) or can mark improper worship of God (Isa 65:7). The root נבל is a particularly important example of this phenomenon. The word means various types of profane actions, including apostasy (Deut 32:21), the misappropriation of taboo sacred property (Josh 7:15), various sexual offenses (Deut 22:21; Judg 20:6, 10; 2 Sam 13:12, 13 [although Lev 20:17 does not demand death in the case of brother–sister incest]; Jer 29:23; and Hos 2:12), and swearing false words in God's name (Jer 29:23). Moreover, the Bible reports that a person who commits another crime within this class of crimes is also capable of committing blasphemy (Isa 8:19–22; cf. Isa 9:16).

35. Westbrook, "Punishments and Crimes," 548. See, e.g., Isa 9:3–20; cf. Pss 10:12; 17:11, 22.

36. See Lev 24:10–23 (by stoning); 1 Sam 3:1–4:22 (through warfare and other acts of God); 1 Kgs 21:1–29 (by stoning); 2 Kgs 19:4–38 and its parallel in 2 Chr 32:17–23 (by assassination); and Dan 3:29 (being torn limb from limb). Where the defendant was indeed executed, the responsibility for his death, what is called his bloodguilt in the Hebrew Bible, rested upon the offender himself and no right of revenge rested in his family. On bloodguilt, see Exod 22:1, 2; Lev 17:4; 20:9, 11, 12, 13, 16, 17; Num 35:27; Deut 19:10; 21:8; 22:8; 2 Sam 21:1; Ezek 33:5; Pss 51:16; 106:38; Prov 28:17.

37. See 1 Kgs 21:1–29; Dan 3:29, although, in the Kings passage, Naboth is also accused of treason, which could independently justify forfeiture of property. For other instances of criminal forfeiture in the Bible, see 1 Sam 22:19; Dan 2:5; Ezra 6:11; 10:8.

38. See 1 Sam 3:1–4:22; 1 Kgs 21:1–29. The destruction of Ahab's line is reported in 2 Kgs 9:25–26.

We thus come to the question of whether the Satan's accusation against Job is a legally sufficient accusation that will initiate litigation. The Satan states in relevant part: "If he does not blaspheme (ברך) you to your face ... !" (1:11). Again, he states: "If he does not blaspheme (ברך) you to your face ... !" (2:4–5). The Satan has accused Job of a crime using the common abbreviated weakened oath formula found in the Neo-Babylonian period: "If he has not done X [the content of the accusation] . . . ."[39] The Neo-Babylonian texts demonstrate that the abbreviated weakened oath formula is one possible formulation of a legal accusation. This lends credence to the view that the Satan is initiating a trial on the crime of blasphemy.

The chief difficulty in accepting this position is that the Satan's accusation concerns a future act rather than a past one. No one accuses Job of having already cursed God. Quite to the contrary, we know that Job is so scrupulous concerning the matter of blasphemy that he regularly offers expiatory sacrifices against the possibility that one of his children might have committed blasphemy in their heart. Conviction for a crime in a human court of law demands that those bringing the case prove that a crime *was* committed. This has two elements: (1) that the defendant had the requisite guilty intention (*mens rea*) to commit the crime; and (2) that the defendant committed the requisite guilty act (*actus reus*) in the past.[40] Criminal accusations always assume that the guilty act of the crime has been completed. Even in the case of criminal attempt, the perpetrator must have accomplished substantial acts in furtherance of the crime.[41] Consequently,

---

39. F. W. Dobbs-Allsopp remarks that it is often difficult to determine when אם־לא represents the oath formula and when it is asseverative ("Genre," 53, relying on W. L. Holladay, *Jeremiah 1* [Hermeneia; Philadelphia: Fortress, 1986], 454). I believe that the oath formula is in use here. This is recognized by Andersen, *Job*, 85; Clines, *Job 1–20*, 26; Good, *In Turns of Tempest*, 195; and Peake, *Job*, 61, among others. See further Conklin, "Means of Marking Oath Content."

40. Both Latin terms, *mens rea* and *actus reus*, derive from the maxim: *actus non est reus nisi mens sit rea* ("the act is not answerable unless the intention should be answerable"). The *actus reus* of a crime is "[a] wrongful deed which renders the actor criminally liable if combined with *mens rea*. The *actus reus* is the physical aspect of a crime, whereas the *mens rea* (guilty mind) involves the intent factor" ("Actus Reus," BLD, 36). *Mens rea* is "an element of criminal responsibility: a guilty mind; a guilty or wrongful purpose; a criminal intent. Guilty knowledge and willfulness" ("Mens Rea," BLD, 985). The ancient legal world had an equal sensitivity to the issue of intent. In Israel one can see this predominantly in the law of homicide (see, e.g., Num 35:9–35; and Deut 19:1–13), but it applied also in the case of personal injury (Exod 21:18–19; and Deut 22:28). For a few of the many discussions of intention in the ancient Near East, see G. Cardascia, "Le caratère volontaire ou involontaire des atteintes corporelles dans les droits cuneiforms," in *Studi in Onore di Cesare Sanfilippo* (ed. D. A. Giuffrè; 8 vols.; Milan: Università di Catania Facoltà di Giurisprudenza, 1985), 4:163–207; Westbrook, *Studies*, 39–88, esp. 70; and idem, "Punishments and Crimes," 550–54.

41. In modern law, a finding of criminal attempt requires "an intent combined with an act falling short of the thing intended. It may be described as an endeavor to do an act, carried beyond mere preparation, but short of execution" ("Attempt," BLD, 127). There must

by human standards, the Satan cannot be accusing Job of having committed blasphemy. The most the Satan can do is to accuse Job of having the *mens rea* of the crime. The Satan's words seem to be an imprecation, the type found in many ancient Near Eastern inscriptions, whose consequence will take effect when the forbidden act occurs.[42] This is the reason so many interpreters suggest that the Satan's plan to withdraw God's blessing and inflict suffering on Job can be no more than some sort of test of Job, a form of divine entrapment.[43]

God, indeed, tests humanity, and he often tests in most uncomfortable ways. The Bible reports incidents of divine testing thirty-three times outside of the book of Job.[44] The verb בחן is used in seventeen of these verses,[45] and the verb נסה in twelve.[46] One verse even has בחן and נסה in parallel.[47] Three verses use the verb חקר, one in parallel to בחן.[48] One has both פקד and צרף in parallel with בחן.[49] Twelve of these thirty-three reports indicate that God specifically tests the heart of humanity.[50] The heart is the seat of

---

generally be four elements present: "1) an intent to commit [a crime]; 2) an overt act toward its commission; 3) failure of consummation; and 4) the apparent possibility of commission" (ibid.). While there are not many attempt cases in the ancient Near East, they do exist. In the Neo-Babylonian period, see, e.g., TCL 12, 117; TCL 13, 219 (= *Nbn* 720), YOS 6, 235, and YOS 7, 97. The same four elements of attempt that we find in the modern world are all also present in these cases, although in YOS 7, 97 a completed act of battery also was involved in the case. In Egypt, the Harem Conspiracy Trial, in which a large number of individuals plotted the death of Ramses III, is the most important example (although, while most scholars believe this is an attempt case, the plot may have been successful and the trial convened not by Ramses III but by Ramses IV) (*ANET*, 214–16; and S. Redford, *The Harem Conspiracy: The Murder of Ramesses III* [DeKalb: Northern Illinois University Press, 2002]). Furthermore, we have narratives concerning trials for attempted crimes in the Hebrew Bible. Joseph is accused and awaiting trial for an attempted rape of a married woman, a forcible adulterous act (Gen 39:14, 17). Mordecai foiled the assassination plot of Bigthan and Teresh, who were then investigated, presumably tried, and executed (Esth 2:21–23).

42. See further S. Gevirtz, "West-Semitic Curses and the Problem of the Origins of Hebrew Law," *VT* 11 (1961): 137–58.

43. The word "entrapment" rarely appears in print in relation to the test, but it is bandied about regularly in discussions by scholars of wisdom and biblical law.

44. Gen 22:1; Exod 15:25; 16:4; 20:20; Deut 8:2, 16; 13:14; Judg 2:22; 3:1, 4; Isa 48:10; Jer 6:27; 9:6; 11:20; 12:3; 17:10; 20:12; Zech 13:9; Pss 7:10; 11:4, 5; 17:3; 26:2; 44:22; 66:10; 81:8; 105:19; 139:23; Prov 17:3; 27:21; Eccl 3:18; 1 Chr 29:17; 2 Chr 32:31; cf. Isa 28:16. Ezek 21:18 might also make reference to a testing of humanity by God, but the verse is obscure and the translation in dispute.

45. Jer 6:27; 9:6; 11:20; 12:3; 17:10; 20:12; Zech 13:9; Pss 7:10; 11:4, 5; 17:3; 26:2; 66:10; 81:8; 139:23; Prov 17:3; 1 Chr 29:17.

46. Gen 22:1; Exod 15:25; 16:4; 20:20; Deut 8:2, 16; 13:4; Judg 2:22; 3:1, 4; Pss 26:2; 2 Chr 32:31.

47. Ps 26:2.

48. Jer 17:10; Pss 44:22; 139:24. Ps 139:24 has חקר in parallel to בחן.

49. Ps 17:3.

50. Deut 8:2; Jer 11:20; 12:3; 17:10; 20:12; Pss 7:10; 17:3; 26:2; 139:23; Prov 17:3; 1 Chr 29:17; 2 Chr 32:31.

human intention in the worldview of the Hebrew Bible.[51] The verb בחן is used in ten of these verses,[52] and נסה in one of the remaining two,[53] while חקר occurs in the other.[54] Additionally, the verb דרש is used to convey God's *searching* or *investigating* the human heart. For example, 1 Chr 28:9 says in part: "for Yahweh searches (דרש) all hearts (לבב), and understands every intent of the thoughts (יצר מחשבות)."[55]

The verbs used to indicate God's testing, however, also have legal force. They relate to conducting a legal investigation in some cases. In Gen 42:14, Joseph accuses his brothers of espionage. In 42:15–16, he devises a way to investigate or prove the matter. The verb בחן is used there.[56] The fact that נסה is parallel to both בחן and ריב ("to sue") indicates its legal force.[57] The legal meaning of חקר becomes evident in Ps 44:22, where apostasy is under God's investigation.[58] The root דרש can also mean to conduct a rational legal investigation, as well as to inquire of God through an oracular procedure.[59] God's testing of the heart, then, is a cosmic investigation of possible faulty or even criminal intention. This is made explicit in Jer 11:20; 20:12; and Pss 7:9–12; 44:22 (cf. Jer 17:10). Thus, any testing of Job is an investigation of his state of mind. Is a faulty intention alone, however, an offense worthy of divine trial and punishment within the worldview of the Hebrew Bible, or must some guilty act have been committed? To answer this question, we must examine the issue of criminal intention.

It is extremely difficult for mortals to discern the intentions of the human heart. We usually cannot know if someone has a criminal intention without some external manifestation of that intention. That is why humans

---

51. See, e.g., Deut 8:2; Jer 11:20; 12:3; 17:10; 20:12; Pss 7:10; 17:3; 26:2; 139:23; Prov 17:3; 1 Chr 29:17; 2 Chr 32:31.
52. Jer 11:20; 12:3; 20:12; Pss 7:10; 17:3; 26:2; 139:23; Prov 17:3; 1 Chr 29:17; 2 Chr 32:31.
53. Deut 8:2.
54. Jer 17:10.
55. Cf. Prov 24:12, where God weighs (תכן) the human heart, watches (נצר) over the soul, and gives the individual what he or she deserves.
56. P. Bovati also believes that בחן means to conduct a legal investigation, citing Jer 6:27; 9:6; 11:20; 12:3; 17:10; 20:12; Pss 7:10; 11:4; 17:3; 26:2; 139:23; Job 7:18; 23:10; Prov 17:3; and 1 Chr 29:17, although he misses a number of occurrences of the verb's legal meaning (*Re-Establishing Justice*, 244–46).
57. See Ps 26:2 (בחן) and Deut 33:8 (ריב). Bovati lists this verb as one of the lesser important investigative words (*Re-Establishing Justice*, 42, 244–45).
58. Ibid. Bovati considers this verb one of the most significant of the investigative words.
59. For instances when the root דרש means "to conduct a rational legal investigation," see Judg 6:29; Deut 13:15; 17:4; 19:18; Ezra 10:17. The root דרש refers to an oracular procedure in Gen 25:22; Exod 18:15; Deut 18:11; 1 Sam 9:9; 28:7; 1 Kgs 14:5; 22:5, 7, 8; 2 Kgs 1:2, 3, 6, 16; 3:11; 8:8; 22:13, 18; Isa 8:19; Jer 21:2; 37:7; Ezek 14:3, 7; 20:1, 3, 31; 1 Chr 10:13, 14; 13:3; 21:30; 2 Chr 18:4, 6, 7; 34:21, 26. For a study of the many uses of דרש, see C. Westermann, "Die Begriffe für Fragen und Suchen im Alten Testament," *KD* 6 (1961): 2–30. See also M. Fishbane, *Biblical Interpretation in Ancient Israel* (Oxford: Clarendon, 1985), 244–45.

generally do not punish evil intentions—we might be mistaken about them. The fact of and the circumstances surrounding the *actus reus* of the crime are often the only evidence we have concerning the actual intention of the alleged perpetrator.[60] Thus, both elements of the crime, the *mens rea* and the *actus reus*, must be present for conviction in a human court.

That the dual requirements for conviction in a human court do not apply to divine courts in the ancient Near East can be seen in the ritual texts. As we observed in chapter 2, one could have committed a sin quite unintentionally, and even unknowingly, and still have been punished through some form of suffering. For example, the priest in the Šurpu Incantations declares that the sufferer "does not know what is a crime against god, he does not know what is a sin against the goddess" (tablet 2, line 32). In these cases, the petitioner assumes that only the *actus reus* was required for conviction. No *mens rea* existed.[61]

Furthermore, the ritual texts disclose that the crime may have involved only possessing bad intention or may have been solely the result of a mental rather than a physical act. For example, the Namerimburruda Incantations list hating, despising, and forgetting the sufferer's personal god as his cause for suffering.[62] While certain guilty acts or omissions may have followed and proven the bad intention, the intention alone is what is subject to punishment. These crimes are in the nature of improper mental activity rather than improper actions or omissions and are distinguished from committing an abomination toward or against a personal god, which are also mentioned in the Namerimburruda Incantations (lines 12–13; cf. 15–20). Similarly, the sufferer in "A Babylonian Prayer to Anūna" wonders whether he may have "not stood in awe of her [Inninna] praise" (line 89).[63] The petitioner asserts further: "I have not been lustful and have not abandoned the truth" (line 107). These, too, are mental or emotional activities. The Šurpu Incantations further reveal that the sufferer believes he may have "scorned the god, despised the goddess" (tablet 2, line 33; cf. line 73). He additionally postulates that he was contemptuous of, or hateful toward, his relatives (tablet 2, lines 35–36). In all these cases, the incantations do not distinguish between the mental act of forgetting, scorning, despising,

---

60. *Black's Law Dictionary* states that intent is "[a] mental attitude which can seldom be proved by direct evidence, but must ordinarily be proved by circumstances from which it may be inferred" ("Intent," *BLD*, 810). It continues that intent may be shown by the "act, circumstances and inferences deducible therefrom."

61. Additionally, both the Šurpu Incantations and the DINGIR.ŠÀ.DIB.BA Incantations indicate that the sins of one's parents may be the cause of the problem. (DINGIR.ŠÀ.DIB.BA, no. 1, lines 115–18; and Šurpu, tablet 3, lines 176–83). Here the punishment is vicarious and entirely unrelated to either the sufferer's state of mind or actions.

62. Geller, "An Incantation against Curses," 133, lines 10–11, 14.

63. Lambert, "A Babylonian Prayer to Anūna," 330.

being contemptuous or hateful toward and doing physical acts or saying clear words to make the negative attitude manifest. The *mens rea* alone must have been sufficient for conviction. Consequently, I suggest that Yahweh and the Divine Council may act similarly, convicting on only one element of a crime.

The Bible is replete with examples of God's distress over a poor mindset. Both 1 Chr 28:9 and Ps 44:22 testify that God does not necessarily require an *actus reus* to judge us guilty and that an evil intention alone may be sufficient. In many instances, God clearly threatens punishment for bad intent. In Lev 19:17–18, Yahweh instructs: "You shall not hate (שׂנא) your kinsfolk in your heart (לבב). Reprove (יכח) your kinsfolk lest you bear sin (חטא) because of him. You shall not take vengeance or bear a grudge against your countrymen." Deut 29:17–19a warns:

> It may be that there is among you a man or woman, or a family or tribe, whose heart (לבב) is already turning away from Yahweh, our God, to serve the gods of those nations. It may be that there is among you a root sprouting poisonous and bitter growth. When a person hears the words of these sanctions, he may fancy himself immune, thinking, "I shall be safe, though I follow my own willful heart (לבב)"—to the utter ruin of moist and dry alike. Yahweh will never forgive him; rather will Yahweh's anger and passion rage against that person. . . .

In this passage, the growing intention toward apostasy and a cavalier attitude toward God are penalized. Additionally, in Isa 29:13–14, God declares that honoring him with the lips and doing worship by rote count but little if he is far from the human heart. In this case, God will bring bafflement upon the people, and wisdom and prudence will fail. Here, too, God judges one more by one's intention than by one's behavior.[64] In Jer 12:2-3, Jeremiah, who is frustrated in much the same way Job is, says to God:

> You plant them, and they take root;
>    they grow and bring forth fruit;
> you are near in their mouths
>    yet far from their emotions.[65]
> But you, O Yahweh, know me;
>    You see me and investigate (בחן) me—my heart (לב) is with you.
> Pull them out like sheep for the slaughter,
>    and set them apart for the day of slaughter.

---

64. In Zech 7:10b and 8:17a, God forbids plotting evil against others. What is not made clear is whether plotting in the heart is sufficient for divine punishment or whether some concrete steps must be taken toward the commission of the plot. Cf. Prov 6:24–25, which warns that one should not desire the beauty of an evil or adulterous woman in one's heart.

65. Literally "kidneys" (כליות). In the Hebrew Bible, the kidneys are the center of human emotion.

The implications of this passage are that Yahweh will slaughter those whose acts are righteous but whose emotions and intentions do not follow suit. Consequently, a guilty intention may open oneself up to divine investigation, trial, and punishment consistent with the ritual texts of the ancient Near East. I suggest that the reason a faulty intention alone justifies God's trial and punishment of humanity is that God, from the point of view of the writers of the Hebrew Bible, can more easily determine the intentions of the human heart than humans can.

Job's ritual expiation for his children's benefit seals our belief that the Satan has accused Job of having a blasphemous mind. In light of 1 Sam 3:14, Job's sacrifices on behalf of his children seem quite odd. Blasphemy cannot be expiated. Nonetheless, Job, a man knowledgeable in the law, does this repeatedly, believing it to be highly effective. Why? I postulated that such sacrifices are reasonable because Job is expiating, not for blasphemous *acts* completed but for a blasphemous *intent*, which he believes can be expiated. In 1:5, Job has no evidence that his children are committing the *actus reus* of the crime of blasphemy by speaking ill words against God with their lips. Rather, he worries that such words are in their hearts, the seat of human intention. Hence, the cause of Job's anxiety is that his children may have a blasphemous intent, which can bring divine punishment. Job performs expiation rituals for his children under the presupposition that guilty intention alone can convict a human before God. Thus, to Job, the ability to expiate appears to turn on whether or not the *actus reus* has been completed.[66] If one has the requisite *mens rea* of blasphemy but has not committed the *actus reus*, then only a lesser offense stands against God, which may be expiated.[67] Once a blasphemous guilty act is coupled with

---

66. A full study of the relationship between criminal culpability and ritual expiation has not, to my knowledge, been undertaken, although most discussions of either biblical crimes or the sacrificial provisions of Leviticus and Numbers touch on the subject. Westbrook's very brief analysis is the most helpful of all such analyses of the issue ("Punishments and Crimes, 546–56).

67. The charge of blasphemous intention might be called a *lesser included offense* within the divine legal system. Under the common law, a lesser included offense is "[o]ne which is composed of some, but not all the elements of a greater offense and which does not have any element not included in the greater offense so that it is impossible to commit [the] greater offense without necessarily committing the lesser offense" ("Lesser Included Offense," *BLD*, 902). In this case, the crime of blasphemy requires the intent to curse God and the act of cursing God. The crime of possession of a blasphemous intent is a crime that has one, but not all, of the elements of the greater crime of blasphemy. Furthermore, conviction for a blasphemous intention does not require proving an element outside of the crime of blasphemy. Hence, it is a lesser included crime. The ancient world did not embrace this concept in the way we moderns do. Their legal philosophy did not allow them to think in quite this way (see further the works of R. Westbrook, including: "Cuneiform Law Codes," 210–22; *Studies*, 1–8, 133–35; "Covenant Code?" 15–36; and "Codification and Canonization," 33–46). Nonetheless, dis-

the requisite guilty intention, blasphemy has occurred and ordinary ritual expiation will not be effective. Death is demanded if the pollution is not to spread to the entire community, which would justify divine punishment of the whole lot. In the worldview of the Joban text, a blasphemous intention alone can subject one to legal charges in the Divine Council.

From a literary perspective, the Satan's concern over Job's blasphemous intent appears to be running parallel to Job's concern over his children's blasphemous intent.[68] The Satan's and Job's responses to their concerns are quite different, but their awareness of the seriousness of the problem is the same. The Satan, having no love for Job and having legal recourse available to him in the Divine Council, may press charges. Job, on the other hand, loves his children and cannot (and does not want to) use the human legal system in order to chastise them for a guilty intention alone or to correct the offense. He can, however, easily employ the sacrificial system to solve his dilemma. Consequently, the Satan is most distressed over Job's blasphemous intention and has issued a formal legal accusation on a recognized substantive crime before the proper court. Such an accusation is correct in its form and is legally effective. This will begin a trial on the charge that Job has a blasphemous intent.

Job 31:9–11 and 26–28 provide additional support for this view. In chapter 31, Job offers an oath of denial. In the midst of it, he swears that he never lusted (אם־נפתה לבי) after a woman or waited by his neighbor's door hoping to meet her (31:9). His self-curse, if he should have done such things, is that his wife will have sexual relations with another (31:10).[69] He follows this up with his reasoning:

> For that is an intended crime (זמה),
>     that is an actionable offense (עון פלילים).[70]

---

tinctions for different levels of culpability and distinctions regarding whether or not the *actus reus* of the crime was completed clearly existed in the ancient world (see nn. 33–34 above). The law of the ancient Near East had a mechanism for dealing with the lesser included crime. Further development of this concept must also wait.

68. M. Weiss notes the parallelism between the sons of Job and the sons of God: "The sons of Job are summoned; in heaven the 'sons of God' appear. Thus, not only is the portrayal of the scene in heaven juxtaposed with that of the scene in the Land of Uz, thereby accentuating the correlation between the two worlds, but in addition, the scenes are described in parallel terms" (*Job's Beginning*, 33). Cf. Habel, *Book of Job: Commentary*, 89.

69. For a full explanation of *grinding* as sexual intercourse rather than milling, see Westbrook, "Lex Talionis," 59 n. 35.

70. I follow Good's translation in 31:11 (*Turns of Tempest*, 132, 133), disagreeing with that of Westbrook, "Lex Talionis," 59. Westbrook suggests that none of the crimes in ch. 31 is subject to human justice, only divine justice, in spite of the use of עון פלילים in 31:11, 28. He therefore translates the relevant material in 31:11b and 28a: "a sin for which I am solely responsible," but this does not account for the attempted crimes represented in 31:9, 26–27.

E. M. Good argues: "*Zimmah* is a technical legal term, sometimes for sexual misconduct (e.g., Lev 18:17; 20:14), sometimes for other kinds of misconduct (Ps 26:10; Hos 6:9)."[71] He continues: "The noun is derived from *zmm*, which has to do with intending, and its use in the plural in 17:11 apparently has the meaning not of a crime but of an intention or purpose."[72] I maintain that the root has to do with both intending and planning, and Job's oath demonstrates this principle.[73] Job refers both to falling into a criminal intention (lusting) and to taking steps to fulfill that intention (waiting for his neighbor's wife by her door) (31:9). The first is actionable before God because it involves guilty intention alone, as in the "Babylonian Prayer to Anūna." The second is actionable before both God and humanity because Job would have taken substantial acts toward the commission of the crime (adultery). Waiting by the door, as an act in furtherance of the crime, would constitute attempted adultery, which is punishable by a human court.[74] Similarly, in 31:26–28, the intention to worship false gods is subject only to divine punishment, but once the perpetrator kisses his hand in homage, he has made an overt act toward the commission of the crime.[75] He is therefore subject to human justice. The Satan's accusation is directed toward Job's possible blasphemous intent, which, if true, is clearly actionable in the Divine Council. The Satan's actions are therefore far more than a test of Job's faith in the modern sense. Rather, we are seeing divine law in action. The council is acting in its judicial capacity. It is hearing a legal accusation against Job. The fact that the council is antagonistic toward Yahweh would not necessarily undermine the position that the Divine Council is serving as a court, because an accuser could serve as a member of the court panel in the Divine Council or in the human law court.

Understanding what we now do about intention and the legal import of the events in the Divine Council, let us look at one last possibility—the possibility that the Satan intends to entrap Job. This is a modern legal term often used by biblical scholars to describe the Satan's actions. The issue of entrapment turns on whether one has a guilty intention. When an individual is on trial for a crime in the American legal system, for instance, he or she may raise the defense of entrapment. The claim is that, although the defendant committed the *actus reus* of the crime, government officials induced its *mens rea* where such had not previously existed. In other words, officials sought to provoke the defendant into committing a crime that he

---

71. Good, *Turns of Tempest*, 132–33.
72. Ibid., 132. Cf. Habel, *Book of Job: Commentary*, 423; and NASB.
73. See further *HALOT* 1:272, 273.
74. See, e.g., the situation of Joseph, who is accused and awaiting trial for attempted forcible rape of a married woman (Gen 39:14, 17). See n. 41 above.
75. For more on the kiss as an act of homage in ancient Mesopotamia, see Dick, "Job 31," 58, 102 n. 129.

or she was not originally contemplating in order to obtain a criminal conviction.[76] Most authorities believe that, for the defendant's defensive plea to succeed, he or she cannot have had a predisposition to committing the crime, that is, a previously standing guilty intent.[77] The Satan, one of the divine government's officers, believes that Job has the requisite guilty intention. Whether or not the Satan is instituting a formal legal charge, he is not, from his point of view, entrapping Job. He is, instead, setting up a sting operation against a man with a guilty mind. He is simply giving Job an opportunity to live out his predisposition to blasphemy so that he can be caught in the act. All police sting operations are based on this principle.

Nonetheless, what the police view as a sting operation, the defendant may see as entrapment because the defendant may not experience him- or herself as having a guilty intention. Certainly Job does not view himself as having one. Furthermore, Job does not raise the issue of entrapment at any point in his speeches because he never admits to having done the *actus reus* of the crime—he protests loudly against any such accusation. Moreover, he never suggests that anyone has or can persuade him toward any inappropriate thought or deed. He defends himself by asserting that he both lacks a guilty intention and has committed no guilty acts. In this manner, he sets forth a traditional defense against the charge. To the extent that he complains against the actions of members of the Divine Council, he uses an entirely different basis for his claim, as we will examine in the next chapter. Consequently, it is not helpful to describe the Satan's actions as *entrapment*. They either give rise to a formal legal accusation on the crime of possession of a blasphemous intent, or they are a sting operation on the crime of blasphemy. Most commentators who suggest that the Satan means to entrap Job are actually arguing that the Satan intends to catch Job in a sting operation designed just for him. Nonetheless, this is the stuff of law, not a mere test of faith. A sting operation assumes that legal consequences will flow to those with a guilty intention and a propensity to do the guilty acts.

If one takes the stance that the Satan's denunciation constitutes a formal legal accusation rather than a sting operation, one wonders: Why does the Satan care whether Job commits the act? Why is this raised as part of the accusation itself? If Job is charged with possession of a blasphemous intent, the crime is completed with the formulation of the thought and the speech act of cursing is irrelevant to a conviction. Job's future conduct is of no consequence to the charge. All that the Satan must prove is that Job has had, or currently has, the requisite guilty mind. Yet how will the Satan prove this to the Divine Council? The state of Job's intention is contested in

---

76. "Entrapment," *BLD*, 532.
77. Ibid.

the Divine Council. The Satan believes it is guilty; Yahweh does not. What evidence will the Satan bring to the court? As discussed above, when human intention is in doubt in the worldview of the Hebrew Bible, God investigates. Job's cursing of God when the divine hedge of blessings is removed will serve, for both God and the Satan, as the best evidence of Job's guilty intention. This divine test is not, therefore, one of faith but rather one of legal culpability. Unfortunately, the act will complete the full crime of blasphemy; thus, this view seems to produce a slight legal anomaly.

The solution to this dilemma ultimately rests in the strained relationship between Yahweh and the Satan, where this lengthy discussion began. In taking the position he does against Yahweh, the Satan seems to be claiming, at a minimum, knowledge superior to that of Yahweh concerning the content of Job's mind. This is challenge enough to a supreme being. Yet the challenge may run far deeper than that; it may involve a challenge to Yahweh's conduct and authority. P. L. Day argues that the primary target of the Satan's accusations is God, who has offered Job unfair "divine patronage."[78] In my opinion, Day is on the right track.

The Satan has a theory as to why the *actus reus*, which one might expect to have followed a guilty mind-set, has not occurred. It is because God has protected Job with a perfect life, filled with innumerable blessings. He claims that, if God would withdraw such favor and strike Job instead, Job would respond with blasphemous acts. It therefore may be that the Satan believes that both he and Yahweh have equal knowledge of Job's mind-set—they both know that Job is capable of blasphemy, but God has intentionally built a protective hedge of blessings around the criminal. In so doing, he has maintained the conditions of blasphemy. Knowing of Job's evil, God created conditions that protected it. He allowed this guilty mind to go unchecked and unpunished. Consequently, the Satan may be accusing God of complicity in the matter: God has aided and abetted this criminal.

The ancient world recognized derivative crimes. Under Neo-Babylonian law, accomplices and aiders and abettors of significant participation were considered criminals equal to the criminal they supported. For instance, in YOS 19, 98, the court indicated that a woman would also be considered a thief of temple property if a witness came forward to prove that she aided and abetted the actual thief, who was named in the conditional-verdict document against her.[79] The same is true under bibli-

---

78. Day, *Adversary in Heaven*, 76, 80–81; quote at 76. Day states further: "I am suggesting that Yahweh is on trial, for his conduct of world order, from the very beginning [of the dispute]" (p. 81; cf. p. 80). She indicates that F. M. Cross and P. Mosca first suggested this idea to her (p. 76 n. 18). Good (*Turns of Tempest*, 195, 411 n. 17) agrees with Day.

79. In TCL 13, 170, a storeroom clerk who reported a theft was under investigation for

cal law.⁸⁰ Furthermore, those who come to know of the crime later but do not report it are, in modern legal terms, accomplices after-the-fact and are subject to criminal penalties.⁸¹ Such individuals were also subject to penalty. Prov 29:24 is instructive in the situation: "One who shares with a thief hates (שׂנא) his own life; he hears the [victim's] curse, but does not accuse (נגד)."⁸² Leviticus 5:1 similarly indicates that one who does not accuse when one has knowledge of a public curse of a victim is subject to punishment. Deut 13:9 declares that one should not shield a lawbreaker. Significantly, in 1 Sam 3:13, God punishes the entire house of Eli because Eli did not rebuke his sons for their blasphemy. The Satan, therefore, may be accusing Yahweh of supporting the criminal conduct of Job. If Job should commit a blasphemous act when God's protective hedge is removed, the act will serve as legally sufficient evidence on the issue of God's succor of one with a guilty intention. The act would prove the element of causation—that God's hedge is that which has protected Job's guilty mind. Thus, if Job falls, God may be condemned for aiding and abetting him. One might argue against this view by noting that God is always the victim of the crime of blasphemy and thus cannot aid and abet a crime that is directed against him. Yet blasphemy is of such a nature that it might offend other members of the Divine Council besides God. Then God's conduct would be actionable.

Even if it were not legally actionable, this would still be an important device on the Satan's part. It may be that, to his way of thinking, God is guilty of doing more than aiding and abetting this one particular individual's guilty intention. Job is instead just one manifestation of God's general failure to maintain the moral economy. Retributive justice demands that

---

aiding and abetting the thief. Cf. TCL 13, 181, where Gimillu's brother, Iddinaya, was probably under investigation for being Gimillu's aider and abettor. Investigations of and convictions on the fencing of stolen goods also exist. Fences are both aiders and abettors to theft and are liable on the separate crime of receiving stolen goods. See, e.g., RA 14, 158 no. 152 and YOS 7, 97.

80. Wells, Law of Testimony, 57–58. Westbrook points out that in the case of theft, there can be differences in penalties between a thief and a receiver of stolen goods ("The Deposit Law of Exodus 22,6–12," ZAW 106 [1994]: 396). He addresses, however, only the case of an innocent receiver of stolen goods (p. 397). I maintain that guilty receivers of stolen goods were treated in the same manner as the original thief. Divine disfavor with aiding and abetting evil is made explicit in Jer 23:14–15.

81. Unless, of course, they have some sort of protection from disclosure for knowledge gained in confidence. These persons would include, under certain conditions, therapists, pastors, and attorneys under the common law.

82. See Wells, Law of Testimony, 78–80; contra Geller, "Šurpu Incantations," 185–86. But see Lev 20:2–5, where the text discusses failure to prosecute the serious offense of worshiping Molech, but does not indicate that any punishment is due to those who remain silent.

God reward right thought, word, and deed with divine blessings and punish wrong thought, word, or deed with disease, disability, and/or disaster: good begets good, bad begets bad. In this case, God gave blessings without justification and brought no suffering upon the suspected perpetrator. The Satan could be averring that God did not make certain that Job was good and true before bestowing blessings upon him. In this manner, God has failed to maintain a fundamental principle of justice. This is a most serious charge. If this has been the nature of the discussion in prior council sessions, it would explain why God raises the "Job question" at all, and why he asserts that Job is a man of "integrity (תם) and uprightness (ישר)" and that he fears God (ירא אלהים) and shuns evil (סר מרע) (1:1a).

Reading the accusations in Job 1–2 as standing against God as well as Job raises another legal question: Can one member of the Divine Council legally charge another with inappropriate conduct? The answer is yes. J. Ackerman explains that, in Psalm 82, Yahweh puts the sons of God on trial for failing to maintain adequate social justice: "In verses 2–4, . . . the indictment Yahweh brings against אלהים is that they had not used their power to assure justice for the weaker members of society."[83] The Divine Council is responsible for trying any being who fails to live up to the heavenly standards of justice. In this case, the Satan claims that Yahweh has subverted justice. While putting God, the head of the council and chief justice, on trial is a brazen move, it may well be possible.[84] It is also possible, however, that members of the Divine Council are not formally charging God with a crime proper. Rather, this might be a political challenge that asserts that God is inconsistent in his application of both blessings and punishments and is "less than zealous in his pursuit of justice where certain favored individuals are concerned."[85] Whether the accusations against God are formal criminal charges or are merely political in nature, one may resolve the anomaly in the Satan's accusation of Job by understanding that the Satan has not brought a suit simply against Job but has also leveled some type of very serious charge against Yahweh. Job is small-fry baited for a bigger catch. As Job goes, so goes God. In all likelihood, God would be stripped of power if Job should blaspheme against God. This event would leave a power vacuum in the council. We can only assume that the Satan intends to fill it.[86]

---

83. Ackerman, "Exegetical Study of Psalm 82," 228.
84. An analogy might be drawn to trying a U.S. President for crimes committed in office. This country has wrestled with that issue twice in recent history, with the cases of Richard Nixon and William Clinton. It is possible but not something done lightly.
85. R. Westbrook, private communication, August 7, 2002.
86. See the work of J. Lévêque, who suggests that the Satan seeks to humiliate God through his questioning of God's confidence in Job (*Job et son Dieu: Essai d'Exégèse et de Théologie biblique* [2 vols.; EBib; Paris: Gabalda, 1960], 1:185, 189).

Many ancient Near Eastern Divine Council reports reflect such power struggles within the council.[87] This situation may be similar.

Such a reading might also explain why God seems to authorize the Satan to strike Job—or at least to acquiesce to the strike—in 1:12 and 2:6. The actions constitute a horrifically cruel deed if all that is at stake is a test of Job's faith. Surely God has other, less invasive and traumatic ways to gather such data. The theological view arising from a focus on the sovereignty and omnipotence of God that God must be in league with the Satan is deeply disturbing. If God is capable of destroying ten children and stripping Job of any human dignity on a bet—on a dare—then he is, to my mind, a very immature, highly insecure, and deeply troubled god, certainly no better than our worst view of the Satan. There is a better solution to the theological conundrum presented by the events in the Divine Council. If we read Job 1–2 with the idea that the Satan has charged God with serious misconduct, then God is also subject to investigation and must allow such investigation to proceed against his will. The withdrawal of all Job's blessings and the imposition of suffering are much more than an investigation of Job's state of mind; they are, more important, an investigation of God. Whether or not Job actually curses God to his face, Job may still be guilty of having a blasphemous intent. His falling is only a matter of the best possible evidence of his intention. But only if Job should fall is God proven, beyond a shadow of a doubt, guilty of disrupting the moral economy. This investigation goes to the very heart of the charges against God, whether those charges be legal or political. It is not a matter of the best possible evidence.

The Satan's point in bringing his charge against God is to enforce the idea that a god of integrity and uprightness does not interfere with or disrupt justice in any manner. Thus, if God should interfere with the trial of Job, he will have once more favored Job and interfered with or disrupted justice. By such an act, he will have proven the case against himself! No accused can stop the machinery of justice once a formal accusation is leveled by simply declaring, "I didn't do it!" If that were the case, every defendant's denial would succeed and trials would never occur. This heavenly legal system is consistent with all earthly legal systems. It does not allow for such an easy escape. Hence, if Yahweh is a defendant, he cannot stop this investigation by merely asserting that the Satan is wrong. Moreover, if God should try such a strategy, God will have favored Job once again by inappropriately stopping the proceedings and be caught in Satan's trap. If Yahweh is to prove that he is a god of justice, he simply must cooperate with the legal process. Accordingly, Yahweh can only find his way out of

---

87. For discussion of this point, see Mullen, *Divine Council*, 46–84; and Polley, "Hebrew Prophecy," 144.

this dilemma by winning at trial. This investigation of Job and, therefore, himself must now proceed.[88] The Satan has very shrewdly dropped God's power and pleasure out of the legal equation.

I do not believe that God is at all pleased with the situation. Nor do I believe that God is actively participating in the investigation, which would undermine the idea that God is one of the accused.[89] This issue is also contested among scholars.[90] Job 1:12 and 2:6–7 seem to indicate that the Satan is completely in charge. Job 1:16 reports, however, that "a fire of God fell from the heavens" to destroy Job's sheep, which may implicate God pursuant to Lev 10:2 and Num 16:35. Furthermore, a great wind, which might have come from God, as in Jonah 1:4, takes Job's children in 1:19. Finally, in 2:3b, God might have assumed ultimate responsibility for the activity against Job when he says to the Satan, "you incited (סות) me against him to overpower him without cause (חנם)." Nevertheless, I do not follow this line of reasoning. My position is based on an analysis of 1 Kgs 22:20–23.

In the case in 1 Kings, Yahweh wished to bring death finally to Ahab for his many sins. He sought a volunteer from members of the Divine Council to entice Ahab into war at Ramoth-gilead so that he would fall. A spirit came forward with a plan to put a lying spirit in the mouths of all Ahab's prophets. Yahweh approved the plan and commissioned the spirit with the words: "You are to entice him, and you shall succeed; go forth and do it" (1 Kgs 22:22).[91] In Job's case, God appears far more reticent in 1:12 and 2:6 than he does in the Kings passage.[92] God does not say the commanding "go forth and do it"; rather he offers, after the first accusation, the more reserved "All that is his is in your hand; only you should not

---

88. E. M. Good points out: "The curse does not bind Yahweh in moral problems at all; Yahweh is helpless to stop the working of the curse, though he can, it seems, put limits on the worker..." (*In Turns of Tempest*, 195).

89. From a legal perspective, it is irrelevant who conducts the investigation if Job is its prime subject. Many persons had investigative powers in the Neo-Babylonian period, even, in some cases, a party to the suit. If the Satan and God are aligned on the fact that Job should be subject to this investigation, either one or both could conduct the investigation. The issue is far more complicated, however, if God is in fact the primary target of the Satan's accusation. It is rare for a criminal defendant to initiate the investigation of his own case, although he was, of course, responsible for complying with its demands under Neo-Babylonian law. If God is a pro-active member of the investigation team, this would argue against his being the primary subject of the accusation and investigation. My thinking on this point would fail in this case.

90. N. C. Habel, for example, contends that the Satan strikes Job alone (*Book of Job: Commentary*, 97). F. I. Andersen, on the other hand, argues that God was directly involved (*Job*, 90–91).

91. In accord, R. B. Chisholm, Jr. "Does God Deceive?" *BSac* 155 (1998): 12–17.

92. According to E. T. Mullen, these words of dispatch are similar to those used to send out messengers in the Ugaritic council myths (*Divine Council*, 206). Deviation from them is, therefore, significant.

stretch your hand against his person" (1:12). He replies similarly after the second accusation: "He is in your hand; only protect his life" (2:6). It appears that God is trying to put the brakes on this investigation to whatever extent possible. Given that the Satan invited God to act in the first place (1:11 and 2:5), God's response seems especially reserved. He is not an enthusiastic supporter of it. Furthermore, in 1 Kgs 22:23, the prophet Micaiah, who is the narrator of the scene in the Divine Council, reports that Yahweh is the primary actor in carrying out the plot: "So, indeed, Yahweh put a lying spirit in the mouth of all your prophets; for Yahweh has decreed disaster upon you." In Job 2:7, however, the narrator reports that the Satan is the primary actor in carrying out the investigation: "So, the Satan departed from the presence of Yahweh and afflicted Job with terrible sores from the sole of his foot to the top of his head." Yahweh is not an eager member of the investigating team. He only participates because the law demands compliance from all those connected to a trial.

In this light, we return to the problem of 2:3b. After the first phase of the investigation in chapter 1, Job holds firm (vv. 13–22). Hence, Yahweh immediately protests to the Satan: "תסיתני against him to בלעו חנם." Some commentators argue that Yahweh appears weak for admitting that the Satan manipulated him.[93] This is not, however, an appropriate characterization. Rather, Yahweh is chastising the Satan for bringing charges against both Job and himself. The charge itself began with the words "Does Job fear God without cause (חנם)?" (1:9). Yahweh hopes to end it by accusing the Satan of being "without cause."

The Hebrew word for "incite," the *hiphil* of סות, can carry a legal connotation. It does not only mean "to provoke," "to cause to happen," and "to stir against"; it can also mean "to cause to bring legal charges" particularly when followed by the preposition ב. This is evident in 1 Sam 26:18-19, where David addresses Saul, demanding:

> Why does my lord pursue his servant? For what have I done? What guilt (רעה) is on my hands? Now, שמע־נא my lord the king the words of his servant. If it is Yahweh who הסותך against me, may he accept an offering; but if it is mortals, may they be cursed before Yahweh, for they have driven me out today from my share in the heritage of Yahweh, saying, "Go, serve other gods."

The context of his speech involves litigation. I begin to prove this point with a word study of the biblical command, שמענה, שמע־נא, or שמעו־נא ("Hear, I pray!"). This expression is often used in legal contexts. It may signify variously (1) the convening of a court; (2) a plea for a favorable judgment; or (3) that an individual's testimony is about to begin. First, I examine

---

93. See, e.g., Habel, *Book of Job: Commentary*, 61, 85.

when "Hear, I pray!" is used to indicate that the court has been convened. For example, in 1 Sam 22:6, this phrase prefaces King Saul's accusation against his servants that they are conspiring with David and that they aid and abet David by not accusing him of known treachery against the king. In the subsequent trial of Ahimelech for conspiracy, Ahimelech responds to his summons to appear and now stands before King Saul. Saul begins the trial with the words: "Hear, I pray, son of Ahitub" (1 Sam 22:12aβ). Ahimelech replies that he is present for trial (הנני אדני) (1 Sam 22:12bβ). Then Saul begins to question Ahimelech (1 Sam 22:13). In Mic 6:1, God requests a hearing of Israel before the mountains and hills, using this phrase. God also uses this phrase before he accuses Miriam for her grumbling against Moses in Num 12:6. Second, "Hear, I pray!" may serve as a call for a decision to be rendered by the court. When Irijah arrested Jeremiah for allegedly defecting to the Chaldeans (Jer 37:13), he was tried before King Zedekiah. At the conclusion of his questioning, Jeremiah said: "And now, hear, I pray, my lord the king! Let my plea come before you, and do not send me back to the house of Jonathan, the scribe, lest I die there" (Jer 37:20). Third, "Hear, I pray!" may be a simple testimony marker. This is the case in Ezek 18:25, where Yahweh responds to a claim of Israel that his justice is unfair with his defense that he is indeed fair and it is Israel who is unfair. His testimony is prefaced by "Hear, I pray."

The *qal* imperative of שמע ("Hear!") and, secondarily, the *hiphil* imperative of אזן ("Listen!"), standing alone, are also used in the Hebrew Bible to these same purposes. For example, in both Jer 2:4 and Mic 1:2, the *qal* imperative announces that the accusations of God against Israel are soon forthcoming. The *hiphil* imperative of אזן is used by the Psalmist to mark his plea to God for a favorable judgment in Ps 17:1 (cf. Pss 5:2; 143:1). I therefore suggest that the use of the *qal* jussive of שמע in this context is also legal. Moreover, David's immediate question concerning his possible guilt, the tenor of this stage of the conflict between David and Saul, which includes the Ahimelech conspiracy trial, and the fact that Saul is pursuing David to execute him together demonstrate that 1 Sam 26:17–24 involves an accusation of a criminal charge of treason against David. David's call to the king, ישמע־נא, therefore, is an announcement of his defense. In this environment, the *hiphil* of סות followed by the preposition ב would mean "to cause to bring a charge against."[94] Thus, David says to Saul in 1 Sam 26:18-19:

> Why does my lord pursue his servant? For what have I done? What guilt (רעה) is on my hands? Now, I pray, let my lord the king hear the words of

---

94. This may not be the case for every occurrence of the *hiphil* of סות followed by the preposition ב, only in clearly legal contexts. See, e.g., 2 Sam 24:1; Jer 43:3.

his servant. If it is Yahweh who caused you to bring a charge against me, may he accept an offering; but if it is mortals, may they be cursed before Yahweh, for they have driven me out today from my share in the heritage of Yahweh. . . .

If we now apply same translation of the *hiphil* of סות to Job 2:3b, the best translation of Yahweh's assertion to the Satan is, "He still holds fast to his integrity even though you caused me to bring a charge against him, without cause, in order to overwhelm him."

This assertion is no confession that the Satan manipulated Yahweh, that Yahweh was in favor of the legal action, or that he participated in Job's investigation. Rather, Yahweh is furious that the Satan forced Yahweh's mechanism of justice to churn against Job by stating a formal legal accusation without cause before the Divine Council, Yahweh's court. Yahweh thinks this is a false suit. This case should end with the same words with which it began—"without cause." It is Yahweh's view that the investigation has been sufficient and the case should be dropped. Unfortunately, this protestation is met head-on by the Satan with a still greater accusation (2:4–5), which obliges God's mechanism of justice to turn once again. The investigation of Job must continue unimpeded. The machinery of justice has been legitimately set in motion; the process simply must advance in accordance with correct legal procedure. No one may subvert the process. God does not, however, have to be pleased about it and is not. No wonder there is tension in the room! The Satan is spearheading a coup. The sons of God have assembled not to serve God but to dethrone him.

Consequently, we see in the Divine Council scene of chapters 1 and 2 that all five elements of legal narrative are present. The Satan is serving as the prime accuser against Job and God. Thus, there are identifiable parties. Both Yahweh and the Satan have different stories to tell regarding the state of Job's mind. Thus, we have multiple, conflicting narratives that offer diverse truth claims and seek to persuade each other and an assembled court, the Divine Council. The stories are structured by correct legal procedure. The Satan offers a formulaic legal accusation on a criminal charge recognized by the court—possessing a blasphemous intent. What is not yet seen with the greatest of clarity is the fragmenting and disordering of each story's linearity by repeated interruptions. We certainly perceive repartee between Yahweh and the Satan, but the text has not yet revealed the full extent of its fragmentation and disarray. That is still to come.

In sum, from our analysis of the interaction of God and the Satan in the Divine Council, it appears that the Satan has brought a valid, formal legal charge against Job, which initiates a trial of Job before the Divine Council. Such a trial is consistent with the worldview of a number of the ritual and wisdom texts of the ancient Near East. This trial is not, however, only about Job. It has another critical dimension. Job's trial is part of a larger attack on

Yahweh, which is why Yahweh cannot stop the proceedings in favor of Job. To do so is to prove the Satan correct. It is to confirm that Yahweh violates the rules of divine justice by continuing to give Job favor before the council determines whether or not it is justified. The Satan has been very cunning in his attack.

## The Satan's Investigation

The ritual incantation and wisdom texts of the ancient Near East remind us that divine trials were often conceived much like human trials. Hence, we wish to explore whether what happens to Job once the Satan levels his accusation is similar to what would have happened under Neo-Babylonian trial law. As noted in the preceding chapter, once a formal legal accusation was brought, some investigation of the matter typically ensued. It was often undertaken early in the trial process and could be hard on a body. A suspect under investigation in the Neo-Babylonian system could have been immediately arrested upon accusation. Investigative measures often involved torturing the defendant. His property could have been seized immediately upon arrest or court summons or later in the trial. What we moderns think of as postconviction punishments might come at any stage of the proceedings—upon arrest, during investigation, during trial, or after conviction. Where the defendant had suffered the pain of a summary or conditional verdict, the decision could be protested, either immediately or after some time.[95] There were provisions for appellate review in the case where the punishment was instituted after a full trial was held, but the execution of the punishment was not necessarily stayed pending appeal.

The Hebrew Bible also testifies to such legal procedures. First, the text records pre-trial arrest. For example, Joseph suffers immediate loss of position and imprisonment for two years awaiting trial on the charge of the attempted adulterous rape of Potiphar's wife (Gen 39:14, 17, 20; 41:1).[96] Joseph imprisons his brothers for three days for their alleged spying and continues to hold Simeon until the arrival of Benjamin, who is to testify in the trial of his brothers (Gen 42:15-20). Jeremiah is repeatedly imprisoned (20:2; 32:2-3; and 37:14-16). Notably, the blaspheming son in Lev 24:12 is imprisoned while awaiting trial.[97] Second, the Hebrew Bible reports the use of physical punishment while a person was incarcerated or under

---

95. For a summary judgment subject to the rejection and appeal of the defendant, see, e.g., *CT* 29, 42–43.
96. Joseph was imprisoned with several other fellows who angered the king (40:1–3). We do not know, however, the exact circumstances of their arrest.
97. For other instances of arrest, see Num 15:32–34; 1 Kgs 22:26–27; cf. Deut 21:19.

investigation. Jeremiah is a case in point. He was imprisoned and beaten to silence him by Pashhur, who clearly had the authority thus to treat those suspected of crimes (20:2). Moreover, Jeremiah was flogged when he was suspected of defecting to the Chaldeans (37:15). Third, pre-trial and mid-trial seizure of stolen property is implied in the Hebrew Bible by the many recorded searches for such property (Gen 31:32-35; 44:8-13; and Exod 22:4). The Hebrew Bible reports instances of several criminal forfeitures of property.[98] Thus, we see adverse consequences falling upon defendants at all stages of the trial proceedings in ancient Israel.

Yahweh's investigations and trials, as reported by the Hebrew Bible, also reflect that suffering might be inflicted at any stage. Yahweh certainly punishes individuals and communities that have directly failed to follow his law. Countless instances of this appear in the Hebrew Bible. Moreover, as discussed previously, in the case of crimes of high moral culpability, such as blasphemy, the community might suffer famine, disease, or military defeat, in addition to any individual consequences that Yahweh might bring upon the perpetrator.[99] Vicarious divine punishment inflicted on the perpetrator's children was also possible.[100] Additionally, divinely given suffering was not always postconviction punishment. Yahweh's investigative measures could have been as harsh as those accorded a defendant in a human court. One illustration of this is Deut 8:2-3, where Moses says to the Israelites:

> Remember the long way that Yahweh your God has led you these forty years in the wilderness, in order to humble you, investigating you (נסה) to know what was in your heart (לבב), whether or not you would keep his commandments. He humbled you by letting you hunger, then by feeding you with manna, with which neither you nor your ancestors were acquainted, in order to make you understand that one does not live by bread alone, but by every word that comes from the mouth of Yahweh.[101]

In Judg 2:22–3:4, Yahweh leaves five tribes of peoples in Canaan "[i]n order to investigate (נסה) Israel, whether or not they would take care to walk in the way of Yahweh as their ancestors" (Judg 2:22).[102] This resulted is ongoing warfare. Again, in both Jer 6:22-30 and 9:1-11, Yahweh will bring warfare and destruction upon Judah during his investigation of those whom he accuses of sinning. Divine investigation of human intention is devastating in these cases. God sums up his policy well in Isa 48:10:

---

98. See n. 37 above.
99. See nn. 33–34 above.
100. Westbrook, "Character of Ancient Near Eastern Law," 36, 74, 79.
101. See also Deut 8:16.
102. The verb נסה is repeated in 3:1, 4.

> See, I have refined you, but not like silver;
> I have tested (בחן) you in the furnace of adversity (עני).

Thus, in Yahweh's court, suffering does not necessarily flow only from a summary or final judgment, as the ritual incantation texts tend to envision. Divine trial investigations could be equally severe.

The adversity that the Satan sends upon Job is consistent both with Yahweh's legal investigations of all those who have faulty intention in the Hebrew Bible and with that which other defendants, under investigation, experienced under Neo-Babylonian trial law. The Satan's investigation of Job's capacity to blaspheme begins immediately (1:12–13; 2:7). The investigation ultimately results in the loss of Job's herds (1:14–17), all but a few of his servants (1:15–17), the house of his firstborn son (1:18–19), all ten of his children (1:19), and his health (2:7–8). All the blessings about which we heard in 1:3, and then some, are extinguished. This investigation is terribly difficult. Job is obviously suffering. Are we truly to believe that this is some cosmic wager wherein Job is treated like a cat's plaything, being batted and battered for sport before the kill. No, this is serious business. The council members are playing for keeps because so very much is at stake.

If this is correct, then a new difficulty arises: In the final analysis, are the ritual incantation texts actually helpful in a study of the book of Job? The incantation texts typically presume that one's suffering is related to divine postconviction punishment, not divine investigation. This should exclude them from consideration and leave us with a paradox: the ritual incantations alert us to the fact that suffering and law are intimately connected in the book of Job but are not, in fact, helpful in our analysis. I reject this seeming paradox. Rather, the ritual incantation texts remain of utmost importance to the study of Job. This is because the question of whether Job's suffering results from a divine investigation of Job or from a prior divine conviction for sin committed drives the dialogue between Job and his three friends. Their points of view on this issue diverge, and much of the dialogue deals with this conflict. To comprehend this fully, we must look at the various characters' points of view. We will undertake the analysis of Job's understanding of the situation and his response in the next chapter.

In conclusion, a clear legal conflict exists within the Divine Council: the Satan disagrees with Yahweh's assessment of Job's integrity and uprightness. The Satan believes that Job possesses the guilty mind of a blasphemer, which is a lesser offense when considered against the crime of blasphemy. Nonetheless, this offense falls within the jurisdiction of the Divine Council. The Satan is not, however, accusing Job to protect the best interests of Yahweh, as we might expect from a third-party private prosecutor or the Eye of the King. Instead, this suit is an effort to discredit Yahweh and is part of a power play against Yahweh in the council. The Satan hopes to accomplish this through his accusation that Yahweh has protected, rather than prosecuted, the guilty Job and has thereby upset the moral economy. The proof of both Job's guilt and Yahweh's succor of the criminal lies in the Satan's investigation of Job, which Yahweh cannot stop without proving the Satan correct. The Satan undertakes this investigation, which devastates Job. This brutal investigation is consistent with the criminal investigations of its day, both human and divine. Job must now come to terms with what is happening to him. He begins that work in chapter 3.

# 6

# Job's Counteraccusation

However the members of the Divine Council might understand the incident in the council, it is entirely hidden from Job and his friends. It is critical to understand that we are party to the proceedings in the Divine Council, thanks to the efforts of the narrator, and we know the events primarily from the narrator's point of view. Job and his friends do not, however, know what readers know. They have no information regarding the events in the Divine Council. As a result, they are forced to speculate about what is happening to Job, based on what they previously know of God and suffering. As a result, they may guess erroneously and/or come to different views of Job's circumstances. In fact, they do not understand precisely what has happened, and they do disagree. Their different opinions regarding Job's situation set up the book's dialogues. This chapter addresses primarily how Job understands his situation and his initial response to it. Job believes that God has brought him to trial unjustly, and he consequently threatens to counter-sue God for this act and other acts that manifest God's abusive use of divine judicial authority.[1]

## The Literary Function of Diverse Points of View

The fact that the earthly characters of the book do not know what has happened in the Divine Council is a most important literary feature of the book. M. Weiss points out that 1:13 does not make reference to "Job's" sons and daughters, but only to "his" sons and daughters.[2] We would normally expect "his" to refer back to the male figure in the preceding verse, the Satan. The seam causes suspicion that 1:7–12 is an addition. Moreover, the repetition of the phrase "one day" in both 1:6 and 1:13 could be a resumptive repetition, leading one to believe that 1:7–12 is an addition for yet

---

1. I attend to the friends' views of Job's condition in chapter 8.
2. Weiss, *Job's Beginning*, 47–50.

another reason. Weiss suggests, however, that this is a rhetorical device and not an editorial device. Picking up in 1:13 as though there were no interruption from 1:5 exposes the fact that, on earth, no one knows what is transpiring in heaven. This ignorance causes all the earthly characters to conjecture the cause of Job's situation. The different perceptual points of view of the various characters make disagreement among them possible.[3] Genesis 42 reflects just how significantly the different perspectives of a story's characters can affect trial proceedings in literature and to what use they can be put literarily.

In Genesis 42, Joseph falsely accuses his brothers of espionage and initiates what is not, from his perspective, a legitimate trial, but what is very much so from the brothers' point of view (Gen 42:6–17). The brothers have not, in fact, committed any guilty acts, nor does any evidence exist that they have the requisite guilty mind. Yet Joseph and his brothers proceed as if a trial has indeed begun. Joseph's position and power, the brother's status as sojourners in a foreign land, and the course of the supposed litigation leave the brothers believing that they are in the midst of a trial on a very serious charge. Joseph, first, initiates what looks, to the brothers, like an investigation (Gen 42:7). He then inquires of his brothers whence they came before he lodges his formal accusations in Gen 42:9 and 12. The point of Joseph's action is not to bring the brothers to actual trial. In that sense, this is not a case of false accusation for which Joseph may be held liable. The proceedings will not go that far. Rather, the goal of the deception is to shake up the brothers in order to get some intended action out of them, that is, to bring Jacob and Benjamin to Egypt (Gen 42:15). Because the brothers see the events of the story from very different angles, Joseph can play the trick. Readers are let in on the joke long before Joseph's brothers are, and it may amuse (or horrify) them.

Job and his friends know only that Job is suffering illness, financial ruin, and the loss of his children. Because they are not privy to the events in the Divine Council, they must speculate as to the cause of Job's suffering. Their perceptions may differ from all those who have witnessed those events and from each other. When Job commences speaking after seven days of silence, he begins to interpret his condition, vent his anger, and strategize about his circumstances before his friends. They also interpret his condition, evaluate and criticize his interpretation and strategy, and offer their own solutions. The dialogues of the book are the result of these thoughts and conversations.

If the book's social world reflects the social world behind the text, these companions would be familiar with the culture's view of suffering. They might very well interpret Job's suffering in harmony with many of the rit-

---

3. Regarding my point of view theorist, see ch. 3, n. 77 above.

ual and wisdom texts of the ancient Near East. If so, they would understand Job's misery as most probably caused by witchcraft, demons, or God. The text informs us that Job and his friends clearly believe that God is the cause of Job's circumstances. They never speculate that a witch, a demon, or the Satan is the source of his problems. The question then becomes whether Job and his friends believe that Job is suffering in connection with some divine trial or whether they believe that God is sending an alternative message. Their speeches are infused with legal language, even more so than the prologue of the book, as the rest of this work will demonstrate. The sheer quantity of such language is an indicator that the worldview of the ancient Near Eastern ritual texts and theodicies is once again operating and that these characters believe that God has brought suit against Job.

We would expect, from what we know of the ritual incantations, that, to the minds of Job and his friends, the trial must be complete and the penalty assessed. We would expect that any investigation associated with the accusation and trial must have been completed before the divine court entered its summary judgment. We would then also expect Job to request a new trial or to appeal the ruling. Yet the characters' language in this regard does not appear to be uniform. Moreover, even if Job and his friends all agree that the trial is complete, they could reasonably hold divergent opinions regarding the sin underlying the dispute and what Job must do about the situation. Furthermore, their opinions might have little to do with what actually happened in the Divine Council because they have no knowledge of those proceedings. This literary aspect of the text has contributed to the profound disagreement among Job and his friends. It also contributes to the profound disagreement among forensic commentators regarding the nature of the legal altercation in the book of Job. Consequently, close study of the positions of each character is justified. I turn first to an analysis of Job's view.

## Job's Understanding of the Investigation

From Job's perspective, knowing nothing of the efforts of the Satan, God is responsible for Job's situation. God is head of the Divine Council. God may, and often does, judge entirely alone. Consequently, Job rationally believes that God has brought the action against him, and he is angry. Job's worst fears have been realized (3:25), and it is entirely God's fault. God is not, from Job's perspective, his aider and abettor. Rather, God is his accuser, investigator, and torturer. Although Job is prepared to defend himself against the charges, as we will discuss in the next chapter, he is not content merely to defend. First, he intends to file a counteraccusation against his legal adversary. He now desires to charge God with wrongdoing, unlike what the narrator reported in 1:22. Job goes on the offensive. His goal is to force God to restore at least some, if not all, of his losses.

When we measure Job's words about his suffering against the conditions for, and methods of, human and divine legal investigations set forth in prior chapters of this study, we discover that Job believes that he is in the midst of an extremely arduous, even torturous, divine trial investigation. This investigation looks very much like one to which an accused might be subject in the ancient Near East, whether in a human or divine court. First, Job's language appears to reflect that he thinks that he has been arrested. He acknowledges that God can arrest in 9:12aα, where he says plainly: "Look! He arrests (יחתף)!"[4] Job complains that God has imprisoned him by reducing him to sitting in one spot on the earth for seven days in a kind of prison without walls (2:8, 13). He continues later:

> You put my feet in the stocks; you watch all my paths;
> to the soles of my feet, you set a bound" (13:27).[5]

There he wastes away (13:28). D. J. A. Clines says of 13:27: "The three cola depict an investigation of Job by God and a restriction on his movement." Clines calls these events "acts of close arrest."[6] E. van Wolde asserts: "Job has an image of God as a supreme jailer."[7] Job also contends that God constrains his movements by sealing off roads of passage (19:8) and by sending troops to surround his camp (19:12). Job believes that he is under arrest. Second, God has confiscated Job's property when he seizes Job's flocks (1:15–17), servants (1:15–17), and children (1:19) through various means of destruction (cf. Josh 7:24–25). Third, Job is being tortured, according to C. Newsom and others.[8] J. A. Wharton calls Job's suffering "inquisitorial

---

4. The usual translation of this rarely attested root is "to snatch away," "to rob," or "to prey upon." See BDB, 368–69; and *HALOT* 1:365. See also Prov 23:28. I suggest that חתף belongs to a constellation of roots meaning 'to seize," "to grasp," and/or "to take possession of." Their semantic ranges also include "to rob," "to prey upon," "to capture," and/or "to arrest." This group would include, for example, the roots אחז, לקח, and תפש. The context of Job 9:12–15 suggests that the best translation of חתף is "to arrest." For exemplars of the meaning "to capture" or "to arrest" for the root אחז, see Judg 1:6; 12:6; 16:21; 2 Sam 4:10; Ps 56:1; for the root תפש, see Josh 8:23; 1 Sam 23:26; 2 Kgs 26:5; Jer 26:8; 37:13, 14; 52:9; for the root לקח, see Jer 39:5.

5. This is generally understood to be the mark of slavery, but Clines points out its improbability (*Job 1–22*, 321–23). For a fuller discussion of slave marks in the Neo-Babylonian period, see Dandamaev, *Slavery in Babylonia*, 229–34, 488–89.

6. Clines, *Job 1–20*, 323.

7. Van Wolde, "Development of Job," 207.

8. C. Newsom, "The Character of Pain: Job in Light of Elaine Scarry's *The Body in Pain*" (paper presented at the annual meeting of the Society of Biblical Literature, Orlando, Florida, November 23, 1998). While Newsom's insights are important, especially those regarding how Job's torture and resistance fit Scarry's theoretical construct (*The Body in Pain: The Making and*

terror."⁹ If I understand this correctly, all the legal investigative consequences that stem from a formal legal accusation in a trial context flow upon Job. The first two effects, arrest and property seizure, seem fairly obvious on the face of the text; the third, inquisitional terror, may not be as evident to all readers as it is to Newsom and Wharton. Hence, this issue of heavenly investigative torture deserves additional study.

The effects of the Satan's investigation are tremendous. Job uses words similar to the words used by torture survivors to describe what is happening to them under inquisitorial torture.¹⁰ Job loses his health (2:7; 7:5; 16:8b; 17:7b; 19:20a; 21:6b; 30:30) and must endure the horrible emotional effects of the death of his children and servants, as well as the loss of his wealth.¹¹ He grieves and weeps much (1:20a; 2:8; 16:15–16a; 20a; 17:7a; 30:31).¹² In fact, he looks so terrible for all this that his friends no longer recognize him, and they weep and mourn when it finally dawns on them that the stranger they approach is Job (2:12). At first, Job speaks little and, finally, not at all (2:10–3:1).¹³ When he regains his ability to speak after seven days of silence, he describes what is happening to him in very vivid terms. He sees himself as the victim of divine violence and reports receiving many wounds (6:4; 7:20b; 9:17; 16:9b–c, 12–14; 19:10–12, 22; 30:18).¹⁴ He suffers relentless pain, anguish, and misery (2:13; 6:2–3, 10; 9:28a; 11:16a; 16:6a; 30:16b, 27b). He groans under the pain (3:24; 23:2). He states that he cannot catch his breath and what little air does come into his chest feels bitter to him (9:18). He speaks wildly at times (6:3b). His sleep is disturbed (3:26; 7:3b–4a, 13; and 30:17; cf. 11:18b–19a). In those few moments of respite, God sends him night terrors (7:14). He has lost his appetite and cannot eat (6:5–7). His bowels churn (30:27). He expresses how overwhelmed he feels (3:24–26). He bemoans the fact that he has no peace, no quiet, no rest, but only anxiety and fear (3:25–26; 21:6a; 30:15; cf. 11:15b). He has developed a specific fear of God (6:4c; 9:35a; and 23:15–16). He has lost

---

*Unmaking of the World* [New York: Oxford University Press, 1985]), I disagree with a number of her conclusions. S. Terrien also calls Job's experience torture (*Job: Poet of Existence* [Indianapolis: Bobbs-Merrill, 1957], 25). Cf. Beach, "More Righteous Than God," 8.

9. Wharton, *Job*, 60.

10. I develop further the concept of Job as torture survivor and the import of God's violence in the divine legal system in "Job's Wife as Hero," 374–423. I rely on that article here and quote from it extensively without the use of quotation marks.

11. See Newsom, "Character of Pain," 4.

12. P. Bovati suggests that the grieving rituals of 2:8 and 2:12 (and, by implication, 1:20) are supplications for a pardon (*Re-Establishing Justice*, 139–41). Although I agree that they often have that meaning in a legal context, they cannot possibly mean that here because Job denies his guilt throughout the book and both God and the narrator report his innocence throughout Job 1–2. Even Job's friends do not think that he is repentant.

13. Cf. Lam 2:10–11, where the same process occurs.

14. Job 6:4 expresses the same sentiments as Lam 3:12.

his success (30:22) and his dignity (19:9; 30:15c, 29). Those of his community revile and abuse him (16:10; 17:6; 19:18); even the despised disrespect him (30:1–14). His friends, family, and servants are all alienated from him (19:13b–17, 19), and he believes that God has tendered him to the wicked (16:11). He suffers terrible shame (10:15). He has lost all trust and much hope (7:6b, 7b; 9:25bα; 11:18a; 17:15–16; 19:10b). His spirit is broken (17:1a; and 27:2b), and his life now feels empty and dark (7:3a; 30:28a; cf. 11:17; 17:12). His friends make his words out to be no more than wind (6:26b). According to Job, God has turned his very life to mere wind (7:7a). He says he has not the strength to go on (6:11–13; 16:17a). He is sure he is dying (16:16b; 17:1b, c, 11–14; 30:16a, 19b, 23). This is no small amount of misery. These physical and emotional experiences are common among torture victims.[15] Job's conviction that he is being tortured is the very reason that he repeatedly declares that he hates his life (9:21c; 10:1), comes to rue the day he was born and curses it (3:3–22),[16] and awaits death longingly (6:8–10a; 7:15–16; 10:18–19). These attitudes do not generally belong to those whose suffering is mild. J. A. Wharton aptly calls the soliloquy in chapter 3 "Job's primal scream."[17] The similarities between Job's sufferings and the torture of real suspects in criminal investigations and the torture of other biblical characters are quite striking. The similarities are such that Job is certain that he is under divine legal investigation.[18]

---

15. See Scarry, *Body in Pain*; and E. Stover and E. Nightingale, *The Breaking of Minds and Bodies* (New York: Freeman, 1985).

16. The roots ארר, ברך, הלא, זעם, חרם, נקב/קבב, and קלל can all mean "to curse." See further F. Rachel Magdalene, "Curse," *EDB*, 301. The root קלל is used in 3:1 and both ארר and קלל in 3:8.

17. Wharton, *Job*, 25.

18. One issue that we should address is: Why is the Satan torturing Job? What purpose does it serve in this case? The commonly understood goal of torture in the context of human litigation is to elicit a confession regarding the past criminal activity under investigation. Torture's ostensible purpose is to provide evidence of guilt and, therefore, to smooth the way for a swift conviction. Torture is expedient. The Satan is not, however, apparently interested in a verbal confession. Rather, he wants to see whether or not Job will commit the blasphemous act itself. This, too, will convict Job, but it is not the type of confession one might expect to acquire from a tortured suspect. Consequently, one might argue that the Satan's actions are truly a sting operation meant to provoke a public criminal act on which the Divine Council can convict Job. This thinking, however, is wrong-headed because confessions in divine courts serve a profoundly different purpose than do confessions in human courts. Extracting a verbal confession is not, in fact, the chief purpose behind torturous divine investigations. An examination of Josh 7:19–20 is helpful here because it records the only investigative confession in the Hebrew Bible where the confession is used as evidence. In that passage, Achan confesses to Joshua that he took חרם. This confession is used as evidence of the identity of the criminal. This evidentiary use of a confession occurs, however, before a human court. It is unnecessary for the divine court (R. E. Clements, "Achan's Sin: Warfare and Holiness," in *Shall Not the Judge of All the Earth Do What Is Right? Studies on the Nature of God in Tribute to James L. Crenshaw* [ed. D. Penchansky and P. L. Redditt; Winona Lake, Ind.: Eisenbrauns, 2000],

Job's language in regard to his sufferings is also reminiscent of the suffering of petitioners in the ritual and wisdom texts of the ancient Near East. For example, his many health complaints (2:7; 7:5; 16:8b; 17:7b; 19:20a; 21:6b; 30:30) are very common to the incantations. Other physical difficulties are shared by Job and the Mesopotamian material. In the Babylonian "Man and His God," the petitioner laments: "You have made a mouth filled (with food) very bitter to me. It . [ . . ] . . has become like stinkwort."[19] In Job, 6:6–7, Job declares:

> Can that which is tasteless be eaten without salt,
>    or is there any flavor in the juice of mallows?
> My appetite refuses to touch them;
>    they are like food that is loathsome to me.

M. Stol observes that Mesopotamian incantations repeatedly discuss financial losses and the cessation of profits.[20] Job certainly suffered those when

---

116–17). Confession, when made before God in the Hebrew Bible, does not fundamentally serve as evidence of the crime. Divine investigations, not confessions, are used to reveal human intentions to God. Rather, it is primarily an act of contrition and, therefore, a mitigating factor in divine punishment (see, e.g., Lev 26:14–42; Num 5:6–7; 2 Sam 24:1–25; Ps 32:3–5; Prov 28:13). J. Milgrom notes a connection between confession and the reduction of divine punishment (*Cult and Conscience: The "Asham" and the Priestly Doctrine of Repentance* [Leiden: Brill, 1976], 117–19; and *Leviticus*, 1:301). He rightly observes that confession is never required of inadvertent sins; expiation alone is sufficient to ward off any difficulties with the deity (see, e.g., Lev 4:1–35; 5:14–15; Num 15:22–29). Confession is necessary only in cases of deliberate sins (see, e.g., Lev 5:1–4; Num 5:6–7). Confession does not, however, as Milgrom asserts, "convert deliberate sins into inadvertences" (*Leviticus*, 1:301; cf. 315). Confession does not affect the *mens rea* that lies behind the finding of guilt. Crimes are not converted into lesser crimes by confession. Rather, confession is a mitigating factor in the assessment of punishment for the crime committed. See Westbrook, *Studies*, 28. Confession as a mitigating factor is not, however, effective in all cases. Sins of highest culpability or with some aggravating factor, such as taking חרם (Josh 7:19–26) or direct disobedience of a divine order (1 Sam 15:12–35), typically cannot be mitigated through confession (see also Num 15:30). Thus, God's mitigation of Ahab's sentence for participating in a false suit involving blasphemy to the lesser vicarious punishment—his children's death—because of his repentance and humility seems most unusual (1 Kgs 21:27–29), especially given that Ahab never spoke words of confession. Some other principle may be operating in this case. On vicarious punishment as a mitigated penalty, see Westbrook, *Studies*, 55–57; and idem, "Punishments and Crimes," 550. The Satan does not want a typical confession about a past guilty act. He wants, instead, the act itself. This is because any acts that proceed from the investigation in Job's situation would be evidence of the criminal *mens rea*. They would not constitute one of the legal elements necessary for conviction of the crime. Torturous investigations of maleficent intention are used to produce hard evidence on the charge of a criminal intent. In summary, God's investigative efforts seek to produce results different from those of human investigations because the goals of God's and humans' legal processes are somewhat different; nonetheless, divine investigations are valuable in obtaining a criminal's ultimate conviction.

19. Translation from Lambert, "Further Attempt," 191, line 29.
20. Stol, "Psychosomatic Suffering," 61–62.

he lost all his livestock (see Job 30:22). Stol also addressed situations in which petitioners feel that they have been abandoned by God and humanity, just as Job expresses (16:10–11; 17:6; 19:13b–19:18; 30:1–14).[21] The incantations additionally speak to the petitioners' fear and the various consequences thereof. SBTU 2 110, no. 22 is just one example. It states that, if a person is "constantly brought into fear, he feels bad day and night . . . the wrath of god and goddess is upon him; god and goddess are angry with him."[22] Job, too, is afraid (3:25–26; 6:4c; 9:35a; 21:6a; 30:15). The Šurpu Incantations request that the gods drive out the petitioner's "restlessness, his gloom . . . woe and lament, . . . his gloom" (tablet 4, lines 84–85). Job complains of depression (7:3a; 17:1a; 27:2b; 30:28a; cf. 11:17; 17:12). The petitioner of the Šurpu Incantations complains of sleeplessness and weariness, as does Job (3:26; 7:3b–4a, 13; 30:17; cf. 11:18b–19a) (ibid.). Odd, unexplained dreams and night terrors occupy both Job (7:14) and the sufferers in the ritual incantations.[23] The similarity of Job's sufferings to those of the petitioners in the incantation texts should cause us to see that Job's sufferings are the outcome of a divine trial process.

Job's laments about his suffering are not, however, the only indication that he believes that he is under legal investigation pursuant to trial. He states both plainly and frequently that he is on trial and under investigation. First, he reports numerous times that he experiences the watchful gaze of God (7:8a; 13:27b; 31:4). He knows he is under scrutiny. Second, Job refers to God's investigation of him four separate times, often making reference to a divinely initiated trial. He first raises the issue in 7:17–19:

> What is a human being that you make so much of him?
>   That you set (שית) your intentions (לב) upon him?
> That you inspect (פקד) him every morning;
>   every moment you investigate (בחן) him?[24]
> How long will it be until you cast your gaze from me;
>   until you let me rest to swallow my spittle?

He uses both פקד and בחן to indicate the legal ramifications of God's inspection of him. Ps 8:5 uses similar language to declare God's greatness in his treatment of humanity:

> What are humans that you remember them,
>   the children of humanity that you examine (פקד) them?

Job is not nearly as impressed with God's treatment of humanity as is the Psalmist.[25] A trope exists in 7:17 between God's setting (שית) his intention

---

21. Ibid., 60–61.
22. Translation by M. Stol, ibid., 61–62.
23. Ibid., 61.
24. Gemser, "*Rîb*-Pattern," 124.
25. See further Fishbane, *Biblical Interpretation*, 285–86.

on humanity and the Satan's roving (שוט), which searches out the just and the unjust. For Job, God is that roving, accusing eye. God conducts hypervigilant legal investigations around the clock, which give about as much dignity to humans as similar inspections give to the flocks (5:24b).[26] God has, in the words of Newsom, "an obsessive and malicious curiosity."[27]

In 10:4–8, Job makes the fact of his investigation still clearer by employing the verbs בקש and דרש in parallel. This time, he links this investigation to a lawsuit against him:

> Do you have eyes of flesh?
>   Is your vision that of a mortal?
> Are your days the days of a mortal?
>   Are your years the years of a human,
> that you seek out (בקש) my iniquity (עון),[28]
>   and you investigate (דרש) my sin (חטאת)?
> You know that I am not guilty (רשע),[29]
>   and that there is none to deliver from your hand.
> Your hands fashioned and made me;
>   now you turn and destroy me! (10:6–8)

Job repeats the assertion in 31:14 that he is under divine investigation, this time, using the verb פקד in parallel with קום:

> What then should I do when God initiates a case (קום)?
>   When he investigates me (פקד), how should I respond?[30]

The semantic range of the verb קום includes certain trial procedures. Deut 19:15–19 makes clear that, in forensic contexts, the root can means "to initiate a case" as an accuser or "to stand at trial" as a witness:[31]

> A single witness will not initiate a case (קום) against a person for any iniquity (עון) or sin (חטאת) in connection with any offense (חטא) that they may commit (חטא). Only by the mouths of two witnesses (עד) or by the mouths of three witnesses (עד) shall a lawsuit (דבר) be initiated (קום). If a malicious witness (עד) initiates a case (קום), testifying (ענה) against any person for

---

26. For a discussion of the legal investigative force of the root פקד, see Bovati, *Re-Establishing Justice*, 245. See also Ps 17:2–3, where פקד and בחן are also coupled.

27. Newsom, "Book of Job," 335.

28. The legal investigative force of בקש is noted by Westermann, "Begriffe für Fragen," 2–30; and Bovati, *Re-Establishing Justice*, 242–43. See Judg 6:29; Jer 50:20; and Esth 2:23; cf. Jer 5:1.

29. D. R. Hillers established that the *hiphil* of רשע means "to condemn" ("Delocutive Verbs in Biblical Hebrew," *JBL* 86 [1967]: 320–24; see also Bovati, *Re-Establishing Justice*, 348–49).

30. Cf. Gemser, "*Rîb*-Pattern," 124.

31. Newsom, "Book of Job," 478; and Hartley, *Book of Job*, 294. See also Jer 50:31–34 and Pss 27:12; 35:11.

wrongdoing (סרה), then both parties to the lawsuit (ריב) shall appear before Yahweh, before the priests and the judges (שפט) who are in office in those days, and the judges (שפט) will investigate (דרש). If the witness (עד) is a false witness (עד), having testified (ענה) falsely against another, ʾthen you shall do to that one as they had meant to do to the other.

This important passage indicates that קום has legal meaning in the context of litigation and therefore probably has a legal meaning in Job 31:14. God has put Job on trial and is investigating him.

Job reiterates that God is watching him in the context of a trial when he says in 14:1–3:

> Furthermore, a mortal, born of woman,
>   few of days and full of trouble,
> comes forth like a flower and withers,
>   flees like a shadow and does not last.
> But upon such a one, you do fix your eyes!³²
> But me, you bring into litigation (משפט) with you!³³

Job specifies repeatedly that God is investigating him in conjunction with a lawsuit filed against him, and this interrogation is torturous.

Job's suffering is consistent in quality with the ritual incantation texts of the ancient Near East. Job's language indicates that he believes that disease, disability, and disaster stem from God's mechanism of justice. Thus, this brutal investigation is consistent with the criminal investigations of its day, both human and divine. As a result, Job rightfully believes that he is in the midst of a divine trial, that he is suffering a horrible investigation, and that he must defend himself.

## The Fact of Job's Counteraccusation and His Summons of God

One of the most baffling aspects of Job's speeches is his repeated movement between defensive and accusatory statements. W. L. Holladay notes with some perplexity: "It is not always clear in the Book of Job who is the

---

32. I follow the NJB in maintaining that the two cola of 14:3 are not questions but instead snide statements.

33. The word משפט is often translated "justice." Its semantic range includes, however, "case," "lawsuit," "litigation," "legal controversy," and "judgment." See BDB, 1048–49; and HALOT 2:651–52. Moreover, משפט is coupled with ריב in a number of verses. In two of these, 2 Sam 15:4 and Ps 35:23, משפט means "lawsuit," "legal controversy," or "case." Scholnick studies the use of משפט in the book of Job and concurs that it often has this meaning ("Lawsuit Drama.")

plaintiff and who is the defendant. Sometimes Job seems to be the plaintiff, taking the initiative to establish his innocence.... Sometimes Job seems to be the defendant in a monstrously unfair suit brought by God.... But the language of the lawcourts is constant....."[34] Most commentators have elected to privilege one set of statements over the other in determining whether it is God or Job who brings suit.[35] During their analysis, some of these commentators completely or substantially ignore those statements that do not fit their understanding of the legal schema of the book. Other commentators clearly acknowledge that Job moves between defensive and offensive positions but resolve the dilemma in favor of one. For example, after discussing Job's status as a defendant, M. Dick states:

> [I]n accordance with Ancient Near Eastern principles God appears to initiate the charges and Job seems to be the defendant. Job's request for a writ of particulars implies that he is the victim of a prior judicial action.... God has afflicted Job with a series of catastrophes because he has apparently been found guilty of sin the nature of which Job does not know."[36]

Later Dick continues: "Job's defense against the judgment implies an indictment of Eloah. In virtue of his defense he becomes a plaintiff!"[37] Hence, Dick suggests that Job is filing a collateral attack on a divine final judgment in the nature of a writ of habeas corpus.[38] S. H. Scholnick asserts that Job may be either a defendant or a plaintiff: "Knowing nothing he has done to warrant such a severe sentence, Job demands litigation with God as plaintiff to charge him formally with specific offenses or as defendant to answer the charge of unlawful seizure of Job's property."[39] Her predominant position is, however, that Job brings the action.[40] Much like Dick and Scholnick, P. Bovati recognizes a reversal from defense to accusation in the book of Job, suggesting that Job is both victim and protagonist in the trial against him. Unfortunately, Bovati's subsequent discussion is somewhat confused.[41] N. C. Habel labels Job's accusation a counterclaim, which would

---

34. Holladay, "Jeremiah's Lawsuit," 286.
35. See, e.g., Chin, "Job and Injustice," 94–95; J. B. Frye, "Use of Māšāl," 63–64; Gemser, "Rîb-Pattern," 135; Gordon, "Legal Background," 30; Greenstein, "Forensic Understanding," 241–43; Many, "Der Rechtsstreit mit Gott," 196; Patrick, *Arguing with God*, 65, 67; Richter, *Studien zu Hiob*, 71; Robertson, "Book of Job," 451; Stamm, "Die Theodizee," 104; Stier, *Buch Ijjob*, 217, 224–51; Wharton, *Job*, 49, 55–56; and Zuckerman, *Job the Silent*, 107.
36. Dick, "Job 31: Form-Critical Study," 38–39.
37. Ibid., 125.
38. Ibid., 40; see also idem, "Legal Metaphor," 40. For more on collateral attack by writ of habeas corpus, see "Habeas Corpus," *BLD*, 709.
39. Scholnick, "Meaning of *Mišpāṭ*," 350.
40. Scholnick, "Lawsuit Drama," viii, ix.
41. He ultimately argues that God never brings a formal accusation and that Job begins the lawsuit proper (*Re-Establishing Justice*, 114–16, citing in particular Job 7:20). Nevertheless,

account for Job's use of both defensive and accusatory language in the same suit.⁴² Yet he does not work fully with the idea and oscillates in his discussion.⁴³ Ultimately, Habel was on the right track in granting priority to Job's accusation over his defense. The best explanation of the seeming contradictions in Job's speeches is that Job seeks to bring a counterclaim in an active, unresolved lawsuit that he believes God has filed against him. Thus, Job sees himself as both the defendant and the counter-plaintiff in the suit.

Counterclaims were permissible in the ancient Near East. The Hebrew Bible also records such a procedure. Indeed, Bovati states: "The fact that a protestation of innocence can be transformed into an accusation against the accuser forms the very structure of a bilateral [legal] encounter [in the Hebrew Bible]."⁴⁴ The most important illustration of this in a trial context is in Gen 31:25–55. There Laban accuses Jacob, before an assembly of kinsmen, of fleeing with his daughters (Gen 31:27) and stealing his household gods (Gen 31:30). Jacob defends himself by saying that he feared that Laban would rob him of Laban's daughters through abuse of legal process (גזל),⁴⁵ but that he himself will kill anyone who has possession of the gods. He permits Laban to conduct a thorough investigative search (Gen 31:31–32). After Laban's search is fruitless (Gen 31:33–35), Jacob counteraccuses Laban of false suit and unfair business deals with him over the prior twenty years (Gen 31:36–42).⁴⁶ At that point, Laban extends a settlement offer to Jacob, which is a mid-trial offer (Gen 31:43–44). Jacob accepts the offer, and they enter into a covenant of settlement (Gen 31:45–54).⁴⁷ Another instance of a counterclaim exists in Jer 2:29, where God countersues Judah with the words:

Why do you bring a lawsuit (ריב) against me?
All of you have rebelled (פשע) against me . . . .⁴⁸

Significantly, Bovati observes that the Psalmist often turns a defense into an

---

Bovati contradicts himself repeatedly on this point and often indicates that Job is responding to an accusation that begins a trial. For example, just five pages after claiming that Job begins the trial, he states, "[Job] earnestly desires that the *rîb* against him should come to an end" (ibid., 120).

42. Habel, *Book of Job: Commentary*, 38.
43. A more complete discussion of Habel's oscillation can be found in ch. 1, n. 30 above.
44. Bovati, *Re-Establishing Justice*, 114.
45. The significance of this will be made apparent in the material that discusses גזל and abuse of authority in nn. 94–101 below.
46. For the basis of Jacob's claims beyond the false suit, see J. J. Finkelstein, "An Old Babylonian Herding Contract and Genesis 31:38f.," in *Essays in Memory of E. A. Speiser* (ed. W. W. Hallo; AOS 53; New Haven: American Oriental Society, 1968), 30–36.
47. For additional discussion of this text as a lawsuit involving a claim and counterclaim, see C. Mabee, "Jacob and Laban: The Structure of Judicial Proceedings (Genesis XXXI 25–42)," *VT* 30 (1980): 192–207.
48. See Westbrook, "Biblical Law," 9.

accusation against God.⁴⁹ These actions, too, are in the nature of a counterclaim. Finally, a counterclaim possibly undergirds the deposit law in Exod 22:6–12.⁵⁰

If Job should intend to countersue God, one must inquire whether anyone can sue God. Does God have a type of divine sovereign immunity or official immunity from suit, as human governments and their officials sometimes have from damage suits?⁵¹ Can an accusation against the deity have legal effect? Jeremiah addresses this question. Distressed at his treatment by the people to whom he prophesies, he feels that God is ultimately responsible for his troubles. He desires to bring a lawsuit against him but fears that Yahweh will be acquitted. Notwithstanding this possibility, Jeremiah is prepared to go forward and issues his accusation in Jer 12:1:

> You will be acquitted (צדק),⁵² Yahweh, if I bring suit (ריב) against you.
> Yet, I would state my case (משפט) against you:
> Why does the way of the wicked prosper?
> Why are all who are treacherous at ease?

In discussing this verse, Holladay says: "Since Jeremiah felt that Yahweh was not properly supporting him in his prophetic activity, the possibility dawned on Jeremiah that Yahweh was not remaining faithful to his part of the bargain, and that if Yahweh could sue Israel for breach of contract, Jeremiah could turn and sue Yahweh for breach of contract as well."⁵³ Jeremiah does not believe that God has sovereign or official immunity; rather, he is just not sure that he can win against such an adversary at law. Job expresses similar sentiments. Jeremiah was not, however, on trial before God and therefore had to initiate a suit for breach of contract against God. Job, on the other hand, is already on trial for a blasphemous intent. Thus, Job must use the counteraccusation to raise his claims against God.

---

49. Bovati, *Re-Establishing Justice*, 115. See, e.g., Ps 44:10–27.

50. Westbrook, "Deposit Law of Exodus," 400–401.

51. For more on the immunity of governments from damages suits (sovereign immunity), see "Immunity: Governmental Tort Immunity," *BLD*, 751; and "Sovereign Immunity," *BLD*, 1396. On the immunity of government officials from suits against certain types of acts (official immunity), see "Immunity: Qualified Immunity," *BLD*, 752; and "Official Immunity Doctrine," *BLD*, 1084.

52. Holladay ("Jeremiah's Lawsuit," 281) and Bovati (*Re-Establishing Justice*, 104) support this translation. See also 2 Kgs 10:9.

53. Holladay, "Jeremiah's Lawsuit," 283. The more common translation of משפט in this verse is "judgment," rendering the line as Holladay maintains: "yet I would pass judgment upon thee" (ibid., 280–81; see also, e.g., NASB; NJB; NRSV; and RSV), relying in part on Jer 39:5. There is justification for this translation in both Jer 12:1aβ; and 39:5. Nevertheless, here the meaning "litigation," or "case," as the NJPS has it, is better. This proposal would give further credence to Holladay's position because he maintains that Jeremiah is not God's judge but his accuser in this instance.

Job makes a number of statements that indicate that he desires to file such a countersuit. He boldly avows his intention to speak out and state his position to God in 7:11:

> What's more, I will not restrain my mouth!
>   Let me speak in the anguish of my spirit!
>   Let me complain (שׂיח) in the bitterness of my soul!

He again states in 10:1 that he will bring a complaint against God:

> My soul loathes my life.
>   Let me loose my complaint (שׂיח)!
>   Let me speak in the bitterness of my soul!

He reiterates the acrimony of his complaint:

> My complaint (שׂיח) is bitter today.
>   My hand is heavy because of my groaning. (23:2)

Moreover, in 21:4, he explains his impatience in the suit by the fact that his complaint (שׂיח) is not lodged against a mere mortal. This complaint is more than an expansion of frustration. It has legal significance. The juridical meaning of שׂיח is apparent from Pss 55:3, 18; and 64:2. We also see its legal significance again in Job 9:27–29a:

> If I say, "I will forget my complaint (שׂיח),
>   I will loosen my sad countenance and smile,"
> I remain afraid of all my suffering,
>   for I know that you will not acquit (נקה) me.[54]
> I will be condemned (רשׁע).

This verse suggests that Job intends to bring a counterclaim against God, in part because he believes he will lose on his defense alone. We will discover in a moment, however, that this is not the only reason for his claim.

Job repeats his desire to contend with God using the root יכח. In 13:3, he asserts:

> Indeed, I would speak to Shaddai.
>   I insist on accusing (יכח) God.

He continues in 13:6:

> Hear now, I pray, my accusations (תוכחת)
>   and listen to the pleadings (ריב) of my lips.

---

54. For more on נקה as indicating an acquittal, see Bovati, *Re-Establishing Justice*, 104, 375 n. 86.

He makes his intention plain in 23:4:

> I will present (ערך) my case (משפט) before him
> and fill my mouth with accusations (תוכחת).⁵⁵

The root יכח in the *hiphil* conveys two primary meanings. First, it can mean "to accuse," "to correct," "to reprove," or "to chastise." It can also mean, however, "to decide a lawsuit," "to judge," or "to adjudicate." Bovati demonstrates that יכח often refers to the act of accusing, and he offers citations to the book of Job to prove the point.⁵⁶ He stresses that the root יכח can serve as a synonym for ריב, as is plain in 13:6.⁵⁷ In the book of Job, the root's predominant meaning is "to accuse." Only secondarily does it means "to judge" or "to reprove." The related noun תוכחת is often translated as "argument" in the book of Job.⁵⁸ It is, however, better translated "accusation" here and in 13:6.⁵⁹

Once Job makes his accusation, he will have to summon the defendant to court, and the defendant will have to answer. As noted in chapter 4 above, the judges of Babylon were often quite explicit about their summoning of the defendant. In the biblical world, the plaintiff might also seize the defendant and bring him to court (Deut 21:18–21), or the court might issue a summons (Deut 25:8).⁶⁰ With regard to the latter procedure, King Saul issued a judicial summons of the defendant, Ahimelech, using the verb קרא, immediately following Doeg's accusation of Ahimelech in 1 Sam 22:9–11. Numerous other biblical passages reveal the legal import of קרא as a legal summons to appear.⁶¹ When issued against a defendant, such a summons demanded that the defendant respond to the charges presented. If he failed to do this, he would lose the case.⁶² In the biblical world, the root ענה, "to answer," signified, among other things, a defendant's formal legal response to a lodged accusation. Ahimelech answers (ענה) Saul's accusation in 1 Sam 22:14.⁶³ Similarly, Job contemplates both summoning God and God's answer to such a summons (9:16), when Job states:

---

55. See Gemser, "*Rîb*-Pattern," 123.
56. Bovati, *Re-Establishing Justice*, 42–48.
57. Ibid., 42–43, 45 n. 30. See, e.g., Hos 4:4; Mic 6:2.
58. Bovati, *Re-Establishing Justice*, 45 n. 31
59. See Hab 2:1; Ps 38:15.
60. See Westbrook, "Biblical Law," 9.
61. Deut 25:8; 1 Kgs 20:7; Isa 59:4; Ps 50:1, 4; cf. Ps 4:2; Amos 7:4. See also Bovati, *Re-Establishing Justice*, 223–25, 326–28; and Westbrook, "Biblical Law," 9.
62. This is true in the Neo-Babylonian data. Bovati asserts this is also the case in biblical trial law (*Re-Establishing Justice*, 342). See Sus 41; cf. Gen 44:16; Isa 53:7; Ps 38:14–15; Neh 5:8.
63. See also Josh 7:20. For further discussion of ענה signifying a trial defense, see Bovati, *Re-Establishing Justice*, 333–34.

> If I summoned (קרא), and he answered (ענה),
> I would not believe that he would listen (אז) to my voice.

Nowhere is Job quite so clear that he intends to file a counterclaim in a suit where God has just filed the accusation against him as he is in 13:22. He dares God to summon him and let him answer. If not, he will go forward immediately with his counteraccusation:

> Then summon (קרא) and I will answer (ענה),
> or I will state my case (דבר)[64] and you may reply (שוב) to me.

This verse does not raise the question concerning who will sue first, as it might seem to do on first glance. To Job's mind God has already accused him. Rather, Job is demanding that he be summoned to the court to be allowed to testify. He objects to a possible summary judgment that would be brought down without benefit of his testimony. He feels that such an outcome would be highly problematic. If he is not permitted to testify, then he will lodge a counterclaim and God can respond.

Job is not the only one who believes that he intends to summon God. Eliphaz is well aware that Job is contemplating filing a counterclaim and mocks him for it in 5:1.[65] Eliphaz believes neither that God will answer Job nor that Job has any judge who will hear his case:

> Summon (קרא), I pray! Is there anyone who will answer (ענה) you?
> To which holy one will you turn?

Later, Job complains about such scorn, but, in so doing, he concedes that he expects to summon God:

> I have become a laughingstock to my friends.
>   I, who summon (קרא) God to answer (ענה) me,
>   an innocent (צדיק), honorable (תם) man, am a laughingstock! (12:4)

Summoning one to answer in a legal setting means that a charge has been filed. In this case, it would have to be a countercharge.

Job expresses several more times that he wants God to answer his counteraccusation, but he doubts that God will. For example, in 9:2–4, while responding to Eliphaz's report that, according to heaven, no human can be acquitted before God (4:17–19),[66] Job frets:

---

64. The verb דבר, "to speak," has a forensic meaning in legal contexts. It may refer to the act of testifying (see Wells, "Law of Testimony," 34–37) or stating one's case by way of accusation (Habel, *Book of Job: Commentary*, 224). See, e.g., Ps 50:7 and Prov 21:28.

65. See M. D. Crook, *The Cruel God: Job's Search for the Meaning of Suffering* (Boston: Beacon, 1959), 30.

66. I disagree with the commentators who suggest that 4:12–21 is Job's revelation, not that of Eliphaz. See, e.g., H. L. Ginsberg, "Job the Patient and Job the Impatient," in *Congress*

> Truly, I know that it is so!⁶⁷
> But how can a mortal be acquitted (צדק) before God?
> If one wished to bring suit (ריב) against him,
> he would not answer him once in a thousand.⁶⁸
> Wise in heart (לבב) and mighty in strength—
> who has argued (קשה)⁶⁹ with him and emerged whole? (9:2–4)

Twice more Job fears that God will not answer him should he bring a claim. He uses a number of words related to "crying" or "crying out," including זעק, צעק, and שוע, in his speeches. These words may all have a forensic meaning. H. J. Boecker recognizes this with respect to the verb צעק.⁷⁰ F. W. Dobbs-Allsopp also notes the use of צעק in petitions for redress before the king.⁷¹ Bovati indicates that, when צעק is coupled with חמס, it constitutes a petition for redress from a serious injustice.⁷² In the book of Job, this coupling represents, not postverdict redress, as is often suggested, but an accusation against a serious injustice. Job 19:7 and 30:20 make this evident, as Job expresses consternation over the fact that God may not answer his suit:

> Lo! I would cry (צעק) violence (חמס), but you will not answer (ענה);
> I would cry out (שוע), but there will be no litigation (משפט) (19:7).
> I would cry out (שוע) to you, but you will not answer (ענה) me;
> I would take my stand (עמד), but you will turn your attention against me. (30:20)

Notwithstanding his fear, Job is prepared to rise and cry out (שוע) before the entire congregation of Israel (קהל) (30:28).⁷³ He also begs that his cry (זעקה) not rest (16:18b). It should live beyond him (16:18a; 19:26). He is prepared to face death in his cause,⁷⁴ as Job exclaims in 13:15:

---

*Volume: Rome, 1968* (ed. G. W. Anderson et al.; VTSup 17; Leiden: Brill, 1969), 98–107; Greenstein, "Forensic Understanding," 258; and Tur-Sinai, *Book of Job*, 88–91.

67. In this colon, Job asserts his own knowledge over that of Eliphaz, who demands that Job take his advice because he knows the truth (5:27).

68. This reading follows that of NJPS and Habel, in tracking the similar language of Elihu (33:13): "He would not answer one charge in a thousand." This translation decision runs contrary to the great majority of translations and scholars, who want to maintain a perfect parallelism in the verse. Unfortunately, the poetry of Job does not always maintain perfect parallelism.

69. Following Gordis (*Book of Job*, 102) and Clines (*Job 1–20*, 211, 216) that קשה in the hiphil means "to argue" or "to dispute," thereby keeping the legal tone.

70. H. J. Boecker, *Redeformen des Rechtsleben im Alten Testament* (WMANT 14; Neukirchen-Vluyn: Neukirchener Verlag, 1963), 67.

71. Dobbs-Allsopp, "Genre," 54 nn. 6, 9.

72. Bovati, *Re-Establishing Justice*, 316–18. On חמס as a crime, see Boecker, *Redeformen*, 6; Dick, "Legal Metaphor," 40 n. 17; cf. Scholnick "Lawsuit Drama," 201, 203, 206.

73. Zophar makes clear the import of קהל as an adjudicating body in 11:10.

74. My argument that Job is willing to martyr himself in his cause is further delineated in, "Job's Wife as Hero," 374–423.

> Though he might slay me, and I should have no hope,
> still, I will accuse (יכח) his conduct (דרך) to his face.⁷⁵

His hope is that his accusation might be heard and judged (30:28).

Job has, on the other hand, times of confidence. In 23:5, he expects God to answer and plots against his adversary's defensive strategy:

> I would learn the arguments (מלה) with which he will answer (ענה) me
> and know what he would say to me.

By the end of his defensive speech, which he seals, Job grows brave. He insists that God now answer his counteraccusation. He also insists that God set his original charges in writing. Job demands in 31:35b–c:

> Here is my mark! Let Shaddai answer (ענה) me,
> and let my adversary at law (איש ריב) draw up (כתב) a bill (ספר)!⁷⁶

Like 13:22, this verse demonstrates that the litigation before us involves both a claim and a counterclaim.

Job and Eliphaz are not, however, the only individuals who believe that Job desires to counteraccuse God. Elihu is convinced that Job has already asserted his claim against God and, therefore, queries Job in 33:13–14:

> Why do you bring suit (ריב) against him,
> claiming: "He will not answer (ענה) my case (דבר)?"
> For God testifies (דבר) time and again⁷⁷
> though people do not perceive it.

He also refers to suit in 35:14:

> How much less when you say you do not see him,
> that the case (דין) is before him and you are waiting for him.

---

75. This verse is one of the most perplexing in the book of Job. Because Job cannot accuse (יכח) based on his own conduct, I. L. Seeligmann proposes emending דרכי to דרכיו ("Zur Terminologie für das Gerichtsverfahren im Wortschatz des biblischen Hebräisch," in *Hebräische Wortforschung: Festschrift zum 80. Geburtstag von Walter Baumgartner* [ed. B. Hartmann et al.; VTSup 16; Leiden: Brill, 1967], 267–68). This is an acceptable solution, given the accusatory focus of 12:16–13:13. I therefore reject the more common solution of reading יכח as "to defend" (see, e.g., Clines, *Job 1–20*, 276, 282), which would then place this verse in Job's defensive repertoire and violate the traditional meanings "to accuse" and "to judge." Habel proposes reading the colon: "I will now argue my case to his face" (*Book of Job: Commentary*, 224). Clines suggest this possibility, as well, although he does not adopt it (*Job 1–20*, 282). I am not convinced, however, that דרך includes "case" in its semantic range.

76. Gemser, "*Rîb*-Pattern," 123–24.

77. "Time and again" is, literally, "in one way and in two." See NJPS.

Furthermore, Elihu is prepared to defend God against the counterclaim:

> Bear with me a little, and I will convince you.
>   There are still more arguments (מלה) on God's behalf!
> I will glean my knowledge from afar,
>   and I will prove (נתן) my maker innocent (צדק).
> In truth, my arguments (מלה) are not false;
>   one with perfect (תם) knowledge is with you. (36:2–4)

Most important, God grants that the nature of Job's actions is a counterclaim in both 40:2 and 8:

> Will a faultfinder bring suit (ריב) against Shaddai?
>   Will the one accusing (יכח) God answer (ענה) him? . . .
> Would you frustrate (פרר) my case (משפט)?
>   Would you convict (רשע)[78] me so that you might be innocent (צדק).

Indeed, the existence of the counterclaim is the very reason God must speak to Job at all. As a counterdefendant, he must answer the counteraccusation or risk the case.

## The Basis of Job's Counterclaim: Abuse of Authority

Job must have some substantive legal basis for counterclaiming against God. Counterclaims will not stand where the defendant's sole argument is that he or she did not do the act. That assertion constitutes a simple defense. The defendant must offer an affirmative charge on a separate legal breach.

I suggest that, in the end, Job will threaten to lodge a complex counteraccusation against God, which will contain three counts on the charge of abuse of authority. These counts will include: (1) abuse of the legal process by initiating a false suit and conducting oneself in an outrageous manner in the course of the trial; (2) violating rather than upholding the fundamental principles of justice as is required of the deity; and (3) failing to create a universe that is orderly, from which justice might flow, as God has promised.

Multiple-count accusations were permissible under Neo-Babylonian law and are also found in the Bible. For example, Jacob's counterclaim against Laban is actually a multi-count accusation, in which one of the

---

78. D. R. Hillers established that the *hiphil* of רשע means "to condemn" ("Delocutive Verbs," 320–24). See also Bovati, *Re-Establishing Justice*, 348–49.

counts charges Laban with false suit (Gen 31:36–42).[79] Job uses similar procedures in charging God. In order to appreciate Job's multi-count counterclaim fully, we must first explore the problem of abuse of authority in the ancient Near East generally, and in ancient Israel specifically.

Westbrook maintains that all legal systems must contend with the challenge that abuse of power poses.[80] People can, at times, stretch the limits of their authority to the point of abuse. The improper action may fall within the strict letter of the law, but the result is nevertheless unreasonable or, even, unconscionable. A legal claim of abuse of authority stands when those with superior economic, political, or legal power use their influence to an unfair advantage and cause harm to a less well-positioned individual.

In the ancient Near East, claims of abuse of authority existed. Such claims stood in several situations, including where the petitioner may have been subject to some sort of unfair financial, administrative, or legal maneuver. The resulting injury may have included loss of property, the deprivation of a legal right or economic benefit owed to the claimant, or other type of damage to his or her welfare.[81] One could complain about an incident of abuse of power through regular legal channels or by extrajudicial petition, but the latter course was preferable. The king, as protector of justice, heard a great many of these cases by petition.[82] This protocol was imperative in cases where the petitioner believed the power of his opponent would render any lawsuit on the matter an exercise in futility.[83] Officials often held both administrative and legal functions.[84] Westbrook maintains that this overlap authorized officials, in some circumstances, to act in a quasi-judicial function with respect to their subordinates. This permitted the officials to decide legal matters that affected their subordinates without instituting formal legal proceedings.[85] This was true even where the superior had a stake in the matter because, in the ancient Near East,

---

79. See the materials at nn. 45–47 above.

80. Westbrook, *Studies*, 9–38, esp. 9–11. See also idem, "Social Justice in the Ancient Near East," 149–63; and his very brief summary of offenses against the legal system in "Punishments and Crimes," 555. This discussion derives almost entirely from his work. Bovati, additionally, has a discussion of abuse of authority (*Re-Establishing Justice*, 306–28). His focus, however, is on the legal procedure associated with the claim and not on the substantive law of abuse of authority itself.

81. On this last category of harm, see, e.g., LH §163, where a soldier's superior may not give him out for hire.

82. Possible Neo-Assyrian abuse of authority petitions include *CT* 54, 463 and 510 (discussed in Parpola, *Letters from Scholars*, 125–27 nos. 163 and 164). A similar kind of petition appears to have been brought before the crown prince in *ABL* 500, discussed in Parpola, *Letters from Scholars*, 128 no. 168.

83. Westbrook, *Studies*, 11–14.

84. See ch. 4, n. 4 above.

85. Westbrook, "Social Justice," 152.

parties could also be judges, particularly where the harm was only economic and the party-judge played an important administrative function in the government. The best course in a case where a superior abused his discretion in this type of situation was to petition the king.[86] Westbrook notes, however, citing LH §34, that lesser officials also had the ability to handle claims of abuse of power.[87] The presiding official, whether the king or one of his subordinates, could have assessed a number of penalties where an individual was found guilty of such abuse. This might have included capital punishment.[88]

Two literary documents from Mesopotamia list the types of abuses that were considered particularly egregious to their writers. In a Neo-Assyrian document entitled, "Advice to a Prince," the ruler is warned against failing to heed justice, improperly convicting a citizen, taking bribes, treating a lawsuit frivolously, improperly imposing fines or imprisonment of his citizens, and taking silver for his own coffers, among other offenses.[89] Furthermore, if his advisors swore false accusations as a means to receive bribes, they would also suffer severe consequences.[90] The Neo-Babylonian

---

86. Ibid.

87. Ibid., 12. Westbrook also notes that there seems to have been, in the Hittite Empire, an itinerant ombudsman to handle such claims ("Punishments and Crimes," 555, citing the Hittite "Instructions to the Border Guard Commander," translated by A. Goetze, *ANET*, 211).

88. Westbrook, "Punishments and Crimes," 555. See LH §34.

89. *BWL*, 110–15. For a history of the copies, transliterations, translations, and analyses of the Nineveh exemplar, see I. M. Diakonoff, "A Babylonian Political Pamphlet from about 700 B.C.," in *Studies in Honor of Benno Landsberger on His Seventy-Fifth Birthday* (ed. H. G. Güterbock and T. Jacobsen; AS 16; Chicago: University of Chicago Press, 1965), 343 nn. 1–2. A very early Neo-Babylonian copy of this document was discovered in the Neo-Babylonian Governor's Archive from Nippur (Nippur 4, 128). S. W. Cole copies, transliterates, and translates this copy, but M. Civil provided a prior transliteration in an appendix to Reiner, "The Babylonian Fürstenspiegel in Practice," *The Neo-Babylonian Elders: Society and Languages of the Ancient Near East; Studies in Honour of I. M. Diakonoff* [ed. M. A. Dandamaev et al.; Warminster: Aris and Phillips, 1982], 320–26, appendix at pp. 324–26. *CT* 54, 212, an early Neo-Babylonian letter to King Esarhaddon, seems to quote from "Advice to a Prince" with some slight deviation from the original. Reiner discusses *CT* 54, 212 in ibid., 320–23.

90. Interestingly, both G. E. Bryce and F. H. Cryer observe the relationship between "Advice to a Prince" and ancient Near Eastern divination texts (F. H. Cryer, *Divination in Ancient Israel and Its Near Eastern Environment: A Socio-Historical Investigation*. [JSOTSup 142; Sheffield: JSOT Press, 1994], 192–93; and G. E. Bryce, "Omen-Wisdom in Ancient Israel," *JBL* 94 [1975]: 23–24). V. A. Hurowitz also notes the connection and observes that, in a number of instances, the punishment for the breach of royal duty is actually *lex talionis* from a philological point of view ("Alliterative Allusions, Nebus Writing, and Paronomastic Punishment: Some Aspects of Word Play in Akkadian Literature," in *Puns and Pundits: Word Play in the Hebrew Bible and Ancient Near Eastern Literature* (ed. S. B. Noegel; Bethesda, Md.: CDL Press, 2000), 83–86. For instance, lines 15–18 of "Advice to a Prince" state: "If (the king) takes silver of the citizens of Babylon and adds it to his own coffers (*ana makkūri ušērib*) . . . Marduk . . . will set his foes upon him, and will give his property and coffers (*makkūrašu*) to his enemy"

document "Nebuchadnezzar King of Justice" also complains about abuse of authority.[91] It addresses the ability of the strong to oppress those who are incapable of obtaining legal redress, a failure of government representatives to assist the widow or the person with a disability before the court, the failure of judges to give rightful legal relief to the deserving, and judges' acceptance of bribes. While this latter document appears to be engorged with hyperbole and the documents of practice do not reflect that these abuses were especially problematic during the reign of any Neo-Babylonian king, the text does reflect legal traditions, procedures, and attitudes of ancient origin.

One Old Babylonian document of practice related to abuse of authority exposes this fact.[92] It is an extrajudicial petition for abuse of legal process in a case where an official had not followed appropriate legal procedure. The suit involved the question: Had the petitioner's contract of purchase been invalidated by a *mīšarum* decree?[93] Representatives of the assembly, which was the lower tribunal, determined that the contract was good and sent the man to a higher official for further proceedings. The official, disagreeing with the lower court, broke the tablet outside of the petitioner's presence, without a hearing. The petitioner returned to the lower court with the tablet shards to complain of his treatment, whereupon they said that they were powerless against the higher official. The victim then petitioned the king for relief. The petition was not based on a claim that the official lacked the authority to overturn the decision of the lower court. Rather, it rested on the fact that the official abused his discretion when he overruled the lower court because he did so without giving the petitioner due process of law.

We have little Neo-Babylonian evidence for claims of abuse of authority. It is possible, however, that the subject matter of the letter CT 22, 160 is

---

(translation is that of Hurowitz, ibid., 83). A less obvious case is: "If (the king) voids their documents and changes their inscribed privileges (*riksīšunu upaṭṭarūma nārêšunu ušannû*) and sends them out on a military campaign and to the treaty [xxx] then, Nabû, scribe of Esagil, inspector of heaven and earth, director of everything, designator of kingship will open the bonds of his land and determine hostility (*riksāt mātīšu upaṭṭarma aḫīta išâm*)" (ibid., 85).

91. CT 46, 45. See further ch. 3 n. 43 above.

92. Published by J. J. Finkelstein, "Some New *Misharum* Material," 233–51. Westbrook makes some modifications to Finkelstein's translation (*Studies*, 13–14).

93. A *mīšarum* decree, as used in this context, is an edict issued by a king for the purpose of economic reform. It might cancel valid debt agreements, release individuals from debt-slavery, reverse forced sales of family domiciles, and relieve other types of economic hardships that were legitimately created before the decree. They were often issued by a king at the commencement of his reign to commemorate an important occasion, or in response to various economic, political, or religious pressures. See M. Weinfeld, "'Justice and Righteousness' in Israel," 158–60, cf. B. F. Foster, "Social Reform in Ancient Mesopotamia," in *Social Justice in the Ancient World* (ed. K. Irani and M. Silver; Westport, Conn.: Greenwood, 1995), 165–75.

a claim of abuse of authority brought before the king. There a representative of the king contacted the *šatammu*-officer at the king's behest about having the overseer of the stonemasons arrested because his subordinates complained that the overseer had not paid them. The letter reflects that the king also ordered that the stonemasons be paid. Apparently, the petitioners were denied an economic benefit that was due them by a superior and petitioned the king, who gave them redress.

Ancient Israel, like its neighbors, had a legal remedy for these types of claims. According to Westbrook's study, the Hebrew Bible employs two roots to express these abuses. The root גזל is used to connote abuse of authority where loss of property results;[94] עשק is used to signify cases where a deprivation of economic benefit or legal right results.[95] As in the rest of the ancient Near East, the king in ancient Israel was the usual recipient of such petitions.[96] Nevertheless, it appears that others within the administration could hear these petitions.[97] The penalty for abuse of authority was typically within the discretion of the official hearing the claim and could have involved financial compensation[98] and/or capital punishment.[99]

The *Meṣad Ḥashavyahu* ostracon must be central to any discussion of abuse of authority in ancient Israel. This document from the time of Josiah is, apparently, the only Hebrew legal document of practice of assured

---

94. For a full discussion of גזל, see Westbrook, *Studies*, 15–38, esp. p. 36. For a few biblical examples, see Gen 31:31; Lev 5:21; 19:13; Deut 28:29; Isa 3:14; 10:2; 61:8; Jer 21:12; 22:3, 17; Ezek 18:18; 22:29; 33:15; Mic 2:2; 3:2–3; Pss 35:10; 62:11; 69:5; Prov 22:22; Eccl 5:7.

95. For a full discussion of עשק, see *Studies*, 35–38, esp. p 36. For a few biblical examples, see Lev 5:21; 19:13; Deut 24:14; 28:29, 33; 1 Sam 12:3–4; Jer 7:6; 21:12; 22:3; Ezek 18:18; 22:7, 12, 29; Hos 5:11; Amos 4:1; Mic 2:2; Zech 7:10; Mal 3:5; Pss 62:11; 72:4; 73:8; 103:6; 146:7; Prov 14:31; 22:16; 28:3; Eccl 4:1; 5:7.

96. Westbrook, *Studies*, 36, citing Jer 21:12; 22:3; and Ps 72:4. For a brief discussion of the king's general judicial powers, see Westbrook, "Biblical Law," 8. Weinfeld observes that the king in Israel was expected to uphold the concept of social justice just as kings were in the greater ancient Near East ("Justice and Righteousness," 492; see Prov 21:3; cf. Isa 16:5). In Hebrew, the hendiadys meaning "social justice" is צדקה ומשפט (see Gen 18:19; Ps 33:5; Prov 21:5).

97. This is discernible from the *Meṣad Ḥashavyahu* ostracon, a Hebrew extrajudicial petition concerning abuse of authority that we will discuss at length momentarily. For literature on this petition, see ch. 1 n. 10 above.

98. Westbrook states: "if the culprit voluntarily confessed, he must restore the property plus a fifth and bring a guilt-offering for sacrifice (Lev 5:21–26)" ("Punishments and Crimes," 555). Westbrook reads a confession into this passage, but it makes no mention of such, as we find in Lev 5:1–4 and Num 5:6–7. He believes this must be implied because the compensation seems much too low for the offenses listed (*Studies*, 15–16). The penalty, therefore, must be mitigated by confession. I believe that the expiation may be the actual mitigating factor in this pericope.

99. See Westbrook, "Punishments and Crimes," 555, discussing 2 Sam 12:1–6.

authenticity that archaeologists have uncovered thus far. While its genre is under dispute, I believe that Westbrook and Dobbs-Allsopp are correct in their assertion that this is an extrajudicial petition grounded in abuse of administrative authority.[100] It was a גזל claim that resulted in the loss of property. In this case, a harvester complained to a royal official that his superior, who, it seems, had the right to take possession of his garment pending completion of his assignment, failed to restore it when the harvester's work was finished. The petition is broken; but I believe that Dobbs-Allsopp successfully reconstructs the document. The petition opens: "Please, may my lord, the official, hear a word of his servant!" This is very similar to the petition of the wise woman of Tekoa in 2 Sam 14:12: "Please, may your servant speak a word to my lord, the king!"[101] Dobbs-Allsopp, using 2 Sam 14:2–22 and Westbrook's understanding of גזל—especially his analysis of the parable of the poor man's ewe-lamb (2 Sam 12:1–14)—restores and translates the last four lines of the ostracon as follows:

> Truly I am innocent of any of[fence, but he unjustly took (גזל)] my garment. Surely it is for the official to re[turn the garment] of your ser[vant. So may you gra]nt him compas[sion and he]ar the [plea of your] servant and do not be silent . . . .

Claims of abuse of authority were an important corrective in the society.

Whenever this system of earthly justice failed, Israel believed that God would rectify the situation and punish the offender. God could initiate his own lawsuits (ריב) against offending persons, institutions, and nations.[102]

---

100. Westbrook, *Studies*, 35 n. 128; and Dobbs-Allsopp, "Genre," 49–55.

101. Dobbs-Allsopp's translation ("Genre," 51). Dobbs-Allsopp also observes similar petition language in 2 Kgs 6:26 and notes that 1 Kgs 20:39–40 may be a petition as well. Both Kings passages indicate the start of petition before the king by use of the verb צעק ("to cry out") ("Genre," 54 nn. 6, 9). See also Boecker, *Redeformen*, 67.

102. There are numerous important writings on God's legal enforcement powers and his ability to bring lawsuits as a part of those powers. See, e.g., R. V. Bergren, *Prophets and the Law* (HUCM 4; Cincinnati: Hebrew Union College Press, 1974); Gemser, "Rîb-Pattern," 120–37; J. Harvey, "Le 'rîb-Pattern': Requisitoire Prophetique sur la Rupture de l'Alliance," *Bib* 43 (1962): 172–96; D. R. Hillers, *Covenant: The History of a Biblical Idea* (Baltimore: Johns Hopkins University Press, 1969), 124–31; H. B. Huffmon, "The Covenant Lawsuit in the Prophets," *JBL* 78 (1959): 285–95; J. Limburg, "The Lawsuit of God in the Eighth Century Prophets" (Th.D. diss., Union Theological Seminary [Virginia], 1969); idem, "The Root ריב and the Prophetic Lawsuit Speeches," *JBL* 88 (1969): 291–304; G. E. Mendenhall, "Samuel's 'Broken Rîb': Deuteronomy 32," in *No Famine in the Land: Studies in Honor of John L. McKenzie* (ed. J. W. Flanagan and A. W. Robinson; Missoula, Mont.: Scholars Press, 1975), 63–74; K. Nielsen, *Yahweh as Prosecutor and Judge: An Investigation of the Prophetic Lawsuit (Rib-Pattern)* (JSOTSup 9; Sheffield: JSOT Press, 1978); H. E. von Waldow, *Der Traditionsgeschichtliche Hintergrund der prophetischen Gerichtsreden* (BZAW 85; Berlin: de Gruyter, 1983); C. Westermann, *Basic Forms of Prophetic Speech* (trans. H. C. White; Philadelphia: Westminster, 1967); E. B. Wilson, "Rîb in Israel's Historical and Legal Traditions: A Study of the Israelite Setting of Rîb-Form" (Ph.D.

The prophets speak repeatedly of such suits.[103] Their view of God arises out of the Israelite understanding that he is the ultimate progenitor and protector of justice.[104] God's enforcement powers were, then, the final check on the problem of abuse of power.[105]

While Westbrook's study focuses on the two most important terms for abuse of authority in the Hebrew Bible, other vocabulary may also signify various types of abuse within this class of offenses. First, Westbrook notes the importance of לקח, which can reflect an abusive taking in such cases.[106] This verb appears in the Meṣad Ḥashavyahu ostracon. It also appears in Samuel's speech before the people in 1 Sam 12:3. According to Westbrook, Samuel is giving "examples of the corrupt practices of a judge."[107] Samuel queries: "Whose ox have I seized (לקח) or whose ass have I seized (לקח)? Or whom have I deprived through abuse of power (עשק)? Whom have I oppressed (רצץ)? Or from whose hand have I taken ransom money or taken a bribe?[108] Testify (ענה) against me! Then I will restore it to you."[109] The people respond that he has done none of these things, using the same three significant verbs (1 Sam 12:4).

---

diss., Drew University, 1970); and G. E. Wright, "The Lawsuit of God: A Form-Critical Study of Deuteronomy 32," in *Israel's Prophetic Heritage: Essays in Honor of James Muilenburg* (ed. B. W. Anderson and W. Harrelson; New York: Harper & Brothers, 1962), 26–67. While most form critics maintain that there is a prophetic lawsuit genre in the Hebrew Bible, there are those who contest this idea. See, e.g., D. R. Daniels, "Is There a 'Prophetic Lawsuit' Genre?" *ZAW* 99 (1987): 339–60; and M. de Roche, "Yahweh's *rîb* Against Israel: A Reassessment of the So-Called 'Prophetic Lawsuit' in the Preexilic Prophets," *JBL* 102 (1983): 563–74.

103. See, e.g., Hos 4:1–2. Consult the bibliography in the preceding note for all instances of these suits.

104. T. Mafico, "Just, Justice," *ABD* 3:1128–29. This is clearly attested in Gen 18:25; Pss 7:6–11; 9:7–9; 17:2; 26:1–3; 28:3–4; 76:9; 94:2–4; 99:1–4; 113:4–9; 119:137, 153–59; 139:23–34; 145:17; and 146:7–9; cf. Ps 97:2. Weinfeld observes that God is deeply connected to the concept of social justice ("Justice and Righteousness," 492). His throne is built upon social justice in Ps 89:15. God loves it in Ps 33:5.

105. Westbrook, *Studies*, 36. See, e.g., Deut 24:14; Isa 3:13–14; Jer 21:12; 22:3; Ezek 22:7, 12–13, 29; Amos 4:1; Mic 2:2; 3:2–3; Zech 7:10; Prov 22:22–23.

106. Westbrook, *Studies*, 35 n. 128. See also 2 Sam 12:4.

107. Westbrook, *Studies*, 19–20.

108. F. H. A. Kemik, "Code of Conduct for a King: Psalm 101," *JBL* 95 (1976): 396–97. For further discussion of the bribe as judicial corruption in the Hebrew Bible, see Bovati, *Re-Establishing Justice*, 195. See, e.g., Exod 23:8.

109. The MT has כפר ואעלים עיני בו, which is usually translated "a bribe to blind my eyes with it" (see, e.g., NASV; and NJPS). The LXX suggests כפר ואעלים עני בי, which makes less sense. R. Gordis ("Naʾalamʾ and Other Observances on the Ain Fashka Scrolls," *JNES* 9 [1950]: 44–47) proposes כפר ונעלם ענו בי based on column 13 of the *Hymns of Thanksgiving* (1QHª) as published by E. L. Sukenik in *Megillot Genuzot* (Jerusalem, 1949; unavailable to this author) and the Greek of Ben Sira 46:19. I follow Gordis's suggestion, as does Westbrook (*Studies*, 19–20). A later version of Sukenik's work can be found in *The Dead Sea Scrolls of the Hebrew University* (Jerusalem: Magnes, 1955, pl. 47).

Moreover, Westbrook points out: "Other terms, such as *dk'* and *rṣṣ*, do not appear in any legal passages and seem to be used figuratively, but they may have had some technical meaning [related to abuse of authority], as in 1 Sam 12:3–4."[110] I believe they clearly have a technical meaning and take up דכא first. In his study of גזל, Westbrook examines Prov 22:22–23:

> Do not abuse power to rob (גזל) the poor because they are poor;
>   Do not crush (דכא) the poor in the gate;
> for Yahweh will sue (ריב) their lawsuit (ריב)
>   and rob (קבע) those who rob (קבע) them of life.[111]

This proverb refers to that situation wherein God will avenge the rights of the oppressed against their abusers. Its chiastic structure (a-b-b'-a'), along with the reference to the gate, reveals that דכא has a connotation related to litigation (ריב) in this pericope. The root דכא, therefore, must signify a legal defeat. Yet it is not just any legal defeat. The fact that גזל and דכא are in parallel in v. 22 helps us to comprehend its nature. It is a defeat dispensed unfairly by an individual using the legal system in an inappropriate, fraudulent, or abusive manner. These two verbs are linked again to another term for litigation in Isa 3:14–15, where God accuses the leaders of Israel of abuses against his people:

> Yahweh will bring a case (משפט)
>   against the elders and officers of his people:
> "It is you who have ravaged the vineyard.
>   The spoil of your abuse (גזלה) of the poor is in your houses.
> How dare you[112] crush (דכא) my people,
>   grind the faces of the poor?" says my lord, Yahweh of the Hosts.[113]

Again, God will enforce justice where it is not otherwise enforced. He will avenge with his own lawsuit those who have been robbed of their property via abuse of authority or who have been handed legal defeats through improper manipulation of the legal system. He will sue the perpetrators of such crimes, the elders and officers of his people, who are in positions of power. God will not tolerate abuse of authority, generally, or abuse that involves the law courts, specifically.

The root רצץ has a connotation similar to דכא in certain passages. רצץ generally means to "break," "crush," or "oppress."[114] It is found coupled

---

110. Westbrook, *Studies*, 38 n.149.
111. See also Isa 3:14–15; Lam 3:34–36.
112. Following the NJPS translation of מלכם.
113. For other instances of דכא with this connotation, see Pss 94:5; 143:2–3; Lam 3:34; cf. Ps 72:4.
114. Bovati acknowledges this as one of the important words related to abuse of authority (*Re-Establishing Justice*, 308).

with עשק in 1 Sam 12:3–4, as discussed above, and in Deut 28:33; Jer 22:17; Hos 5:11; and Amos 4:1. Just as there is a poetic link established between גזל and דכא, there is an analogous link created between עשק and רצץ. Moreover, just as גזל and דכא were connected to משפט in Isa 3:14–15, עשק and רצץ are connected to משפט in Hos 5:11, where Yahweh says: "Ephraim is abused (עשק) and crushed (רצץ) in a lawsuit (משפט)." Consequently, I believe that both דכא and רצץ relate specifically to an abuse of the legal system. In the case of דכא, it results in the loss of property. In the case of רצץ, it results in the deprivation of an economic benefit or legal right. In light of this information, Westbrook's translation of 1 Sam 12:3 should be revised slightly to: "Whose ox have I seized or whose ass have I seized? Or whom have I deprived through abuse of power? Whom have I defeated in court through abuse of the legal process? Or from whose hand have I taken ransom money or taken a bribe? Testify against me! Then I will restore it to you." Samuel's list spells out several profound breaches of judicial fiduciary duty in ancient Israel. Deut 16:19; Ps 82:2; Prov 24:23–24; and 2 Chr 19:7 designate two other such breaches, that is, being partial in decisions and judging wrongly.[115] All these abuses are important in the book of Job.

On a related note, scholars have also observed that a scoundrel (בליעל or בן בליעל) is one who disrupts the social order.[116] These people are architects of chaos and often participate in abuse of legal process. For example, two scoundrels (בן בליעל) falsely accuse Naboth of the crime of blasphemy in 1 Kgs 21:10, 13. Moreover, Prov 19:28 uses this term to describe a witness who subverts the legal process (עד בליעל יליץ משפט). They may not, however, be explicitly abusing a position of power.

Finally, the root בצע is also tied to abuse of authority in some verses. In its nominal form, בצע usually represents illicit financial gain, the taking of which serves to ruin the victim.[117] In its verbal forms, בצע may describe the fraudulent, violent, or abusive process by which one ruins another or the state of being greedy for such gain.[118] While בצע does not confine its meaning to situations of abuse of authority, several verses bear witness to its use in these contexts. In Ezek 22:12–13, 27 and Prov 28:16, officials use their authority to receive illicit gain. Only those men who hate בצע may serve as judges (Exod 18:21). Moreover, בצע is coupled with the other vocabulary of abuse of authority in quite a number of verses. It is associated with עשק in Isa 33:15; Ezek 22:12; and Prov 28:16. It is connected to both עשק and רצץ in

---

115. For a fuller discussion of judicial corruption in the Hebrew Bible, see ibid., 194–201.

116. T. J. Lewis, "Belial," *ABD* 1:655.

117. See, e.g., Gen 37:26; Exod 18:21; 1 Sam 8:13; Isa 33:15; 57:17; Jer 6:13; 8:10; 22:17; Ezek 22:13, 27; 33:31; Hab 2:9; Pss 10:3; 119:36; Prov 1:19; 28:16; cf. Isa 56:11.

118. See, e.g., Jer 6:13; 8:10; Ezek 22:12, 27; Hab 2:9; Prov 1:19; 15:27.

Jer 22:17. It is also connected to the taking (לקח) of bribes in 1 Sam 8:3 and Ezek 22:12 and to the holding of bribes in Isa 33:15.[119] It is additionally linked to the perverting of justice (משפט) in 1 Sam 8:3. Hence, there are circumstances when illicit gain is derived from abuse of authority, in which case it is marked by the use of the root בצע. In conclusion, there is a broad range of vocabulary dedicated to the problem of abuse of power, including abuse of the legal process, in Hebrew.[120] This fact indicates that the offense was of utmost concern in ancient Israel.

Israel invested considerable time delineating which actions would constitute proper social justice and which would constitute abusive actions that violated the principles of social justice and were, therefore, grounds for petition.[121] The Hebrew prophets, and Proverbs in particular, offer many instructions and admonitions on this point. Samuel was not the only personality in the Hebrew Bible who made such lists. Isaiah 1:17 is an excellent exemplar:

> Learn to do good;
> seek (דרש) justice (משפט);
>   reprove (אשר) the ruthless;
> judge (שפט) for the orphan;
>   bring lawsuits (ריב) for the widow.

This verse speaks to a number of the issues that the Neo-Babylonian document "Nebuchadnezzar King of Justice" also takes up. Israel was very similar to its neighbors in its view of what proper justice demanded.

As the greater ancient Near East had admonitions against its kings falling into the trap of abuse of authority, so had Israel. The events of 2 Sam

---

119. The root בצע is also contrasted with the hating of bribes in Prov 15:27.

120. P. Bovati would add בזז, which typically has the meaning "to make prey" or "to take plunder," to this lexicon of abuse of authority (*Re-Establishing Justice*, 308 n. 122). He rests his case on Isa 10:2, where בזז is coupled with גזל. Indeed, it appears to take on this connotation in this passage, as well as in Ps 109:11. Yet, in these cases, בזז seems to be more metaphorical than reflective of the technical vocabulary of law. Hence, I would not include it.

121. For background materials on social justice in Israel and its ancient Near Eastern neighbors, see generally B. Birch, *Let Justice Roll Down: The Old Testament, Ethics, and Christian Life* (Louisville: Westminster John Knox, 1991); L. Epsztein, *Social Justice in the Ancient Near East and the People of the Bible* (trans. J. Bowen; London: SCM, 1986); F. C. Fensham, "Widow, Orphan, and the Poor in Ancient Near Eastern Legal and Wisdom Tradition," *JNES* 21 (1962): 129–39; Foster, "Social Reform," 165–75; H. Havice, "The Concern for the Widow and Fatherless in the Ancient Near East" (Ph.D. diss., Yale University, 1979); Mafico, "Just, Justice," 1127–29; B. V. Malchow, *Social Justice in the Hebrew Bible: What Is New and What Is Old* (Collegeville, Minn.: Liturgical Press, 1996); H. E. von Waldow, "Social Responsibility and Social Structure in Early Israel," *CBQ* 32 (1970): 182–204; Weinfeld, "Justice and Righteousness," 491–519; idem, *Justice and Righteousness in Israel and the Nations*; idem, *Social Justice in Ancient Israel and in the Ancient Near East* (Minneapolis: Fortress, 1995); and Westbrook, "Social Justice," 149–63.

12:1–24 and 14:2–22 demonstrate that means existed to chastise the king for any abuse of authority on his part.[122] It was assumed, however, that the ultimate defender of justice, Yahweh, would never participate in such inappropriate conduct. For example, Deut 10:17–18 teaches: "For Yahweh, your God, is God of gods and Lord of lords, the great God, mighty and awesome, who is not partial and takes no bribe. He executes justice for the orphan and the widow and loves the stranger, providing them food and clothing."

Job's problem is that, in his experience, God is violating the very principles of justice that he is supposed to be upholding as the court of final recourse. Instead of God serving as the final defender of social justice, he has become the greatest perpetrator against it. He is the very one whom Job believes is abusing his power. He is the corrupt judge. He is the one bribing witnesses. He is the one who has failed to protect the orphan and widow and supply the stranger. He is the one who created and maintains a corrupt justice system. Job believes that the law ought to apply equally to God.[123] Thus, the problem of abuse of authority is at the heart of Job's claim against God.

This is made unequivocal in 10:2–3 where Job says:

> Let me say to God, "Do not condemn (רשע) me;
>   make known to me why you bring suit (ריב) against me.
> Does it seem good to you to oppress (עשק),
>   that you reject the work of your hands,
>   but the designs of the wicked you favor?

This is a critical part of his speeches. He expects clarity on all charges. He demands a bill of particulars from God concerning the original charges against him (10:2). His use of the root ריב makes patent that Job knows beyond doubt that he is involved in a trial. We would expect that a charge of blasphemy would be on his mind due to his wife's remarks (2:9), but he wants to know the exact acts that constitute God's claim because he, frankly, cannot imagine what he might have done to cause God to file suit.

---

122. Psalms 18 [= 2 Samuel 22] and 101, which are royal psalms, also subtly indicate the role of the king in maintaining social justice. In them, the king is admonished to do justice.

123. F. Stier says of this: "Das Recht ist stärker als das 'Rechts des Stärkeren'. Das letztere hat Ijjob erfahren. Der Versuch seiner Freunde, ihm diese Erfahrung als Irrtum auszureden, ihm weiszumachen, daß Gott gerechtes Gericht, nicht Gewalt an ihm übe, ist gescheitert. Der 'Reinigungseid', die konkrete Entfaltung des *'tam'anî'*, [9, 21], setzt die Überzeugung voraus, daß das Rechtsein des Menschen kraft des status innocentiae im ethischen wie forensischen Sinne ein auch für Gott, verbindliches Recht schaffe, an das Gott gehalten sei, und daß er, sich nicht daran haltend, im Namen des Rechts zur Verantwortung und Wiedergutmachung des Unrechts gefordert werden können" (*Das Buch Ijjob*, 235).

He also names his fundamental legal claim against God in 10:3 with the verb עשק: abuse of authority.[124] Job's words have the same flavor as those of Jeremiah's accusation against God in Jer 12:1.

The language of abuse of authority is seen in other verses as well. In 6:8–9, Job utters words of desperation in response to his pain, saying:

> Would that my request find fulfillment,
>   that God grant my desire,
> that God would determine to crush (דכא) me,
>   that he would let loose his hand and ruin (בצע) me.

In chapter 19, when Job chastises his friends for the way they are treating him and requests that they assist him in his claims against God, he asks:

> How long with you grieve my soul,
>   and crush (דכא) me with arguments (מלה).

Job complains that God does not punish the wicked in 24:1–12. Twice Job uses גזל to demonstrate that the wicked abuse the poor:

> They remove boundary stones.
>   They seize flocks abusively (גזל) and pasture them . . . .
> They snatch (גזל) the orphan from the breast,
>   and distrain (חבל) upon the poor. (24:2, 9)[125]

God's failure to confront this wrong constitutes, from Job's perspective, God's own abuse of authority.

Others use the language of abuse of authority, as well. For example, in chastising Job, Eliphaz proclaims that the children of the fool cannot be successful and that his sons "are defeated (דכא) in the gate with no one to rescue them" (5:3b–4, quote at v. 4b). In chapter 20, Zophar defends God, using both גזל and רצץ to indicate that the wicked will not ultimately prosper:

> Because they legally defeated (רצץ) and disregarded the poor,
>   [because] they have gained through abuse of authority (גזל) a house
>     they did not build,
>   they knew no quiet in their bellies,
>     in their greed, they let nothing escape.

---

124. Westbrook states of this verse: "Job here pleads his case with God, asking why God has found against him while accepting the arguments of the wicked. In saying, 'Does it seem good to you to oppress ('šq)? (v. 3), Job is suggesting that that is what God's judgment in his case amounts to" (*Studies*, 35 n. 134). I agree that abuse of authority is the claim, but disagree that Job seeks postverdict relief.

125. Westbrook points out the significance of this verse for abuse of authority (*Studies*, 36). I follow his translation.

> There was nothing left after they had eaten;
> therefore, their prosperity will not endure. (20:19–21)

Zophar employs this vocabulary intentionally to transfer liability for suffering from God to the wicked. Bildad plays with alternative meanings of גזל when he asserts that God will bring judgment to the wicked:

> As drought and heat rob (גזל) snow waters,
>     so Sheol, those who have sinned (חטא). (24:19)[126]

The characters' use of the vocabulary of abuse of authority supports my claim that Job countersues God on these grounds.

We now examine the precise basis for Job's counterclaim. Ultimately, Job seeks to charge God with three specific counts of breaches of his divine juridical authority: (1) initiating a false suit; (2) violating the fundamental principles of social justice; and (3) failing to create an orderly universe from which justice should stem.[127]

Under Neo-Babylonian law, one could countersue for false accusation. The defendant argued, in these cases, that there was no reasonable basis on which to charge him with wrongdoing. The accuser did not have to be certain that the suspect perpetrated the specific harm alleged before he or she

---

126. I attribute 24:13–25 to Bildad, not Job. See ch. 1, n. 32 above.

127. In seeking to file a counterclaim against God on these three counts, Job makes an unintentional error owing to his ignorance concerning the incident in the Divine Council. He intends to charge God with the false suit when the Satan is the actual plaintiff in Job's case. The counterclaim on the first count should run against the Satan. Job's other two counts are rightfully brought against God. These two counts are not, however, technically counterclaims in American legal parlance. They are either cross-claims or impleader actions. A cross-claim is an accusation lodged by a party against his or her co-plaintiff or a co-defendant in a suit (BLD, 375). If God is also criminally charged for aiding and abetting Job, then these are cross-claims against his co-defendant in the suit. If God is only under political attack, then Job has impleaded God, who was a party outside the original suit, in order to bring related claims against him. For more on impleader accusations, see ch. 3, n. 52 above. We do not have a clear instance of a cross-claim among the Neo-Babylonian records in our document sample. This lack may result from the separation of such suits, or it may be attributable to the brevity of the records and the fact that they are typically written for the benefit of the ultimate winner of the case. It is possible that some of what appear to be impleader accusations are actually cross-claims. Which they might be turns on exactly when a given party enters a suit and when the accusation is made, because impleader accusations run against non-parties for the purpose of joining them to the suit and cross-accusations run against persons already made parties to the suit. The Neo-Babylonian records are not always clear with regard to such matters. In spite of how we readers might understand the legal nuances of the situation because we are aware of the events in the Divine Council, Job thinks that God is his plaintiff. Job, therefore, brings a three-count counteraccusation against him. The friends also understand Job's suit in this way. Consequently, we will examine Job's specific allegations from the perspective of the human characters. Later, however, we will see that God, knowing the true story, will respond accordingly.

brought suit; he or she did, however, have to have reasonable grounds upon which to sue. If none existed, a false-suit claim would stand.

The Hebrew Bible also prohibits false suit (Exod 20:16; 23:7; Deut 19:16–21; and Prov 19:5, 9).[128] The principle of *lex talionis* operated in such suits; the accuser might suffer the same penalty that his victim would have suffered had he been convicted (Deut 19:19), although the victim could elect to reduce the penalty of his false accuser (Deut 22:13–21).[129] The threat of false-suit penalties is what gives Jacob the ability to demand of Laban that he back up his accusation with a suit before the assembly of kinsmen on Jacob's alleged theft of his household gods (Gen 31:36–37). It is also what provokes Laban into signing a covenant to settle the matter (Gen 31:44).[130]

We see the law of false suit applied in a situation involving blasphemy in 1 Kgs 21:1–29. There Queen Jezebel, in an abuse of Ahab's and her authority, instigates a false suit against Naboth on a charge of blasphemy in order to secure his death and obtain his vineyard for King Ahab through the action of legal forfeiture. Naboth and his sons were executed in accord with the rule that both the blasphemer and his line are subject to capital punishment.[131] After Ahab acquired the vineyard, God confronted him through the prophet Elijah on his complicity in the murder. Although he was not confronted directly on the means used in the murder—that is, the false suit—Ahab had to suffer the consequences of participating in the false suit. He and Jezebel were subject to death and the destruction of their line (1 Kgs 21:19–24; 2 Kgs 9:1–10:17). Just as the dogs licked up Naboth's blood, so the dogs must lick up the blood of Ahab, Jezebel, and their line (1 Kgs 21:19, 23–24; 2 Kgs 9:36–37; cf. 2 Kgs 9:26). Only Ahab's repentance mitigated the actual punishment levied against him (1 Kgs 21:27–29).

Job and God stand in opposite positions from those of Ahab and God. Job counteraccuses God for false suit because he believes that God has no reasonable basis for his suit—a blasphemy suit at that—against Job.[132] Job begins his legal attack on the first count, false suit and abuse of the legal process, immediately upon speaking. His "primal scream" in chapter 3 is more than a venting of his intense pain; it begins his confrontation of God using legal means. From the minute he opens his mouth in 3:1, Job builds toward a countersuit against God on abuse of authority. He enters, in the words of J. A. Wharton, a "titanic struggle with God."[133] In order to com-

---

128. Cf. Zech 8:17b; Prov 12:17; 14:5; 21:28; 25:18. See further Wells, *Law of Testimony*, 134–57.
129. Ibid., 155–57.
130. See Mabee, "Jacob and Laban," 192–207.
131. The sons' deaths are revealed in 2 Kgs 9:25–26.
132. See Bovati, *Re-Establishing Justice*, 115.
133. Wharton, *Job*, 4.

prehend the legal character of Job's first major speech, we must compare it to Jeremiah's speech after Jeremiah's groundless arrest and flogging by Pashhur. In Jer 20:7a, Jeremiah cries out to God:

> You ensnared (פתה) me, O Yahweh, and I was ensnared (פתה);
> You overpowered (חזק) me and you prevailed (יכל).

He feels trapped by the word of Yahweh that burns within him and causes him to be subject to public scorn and false legal accusations and trial (Jer 20:7b–10). Verse 10 is especially important:

> I heard many whispers of the crowd—
>   terror surrounding:
> "Accuse (נגד) him! Let us accuse (נגד) him!"[134]
>   All my friends,
>   watching for me to stumble, say:
> "Perhaps he can be ensnared (פתה),
>   and we can prevail (יכל) against him
>   and take our vengeance on him.

There is a profound connection between Yahweh's call on him and the people's groundless legal charges. The first causes the second. Yahweh is setting him up for the suits that flow from Jeremiah's unpopular prophetic speeches. To Jeremiah's way of thinking, the result is that both Yahweh and the people have ensnared (פתה) him and both will prevail (יכל). God, therefore, is the ultimate cause of his legal entanglements. This hurts Jeremiah even more because Yahweh is obligated to protect him from harassing lawsuits that involve abuse of the legal process, not cause such suits.[135] Nonetheless, Jeremiah continues to hope that God will honor their agreement and bring him victory in these harassing earthly lawsuits. Jeremiah demands that Yahweh, "who investigates (בחן) the innocent (צדיק), who sees the emotions (כליות) and the intentions (לב)" of humanity, bring Jeremiah's vengeance (20:12).[136] Jeremiah clearly expects Yahweh, when summoned, to investigate the parties' respective guilt and innocence and to decide in his favor. As T. Mafico observes:

> Since God requites all people according to their just deserts [sic], those who felt innocent of any wrongdoing against other people, and who had

---

134. The verb נגד, in both the *hiphil* and *hophal*, marks a legal accusation; it means to inform a judicial authority of an legally inappropriate act (Bovati, *Re-Establishing Justice*, 71, 74). See, e.g., Gen 31:22; 38:24; Deut 17:4; Josh 2:14, 20; 1 Sam 14:33; 1 Kgs 2:41; Prov 29:24; cf. Esth 2:22; Lev 5:1.

135. This is discussed more fully in the material at nn. 67–70 above.

136. See further 20:11–13. The kidneys (כליות) were the seat of the emotions in the worldview of the ancient Israelites.

not transgressed God's law, summoned God to test, try, or examine them to verify their uprightness in order that he might judge (*špṭ*) them accordingly (Ps 139:23–24). In making this summons, God was invoked to reward the wicked according to their wickedness and the upright in heart according to their righteousness (Ps 94:1–3).[137]

God should investigate Jeremiah's claims and declare him victorious.

Whatever Jeremiah's hopes and expectations might be, the fact remains that he is in enormous legal trouble and physical pain now. Consequently, from 20:14 to 20:18, he curses both the day he was born and the man who announced his birth. Jeremiah desires, no less than Job, to have died in the womb. He believes that his tortuous legal troubles are the direct result of an unfair, unjustified legal process and that God has failed him in obtaining its resolution. Through his curse and longing, Jeremiah places responsibility for his troubles squarely on God, and he expects God to resolve the matter.[138] Jeremiah's speech, therefore, informs us about Job's thinking when he, too, curses the day of his birth and wishes that he had suffered his demise on that day (3:3–22).

Job addresses both his unwarranted arrest and unsupportable, tortuous investigative process in his speeches. He is quite explicit about his upset over God's uncontrollable arrest powers in 9:12a: "Look! He arrests (חתף)! Who can restrain (שוב) him?" He continues in 12:14b: "If he imprisons (סגר), none can release." Zophar agrees with Job concerning this matter:

If he passes by and imprisons (סגר)
and calls one to the assembly (קהל),[139]
who can restrain (שוב) him? (11:10)

Clines acknowledges, when speaking about Job's de facto imprisonment in 13:27, that Job is concerned about improper trial procedure: "Such acts of close arrest carry legal implications: God should follow up his arrest with the formulation of charges, but if that does not happen, he is behaving like a gangster...."[140] Actually, Job considers God a gangster for arresting him in the first place and bringing all the subsequent horror down upon his head.

With regard to God's investigative powers, Job complains that God's inspections are excessive and do not produce the proper results (7:17–19;

---

137. Mafico, "Just, Justice," 1128–29.
138. Holladay maintains that the book of Job builds on the Jeremiah passages and not the reverse ("Jeremiah's Lawsuit," 285). The fullness of the Job passages in comparison to those in Jeremiah would lead to this conclusion (see ibid.). I concur. For discussion of the dating of the book of Job, see ch. 1 n. 13 above.
139. For judgment.
140. Clines, *Job 1–20*, 323.

10:6–7). Job recounts God's great power over his life and the time when God seemed to use that power to the good (10:9–12). God was, however, really lying in wait for him:

> Yet this was your secret intention (צפן בלבבך),
> I know this was your purpose,
> that, if I sinned (חטא), you would mark (שמר) me,
> and would not acquit (נקה) me of my iniquities (עון)! (10:13–14)

Verse 14 is to be compared with Ps 130:2–3, where the Psalmist asserts:

> Lord, hear my voice!
> Let your ears be attentive to the voice of my petition (תפלה)!<sup>141</sup>
> If you, O Yah, Lord, would mark (שמר) iniquities (עון),
> who could stand (עמד)?

Job knows that no good can come of God's hyper-vigilant inspection. Job reports that God treats him as though he were chaos itself:

> Am I the Sea or the Dragon,
> that you set a guard (משמר) over me? (7:12)<sup>142</sup>

Additionally, Job's many laments about his condition indicate that he believes that his pain is excessive.

Job also thinks that God is overly demanding with respect to compliance with his law. He should be more forgiving. He leaves no room for reasonable error (7:20–21; 13:26). Instead of tossing Job into this abusive legal action, God should treat Job with the care expected of the deity.

> O that you would hide me in Sheol,
> conceal me until your anger relented (שוב),
> set an appointed time to remember me.
> If a mortal dies, can he live again?
> All the days of my service, I would wait until my release comes.
> You would call (קרא), and I would answer you (ענה);
> you would long for your handiwork.
> Then you would [not] count my steps,
> or mark (שמר) my sin (חטאת).
> Sealing my transgression (פשע) in a pouch,
> you would cover over my iniquity (עון). (14:13–17)

Twice in Isaiah, God says that, if called, he will answer (58:9; 65:24). The Psalmist informs us three times that God will answer if called (Ps 3:5; 17:6–

---

141. On the legal significance of תפלה, see the material at nn. 152–54 below.
142. See further R. Raphael, "Things Too Wonderful: A Disabled Reading of Job," *PRSt* 31 (2004): 399–424.

7; and 120:1–2). Once the Psalmist calls on God to answer (4:2).[143] Job remembers the loving response of Yahweh. He therefore believes that God should call to him with loving-kindness instead of summoning him before a court. God should let him answer out of devotion instead of demanding a legal answer. God should look the other way when he commits infractions instead of expecting scrupulous conduct because such infractions could only have been unwitting, minor, or done in the folly of youth (6:24b; 13:26; and 19:4).[144] God should treat him as the creature of God that he is (10:8a, 9–12; 12:9–10; 30:19; and 31:15) instead of treating him like a legal adversary (איב) worthy of inspection and destruction (13:24; cf. 10:8b).[145] As Job understands it, God owes him a duty of care because he is Job's creator; God is breaching that duty.

Moreover, Job does not believe that God has grounds for the suit. He accuses God of false suit while protesting his innocence. Repeatedly, Job declares that God is attempting to convict him even though he is guiltless. He says in 9:20b: "[Though] I am honorable (תם), he would make me crooked (עקש)." The word for "crooked," עקש, twists and, thereby, plays anagrammatically off of one of the prime words meaning "abuse of authority," עשק. God's twisted accusation that Job is crooked is the abuse. Furthermore, Job asserts, in 9:30–31, that no matter how he tries to cleanse (זכך) himself, God will still cast him into the pit and, in that state, even his clothing would abhor him. Job uses a double antanaclasis to get his point across. First, the metaphor of washing, marked with the root זכך, is often used as a declaration of innocence in the Hebrew Bible.[146] Second, the word שחת can refer to a pit in the dirt.[147] As a result, some translate this word as "muck," consistent with the idea that Job cannot get clean and that even his clothes would find him disgusting in this condition. The word שחת can also signify, however, the Pit of Sheol.[148] Thus, Job thinks that he cannot ever be guilt-free (זך) under God's jurisdiction and, therefore, God will condemn him to the Pit.

Significantly, Job unintentionally plays on the dispute between God and the Satan regarding cause in 1:9 and 2:3, when he contests this suit against him:

---

143. We also learn in Proverbs, however, that God will not answer the wicked if called (21:12–13).

144. See further ch. 7 below.

145. J. Milgrom, "The Cultic שגגה and Its Influence in Psalms and Job," *JQR* 58 (1967): 115–25. Bovati notes that איב does not, in this context, mean "enemy" but "legal adversary" (*Re-Establishing Justice*, 296). Many have spoken on the play between Job's name and this word; understanding איב as a legal adversary makes this wordplay more apparent.

146. On the use of the metaphor of washing as a declaration of innocence in the Hebrew Bible, see Bovati, *Re-Establishing Justice*, 113.

147. See, e.g., Pss 7:16; 9:16; 35:7; 94:13; Prov 26:27.

148. See, e.g., Pss 16:10; 49:10; 55:24; Isa 51:14; Ezek 28:8; Jonah 2:7.

> For he crushes (שׁוּף) me with a tempest,
> and multiplies my wounds without cause (חנם). (9:17)

No grounds for this suit exist. Job emphasizes this point in 16:9a when he says that God "hates" (שׂטם) him (16:9a). This root is a by-form of the root שׂטן, from which the Satan's name originates.[149] Certainly the meaning of the two roots includes *to hate* or *to be opposed*.[150] They also signify, however, "to accuse legally."[151] Thus, another double entendre exists because of the two meanings of the word. God hates Job in his rage, but God also accuses him in his rage. God is, from Job's perspective, the Satan, and he brings this suit with no justification. It is nothing but harassment (13:25–26).

The confusion of God with the Satan on account of Job's ignorance concerning the incident in the Divine Council is not surprising and has not clearly been acknowledged in the text. As a result of the divine suit, Job has wrongfully been stripped of his dignity and the respect of others, and shame has replaced pride (10:15; 16:10–11; 17:6; 19:9, 13b–19; 21:1–30; 29:2–17, 21–25; 30:1–14, 15c, 21–22, 26, 29). Job expected to live out his life in full vigor with his family (29:18–20), but it does not look like that will happen now. This result should be for the guilty (31:3), not for Job because he knows:

> ... there is no violence (חמס) in my hands,
> and my petition (תפלה) is guilt-free (זך) (16:17).

Job has perpetrated injustice on no one.

This verse holds significance deeper than its protestation of innocence. It is also a call for justice. Z. W. Falk observes:

> Some forms of biblical prayer were clearly influenced by legal procedure. Hebrew thought ... described the relations between God and man under the rule of law, and from there resulted some specific patterns of worship. The usual term for prayer, *tefilah*, was derived from the root *palal*, meaning to judge, to assess, to estimate, and to intervene. Originally a person praying to God asserted his righteousness and asked God to do justice.[152]

---

149. See Gen 27:41; 49:23; 50:13; Hos 9:8; Ps 55:3; cf. Gen. 26:21.
150. See Num 22:22, 32; 1 Sam 29:4; 1 Kgs 5:18; 11:14, 23, 25.
151. See 2 Sam 19:23; Zech 3:1–2; Pss 38:21; 71:13; 109:4, 6, 20, 29; Ezra 4:6.
152. Z.W. Falk, *Hebrew Law in Biblical Times* (Jerusalem: Wahrmann Books, 1964), 52, citing Gemser, "*Rîb*-Pattern," 126; E. A. Speiser, "The Root *pll* in Hebrew," *JBL* 82 (1963): 301–6; and D. R. Ap-Thomas, "Notes on Some Terms Relating to Prayer," *VT* 6 (1956): 230–31. The relationship between law and prayer in the lawsuit genres is more fully developed by S. H. Blank, "The Confessions of Jeremiah and the Meaning of Prayer," *HUCA* 21 (1948): 337–38; and A. Laytner, *Arguing with God: A Jewish Tradition* (Northvale, N.J.: Jason Aronson, 1990), xvii–xviii, 1–39.

P. Bovati explains that the word תפלה is typically connected to supplication for a pardon.[153] He continues, however: "The prayer that asks for amnesty . . . can be transformed into a complaint against the executor of justice."[154] This would hold true in cases of abuse of authority. Job's claim is that a terrible injustice is being done to him, and God should right it or pay the cost.

The case is not only false; it is rigged according to Job. This rigging is highly reminiscent of Jezebel's work in 1 Kings 21. Job testifies that God abuses the legal process in a number of ways in order to get his desired results. First, God will not really listen to Job's defense and give him justice. Job 27:2 comes in the midst of Job's defense. He complains:

> The living God has deprived me of my case (משפט)!
> and Shaddai has embittered my soul (27:2).

Second, God will not necessarily answer Job's summons (4:18; 19:7; 30:20). Even if he did answer, he might not really hear what Job has to say (9:16), presumably giving Job an inadequate answer. Third, God even goes so far as to twist Job's words in order to get a conviction: "Though I am innocent (צדק), my mouth would condemn (רשע) me" (19:20a). The meaning of this verse is clarified by 16:7b–8a, where Job says to God: "You have destroyed my witness-testimony. / You have seized me to be a witness [against myself]."[155] God is powerful, relentless, cruel, and unpredictable (9:12–13; 10:16; 12:10, 16; 24:1; 30:21; 31:23). He continually renews his witness against Job (10:17).[156] Job even goes so far as to imply that God bribes Job's friends with a share of his property for their false testimony against him (17:5), thereby turning them into the scoundrels (בני־בליעל) of Ahab's court.

---

153. Bovati, *Re-Establishing Justice*, 126, 154, 311.
154. Ibid., 311–12 n. 128.
155. Here I reject the traditional reading of עדה in 16:7b as "community" in favor of "witness-testimony," which maintains the wordplay between עדה and עד. Furthermore, in 16:8a, I follow the usual translation of קמט, "to seize," instead of the proposed and readily accepted "to shrivel."
156. Job asserts that God continues to hunt him down like prey (10:16a) and renews his "witnesses against him" (10:17a). For this translation, see, e.g. Clines, *Job 1–20*, 215, 222. God increases his anger toward Job (10:17b) and sends "an ever-changing array of hosts against him" (10:17c) (following Habel, who reads the literal "change and a host" as a hendiadys, meaning "changing array of troops" [*Book of Job: Commentary*, 181, 184]). These metaphors seem incongruous, which has led several commentators to emend the first and last colon of 10:17; however, this is not necessary. According to Bovati, both hunting and military metaphors are used to describe legal contests (*Re-Establishing Justice*, 265 n. 21, 296–98, 302 n. 107). He notes that the adversary may be presented as a fierce animal. He cites Job 4:10–11; 5:15; 10:16–17; and 29:17 in support of his contention. Thus, a legal shadow is cast over 10:16–17. Job's reference to God's renewal of witnesses against him is significant. Job is expressing how overwhelmed he is by the prosecution. It is powerful, and it is abusive.

God's anger is immense (9:5b, 13; 10:17; 14:13; 16:9; 21:17; 36:33). God is terrifying (23:15–16). His hand is dangerous and highly intimidating. Job demands:

> Only stop doing two things to me,
>   then I will not hide myself from your face!
> Withdraw your hand far from me,
>   and let not dread of you terrify me. (13:20–21)

Under these conditions alone can Job square off fairly with God. God's divine status also puts him in a different class of being, which makes it difficult for Job to sue him (9:32; 10:4–5; 21:22). Additionally, God hides from Job and is not easily confronted (9:11; 23:3–9; cf. 13:24). Between the disparity in their power and all this trickery, the case's probable outcome is that Job will be wrongfully convicted. God appears to be unstoppable (23:14).

Yet another cause of Job's likely conviction exists: there is no judge to protect Job from God. Eliphaz is, remarkably, the first to acknowledge that it will take some outsider to hear Job's claim, when he asks, in 5:1b, "To which holy one will you turn?" He is not referring here to the one who might answer Job in the role of defendant. God is the counter-defendant here. Rather, Eliphaz is inquiring as to who might hear Job's case. Under Neo-Babylonian law, parties with this much authority could be judges, although the disputes usually involved only economic harm. In the ancient world, however, the type of harm was not the most important criterion in determining whether a party could be a judge. It was the power and status of the plaintiff. God or the king could serve as a judge in a case where an underling had injured him (e.g., 1 Sam 22:11–16; Isa 3:13–15).[157] Such "hierarchal" trials were quite common in the ancient Near East.[158] God certainly is Job's superior in this case. Nonetheless, one could not judge a claim of abuse of authority lodged against oneself because the plaintiff would be most unlikely to gain relief. Because of this difficulty and because these claims were so critical to the proper functioning of ancient society, the king himself heard most of these claims. God heard all claims against the king. Who, however, can hear Job's claim? There is no one above God. He is the king above all other kings. Thus, Eliphaz taunts Job that, indeed, no one can hear his claim. Consequently, Eliphaz asserts that it is sheer foolishness to bring it. Job, too, admits the problem.[159] In 9:19 he despairs of one to convene the court for him:

---

157. This rule applies in cases of other injured hierarchical superiors as well (see Westbrook, "Biblical Law," 10).

158. Ibid.

159. On the impossibility of finding a judge to hear this claim, see Bovati, *Re-Establishing Justice*, 34, 81; cf. Dick, "Legal Metaphor," 45–49. See further F. R. Magdalene, "Who Is Job's Redeemer? Job 19:25 in Light of Neo-Babylonian Law," *ZABR* 10 (2004): 292–316.

If this is a trial of strength—he is the strong one.
If this is a court case (משפט)—who can convene [it] for me?[160]

He returns to this idea, despairing of a judge who will protect him from God's violence:

There is no judge (מוכיח) between us,[161]
   who might lay his hand upon us both,
that he might take his rod away from me,
   and that dread of him might not terrify me,
Thus, I will speak and fear him not,
   for I am not my usual self. (9:33–35)

He despairs of one to rescue him from God's hand (10:7b). He again laments the seeming lack of a judge in 31:35a: "O that I had someone to judge (שמע) for me."[162] To what court can he truly turn? Job knows that this lack is a major hindrance to his cause. Job, therefore, wonders why he should bother at all with the cards stacked against him as they are:

---

160. The vast majority of commentators suggest that the translation of מי יועידני should be "who can summon him?" This takes the *hiphil* of יעד as "to summons," as in Jer 49:19 [= 50:44]. One problem with this proposal is that this line of Job's worrying follows closely his concern over what will happen should he summon his opponent (19:16). Job has not been fretting over the logistics of his issuance of the summons but, rather, the effect of any summons he might issue. It does not make complete sense to argue that Job now does not suppose that he or anyone else can summon God at all. His statements up to this point indicate that he believes he can. Further, the usual translation proposal requires emendation of the first common singular pronominal suffix to the third masculine singular, against the MT and the LXX. As a result, Habel suggests that the suffix be taken as dative: "—who will arraign [him] for me" (*Book of Job: Commentary*, 182–83). It is more likely that Job is now shifting his thoughts, for a moment, to the logistics of the case itself, that is, who has the power to hear the case. The phrase מי יועידני may refer to the summons power of the court, as the Neo-Babylonian records reflect. I propose that Job is really asking: What court can summon God for me? In order to use language that is clearer to the English reader, we turn to Bovati. He believes יעד signifies "to convene before a court" (*Re-Establishing Justice*, 223 n. 8). I suggest that Job uses יעד to signify "convening a court."

161. Most translate מוכיח as "umpire," "mediator," or "arbiter." See, e.g., Clines, *Job 1–20*, 215; Good, *In Turns of Tempest*, 75; Habel, *Book of Job: Commentary*, 180; NIV; NJB; NJPS; NRSV; and NASV. This reduces the power of this individual in the minds of English readers. As discussed in the material at nn. 21–23 above, the root יכח in the *hithpael* conveys two primary meanings. First, it can mean "to accuse," "to correct," "to reprove," or "to chastise." It can also mean, however, "to decide a lawsuit," "to judge," or "to adjudicate." See, e.g., Gen 31:37, 42; Isa 2:4 [= Mic 4:3]; 11:3; Ps 94:10. Although the second meaning of the root is not the most common meaning of יכח in the book of Job, it is in operation here. It is a synonym of שפט (see esp. Isa 2:4 [= Mic 4:3]). Hence, the best translation of מוכיח in this instance is "judge" or "adjudicator." The author's choice of מוכיח instead of שפט is probably intentional. It plays on the wisdom/law duality that can be found throughout the book.

162. A hearer (שמע) was a judge in ancient Israel. See, e.g., Deut 1:16; 2 Sam 15:3; 1 Kgs 3:11.

I will be convicted (רשע).
Why then should I labor in vain? (9:29)[163]

Thus, Job believes that God has brought a false suit against him, one that he cannot possibly win because the legal system is so heavily under the influence of God.

Job is distressed not only by God's handling of his situation; he is also distressed by God's relationship with social justice and the legal system as a whole. The second count of Job's claim relates to his perception that God violates rather than upholds the fundamental principles of justice. God is expected, in ancient Israel, to maintain social order and eradicate inequities, not cause them.[164] R. V. Bergren observes that the prophets stand for the proposition that God's law "has teeth."[165] In Psalm 82, God sues members of the Divine Council for failing to maintain social justice. There the Psalmist says:

> ... God has taken his place in the Divine Council,
>     among the gods he judges:
> "How long will you judge falsely
>     and be biased toward the wicked? ..." (vv. 1–2)

God orders the "gods, children of the Most High" (v. 6), to:

> Judge [fairly] (שפט) the weak and the orphaned;
>     vindicate (צדק) the right of the lowly and the poor!
> Rescue the weak and the needy!
>     Deliver them from the hand of the wicked!
> They have neither knowledge nor understanding,
>     they go about in darkness;
>     all the foundations of the earth are shaken. (vv. 3–5)

---

163. Some translate this phrase to mean that Job recognizes that he has already suffered judgment from God (i.e., "I am convicted" or "I was convicted" [see, e.g., NASB, NCV, NIV, NJB]), but this is inconsistent with the concern Job has for defending the suit, which he exhibits in 9:14–15 and in the rest of his speeches. Job worries constantly about whether his counterclaim and defense can be successful, but this presumes that he still has the opportunity to try the case. This file is open, and Job intends to respond to the pending charges and to challenge God's abuse of the legal process.

164. See Mafico, "Just, Justice," 1129. Inequities were not, however, necessarily inequalities. Westbrook correctly notes: "The concept of social justice in such a society was not at all one of equality, nor was it identified with the relief of poverty as such. . . . Social justice was conceived rather as protecting the weaker strata of society from being unfairly deprived of their due: the legal status, property rights, and economic condition to which their position on the hierarchical ladder entitled them" ("Social Justice," 149). The principles of social justice did not seek to alter that hierarchy.

165. Bergren, *Prophets and Law*, 89.

The verdict against them strips them of their immortality (vv. 6–8). Job wants the protection of justice from God no less than the deity expects it from his children.

Yet Job's experience tells him that God does not, in fact, protect those whom he should protect. Rather, he has the characteristics of a corrupt judge, and he perverts justice generally. God abuses his authority not only with respect to Job but with respect to all humans. Job repeatedly challenges God on whether he is fulfilling the basic guidelines of social justice. Job believes he is entitled to prosecute this issue because he claims that he is a witness to God's violations of social justice:

> Indeed, my eye has seen all this;
>   my ear has heard and understood it. (13:1)

B. Wells has pointed out that when a witness sees with the eye or hears with the ear, he or she is an eyewitness.[166] Job has great knowledge because he is a direct observer of God's failure. Moreover, he is not the only one who is a witness to God's breach of social justice. Even the beasts, birds, fish, and earth know that God lets the guilty go free (12:6–10).

Job accuses God of failing in his general duty of care when he says regarding his own situation:

> Is not calamity for the iniquitous (עון);
>   misfortune, for the wrongdoer (און)? (31:3)

He asserts that God does not distinguish between the innocent and the guilty. God destroys the honorable and the guilty alike:

> It is all one; therefore, I say,
>   he destroys both the honorable (תם) and the guilty (רשע). (9:22)

These words are reminiscent of Abraham's when he argued for the salvation of Sodom:

> Then Abraham came forward and said, "Will you indeed sweep away the innocent (צדיק) with the guilty (רשע)? Suppose there are fifty righteous within the city; will you then sweep away the place and not forgive it for the fifty righteous who are in it? Far be it from you to do such a thing, to slay the innocent (צדיק) with the guilty (רשע), so that the innocent (צדיק) fare as the guilty (רשע)! Far be that from you! Shall not the judge (שפט) of all the earth do justice (משפט)?" (Gen 18:23–25)

God is not holding up his end of the bargain.

---

166. Wells, *Law of Testimony*, 64–66, 78. One who knows is typically a hearsay witness, although on occasion one who hears is also a hearsay witness (see further, "שמע," *HALOT*, 1575).

Moreover, Job alleges that both the fortunate and the unfortunate come to the same end: death (24:23–26). He says that, if some roving, scourging natural disaster (שׁוֹט) "causes sudden death, God mocks the calamity of the innocent (נקה)" (9:23).[167] Job devotes a great deal of attention to God's apparent favoring of the wicked. He delivers the earth into their hands (9:24a). He smiles on their counsel (10:3). The tents of robbers are at peace (12:6a). Those who provoke God are secure (12:6b). They are under God's protection (12:6c).[168] God controls both those who stray and those who lead astray (12:16b). Job indulges in a long discourse on God's failure to punish the wicked (21:7–22, 30–33, esp. v. 9b). In 21:7, he complains much like Jeremiah in Jer 12:1b:

> Why do the wicked live on,
> reach old age, and grow mighty in power?

Job re-emphasizes a few of these points in 24:2–4a. God's failure has severe consequences according to Job:

> ... all the poor of the land are forced into hiding.
> Like the wild asses of the wilderness,
>     they go about their toil,
> seeking prey in the wasteland,
>     food for their young.
> They harvest fodder in the field,
>     and glean in the vineyards of the wicked.
> They pass the night naked, for lack of clothing,
>     and have no covering against the cold.
> They are drenched by the mountain rains,
>     and huddle against the rock for lack of shelter.
> They snatch (גזל) the orphan from the breast,
>     and distrain (חבל) upon the poor.

---

167. We notice that God also caught the virtuous Job in his destructive net and that the roving Satan sent roving disasters upon Job. Count 1 is not terribly far from Job's mind. This is made especially obvious in the use of the word מסת in 9:23b. Commentators have discussed at length whether מסת is from the root מסס, thereby giving the meaning "to despair" or "to fail" (see, e.g., NAB; NASB; NIV; NJB; and Pope, *Job*, 69), whether it is "what causes one to fail or despair," that is, "a calamity" (see, e.g., Clines, *Job 1–20*, 214, 218; JB; JPS; NEB; RV; and Rowley, *Job*, 96), or whether it is from the root נסה, "to test" or "to investigate" (see, e.g., Kissane, *Book of Job*, 49; KJV; NRSV; and RSV). I believe that "calamity" makes the most sense here in order to maintain the parallelism of the verse, but I doubt that the wordplay, based on the root נסה, was lost on the author of Job. In the ancient world, calamities were often thought of as tests from, or investigations by, the divine, and they certainly constitute part of God's investigation of Job.

168. Following Clines, *Job 1–20*, 291–92.

> They go about naked for lack of clothing,
>> though, hungry, carry sheaves.
> Between rows [of olive trees], they make oil,
>> they tread the winepresses though thirsty.
> From the city, the dying groan,
>> and the souls of the fatally wounded cry out (שׁוע) .... (24:4b–12b)

Notwithstanding these dreadful effects, Job claims that "God pays no attention to their petition (תפלה)"[169] (24:12c). The lowly, the poor, and the hurt cry out in judicial protest, but God does not answer. God does not protect them. Rather, he blesses the strong (24:22–23).[170] What is happening to Job is happening to the many.

God is not, to Job's mind, the great equalizer. Death is. When Job is wishing for death in 3:11–19, he is doing more than putting God on notice that he will countersue on the first count. He is also testifying about the inequalities of life and how it is death, not God's justice, that finally levels the uneven playing field. Job claims that, in death, the wicked cease their raging (3:17a) and the weary of strength get their rest (3:17b). Prisoners no longer must contend with their taskmasters' voices and are finally at ease (3:18). Slaves are also free from their masters (3:19b). There the small and the great are alike (3:19a). This is noteworthy because the phrase "small and great" is similar to the expression "old and young" used in Neo-Babylonian documents to signify an assembly of the people who have gathered for some important purpose, such as to hear a message from the king.[171] Everyone is there. R. N. Whybray observes:

> Job sums up all of humanity in terms of three socio-economic classes: two kinds of free persons, small and great (that is powerless and powerful) and the slaves. It is to the last of these that death comes as the greatest relief.... Job identifies himself with the most wretched of all human beings, for whom death would be preferable to life. The whole passage (vv. 18–23) is remarkable in that it gives indirect expression to the voice of the oppressed.[172]

---

169. Reading with the Syriac. Habel notes that repointing the MT loses "the ironic interplay with 1:22" (*Book of Job: Commentary*, 354), but I believe that the connection between שׁוע and תפלה is the more significant interplay.

170. Job 24:13–17, 21 also address the wicked. A more literal rendering of 24:18–20, 24, as represented by the RSV and NRSV, seems to indicate a contradiction in Job's words, suggesting that the blessings of the wicked are short-lived. The solution of the NJPS, wherein these verses represent what Job thinks ought to happen, is the better rendering; however, these verses are not included in the main discussion here because of their difficulty.

171. See the material at ch. 3 n. 27 above.

172. Whybray, *Job*, 39.

God has failed to bring justice to the people. Death is the real hero, and Job longs for it in 3:20–26.[173] S. Terrien states Job's view beautifully: "Death is the only genetrix of man's hollow desires for liberty, fraternity, and equality."[174]

God not only abandons the innocent in favor of the wicked; he disrupts nations, governments, and judicial structures. He leads once-great nations astray, scattering some, destroying others (12:23). He strips kings of the symbols of their power (12:18). He deranges the minds of the peoples' leaders, and they wander aimlessly in the dark or like drunkards (12:24–25). He pours contempt on the great (12:21a). He makes counselors wander naked (12:17a). He blindfolds the earth's judges that they may be corrupt (9:24b). He also makes them go mad (12:17b). He takes away the discernment of elders that they may not judge (12:20b). He subverts temple officials (12:19b). He causes priests to wander naked (12:19a). He weakens the valiant (12:21b). He renders the trusted speechless (12:20a). When God acts, his work cannot be reversed: "If he tears down, none can rebuild" (12:14a). God is a terrible force with which to contend. He will have his way—and that is anything but just.

Job's third count is the most important of all. It speaks to whether God really is the font of justice. Job contends that the very structure of the universe does not denote that God, in fact, stemmed chaos and brought order to the cosmos. Rather, it is bedlam. How can God possibly create justice from such a genesis as this? N. C. Habel asserts that in chapter 3 Job summons, via incantations, "forces of darkness against his origin and makes nasty allegations about God's *modus operandi* in the design of human life."[175] E. F. Beach declares:

> Job's cursing the day of his birth does call into question God's management of the cosmos. . . . Job learns from the Yhwh speeches that most of the cosmos is *not* subject to meaningful justice; good fortune may come like rain to the desert (38:26), and misfortune may come like the fate of the trampled ostrich egg (39:14–15).[176]

The result of God's work is human misery. God is its first cause.

---

173. Job's complicated and unusual relationship with death is well explained by S. Boorer, "A Matter of Life and Death: A Comparison of Proverbs 1–9 and Job," in *Prophets and Paradigms: Essays in Honor of Gene M. Tucker* (ed. S. B. Reid; JSOTSup 229; Sheffield: Sheffield Academic, 1996), 187–204. Whybray also notes that Job's view of death "is virtually without parallel in the Old Testament" (*Job*, 38).

174. S. Terrien, *Job: Poet of Existence* (Indianapolis: Bobbs-Merrill, 1957), 47.

175. Habel, *Book of Job: Commentary*, 102, relying on M. Fishbane, "Jeremiah 4:23–26 and Job 3:3–13: A Recovered Use of the Creation Pattern," *VT* 21 (1971): 151–67.

176. Beach, "More Righteous than God," 9–10.

This misery has, to Job's mind, everything to do with the quality and quantity of human existence. Job asserts that life is suffering and embitters the spirit (3:20). God created humanity blind (3:23a). He hedges us in:

> [Why is life given] to those whose way is hidden,
>   whom God has hedged (סוך) in? (3:23b)

God's hedge is not at all what the Satan claims (1:10). God is not giving succor to Job or to any human being. Human life is hard labor:

> Do not human beings have a hard service on earth,
>   and are not their days like the days of a laborer?
> Like a slave who longs for the shadow,
>   and like laborers who look for their wages,
> so I am allotted months of emptiness,
>   and apportioned nights of misery. (7:1–3)

Part of human suffering is how short life really is. Death is not a happy event, even if it is the great equalizer. Throughout chapter 14, Job complains bitterly about the shortness of life and its effects:

> Furthermore, mortals, born of woman,
>   few of days and full of trouble,
> come forth like a flower and wither.
> They flee like a shadow and do not last . . . .
> If their days are determined,
>   the number of their months in you,
>   you appoint their bounds that they cannot pass.
> Look away from them and desist,
>   that they may enjoy their days like laborers. (14:1–2, 5–6)[177]

Even a life of effort is better than the pain of death. Death deprives humanity of joy and honor. God is responsible. He tears away the hope of humanity:

> Mountains collapse and crumble,
>   and rocks are dislodged from their place.
> As water wears away stone,
>   torrents wash away the soil of the earth,
>   so you destroy the hope of mortals,
> You overpower them forever and they perish.
>   You alter his visage and dispatch him.
> Their children attain honor, and they do not know it.
>   They are humbled, and it goes unnoticed.
> They feel only the pain of their flesh,
>   and their souls mourn for themselves. (14:18–22)

---

177. These words suggest those in 10:20, where Job asks God to cease and desist his attack on Job.

The major failing of God is that he has given humanity a difficult choice: a hard life or no life at all.

One of the harshest things about death, according to Job, is its permanence; humans do not return from the dead (7:9–10; 14:7–12, 14a; cf. 10:21a). Death is a land where creation is reversed. Light turns to darkness and order returns to disorder:

> Are not few my days?
>   Cease! Direct your attention away from me!
>   Let me smile a little,
> before I depart—never to return—
>   to the land of gloom and death's shadow,
>   to a morbid land, like the darkness of death's shadow,
>     without order, where light shines like darkness! (10:20–22)

Job laments his own coming death frequently (7:6–7a, 8b, 16bß, 21b; 9:25–26; 10:20aα; 16:22; 30:23; cf. 6:11b).[178] If God were truly just, he would hide Job in Sheol for later recall (14:13). God rejects the work of his hand, not only through oppressive litigation (10:3) but also through death. Throughout chapter 14, Job plays on creation imagery to confront God about his failure to bring final order to the universe. God seems constantly engaged in destroying whatever he once created. This is especially evident in 14:18–19. Job's confrontation of God on this point is not, however, contained entirely within chapter 14. Job states that God will soon turn what was once clay (חמר) to dust (עפר) (10:8–9; cf. 7:12; 17:15; 21:26; 30:19).[179] God's decision to begin and end humanity in the dirt (Gen 3:19; cf. 2:7) is under attack by Job. Job knows that the breath of God (רוח), first given to us at the creation (cf. 12:10; 27:3; Gen 1:2), will ultimately be withdrawn.

From Job's perspective, problems beyond death exist in God's creation. Across Job's speeches, he uses creation imagery to reject the idea that God is fundamentally good and that he conquered chaos during the creation. Things often seem topsy-turvy in Job's world. For example, Job reverses standard thinking about God's use of light and darkness. To Job's way of thinking, God draws darkness out of Sheol in order to shroud the light of the world (12:22). In so doing, he deprives leaders of light (12:25). God does

---

178. Although Job laments his coming death frequently, he also desires it in some ways to end his pain and uses the possibility of death to put pressure on God to settle the case. He, like most tortured possible martyrs, has conflicted feelings about death. See further my "Job's Wife as Hero," 242–57.

179. On Job's use of the word "dust" as a challenge to the order of the universe, see H.-J. Hermisson, "Observations on Creation Theology in Wisdom," trans. B. Howard, in *Israelite Wisdom: Theological and Literary Essays in Honor of Samuel Terrien* (ed. J. G. Gammie et al.; Missoula, Mont.: Scholars Press, 1978), 51; cf. L. G. Perdue, "Metaphorical Theology in the Book of Job: Theological Anthropology in the First Cycle of Job's Speeches (Job 3; 6–7; 9–10)," in *The Book of Job* (ed. W. A. M. Beuken; BETL 104; Leuven: Leuven University Press, 1994), 155.

not confront and punish those who reject or abuse the light and reap benefits from the dark (24:13–17, 23). Job once knew the light of God's guidance and blessing (29:3; cf. 19), but now it is withdrawn:

> I looked forward to good fortune, but evil came
> I hoped for light, but darkness came. (30:26)

God gives light and life where he should not (3:4, 9, 16, 20). There are times when darkness ought to reign, but it does not (3:5–6, 9). When Job's friends testify falsely for God's benefit, they, too, reverse the lighting of creation:

> They say that night is day,
> that light is here, in the face of darkness. (17:12)

Day turns to night and vice versa, scrambling God's creation of the day and night (Gen 1:5). The outcome of God's work is that the days of many people are hard (30:35), and the day of Job's creation was anything but good (cf. Gen 1:4, 18, 31). That day ought to be undone (3:3–5). Nights, according to Job, are no better (3:6–7; 7:3–4; 24:7; 30:17). God created for six days and then rested in celebration on the seventh (Gen 2:2); Job, on the other hand, sat in silence for seven, mourning God's destruction in his life (2:13).

Light and dark, day and night, and the dust of creation are not the only creation images that Job parodies. To give just a few of the innumerable examples: first, the formlessness of creation (תהו) (Gen 1:2) resurfaces as the wastelands to which Job refers (6:18 and 12:24). Second, in 12:13–15, Job addresses God's wisdom, understanding, design, and power. He indicates that God's efforts to destroy or to imprison cannot be undone. He finally charges God with manipulating the waters of the earth to wreak havoc. By this rhetorical move, Job connects the wisdom, creation, and violence of God. Habel says of these verses: "This God, according to Job's portrayal, promotes cosmic destruction and social disorder rather than peace, order, and stability. His *modus operandi* is an exercise in anarchy, his style fosters violence, and his governance seems to negate the very nature of wisdom as the ordering principle of the cosmos and society."[180] T. N. D. Mettinger states that Job's hymn from 12:7–15 reflects Job's view that God created "a world devoid of meaning. . . . To Job, creation conforms to no moral pattern, and existence has no structure."[181] Third, the doxology that

---

180. N. C. Habel, "In Defense of God the Sage," in *The Voice from the Whirlwind: Interpreting the Book of Job* (ed. L. G. Perdue and W. C. Gilpin; Nashville: Abingdon, 1992), 29.

181. T. N. D. Mettinger, "The God of Job: Avenger, Tyrant, or Victor?" in *The Voice from the Whirlwind: Interpreting the Book of Job* (ed. L. G. Perdue and W. C. Gilpin; Nashville: Abingdon, 1992), 43.

Job sings to God's superiority and abusive ways in 9:5–13 is a satire on creation theology.[182] Here Job recounts God's power, invisibility,[183] and anger. The deity overturns mountains (9:5), shakes the earth from its foundations (9:6), and commands the sun not to rise (9:7). Habel states of this pericope: "in the hands of this poet they [the hymnic passages] are reoriented to announce the violent ways of a Creator bent on disrupting his created order and producing chaos in society and nature."[184] By such acts, God not only undoes creation; he undoes justice. Habel observes:

> In Israel there was a strong tradition that justice was fundamental to the maintenance of the cosmic order. If injustice was rife, the foundations of the earth shook (Ps. 82:1–5). When Yahweh reigned and judged with equity, the earth was established and did not move (Ps. 96:10). By designating El as one who "overthrows" (*hpk*; cf. 12:15) mountains in the way that Sodom and Gomorrah were overthrown (Gen 19:29), Job is characterizing his adversary as one who initiates chaos rather than one who maintains just order.[185]

When God sued the members of the Divine Council for their failure to protect social justice, the earth trembled (Ps 82:5). Now that God has similarly failed, the earth shakes once again. Fourth, the inversion of the chaos battle tradition of creation is seen acutely when Job asks God whether Job is the Sea or the Dragon (7:12).[186] Job returns repeatedly to creation imagery to contest God's ordering of the universe and the quality of the justice that flows therefrom. As Mettinger puts it, God, from Job's point of view, is "an omnipotent tyrant, a cosmic thug."[187] The same God who brings false suits against him for blasphemy disrupts the cosmic order. God is, in Job's mind, a בן בליעל, a scoundrel.

Job also uses more subtle means through which to challenge God's ordering of the universe and justice. For example, L. G. Perdue notes: "Wild animals were at times regarded as the incarnations of chaos that threatened creation and society. To hunt and kill them ritually was a means of securing the structures of life. However, Job, not the embodiment of chaos, is the prey of the Divine hunter."[188] In the Hebrew Bible, the hunter is also

---

182. Job 9:8a is equivalent to Isa 44:24; Job 9:8b is equivalent to Amos 4:13bβ; and Job 9:9a is equivalent to Amos 5:8a.
183. Although Job sees trouble (3:10), he does not see God (9:11).
184. Habel, *Book of Job: Commentary*, 43. See also Job 12:13–25.
185. Habel, *Book of Job: Commentary*, 190; see also Hermisson, "Observations on Creation Theology," 51.
186. Mettinger offers still other examples, including 9:17; 10:8; 16:12 ("God of Job," 43–44).
187. Ibid., 44.
188. L. G. Perdue, *Wisdom in Revolt: Metaphorical Theology in the Book of Job* (JSOTSup

a metaphor for a legal adversary.[189] Consequently, when Job accuses God of hunting him in 10:16, he alleges that God has confused him with chaos and is attempting to control it through legal maneuvers rather than as the divine warrior should. This is a significant cosmological failure that has juridical implications.

In sum, then, Job intends to counterclaim against God, hoping to restore at least some of his losses. He therefore charges God with abuse of authority. Job believes that God uses his power and authority to obstruct justice in three ways. First, God sues Job for unspecified wrongs without reasonable basis. During the course of this litigation, he uses his superior strength and acts in legally contemptible ways in order to secure his victory. Second, God does not generally support social justice, as is his duty. The innocent fail and the wicked prosper. Third, God's creation is devoid of the order and justice that God represents that it has. God really does both give and take away (1:21b)—and Job has decided that it is not so tolerable after all. The chaos of the universe is the fundamental problem from which all failures in God's justice flow. Hence, the three counts move from the particular expression of God's injustice in Job's case to the very cause of the failure of justice in the world.

---

112; Sheffield: Sheffield Academic, 1991), 155, relying on the work of O. Keel, *Jahwes Entgegnung an Ijob* (FRLANT 121; Göttingen: Vandenhoeck & Ruprecht, 1978), 62–63.

189. See n. 116 above.

# 7

# Job's Defense and Demand

Because the textual evidence is so strong in support of the position that Job sues God for redress, most forensic commentators take the view that Job initiates the suit in the book. They often aver that Job believes he has already been condemned at trial, has received his punishment, and is petitioning God for redress against this summary judgment.[1] This position is consistent with the sufferer's claim in the ritual incantation texts of Mesopotamia. The book of Job is not, however, fully consistent with any typical structure. One must watch for deviations. Moreover, the evidence for Job's claim against God does not stand alone. Even as Job formulates his accusations, he asserts that he is now on divine trial and recognizes a need to defend himself against God's allegations if he hopes to win. This chapter will focus on Job's defense and a number of issues that arise out of it, including his settlement demand.

## Job's Acknowledgment of God's Suit and the Need to Defend

Job makes many statements reflecting his concern over the need to answer charges. Job expects that God will produce a summons for him to appear in the trial so that he may answer. Job also acknowledges that, if he should not answer, his losses will remain. He may even face death. His language indicates additionally that a verdict is still forthcoming. When taken together, these statements reflect Job's conviction that he is facing charges that he must answer. Thus, he is not initiating a request for rehearing on, or pardon of, a divine summary verdict. Rather, he is defending a pending case.

Job's understanding that he is still facing the trial itself can be seen, first, in his anxiety about his legal matters, especially in 9:14–32. He wor-

---

1. See ch. 1, nn. 16–17, 20 above.

ries, not only over a potential suit against God, but also frets over his coming defense. Job offers the earliest and clearest of his comments regarding the fact of, and problems in, his defense in 9:14–15a:

> How then can I answer (ענה) him,
>   choose my words against him?
> Though I am innocent (צדק), I cannot answer (ענה).

Job is clearly concerned here with how to formulate the legal answer required of a defendant in a trial.[2] This anxiety demonstrates his awareness that he is facing unresolved charges. Job is also deeply concerned that he may be in a kangaroo court:

> If I say, "I will forget my complaint (שיח),
>   I will loosen my sad countenance and smile,"
> I remain afraid of all my suffering,
>   for I know that you will not acquit (נקה) me.
> I will be condemned (רשע). (9:27–29a)

Job alleges that in God's court he would be found guilty rather than innocent, which is why he needs another judge for his case.[3] All of this refers to future not past action.[4] Additionally, Job closes this section of his speech by articulating the source of this fear: his adversary is not human:

> For he is not a mortal as I am, that I might answer,
>   that we might come to trial (משפט). (9:32)

Job does not know how to formulate a legal answer to a divine adversary at law. In this manner, he reiterates the fear he expressed in 9:14–15a. Job agonizes over this at times. The inequality in the power of the two con-

---

2. See the material at ch. 6, nn. 60–63 above.

3. See ch. 6, nn. 157–62 above.

4. One verse appears to contradict my position. In 7:20–21, Job queries God regarding his past transgression: "[If] I have sinned (חטא), what have I done to you, watcher of humanity? / Why do you make me your target? / Why have I become a burden to you? / Why do you not pardon (נשא) my transgression (פשע) / and forgive (עבר) my iniquity (עון)? / For soon I shall lie in the ground; / you will search diligently (שחר) for me, but I shall not be." This might mean that Job believes he has suffered a final verdict and is requesting a pardon. Bovati claims, however, that this is, once again, a protestation of Job's innocence (*Re-Establishing Justice*, 111). I agree—this denotes a preemptive move on Job's part. In other words, Job is suggesting that, if God should later find him guilty, his sins are such that he should be pardoned anyway. Consequently, there is no point to the investigation. For other biblical references to God as watcher, see Zech 12:4; Prov 22:12; cf. Pss 11:4; 91:8; and Prov 15:3. Ps 11:4a–5b is particularly important in this context because it says that Yahweh's "eyes behold, his eyelids investigate (בחן) the children of humanity. Yahweh investigates (בחן) the righteous and the wicked. . . ."

testants places Job's ability to win in peril. Such a response is most natural in a world where sufferers rarely challenge the deity before a summary verdict had been issued, and even then do so with fear, trembling, and trepidation. Job has few role models on whom to rely. The paradox is that this inequality is the very thing that offers Job his solution—a counterclaim for abuse of that power differential—which he recognizes.

This paradox fuels Job's courage. In 13:22, Job actually urges God to summon him so that he might answer; if he does not, Job will proceed with his countersuit immediately:

Then summon (קרא) and I will answer (ענה),
    or I will state my case (דבר) and you may reply (שוב) to me.

He wants to get the trial rolling even if he has no idea how he will, in fact, answer or accuse God. Somehow, he must, he will, find a way. The presence of this summons is important for yet another reason. Such summons language is most unusual in the ritual incantations. Job's strategy does not track the ritual incantations entirely.

In order to answer God, Job needs the charges specified. Job indicates repeatedly that he is unsure of the nature of God's allegations. In this, he is similar to the petitioners of the Šurpu Incantations and the DINGIR.ŠÀ.DIB.BA incantation texts. In both texts, the petitioner requests a bill of particulars that the sufferer might offer the appropriate confession and request for pardon.[5] Job is not, however, seeking such information in order to beg pardon of the deity. Rather, he needs it in order to offer a careful answer to his divine legal adversary. Job believes that he is entitled to know the specifics of the charges against him in order to make a proper defense. God's seeming readiness to issue a verdict against Job without having tendered a sign identifying his exact sin and allowing Job to respond is highly problematic to Job and constitutes an important reason why Job feels that God is an abusive party who must be stopped through a counterclaim.

Job's need for clarification is first noticed in 10:2, where he most strongly advocates for bringing a counterclaim:

I will say to God, "Do not condemn (רשע) me!
    Make known to me why you sue (ריב) me!"

Job returns to this call for a specification of the charges in 13:23, when he demands:

---

5. A modern bill of particulars gives the defendant notice "of the [details of the] offenses charged in the bill of indictment so that he may prepare a defense, avoid surprise, or intelligently raise pleas" related to any statutory prohibition against trial of the accused ("Bill: Bill of particulars," *BLD*, 165). Without a specific delineation of the charges, it is often impossible to defend the case.

> How many are my iniquities (עון) and sins (חטאת)?
> Advise me of my transgression (פשע) and sin (חטאת)![6]

In God's failure to delineate the charges, he is both hiding his face from Job and disrespecting Job by treating him as an enemy (13:24). Job deserves better. Finally, Job demands, toward the end of his oath of denial, a written bill of particulars on the charges In 31:35b-c, Job declares:

> Here is my mark! Let Shaddai answer (ענה) me,
> and let my adversary at law (איש ריב)[7] draw up (כתב) a document (ספר)!

It is possible to argue that this language cannot refer to a forthcoming written bill of particulars because, in 13:26a, Job accuses God of having already written one against him:

> For you write (כתב) bitter things against me,
> and make me reap the iniquities (עון) of my youth.

Is Job suggesting, however, that God has issued a written verdict on the charge, with Job's youthful sins as its reasoning?[8] In the alternative, does Job mean to say that God has already produced a written indictment or bill of particulars on the charge based on his juvenile follies? Or does Job refer to an investigative report of his follies, as we find in the Neo-Babylonian litigation corpus?[9] Consideration of both 19:23 and 31:35 suggests that Job expresses the belief that God has issued some written investigative report against him in 13:26a.

In 19:23–24, Job cries out:

> Oh, if only my arguments (מלה) were recorded (כתב)!
> Oh, if only they were inscribed (חקק) on a stele (ספר),[10]
> with an iron stylus and with lead,
>     carved on rock forever!

This verse follows a long list of allegations against God. In 19:6a, Job declares to his friends: "Know that God has wronged me." He then specifies those wrongs in 19:16b–20. In 19:21–22, he asks for his friends' support rather than their abuse. Consequently, in 19:23–24, Job exclaims his desire

---

6. B. Halpern, "YHWH's Summary Justice in Job XIV 20," *VT* 28 (1978): 474.
7. Gemser, "*Rîb*-Pattern," 123. Note the similarity between the *bēl dabābi* and the איש ריב. See ch 4, nn. 69–70 above.
8. The NJPS takes this view, but it is inconsistent in its translation of 31:35.
9. See, e.g., *CT* 2, 2.
10. The word ספר means typically, "scroll," "document," or "book." Nonetheless, the references in the rest of the verse to an iron stylus and a rock indicated that Job refers to a stone inscription. In this understanding I follow Habel (*Book of Job: Commentary*, 290, 303).

to write his own indictment against God. Many other interpreters also understand this document to be a written indictment, which is consistent with Job's remark in 19:23–24.[11] After Job's lengthy and broadly scattered defense in chapter 31, he wants God similarly to specify the exact nature of the charges in a written bill (31:35). Job 24:1 lends additional support for this position because there Job states that the time of Shaddai's judgment is unknown; the date of possible conviction seems to remain open. Thus, the writing in 13:26 is unlikely to refer to a final or summary verdict.

Although we have eliminated the view that 13:26 refers to a judgment, two options remain: the writing is either an indictment or an investigative report. If Job is perfectly consistent when he is referring to writings, 13:26 would be an indictment. This interpretation would create, however, a different inconsistency: that is, Job says that he has an indictment in 13:26 and that he does not have one in 31:35. Apparently Job wants to see a written investigative report in 13:26, as existed in the Neo-Babylonian period. In the passages of chapters 19 and 31, Job indicates his desire to set this legal altercation in writing as was typically done in the ancient Near East.

Another indicator that the trial is, to Job's mind, still in process is that Job discusses a future possible verdict in a number of other contexts. For example, he experiences his friends to be supporting witnesses in God's suit against him. He has fears that he will be convicted if his friends do not come to his defense:

Relent (שוב), I pray! Let there not be injustice;
Again, relent (שוב)! In it lies my acquittal (צדק). (6:29)

He calls on them to stop their assault on him so that God will not be victorious.

Moreover, in spite of his fears, Job expresses hope concerning his case. In 13:18, he declares that he has readied his defense and claims a win in the making:

Indeed, I have prepared (ערך) a case (משפט).[12]
I know that I will be found innocent (צדק).

This assumes that he is currently on trial.

Many of Job's statements indicate that he believes that God first filed suit against him and that he must now offer a legal defense or be convicted. No matter what his fears or his hopes concerning his answer and its effect, he must come forward to defend. Within his speeches, he rises to the chal-

---

11. See, e.g., Boecker, *Redeformen*, 14; Dick, "Job 31," 20, 73–74; and Westbrook, "Biblical Law," 9.
12. See Gemser, "*Rîb*-Pattern," 123; see also Ps 1:21.

lenge and prepares his defense. Job's language continually makes clear that the dispute is very much in progress, he is under investigation, nothing has been determined summarily, he must answer the charges, and he will bring his counterclaim on abuse of judicial authority. The view that Job believes that he is suffering from a divine summary judgment and is, therefore, appealing the judgment or attacking it collaterally remains untenable.

In sum, four difficulties with this view now exist. First, Job seems quite focused on God's investigation and his need to answer. These predominant themes in Job's argument tend toward the view that the case is unresolved. Second, Job demands that God summon him to answer, which is not typical of the ritual incantation texts. Third, Job lacks contrition and contemplates a combative counterclaim. Such things are out of character with the tone of the Šurpu Incantations and similar ancient Near Eastern references. Fourth, Job does not appeal to his judge for a reversal of his decision, as happens in *KAR* 184. Rather, he calls upon an independent judge to hear his defense and counterclaim (9:19b, 33–35; 10:7b; 31:35a), a point to which I will return in chapter 9. Still another difficulty with this view will arise shortly. As will be revealed in the discussion of the friends' speeches in chapter 8 below, the friends believe, indeed, that Job has suffered either a justified divine summary or final judgment and that he should act with the appropriate deference to his judge during appeal. The friends also suggest that Job should follow procedures similar to those of the incantations to resolve his case. Job vehemently opposes their ideas and suggestions. While the worldview of the ritual incantations is affecting the thinking of all these characters, Job does not wholly accept its view. He is not attempting to attack an unfair summary judgment as is normally done via the incantations. Rather, he sees himself as defending a trial in progress that began with a burdensome investigation.

The discussion above makes clear how closely connected Job's answer and threatened counterclaim are. They go hand in hand throughout the book. Ignoring one for the benefit of the other fails to explain the book in its entirety. This reading strategy has contributed to the reliance on diachronic methods to explain the book's seeming inconsistencies. There is, however, a legal solution that is more consistent with a synchronic reading of the book: the presence of both a legal claim that Job must answer and a counterclaim that he wishes to allege against God. Job is then both defendant and counter-plaintiff. He then reasonably makes both defensive statements and accusations consistent with this dual position. Further, such statements do not stand independently; rather, Job ties his various offensive and defensive statements together in three critical passages (9:27–29a; 13:22; 31:35b-c). Job intends both to defend this suit on its merits and counterclaim on abuse of authority. His need to do the first is the ground for his need to do the second.

## The Basis of Job's Defense

Because God never does reveal the exact nature of the charges against Job, Job must defend on multiple grounds, hoping that he will hit the mark.[13] This defense strategy turns the priests' actions in the Šurpu Incantations and the DINGIR.ŠÀ.DIB.BA Incantations on their head. The priests in both of those incantation texts recite a long list of possible offenses, anticipating that they would name the correct one for the suffering petitioner so that the petitioner could seek a pardon from the gods. Job, on the other hand, defends against a lengthy list of possible offenses, expecting to meet the relevant allegation with the appropriate response. Job goes still further, however, in that he also avows a broad spectrum of righteous behavior, hoping to offer the correct argument to resolve the dispute. Here he plays on the more involved course of the DINGIR.ŠÀ.DIB.BA Incantations. There, the petitioner hopes to convince the deity that he is a good man who has done many good acts and therefore deserves pardon for any possible indiscretion that he may have committed. Job uses this strategy defensively to explain that he could not possibly be guilty of any charge and never should have been subject to suit in the first place.

The foundation of Job's multipronged defense is his innocence/righteousness (צדק), which he declares frequently. With regard to this case specifically, he asserts his innocence while worrying over his ability to answer God (9:15a). He repeats his innocence while accusing God of twisting his testimony (9:20a). In 12:4, he alleges that his friends mock him for declaring his innocence (צדיק). In 29:14, Job claims righteousness of longstanding:

> I put on righteousness (צדק)
>   and it clothed me like a robe.
> Justice (משפט) was my diadem.

Job holds to his innocence tenaciously. He states:

> I hold fast (חזק) to my innocence (צדק), and will not let it go.
> My intention (לבב) does not reproach me at any time. (27:6)

Just as God and Job's wife observed that Job holds fast (חזק) to his integrity (תם) (2:3, 9), Job claims that he holds fast to his innocence. His intention (לבב) is pure (27:6).

Second, Job defends himself on the same grounds that Yahweh defended Job in the Divine Council. Job asserts several times that he is a man of integrity (תם) (9:20b; 9:21a; 12:4; 31:6). It is not just to his innocence that Job clings. He declares to God:

---

13. God's failure is addressed in chapter 10 below.

> Far be it from me to say you are right (צדק)!
> Until I die, I will not put away my integrity (תם). (27:5)

Job will not surrender the case easily. He proves both God and his wife correct in their understanding of him (2:3, 9): he does hold fast to his integrity. Moreover, he subtly refers to himself as upright (ישר) in 23:7. Job also professes indirectly that he is a God-fearing man when he avers that he can approach God to accuse him because he is not a godless man (חנף) (13:15–16).

His devotion to God is evident in the fact that he has always followed God's law. This is his third defense. In 6:8–9, using the language of abuse of authority, Job utters words of desperation in response to his pain:

> Would that my request find fulfillment,
>   that God grant my desire,
> that God would determine to crush (דכא) me,
>   that he would let loose his hand and ruin (בצע) me.

Nonetheless, he immediately declares that his compliance with God's commands is his consolation:

> Then this consolation could still be mine
>   (even while I recoiled in unrelenting pain):
> that I have not denied the words of the Holy One. (6:10)[14]

He reasserts this position in 23:11–12:

> My foot has held fast (אחז) to his steps.
>   I have kept his way without turning aside.
> I have not deviated from the commandments (מצות) of his lips.
>   I have treasured his words beyond that required (חק) of me.[15]

Job is obedient to God's law. It is here that we can so plainly see that Job agrees with the other characters of the book regarding how justice ought to work: the good ought to be blessed and the wicked made to suffer. The points of contention between the characters involve whether justice actually does work this way and, if it does not, whether God ought to be held responsible.[16]

---

14. The translation of 6:10 is based on that of Clines, *Job 1–20*, 156.
15. Following Habel, *Book of Job: Commentary*, 344, 345–46.
16. God and the Satan also support the proposition that retributive justice ought to hold. None of the characters denies that this is a fundamental element of justice. The book examines whether this justice actually does undergird reality in a trial of both Job and God. C. Newsom states this particularly well: "Throughout the long dialogues between Job and his friends, theological issues and options are set up as alternatives between traditional positions cham-

Fourth, Job asserts that he has maintained proper social justice. Because Job has filed charges against God on his maintenance of social justice, he may feel that it is appropriate to defend himself with respect to any similar allegations. Moreover, two proverbs indicate that to mistreat the poor is to insult one's maker (Prov 14:31; 17:5). Job may fear that his treatment of the less fortunate is also part of the problem. Job therefore covers this issue in his defense. In chapter 29, he looks back over his blessings and past conduct. This gives him the perfect opportunity to explain how good his behavior on this front has been:

> For I saved the poor who cried out (שׁוע),
>   and the orphan who had none to help.
> The blessing (ברך) of those soon to die came upon me,
>   and I made the widow's heart to sing for joy. . . .
> I was eyes to the blind
>   and I was feet to the lame.
> I was a father to the needy,
>   and I investigated (חקר) the lawsuit (רב) of the stranger.
> I broke the jaws of the iniquitous (עול),
>   and I wrested prey from his teeth. (29:12–13, 15–17)

He adds in 30:24–25:

> I did not strike those in ruin (עי)
>   when they cried out (שׁוע) to me in their disaster.
> Did I not weep for the unfortunate?
>   Was my soul not grieved for the needy?

Job contends that his support for social justice has been rigorous (29:14b). God has no need for concern. Job was blessed, in his mind, because he did all these things and more. He cannot imagine why he has been stripped of all his blessings when his past conduct has been impeccable. He should not be on trial.

Job's fifth line of defense is that any sins that he might have committed were entirely unintentional. The verbal, nominal, and adjectival forms of the roots שׁגג and שׁגה refer to unwitting offenses repeatedly in the Hebrew

---

pioned by the friends and the radical challenges posed by Job. The friends argue for the goodness of God, the moral order of the world, the purposiveness of suffering, and the importance of humble submission to God. Job questions the justice of God, describes the world as a moral chaos, depicts suffering in terms of victimization, and stakes his life on the possibility of legal confrontation with God. What goes largely unnoticed is the extent to which both positions depend on the same paradigm of understanding. They both take as unquestionable the assumption that justice, specifically retributive justice, should be the central principle of reality. They disagree only as to whether such justice is operative in the world or whether God should be called to account for failing to enforce such justice" ("Book of Job," 336).

Bible.¹⁷ Less frequently do these roots mean "to err," "to stray," or "to swerve."¹⁸ In some cases, the error, straying, or swaying is caused by foolishness, drunkenness, or love.¹⁹ Only rarely do these roots signify a willful wrong. The author of Job seems to have played with the multiple meanings of this root. In 12:16, the verb clearly means "to stray" when Job uses it to accuse God of leading once-great nations astray. In 6:24 the root שגג seems to signify "to err willfully," where Job challenges his friends:

> Teach me and I will be silent!
> Make me understand how I have erred (שגג)!

Job invites his friends to try to find any intentional wrongs that he has done. The implication of these words is that they cannot; all they will ever be able to find is unintentional errors.²⁰ Job makes this more explicit in 19:4:

> Even if it were true that I have erred (שגה)
> my error (משוגה) stays with me.

An intentional error could hardly stay with him and remain unpunished. Thus, Job is asserting here that, if he has erred, he has done so unintentionally. Such errors, while capable of producing sickness and calamity and while subject to the need for sin offering and atonement, are easily pardoned under the laws of the Hebrew Bible.²¹ Job claims here that he could not possibly be guilty of anything but minimal accidental errors. Job 6:24 and 19:4 only add to Job's declaration in 27:6b that his intentions are pure.

Job believes that he has generally been an upright citizen and devoted follower of God. He summarizes: "There is no crime (חמס) in my hands" (16:17a). The word חמס often means "violence," but, in this setting, it is better translated "crime." Although this statement comes in the midst of his counteraccusations, it is critical to his defense. The thrust of all his remarks is that he has shunned evil. Job is therefore hopeful that he can survive any divine inspection:

> Surely, he knows my conduct (דרך).
> If he assayed (בחן) me, I should emerge [pure] as gold. (23:10)

---

17. See, e.g., Lev 4:2, 22, 27; 5:15, 18; 22:14; Num 15:22, 24–29; 35:11, 15 (= Josh 20:3, 9); Deut 4:42; 19:4; Ezek 45:20; Eccl 5:5; 10:5.
18. "To err" (Gen 43:12; Ps 19:13; Prov 5:23); "to stray" (Deut 27:18; 1 Sam 26:21; Ezek 34:6; Ps 119:21, 118; Prov 19:27; 28:10); and "to swerve" (Isa 28:7; Prov 5:19–20; 20:1).
19. "Foolishness" (Prov 5:23); "drunkenness" (Isa 28:7; Prov 20:1); and "love" (Prov 5:19-20).
20. Bovati avers that, through this statement, Job reminds Eliphaz of Job's own role in teaching others (4:3) and actually asserts his innocence (*Re-Establishing Justice*, 111).
21. See, e.g., Lev 4:2, 22, 27; 5:15, 18; 22:14; Num 15:22, 24–29; 35:11, 15 (= Josh 20:3, 9); and Deut 4:42; 19:4. See further the material in ch. 8, between nn. 35 and 36 below.

## Job's Defense and Demand    187

The use of the verb בחן here works with the investigative theme that exists throughout the book. Job thinks God is inspecting both his intentions and his conduct, and he must defend accordingly when the time is ripe.

None of these defensive statements, however, goes directly to the issue of blasphemy, which is the Satan's charge. One would think that Job might at least suspect that this is the core charge, since his wife raised the issue (2:9). Her words might have been adequate to put him on notice regarding this. It is possible, however, that his intensely scrupulous and demanding behavior in regard to blasphemy (1:5; 2:10) has driven this possibility far from his mind. Job's only references to it seem circumspect. For example, in 6:28–30, when Job is pleading to his friends to help his cause, he states:

> Now be so good as to turn (שוב) to me.
>   If I lie to your face, . . .
> Relent (שוב), I pray! Let there not be injustice.
>   Again, relent (שוב)! In it lies my acquittal (צדק).
> Is iniquity (עולה) on my tongue?
>   Can my palate not discern calamity? (6:28–30)

Here Job swears an oath that he is not lying to his friends. He wants them to support him and cease testifying for God. He fears that their testimony will damage his case. In the end, he asks two critical rhetorical questions of them regarding whether he speaks in an inappropriate manner. By this technique he is emphasizing that he is not lying to them. Furthermore, he is subtly asserting that his words are pure and true. While the words are not as explicit as one might like, the implication is that Job has a mouth that will not blaspheme. In 27:3–4, Job is a little less veiled when he pronounces:

> As long as my breath is in me,
>   and God's breath is in my nostrils,
> my lips will speak (דבר) no iniquity (עולה),
>   nor my tongue utter (הגה) deceit (מרמה).

Job's claim that his lips speak no iniquity (עולה) is similar to the narrator's claim that Job does not sin (חטא) with his lips (2:10). Again, the implication is that Job denies ever having blasphemed God. One might still query, however, whether this assertion is enough to clear him of the actual charge of possession of the guilty mind of a blasphemer because he does not address this specifically. One can have a guilty mind and not do the deed. Are his general claims of having a pure state of mind and a pure mouth sufficient for a finding of *not guilty* on the Satan's charge? They may be. The list of crimes Job names is certainly not as exhaustive as the Šurpu Incantations seek to be. Nevertheless, Job is attempting to offer a broad defense in the spirit of the incantations' request for pardon. One might wish, however, that his defense were more directly on target.

For all the statements Job makes on his behalf throughout chaps. 3–29, he seems not to feel that these are sufficient, because he offers an exculpatory oath in chap. 31.[22] This oath cannot be formal, as some assert.[23] First, it is not court-ordered; Job offers it voluntarily and spontaneously. Second, it is not taken in the name of Yahweh. Third, it does not end the case. Neither God nor the Satan concedes the trial at the oath's conclusion, as a formal oath would demand. The oath, therefore, is nondispositive. It does, however, have legal import because it is a weakened oath, which was prevalent during the Neo-Babylonian period. Job's oath functions to strengthen considerably his declarations of innocence. It adds more evidentiary weight to his words. He wants a big finish. Because the oath concludes Job's remarks (31:40c), it accomplishes this goal for him.

The oath is long and complicated. It begins with some introductory remarks. First, Job indicates that he has "made a covenant with his eyes," and therefore he does not gaze upon a maiden (31:1). This is the only statement of this kind in the chapter. Then, in 31:2–4, through a series of rhetorical questions, Job ponders what lies in store for him, reiterates the standard thinking with regard to retributive punishment, and recognizes that God is watching him. He cries out in 31:6:

> Let him weigh (שקל) me on the scales of righteousness (מאזני־צדק)[24]
> and let God know my integrity (תם)!

By this exclamation, he asks God to consider his defensive oath seriously.

Then Job gets to the heart of his oath by issuing a series of self-imprecations beginning with "if" (אם). The formal characteristics of the oath demonstrate the characteristics of oaths in the Neo-Babylonian period. There are three full oath formulae, with a simple protasis and sanctioning apodosis: "If I have done X, then may Y happen to me" (31:5–6, 7–8, 9–10). In 31:5–6, the sanction mentions God and permits God to judge Job and, by implication, to impose an unspecified sanction. In 31:9–10, the apodosis has a sanction that is directly related to the crime mentioned in the protasis. In 31:7–8, the sanction is not directly connected to the crime. In two of the formulae, the oath has a complex protasis with multiple elements and

---

22. For detailed studies of Job's oath of innocence, see R. A. Aytoun, "A Critical Study of Job's Oath of Clearance" *Interpreter* 16 (1919–20): 291–98; Dick "Job 31: A Form-Critical Study"; idem, "Legal Metaphor," 37–41; idem, "Job 31, Oath of Innocence," 31–53; and D. T. Stewart, "Comparison of the Legal Tradition of Job's Oath of Clearance and Ancient Near Eastern Legal Codes" (paper presented at the annual meeting of the Society of Biblical Literature in Washington, DC, November 22, 1992).

23. This position is argued by several, including, among others, G. Fohrer, "The Righteous Man in Job 31," in *Essays in Old Testament Ethics* (ed. J. L. Crenshaw and J. T. Willis; New York: Ktav, 1974), 10; and Habel, *Book of Job: Commentary*, 429.

24. Or "a just balance."

a sanctioning apodosis (3:19–22, 38–40b). In 31:38–40b, the sanction is directly related to the crime. In 3:19–30, the sanction is related only to the last element of the protasis. One of the protases is followed by a rhetorical question that implies that Job should be punished if the stated condition has been met (31:13–14). In 31:13–15, God is mentioned as the one to whom Job must account when tested. Some of the formulae use the abbreviated form, wherein the apodosis is unstated (31:16–17, 29, 31, 33). In 31:24–27, the abbreviated formula contains a complex protasis. In some instances, the reasons for taking the oath, or for suffering the punishment, follow the apodosis (or the protasis where no apodosis is supplied) (31:11–12, 15, 18, 23, 28). Usually, the reason is stated in the declarative (31:11–12, 18, 23, 28, 32), but it is in the interrogative form once (31:15). The reasons include a specific fear of God (31:23), a fear of a human assembly (31:34), and the justness of the sanction (31:11–12, 15, 28). In three cases, the reason for the oath is the fact that Job never did such conduct (31:18, 30, 32). In 31:34, a reason is also given, but it is related to why a person might do the crime rather than to why the oath is given or the punishment justified. It is, therefore, quite different from the others and feels more like part of the protasis.

By Job's sworn statements in 31:5–40, he both reiterates some of his prior assertions of innocence and supplements his prior defense. Job states that he has neither bad nor lustful intentions in 31:7b, 9a, 26, 27. Job 31:27, where he swears that his intention (לבב) has never been secretly enticed (פתה בסתר), is particularly striking. In 31:7c, Job denies doing any bad acts generally with his hands. He then becomes specific about which offenses he has attempted to avoid. They include lusting after women (31:1, 9), deceiving persons (31:5), walking inappropriate paths (31:7a), putting his faith in riches or celebrating them too proudly (31:24–25), not paying the full measure for goods he has used (31:39–40), mistreating the land (31:38), or rejoicing over the misfortunes of his enemy (31:29). Job asserts again that he has treated well those of lowly position, including his servants, the poor, the orphan, the widow, the hungry, and the stranger (31:13, 16–17, 19–21, 31–32).[25] Finally, he asserts that he has not concealed his transgressions out of fear but has confessed all errors (31:33–34). He means, of course, only minor and unwitting sins.[26] Through this lengthy oath, Job again attempts to deny all possible crimes.[27]

---

25. Westbrook maintains that none of the crimes can be punished in a human tribunal and are matters of first instance for the divine court ("Lex Talionis," 59). I agree, except in the case of not paying the full measure for used goods (31:39–40). This is a form of theft, which is justiciable.
26. See the material at ch. 6 n. 48 above.
27. Stewart makes the case that Job's oath comports well with a great many of the ancient

Once more, however, Job does not explicitly address the issue of blasphemy. The only reference to whether his mouth has ever sinned is his denial in 31:30 of cursing his enemy:

I have never let my mouth sin (חטא)
   by asking for his life with a curse (אלה).

He ignores whether or not he has the *mens rea* for the crime of blasphemy. Job's extensive assertions of innocence, intended to cover all crimes, omit the most important one of all. The omission of a blasphemous intention from his statements and his oath may do damage to his defense.

Job 31:35–37 is distinct in character from the rest of the material in 31:5–40. These verses are concluding in nature and probably originally followed 31:38–40b. In that case, the concluding elements contained in 31:35–37 and 31:40c would have stood together. Consequently, I take these verses together as the closing unit of Job's defense. Verse 35 has four elements. First, Job laments that he has no judge to hear his case. Second, he indicates that he ends his defensive statements and approves its final form by putting his mark on them. Third, Job demands an answer to his counterclaim from God. Fourth, Job demands his formal indictment from God. By the abbreviated oath formula in 31:36, Job swears that he will carry the indictment on his shoulder as a reminder of his possible guilt during the process of judgment. He indicates in 31:37 that, if God should come down with his bill of particulars, Job would give a full accounting of his conduct to God with the honor and respect due a prince. This ends his denial of liability (31:40c).

## Job's Settlement Demand upon God

Job's oath contains a curious element: his request for a bill of particulars (31:35c). Most forensic commentators argue both that Job files his claim against God in either chapter 9 or chapter 13 and that his oath in chapter 31 closes his defense.[28] This leads to two important questions. First, why does a man who files an accusation or petition need to defend himself at all? The difference between an accusation and a defense is an important legal distinction. Second, if Job should indeed be defending himself in a divine trial, why would a man who has just closed his defense now ask for a bill of particulars on the charges? The timing of such a request is inappropriate. A defendant, whether ancient or modern, cannot lodge a defense

---

Near Eastern and biblical law codes—especially H and D—in both content and, at times, form ("Comparison," 1–33). I would affirm that position.

28. See ch. 1 n. 22 above.

until he or she knows the particulars of the charges. Thus, Job's request is odd coming when it does. It is strangely out of order.

The answer to this conundrum is that the trial has not yet progressed beyond the initial accusation and investigation. From chapter 3 to chapter 31, Job has simply considered how he will deal with the coming trial. The characters typically speak about Job's case in the future or the hypothetical—they address what would happen if Job should try to answer or if he should file his counterclaim.[29] His speeches and those of Eliphaz, Bildad, Zophar, and Elihu are, however, more than mere ponderings. They are an organized rehearsal of the trial that does not leave any procedural stone unturned. Job's speeches, in particular, put God and his friends on notice as to the course Job intends to take at trial. Job is making a demand on God to cease and desist, in the nature of the pre-trial or early-trial demands of Neo-Babylonian litigation and is initiating settlement negotiations with God.

The existence of such demands in ancient Israel is implied in Judg 20:22. Additionally, an implied demand for a settlement of the claim exists when Abraham lodges an accusation (יכח) against Abimelech about his servants' improper taking (גזל) of Abraham's well (Gen 21:25–27). Abimelech responds that he had no knowledge of this. As a result, Abraham and Abimelech enter into a settlement agreement or covenant.

Three times, Job makes a demand upon God to abandon his attack on Job and other mortals, and once he even backs the demand up with a threat to die rather than to submit to Yahweh's will:

> I would choose strangling,
>     my soul, death,
>         rather than this body.
> I reject my life!
>     I will not live forever!
>     Let me alone, for my days are but a breath! (7:15–16)
>
> Are not few my days? Cease!
>     Direct your attention away from me!
>     Let me smile a little
> before I depart—never to return—
>     to the land of gloom and death's shadow,
>     to a morbid land like the darkness of death's shadow,
>         to a land without order where light shines like darkness!" (10:20–22)[30]

---

29. The extensive use of the imperfect by the author of Job supports this reading. While Hebrew poetry is generally no respecter of verb tenses, in the book of Job, the tenses generally follow the prose pattern.

30. Some have argued that this pronouncement is the whimpering of a weak, defeated man (see, e.g., Clines, *Job 1–20*, 251–52). I disagree. Job 7:15–16 and 10:20–22 are part of the

> Look away from them [mortals] and desist,
>   that they may enjoy their days like a laborer (14:6).

Job takes advantage of the public demand to give God one last chance to avert a still greater legal conflict.

Not all accusations end up requiring litigation before a court for resolution. Demands are typically a means to initiate a pre-trial or early-trial settlement of the claim, as in Gen 21:25–27. Such a demand may bring the parties into conversation so that restitution can be made and the parties reconciled quickly. Such a conversation is a settlement negotiation. Statements made within the confines of settlement negotiations seek to achieve four fundamental goals: (1) they typically disclose one's coming trial strategy and the testimony that one will offer; (2) they assess the relative strengths and weaknesses of each party's case; (3) they advocate for the rightness of one's cause; and (4) they attempt to resolve the matter.

These attributes are present in Job's statements. Job informs the other characters about his intended trial strategy: to file a counterclaim and defend against the original charge. He discloses his coming testimony throughout his speeches. He assesses the relative merits of both sides of the dispute by reviewing all the assets and liabilities of his case. His bravado and anxiety are not simple expressions of his feelings; they disclose his position relative to God's. Job repeatedly claims that his cause is just. Finally, he seeks reconciliation with God. This last point needs further explication.

Job 9:15 is particularly important in Job's quest for settlement and reconciliation with God. This verse is difficult to translate. The primary issue has involved how למשפטי ought to be rendered. Today, most follow the MT, taking this as a *poel* participle, meaning *my adversary*.[31] Because this is a strange construction for a strong verb, a few translators render it "my judge," usually emending the MT to למו שפטי.[32] A few suggest למשפטי, "my right."[33] Habel, noting that Job never considers God his judge, translates 9:15b, "I would plead for mercy to my adversary at law."[34] Many others

---

backup plan first suggested by Job's wife: to martyr himself rather than submit to God's abusive authority. He thereby puts additional pressure on this opponent. See further, my "Job's Wife as Hero," 374–423.

31. See, e.g., Clines, *Job 1–20*, 215, 217–18; Driver and Gray, *Book of Job*, 90; Good, *In Turns of Tempest*, 72; Gordis, *Book of Job*, 106; Habel, *Book of Job: Commentary*, 182; NEB; NRSV; Pope, *Job*, 69, 72; Rowley, *Job*, 94; and RSV. See also GKC §55b.

32. See, e.g., M. Jastrow, *The Book of Job: Its Origin, Growth, and Interpretation* (Philadelphia: Lippincott, 1920), 228; NIV; NJB; NJPS; and NASB. Some argue, however, that משפטי means "my judge" and do not emend the verb to reach this result (see, e.g., *HALOT*, 1626).

33. See the extensive bibliographies in Clines, *Job 1–20*, 218; and Gordis, *Book of Job*, 106.

34. Habel, *Book of Job: Commentary*, 182, 179.

are in accord.³⁵ Although I believe that the object of the preposition is most likely "my adversary," I struggle with the idea that Job would plead with God at all—whether he is Job's judge or adversary—given Job's complex counteraccusations against God and the many defensive statements that he ultimately offers.³⁶ I propose an alternative rendering of the *hithpael* imperfect of חנן in this instance, even though the use of חנן in numerous forensic contexts refers to an appeal or request for pardon.³⁷ In this verse the best translation of this verb is "to seek a settlement."

In support of this translation, we turn to Judg 21:20–23. There the Benjaminites plan to capture the maidens of Shiloh for wives.³⁸ They agree among themselves that, if the men of Shiloh should come to initiate a lawsuit (ריב) over the capture, they will say to the men: חנונו אותם (Judg 21:22). This is often rendered "give them to us voluntarily"³⁹ or "be generous and allow us to have them."⁴⁰ The Benjaminites are apparently planning to ask for a resolution of the case before the case is filed. A pre-trial act of forgiveness usually results in some form of formal or informal pre-trial settlement. This is precisely what the Benjaminites are seeking: a pre-trial settlement of the threatened lawsuit, and this phrase should be translated: "Grant them in settlement to us." Similarly, in Hos 12:3, the text relates that God has sued Judah (ריב) and "will punish (פקד) Jacob according to his conduct (דרך) and return (שוב) to him according to his deeds (מעלל)." During the following description of the history between God and Jacob, the text reports the striving between Jacob and the angel at the Jabbok (Gen 32:23–33) and relates that Jacob יתחנן לו (Hos 12:5). While the original encounter is not in the nature of a lawsuit, the description of Jacob's actions is not reasonably recounted as "seeking mercy" or "requesting a pardon" from the angel. In fact, the angel had "not prevailed" (יכל) in the matter (Gen 32:26a; cf. Hos 12:5). After wrenching Jacob's hip from its socket to land a last blow against his successful adversary, the angel asked to be set free (Gen 32:26b–27a). In response, Jacob insisted on receiving a blessing (Gen 32:27b). Only after obtaining it, did he let the angel go (Gen 32:28–30). Jacob was the winner in the dispute, which Hos 12:5 acknowledges. He had no need to seek mercy or pardon. He was not, however, a gloating conqueror. Hosea 12:5 reports that Jacob wept after he prevailed. Jacob's demand was not meant

---

35. See n. 31 above.
36. If this is best translated "judge," then it would lend support to the proposition that Job believes that he is appealing a summary judgment, but I think that this is the least likely alternative.
37. Bovati, *Re-Establishing Justice*, 126, 153–55.
38. Interestingly, Judg 21:23 reports that the Benjaminites did, in fact, carry the women off as booty, using גזל in one of its other senses.
39. See, e.g., NASB; cf. RSV.
40. See, e.g., NRSV; cf. NIV; NJPS.

to extract one last victory from the angel. Rather, he wished to reconcile with the angel, which is why he asked for his blessing.[41] Jacob wanted them to part resolved and in relationship. Thus, the use of the *hithpael* imperfect of חנן, in this instance, is meant to signify that Jacob requested a post-victory reconciliation, or settlement of the dispute, with the angel. The connection between Jacob's striving and God's lawsuit with Judah that the Hosea text establishes further supports this contention. Thus, Job 9:15b should be rendered: "I will seek a settlement with my adversary." Job relates here his intention to negotiate some form of settlement with God and to be reconciled with him.

Remarks made during settlement negotiations are not testimony proper. They do have, however, juridical character. They serve a critical function in the legal process by allowing discovery of the other person's case and by facilitating the resolution of disputes. The same literary forms that mark trial testimony often mark them. This is also true within the book of Job. The characters use much forensic vocabulary as part of their speeches to indicate the legal character of their conversation.

B. Wells, in his study of testimony in the Hebrew Bible, maintains that three verbs express the giving of testimony by witnesses.[42] The first is ענה;[43] the second is the *hiphil* of נגד;[44] and the third is דבר.[45] The characters of the book of Job use these verbs quite commonly. Most of the speeches, once we leave the Divine Council, are introduced with the expression, "X answered (ענה) and said" (Job 3:2; 6:1; 9:1; 12:1; 16:1; 19:1; 21:1; 23:1; 26:1; Eliphaz: 4:1; 15:1; 22:1; Bildad: 8:1; 18:1; 25:1; Zophar: 11:1; 20:1; and Elihu: 32:6a; 34:1; 35:1). Job's short responses to God begin with "Job answered (ענה) Yahweh and said" (40:3; 42:1). One of Yahweh's speeches begins with "Yahweh answered Job and said" (40:1). Two others begin with "Yahweh answered Job out of the whirlwind and said" (38:1; 40:6). Only Job's speech beginning at 29:1 leaves out the word "answered" in favor of "added." This structure is legally significant. As indicated previously, the root ענה, "to answer," may have the forensic meaning "to answer an accusation by way

---

41. This is consistent with the view that a blessing is a relationship marker; see further the material at ch. 10, n. 38 below.

42. Wells, *Law of Testimony*, 25–32.

43. Wells cites Exod 20:13; 23:1–2; Num 35:30; Deut 5:17; 19:16, 18; 31:21; Job 16:8; and Prov 25:18.

44. Wells cites Lev 5:1; Prov 12:17; see also Seeligman, "Terminologie," 261–62.

45. Wells cites, e.g., Ps 50:7; Prov 21:28. He continues: "One other verb that should be mentioned in this regard is *ʾiššēr* ("to bless, call happy"). Job 29:11 uses it in parallel with *ʿûd*. The verse is interesting because it attributes the act of testifying, signaled by the two verbs *ʾiššēr* and *ʿûd*, to people who have already heard (*šāmaʿ*) and seen (*rāʾâ*), that is, people who have already performed the function of an observing witness" (*Law of Testimony*, 27 n. 40).

of defense." We saw this use of ענה in our discussion of Job's counterclaim and defense. As Wells demonstrates, however, the root ענה has a second legal use. It is one of the key terms meaning "to testify."[46] 1 Samuel 12:3, which we examined in chapter 6, is another exemplar of this usage. Zophar (11:2; 20:3b), Elihu (32:12, 15–17, 20; 33:12), and the narrator (32:5) all use ענה to refer to their conversations. In most of these instances, the speaker is addressing whether or not prior statements offered were relevant to, or sufficient evidence on, the outstanding charges. Additionally, the characters use the two other verbs that mark the giving of testimony, נגד (in the *hiphil*) and דבר, to refer to the settlement statements and coming testimony of the others. For example, in 17:5, Job accuses his friends of accepting God's bribe for their testimony using the root נגד in the *hiphil*. Elihu says that thunder testifies to God's anger against iniquity using this same verb form in 36:33. In 33:14, Elihu states that God testifies (דבר) repeatedly even though Job seems not to hear him. He also accuses Job of testifying without knowledge and understanding, using the root דבר in 34:35.

The characters use still other testimony markers throughout the book. In order to understand this better, we return to the legal significance of the verbs שמע and אזן. We have already delineated in chapter 5 that the biblical command, "Hear, I pray!" (שמענה, שמע־נא, or שמעו־נא), is used variously to signify the convening of a court, a plea for a favorable judgment, or that an individual's testimony is about to begin. The *qal* imperative of שמע ("Hear!") and the *hiphil* imperative of אזן ("Listen!") are also used in this way. The characters in the book of Job use these verb forms throughout their speeches. Eliphaz concludes his first speech with a call to hear (שמענה) in 5:27b. He repeats his call for the others to hear (שמע) in 15:17b. Job demands in 13:6:

> Hear my accusations, I pray, (שמעו־נא תוכחתי),
> and listen (קשב) to the complaints (ריב) of my lips

He continues:

> Hear carefully (שמעו שמוע) my arguments (מלה),
> and let my declaration (אחוה) be in your ears. (13:17)

Furthermore, Job repeats the language of 13:17a in 21:2a. In reiterating God's challenge to him as he concedes the case, Job uses שמע־נא (42:4). Elihu, however, is the character who uses these expressions most frequently. He employs various forms of the *qal* imperative of שמע ("Hear!") in 32:10; 33:1; and 37:2, and he uses the *hiphil* imperative of אזן ("Listen!") in 33:1 and 37:14 to give notice as to the legal import of God's and his words.

---

46. Wells, *Law of Testimony*, 25–27; see also Frye, "Use of Māšāl," 62–63.

Hence, Job's efforts from chapters 3 to 31 represent his part in settlement negotiations. Job, his friends, and Elihu all participate in these negotiations. Eventually God enters the scene as well. The speeches have a testimonial character, marked by the verb forms of testimony, while not being testimony proper. The fact that the characters are involved in negotiations does not diminish the legal import of their statements in any way. Their statements represent fairly their legal positions.[47] During their speeches, each character takes up his coming role at trial and verbalizes his future testimony. Each seeks to assess the relative strengths and weaknesses of the parties' cases. Each advocates for the rightness of his cause. Each attempts to resolve the matter in his own way. During the process, they proceed in much the way that they would in an actual trial. Furthermore, Job's oath is quite real. It is, however, a means by which to head off the rest of the actual trial, not to conclude it. He wants to nip this trial in the bud. He has suffered quite enough.

While we have little Neo-Babylonian documentation of lengthy settlement negotiations like the one in the book of Job owing to the scribes' need to be brief, fragments of them do exist. Settlements of some of the larger cases, such as that in *BE* 10, 9, may have taken a great deal of negotiating to produce.[48] One can also see a little of this in the record of the trial proceedings and settlement between Jacob and Laban in Gen 31:25–55. Consequently, this understanding of the character of the speeches from Job 3:1 to 42:6 is quite plausible. Henceforth, when I refer to the characters as "witnesses," I mean that they are potential witnesses in the trial. When I refer to the characters' "testimony," I mean their statements regarding their views of Job's situation and their possible testimony at the coming trial.

Understanding that most of the book is a settlement negotiation gives, greater meaning to 23:3–7, where Job states:

> Oh, that I knew where I might find him,
>   that I might come to his dwelling!
> I will present (ערך) my case (משפט) before him
>   and fill my mouth with accusations (תוכחות).[49]
> I would learn the arguments (מלה) with which he will answer (ענה) me
>   and know what he would say to me.
> In the greatness of his power, would he litigate (ריב) with me?
>   Surely, he would not convict (שׂים ב) me![50]

---

47. Frye notes the frequent use of the *māšāl* in the course of the various witness statements and believes that this argues for the statements being testimony ("Use of Māšāl," 62). I suggest that this aspect makes the speeches more in the nature of a settlement discussion rather than actual testimony.

48. See further, ch. 4, n. 193 above; and the material at ch. 10, n. 40 below.

49. Gemser, "*Rîb*-Pattern," 123.

50. The root שׂים with the preposition ב or ל may have the sense of either "to accuse"

> There the upright (ישר) could reason with him,
>> and I would escape forever from my lawsuit (משפט). (23:6–7)

Thus far, Job has been delivering his demand and trying to negotiate with a hidden being. Job prefers to sit down face to face with God to work the problem out before full fruition of the litigation. M. B. Dick recognizes that 23:6–7 addresses Job's wish to settle the case: "Job would prefer to confront Shaddai directly (23:4–5), but the inaccessibility of God precludes an out-of-court settlement. Job is confident that, if he could only face Eloah, reconciliation could be effected (13:15–16)."[51] I argue that God's invisibility makes a settlement more trying but not impossible. Job wants to reconcile with God, and his use of the *hithpael* imperfect of חנן in order to express his desire to settle is no accident. Just as a pardon brings about reconciliation with God after a verdict has been rendered, so a pre- or mid-trial settlement will bring about when reconciliation the case has not yet ended. This is Job's situation. Reconciliation with God is his ultimate agenda.

The view that Job is engaged in a settlement negotiation also helps to explain 31:37, another curiosity. Here Job swears that he will give a full accounting of his conduct to God with the honor and respect of a prince. This is peculiar if Job has, in fact, concluded his actual trial defense, as many maintain. It is true that, from Job's perspective, his defensive remarks are complete. He has put his mark on them, signifying his acceptance of them. Furthermore, the narrator tells us shortly thereafter that Job's words are ended (31:40c). He has nothing to add. Interestingly, even when God demands in 38:3:

> Gird your loins like a man, I pray!
>> I will interrogate (שאל) you, and you will confess (ידע) to me!

Job rejoins in 40:4–5:

> Certainly, I am small; how can I respond (שוב) to you?
>> I lay my hand to my mouth.
> I have spoken once, and will not answer (ענה);
>> twice, and will do so no more.

One could understand this reply as an early sign of Job's coming submission because, when God asks this same question again in 40:7, Job concedes the case (42:2–6). Nevertheless, Job holds out until the last minute.

---

(Deut 22:14) or "to convict" (1 Sam 22:15). I believe that "convict" best fits the context here and in 4:18b, where Eliphaz says that God "convicts" even "his angels of error." Job is clear that God has already accused him. That cannot lie in the future. Thus, "convict" is the most appropriate meaning in 23:6.

51. Dick, "Legal Metaphor," 45.

His reason will become apparent later.⁵² Right now, all Job does is acknowledge his smallness in the face of such an immense adversary. This is all the more reason to read courage in Job's words. If Job's statement in 40:5 is read with such courage in mind, it means that Job has spoken as often in his defense as he intends to speak. He will not answer further questions. He will make no confession. This is his last stand.⁵³ If this is true, then the puzzle of 31:37 may be solved. Job is swearing in this verse that, if settlement negotiations should fail and God gives Job a bill of particulars, as required, then Job will answer fully all charges with due honor at trial. Job will act as the perfect gentleman. The effect is, tactfully, to call his opponent to task for his outrageous trial conduct.

In conclusion, Job's many catastrophes cause him to believe that he is under divine indictment and investigation for still unspecified crimes. Consequently, Job begins to plan his legal strategy. First, he plans a counteroffensive, in which he will charge God with three counts of abuse of authority. Next he plans a broad-ranging defense in order to attempt to cover all possible charges, employing the thinking of the ritual incantations of the ancient Near East for his own use. He sets none of this into motion, however. Job elects, instead, to make an early demand on God to settle the case. He therefore begins to set forth his strategy and his case's strengths and weaknesses before the trial's other participants in the hopes of reaching a favorable conclusion. Chapter 31 indicates that Job is quite serious in the matter and is prepared to go to trial. Nevertheless, he has great hopes that the whole affair can be resolved quickly through settlement.

---

52. See the material before and at ch. 10, nn. 24–30 below.
53. See the material referenced in the preceding note.

# 8

# The Friends as God's Witnesses

We have, heretofore, concentrated on the interactions between the Satan, God, and Job, the parties to this suit. The other characters do not, however, remain silent. While Job is relating both his defensive and offensive positions, his friends offer him immediate responses. They contribute their views on the nature of Job's situation and on what he ought to do about it. In the course of their speeches, they suggest that Job has violated God's law, and they defend God's actions, asserting that God gave Job less than he actually deserved. Additionally, they attempt to discount Job's testimony in the manner of impeachment at trial. In all this, they disclose their coming testimony for God and against Job, and they assess the relative strengths and weaknesses of each party's case. They advocate for the rightness of God's cause. Finally, they offer their own settlement proposal for Job to consider. By these acts, Eliphaz, Bildad, and Zophar play a significant role in the settlement negotiations and demonstrate that they will serve as God's third-party witnesses if the trial should continue. Elihu also chimes in on God's side, but his remarks have a slightly different character from those of the others. Thus, we will deal with them separately.[1] Job does not accept his friends' contributions to the conversation without comment but replies at every chance. Such give-and-take is common to settlement negotiations. In this chapter, we will investigate the friends' contribution to the settlement negotiations and Job's response.

## The Friends as God's Future
## Third-Party Witnesses: Assailing Job

The friends adopt wholeheartedly the worldview of the Šurpu Incantations: if one is suffering, it is because one has violated God's law, intentionally or otherwise. God gives one only what one deserves. Job's suffering

---

1. See ch. 9 below.

is the result of some sin that he has committed. Consequently, Job must inquire of God to reveal the sin and ask for mercy.

Eliphaz is certain that Job is at fault. He is, after all, a part of sinful humanity. For example, Eliphaz says, in 4:8–9:

> As I have seen, those who plow iniquity (און)
>   and sow trouble (עמל) reap the same.
> By the breath of God, they perish,
>   and, by the blast of his nostrils, they are consumed.[2]

Both humans and angels are untrustworthy, and God may crush them:

> Can mortals be acquitted (צדק) before God?
>   Can human beings be pure (טהר) before their maker?
> He puts no trust even in his servants,
>   and he convicts (שׂים ב)[3] his angels of error (תהלה);
> how much more those who live in houses of clay,
>   whose foundation is in the dust,
>   who are crushed like a moth.
> Between morning and evening, they are destroyed;
>   they perish forever without any regarding it.
> Their tent-cord is plucked up within them,
>   and they die devoid of wisdom. (4:17–21)

Eliphaz reiterates the above when he says:

> What are mortals that they should be cleared of guilt (זכה)[4];
>   those born of women that they be acquitted (צדק)?
> God puts no trust even in his holy ones,
>   and the heavens are not guiltless (זכך) in his sight.
> How much less one who is abominable (תעב) and corrupt (אלח),
>   one who drinks iniquity (עולה) like water! (15:14–16)[5]

He continues the theme in 25:4–6:

> How can a mortal be acquitted (צדק) before God?
>   How can one born of woman be cleared of guilt (זכה)?
> Even the moon is not bright,
>   and the stars are not free of guilt (זכה) in his sight.

---

2. This is to be contrasted to Job, who sees only trouble (3:10). Job 4:8 is similar to Prov 22:8; cf. Job 5:3a.

3. For my justification of the translation "convicts," see ch. 7, n. 50 above.

4. See further L. R. Fisher, "An Amarna Age Prodigal," *JSS* 3 (1958): 115.

5. I do not accept the view that 15:13b is a formulaic introduction of direct speech and that therefore Eliphaz is quoting back Job's view in 15:14–16. In accord are Clines (*Job 1–20*, 341); Habel (*Book of Job: Commentary*, 245); Hartley (*Book of Job*, 247); and Pope (*Job*, 112). The similarity between 4:17–21; 15:14–16; and 24:4–5 makes the position unlikely.

How much less a mortal, a worm,
  the child of humanity, a maggot.⁶

Eliphaz is convinced that Job is guilty simply because he is human.⁷

Eliphaz thinks Job is a fool, and the fool suffers terrible things justly (5:4–6). When Eliphaz demands in 5:1a, "Summon (קרא), I pray! Is there anyone who will answer (ענה) you?" he taunts Job theologically as well as legally. Recalling the view that God will answer the righteous if called (Isa 58:9; 65:24; Pss 3:5; 4:2; 17:6–7; 120:1–2) but not the wicked (Prov 21:12–13), Eliphaz states here that God will not answer Job in this situation if Job should call upon him. In fact, no one in the Divine Council will hear Job's claim. The implication is that Job can sue God, but he is wicked and foolish for doing so. Job 5:2–3 make it absolutely clear that, from Eliphaz's point of view, Job's possible suit is foolishness. Eliphaz speaks in a proverb in 5:2. The fool's resentment is not only readily apparent (Prov 12:16a); it also kills. Job's resentment is no different. It is destroying him. More, it has already destroyed his children.

In 5:4, Eliphaz proclaims that the children of the fool cannot be successful and that his sons "are crushed (דכא) in the gate with no one to rescue them" (5:3b–4). On the personal level, this is a cruel verbal blow to Job, whose ten children were crushed when the house of his oldest son fell in upon them.⁸ We can only imagine them running toward the gate of the house in an effort to escape. The house is accursed; the children are crushed.⁹ Yet, as revealed by Prov 22:22b, this remark has legal significance. Eliphaz maintains his insulting assessment of Job's situation: the fool and his sons will suffer. As the angels are convicted, so will Job be convicted. The punishment is that his sons will meet a solid defeat in court—one gained through the exercise of raw, unbridled power. Eliphaz knows this to be true. His proof? The children are, in fact, dead—dead because the sins of the father are to be visited upon the children and because of the rightful exercise of God's fantastic, uncheckable power.¹⁰ Job deserves his

---

6. Because of the similarity between 4:17–21; 15:14–16; and 25:4–6, I attribute 25:2–6 to Eliphaz and not to Bildad. See further ch. 1, n. 32 above.

7. According to R. N. Whybray, Eliphaz introduces a "doctrine of relative guilt shared by all," which is "a new perception of retributive justice. It was the lot of human beings to suffer misfortune; and so, by implication, Job was no exception" (*Job*, 45). Eliphaz's words are, however, reminiscent of those of Ps 143:2, where the Psalmist begs: "Do not bring a lawsuit (משפט) against your servant, for no living thing can be acquitted (צדק) before you."

8. Crook, *Cruel God*, 32.

9. Cf. Prov 15:23a: "Yahweh will tear down the house of the proud . . . ."

10. The vicarious liability that may be imposed on the child is well known in ancient Israel. See Exod 20:5; Deut 5:9; Isa 14:21; Jer 31:29; and Ps 7:8; cf. 2 Sam 21:1–10. The incident in 2 Sam 21:1–10 has some special factors that are involved in the sons' deaths. As M. Greenberg points out: "Saul's sons were executed under extraordinary circumstances: their father

fate, which is already sealed in the blood of his children. There is no point in contesting anything, as Prov 24:7 advises:

> Wisdom is too high for fools;
> in the gate, they do not open their mouths.

The fool should not speak in the gate of justice. For Eliphaz, Job is that fool. He disdains any action by Job in order to gain redress.

Eliphaz does more, however, than simply tell Job to abandon his claim on the basis of God's rights and powers. He additionally addresses some of the specific counts that Job is formulating in his mind. First, Eliphaz contests Job's assessment that God is the cause of human suffering (3:20–23). Rather, humans create their suffering:

> For trouble does not originate from the dust
> and suffering does not sprout from the ground.
> But humans beget trouble[11]
> just as sparks fly upward from the flame. (5:6–7)[12]

Consequently, he argues that Job, because he is ultimately responsible for what is happening to him, should inquire of God through an oracular procedure and, in this manner, hand his legal dispute over to God:

> But I would inquire (דרש)[13] of God.
> I would lay (שים) my case (דברה) before God. (5:8)[14]

---

had violated a sacred national oath; for which divine wrath had later struck Israel; Saul was already dead, and the Gibeonites expressly rejected composition" ("Crimes and Punishments," 736). This might also be a mitigated punishment against Job. Westbrook demonstrates that the death of the child of a head of household is often a mitigated punishment (*Studies*, 55–57).

11. The MT's יולד is not consistent with Eliphaz's worldview, particularly as expressed in 5:6 above. I revocalize to a defective *hiphil* יולד. For those who take this position, see Clines, *Job 1–20*, 116.

12. The meaning of 5:7b is highly contested. I have utilized the older translation tradition in order to maintain a more complete parallelism. Others contend that בני־רשף refers to the sons of Resheph, the Phoenician god of pestilence. Clines states: "On this view, Eliphaz is saying that when humans beget trouble for themselves they let loose (metaphorically speaking) the underworld demons of pestilence to fly high to earth in order to attack mortals. V 7b then is not strictly parallel to v 7a but rather its consequence" (*Job 1–20*, 142). Concurring are Pope, *Job*, 40, 42–43; Whybray, *Job*, 46; and Zuckerman, *Job the Silent*, 241 n. 249. K. H. Richards says that Resheph may be mentioned in this verse ("Death," *ABD*, 2:109). Either translation is plausible, and once again the author of Job may have intended a double meaning. For background bibliography on Resheph and his connection with death, see Clines, *Job 1–20*, 142.

13. For דרש as an oracular procedure, see ch. 5, n. 59 above.

14. For more on דברה and דבר as a legal dispute and this particular idiom, see Bovati, *Re-Establishing Justice*, 212–13; cf. B. S. Jackson, *Theft in Early Jewish Law* (Oxford: Clarendon, 1972); and S. M. Paul, "Unrecognized Biblical Legal Idioms in Light of Comparative Akkadian

Job is convicted of sin. He therefore should inquire of God as to the crime, presumably, that he may petition for relief through expiation. Job 5:8 contains another legal-theological double entendre because, while the Hebrew Bible links דרש rarely outside of the book of Job to settling a lawsuit (e.g., Exod 18:15; cf. Ezek 20:1–4, 31), in several instances it links דרש to gaining a word of God.[15] This type of play on דרש is employed also in 1 Chr 28:9, where David says to Solomon: "know the God of your father, and serve him with a whole heart (לב) and a willing soul; for Yahweh investigates (דרש) all hearts (לבב), and understands every intent of the thoughts (יצר מחשבות). If you seek (דרש) him, he will let you find him; but if you forsake him, he will reject you forever." God need not seek (דרש) the day of Job's birth (3:4) or anything else.[16] Job must seek God. The Hebrew Bible repeatedly affirms the idea that, if one seeks God, blessings will come upon the seeker, and, if one does not, terrible things will follow.[17] Amos 5:6 is especially significant in this context:

> Seek (דרש) Yahweh and live,
>   or else he will advance against the house of Joseph like fire,
>   and it will devour Bethel, with no one to quench it.

The point of Eliphaz's speech is that Job should not contend with God but rather seek the cause of God's judgment. The fire that Job suffered resulted from his failure to seek God adequately in his day-to-day life. Further, Job should seek God immediately because God is the doer of great, incomprehensible deeds (5:9–10); he is the protector of the lowly and the comforter of those who mourn (5:11), and he is absolutely just (5:12–16). This God gives order to the universe. Job's third count cannot stand. Eliphaz emphasizes that God's deeds are unsearchable, beyond human legal investigation (חקר); his justice is beyond human understanding (5:9). God's perfect justice brings "hope for the wretched" and stops "the mouth of wrongdoing" (5:16). This idea originates in Ps 107:42, where God stops the mouth of the wicked. The wise heed this and focus on God's steadfast love (Ps 107:43). Eliphaz insinuates that Job has such a mouth, although he does not directly accuse Job of blasphemy. Job is not wise; rather, he is a self-centered, ungrateful fool who deserves his fate. Job's only hope lies in seeking God.

---

Expressions," *RB* 86 (1976): 235–36. On this particular use of דברה, see Bovati, *Re-Establishing Justice*, 212 n. 105.

15. See, e.g., 1 Kgs 22:5; 2 Kgs 1:16; Ezek 20:1–2; and 2 Chr 18:4; cf. 2 Kgs 3:11. The Akkadian equivalent of דבר, *dabābu*, also has this double meaning. For its legal usage in the Neo-Babylonian period, see, e.g., *Nbn* 52.

16. דרש is used here in is nontechnical meaning.

17. See, e.g., Jer 10:21; Ps 9:11; 34:5, 11; 69:33; 77:03; 105:4 [= 1 Chr 16:11]; 119:155; Prov 10:4; and 2 Chr 15:02; 16:12; 26:5.

Eliphaz solidifies his view that Job should accept his guilt and God's punishment when he states in 5:17:

> How happy (אשר) is the one whom God reproves (יכח)![18]
> Therefore, do not reject the discipline (יסר) of Shaddai.

This is a partial reiteration of Ps 94:12–13:[19]

> How happy (אשר) is the mortal whom you discipline (יסר), O Yahweh,
>    the person you instruct in your law (תורה),
> to give him tranquility in times of misfortune,
>    until a pit be dug for the wicked.

Moreover, according to Prov 15:31–33, the wise allow God to offer them reproof, and those who will not subject themselves to such discipline hate their lives:[20]

> The ear that hears the reproof (תוכחת) of life,
>    lodges among the wise.
> Those who spurn discipline (מוסר) hate (מאס) their lives;
>    but the one who hears reproof (תוכחת) gains understanding (לב).
> The fear of Yahweh is the discipline (מוסר) of wisdom.
>    Humility precedes honor.

This makes them as bad as those aiders and abettors in Prov 29:24 who do not accuse known criminals.[21] Eliphaz considers Job to be just such a lowlife.

Eliphaz continues his argument that Job should submit himself to the discipline of God. He realizes that God's correction is not always pleasant, but he maintains, as Job once did: you must take the good with the bad:

> For he himself inflicts pain and bandages [wounds];
>    he wounds, but his hands heal. (5:18)

This language is reminiscent of Hos 6:1; Deut 32:39; and Lam 3:31–32. Hosea 6:1 is clear that one must return to God for repentance of sins. Deuteronomy 32:39 uses such language in God's discourse on his power. Eliphaz believes both propositions: God is powerful, and one must return to him for the repentance of sins. Lamentations 3:31–32, while not being

---

18. The use of יכח here and in Prov 15:31–33 below plays on the multiple meanings of the root. God reproves through his accusations. See the material at ch. 6, nn. 55–59 above.
19. See also Prov 3:11.
20. Cf. Prov 15:12, where the scoffer will not turn to the wise for reproof (יכח).
21. For the similarity of this culpability to those who aid and abet a criminal by not disclosing his or her crime, see ch. 5, nn. 81–82 above.

quite as similar to the vocabulary of 5:18, may be the most instructive as to Eliphaz's thinking:

> For the Lord does not
> reject forever,[22]
> but first afflicts (יגה), then pardons (רחם)[23]
> in his abundant loving-kindness.

This is the essence of Eliphaz's message: God is a forgiving God; submit to his authority, and know his kindness again.

There may be, however, still more lying beneath Eliphaz's words if he is indeed following the thinking of Lamentations. This is because Lam 3:33–36 continues:

> For he does not intentionally (מלבו) violate (ענה)[24]
> or afflict (יגה) humanity,
> crushing (דכא) under his feet
> all the prisoners of the earth.
> To deflect the case (משפט) of a mortal
> before the Most High,
> to subvert a human in their lawsuit (ריב),
> [this] the Lord does not choose.

In Eliphaz's view, God always has cause when he metes out punishment. He never abuses his authority. While the fool and his children may seem to suffer what appears to be an abuse of authority, it is, in actuality, only what they deserve. Thus, in attacking Job in this manner, Eliphaz also defends God by denying generally Job's claim of abuse of authority.

In explaining his view of God to Job and advising Job as to the right course of action, Eliphaz uses words that cut to the quick. He snorts that God "lifts mourners to safety" (5:11b) and retorts that God ensnares the cunning and thwarts the plan of the perverse (5:12–13), who, he adds, "encounter darkness in the daytime and grope along at noon as if it were night" (5:14). He assaults Job's longing for the darkening of the day of his birth (3:4–5, 9), calling it perversity. The implication of 5:17–18 is: How happy is he who allows God to wound and heal. Eliphaz thereby both

---

22. See also 1 Chr 28:9, which contains this same language and additionally employs the דרש wordplay discussed previously at ch. 5, n. 59 above.

23. Following the NJPS. "To pardon" is within the semantic range of רחם. See, e.g., Deut 13:8; 1 Kgs 8:50; Ps 79:8; and Mic 7:19.

24. Interestingly, the Hebrew root meaning "to violate," ענה, which is found in both in Lam 3:33 and Job 37:23, appears to be identical to the root that means "to answer." While they probably originate in different Proto-Semitic words, the two Hebrew roots are homonyms. This creates a wordplay, suggesting that God neither violates nor answers to anyone. No one should expect God to answer, not even Job.

explains away Job's pain and reinforces the idea that Job had it right the first time when he said: "Yahweh has given and Yahweh has taken away. Let the name of Yahweh be blessed" (1:21b).

From 5:19–26, Eliphaz recounts the successes of those who submit in this way to God. Among the successes are rescue from trouble and harm (5:19), redemption (פדה) from starvation in famine and death by sword in war (5:20), shelter from the roving, scourging (שוט) tongue (5:21a), freedom from fear in the face of destruction (5:21b), a peaceful home (5:24a), successful inspections (פקד) of the herds (5:24b), many offspring (5:25), and the maintenance of one's vigor right until death (5:26). Job, of course, has few of these things any longer. Again, he deserves his fate.

With these unkind sentiments expressed, Eliphaz closes his speech:

Indeed, we have investigated (חקר) this [matter], and so it is;
Hear, I pray, (שמענה) and know it for yourself (ואתה דע־לך)! (5:27)

These words are not, however, just a simple summation and admonition to Job to listen to Eliphaz's sage advice. Eliphaz claims to have been part of the Satan's investigative team by his use of the verb חקר; his remarks are based on those findings (כן־היא).[25] God is just. Humanity is sinful. Job, therefore, cannot be in the right. Job must be suffering correction for sins committed. He predicts that Job will lose his suit. Thus, with the words "Hear, I pray!" Eliphaz is calling for Job's acquiescence to God's charges.[26]

Eliphaz's second speech continues in like vein. In 15:4, Eliphaz asserts that Job subverts both piety and petitions (שיחה) before God.[27] In 15:5–6, Eliphaz returns to the theme that Job's mouth condemns him and that his lips testify against him:

Your iniquity (עולה) dictates your mouth,
  so you choose crafty language.
Your own mouth condemns (רשע) you, not I.
  Your lips testify (ענה) against you.

Eliphaz suggests that Job has no right to contend with God because he was not the first mortal born and was not at the creation (15:8), foreshadowing God's defense against Job's claims as set forth in 38:4. Eliphaz maintains that, in Job's opinion, God's consolations are too small for him, which is why he will not submit himself to God (15:11a). He also suggests that Job

---

25. Bovati, *Re-Establishing Justice*, 253.
26. Ibid., 83. See also Jer 3:13; cf. 1 Sam 12:17; Jer 2:23; 3:2.
27. The word שיחה may have the meanings "complaint," "a meditation," or "talk." It most often holds the first meaning in the book of Job. In 15:4, it indicates appropriate petitions of the deity rather than Job's complaints.

does not find God's gentle words adequate (15:11b). Job, on the other hand, hardly considers Yahweh's word gentle. Eliphaz additionally maintains that Job has turned his spirit away from God and issued arguments from his mouth:

> How your mind (לבב) has carried you away,
>   how your eyes have failed you,[28]
> that you vent your anger against God,[29]
>   and let such arguments (מלה) out of your mouth! (15:12–13)

In 15:20–35, Eliphaz argues that the wicked—those who trust in emptiness, the assembly of perverts, those conceiving evil—all suffer hardships, many of which look like Job's. For example, the wicked writhe in torment (v. 20); robbers fall upon them (v. 21b); they are overcome by anxiety (v. 24a); their houses become rubble (v. 28b–c); they will lose their wealth (v. 29); they will not escape darkness (v. 30b); and fire will devour the tents of bribers (v. 34b). Job has known these hardships and more.

Eliphaz continues his assault on Job in the third cycle and argues that Job is suffering this lawsuit because of his crimes:

> Can the mighty be of use to God,
>   the wise benefit him?
> Does Shaddai profit if you are innocent (צדק)?
>   Does he gain (בצע) if your conduct is in integrity (תמם)?
> Is it because of your piety that he accuses (יכח) you,
>   and enters into a lawsuit (משפט) with you? (22:2–4)

Eliphaz then presents a list of Job's alleged crimes:

> You know that your wickedness is great,
>   and that your iniquities have no limit.
> You exact pledges from your fellows without reason,
>   and leave them naked, stripped of their clothes;
> You do not give the thirsty water to drink.
>   You deny bread to the hungry.
> The land belongs to the strong.
>   The privileged occupy it.
> You have sent away widows empty-handed.
>   The strength of the fatherless is broken. (22:5–9)

Job violates some of the most important principles of social justice according to Eliphaz. Consequently, for this reason too, Job deserves his fate (22:10–11). Moreover, Job challenges the omniscience and wisdom of God:

---

28. Following NJPS for 15:12; cf. Pope, *Job*, 112.
29. Hartley, *Book of Job*, 224; citing Fisher, "Amarna Age Prodigal," 115; cf. Pope, *Job*, 112.

> God is in the heavenly heights.
>   See the highest stars, how lofty!
> You say, "What can God know?
>   Can he judge (שפט) through the dense cloud?
> The clouds screen him so he cannot see
>   as he moves about the circuit of heaven."
> Have you observed the immemorial path
>   that the evil have trodden;
> how they were shriveled up before their time
>   and their foundation poured out like a river?
> They said to God, "Leave us alone (סור)!
>   What can Shaddai do about it?" (22:12–17)

This last statement is particularly telling. Job has demanded of God, in both 7:16c and 10:20a–b, that God leave him alone using the verbs חדל and שית. These are critical statements in Job's demand on God to settle the case. Here Eliphaz mocks Job, using the verb סור. Eliphaz believes that Job's legal demand on God is part of Job's wickedness. Job should admit his liability and offer an oracle in order to determine the exact nature of his crime. In lieu of that, Eliphaz will propose possible crimes that Job has committed, thereby substituting himself for the priest using the Šurpu and DINGIR.ŠÀ.DIB.BA incantations. In line with the thinking of the incantations, Eliphaz probably believes that Job should also offer expiation to solve the problem, although he never states this explicitly.

Bildad, on the other hand, is clear about Job's need to expiate the crime. The essence of Bildad's coming testimony is that God is a just god:

> Does God pervert justice (משפט)?
>   Or does Shaddai pervert a right cause (צדק)? (8:3)

These remarks are reminiscent of Ezek 18:25 and 29, in which God maintains his own justice as against Israel's in the face of its complaint that he is unjust. In this assertion, Bildad agrees with Eliphaz (4:17). Bildad, however, believes that Job's children are dead because they sinned (חטא) against God (8:4). They got what they deserved. Bildad disputes, not only Job's interpretation of the children's death—that is, God caused his children to die unwarrantedly—but also contests Eliphaz's interpretation. Eliphaz attributes their death to the sins of their father (5:4). Bildad thinks the children died on their own merit—or lack thereof. He expresses the position of Deut 24:16; Ezek 18:1–32; 1 Kgs 14:6 (= 2 Chr 25:4); and Jer 31:30, which reject the idea that a child might die for the sins of his or her father. Possibly Bildad thinks they actually committed the blasphemy about which Job worried, although their crime remains unspecified. Bildad's speech creates conflict among the views of the third-party witnesses of the dispute. Those who will be testifying on God's behalf do not necessarily agree with each other. Such intra-position trial controversies typically help the opposing side.

While Bildad would attribute the deaths of Job's children to their own errors, he is deeply concerned about Job's reaction to this event. For that, Job is personally responsible. He is suffering and will continue to suffer his own punishment for his unsuitable response. Bildad maintains that the solution to what ails him is to "search diligently" (שׁחר) for God and then אל־שׁדי תתחנן (8:5). This latter phrase is normally translated "to make supplication to Shaddai"[30] or "to make an appeal to Shaddai."[31] Thus, Bildad's view again falls within the purview of the ritual incantations. Furthermore, those who were clearly guilty of sin or convicted of crime in ancient Israel might well be encouraged to make confession and supplication (Josh 7:20; 1 Kgs 8:33, 47 [= 2 Chr 6:24, 37]).[32] Bildad is advising Job to plead with God for a clarification of the sin already committed and for clemency regarding the error.[33] Here Eliphaz and Bildad agree that Job should turn to God. Bildad is just more explicit in his assertion that Job should throw himself on the mercy of God to receive pardon.

There is, however, a hint of something else in Bildad's words. In urging Job to make supplication regarding the sins he has allegedly committed, Bildad is using the language of settlement, תתחנן.[34] In this manner, Bildad acknowledges the heavenly suit against Job and suggests settling the case. Bildad thinks this would be in the nature of a post-trial settlement, not a mid-trial settlement as Job avers. To Bildad's way of thinking, Job and God can still come to terms in spite of the prior finding of Job's guilt. Tensions need not exist forever. The full measure of the punishment need not fall upon Job. Neo-Babylonian litigation records make plain that a post-trial settlement of claims was a viable means by which to restore positive relations. This is also reported in the Hebrew Bible. For example, Gen 44:18–34 reports a settlement negotiation between Joseph and Judah that occurs after Benjamin's conviction on the theft of Joseph's silver goblet. Therein Judah proposes that he suffer Benjamin's punishment. The concept of a post-trial settlement between adverse parties and the idea of an

---

30. See, e.g., NRSV; cf. NJPS.
31. Cf. NASB; NIV; and NJB; also Gen 42:21; Ps 30:9.
32. Although in the case of Josh 7:20, the death penalty was not averted by confession, as might be expected under the rules of mitigation. See ch. 6, n. 18 above.
33. See, e.g., Bovati, *Re-Establishing Justice*, 126.
34. Z. W. Falk indicates: "Some forms of biblical prayer were clearly influenced by legal procedure. Hebrew thought . . . described the relations between God and man under the rule of law, and from there resulted some specific patterns of worship" (*Hebrew Law in Biblical Times*, 52, citing Gemser, "*Rîb*-Pattern," 126). The relationship between law and prayer in the lawsuit genres is more fully developed by S. H. Blank, "Confessions of Jeremiah," 337–38; and A. Laytner, *Arguing with God*, xvii–xviii, 1–39.

executive pardon are merged in Bildad's counsel because, for Bildad, God is both prosecutor and judge. Bildad believes that, if Job is truly "pure and upright" (זך וישר) and approaches God in this manner, God will restore him to "your rightful estate" (נות צדקך) and make his past prosperity seem small in comparison to his future (8:6–7).

Zophar joins in the chorus of voices charging Job with guilt. In his first speech, he objects that Job inappropriately boasts and derides, maybe even blasphemes;[35] yet none rebukes Job (11:3). Zophar maintains that Job's protestations that he is pure (זך) and his teaching right (בר) are in error (11:4). Zophar suggests that God should speak directly to Job and explain matters to him (11:5–6a). Most importantly, Zophar offers to Job that "God has made you forget your transgression" (11:6b). This is similar to the situations in Lev 5:2–4 in which the individual in question is at first unaware of his or her guilt (נעלם ממנו), but becomes aware of it (והוא ידע), presumably because the sin is making itself known through some problem according to the understanding of the ritual incantations. In those cases, the individual is guilty (Lev 5:2–4). Consequently, he or she must make confession and make a sin offering to remove the guilt (Lev 5:5–6). In some of these assertions, Zophar's position is quite similar to that of his companions. The main differences are Zophar's clear acknowledgment that Job may not be aware of his guilt and his emphasis on the mercy of God. For example, he instructs: "Know then that God exacts of you less than your guilt deserves." He continues that Job cannot know the mystery and limits of God (11:7–9), and concludes:

> But an empty-headed person will get understanding
>   when a wild ass is born human. (11:12)

Job is, by implication, an ass. Zophar's mercy is apparently far less than God's. To Zophar's way of thinking, Job should set his intention (לבב) right, remove his iniquity (און) from his hand and dwelling, and stretch out his hands in supplication to God in accord with Lev 5:2–6 and the ritual incantations of the ancient Near East. The results of this act will be quite favorable to Job.

> If you set aright (כן) your intention (לבב)
>   you will stretch out your hands toward him.
> If iniquity (און) is in your hand, put it far away,
>   and do not let wickedness reside in your tents.
> Surely then you will lift up your face without blemish.
>   You will be secure and will not fear.
> You will forget your misery.
>   You will remember it as waters that have passed away.

---

35. See ch. 5, n. 33 above.

And your life will be brighter than the noonday;
  its darkness will be like the morning.
And you will have confidence, because there is hope.
  You will be protected and take your rest in safety.
You will lie down, and no one will make you afraid.
  Many will entreat your favor.
But the eyes of the wicked will fail.
  All way of escape will be lost to them,
  and their hope is to breathe their last. (11:13–20)

If he does not, however, he will suffer the fate of all the wicked.

In his second speech, Zophar continues his attack on Job. He asserts throughout chapter 20 that the wicked pursue evil (20:12–13), and thus God sends punishment upon them (20:15b, 23b–c, 28b–29). The wicked fall rapidly under God's judgment (20:4–11, 14–15a, 16–23a; 24–28a). Job is implicated as guilty in several of Zophar's assertions. In 20:10b, the wicked must give back their wealth (cf. 20:20–21). In 20:14, their food turns in their stomachs. In 20:22–25, they will be filled with misery and experience themselves as shot through by God's arrows. In 20:26, fire will consume their possessions. Finally, in 20:28, their possessions will be dragged away. Job has complained of all these things. To add insult to injury, Zophar implies that Job is the one who abuses his authority, not God:

> Because the wicked[36] legally defeated (רצץ)[37] and disregarded the poor,
>   [because] they have gained through abuse of authority (גזל) a house
>     they did not build,
> they knew no quiet in their bellies,
>   in their greed, they let nothing escape.
> There was nothing left after they had eaten.
>   Therefore, their prosperity will not endure. (20:19–21)

Job is wicked and deserves far more than he got. God is a merciful god. In fact, Job ought to be glad that he did not suffer worse.

In Zophar's third speech, he persists in his assertion that, if Job would only accept God's instructions, banish iniquity (עולה) from his tent, and pray to God, then God would reward him:

> Submit to God and be at peace with him;
>   in this way, prosperity will come to you.
> Accept instruction (תורה) from his mouth;
>   lay up his words in your mind (לבב).

---

36. Literally, "they"; the referent is found in 20:5.
37. I translate רצץ as "legally defeated," rather than with one of its meanings that is unrelated to abuse of authority, because it is linked to גזל in this pericope. See the material at ch. 6, nn. 114–15 above.

> If you return to Shaddai, you will be restored.
>     If you banish iniquity (עולה) from your tent,
> if you regard gold as dust,
>     Ophir-gold as stones of the wadi,
> and Shaddai be your gold
>     and as precious silver to you,
> when you delight in Shaddai
>     and lift up your face to God,
> you will pray to him, and he will hear you,
>     and you will pay your vows.
> You will decree and it will be fulfilled,
>     and light will shine upon your affairs. (22:21–28)[38]

God is merciful to the guilty (אי־נקי) who supplicate themselves for crimes committed. Their hands will become clean (בר), and they may become advocates of the humble and guilty before God (22:29–30). This is the best course of action for Job in Zophar's mind.

Hence, the friends attack Job repeatedly as being wicked, although only Eliphaz is direct in his legal assault. They believe he is deserving of whatever suffering he has endured. Each witness builds upon the prior witness's testimony to propose a collective solution for Job: that is, to determine the exact nature of the wrong through an oracle and to throw himself on the mercy of God through expiation. This is not, however, the friends' only contribution to the trial. They also stand with God in his defense against Job's claim.

## The Friends' Statements in Support of God

All three of Job's friends assert that God is majestic and powerful. His ways may be unknowable, but he is always just. For example, as to God's greatness, Eliphaz argues that God does great deeds (5:9), creates fair weather (5:10), resides in "the heavenly heights" (22:12a), and is of great power (25:2–3a).[39] He spends considerable time explaining God's justice to Job. He asserts that the wicked reap what they sow (4:8). God thwarts and destroys the wicked (4:9–11, 20–21; 5:12–14; 22:16, 20). They have no hope of relief:

---

38. I maintain that 22:21–30 belong to Zophar's speech, not that of Eliphaz, based on the similarity between 11:15 and 22:26, and the use of בר in both 11:4 and 22:30, the removal of unrighteousness in 22:23, as well as the overall sense of Zophar's position in chs. 11 and 20 (see further ch. 1, n. 32 above).

39. I maintain that 25:2–6 belong to Eliphaz's speech, not that of Bildad, based on the commonalities among 4:17–19; 15:14–16; and 25:4–6 (see further ch. 1, n. 32 above).

> For what hope has the godless when cut down,
>> when God takes away their life?
> Will God hear their cry (צעקה)
>> when trouble comes upon them?
> Will he take delight upon Shaddai?
>> Will he call (קרא) upon God at all times? (27:8–10)[40]

God delivers the good and bestows blessings upon them (5:19–26). He promotes social justice (5:15–16). The suffering that God inflicts as discipline should be received happily because God wounds and heals justly (5:17–18). God is fair to the wicked and the wicked should appreciate God's disciplining. Eliphaz believes that God's actions are always justified and suffering always deserved.

Bildad thinks similarly. One of his earliest legal maneuvers is to argue that God supports justice and upholds the innocent (8:3). He asserts that those who are not aligned with God prosper for only a short time and then wither, just as Job has apparently done (8:11–19). One cannot be cut off from the source of life and survive (8:11). Bildad argues that those who do evil are like the weed that, when ripped from its bed against a house, will be denied by the house with the words "I never saw you" (8:18b). The impious have no real hope (8:13). Bildad is certain of the outcome because:

> Indeed, God does not reject the person of integrity (תם)
>> nor does he grasp the hand of the evil. (8:20)

If Job is truly a pure, upright man of integrity, he will be restored manifoldly when he turns to God. In this particular stance, Bildad and Eliphaz agree. According to Eliphaz, Job's integrity is his hope (5:6). Bildad concurs that Job will be well if he is what he claims to be. Seeking God and asking for pardon is how he will demonstrate his integrity and purity now. Only by returning to God in a surrendered approach can Job bring joy to his life, which will fill his "mouth with laughter" and "his lips with shouting" (8:21). Such a mouth would not, of course, be capable of blasphemy.

In Bildad's second speech, he reiterates these ideas. He claims that Job tears himself up in unjustifiable rage; it is not God who is unjustly angry:

> You who tear yourself to pieces in anger—
>> will earth's order be disrupted for your sake,
>> will rocks be dislodged from their place? (18:4)

Bildad is arguing that the cosmos has an order that Job seeks to disrupt. He is the scoundrel, not God. The wicked, the ungodly, those who do not know

---

40. I maintain that 27:8–12 belongs to Eliphaz's speech, not that of Job owing in part to the idea of calling or summoning God expressed in both 5:1 and 27:10 (see further ch. 1, n. 32 above).

God, are their own undoing (18:7b–10, 21). Bildad lists a number of calamities that fall upon the wicked (18:5–7a, 11–20), a few of which have already happened to Job. For instance, Bildad has a reference to the wicked living in darkness (18:18) and the loss of their offspring (18:19).[41]

Bildad again asserts, in this third speech, that the wicked get their due (24:13–22).[42] They become insignificant (24:18a); their portion is cursed (24:18b); they die young and are not remembered (24:19–20); however powerful they may seem, eventually life will turn on them (24:22). God will bring them to justice:

> God may let them feel safe and secure,
>   but his eyes are on their ways.
> They may be exalted for a while, then they are gone.
>   They are laid low, and shrivel like mallows,
>   and wither like the heads of grain. (24:23–24)

At the last, Bildad addresses Job's third claim, defending God as a powerful creator and sustainer of the cosmos:

> The shades tremble
>   beneath the waters and their denizens.
> Sheol is naked before him;
>   Abaddon has no cover.
> He stretches out Zaphon over the void,
>   who suspended earth over emptiness.
> He wrapped up the waters in his clouds,
>   yet, no cloud burst under their weight.
> He shuts off the view of his throne,
>   spreading his cloud over it.
> He drew a boundary on the surface of the waters
>   at the extreme where light and darkness meet.
> The pillars of heaven tremble,
>   astounded at his blast.
> By his power, he stilled the sea.
>   By his skill, he struck down Rahab.
> By his wind, the heavens were calmed.
>   His hand pierced the fleeing serpent.
> These are but glimpses of his rule,
>   the mere whisper that we perceive of him.
> Who can absorb the thunder of his mighty deeds? (26:5–14)[43]

---

41. Bildad's reference to darkness in 18:18 is similar to that of Eliphaz in 15:30b.

42. I maintain that 24:13–25 belongs to Bildad's speech, not that of Job, because of the plant metaphors in use similar to those in 8:11–12, 16b–18 and 18:16 (see further ch. 1, n. 32 above).

43. I maintain that 26:5–14 belongs to Bildad's speech, not that of Job. The general sense of the pericope and the flow of all the misplaced sections point toward Bildad, although its

Bildad foreshadows God's primary defense against Job's third claim. God is powerful and has control over the universe. God is the master of both the void (26:7) and chaos (26:12). The world is orderly. It is a place where social justice can prevail.

Zophar, too, avows that God is just. He claims that God knows iniquity (און) and evil persons (11:11) and destroys them (11:20). The good are rewarded and the evil punished (11:15–20). In his third speech, Zophar spends considerable time explaining the portion allotted to the evil, the ruthless, and the greedy by God. Their sons are marked for death; their descendants will go hungry and die of the plague (27:14–15a). Even their widows will not weep (27:15b). Their riches will go to the righteous or fail entirely (27:17–19). Terror will overtake them (27:20a). The wind will blow them away (27:20b–23). Zophar trusts in the social justice of God. It is fairly applied to Job in the loss of his sons and riches, as well as in the terrors that have overtaken him.

The friends declare, in combination, the power and wonder of the creator. They believe that the cosmos is orderly and that justice prevails within it. They believe that Job is guilty of some crime and deserving of his fate. Thus, they have defended God on all three counts of Job's accusation.

## Impeaching Testimony

Job's friends stand opposed to Job on a number of fronts. The substantive legal conflict among the characters' stories is clear. Yet legal conflict is seen not only through examining the content of the different stories of the parties and witnesses but also through investigating the manner in which the characters deal with each other. It is not enough simply to tell one's own story in court. One must impeach the character and veracity of the witnesses on the other side and cast doubt on the story they tell. Legal stories are fraught with repartee. This dynamic is evident in the book of Job.

The characters seek repeatedly to impeach each other during the course of the negotiations. The friends attack Job frequently to this purpose. For example, Bildad calls Job's complaints mere wind (8:2), thus mocking Job's cry that God renders Job's words and life as mere wind (6:26a; 7:7a). Job's words are certainly wind to Bildad's way of thinking, but this is Job's doing, not God's. Eliphaz agrees, maintaining that Job supports his claims with windy, useless words (15:2–3). Zophar, falling in line, asks whether a spate of words should go unanswered (11:2a). He also asks whether verbose people are always in the right (11:2b). He calls Job's words

---

ideas and vocabulary might be attributed to any of the friends (see further ch. 1, n. 32 above).

babble (11:3a). Bildad believes that Job is setting word snares—playing word games (18:2).[44] Eliphaz accuses Job of having had his passions carry him away (15:12). Bildad suggests that Job needs to come to his senses (18:2b). Eliphaz attacks Job's source of knowledge by saying that Job did not exist at the beginning of time and has not stood in the Council of God (15:7–8). Eliphaz, on the other hand, knows and will teach Job what God thinks (27:11). He also suggests that the friends know more than Job because they are older and therefore wiser (15:9–10). Job's words are nonsense (27:12b).

In the latter part of chapter 6, Job begins his impeachment of the witnesses. He argues that the friends are disloyal (6:14), disingenuous (6:15a), fickle (6:15b–18), and unreliable (6:19–21a).[45] They are fearful and, by implication, cowardly (6:21b). He contends that they are the ones who reprove (יכח), not God, as Eliphaz claimed in 5:17 (6:25b). Such rebukes (יכח) are completely futile (6:26a). Moreover, Job claims that the friends are insensitive brutes because they treat his despairing words as empty wind (6:26b), although they do not actually accuse him of this until later (8:2; 15:2–3). In Job's mind, the real wind here is coming from Eliphaz. Finally, Job challenges their integrity (6:27).

Job follows up his attack on his friends in chapter 6 with more impeaching allegations. He acknowledges that his friends think they are superior to him (19:5a), but claims that in fact they are not. First, Job maintains that he is at least as smart as they are. Chapter 12 contains a number of impeaching statements. Job 12:3b and 13:2b form an *inclusio* around this material. In them, Job states:

> But I have understanding as well as you.
> I am not inferior to you.
> Who does not know such things as these? (12:3)

> What you know, I also know.
> I am not inferior to you. (13:2)

By this *inclusio*, Job rejects Eliphaz's imperative to accept his words as truth (5:27bβ). Job takes his claim still further, by arguing that his friends are

---

44. Following Habel, *Book of Job: Commentary*, 279, 280–81.
45. The translation of 6:18–19 is under dispute. Typically, "the ways" (אָרְחוֹת) is repointed to "caravans" (אֹרְחוֹת) in both verses (see, e.g., NAB; NEB; NJB; NRSV; RSV; and Clines, *Job 1–20*, 156). I believe that the first of the two occurrences should remain unchanged; the second should be emended to "caravans." In this choice, I follow the NASB; KJV; NJPS; A. Weiser (*Das Buch Hiob* [4th ed.; ATD13; Göttingen: Vandenhoeck & Ruprecht, 1963], 55, 60); and R. Gordis (*The Book of Job: Commentary, New Translation, and Special Notes* [Moreshet Series 2; New York: Jewish Theological Seminary, 1978], 64, 75). This translation makes better sense of the two verses. It conveys two different aspects of the friends' unreliability as witnesses. Furthermore, the wordplay serves to mark and smooth the important transition between the verses.

ignorant and legally unsophisticated. He says wisdom will die with them (12:2b). Even the beasts, the birds, the fish, and the earth can teach them about God's abusive ways (12:7–8). Job's friends have not really investigated (בחן) the legal arguments with their ears (12:11). Job contends that God has hidden understanding from them (17:4a). They are simply not wise (17:10). He scolds his friends for giving advice without wisdom (26:3). Job's view is that the friends' wisdom is old and stale (12:12). He does not believe that it comes with age as Bildad maintains (8:8–10). The friends rely on musty proverbs and clay defenses (13:13). They are poor comforters and healer-counselors (13:4b; 16:2, 4–5). The friends are simply ineffective (26:2). The best course for them would be to remain silent (13:5, 13a).

The friends are, according to Job, doing more damage than spewing forth old and ineffective wisdom. Returning to some of his assertions in chapter 6, Job claims that they are not upright or innocent (17:8). They are deceptive (13:4a) and disloyal (17:3). They take bribes for false testimony (17:5). They also fail to maintain social justice (12:5). His friends, not Job, make a great wind by their words (16:3a). They appear to be afflicted (16:3b). They are certainly cruel. They torment Job (19:2a), crush him with arguments (19:2b), humiliate him (19:3a), are unashamed to abuse him (19:3b), justify his disgrace (19:5b), mock him (12:4; 17:2; 21:3a), and plot against him (21:27). They are dangerous people, unworthy of any trust on the court's part.

Many of these allegations and the questions meant to elicit information regarding these aspects of the friends' dealings go strictly to their character and general reliability. Others address more directly their capacity for truthfulness, a critical issue in a trial. Some of the allegations, however, confront specific behaviors related to the veracity of their testimony in this case: for example, the allegation that they take bribes for false testimony. Job probes their bias more deeply in a cross-examination of his friends in 13:7–11.[46] He wants to know whether they will give truthful and unbiased testimony in the case:

> Will you testify (דבר) falsely on God's behalf?
>   Will you testify (דבר) deceitfully for him?
> Will you be biased (נשא) toward him?[47]
>   Will you sue (ריב) God's cause?

---

46. E. L. Greenstein observes the sequence of testimony in Ps 18:17: "The one in the right is first in his litigation; Then his companion comes and cross-examines him" ("Forensic Understanding, 251). Greenstein then goes on to remark: "This sequence is reflected, perhaps not accidentally, in the overall structure of the book of Job" (ibid.). I think this is correct, although I do not agree with his understanding of who is the accuser and who is the defendant in this case.

47. Literally, "lift up the face," either to win favor or benefit from a bribe per Habel, *Book of Job: Commentary*, 225. See also 13:10 below.

> Will it be well when he examines (חקר) you?
>   Or, as one deceives a person, will you deceive him?
> Will he forcefully accuse you (יכח)
>   if, in secret, you are biased (נשא) toward him?[48]
> Will not his eminence terrify you,
>   and dread of him overwhelm you?

Such questions go to the heart of the friends' value as witnesses before the court. As P. Gewirtz reminds us, all witnesses have their biases.[49] The trick is to appear to be the more objective witness with the most accurate information. Job challenges his friends' capacity to deliver adequate testimony to the court. He suggests that, in the end, his friends will be punished for pursuing him and blaming him for his trouble (19:28–29), for they have participated in a false suit against him.

While Job is assaulting his friends' juridical integrity, he is attempting to maintain his own. He, therefore, queries them:

> Have I said, "Make me a gift"?
>   Or, "From your wealth offer a bribe for me"?
> Or, "Save me from the clutches of my enemy"?
>   Or, "Ransom (פדה) me from the clutches of the ruthless"? (6:22–23).

By this strategy, Job establishes a contrast between his appropriate judicial conduct and the inappropriate conduct of his friends (17:5). Job looks like the unbiased one in the case. He plays fair; his friends do not.

The friends have not sat quietly through Job's attack on their testimony. For example, Eliphaz reiterates that the friends know more than Job because they are older and wiser (15:9–10). Bildad's claim, in 8:2, counters Job's assertion to the contrary in 12:12 and 13:13. Additionally, Bildad contests vehemently, in 18:3, being counted among the beasts and deemed stupid in Job's eyes (12:7–8). Bildad challenges Job to prove him a liar in 24:25. Zophar says that Job's insults, rebukes, and humiliating remarks cause Zophar anxiety that necessitates a reply (20:2–3a). Thus, one can see the legal confrontation between Job and God's third-party witnesses on this rhetorical level, as well as by the legal content of what they say.

## Job's Efforts to Secure a Second Accuser in His Case

Job's verbal repartee with his friends is directed not only at impeaching them but also at persuading them to switch sides and support him as a sec-

---

48. Job 13:7–9 and 13:11 all begin with the interrogative ה. Hence, I carried the interrogative force through, following Gordis (*Book of Job*, 130, 142) and Habel (*Book of Job: Commentary*, 223, 225), against Clines (*Job 1–20*, 276, 281) and Good (*In Turns of Tempest*, 83).

49. See ch. 3, n. 68 above.

ond accuser in his case against God. As we recall from our discussion of Neo-Babylonian law, the fact that formal oaths were disfavored in the period created a more intense need for additional rational evidence in trials. A second accuser or some evidence beyond the accusation was usually required for conviction where the defendant did not confess. This requirement might also be imposed on the defendant where he or she bore the burden of proof. We often see this same need for a second accuser for a conviction in the Hebrew Bible. Numbers 35:30 calls for such in the context of a murder case. Deuteronomy 17:6–7 demands such in the case of apostasy.[50] Deuteronomy 19:15 refers to such a requirement with respect to any iniquity or sin. Of utmost importance to the book of Job is that two witnesses accuse Naboth of blasphemy (1 Kgs 21:13).[51] B. M. Levinson argues that, in the Deuteronomic reforms, the need for two witnesses to secure a conviction became the rule in the local courts in order to avoid the need for parties to come to Jerusalem to take the oath.[52] While I would dispute Levinson's view that this is an innovation meant to undermine the power of the assembly of elders and to centralize legal process in Jerusalem, based on comparative Neo-Babylonian data, two witnesses may have been needed for conviction in most situations by the exilic period. B. Wells has argued convincingly, in his study of testimony in the Hebrew Bible, that the two-witness rule was growing in importance through the Neo-Assyrian period until it reached ascendancy in the Neo-Babylonian period. This pattern was imitated in Israelite law.[53] Consequently, Job's case against God will fail if he does not obtain a second accuser or a corroborating witness. He goes to great lengths to try to convince one or more of his friends to side with him.

Job begins his quest by attempting to turn them away from their efforts to demonstrate his guilt. In 6:29, Job begs:

Relent (שוב), I pray! Let there not be injustice!
Again, relent (שוב)! In it lies my acquittal (צדק).

---

50. But see Deut 13:7–12, where summary execution is permitted in the case of apostasy. I do not believe that this apparent conflict is a reflection of different legal strata. For a discussion of Deut 17:2–7 as a later revision of Deut 13:7–12, see B. M. Levinson, *Deuteronomy and the Hermeneutics of Legal Innovation*, 117–27. Rather, Deut 13:7–12 reflects a case where one is caught in the act of apostasy and is in immediate danger of falling under the spell of such. In this circumstance, the law permits summary justice to prevail. The reasoning here is similar to that of R. Westbrook in the situation where immediate execution of the discovered wife and paramour is allowed in the case of adultery ("A Matter of Life and Death," *JANES* 27 [1997]: 61–69). I thank B. Wells for his insights with regard to the question of summary justice.

51. Although, in this instance, justice failed. The pericope may, therefore, have been a critique of the efficacy of two-witness rule.

52. Levinson, *Deuteronomy and the Hermeneutics of Legal Innovation*, 117–33.

53. Wells, *Law of Testimony*, 83–132.

He seeks to turn his friends away from cooperating in God's cause. The next phase of Job's strategy is to attempt to shame his friends into assisting his cause. He argues that even the beasts, birds, fish, and earth know that God lets the wicked go free. They will teach the friends this (12:7–9). Job then suggests that the friends buttress God's case only because they have not really investigated (בחן) the arguments with their ears (12:11). Job later expands this idea in 21:28–30, where he accuses his friends of failing to do a sufficient inquiry regarding the question concerning whether the wicked prosper. He asks whether they have heard the statements of possible third-party witnesses in the case, the wayfarers, who can testify that the dwelling of the wicked remain (21:29). Surely, if his friends would consider the matter more carefully, they would come to realize that he is right and switch sides. In chapter 17, Job becomes more brazen in his efforts to turn his friends. In 17:8–9, Job tells his friends how good people—the blameless (ישר), the guilt-free (נקי), the innocent (צדיק) and those who have clean hands (טהר־ידים)—would respond to his situation. His friends should be horrified (21:5), but they are not. He calls on them to relent once again and come to his defense, but he despairs of his quest:

> But all of you, relent (שוב) and come, I pray!
> But I shall not find a wise one among you. (17:10)

Still, he does not give it up. His battle for the minds of his friends continues. In 19:2–6a, Job expresses anger and sadness concerning his friends' participation in this wrongful suit. He begins his discussion using the vocabulary of abuse of the legal process, דכא:

> How long will you grieve my soul,
>   and crush (דכא) me with arguments (מלה)? (19:2)

Next, Job offers them specifics of his first count against God (9:6b–20). Finally, he pleads with them to join him and warns them of the impending doom they face if they should not:

> Pity me, pity me! O you my friends!
>   For the hand of God has struck me!
> Why do you pursue me like God,
>   slandering me continuously?[54]
> Oh, if only my arguments (מלה) were recorded (כתב)!
>   Oh, if only they were inscribed (חקק) on a stele (ספר),[55]
> with an iron stylus and lead,
>   carved on rock forever!

---

54. The idiom "to eat the flesh of PN" means "to slander PN" in Akkadian, Arabic, and Aramaic (Habel, *Book of Job: Commentary*, 292).

55. See ch. 7, n. 10 above.

> For I know that my redeemer (גאל) lives,
>> and, at last, he will stand upon the earth;
> possibly, even after my skin has been stripped off.
>> Yet, I, while still in my flesh, would behold God.
> I myself would behold him.
>> My eyes shall behold, not another!
>> My heart (כליה)[56] faints within me!
> If you say, "How we will persecute him!"
>> and, "The root of the suit (דבר) is found in him!"
> be in fear of the sword,
>> for wrath is iniquity (עולה) worthy of the sword!
>> Know there is judgment (שדון)! (19:21–29)

Job's redeemer, in 19:25a, is probably his second accuser, not his judge (and certainly not God), as almost all scholars have maintained.[57] M. H. Pope notes the improbability that God is Job's redeemer, stating simply: "The application of the term *gô'ēl* to God in this context is questionable since elsewhere in Job's complaint it is God himself who is Job's adversary rather than defender."[58] I agree. Further, I doubt that this colon refers to a judge at all. Proverbs 23:11 (cf. Ps 72:14) is the primary support for this view. There the orphans' redeemer sues on their behalf when their legal rights have been violated:

> For their redeemer (גאל) is strong;
> he will sue (ריב) their lawsuits (ריב) against you.

The redeemer in this passage is a third-party private prosecutor, who will accuse for the benefit of wronged orphans. Hence, since Job is prepared to bring his own suit, his redeemer must be the second accuser in the case. Job seeks someone to join him in his accusation against God. If he does not find a second accuser or corroborating witness, he will surely lose, and, from his perspective, a great injustice will be done. Job knows he is in the right. Job is begging his friends to join him; his great pathos is palpable. He therefore cries out that eventually his second accuser will come forward, even if it is after his death.

This view is additionally supported by Job's cry in 16:18–22:

> Earth, do not cover my blood!
> Let there be no resting place for my cry (זעקה)!

---

56. Literally, "kidneys," which is the seat of human emotion in the worldview of ancient Israelites.

57. I first published these ideas in "Who Is Job's Redeemer?" The reader should consult that work for a review of the literature on Job's redeemer (ibid., 292–93).

58. Pope, *Job*, 146.

> Even now my witness (עד) is in heaven;
>     my witness (שהד) is on high.
> My advocate (מליץ) is my friend (רע);[59]
>     for my eyes shed tears because of God.
> He will accuse (יכח) God on behalf of a human;
>     and as between one human being and another.
> For a few more years will pass,
>     and I shall go the way of no return.

Job believes, with all his heart, that someone, even if it be a heavenly figure, will eventually come forward to stand behind him as his second accuser. Yet he must proceed now. The case is ripe. Whatever the outcome of his plea may eventually be, he must go forward. Thus, Job demands a face-to-face confrontation with God. With or without his second accuser, he will contend with God.

Finally, we confront an issue that is related to Job's quest for a second accuser, that is, Job's request for a surety in 17:3. In 17:2–3, Job is once again chastising his friends for their disparagement of him and their defense of God. He calls on his friends to stand surety for him:

> Surely, mockery is all about me,
>     and my eye dwells on their provocations.
> Put down [a pledge] (שים), I pray! Go surety (ערב) for me!
>     Who will be a guarantor (תקע) for me?[60]

Job is not using this term in the same way that Neo-Babylonian courts used it. Rather, L. R. Freedman has correctly shown that this metaphor comes out of the world of ancient commercial law. Freedman asserts:

> Common legal practice does however envision that a surety may become a creditor. As just noted, this often occurs upon the debtor's default when the surety pays off the creditor; the surety's right of recourse against the debtor effectively transforms him into a creditor in regard to the debtor and his original loan. As we have demonstrated elsewhere in the connection with the analysis of Prov. 20:16 (= Prov. 27:13), it was not uncommon for a surety in risky ventures in the ancient Near East to make sure that a debtor had sufficient security in order to protect him in the event of the

---

59. This verse is extremely difficult to translate. I read מְלִיצִי for מְלִיצַי as per Clines, *Job 1–20*, 371; Gordis, *Book of Job*, 268, 269; and Pope, *Job*, 122, 125. Further, I emend רֵעִי to רֵעַי.

60. The idiom "to strike with the hand" in Hebrew means "to serve as guarantor" (Prov 11:15; 17:18; 22:26). We see similar idioms in Akkadian. In the Neo-Babylonian period, the idiom used is "to lift the forehead." In Nuzi, the idiom is "to strike the forehead" (see, e.g., HSS 19 89). See further Fisher, "Amarna Age Prodigal," 115–16; and M. Malul, *Studies in Mesopotamian Legal Symbolism* (AOAT 221; Neukirchen-Vluyn: Neukirchener Verlag, 1988), 252–68.

debtor's default. What riskier venture can be imagined than siding with Job in his assertion of his freedom from indebtedness against YHWH, who is obviously claiming the opposite?! Therefore, Job pleads with Eliphaz and his friends not to side with YHWH and conventional wisdom but to accept his position and support him by going surety for him. To induce them to secure their risk, Job offers a pledge. Thus he addresses the friends saying, "Please put aside my pledge! Who (else) will go surety for me?!"[61]

Although I think Job is asking his friends to put down the pledge and not put it aside, I agree that Job is pleading for his friends to stand with him against God. In this case, the guarantor is Job's second accuser.[62]

In conclusion, Eliphaz, Bildad, and Zophar state their views of the case during this long settlement negotiation. They believe, in line with the ritual incantations of the ancient Near East, that God has convicted Job of one or more sins. They suggest that God is a merciful god and, therefore, Job ought to make ritual reparations to Yahweh. If Job should do this, God will grant Job relief. The friends also defend God against Job's charges. God is good, gives only less than or equal to that which one actually deserves, and is the source and protector of social justice. All three of Job's counts fail to their minds. The judge of this case ought to believe God rather than Job. Job, on the other hand, attempts to challenge the credibility of God's witnesses in a variety of ways. He also pleads with these witnesses to do right and defect to his side that they may serve as second accusers against God. He fails to convince them. With matters standing thus, Elihu begins to speak.

---

61. L. R. Freedman, "Biblical Hebrew *'rb*, 'To Go Surety,' and Its Nominal Forms," *JANES* 19 (1989): 25–29, here 29.

62. If this is accurate, it would lend credence to the translation of 19:25b proposed by S. Mowinckel ("Hiobs *go'el* und Zeuge im Himmel," in *Vom Alten Testament* [ed. K. Budde; BZAW 41; Giessen: Alfred Töpelmann, 1925], 211); and Pope (*Job*, 139, 146). They view אַחֲרוֹן as a substantive and take its meaning as "one who stands behind," or "guarantor" from the Mishnaic and Talmudic term אַחֲרָאִי. If one were to use that meaning of אַחֲרוֹן, one would read 19:25 as follows: "For I know that my redeemer lives, and that a guarantor will stand upon the earth." This would place two of the signifiers of Job's second accuser, "redeemer" and "guarantor," in parallel. I am not completely committed to this translation, but it is not as easily dismissed as some suggest (see, e.g., Clines, *Book of Job*, 433).

# 9

# Elihu as God's Second Accuser-Prosecutor

Elihu's appearance is sudden and late in the book of Job. He is not mentioned in either the prologue or the epilogue. Neither the friends nor Job refers to him. Moreover, the style of his speeches seems somewhat different from that of the speeches of Job and his friends. For these reasons, the great majority of commentators maintain that Elihu's speeches are a later addition.[1] Neo-Babylonian legal procedure demonstrates, however, that Elihu's speeches constitute a critical component of the trial because he identifies the court and seeks to bring the proceedings to closure there. He is not interested in resolving the matter in the way that Job and his friends have attempted. He is not concerned with the reconciliation of the parties. Instead, he seeks Job's conviction. In fact, Elihu's speeches offer something quite rare in literature this ancient: a prosecutorial speech before a legal assembly and a call for judgment. Elihu knows that Job is on trial. He is also keenly aware that Job intends to counteraccuse God. He believes that Job's counterclaim and all his supporting statements are derisive to God. In stating matters thus, Elihu brings the case back to court and serves as God's second accuser-prosecutor in the trial of Job. Additionally, he offers a fuller and more direct defense of God, foreshadowing a number of the arguments that God will make in his own defense. For these reasons, Elihu is an essential part of the proceedings and makes an unlikely afterthought.

## Elihu's Role as Accuser-Prosecutor

After the close of Job's defensive statements (31:40c), the narrator informs us that the three friends "ceased to answer (ענה) Job because he was inno-

---

1. See, e.g., C. Newsom's discussion of Elihu's speech as an accretion ("Book of Job," 321–22). Even E. Good, who is most vehement about how one ought to read Job synchronically, argues that the speech is a late addition (*In Turns of Tempest*, 8, 182–85).

cent (צדיק) in his own eyes" (32:1). The closing of both Job's defense and the friends' statements ends the rehearsal of the case. This constitutes a legal crisis for Elihu because he does not believe that the friends have confronted Job adequately. This fact provokes his anger. The narrator reports in 32:3: "He was angry at his three friends because they had not found an answer (מענה) although they had declared Job to be in the wrong" (32:3). The narrator reiterates in 32:5: "When Elihu saw that there was no answer (מענה) in the mouths of these three men, he became angry." If the case should end now, Job will have the final word. The friends obviously did not dissuade him from his course (32:2). Moreover, the friends made no rebuttal to his oath. In the Neo-Babylonian period, defendant oaths of denial, though not dispositive, placed the declarant in a position of strength. Such oaths, therefore, generally demanded some rebuttal if the plaintiff were to overcome it. In 32:6–16, Elihu cries out in frustration at the poor quality of the friends' assertions against Job. Elihu claims that he has listened patiently throughout the friends' remarks, but they did not do what they were required to do. Elihu had deferred to age and waited to speak (32:4, 6–7, 16), but he now regards his silence as a mistake. Understanding comes not from age according to Elihu:

> But truly it is the spirit in humanity
>   and the breath of Shaddai that gives them understanding.
> It is not the aged who are wise;
>   the elders, who understand litigation (משפט). (32:8–9)

Eliphaz, Bildad, and Zophar do not seem to appreciate what is needed in the case. Their ignorance of litigation is obvious from Elihu's point of view. Elihu asserts that the friends' arguments are weak and that they have not offered the level of legal assault demanded. Job's oath stands as the last word. Someone must step forward at this most critical juncture, or Job will keep the upper hand. Thus, Elihu must speak out.

In four instances, Elihu acknowledges that Job is the defendant in a divine lawsuit. First, in 33:8–11, he recaps some of Job's assertions of innocence and charges against God:

> Indeed, you have stated in my hearing,
>   and I heard the arguments (מלה) spoken:
> "I am guiltless (זך), without transgression (פשע);
>   I am pure (חף), without iniquity (עון).
> But he finds reasons to oppose me,
>   he counts me as his enemy.[2]

---

2. Colon 33:10b is a quotation of 13:24b.

> He puts my feet in stocks
> and watches all my ways."³

Later, Elihu says:

> He is accused (יכח) by pains on his bed,
> and by a constant trial (ריב)⁴ in his bones;
> so that his being loathes food;
> and his soul, the choicest meal;
> his flesh wastes away until it cannot be seen,
> and his unseen bones become visible;
> his soul draws near the Pit,
> his life unto death. (33:19–22)

In 35:13–14, Elihu rejects Job's claims, again acknowledging the suit:

> Surely El does not hear an empty cry (שוא),
> nor does the Shaddai regard it.
> How much less when you say you do not see him,
> that the case (דין) is before him and you are waiting for him.

Furthermore, in 36:21, Elihu warns Job:

> Beware! Do not turn to iniquity (און);
> for to this end you have been investigated (בחר)⁵ by affliction (עני).

One observes the worldview of the ritual incantations operating again in Elihu's linkage of legal language and suffering in both 33:9 and 36:21. Elihu understands that God's investigations, accusations, and trials may all be marked by pain and affliction. Disability, disease, and disaster may not only reflect a divine summary judgment.

On this basis, Elihu separates himself from his friends. He regards the trial of Job as still in progress. Elihu reasons that Job's pain is part of the investigation, accusation, and trial processes. This is why the friends should not have given up when they did. To Elihu's way of thinking, their legal role was not to encourage Job to seek a pardon. Rather, it was to accuse Job of improper speech before God as soon as he threatened his counterclaim and to defend God more fully. The friends failed in their task.

---

3. Job 33:11 is a quotation of 13:27b.
4. Qere reads רוב.
5. Following Dhorme (*Commentary on the Book of Job*, 550) and Pope (*Job*, 267, 272) in emending בָּחַרְתָּ to בְּחַרְתָּ. This reading follows the Syriac. It reads the verb in its Aramaic sense of "to examine," "to test," or "to investigate." It is equivalent to the Hebrew root בחן.

They saw the heavenly trial as involving a crime of limited moral culpability, not blasphemy, and as complete; therefore, they encouraged Job to seek post-verdict relief in accord with the ritual incantations. As a result of their legal misconceptions, they served as neither accusers nor defenders at trial. Furthermore, they did not protect the community from Job's polluting act by accusing Job of this significant violation of God's law.[6] Elihu attacks vigorously the quality of the friends' legal strategy:

> Here I have waited out your legal arguments (דבר),
>   I have given ear to your insights
>   while you searched (חקר) for arguments (מלה).
> But as I attended to you,
>   I saw that there was no accuser (מוכיח) against Job,
>   or a defender (עונה) against his statements (אמרה).
> I fear you will say, "We have found wisdom.
>   God will defeat him, not mortals."
> He did not set out his arguments (מלה) against me,
>   nor shall I use your statements (אמרה) to answer (ענה) him.
> They have been broken and can answer (ענה) no more;
>   arguments (מלה) fail them.
> I waited until they stopped speaking,
>   until they ended and answered (ענה) no more. (32:11–16)

The word מוכיח may mean either "judge" or "accuser" depending on its context,[7] although a number of scholars read מוכיח as "arbiter" in all cases.[8] The *hiphil* of יכח is used most often in the book of Job to indicate the action of accusing rather than judging. Moreover, in 32:12, the word is in antithesis to עונה, which means "an answerer" or "defender." If one translates מוכיח as "judge" in this verse, the reading would destroy the balance in the poetic line and would fail to acknowledge that both claim and counterclaim exist in this suit. Elihu is objecting to the fact that the friends have not served as a proper accuser of Job or defender of God. They said Job was wicked and described at length what that means in terms of God's justice. They did not, however, offer definitive proof of Job's guilt. Only Eliphaz sought to recount Job's specific behavior (22:5–9). Additionally, they never accused him of the more serious charge of blasphemy. Finally, they never offered God a solid defense against Job's threatened counterclaim. Elihu is

---

6. See further the material at ch. 5, nn. 34–35 above.

7. In 9:33, the word מוכיח has the meaning of "judge," reflecting one of the root's meanings, "to adjudicate" (see ch. 6, n. 161 above).

8. For example, Good renders מוכיח as "arbiter" here and would translate this verse: "And I examine you, and there! Job has no arbiter, one answering his statements, among you" (*In Turns of Tempest*, 137–38). Judges do not, however, answer. Defendants and witnesses answer.

dismayed by the fact that the friends seem to rely on God's coming testimony to vanquish Job. If it is true that Job has said derisive things about God, the community has an absolute duty to bring charges. They have failed to assist God on both the claim and the counterclaim. Consequently, Elihu has stepped forward to serve those essential legal functions.

Elihu asserts strongly and urgently both his right and his desire to testify in the matter. He states in 32:10:

> Therefore, I say, "Hear (שמעה) me!
> I would speak my mind. Yes, I would!"

Elihu continues in 32:17–20:

> Now I also would answer (ענה);
> I, too, would speak my mind. Yes, I would!
> For I am full of arguments (מלה).
> The wind in my belly presses me.
> My belly is like wine not yet opened,
> like jugs of new wine ready to burst.
> I must testify (דבר) that I might find relief.
> I must open my lips and answer (ענה).

He adds in 33:1–2

> But now, hear, I pray (שמע־נא), my arguments (מלה), Job,
> and listen (האזינה) to all my testimony (דבר).
> Now I open my lips;
> my tongue testifies (דבר) in my mouth.

Job 36:2 and 37:14 contain similar assertions. Elihu is prepared to testify in this case.

Consistent with his view that he is an accuser, Elihu claims a level of authority and an importance not assumed by the other witnesses. For instance, N. Habel points out: "Unlike the friends, he [Elihu] tends to quote Job directly and summon him by name, a practice consistent with court procedure elsewhere (cf. Micah 6:1–5; Jer. 26:9, 18)."[9] Elihu understands himself as God's stand-in. We first see this in 33:5, where Elihu says to Job:

> Turn me (שוב), if you can!
> Present your suit (ערך) before me. Take your stand (יצב)!

This suggestion is confirmed by Elihu's statement in 33:32:

> If you have arguments (מלה), respond to me;
> Testify (דבר) for I am eager to vindicate (צדק) you.

---

9. Habel, *Book of Job: Commentary*, 36.

He will receive Job's answer. Elihu seems, at first glance, to be usurping the role of judge.[10] This understanding, however, is erroneous. Several things militate against this view.

First, we have already noted Elihu's use of the language of testimony rather than judgment in his speeches. He uses the *qal* imperative of שמע, "hear," as a testimony marker in 32:10 and 33:1; and he uses the *hiphil* imperative of אזן, "listen," in 33:1 and 37:14. He employs ענה, "answer," in 32:14, 17, and 20. He also claims that he will דבר, "testify," in 32:20 and 33:2, 32. All of this vocabulary indicates that Elihu believes he is testifying. Elihu, therefore, is not insisting that he is a judge; on the contrary, he is declaring that he is a witness.

Second, when Elihu commands in 33:33 that Job be silent so that Elihu may teach him, Elihu takes up Job's dare of 6:24a: "Teach me, and I will be silent." Elihu also reiterates the language of Eliphaz in 27:11a: "I will teach you what is in God's power."[11] Elihu acts similarly to Eliphaz in this instance, more like a witness than a judge.

Third, Elihu asserts his integrity and authority as a witness in the suit. Job attempted to impeach the credibility of the friends through a series of rhetorical questions meant to assert that his friends are partial:

> Will you testify (דבר) falsely on God's behalf?
>   Will you testify (דבר) deceitfully for him?
> Will you be biased (נשא) toward him?
>   Will you sue (ריב) God's cause? (13:7–8)

In response, Elihu swears an oath that his testimony is impartial:

> I will not be biased (נשא) toward any mortal
>   nor to any human will I offer flattery.
> But if I know how to flatter,
>   my maker will quickly put an end to me.[12] (32:21–22)

---

10. A few scholars contend that Elihu understands himself as Job's judge or the arbiter of the case. For example, Habel argues: "Elihu enters the scene as an arbiter, not as one of the friends. His appearance is a logical response to Job's call for an arbiter to handle his case (31:35). There is no reason, therefore, to expect Elihu to be mentioned in the prologue. His speeches reflect his role, and his language is consistent with that role" (*Book of Job: Commentary*, 36; cf. R. H. Pfeiffer, *Introduction to the Old Testament*, 673).

11. I assign this verse to Eliphaz, not Job; see ch. 1, n. 32 above.

12. Many translate 32:22: "For I do not know how to flatter, else would my Maker soon put an end to me" (see, e.g., NASB and RSV; cf. NJPS). Others suggest, however, that לֹא be emended to a conditional לָא (= לוּ) and the material read as "for if." See, e.g., Habel, *Book of Job: Commentary*, 443, following Gordis, *Book of Job*, 371. This emendation allows for clarity in the protasis of the oath. If this emendation is correct, however, there might be a better way to translate the verse. The idiom כִּי אִם often used in oath formulas to understand an exception (see, e.g., Gen 32:27 and Lev 22:6; BDB 474–75). If we understand the כִּי לֹא as being functionally equivalent to כִּי אִם, the preferred reading might be "but if."

Elihu's assertions here are a direct response to Job's similar claims. This is seen again in 33:3-4:

> My statements (אמרה) declare the uprightness (ישר) of my intention (לבב).
> My lips utter (מלל) insight sincerely (ברר).
> The spirit of God formed me.
> The breath of Shaddai sustains me.

The spirit and the breath also bring knowledge (32:8); consequently, he is possessed of that which gives real wisdom. Elihu professes perfect (תם) knowledge and truth in all his arguments. He claims that he is the truth-teller in this trial:

> In truth, my arguments (מלה) are not false.
> One with perfect knowledge is before you (36:4).

Job, by contrast, is the one who lacks integrity and uprightness. By responding in this manner, Elihu sets himself above Job and apart from Eliphaz, Bildad, and Zophar as the most faithful witness. The language of integrity might cause us to believe that Elihu is a judge because we moderns, especially those who are familiar with adversarial legal systems, are very concerned about the impartiality of judges, not that of witnesses. As Gewirtz indicates, those under adversarial systems *expect* witnesses to be biased for one side or the other.[13] Consequently, Elihu's words regarding his impartiality send our minds spinning toward images of judges posed for judgment. Nonetheless, it is different in the ancient Near East, where parties might well be judges. In this inquisitorial legal system, the emphasis is on the honesty and integrity of its witnesses rather than on that of its judges, even though there are clear strictures against corrupt judges.[14] Elihu maintains, by the assertion of his integrity, that he will be a righteous witness, not a righteous judge.

While Elihu is a witness rather than a judge, he is a special kind of witness. He is the second accuser against Job. Job asks the friends in 13:8b: "Will you sue (ריב) God's cause?," meaning "will you accuse me along with God?" Elihu responds that he will. We see this not only in the special authority he claims but also in his use of the *qal* imperative of שמע, "hear," in 33:31–33:

> Pay heed, Job, and hear me (שמע)!
> Be still, and I will testify (דבר) . . . .
> If you have arguments (מלה), reply to (שוב) me.
> Testify (דבר) for I am eager to vindicate (צדק) you.

---

13. See ch. 3, n. 68 above.
14. See LH §5.

> But if not, hear me (שְׁמַע)!
> Be silent, and I will teach you wisdom.

As we noted in chapter 5, the *qal* imperative of שׁמע can also mark the beginning of a trial and the lodging of an accusation. Saul began the trial of Ahimelech with the words: "Hear, I pray, son of Ahitub" (1 Sam 22:12aβ), which he followed up with an accusation (1 Sam 22:13). Although a heavenly trial is already under way, no earthly trial has begun. Elihu is preparing to lodge an accusation to begin an action on earth. He uses the *qal* imperative of שׁמע to announce that coming accusation. This explains the odd remark in 33:32. Elihu is calling for Job to answer his earthly summons. If he can, then Elihu will drop the charges, thereby, vindicating Job.

This accusation will function as the earthly trial's first accusation. It will also serve as the heavenly trial's second accusation. Elihu sees himself as God's private prosecutor and defender. He is not simply supplementing the weak offensive and defensive testimony that Eliphaz, Bildad, and Zophar will offer at trial. Elihu assigns more importance to himself than that. He believes that he is a שָׂטָן, God's second accuser in the case. Elihu believes that he searches for the just and the unjust, accuses defendants, hears their answers, and defends counterclaims, all on God's behalf. As the Satan accused Job in the celestial plane, Elihu will accuse Job on the terrestrial plane. Elihu will pick up where the heavenly Satan left off and complete the accusations begun in the Divine Council. The Satan alleged that Job would curse God during the investigation. Elihu is preparing himself to say that Job has in fact. Elihu is about to become the second שָׂטָן.

If this assertion is correct, Elihu's role as an accuser may explain why he does not appear earlier in the text. First, it is only by listening to Job's statements made in the course of settlement negotiations that the earthly accusation becomes ripe. Second, he says that he has deferred to age to allow the friends to accuse Job; only because they do not act, does Elihu take the lead (33:4, 6–7, 11–16). Third, in the Neo-Babylonian period, the documents reveal that second accusers often waited to speak until after the defendant finished his or her defense in order to offer a final rebuttal to the defense. The maneuver was intentional. Second accusers did not wait in all cases, but it was a common phenomenon. Furthermore, when a second accuser spoke late in the proceedings, he or she was rarely mentioned in the document before he or she made the accusation. Legally speaking, then, Elihu's timing is impeccable. He is cunning. He is lying in wait for Job with the second accusation. As the heavenly case's second accuser, Elihu may not be mentioned earlier in the text because it simply is not necessary from a legal standpoint to mention him sooner. Doing so probably would have disrupted the normal flow of the proceedings for the ancient reader.

The order of appearance of witnesses in Neo-Babylonian trial records may also answer why it is that the Satan disappears after the prologue. In the Neo-Babylonian period, first accusers rarely reappeared in litigation after they lodged their complaints. The primary accuser typically disappeared from the case unless a defensive maneuver remained unchallenged or the accuser had somehow managed to implicate himself in the course of his accusation of another, which he then needed to explain. It is most unusual for a first accuser to appear twice, in a litigation record, where a second accuser is explicitly named. Thus, Neo-Babylonian trial records may explain the Satan's and Elihu's comings and goings from the text.

Elihu is still more than just a second accuser in God's lawsuit. He is also God's primary defender against Job's threatened counterclaim, usurping whatever role the three friends claimed in that task. Let us look at this issue in more detail. First, Elihu recognizes that Job is prepared to counter-sue on the grounds that God has abused his authority. For example, Elihu says to Job in 33:13:

> Why do you bring a suit (ריב) against him,
> because [you claim]: "He will not answer any of my charges (דבר)?"

Again, he acknowledges the suit when he asserts in 34:5–6:

> For Job has said, "I am innocent (צדק).
> God has deprived me of justice (משפט).
> In my own litigation (משפט), I am called a liar.
> My arrow-wound is deadly, though I am free from transgression (פשע)."

Elihu continues in 36:17:

> You are full of a lawsuit (דין) of the wicked.
> Lawsuit (דין) and litigation (משפט) obsess you.

Second, Elihu apparently feels some internal pressure to defend God. For instance, immediately after 33:5, wherein Elihu challenges Job to present his suit before him, Elihu assures Job:

> Behold I, like you, am from God.
> Yes, I too was nipped from clay.
> So my terror need not dismay you.
> My hand need not oppress[15] you. (33:6–7)

These are most significant words. Back in 9:3–35, when Job was contemplating bringing his counterclaim against God, Job said that he was afraid to accuse God and come to trial together with him because God is "not a

---

15. Habel's translation (*Book of Job: Commentary*, 455).

man as I am" (9:32). By these words, Job proclaimed his fear of the power of divine words against his mere mortal words in the legal contest. He feels that his accuser-opponent has the edge. In 32:6–7, Elihu recalls these words and states his own position vis-à-vis Job—that is, he is also human. The result is an equal contest of words with Job. It could be argued that Job fears God as judge in 9:32 and that Elihu, in recalling these words, is placing himself in the role of judge. That reading does not, however, account for the fact that Job's expression of fear is followed by his call for a judge to resolve the claims and counterclaims between God and himself in 9:33, a call that Job repeats twice thereafter (10:7b; 31:35a). This recurring demand for a judge clearly throws into question the traditional view that Job acknowledges God as his judge. Moreover, the fact that Elihu does not reference that call for a judge at this point but instead tries to assuage Job's fear by substituting himself for God as Job's opponent indicates that Elihu does not believe that either God or he is Job's judge in this particular matter. Elihu is conveying to Job: "I am human, so you may accuse me in God's place. Let me answer for him."

Third, Elihu makes plain his intention to defend God in two other places. After repeating Job's assertion that God has brought a false suit against him in 33:9–11, Elihu advises Job:

> In this, you are not innocent (צדק).
> I will answer (ענה) you: God is greater than any mortal (33:12).

We see this still more clearly in 36:2–3, where Elihu avows before Job:

> Bear with me a little and I will convince you.
>   There are still more arguments (מלה) on God's behalf.
> I will glean my knowledge from afar;
>   and I will prove my maker innocent (נתן צדק).

Elihu is God's advocate not only in attempting to convict Job but also in proving God innocent.

## The Content of Elihu's Prosecution and Defense

Elihu has three basic tasks in his self-appointed role: to accuse Job, to defend God, and to impeach Job.[16] We address Elihu's accusations first. Elihu accuses Job of making blasphemous statements during his speeches,

---

16. Cf. R. G. Albertson, who states that Elihu has three arguments: "a reproof of Job, a justification of God, and a final defense of retribution" ("Job and Ancient Near Eastern Wisdom," 230).

although his charge of blasphemy is stated in indirect terms. He repeatedly asserts that Job's complaint is itself a sin. For instance, in 34:7–9, Elihu asks:

> What mortal is like Job,
>   who drinks up derision (לעג) like water,
> who goes in company with evildoers
>   and walks with the wicked?
> For he has said, "It profits one nothing
>   to take delight in God."

To Elihu, the countercharges against God constitute derision (לעג) of God. Elihu uses the language of derision again in 36:17–21 and connects it to Job's lawsuit:

> You are full of a lawsuit (דין) of the wicked.
>   Lawsuit (דין) and litigation (משפט) obsess you.
> Beware that wrath does not entice you into derision (לעג),
>   and do not let a large bribe (כפר) turn you aside.[17]
> Will your cry (שוע) avail to keep you from distress,
>   or all the force of your strength?
> Do not long for the night
>   when peoples vanish where they are.
> Beware! Do not turn to iniquity (און);
>   for to this end you have been investigated (בחר) by affliction (עני).

BDB states that the noun לעג, as it is used in 34:7 and 36:18, "nearly = blasphemy" (514). R. L. Harris and G. L. Archer agree that לעג belongs in the constellation of roots meaning blasphemy and slander.[18] Elihu is suggesting that Job's counterclaim and his testimony in support of it are blasphemous and will not protect him from God's investigation and ultimate punishment. Although Zophar also indicates that Job's words deride (11:3), Elihu connects these verbal outrages to the litigation itself.

These two instances are not the only time that Elihu maintains that Job's claim is blasphemous. Elihu continues his attack throughout chapter 34. In 34:30, he argues that Job is impious. Then Elihu pronounces what a righteous person should do; this is, by implication, what Job has not done:

---

17. In chapter 5, I argued that the *hiphil* of סות when followed by the preposition ב + PN in legal settings can mean "to cause to bring a charge against." I also indicated that this is not the best translation for every occurrence of the *hiphil* of סות when followed by the preposition ב, but only in clearly legal contexts (see, ch. 5, n. 94). Job 36:18 is an instance where "entice into" is the better translation because the ב is not followed by a person or personal pronoun. I think, however, that the possible dual meaning is not lost on the author of Job. Elihu contends that Job's wrath has caused him to bring a charge against God and that such charge is derision.

18. *TWOT*, 1:480. See further ch. 5, n. 33 above.

> Has he said to God,
> "I will bear (נשא) [my guilt] and offend no more.
> What I cannot see, teach me.
> If I have done iniquity (עול), I shall not do so again"? (34:31–32)

Elihu alludes to the common expression "to bear guilt" (נשא עון) in 34:31. The expression "to bear sin" (נשא חטא) is similar. Several scholars have discussed the import of these idioms as indicators of actual or possible guilt, especially on a charge that remains unspecified or unknown. For example, P. Bovati maintains that these idioms may mean "to be guilty," "to be chargeable with a crime," or "to run the risk of a crime."[19] B. Wells points out that:

> Many of the texts that use the expression do so in a theological context, where the focus is upon the Israelites' relationship with their deity, Yahweh. It is not surprising, therefore, that Yahweh frequently seems to be the one who will inflict the punishment. In the two texts mentioned above that stipulate death for someone whose guilt is indicated with the phrase "he shall carry his iniquity/sin" (Exod 28:43 and Num 18:22), it is implied that the one who will inflict death is Israel's deity. This is not always the case, however, as revealed by Lev 24:15–16. There, the person who commits blasphemy must "bear his sin" (v. 15). The text then indicates the punishment for having such guilt. This time, it is not a divinely caused death. The guilty person is to be stoned to death by the kōl hāʿēdâ ("the whole community").[20]

Elihu is cognizant of the fact that those who blaspheme should bear their iniquity. Thus, he says in 34:36–37:

> Would that Job were investigated (בחן) to the limit
> for responses (תשובה) that befit those of iniquity (און).
> He adds to his sin (הטאת).
> He increases his transgression (פשע) among us.
> He multiplies his statements (אמרה) against God.

Both Job's defense and his counterclaim are transgression and sin. A wordplay reinforces the idea that Job's responses give rise to the highest order of culpability. The word for "response," תשובה, is very close to the word for "apostasy," משובה, another of the great polluting crimes.[21] Job's words are blasphemous.

---

19. Bovati, *Re-Establishing Justice*, 145. See similarly B. Schwartz, "The Bearing of Sin in the Priestly Literature," in *Pomegranates and Golden Bells: Studies in Biblical, Jewish, and Near Eastern Ritual, Law, and Literature in Honor of Jacob Milgrom* (ed. D. P. Wright, D. N. Freedman, and A. Hurvitz; Winona Lake, Ind.: Eisenbrauns, 1995), 8–9. Exod 28:43; Lev 5:1, 17; 17:16; 24:15; Num 5:31; 14:34; 18:22; 30:16; Ezek 14:10; 18:20; and 44:10, 12 are all examples of this.

20. Wells, "Law of Testimony," 61–62.

21. See further the material at ch. 5, nn. 34–35 above.

Furthermore, in 35:2–8, Elihu challenges Job's defensive assertions of innocence and reminds Job that his conduct is of no real consequence to God; it does, however, sway humans:

> Do you think it justice (משפט)
> to claim, "I am innocent (צדק) against God"?
> If you ask how it benefits you—
> "What have I gained from not sinning (חטאת)?"—
> I will reply (שוב) to your arguments (מלה)
> and those of your friends.
> Behold the heavens and sea;
> look at the skies high above you.
> If you sin (חטא), what do you do to him?
> If your transgressions (פשע) are many, how do you affect him?
> If you are righteous (צדק), what do you give him;
> what does he receive from your hand?
> Your wickedness affects humans like yourself;
> your innocence (צדק), mortals.

Job is setting a terrible moral example.

Elihu, then, scolds Job, saying that people suffering abuse of authority cry out to God for help. They do not chastise God under such circumstances:

> Under great oppression (עשוקים) the abused cry out (זעק);
> They call for help (שוע) against the arm of the mighty.
> But none says, "Where is my God, my maker,
> who gives songs in the night,
> who gives us more knowledge than the beasts of the earth,
> and makes us wiser than the birds of the sky?" (35:9–11)

Job is not acting in a manner fitting a man of integrity. Furthermore, Job may wait a very long time for God's answer to his complaint, even if legitimate, because he does not answer the abused directly. Job's complaint will only serve to silence God further:

> There they cry (צעק), but he does not answer (ענה)
> because of the arrogance of evil men.
> Indeed, God does not hear deceit,
> Shaddai does not regard it.
> How much less when you say you do not see him,
> that the case (דין) is before him and you are waiting for him.
> But, still, his anger does not punish (פקד),[22]
> and he clearly does not acknowledge transgression (פש).

---

22. The root פקד typically means "to inspect," "to investigate," or "to test" in Job (see, e.g., 7:18; 31:14). Here, however, it takes the meaning "to punish." See, e.g., Jer 6:15; 49:8; 50:31; and Ps 59:6.

> Yet, Job opens his mouth in vain
> and multiplies arguments (מלה) without knowledge. (35:12–16)

According to Elihu, Job is completely unjustified in his complaint. In fact, Job deserves more punishment than he is getting. Indeed, if Job is blaspheming God, he deserves death. God is being merciful. In such an assertion, Elihu sounds much like Zophar.

In these allegations, Elihu goes beyond anything that the friends accuse Job of doing. To the friends' minds, Job has done some crime of lesser moral culpability that justifies the summary punishment he is suffering at the hand of God in accord with the worldview of the ritual incantations. Elihu, on the other hand, is cognizant of the investigatory nature of Job's suffering. He believes that Job has failed the investigation and has blasphemed God through his countercharges. Thus, Elihu completes the Satan's initial charges. The Satan accused Job of having a blasphemous intent, which might be proven in an investigation that should serve to provoke Job's cursing of God. Elihu charges Job with having failed that investigation and done the deed. He, therefore, concludes the prosecution of Job.

Elihu, however, also defends God against Job's countercharges. He wants to make clear that Job's position is unwarranted. Elihu begins his defense in 33:12. He says that Job's claim of innocence is not correct (33:9–12aα). He continues that he will answer Job's charges (33:12aβ). He claims that God speaks even though people do not perceive it (33:14–15). God's justice is painful (33:19–22). Humanity suffers under God's accusations just as Job is suffering. They will come to loath (זהם) their lives. He does this, however, for their own good:

> Then he opens the ears of humanity,
>     and, through discipline (מוסר), leaves his seal (חתם),
> that he may turn humanity aside (סור) from their deeds,
>     and keep them from pride,
> to spare their souls from the Pit,
>     their lives from traversing the River.[23] (33:16–18)

Elihu returns to this idea in 36:7–12:

> He does not withdraw his eyes from the innocent (צדיק);
>     but with kings on thrones
>     he seats them forever, and they are exalted.
> If they are bound in fetters
>     and caught in cords of affliction (עני),
> he declares to them what they have done
>     and that their transgressions (פשע) are arrogant.

---

23. Following Dhorme, *Commentary on the Book of Job*, 496; Pope, *Job*, 250; Gordis, *Book of Job*, 375–76; and the NRSV.

> He opens their ears to discipline (מוסר),
>> and orders them back from iniquity (און).
> If they will serve obediently,
>> they shall spend their days in prosperity,
>> their years in delight.
> But, if they are not obedient,
>> they shall transverse the River,
>> and die in ignorance.

The trials of humanity are required to correct a fundamentally immature or corrupt nature. In this, Elihu agrees with Eliphaz. Job suffers only what he needs to suffer. God rewards those who receive their discipline well:

> Indeed, he draws you away from the brink of distress
> to a broad place where there is no constraint.
> Your table is laid out with rich food. (36:16; cf. 36:21)

Elihu, then, proceeds to testify as to God's true character. God is far greater than humanity (33:12bβ; 36:26–30; 37:23a). He is the first actor, the primordial creator (34:4a, 13, 19c; 36:26–30; cf. 37:6–13). God is powerful (36:5, 22a; 37:6–13, 23b). He sustains life; without him, all things would wither (34:4b, 14–15, 20). His voice is grand and controls cosmic forces (37:1–7). His universe is orderly (36:26–30; 37:6–13; cf. 34:20b). God acts in constructive ways (36:5aα; 37:23cβ). God is not wicked:

> Therefore, people of understanding, hear (שמעו) me!
>> Wickedness is far from God,
>> injustice (עול), from Shaddai. (34:10)

Nevertheless, he may give both what seems good and what seems evil (37:13). God is simply beyond understanding (37:15–18, 31). He is absolutely just:

> For he pays humans according to their actions,
>> and he requites them according to their conduct.
> In truth, God does not act wickedly.
>> Shaddai does not pervert justice (משפט). (34:11–12)

> He is not partial to princes;
>> the noble are not preferred to the wretched;
>> for all of them are the work of his hands. (34:19)

> Shaddai, we cannot attain to him.
>> He is great in power and justice (משפט)
>> and abundant in righteousness (צדקה);
>> he does not violate (ענה).[24] (37:23)

---

24. As I pointed out in ch. 8, n. 24 above, the wordplay on the Hebrew dual root ענה

Elihu offers extensive renditions of God's social justice in both 34:21–30 and 36:6–15. Elihu's assertions about God's use of his trial powers in his maintenance of social justice are of particular interest:

> For his eyes are upon a person's ways.
>   He observes all their steps.
> Neither deep gloom nor deep darkness offers
>   a hiding-place for evildoers.
> He has no set time (שִׂים) for one
>   to appear before God in litigation (מִשְׁפָּט).
> He shatters the mighty without investigation (חֵקֶר)
>   and appoints others in their place.
> Truly, he knows their deeds.
>   He overthrows (הָפַךְ) by night, and they are crushed (דָּכָא). (34:21–25)

God is good, however it might appear. The seeming oppression of humanity is actually necessary for the maintenance of social justice. The divine legal system is for God's use alone. He will set the time of litigation. He will decide summary judgments without investigation if he pleases. God is not open to criticism. No one can correct him:

> Who appoints his way for him?
>   Who says, "You have done wrong"? (36:23)

He is the great teacher (36:22b). God is majestic (37:22) and is to be exalted (36:24–25). God is the ultimate judge. Elihu asks: "When he is silent, who will condemn (רָשַׁע)?" (34:29a). He continues later:

> By these things [clouds, rain, and thunder], he judges (דִּין) peoples.
>   He gives food in abundance.
> Lightning fills his palms.
>   He orders it to hit the mark.
> Its thunderclap tells of him.
>   The storm is his anger against iniquity (עוֹלָה).[25] (36:31–33)

Elihu also defends God's mercy, as did Zophar before him. In so doing, however, he mocks Job's assertion that he has a heavenly advocate who will serve as his second accuser in his counterclaim against God (16:19–21; 19:25a):

> If there is an angel for a mortal,
>   an advocate (מֵלִיץ), one of the thousand
>   to vouch for a person's uprightness (יֹשֶׁר),

---

suggests that God neither violates nor answers to anyone. Job should not expect God to answer to him.

25. Emending עוֹלֶה to עַוְלָה, following Gordis, *Book of Job*, 506, 507.

> then he will be gracious to that person and say:
>> "Redeem (פדע) them from descending to the Pit,
>> for I have obtained a ransom (כפר).
> Let their flesh be healthier than in their youth.
>> Let them return to their youthful vigor."
> They will pray to God and he will accept them;
>> that they may come into his presence with joy,
> and he may restore the person's innocence;
>> that one sings aloud before mortals:
> "I have sinned (חטא); I have perverted what was upright (ישר);
>> but I was not paid back for it.
> He redeemed (פדה) my soul from passing into the Pit;
>> and my life will see the light."
> Truly, God does all these things
>> two or three times to humans,
> to bring them back from the Pit,
>> that they may be lighted with the light of life. (33:23–30)

Elihu mocks Job: Job has no redeemer; no one in heaven or on earth will defend him against God's claim; no one will stand as second accuser in his threatened suit against God. If such a being actually existed, God's mercy would surely have produced a result happier than Job currently is experiencing. Job needs to admit his guilt before God that he may be spared capital punishment and the Pit. Thus, Elihu's statements in 33:23–30 work both to defend God against Job's claim and to instruct Job as to the right course of action.

Elihu, like all good witnesses, also seeks to impeach Job's prior testimony in the suit. Throughout Elihu's statements, he disparages Job's protestations of innocence. For instance, he rejects Job's assertions that he is guilt-free (זך), pure (חף), without transgression (בלי פשע), and without iniquity (לא עון) (33:9–12). He avows that:

> Job does not testify (דבר) with knowledge;
>> his words lack understanding. (34:35)

He chides:

> Yet, Job opens his mouth in vain
>> and multiplies arguments (מלה) without knowledge. (35:16)

Elihu instructs Job to "consider the marvels of God" (37:14) and asks him a series of questions regarding whether Job understands the workings and power of God (37:15–17) and whether Job can assist God in doing his job (37:18). Scorning Job's supposed knowledge and his lawsuit, Elihu asks of Job in 37:19–20:

> Teach us, then, what we should say to him.
>   We cannot prepare a case (ערך)²⁶ in the dark.
> Is anything conveyed to him when I testify (דבר)?
>   Can one say anything when overwhelmed (בלע)?

Elihu is unimpressed by Job's claims. Job is a blasphemous fool. The evidence against Job is overwhelming. He should ask for God's mercy and be restored to wholeness.

## Elihu's Identification of the Court

Elihu's speeches raise another critical question: Who is the judge of this case? All the characters assent at given moments to the proposition that God is the greatest of all judges. Nonetheless, Job has demanded another judge in this instance because he claims that God is abusing his judicial authority (9:32–35; 31:35). Eliphaz mocked Job's request, noting that no one would hear his claim (5:1b). Even Job worries that no one can hear his claim (10:7b; 19:19). The question of who is this trial's judge creates some anxiety for a number of the book's characters. It has also been a perplexity to interpreters of the book. A broad range of proposals have been offered, including God, Job, the friends, Elihu, and readers external to the story.²⁷ In spite of Elihu's obvious support of the proposition that God is the final arbiter of behavior, Elihu's speeches demonstrate that the jurisdiction of the dispute has moved from the Divine Council, where the case began, to an earthly assembly of the wise. Such a mid-trial transfer of jurisdiction is consistent with trial practice in the Neo-Babylonian period.

Chapter 5 of this study showed that a trial was initiated in the Divine Council when the Satan brought charges against Job for having the guilty mind of a blasphemer and some type of legal or political complaint against God for favoring Job. Little question exists in the minds of those who constitute the Divine Council that they will be deciding matters. The Divine Council has the power to try cases against its members and human beings.²⁸ The suit is brought in that forum. They are the investigating body. It is only natural to conclude that they will determine the outcome of the case. Throughout the book, the presence of the Council remains in the mind of the reader: What will they think of Job's behavior? Is it blasphemous or not? Will Elihu ultimately be convincing? Nonetheless, the human characters of the story never address themselves to that august body. God

---

26. See also 13:18; 23:4.
27. For citations of scholars who take these various positions, see ch. 1, nn. 23–27 above.
28. See ch. 5, nn. 23–24, 30–31 above.

alone is on their minds and in their conversations. It does seem, however, that it would be most inappropriate for God to judge this case given the fact that Job has charged him specifically with abuse of judicial authority. Elihu reveals the solution to this terrible literary and legal dilemma.

Elihu specifically calls for human judges to hear the case. These judges are the assembly of the wise. For example, in 34:2–10 he calls on them to hear, and to choose between, the competing claims:

> Hear (שמעו) my arguments (מלה), you wise ones;
>    and listen (האזינו) to me, you who know;
> for the ear tests (בחן) arguments (מלה)
>    as the palate tastes food.
> Let us choose what is justice (משפט).
>    Let us determine among ourselves what is good.
> For Job has said, "I am innocent (צדק).
>    God has deprived me of justice (משפט).
> In my own litigation (משפט), I am called a liar.
>    My arrow-wound is deadly, though I am free from transgression (פשע)."
> What mortal is like Job,
>    who drinks up derision (לעג) like water,
> who goes in company with evildoers
>    and walks with the wicked?
> For he has said, "It profits one nothing
>    to take delight in God."
> Therefore, people of understanding, hear (שמעו) me!
>    Wickedness is far from God,
>    Injustice (עול), from Shaddai.

While Elihu often uses the *qal* imperative of (שמע), "hear," in its first legal function—that is, to mark his testimony—this is not the only use to which he puts the word. In 33:31 and 33, Elihu uses the *qal* imperative of שמע in its second legal function, as a means to indicate that he is accusing Job. Here, however, he calls on an earthly assembly of people to decide the case, much in the way that Jeremiah calls for a decision from King Zedekiah at the conclusion of his testimony in his trial (Jer 37:20). This is the third legal function of the *qal* imperative of שמע. Elihu is making a strong argument against Job's position in favor of God's. He invites the wise, in which he is included, to choose what is good and just in this case.

He implores those with understanding to hear him and asks whether they will condemn God and let one who hates justice—namely, Job—govern:

> If you have understanding, hear (שמעה) this.
>    Listen (האזינה) to what I say.
> Shall one who hates justice (משפט) govern?
>    Will you condemn (רשע) one who is righteous (צדיק) and mighty,

> who says to a king, "You scoundrel!"
> and to princes, "You wicked men!";
> He is not partial to princes;
> the noble are not preferred to the wretched;
> for all of them are the work of his hands.
> In a moment they die;
> at midnight the people are shaken and pass away,
> and the mighty are taken away by no human hand. (34:16–20)

Elihu argues strongly against a finding of guilty for God and not guilty for Job. He intimates that there will be a horrible outcome to such verdicts. Elihu continues this line of argument in 34:29–30, where he says that God will be silenced and an impious person will rule. This cannot happen.

Consequently, in 34:34–35, Elihu declares that the assembly should find for God and state that Job's testimony was not convincing:

> People of understanding should say to me,
> and so also the wise one who hears:
> "Job does not testify (דבר) with knowledge;
> his words lack understanding."

Elihu follows up this statement concerning the right result with the plea for Job's conviction for blasphemy:

> Would that Job were investigated (בחן) to the limit
> for responses (תשובה) that befit those of iniquity (און).
> He adds to his sin (הטאת).
> He increases his transgression (פשע) among us.
> He multiplies his statements (אמרה) against God. (34:36–37)

Elihu wants the assembly to give the win to God.

Elihu apparently rejects the Divine Council as the appropriate adjudicating body. The divine king's royal judges are not to hear this case. Instead, an assembly of the people will hear it. Elihu follows Lev 24:15–16: the whole congregation (כל־העדה) should punish for blasphemous remarks and not leave the matter to God alone (32:13). His position naturally flows from the view that blasphemy is a high-culpability crime that demands congregational punishment in order to avoid God's wrath falling upon all of Israel.

The record of Elihu's argument before the assembly and call for decision is most unusual. We rarely find evidence of a lengthy prosecutorial speech in ancient Near Eastern trial reports. The Nippur Homicide Trial[29] and Jeremiah's trial before the officials of Judah and the people (Jer 26:10–

---

29. For some of the important literature on this text, see ch. 4, nn. 75, 85 above.

11) are the only two exemplars known to me.³⁰ This facet of Elihu's speeches is most significant from a legal historical point of view.

The question remains: Who makes up the assembly? Is it Elihu and Job's three friends? Is it Elihu and the elders who have gathered for such purposes? Or does it include the witnesses to the proceedings who stand outside the text, that is, the book's readers?³¹ I doubt that it is Elihu and Job's three friends alone, because Elihu has disavowed the legal knowledge and ability of the friends to try the case adequately (32:6–16). It could be a larger body of elders who have now assembled to hear the case. From 29:2 to 30:15, Job indicates that the assembly of the aged treated him with respect when he had God's favor and stood at the gate. Now the same people treat him poorly. The implication is that they have gathered around him once again. Job also refers to the fact that he is standing in the congregation of Israel for judgment: "I rise in the congregation (קהל) and cry out for help (שוע)" (30:28b). That may explain his charge that the elders are under the influence of a corrupt God (12:20). He does not trust this group for judgment. He wants a different court, as indicated in 9:32–35 and 31:35. Elihu's vision of the assembly may, however, be still greater than simply the assembly of elders in the book of Job. The book's readers may be in that group of wise ones to which Elihu refers and in the congregation of Israel to which Job refers. This last possibility will be explicated more fully in chapter 11.

In conclusion, Elihu's lengthy accusation against Job and defense of God before the assembly of the wise is an extremely important part of the book of Job. Elihu's speeches constitute a foundational component of the trial. When Elihu decides that Job has blasphemed, he convenes an earthly assembly to try Job on such grounds as required by Israelite law. In so doing, he completes on earth what the Satan began in heaven. The Satan accuses Job before the Divine Council of having the guilty mind of blasphemer, which will be revealed once God's blessings are withdrawn. Elihu argues that Job has proven the case through his own derisive words that were spoken after the withdrawal. In furtherance of this position, Elihu recounts Job's sins and blasphemy, how other afflicted persons do not succumb to such things, the wonders of God, and how Job ought to be responding. The speeches are an extensively argued prosecution of Job and defense of God. In this way, he becomes the required second accuser in the original case. In fact, Elihu's accusation is the reason that Job ultimately surrenders the case: Job does not have a second accuser as does God (or the Satan). This last point will become even more apparent as we explore God's

---

30. Such an account is also found in the Iliad; see Westbrook, "Trial Scene," 53–76.
31. Both D. Cox and S. Lasine propose that the reader is the final judge of the book. See ch. 1, n. 27 above.

remarks in chapter 10. Elihu's speeches add a great deal to the book from both legal historical and literary points of view. Most importantly, they bring the legal materials of Job into a cohesive unit. Although it is conceivable, from a literary perspective, that the Elihu speeches are a Neo-Babylonian or Persian-period addition to an earlier text, from a legal perspective they are much more likely to be original to the text.[32]

---

32. Agreeing with Albertson, who states: "The so-called insertion of Elihu at this point becomes an integral feature of the book-reclaiming-its-unity when it is seen in the structure of the *rîb* pattern. . . . Elihu illustrates the formal and proper use of disputation in debate, controlled controversy" ("Job and Ancient Near Eastern Wisdom," 230).

## 10

# God's Defense and Settlement of Claims

Now that Elihu has served as the heavenly trial's second accuser, brought charges against Job on earth, argued the case before the assembly, and called for a decision in God's favor, the case against Job is almost complete. The Satan has obtained the critical second accuser for his case. Elihu's testimony and argument before the assembly are highly damaging to Job. Although Job has offered an extensive defense, it was not as strong as it might have been because he never specifically denied having the guilty mind or mouth of a blasphemer. Furthermore, Job has not, in spite of his best efforts, lined up a second accuser for his counterclaim. Nonetheless, two impediments to a successful prosecution of Job remain. First, no one has yet stepped forward to be the all-important second accuser of Job on the earthly plane. Humans, therefore, may not yet convict Job of blasphemy. All punitive action will have to come from the heavenly court. Second, Job's threat of a counterclaim remains outstanding. He has not withdrawn it. Because all defendants in this inquisitorial legal system must speak to the charges or risk losing the case, Yahweh must be prepared to offer some defense. Hence, Yahweh comes forward to respond to the countercharge, appearing out of the tempest to speak to Job (38:1; 40:6). Yahweh must, however, not only defend against Job; he continues to face the Satan's allegation that he applied justice unfairly and assisted Job in his crimes. Yahweh must defend against this outstanding charge as well or be subject to action in the Divine Council. It would not be beneficial to Yahweh's cause in the council to appear to be conspiring with Job by failing to defend himself with great diligence. As a result, Yahweh offers a lengthy defense of himself, attacking Job in the process.

## Yahweh's Counterdefense

In his speeches, Yahweh grants twice that Job is prepared to countersue him:

> Will a faultfinder (יסור) bring suit (ריב) against Shaddai?
> Will the one accusing (מוכיח)[1] God answer (ענה) him? (40:2)
>
> Would you frustrate (פרר) my case (משפט)?
> Would you convict (רשע) me so that you might be innocent (צדק)? (40:8)

Yahweh is clear that Job has not actually filed suit. Job could have instituted formal charges against God at the conclusion of Elihu's testimony and prosecutorial argument because Elihu brought the case back to court. Job, however, did not. Instead, Yahweh began to speak immediately. Consequently, Yahweh's remarks address a potential claim, not an actual indictment, and they must be in the nature of statements made within the confines of settlement negotiations. Nevertheless, Yahweh puts forward a rigorous defense, keeping the Satan's attack ever in mind.

Yahweh is an extremely good legal tactician. He uses two fundamental strategies to defend. First, he attempts to impeach Job's credibility as a witness. Second, he offers an aggressive defense on Job's second and third counts.[2] He does not address the first count, that is, Job's charge of false suit. This may be for one of two reasons. First, the false-suit charge is subsidiary to the second two. In other words, if Yahweh can prove that he is the source and protector of order and social justice and that all is right in the world, then Job's specific situation must be fair. It would be more satisfying to many readers if Yahweh had actually addressed Job's specific complaint with regard to his treatment, but legally it is not mandatory. In the alternative, it may be that any demonstration of weakness would undermine Yahweh's authority in the Divine Council. The speeches of Yahweh must be powerful and bold. Moreover, Yahweh simply cannot claim forthrightly that Job's situation is fair because he made it absolutely clear in 2:3b that he did not think the charges were fair. He therefore must appear to intimidate Job while never addressing Job's complaint with regard to his current circumstances.[3] We will examine more carefully Yahweh's efforts to clear himself, beginning with his attempt to impeach Job.

Quickly Yahweh establishes an important rhetorical strategy, which he will use throughout his speeches. He says to Job:

---

1. I disagree with Good that in this context מוכיח means "arbiter" (*In Turns of Tempest*, 163, 348–49). As I indicated in ch. 9, n. 8 above, judges do not answer; parties and witnesses answer. Thus, מוכיח takes on its other meaning, "accuser."

2. See Greenstein, "Forensic Understanding," 252–54; he carefully notes the military metaphors and general hostility of Yahweh's approach in his speeches (pp. 248–50).

3. As B. Vawter puts it: "At first glance, Yahweh's response to Job in chaps. 38–41 seems to be the performance of a god who is merely the caricature of the one against whom Job has complained, a bully fighting a foredoomed battle with superior weapons" (*Job and Jonah: Questioning the Hidden God* [New York: Paulist, 1983], 84).

> Gird your loins like a man, I pray!
> I will interrogate (שאל) you, and you will confess (ידע) to me. (38:3)

He reiterates these words without change in 40:7 at the beginning of his second speech. This justifies Yahweh's use of rhetorical questions throughout his speeches. As God, he questions, he instructs, and he is not called to task by humans. He therefore rapid-fires a barrage of questions meant to undermine Job's position. S. H. Scholnick argues that Yahweh's questions are "a series of cross-examining interrogatories" meant to subvert any claim that Job might have over title to the universe.[4] While this last point is not correct, Scholnick does capture the essence of Yahweh's rhetorical plan.[5] The questions seek to impeach and intimidate Job and, thus, are similar to modern cross-examination in adversarial legal systems. In inquisitorial systems, however, the investigating magistrate or judge often performs such questioning. While Yahweh is not the judge of the case because he is accused of being a corrupt one, Yahweh attempts to assume a judgelike stance in order to assert his authority. He will not be dragged into court by this human. Yahweh attempts through this strategy to knock Job off the offensive and put him back into a defensive stance.

Yahweh uses his superior age, creativity, and knowledge to undermine Job's credibility as a witness. In particular, Yahweh levels many challenges at Job's knowledge and wisdom, beginning in his opening move:

> Who is this that darkens counsel
> with arguments (מלה) without knowledge? (38:2)

This launches a pattern of impeachment based on Job's lack of knowledge and wisdom when compared with Yahweh.

In his questioning of Job, Yahweh refers repeatedly to himself as the creator of the universe and compares his creature Job unfavorably to himself. Yahweh chastises Job for failing to be the creator, and he impugns Job's knowledge because Job was not present at the creation of the universe:

> Where were you when I laid the earth's foundations?
>   Tell me, if you have understanding.
> Do you know who fixed its dimensions
>   or who measured it with a line?
> Onto what were its bases sunk?
>   Who set its cornerstone
> when the morning stars sang together
>   and all the divine beings shouted for joy?

---

4. Scholnick, "Poetry in the Courtroom," 427.
5. This view comes from her understanding of the force of עשק as the misappropriation of property (ibid., 425). I believe Westbrook has the better view; see ch. 6, n. 95 above.

> Who closed the sea behind doors
> when it gushed forth out of the womb,
> when I clothed it in clouds,
> swaddled it in dense clouds,
> when I prescribed my limit (חק)[6] for it,
> and set up its bar and doors,
> and said, "You may come so far and no farther.
> Here your surging waves will stop"? (38:4–11)

This same strategy can be seen in 38:16–23:

> Have you penetrated to the sources of the sea,
> or walked in the recesses of the deep?
> Have the gates of death been disclosed to you?
> Have you seen the gates of deep darkness?
> Have you surveyed the expanses of the earth?
> If you know of these, tell me—
> which path leads to where light dwells,
> and where is the place of darkness,
> that you may take it to its domain
> and know the way to its home?
> Surely you know, for you were born then
> and the number of your years is many!
> Have you penetrated the vaults of snow,
> seen the vaults of hail,
> which I have put aside for a time of adversity,
> for a day of war and battle?

Yahweh uses legal language in his attack in 38:24–34:

> Do you know the laws (חק)[7] of heaven
> Or impose (שׂים) its authority (משׁטר) on earth? (38:33)

Yahweh continues to minimize Job's knowledge in 39:1–3.

> Do you know when the mountain goats give birth?
> Do you observe the calving of the deer?
> Can you number the months that they fulfill,
> and do you know the time when they give birth,
> when they crouch to give birth to their offspring,
> and are delivered of their young?

Yahweh also minimizes Job's wisdom several times; for example, in 39:26–30, Yahweh asks:

---

6. See the material at n. 16 below.
7. Ibid.

> Is it by your wisdom that the hawk grows pinions,
>   spreads his wings to the south?

Moreover, in 38:36–37a, Yahweh queries Job:

> Who put wisdom in the hidden parts?
>   Who gave understanding to the mind?
> Who is wise enough to give an account of the heavens?

Yahweh alone, that is who.[8] Job is not wise enough to challenge Yahweh in this fashion. The pièce de résistance is Yahweh's reference to the mother ostrich in 39:13–18. He notes that she does not protect her eggs adequately and declares:

> For God deprived her of wisdom,
>   gave her no share of understanding,
> else she would soar on high,
>   scoffing at the horse and its rider. (39:17–18)

The implication is that God also deprived Job of wisdom. Job cannot charge God with these crimes because Job has no ability to assess the situation. He makes a very poor witness.[9]

One of the most important scholarly conversations around Yahweh's speeches is whether or not he responds to Job in any meaningful way. J. G. Williams states this position particularly well:

> Yet the speeches of God are strange and elusive. In terms of the verbal level it is simply a fact that Yahweh makes no affirmation about himself that Job has not already expressed in the dispute: God is omnipotent, omniscient, omnipresent, etc. Neither does the Voice directly respond to Job's questions, complaints and laments. Is it true or not that there is no moral order in the universe? That Elohim is terrible, the Almighty a supernatural tyrant who acts capriciously, unwisely, and unjustly? Is it true that the doctrine of retribution is an illusion, that the just man is not rewarded nor the wicked punished? Yahweh does not address himself to these questions.[10]

I suggest that, even though Yahweh does not respond point by point, he does offer a legally significant answer to Job's charges. Yahweh's string of

---

8. C. J. Labuschagne argues that God's rhetorical questions throughout chs. 38 and 39 are meant to evoke the response, "None but Yahweh alone" (*The Incomparability of Yahweh in the Old Testament* [Leiden: Brill, 1966], 27; cf. 19).

9. See further Greenstein, "Forensic Understanding," 241–58.

10. J. G. Williams, "Deciphering the Unspoken: The Theophany of Job," in *Sitting with Job: Selected Studies on the Book of Job* (ed. R. B. Zuck; Grand Rapids: Baker, 1992), 364. See also A. Brenner, "God's Answer to Job," *VT* 31 (1981): 129.

rhetorical questions serves not only to impugn Job's integrity as a witness but also to respond to Job's challenge that God is an extremely poor defender of justice, his second count, and that God never created a beneficent order in the universe, Job's third and most significant charge. We take up count 2 first.

T. N. D. Mettinger argues that Yahweh defends his righteousness in 40:7–14.[11] In particular, Yahweh maintains that he is a good defender of justice. In 40:10–14, Yahweh commands Job:

> Deck yourself now with grandeur and eminence.
>   Clothe yourself in glory and majesty.
> Scatter wide your raging anger.
>   See every proud human and bring him low.
> See every proud human and humble him,
>   and bring them down where they stand.
> Bury them all in the earth.
>   Hide their faces in obscurity.
> Then even I would praise you
>   for the triumph your right hand won you.

In his references to bringing the proud low and humbling them, Yahweh asserts that he is maintaining social justice and that Job is incapable of doing such (cf. 1 Sam 2:7; Isa 2:17).

Yahweh also claims to have produced natural phenomena that assist in this task. For example, in 38:12–15, he says:

> Have you commanded the morning since your days began,
>   and caused the dawn to know its place,
> so that it might take hold of the skirts of the earth,
>   and the wicked be shaken out of it?
> It is changed like clay under the seal,
>   and it is dyed like a garment.
> Light is withheld from the wicked,
>   and their uplifted arm is broken.

Habel says of this: "The morning is on standing orders to make a regular appearance and keep the wicked in check."[12] Thus, it plays a role in the maintenance of justice.

Yahweh spends more time defending himself against count three.[13] In 38:4–11, during Yahweh's severe questioning of Job concerning whether he

---

11. Mettinger, "God of Job," 45.
12. Habel, "In Defense of God the Sage," 35.
13. See ibid. A number of other commentators have suggested that the speeches argue for the existence of a beneficent cosmic order. See, e.g., Gordis, *Book of God and Man*, 133; and Mettinger, "God of Job," 45.

was at the making of the foundations of the earth, Yahweh demonstrates the wonder of the earth's land, sea, and rain, which he created. As Habel suggests:

> God commences his defense by pointing to the primordial structures of the universe, which reflect its cosmic design (38:4–7). The earth is a stable edifice with a blueprint, exact measurements, and solid foundations. Wisdom is required for an artisan to construct a house, and "discernment for those who establish it" (Prov. 24:3). God becomes the wise artisan of the cosmos, the architect of a universe hailed by the court of heaven as a finished masterpiece (cf. Zech. 4:7). Here is a God concerned about stability and precision, not anarchy and disorder.[14]

There is an implication in 38:10 that even the primordial waters are subject to Yahweh's law because the word "limit" (חק) in 38:10 also means "law," "decree," or "statute," as in 38:33.[15] When Yahweh asks in 38:31–32, 34–35,

> Can you tie cords to Pleiades
>   or undo the reins of Orion?
> Can you lead out Mazzaroth in its season,
>   conduct the Bear with her sons? . . . .
> Can you send up an order to the clouds
>   for an abundance of water to cover you?
> Can you dispatch the lightning on a mission
>   and have it answer you, "I am ready"?

he is arguing that the fact that the stars remain in the heaven but rotate through the seasons reflects divine order; the fact that the clouds pour out rain to sustain life is part of that same beneficent order. Similar thinking lies behind 38:24–30, where Yahweh queries:

> By what path is the west wind dispersed,
>   the east wind scattered over the earth?
> Who cut a channel for the torrents
>   and a path for the thunderstorms
> to rain down on uninhabited land,
>   on the wilderness, where no mortal is,
> to saturate the desolate wasteland
>   and make the crop of grass sprout forth?
> Does the rain have a father?
>   Who begot the dewdrops?
> From whose belly came forth the ice?
>   who gave birth to the frost of heaven?

---

14. Habel, "In Defense of God," 34; see also, Good, *In Turns of Tempest*, 346–47.
15. See BDB, 349; cf. Habel, "In Defense of God," 34–35.

Water congeals like stone,
  and the surface of the deep compacts.

In 38:27, Yahweh maintains that this order produces food for humans and animals alike when the grass sprouts. We see this argument again in 38:39–41:

Can you hunt prey for the lion
  and satisfy the appetite of the king of beasts?
They crouch in their dens,
  lie in ambush in their lairs.
Who provides food for the raven
  when his young cry out to God
  and wander about without food?

This demonstrates Yahweh's goodness.[16]

Yahweh provides other resources for mortals beyond food. For example, in 39:19–25, Yahweh gives us the horse, which can be used in battle:

Do you give the horse his strength?
  Do you clothe his neck with a mane?
Do you make him leap like the locust?
  Its majestic snorting is terrible.
He paws with force, he runs with vigor,
  charging into battle.
He scoffs at fear; he cannot be frightened.
  He does not recoil from the sword.
A quiverful of arrows whizzes by him,
  and the flashing spear and the javelin.
Trembling with excitement, he swallows the land.
  He does not turn aside at the blast of the trumpet.
As the trumpet sounds, he says, "Aha!"
  From afar he smells the battle,
  the roaring and shouting of the officers.

Humanity's ability to tame wild oxen to toil in our fields results from Yahweh's efforts:

Would the wild ox agree to serve you?
  Would he spend the night at your crib?
Can you hold the wild ox by ropes to the furrow?
  Would he plow up the valleys behind you?
Would you rely on his great strength
  and leave your toil to him?

---

16. In accord is B. L. Newell, "Job: Repentant or Rebellious?" in *Sitting with Job: Selected Studies on the Book of Job* (ed. R. B. Zuck; Grand Rapids: Baker, 1992), 446.

Would you trust him to bring in the seed
and gather it in from your threshing floor? (39:9–12)

Moreover, Yahweh offers freedom, rather than the bondage of servitude, to many animals, which is another sign of his goodness:

Who sets the wild ass free?
    Who loosens the bonds of the onager,
whose home I have made the wilderness,
    the salt land his dwelling-place?
He scoffs at the tumult of the city;
    he does not hear the shouts of the driver.
He roams the hills for his pasture;
    he searches for any green thing.
Does the eagle soar at your command,
    building his nest high,
dwelling in the rock,
    lodging upon the fastness of a jutting rock?
From there he spies out his food.
    From afar his eyes see it.
His young gulp blood.
    Where the slain are, there is he. (39:5–8, 27–30)

The implication is that free humans owe a debt of gratitude to Yahweh for their freedom, as well.[17]

The very fact of life and death depend on Yahweh. This is supported by Yahweh's remarks concerning the birth of mountain goats and calves in 39:1–4 and the location of the gates of death in 38:17.[18] Yahweh controls all facets of existence from beginning to end.

Yahweh commands the very forces of chaos in the universe, as represented by the Behemoth (40:15–24) and the Leviathan (40:25–41:2; 41:4–26).[19] Yahweh's lengthy discourse regarding these two creatures seeks to convince Job that he can subdue chaos because it is the first creation of Yahweh (40:19a). As Mettinger phrases it: "His supremacy over the chaotic forces is pointed up with formulations marked by Hebrew humor: The chaotic waters are described as a child in her swaddling bands (38:8–11),

---

17. It is interesting to note, however, that while God offers great attention to animals in his speeches, the deity shows little direct concern for humans. Job must infer such from the treatment of animals.
18. See Habel, "In Defense of God," 35.
19. Many have noted the connection between the Behemoth, the Leviathan, and chaos. They maintain that God's discussion of them indicates his power to control and structure chaos during the creation and beyond. See, e.g., Mettinger, "God of Job," 45–46. Mettinger also suggests that these creatures stand in for the proud and the wicked, thereby reinforcing the idea that God is a god of social justice (p. 47).

and Leviathan as a pet animal (40:29; cf. Ps. 104:26)."[20] Yahweh orders the universe. Yahweh is good in his exercise of power. He is a god of care and protection.[21]

Although Yahweh asserts this view, it might be difficult for Job to accept it when he is being intimidated by this hail of questions. Yahweh plays the power card repeatedly. Yahweh asserts his control of, and authority over, the universe by his questions. He mocks Job's powerlessness. For instance, Yahweh asks whether Job can control the stars, clouds, and lightning in 38:31–32, 34–35. Similarly, in 38:12–14, Yahweh queries whether Job can command the day to break and thereby control the wicked. He again mocks Job by commanding him to attempt to equal Yahweh's grandeur and anger and to enforce social justice himself in 40:10–14. He dishes out more of the same in 38:16–23, 37b–41; 39:5–8, 27–30; and 40:27–41:26. Only Yahweh can command the trust and servitude of the beasts of the earth (39:9–10). Job is weak in Yahweh's eyes:

> Have you an arm like God's?
> Can you thunder with a voice like his? (40:9)

Yahweh's point is that Job is no match for an adversary such as this.

Especially interesting are Yahweh's inquiries of Job regarding the Leviathan in 40:27–28:

> Will he negotiate at length (רבה תחנון) with you?
> Will he speak soft words to you?
> Will he make a covenant (ברית) with you
> to be taken (לקח) as your lifelong slave?

Here Yahweh asserts his legal power. Even the great Leviathan, a representative of chaos itself, will negotiate a settlement (תחנון) with Yahweh. Even the great Leviathan will surrender his cause in the face of Yahweh and become a slave. If no one can stand against the Leviathan and the Leviathan cannot stand against Yahweh, who is Job to imagine that he can stand against Yahweh?

> Any hope of subduing him [the Leviathan] is false;
> the mere sight of him is overpowering.
> No one is so fierce as to rouse him;
> who then can take their stand before my face?
> Whoever confronts me I will requite,
> for everything under the heavens is mine.

---

20. Mettinger, "God of Job," 47; cf. R. Raphael, "Things Too Wonderful: A Disabled Reading of Job," *PRSt* 31 (2004): 399–401.

21. Raphael, "Things Too Wonderful," 399–401; and Newell, "Job: Repentant or Rebellious?" 446.

> Did I not silence his boasting
>> his mighty word (דבר) and his persuasive case (חין ערכו)²²? (41:1–4)

Yahweh informs Job that even divine beings are afraid of the Leviathan (41:17). In the final analysis, Yahweh's questions are not just a representation of the examination he will deliver at trial in an attempt to impeach Job; they are a means to induce Job to cave in during settlement negotiations.

Although the pressure is intense, Job is no fool. He does not take the bait. As we have already discussed in chapter 7, Job answers Yahweh's first onslaught, in 40:4–5, with the words:

> Certainly, I am small; how can I respond (שוב) to you?
>> I lay my hand to my mouth.
> I have spoken once, and will not answer (ענה);
>> Twice, and will do so no more.

Job is humble in his short speech. He acknowledges his smallness. He does not try to go head to head with God. He long ago asserted that no one can cause God to respond or relent (9:12–13). No one can win a case against God (9:2). He does not try to force God's hand now.²³ Nonetheless, Job is not surrendering here as so many maintain.²⁴ Instead, Job is responding negatively to Yahweh's demand (38:3) that Job answer him again. Yahweh orders Job to answer these many questions by way of confession. Job puts hand to mouth in order to demonstrate that he will not speak in answer.²⁵ Job's reply is essentially, "I have answered completely. I am done." I concur with A. E. Steinmann that the author's use of graded numerical sayings marks "important junctures in the structure of the book."²⁶ Nevertheless, I do not agree that the references to having spoken twice are enumerative in the manner Steinmann maintains. If it is enumerative at all, the "once" must refer to Job's declarative statements as to his innocence and the "twice" must refer to his oath. It is not necessary, however, to interpret the

---

22. Following Habel, *Book of Job: Commentary*, 555.
23. See ibid., 549.
24. See, e.g., B. Vawter, who states: "How can Job claim to command a respectable hearing as a man of wisdom in his own constituency if he has failed to make a satisfactory response and can but stand mute. And stand mute he does, first overtly in 40:3–5, and, somewhat ambiguously, in 42:1–6" (*Job and Jonah*, 85). Gordis says of this passage: " He [Job] sets forth his weakness and insignificance and his determination to remain silent" (*Book of Job*, 466). I disagree.
25. Newell has a lengthy discussion of this gesture as an indicator of silence ("Job: Repentant or Rebellious?" 449–50).
26. A. E. Steinmann, "The Graded Numerical Sayings in Job," *Fortunate the Eyes That See: Essays in Honor of David Noel Freedman in Celebration of his Seventieth Birthday* (ed. A. B. Beck, A. H. Bartelt, P. R. Raabe, and C. A. Franke; Grand Rapids: Eerdmans, 1995), 297.

statement as enumerative to understand its force. It could be purely rhetorical. B. Jackson points out that the expression "x or x+1" in law can represent a sense of completeness.[27] I believe that the graded numerical statement in this context also signifies a sense of completeness. Job is asserting the fact that he closed his defense against the charges with his oath of innocence. Moreover, Job is using the expression to respond to Elihu's assertion (33:14) that God "speaks in one way, even in two ways, without people noticing it." It seems that Job has spoken in one way and two without God having noticed it. Elihu continues that God settles matters favorably with people "two or three times" (33:19). By Job's use of his graded numerical saying, he is suggesting that the time for settlement is upon them. Job has neither duty nor need to answer Yahweh again in this particular legal context. By refusing to be intimidated, he insists that Yahweh continue with this defense or settle the matter immediately.[28] Yahweh elects to continue with his defense.

Eventually, however, Job does concede the case. At the end of Yahweh's second speech, Job gives it up. There are two accusers against Job, while he has been unable to find a second accuser for his claim against Yahweh. Yahweh has defended on the second and third charges. Job's first count against God fails on God's success on the other two. Job has not apparently been able to cause God to respond in the way he had hoped. Consequently, Job states:

> I know that you can do everything
>   and that no scheme of yours can be thwarted (בצר).
> [You said:] "Who is this who obscures counsel without knowledge?
> Indeed, I spoke without understanding
>   of things beyond me, which I did not know."
> [You said:] "Hear, I pray (שמע־נא), and I will speak.
>   I will interrogate (שאל) you, and you will confess (ידע) to me."
> I had heard you with my ears,
>   But now I see you with my eyes.
> Therefore, I retract [my case],[29]
>   and repent of dust and ashes. (42:2–6)

---

27. B. S. Jackson, "'Two or Three Witnesses,'" in *Essays in Jewish and Comparative Legal History* (SJLA 10: Leiden: Brill, 1975), 153–71; although, with regard to the exact analysis of the expression "two or three witnesses" in the Pentateuch, I follow B. Wells (*Law of Testimony*, 83–132). I also disagree that the rhetorical device only means to say *several* as maintained by some; see, e.g., Good, *In Turns of Tempest*, 352.

28. Good states that Job's refusal to speak again is "a mild dig at the deity" (*In Turns of Tempest*, 352).

29. Following Scholnick, "Meaning of *Mišpāṭ*," 357; and Habel, *Book of Job: Commentary*, 576; contra Greenstein, "Forensic Understanding," 253.

Whatever Job once heard and saw to make him threaten to bring his counterclaim (13:1), he now sees differently. He sees that he truly cannot win against such an opponent as this. He cannot answer the questions that Yahweh puts to him.

Job does not, however, concede without some protest. The word בצר, "to thwart," is a word play on בצע, "to gain by violence."[30] Job cannot stop God's abuse of him. He further acknowledges this by his reiteration, in 42:3–4, of both Yahweh's impeachment and intimidation of him in 38:2–3 and 40:7. Job has had his opportunity to confront Yahweh face-to-face (42:5), but it was in vain. Vawter concludes: "The God who spoke to Job out of the whirlwind has overwhelmed him with his all-presence and all power, but he has offered no path by which man may seek the divine."[31] Job is beaten. While Job must concede, he is not convinced.[32] God never did state the charges against Job. God never did directly defend against the false suit. Job still believes he has been treated unjustly. He speaks with frustration in his voice.

## The Lawsuit's Settlement

We should now expect that Job's concession would bring punishment upon his head. The sanction for blasphemy is death; yet Job does not die. Instead, Yahweh unexpectedly launches into an attack on Eliphaz and the other friends. Yahweh tells Eliphaz that he is angry with the friends because they have misrepresented him: they have not spoken the truth about him (כי לא דברתם אלי נכונה כעבדי איוב) (42:7, 8). *Their* actions have bordered on the blasphemous (נבלה) (42:8)! Yahweh supports Job's position and calls Job once more by his honorific title, "my servant" (42:7, 8). He commands the friends to offer a burnt offering of seven bulls and seven rams before Job as though before a priest. He asks Job to pray for the friends and says that

---

30. Note also the probable play on Gen 11:6; see Greenstein, "Forensic Understanding," 254.
31. Vawter, *Job and Jonah*, 86.
32. Several commentators maintain that Job's surrender seems inconsistent with the entire course of the book. See, e.g., J. B. Curtis, "On Job's Response to Yahweh," *JBL* 98 (1979): 497–511; K. Fullerton, "The Original Conclusion to the Book of Job," *ZAW* 42 (1924): 125–28; C. G. Jung, *Answer to Job* (New York: Pastoral Psychology Book Club, 1955), 31; and Robertson, *Old Testament*, 52; idem, "Book of Job," 466. Robertson goes so far as to say that Job's submission is a fraud. Curtis claims that Job simply does not submit. See also E. L. Greenstein, "In Job's Face/Facing Job," in *The Labor of Reading: Desire, Alienation, and Biblical Interpretation* (ed. Fiona C. Black, Roland Boer, and Erin Runions; Semeia Studies 36; Atlanta: Society of Biblical Literature, 1999), 301–17. Job's submission is real because of the legal position in which he finds himself, although he is not pleased about it. This is no happy or wizened concession.

he will not treat them with contempt (42:8). The burnt offering indicates that, in Yahweh's mind, the friends erred unintentionally even if the conduct was wrongful according to the Levitical laws.[33] In the story, the friends did as Yahweh commanded them (42:9).

Yahweh's assessment that the friends spoke wrongly and that they should humble themselves before Job as one would before a priest is his concession of the case.[34] Yahweh is not the judge of this case and therefore has no ability to declare a verdict here. Consequently, he does not use the Hebrew legal formula that declares a winning verdict: "You are innocent" (צדיק אתה).[35] He does, however, have the power to settle the dispute and does so by declaring Job in the right, even if he does say this to Job's friends rather than to Job himself.[36] The narrator also deems Yahweh guilty as charged when he reports that Job's relatives and friends "consoled and comforted him for all the evil Yahweh had brought upon him" (42:11b).

Consequently, Yahweh states forcefully (42:8) that he will show favor to Job (כי אם־פניו אשא) and carries that out in 42:9. Yahweh blesses the latter years of Job's life (42:12), giving him ten more children and double his property (42:10, 12–13). The blessing is significant. According to K. H. Richards:

> Bless/blessing has been most frequently understood in terms of benefits conveyed—prosperity, power, and especially fertility. This focus on the content of the benefit is now being viewed as secondary. The primary factor of blessing is the statement of relationship between the parties. God blesses with a benefit on the basis of the relationship. The blessing makes known the positive relationship between the parties. . . .[37]

God's blessing of Job indicates that Job and God are reconciled. In the legal arena, this often happens through a settlement agreement, just as Job requested. The restoration of Job's children and double his property are the terms of that agreement.

A settlement for twice the amount of the damage is not unusual. We see penalty provisions in multiples of one, two, ten, and thirty in the Neo-

---

33. See the material in ch. 8, between nn. 35 and 36 above.

34. Bildad apparently foreshadowed this possibility when he said that, after Job settles with God, those who hate (שׂנא) Job will come to shame (בשׁת) and have their own dwelling destroyed (8:22). Now it is Job's friends who must make supplication for their unwitting errors.

35. R. Westbrook notes: "The verdict in actions in personam was a formula directed to the winning party: 'You are in the right' . . . " ("Biblical Law," 10, citing Prov 24:24).

36. See Beach, "'More Righteous Than God,'" 11.

37. K. H. Richards, "Bless/Blessing," ABD 1:754; see also F. R. Magdalene, "Bless/Blessing," EDB, 192; J. Ries, "Blessing" (trans. J. C. Haight and A. S. Mahler), The Encyclopedia of Religion (ed. M. Eliade; 16 vols.; New York: Macmillan, 1987), 2:247; and J. Scharbert, "brk," TDOT, 2:284.

Babylonian trial documents and in multiples of two, seven, and ten in the Hebrew Bible.[38] Double penalties can be found in Exod 22:3, 6, 8; Isa 40:2; and Jer 17:18 (cf. Gen 43:12, 15). Settlement provisions could also equal the appropriate multiplied damage figure. This settlement seems reasonable from a legal standpoint.

Furthermore, a direct concession of liability was not required in order to enter into a settlement agreement. Cases exist in the Neo-Babylonian period where a very powerful party refused to admit liability but paid a substantial settlement amount. For example, in *BE* 10, 9, a group of Nippurians apparently invaded and looted the town of Rabiya. One Baga'data accused a certain Bel-nadin-šumi, an individual of the economically important house of Murašu, and his servants of trespassing in and looting his property during the raid. Bel-nadin-šumi denied liability. In spite of his denial, Bel-nadin-šumi paid a large amount, including 20 oxen, 200 female sheep, 350 gur of barley, 200 gur of dates, 50 gur of wheat, 1 gur of spelt, 50 jars old wine with bottles, 50 jars of new wine with bottles, and 5 talents of wool — a healthy sum — in consideration for dropping the suit. Thus, one does not have to admit liability to pay a most liberal settlement. In the book of Job, Yahweh does admit liability, just not directly to Job.[39] The friends are the recipients of Yahweh's concession. In spite of the misdirected admission of guilt, Yahweh pays a large settlement amount, restores Job's honorific title, and commands the friends to make sacrifices before Job to clear their error. Job's children, property, honor, and positive relationship with his fellows are restored. With that, Yahweh and Job are reconciled.

I must admit that the divine speeches cause one to be surprised by the settlement. One has to ask: Why would Yahweh settle the matter when (1) he has apparently proven that he is the font and guardian of justice; (2) he has lambasted Job, leaving him in no position to question that position in any case; and (3) Job has, in fact, conceded the suit? The answer lies at the start of the book: because Yahweh knows that Job is a man of "integrity (תם) and uprightness (ישר)" (1:1aα). He fears God (ירא אלהים) and shuns evil (סר מרע) (1:1aβ). Yahweh always believed in Job's innocence. He cooperated with this suit because the Satan instituted a formal charge. The integrity of the legal system demanded that God respect the process. Furthermore, if he had tried to subvert it for Job's benefit, he would have proven the case against himself and fallen in the Divine Council. The lambasting of Job was necessary to prove the Satan wrong with respect to the

---

38. For seven see, e.g., Ps 6:31 and Prov 1:30–31; for ten, see, e.g., Gen 4:15, 24; Lev 26:18, 21, 24, 28; and Prov 6:31.

39. Beach likens what Yahweh does to the modern *nolo contendere* plea, where no guilt is admitted ("'More Righteous Than God,'" 11). This is exactly the case in *BE* 10, 9. It is not, however, the Joban situation.

allegations against God. It had little to do with Job. Yahweh's focus on his power, control, and authority put all challengers in their place. Interestingly, even after Job completed his statements and Elihu lodged his accusation, Yahweh never accused Job of blasphemy. Yahweh never came to believe that Job had the guilty mind of a blasphemer or that his counterclaim constituted the act. He never denied his original assertions of Job's integrity and uprightness. This solves the riddle of why God never answered Job's first charge of false suit. God could not because he, too, thought it was a false suit and to have conceded that point was possibly to fall into the Satan's trap. In the end, the suit against Job was proven to have no merit, and, therefore, restoration of Job's losses was in order. Elihu's accusation died on the vine along with the Satan's. Once the Satan's defeat was in hand, Yahweh could get on with the business of clearing matters up with Job.

The fact that Yahweh respected the Satan's claim, let the case proceed, and satisfied Job's losses are all indications that God has a deep commitment to order and fairness. I therefore disagree with those commentators who suggest that God is not faithful to the principles of retributive justice.[40] Given all that occurs in this tale, however, that justice might better be called restorative or reconciling justice.

In summary, when Elihu finishes his impassioned argument before the assembly of the wise, the case against Job looks strong. Because of the threatened counterclaim, Yahweh feels that he must respond at this point. If he should not, Job might just file those charges and Yahweh would be forced to respond formally as a counterdefendant. Yahweh offers a scathing attack on Job's wisdom and knowledge, but never returns to his integrity or uprightness. Nor does he accuse Job of having a blasphemous mind or mouth. Instead, he defends himself on the grounds that he is the ordering principle of the universe and the absolute source and protector of social justice. Job concedes the case after Yahweh is finished because he must. The case against Job is complete. Yahweh has revealed his hand. He has dispatched the Satan's charges against him; he has humbled Job. Nonetheless, this god of justice remains convinced that Job is a man of integrity and uprightness. Consequently, Job must be fully restored through a mid-trial settlement. Yahweh pays Job double his losses and restores his children and his honor, thus proving even to Job that Yahweh is just. All's well that ends well.

---

40. See, e.g., M. Tsevat, "The Meaning of the Book of Job," *HUCA* 37 (1966): 105.

# 11

# Conclusions

I have attempted to demonstrate in this study that a comparison of the book of Job with Neo-Babylonian trial transcripts is a most fruitful exercise. It offers us a new avenue by which to explore the book of Job. It has the potential for answering a number of the outstanding legal, literary, and theological puzzles of the book. Most important, it may explain the great divergence in readings that readers have generated over the millennia.

My particular reading is informed, in part, by the ritual incantations of the ancient Near East. As other commentators have noted, suffering was often cast in terms of trial law in the healing incantations of the region. Those who experienced a calamity saw themselves as subject to a divine trial that might result in a difficult investigation or harsh punishment. The author of Job explores this understanding using a sophisticated literary trial. In the course of this trial, Job's friends accept the worldview of the incantations wholeheartedly. Job, on the other hand, accepts it only in part. Where he does acknowledge its view, he uses the incantations to his own ends. Thus, the trial that the author embeds in the story is of special importance: it structures the book. The trial of Job and God is precisely where the issue of whether divine justice is administered fairly will be determined.

Using the methods of the law-as-literature movement, I have shown that, in the author's attempt to structure a trial in the book, the book mimics to some degree the very form of ancient Near Eastern trial transcripts and the legal stories in them. The author produced a tale that includes all five common features of trial narrative. (1) It contains multiple narrative strands, which are the statements of the parties and witnesses. (2) These narrative strands are in conflict and competition. (3) They seek to persuade. (4) Moreover, these strands are fractured by the dialogue format and the many textual breaks of the text. (5) They are, additionally, structured by legal metaphors that are very similar to Neo-Babylonian legal procedure. In these regards, the book follows common legal narratological conventions, whether ancient or modern. The book of Job has, however, one other feature that is particular to ancient trial records, or, at least, Neo-Babylonian trial records. In Job's case accusers appear and disappear in a manner similar to that of accusers in Neo-Babylonian trial documents. In all six of these respects, the book of Job mimics to an important degree ancient Near Eastern legal documents of practice.

The trial itself, as we read it in the comparative light of Neo-Babylonian trial procedure, is complex. The Satan brings, by his oath, an authentic legal charge against Job in the Divine Council, namely, possession of a blasphemous mind. The Satan also accuses God of applying his justice unfairly, aiding and abetting Job by allowing Job's guilty mind to go unchecked and upsetting the moral economy. The Satan's goal is to undermine God's authority in the council so that he can gain more power. Because God also stands accused, he cannot avert the trial. It must proceed. Job suffers a tortuous legal investigation during which he loses his children, servants, wealth, health, and honor. The Satan's hope is to hear Job blaspheme God to his face. Based on what we know of divine investigations and trials in the worldview of the Hebrew Bible, Job's blasphemy of God would be the best evidence on the charge before the council. Job, however, not knowing that the Satan has brought the charges against him, assumes that God is the accusing party in line with the ritual incantations. Job therefore threatens to counter-sue God for abuse of judicial authority based on three counts: (1) initiating a false suit and conducting himself in an outrageous manner in the course of the trial; (2) violating rather than upholding the fundamental principles of justice as is required of the deity; and (3) failing to create a universe that is orderly from which justice might flow. He demands justice.

Job's demand begins a lengthy settlement negotiation, in which both parties and their supporters jockey for position. Job and his friends state their views. In so doing, they reveal their legal strategies—what their testimony will be if the trial should need to continue—advocate for their position, and seek reconciliation between the parties. Job is in the position where he must defend himself against the charges, but they are unknown to him. He therefore insists on a clarification of the charges, as would be expected according to the ritual incantations. Not having a response from God as to the allegations, Job defends against a broad range of possible charges through both defensive statements and a lengthy oath of denial. Using a multipronged strategy similar to the petitioners of the DINGIR.ŠÀ.DIB.BA incantations, he claims not only that he is free from wrong but also that he is a righteous man of integrity who follows God's law and supports social justice. Unfortunately, Job never specifically defends against blasphemy.

During the negotiations, Job also seeks to find someone to join his claim as a second accuser against God. No one is willing. Instead, the three friends seek to impeach Job and impugn his integrity, uprightness, upholding of social justice, and innocence. They also defend God. They believe that Job's punishment is an appropriate divine response to a sin that he must have committed. Job's suit is folly. His best course of action would be to seek God's pardon in a post-trial settlement of the dispute.

Elihu, who has been standing on the sidelines, thinks that the friends' responses to Job are wholly inadequate. Elihu avers that Job's speeches constitute blasphemy, and he believes that the friends should have filed an accusation against Job to protect the community against this pollution. Elihu therefore accuses Job of derisive speech before an assembly of wise persons and offers one of the great prosecutorial speeches recorded in the ancient Near East. In this manner, Elihu becomes the heavenly trial's second accuser and transfers the case to an earthly court. He thereby picks up where the Satan left off. The heavenly case against Job is now complete.

Nevertheless, God must prepare himself to defend against Job's claim or risk both Job's and the Satan's cases against him. God attempts to impeach Job's testimony and defends himself against both Job's second and third counts, as well as the Satan's accusations. In order to confront the Satan's allegations, God must act with complete integrity during his speeches. He must defend himself to the best of his ability. Unfortunately, he can only defend on counts 2 and 3 because he agrees with Job that the suit is unfair. Nonetheless, the defense is rigorous. Job, believing that God is too strong an opponent after hearing God's defense, concedes the case. He levels, however, a strong protest in so doing.

In spite of Job's surrender, God admits liability in a speech to Eliphaz and settles the case by returning Job's children, property, and honor. The property is restored in double, a common penalty figure in the ancient Near East. Although the suit was not God's doing, Job must be restored to wholeness under the terms of the legal system. Furthermore, Job and God need to be reconciled. Consequently, God settles the case fairly.

According to this reading, the book offers a happy ending, where God's retributive justice prevails, Job's losses are restored, and all the characters but the Satan are reconciled. This, I must acknowledge, is not, however, the only possible reading of the text. In fact, readers throughout the millennia have felt that the book of Job leaves many disturbing questions. I doubt that my reading erases them. It is this conviction that leads me to argue that readers throughout the millennia have judged the situation for themselves. They have offered their own views of the characters' various statements and whether the result is correct. They have adjudicated the dispute; they have approved or disapproved of the settlement just as ancient courts could do. The book's very mimicry of the trial form begs readers to adjudicate the dispute. This demonstrates further just how important Elihu's role in the book is. He is the one who invites the reader into the assembly of the wise to decide finally who is right and what is fair. Thanks to Elihu, Job gets his court of last resort: it is us.

# Appendix A

# List of Neo-Babylonian Trial and Related Documents in Sample

This study used the following Neo-Babylonian texts in assessing the Neo-Babylonian litigation system, although not all these documents were cited in the report of findings. See the Index of Citations for the list of those documents, both Neo-Babylonian and otherwise, actually cited in this study.

| | | |
|---|---|---|
| AfO 17, 2 | BE 10, 9 | CT 2, 2 |
| AfO 44, 76 | BE 10, 10 | CT 22, 40 |
| AfO 44, 78 | BE 10, 11 | CT 22, 56 |
| AfO 44, 81 | BIN 1, 23 | CT 22, 66 |
| AfO 44, 83 | BIN 1, 28 | CT 22, 74 |
| AfO 44, 88 | BIN 1, 43 | CT 22, 80 |
| AfO 44, 89 | BIN 1, 49 | CT 22, 82 |
| AfO 44, 91 | BIN 1, 54 | CT 22, 85 |
| AfO 44, 92 | BIN 1, 73 | CT 22, 87 |
| AnOr 8, 21 | BIN 1, 87 | CT 22, 105 |
| AnOr 8, 27 | BIN 1, 113 | CT 22, 113 |
| AnOr 8, 39 | BIN 1, 122 | CT 22, 114 |
| AnOr 8, 50 | BIN 1, 141 | CT 22, 144 |
| AnOr 8, 56 | BIN 1, 142 | CT 22, 160 |
| BaghM 5, 14 | BIN 1, 169 | CT 22, 168 |
| BaghM 5, 15 | BIN 2, 108 | CT 22, 174 |
| BaghM 5, 29 | BIN 2, 116 | CT 22, 201 |
| BE 8/1, 2 | BIN 2, 132 | CT 22, 202 |
| BE 8/1, 42 | BIN 2, 134 | CT 22, 210 |
| BE 8/1, 123 | Camb 85 | CT 22, 227 |
| BE 8/1, 139 | Camb 315 | CT 22, 228 |
| BE 9, 24 | Camb 321 | CT 22, 229 |
| BE 9, 57 | Camb 412 | CT 22, 230 |
| BE 9, 69 | CM 20, 166 | CT 22, 231 |

268  Appendix A

CT 22, 234
CT 22, 235
CT 22, 236
CT 22, 240
CT 22, 247
CT 46, 45
CT 55, 91
CT 55, 110
CT 55, 191
Cyr 128
Cyr 146
Cyr 281
Cyr 307
Cyr 311
Cyr 312
Cyr 328
Cyr 329
Cyr 332
Dalley Edinburgh 69
Dar 53
Dar 128
Dar 358
Dar 375
Dar 468
Dar 551
Durand Textes
 babyloniens 6
Durand Textes
 babyloniens 58
Durand Textes
 babyloniens 60
EE 91
EE 109
Fs. Walker 356
Fs. Sjöberg 482–83
GCCI 1, 57
GCCI 1, 108
GCCI 1, 120
GCCI 1, 229
GCCI 1, 275
GCCI 1, 307
GCCI 1, 380
GCCI 1, 411

GCCI 2, 115
GCCI 2, 65
GCCI 2, 103
GCCI 2, 350
GCCI 2, 395
GCCI 2, 400
IMT 105
Iraq 13, 96
Iraq 41, 138
Iraq 54, 123-24
Iraq 59, 155
JCS 9, 26
JCS 28, 45
JCS 28, 198-99
NBDM 28
NBDM 49
Nbk 52
Nbk 104
Nbk 183
Nbk 359
Nbk 361
Nbk 363
Nbk 365
Nbk 366
Nbk 419
Nbn 13
Nbn 64
Nbn 314
Nbn 343
Nbn 495
Nbn 626
Nbn 665
Nbn 668
Nbn 679
Nbn 682
Nbn 720
Nbn 954
Nbn 1113
Nbn 1128
NCBT 518
NCBT 609
PBS 2/1, 17
PBS 2/1, 21

PBS 2/1, 85
PBS 2/1, 140
RA 1, 4
RA 12, 6-7
RA 14, 158
RA 41, 102
RA 67, 148-49
RawlCu 5, 5
ROM 2, 36
ROM 2, 38
Sack 79
Sack 80
Stolper 399-400
TCL 9, 48
TCL 9, 94
TCL 9, 100
TCL 9, 107
TCL 9, 137
TCL 12, 4
TCL 12, 14
TCL 12, 24
TCL 12, 43
TCL 12, 50
TCL 12, 60
TCL 12, 70
TCL 12, 77
TCL 12, 80
TCL 12, 86
TCL 12, 89
TCL 12, 96
TCL 12, 106
TCL 12, 115
TCL 12, 117
TCL 12, 119
TCL 12, 120
TCL 12, 122
TCL 13, 125
TCL 13, 131
TCL 13, 132
TCL 13, 134
TCL 13, 137
TCL 13, 138
TCL 13, 151

| | | |
|---|---|---|
| TCL 13, 154 | YOS 3, 182 | YOS 7, 3 |
| TCL 13, 160 | YOS 6, 28 | YOS 7, 7 |
| TCL 13, 170 | YOS 6, 57 | YOS 7, 10 |
| TCL 13, 179 | YOS 6, 60 | YOS 7, 15 |
| TCL 13, 181 | YOS 6, 71 | YOS 7, 24 |
| TCL 13, 212 | YOS 6, 72 | YOS 7, 25 |
| TCL 13, 215 | YOS 6, 77 | YOS 7, 26 |
| TCL 13, 219 | YOS 6, 105 | YOS 2, 28 |
| TCL 13, 222 | YOS 6, 108 | YOS 7, 31 |
| TMH 2/3, 203 | YOS 6, 113 | YOS 7, 42 |
| UCP 9/1 2 37 | YOS 6, 116 | YOS 7, 50 |
| UrET 4, 171 | YOS 6, 119 | YOS 7, 58 |
| UrET 4, 186 | YOS 6, 122 | YOS 7, 61 |
| UrET 4, 191 | YOS 6, 129 | YOS 7, 66 |
| UrET 4, 201 | YOS 6, 131 | YOS 7, 69 |
| VAS 4, 87 | YOS 6, 134 | YOS 7, 77 |
| VAS 4, 192 | YOS 6, 137 | YOS 7, 78 |
| VAS 4, 252 | YOS 6, 144 | YOS 7, 88 |
| VAS 6, 38 | YOS 6, 148 | YOS 7, 91 |
| VAS 6, 43 | YOS 6, 152 | YOS 7, 96 |
| VAS 6, 66 | YOS 6, 153 | YOS 7, 97 |
| VAS 6, 82 | YOS 6, 156 | YOS 7, 107 |
| VAS 6, 97 | YOS 6, 165 | YOS 7, 115 |
| VAS 6, 99 | YOS 6, 169 | YOS 7, 116 |
| VAS 6, 127 | YOS 6, 175 | YOS 7, 137 |
| VAS 6, 128 | YOS 6, 179 | YOS 7, 141 |
| VAS 6, 182 | YOS 6, 184 | YOS 7, 144 |
| VAS 6, 243 | YOS 6, 186 | YOS 7, 146 |
| VAS 6, 274 | YOS 6, 191 | YOS 7, 152 |
| YNER 1, 2 | YOS 6, 193 | YOS 7, 159 |
| YOS 3, 6 | YOS 6, 203 | YOS 7, 187 |
| YOS 3, 8 | YOS 6, 208 | YOS 7, 189 |
| YOS 3, 35 | YOS 6, 212 | YOS 7, 192 |
| YOS 3, 40 | YOS 6, 213 | YOS 7, 196 |
| YOS 3, 57 | YOS 6, 214 | YOS 7, 198 |
| YOS 3, 67 | YOS 6, 223 | YOS 17, 32 |
| YOS 3, 87 | YOS 6, 224 | YOS 17, 320 |
| YOS 3, 95 | YOS 6, 225 | YOS 19, 64 |
| YOS 3, 113 | YOS 6, 230 | YOS 19, 65 |
| YOS 3, 116 | YOS 6, 231 | YOS 19, 66 |
| YOS 3, 125 | YOS 6, 235 | YOS 19, 90 |
| YOS 3, 145 | YOS 6, 273 | YOS 19, 91 |
| YOS 3, 165 | YOS 6, 288 | YOS 19, 92 |

YOS 19, 93
YOS 19, 94
YOS 19, 95
YOS 19, 97

YOS 19, 98
YOS 19, 100
YOS 19, 101
YOS 19, 112

YOS 19, 263
*ZA* 2, 168
*ZA* 3, 224

# Abbreviations

| | |
|---|---|
| AAASH | *Acta Antiqua Academiae Scientiarum Hungaricae* |
| AASOR | Annual of the American Schools of Oriental Research |
| AB | Anchor Bible |
| ABAW | Abhandlungen der Bayerischen Akademie der Wissenschaften |
| AbB | *Altbabylonische Briefe in Umschrift und Übersetzung.* Edited by F. R. Kraus, Leiden, 1964– |
| ABD | *Anchor Bible Dictionary.* Edited by D. N. Freedman. 6 vols. New York, 1992 |
| ABL | *Assyrian and Babylonian Letters Belonging to the K(ouyunjik) Collection(s) of the British Museum.* Edited by R. F. Harper. 14 vols. Chicago, 1892–1914 |
| ADD | *Assyrian Deeds and Documents.* C. H. W. Johns. 4 vols. Cambridge, 1898–1924. |
| AfO | *Archiv für Orientforschung* |
| AfO Beihefte | Archiv für Orientforschung: Beihefte |
| AHw | *Akkadisches Handwörterbuch.* W. von Soden. 3 vols. Wiesbaden, 1965–1981 |
| AJBA | *Australian Journal of Biblical Archaeology* |
| AJSL | *American Journal of Semitic Languages and Literature* |
| Akkadica Supp | Akkadica Supplement |
| Alalakh | *The Alalakh Tablets.* D. J. Wiseman. British Institute of Archaeology in Ankara Occasional Publications 2. London, 1953 |
| ALUOSASup | Annual of Leeds University Oriental Society Annual Supplement |
| AnBib | Analecta biblica |
| ANET | *Ancient Near Eastern Texts Relating to the Old Testament.* Edited by J. B. Prichard. 3rd ed. Princeton, 1969. |
| ANETAS | Ancient Near Eastern Texts and Studies |
| AnOr | Analecta orientalia |
| AnSt | *Anatolian Studies* |
| Anton | *Antonianum* |
| AOAT | Alter Orient und Altes Testament |
| AoF | Altorientalische Forschungen |
| AOS | American Oriental Series |
| ArBib | The Aramaic Bible |
| ArOr | *Archiv Orientální* |

## 272  Abbreviations

| | |
|---|---|
| AS | Assyriological Studies |
| *ASTI* | *Annual of the Swedish Theological Institute* |
| *ATD* | *Das Alte Testament Deutsch* |
| *AUSS* | *Andrews University Seminary Studies* |
| *BA* | *Biblical Archaeologist* |
| *BaghM* | *Baghdader Mitteilungen* |
| *BAR* | *Biblical Archaeology Review* |
| BAR International Series | Biblical Archaeology Review International Series |
| *BASOR* | *Bulletin of the American Schools of Oriental Research* |
| *BBSt.* | L. W. King. *Babylonian Boundary Stones*. London, 1912 |
| BDB | Brown, F., S. R. Driver, and C. A. Briggs, *A Hebrew and English Lexicon of the Old Testament*. Oxford, 1907 |
| BE | The Babylonian Expedition of the University of Pennsylvania. Series A: Cuneiform Texts |
| BEATAJ | Beiträge zur Erforschung des Alten Testaments und des antiken Judentum |
| BETL | Bibliotheca ephemeridum theologicarum lovaniensium |
| *BHS* | *Biblia Hebraica Stuttgartensia*. Edited by K. Elliger and W. Rudolph. Stuttgart, 1983. |
| *Bib* | *Biblica* |
| *BibInt* | *Biblical Interpretation* |
| BibOr | Biblica et orientalia |
| *BIN* | *Babylonian Inscriptions in the Collection of J. B. Nies* |
| *BJRL* | *Bulletin of the John Rylands University Library of Manchester* |
| BJS | Brown Judaic Studies |
| BLD | *Black's Law Dictionary*. H. C. Black, J. R. Nolan, J. M. Nolan-Haley, M. J. Connolly, S. C. Hicks, and M. N. Alibrandi. 6th ed. St. Paul, 1990 |
| BM | Tablets in the collections of the British Museum |
| BMS | L. W. King. *Babylonian Magic and Sorcery*. New York, 1975 |
| *BN* | *Biblische Notizen* |
| BO | *Bibliotheca orientalis* |
| BRM | Babylonian Records in the Library of J. Pierpont Morgan |
| *BSac* | *Bibliotheca Sacra* |
| BT | The Bible Translator |
| BWA(N)T | Beiträge zur Wissenschaft vom Alten (und Neuen) Testament |
| *BWL* | *Babylonian Wisdom Literature*. W. G. Lambert. Oxford, 1960 |
| BzA | Beiträge zur Assyriologie |
| BZABR | Beihefte zur Zeitschrift für Altorientalische und Biblische Rechtsgeschichte |
| BZAW | Beihefte zur Zeitschrift für die alttestamentliche Wissenschaft |
| CAD | *The Assyrian Dictionary of the Oriental Institute of the University of Chicago*. Edited by I. J. Gelb, A. L. Oppenheim, E. Reiner, M. T. Roth, and R. D. Biggs. Chicago, 1956– |
| CahRB | Cahiers de la Revue biblique |
| *Camb* | *Inschriften von Cambyses, König von Babylon (529–521 v. Chr.)*. J. N. Strassmaier. Leipzig, 1890 |

| | |
|---|---|
| CANE | *Civilizations of the Ancient Near East*. Edited by J. Sasson. 4 vols. New York, 1995 |
| CAT | Commentaire de l'Ancien Testament |
| CBC | Cambridge Bible Commentary |
| CBQ | *Catholic Biblical Quarterly* |
| CH | Code of Hammurabi |
| CKLR | *Chicago-Kent Law Review* |
| CM | Cuneiform Monographs |
| ConBOT | Coniectanea biblica: Old Testament Series |
| Cowley | A. E. Cowley, *Aramaic Papyri of the Fifth Century B.C.* 1923. Innsbruck, 1967. |
| CRRA | Compte Rendu Rencontre Assyriologique |
| CT | *Cuneiform Texts from Babylonian Tablets in the British Museum* |
| CTMMA | *Cuneiform Texts in the Metropolitan Museum of Art* |
| Cyr | *Inschriften von Cyrus, König von Babylon (538–529 v. Chr.)*. J. N. Strassmaier. Leipzig, 1890 |
| Dalley Edinburgh | S. Dalley, ed. *A Catalogue of the Akkadian Cuneiform Tablets in the Collections of the Royal Scottish Museum, Edinburgh, with Copies of the Texts*. Royal Scottish Museum Art and Archaeology 2. Edinburgh, 1979. |
| Dar | *Inschriften von Darius, König von Babylon (521–485 v. Chr.)*. Edited by J. N. Strassmaier. Leipzig, 1897 |
| DN | divine name |
| Durand *Textes babyloniens* | *Textes babyloniens d'époque récente*. J.-M. Durand. Recherche sur les grandes civilisations 6. Paris, 1981 |
| EBib | Etudes bibliques |
| EDB | *Eerdmans Dictionary of the Bible*. Edited by D. N. Freedman et al. Grand Rapids, 2000 |
| EE | *Entrepreneurs and Empire: The Murašû Archive, The Murašû Firm, and Persian Rule in Babylonia*. M. W. Stolper. Uitgaven van het Nederlands Historisch-Archaeologisch Instituut te Istanbul. Leiden, 1985 |
| EncJud | *The Encyclopaedia Judaica*. Edited by C. Roth. 16 vols. Jerusalem, 1972 |
| EPE | *The Elephantine Papyri in English: Three Millennia of Cross-Cultural Continuity and Change*. B. Porten. Documenta et Monumenta Orientis Antiqui, Studies in Near Eastern Archaeology and Civilization 22. Leiden, 1996 |
| EPHE | *Documents Cunéiformes de la IV$^e$ Section de L'Ecole pratique des Hautes Etudes*. J.-M. Durand. Hautes Études Orientales 18. Geneva, 1982 |
| EvT | *Evangelische Theologie* |
| ExpTim | *Expository Times* |
| FCB | Feminist Companion to the Bible |
| FOTL | Forms of the Old Testament Literature |
| FRLANT | Forschungen zur Religion und Literatur des Alten und Neuen Testaments |

| | |
|---|---|
| Fs. Borger | *Festschrift für Rykle Borger zu seinem 65. Geburtstag am 24. Mai 1994.* Edited by S. M. Maul. Cuneiform Monographs 10. Groningen, 1998 |
| Fs. Oelsner | *Assyriologica et Semitica: Festschrift für Joachim Oelsner anläßlich seines 65. Geburtstages am 18. Februar 1997.* Edited by J. Marzahn and H. Neumann. Alter Orient und Altes Testament 252. Münster, 2000 |
| Fs. Sjöberg | *DUMU-E$_2$-DUB-BA-A: Studies in Honor of Åke W. Sjöberg.* Edited by H. Behrens, D. Loding, and M. T. Roth. Occasional Publications of the Samuel Noah Kramer Fund 11. Philadelphia, 1989 |
| Fs. Walker | C. Wunsch, ed. *Festschrift for Christopher Walker.* Dresden, 2002 |
| GBS | Guides to Biblical Scholarship |
| GCCI | Goucher College Cuneiform Inscriptions |
| GKC | *Gesenius' Hebrew Grammar.* Edited by E. Kautzsch. Translated by A. E. Cowley. 2nd ed. Oxford, 1910 |
| HALOT | *The Hebrew and Aramaic Lexicon of the Old Testament.* L. Koehler, W. Baumgartner, and J. J. Stamm. 4 vols. Leiden, 1994–1999. |
| HAR | *Hebrew Annual Review* |
| HAT | Handbuch zum Alten Testament |
| HBT | *Horizons in Biblical Theology* |
| HdO | Handbuch der Orientalistik |
| HL | Hittite Laws |
| HS | *Hebrew Studies* |
| HSCP | *Harvard Studies in Classical Philology* |
| HSM | Harvard Semitic Monographs |
| HSS | Harvard Semitic Studies |
| HTR | *Harvard Theological Review* |
| HUCA | *Hebrew Union College Annual* |
| HUCM | Monographs of the Hebrew Union College |
| IB | *The Interpreter's Bible.* Edited by G. A. Buttrick et al. 12 vols. New York, 1951–1957 |
| IBC | Interpretation: A Bible Commentary for Teaching and Preaching |
| ICC | International Critical Commentary |
| IDB | *The Interpreter's Dictionary of the Bible.* Edited by G. A. Butterick. 4 vols. Nashville, 1962 |
| IEJ | *Israel Exploration Journal* |
| IMT | *Istanbul Murašu Texts.* Edited by V. Donbaz and M. W. Stolper. Uitgaven van het Nederlands Historisch-Archaeologisch Instituut te Istanbul 79. Istanbul, 1997 |
| Int | *Interpretation* |
| IOS | *Israel Oriental Studies* |
| ITC | International Theological Commentary |
| JAAR | *Journal of the American Academy of Religion* |
| JANES | *Journal of the Ancient Near Eastern Society of Columbia University* |
| JAOS | *Journal of the American Oriental Society* |
| Jas | R. M. Jas. *Neo-Assyrian Judicial Procedures.* State Archives of Assyria Studies 5. Helsinki, 1996 |
| JB | Jerusalem Bible |

| | |
|---|---|
| JBL | *Journal of Biblical Literature* |
| JBQ | *Jewish Bible Quarterly* |
| JCS | *Journal of Cuneiform Studies* |
| JDT | Jahrbuch für deutsche Theologie |
| JEOL | *Jaarbericht van het Vooraziatisch-Egyptisch Gezelschap (Genootschap) Ex oriente lux* |
| JESHO | *Journal of the Economic and Social History of the Orient* |
| JJS | *Journal of Jewish Studies* |
| JNES | *Journal of Near Eastern Studies* |
| JNSL | *Journal of Northwest Semitic Languages* |
| JPS | Jewish Publication Society Bible |
| JQR | *Jewish Quarterly Review* |
| JRAS | Journal of the Royal Asiatic Society |
| JSOT | *Journal for the Study of the Old Testament* |
| JSOTSup | Journal for the Study of the Old Testament: Supplement Series |
| JSS | *Journal of Semitic Studies* |
| JTS | *Journal of Theological Studies* |
| K | tablets in the Kouyunjik collection of the British Museum |
| KAI | *Kanaanäische und aramäische Inschriften.* H. Donner and W. Röllig. 2nd ed. Wiesbaden, 1966–1969 |
| KAR | *Keilschrifttexte aus Assur religiösen Inhalts.* Edited by E. Ebeling. Leipzig, 1919–1923 |
| KAT | *Kommentar zum Alten Testament* |
| KD | *Kerygma und Dogma* |
| KJV | King James Version |
| Kraeling | E. G. Kraeling. *The Brooklyn Museum Aramaic Papyri: New Documents of the Fifth Century B.C. from the Jewish Colony at Elephantine.* New Haven, 1953 |
| LE | Laws of Eshnunna |
| LH | Laws of Hammurabi |
| Lindenberger | J. M. Lindenberger, *Ancient Aramaic and Hebrew Letters.* Society of Biblical Literature Writings from the Ancient World 4. Atlanta, 1994 |
| LKA | E. Ebeling. *Literarische Keilschrifttexte aus Assur.* Berlin, 1953 |
| LSS | *Leipziger semitische Studien* |
| LXX | Septuagint |
| MAL | Middle Assyrian Laws |
| MBPF | Münchener Beiträge zur Papyrusforschung und antiken Rechtsgeschichte |
| MDAIK | *Mitteilungen des Deutschen Archäologischen Instituts Abteilung Kairo* |
| MDOG | *Mitteilungen der Deutschen Orient-Gesellschaft* |
| MT | Masoretic Text |
| NAB | New American Bible |
| NABU | *Nouvelles assyriologiques breves et utilitaires* |
| NASB | New American Standard Bible |
| NBDM | *Neo-Babylonian Documents in the University of Michigan Collection.* E. W. Moore. Ann Arbor, 1939 |

| | |
|---|---|
| *Nbk* | *Inschriften von Nabuchodonosor, König von Babylon (604–561 v. Chr.)*. J. N. Strassmaier. Leipzig, 1889 |
| NBL | Neo-Babylonian Laws |
| *Nbn* | *Inschriften von Nabonidus, König von Babylon (555–538 v. Chr.)*. J. N. Strassmaier. Leipzig, 1889 |
| NCB | New Century Bible |
| NCBT | Signatur Newell Collection of Babylonian Tablets, New Haven |
| NCV | New Century Version |
| *NEA* | *Near Eastern Archaeology* |
| NEB | New English Bible |
| *Ner* | *Inscriptions of the Reigns of Evil-Merodach (B.C. 562–559), Neriglissar (B.C. 559-555) and Laborosoarchod (B.C. 555)*. B. T. A. Evetts. Babylonische Texte 6B. Leipzig, 1892 |
| *NIB* | *New Interpreter's Bible*. Edited by L. E. Keck. 12 vols. Nashville, 1994– |
| NICOT | New International Commentary on the Old Testament |
| *Nippur 4* | *Nippur IV: Early Neo-Babylonian Governor's Archive from Nippur*. S. W. Cole. Oriental Institute Publications 114. Chicago, 1996 |
| NIV | New International Version |
| NJB | New Jerusalem Bible |
| NJPS | New Jewish Publication Society Bible |
| NKJV | New King James Version |
| *NKOB* | *Neriglissar—King of Babylon*. R. H. Sack. Alter Orient und Altes Testament 236. Kevelaer and Neukirchen-Vluyn, 1994 |
| *NovT* | *Novum Testamentum* |
| NRSV | New Revised Standard Version |
| OBC | Orientalia Biblica et Christiana |
| OBO | Orbis biblicus et orientalis |
| OCuT | Oxford Editions of Cuneiform Texts |
| OIP | Oriental Institute Publications |
| *Or* | *Orientalia* |
| *OrAnt* | *Oriens antiquus* |
| *OrNS* | *Orientalia (NS)* |
| OTG | Old Testament Guides |
| OTL | Old Testament Library |
| OTS | Old Testament Studies |
| PBS | Publications of the Babylonian Section, University Museum, University of Pennsylvania |
| *PEGLMBS* | *Proceedings of the Eastern Great Lakes and Midwest Biblical Societies* |
| PN | personal name |
| *PRSt* | *Perspectives in Religious Studies* |
| *PSBA* | *Proceedings of the Society of Biblical Archaeology* |
| RA | Revue d'assyriologie et d'archéologie orientale |
| *RawlCu* | *The Cuneiform Inscriptions of Western Asia*. Edited by H. C. Rawlinson. London, 1891 |
| RB | *Revue biblique* |
| *ResQ* | *Restoration Quarterly* |

| | |
|---|---|
| *RevQ* | *Revue de Qumran* |
| *ROM* | *Royal Ontario Museum Cuneiform Texts* |
| RS | Ras Shamra |
| RSV | Revised Standard Version |
| SAA | State Archives of Assyria |
| *SAAB* | *State Archives of Assyria Bulletin* |
| SAAS | State Archives of Assyria Studies |
| Sack | R. H. Sack. *Cuneiform Documents from the Chaldean and Persian Periods*. London, 1993 |
| SANE | Source from the Ancient Near East |
| SAOC | Studies in Ancient Oriental Civilizations |
| SB | Sources bibliques |
| SBAW | Sitzungsberichte der bayerischen Akademie der Wissenschaften |
| SBLBSNA | Society of Biblical Literature Biblical Scholarship in North America |
| SBLDS | Society of Biblical Literature Dissertation Series |
| SBLMS | Society of Biblical Literature Monograph Series |
| SBLSBS | Society of Biblical Literature Sources for Biblical Study |
| SBLSP | Society of Biblical Literature Seminar Papers |
| SBLSymS | Society of Biblical Literature Symposium Series |
| SBLWAW | Society of Biblical Literature Writings from the Ancient World |
| SBS | Stuttgarter Bibelstudien |
| SBT | Studies in Biblical Theology |
| *SBTU* | *Spätbabylonische Texte aus Uruk* |
| ScrHier | Scripta hierosolymitana |
| *Sem* | *Semitica* |
| SJLA | Studies in Judaism in Late Antiquity |
| SOFS | Symbolae Ostoenses Fasciculi Suppletorii |
| SOTSMS | Society for Old Testament Studies Monograph Series |
| *Sound* | *Soundings* |
| Spar | I. Spar. "Three Neo-Babylonian Trial Depositions from Uruk," Pages 157-72 in *Studies in Honor of Tom B. Jones*. Alter Orient und Altes Testament 203. Kevelaer, 1979 |
| *SR* | *Studies in Religion* |
| SSS | Semitic Study Series |
| *Stolper* | M. W. Stolper "Management and Politics in Later Achaemenid Babylonia: New Texts from the Murašû Archive." Ph.D. diss., University of Michigan, 1974. |
| TAD | *Textbook of Aramaic Documents from Ancient Egypt*. Edited by B. Porten and A. Yardeni. 2 vols. Winona Lake, 1989 |
| *TAPA* | *Transactions of the American Philological Society* |
| TB | Theologische Bücherei: Neudrucke und Berichte aus dem 20. Jahrhundert |
| TCL | Textes cunéiformes. Musée du Louvre |
| TDNT | *Theological Dictionary of the New Testament*. Edited by G. Kittel and G. Friedrich. Translated by G. W. Bromiley. 10 vols. Grand Rapids, 1964–1976 |

| | |
|---|---|
| TDOT | *Theological Dictionary of the Old Testament*. Edited by G. J. Botterweck and H. Ringgren. Translated by J. T. Willis, G. W. Bromiley, and D. E. Green. 8 vols. Grand Rapids, 1974– |
| ThArb | Theologische Arbeiten |
| ThWAT | *Theologisches Wörterbuch zum Alten Testament*. Edited by G. J. Botterweck and H. Ringgren. Stuttgart, 1970– |
| TLZ | *Theologische Literaturzeitung* |
| TMH | Texte und Materialien der Frau Professor Hilprecht Collection of Babylonian Antiquities im Eigentum der Universität Jena |
| TOTC | Tyndale Old Testament Commentaries |
| TRE | *Theologische Realenzyklopädie*. Edited by G. Krause and G. Müller. Berlin, 1977– |
| TWOT | *Theological Wordbook of the Old Testament*. Edited by R. L. Harris and G. L. Archer, Jr. 2 vols. Chicago, 1980 |
| TynBul | *Tyndale Bulletin* |
| TZ | *Theologische Zeitschrift* |
| UCP | University of California Publications |
| UrET | Ur Excavations: Texts |
| VAB | Vorderasiatische Bibliothek |
| VAS | Vorderasiatische Schriftdenkmäler der Königlichen Museum, Berlin |
| VAT | Vorderasiatische Abteilung Tontafel. Vorderasiatisches Museum, Berlin |
| VDI | Vestnik drevnej istorii |
| VE | *Vox evangelica* |
| VT | *Vetus Testamentum* |
| VTSup | Supplements to Vetus Testamentum |
| WBC | Word Biblical Commentary |
| WMANT | Wissenschaftliche Monographien zum Alten und Neuen Testament |
| WTJ | *Westminster Theological Journal* |
| WVDOG | Wissenschaftliche Veröffentlichungen der deutschen Orientgesellschaft |
| WZKM | *Wiener Zeitschrift für die Kunde des Morgenlands* |
| YNER | Yale Near Eastern Researches |
| YOS | Yale Oriental Series, Texts |
| YOSR | Yale Oriental Series, Researches |
| ZA | *Zeitschrift für Assyriologie* |
| ZABR | *Zeitschrift für altorientalische und biblische Rechtsgeschichte* |
| ZAW | *Zeitschrift für die alttestamentliche Wissenschaft* |
| ZKT | *Zeitschrift für katholische Theologie* |
| ZSS | *Zeitschrift der Savigny-Stiftung für Rechtsgeschichte* |

# Bibliography

Abusch, I. Tzvi. *Babylonian Witchcraft Literature: Case Studies*. Brown Judaic Studies 132. Atlanta: Scholars Press, 1987.
———. "'He Should Continue to Bear the Penalty of That Case': An Interpretation of Codex Hammurabi Paragraphs 3–4 and 13." Pages 77–96 in *From Ancient Israel to Modern Judaism: Essays in Honor of Marvin Fox*. Edited by J. Neusner, E. S. Frerichs, and N. M. Sarna. Brown Judaic Studies 159. Atlanta: Scholars Press, 1989.
———. "Mesopotamian Anti-Witchcraft Literature: Texts and Studies, Part I: The Nature of *Maqlu*: Its Character, Divisions, and Calendrical Setting." *Journal of Near Eastern Studies* 33 (1974): 251–62.
———. "Studies in the History of Interpretation of Some Akkadian Incantations and Prayers." Ph.D. diss., Harvard University, 1972.
———. "Witchcraft and the Anger of the Personal God," Pages 83–121 in *Mesopotamian Magic: Textual, Historical, and Interpretive Perspectives*. Edited by T. Abusch and K. van der Toorn. Groningen: Styx, 1999.
Abusch, I. Tzvi, J. Huehnergard, and P. Steinkeller, eds. *Lingering over Words: Studies in Ancient Near Eastern Literature in Honor of William L. Moran*. Harvard Semitic Studies 37. Atlanta: Scholars Press, 1990.
Abusch, I. Tzvi, and K. van der Toorn, eds. *Mesopotamian Magic: Textual, Historical, and Interpretive Perspectives*. Groningen: Styx, 1999.
Ackerman, J. "An Exegetical Study of Psalm 82." Th.D. diss., Harvard University, 1966.
Ackroyd, P. R. *Exile and Restoration: A Study of Hebrew Thought of the 6th Century B.C.* Old Testament Library. Philadelphia: Westminster, 1968.
———. "The Written Evidence for Palestine." Pages 207–20 in *Centre and Periphery: Proceedings of the Groningen 1986 Achaemenid History Workshop*. Edited by H. Sancisi-Weerdenburg and A. Kuhrt. Achaemenid History 4. Leiden: Nederlands Insituut voor het Nabije Oosten, 1990.
Ahlström, G. W. *The History of Ancient Palestine from the Palaeolithic Period to Alexander's Conquest*. Edited by D. Edelman, with a contribution by G. O. Rollefson. Journal for the Study of the Old Testament: Supplement Series 146. Sheffield: Sheffield Academic, 1993.
Albertson, R. G. "Job and Ancient Near Eastern Wisdom Literature." Pages 215–30 in *Scripture in Context II: More Essays on the Comparative Method*. Edited by W. W. Hallo, J. C. Moyer, and L. G. Perdue. Winona Lake, Ind.: Eisenbrauns, 1983.
Allam, S. *Hieratische Ostraka und Papyri aus der Ramessidenzeit*. Urkunden zum Rechtsleben im alten Ägypten 1. Tübingen: Mohr, 1973.
Alonso Schökel, L. "Toward a Dramatic Reading of Job," *Semeia* 7 (1977): 45–61.

Alonso Schökel, L, and J. L. Ojeda. *Job*. Los Libros Sagrados 16. Madrid: Ediciones Cristiandad, 1971.

Alter, R. *The Art of Biblical Narrative*. New York: Basic Books, 1981.

———. *The Art of Biblical Poetry*. New York: Basic Books, 1985.

American Law Institute. *Model Penal Code*. Philadelphia: American Law Institute, 1961.

Andersen, F. I. *Job: An Introduction and Commentary*. Tyndale Old Testament Commentaries. Downers Grove, Ill.: InterVarsity, 1976.

Anderson, B. W. *Understanding the Old Testament*. 4th ed. Englewood Cliffs, N. J.: Prentice Hall, 1986.

Anderson, B. W., and W. Harrelson, eds. *Israel's Prophetic Heritage: Essays in Honor of James Muilenburg*. New York: Harper & Brothers, 1962.

Anderson, G. A. "Sacrifice and Sacrificial Offerings (OT)." Pages 870–86 in vol. 5 of *The Anchor Bible Dictionary*. Edited by D. N. Freedman. 6 vols. New York: Doubleday, 1992.

———. *Sacrifices and Offerings in Ancient Israel: Studies in their Social and Political Importance*. Harvard Semitic Monographs 41. Atlanta: Scholars Press, 1987.

Anderson, G. W., P. A. H. de Boer, G. R. Castellino, H. Cazelles, E. Hammershaimb, H. G. May, and W. Zimmerli, eds. *Congress Volume: Rome, 1968*. Vetus Testamentum Supplements 17. Leiden: Brill, 1969.

Ap-Thomas, D. R. "Notes on Some Terms Relating to Prayer." *Vetus Testamentum* 6 (1956): 230–31.

Armstrong, J. A. "The Archaeology of Nippur from the Decline of the Kassite Kingdom until the Rise of the Neo-Babylonian Empire." Ph.D. diss., University of Chicago, 1989.

Arnaud, D. "Un Document Juridique Concernant les Oblats." *Revue d'assyriologie et d'archéologie orientale* 67 (1973): 147–56.

Augapfel, J. *Babylonische Rechtsurkunden aus der Regierungszeit Artaxerxes I und Darius II*. Denkschriften der kaiserliche Akademie der Wissenschaften in Wien philosophisch-historische Klasse 59. Vol. 3. Vienna: Alfred Hölder, 1917.

Avalos, H. *Illness and Health Care in the Ancient Near East: The Role of the Temple in Greece, Mesopotamia, and Israel*. Harvard Semitic Monographs 54; Atlanta: Scholars Press, 1995.

———. Review of B. M. Levinson *Theory and Method in Biblical and Cuneiform Law: Revision, Interpolation, and Development*. *Hebrew Studies* 37 (1996): 156.

Aytoun, R. A. "A Critical Study of Job's 'Oath of Clearance.'" *Interpreter* 16 (1919–20): 291–98.

Azzoni, A. "The Private Life of Women in Persian Egypt." Ph.D. diss., The Johns Hopkins University, 2000.

Bakon, S. "God and Man on Trial," *Jewish Bible Quarterly* 21 (1993): 226–35.

Ball, M. A. *The Word and the Law*. Chicago: University of Chicago Press, 1993.

Barstad, H. M. "History and the Hebrew Bible." Pages 37–64 in *Can a "History of Israel" Be Written?* Edited by L. L. Grabbe. European Seminar in Historical Methodology 1. Journal for the Study of the Old Testament: Supplement Series 245. Sheffield: Sheffield Academic, 1997.

———. *The Myth of the Empty Land: A Study in the History and Archaeology of Judah*

*during the "Exilic" Period.* Symbolae Osloenses Fasciculi Suppletorii 28. Oslo: Scandinavia University Press, 1996.
Barr, J. "The Book of Job and Its Modern Interpreters." *Bulletin of the John Rylands University Library of Manchester* 54 (1971–72): 28–46.
Barth, J. *Nominalbildung in den semitischen Sprachen.* 2nd ed. Leipzig: Hinrichs, 1894.
Barton, J. *Reading the Old Testament: Method in Biblical Study.* 2nd ed. London: Darton, Longman & Todd, 1996.
Barton, J. H., J. L. Gibbs, V. H. Li, and J. H. Merryman. *Law in Radically Different Cultures.* American Casebook Series. St. Paul: West Publishing, 1983.
Baumgärtel, F. *Der Hiobdialog: Aufriss und Deutung.* Beiträge zur Wissenschaft vom Alten (und Neuen) Testament 61. Stuttgart: Kohlhammer, 1933.
Beach, E. F. "More Righteous than God? A Legal Formula (*zedek min*) and Theological Conundrum in Job." Paper presented the annual meeting of the Chicago Society for Biblical Research, Chicago, Ill., April 19, 1997.
Beaulieu, P.-A. "The Descendants of Sîn-lēqi-unninni." Pages 1–16 in *Assyriologica et Semitica: Festschrift für Joachim Oelsner anläßlich seines 65. Geburtstages am 18. Februar 1997.* Edited by J. Marzahn and H. Neumann. Alter Orient und Altes Testament 252. Münster: Ugarit, 2000.
———. *Late Babylonian Texts in the Nies Babylonian Collection.* Catalogue of the Babylonian Collections at Yale 1. Bethesda, Md.: CDL, 1994.
———. *Legal and Administrative Texts from the Reign of Nabonidus.* Yale Oriental Series, Texts 19. New Haven: Yale University Press, 2000.
———. "New Light on Secret Knowledge in Late Babylonian Culture." *Zeitschrift für Assyriologie* 82 (1992): 98–111.
———. "A Note on the River Ordeal in the Literary Text 'Nebuchadnezzar King of Justice.'" *Nouvelles assyriologiques breves et utilitaires* (1992–93): 58–60.
———. *The Reign of Nabonidus, King of Babylon—556–539 B.C.* Yale Near Eastern Researches 10. New Haven: Yale University Press, 1989.
Bechtel, L. M. "A Feminist Approach to the Book of Job." Pages 222–51 in *A Feminist Companion to Wisdom Literature.* Edited by A. Brenner. Feminist Companion to the Bible 9. Sheffield: Sheffield Academic, 1995.
Beck, A. B., A. H. Bartelt, P. R. Raabe, and C. A. Franke, eds. *Fortunate the Eyes that See: Essays in Honor of David Noel Freedman in Celebration of His Seventieth Birthday.* Grand Rapids: Eerdmans, 1995.
Becking, B., and M. C. A. Korpel, eds. *The Crisis of Israelite Religion: Transformation of Religious Tradition in Exilic and Post-Exilic Times.* Old Testament Studies 42. Leiden: Brill, 1999.
Behrens, H., D. Loding, and M. T. Roth, eds. *DUMU-E$_2$-DUB-BA-A: Studies in Honor of Åke W. Sjöberg.* Occasional Publications of the Samuel Noah Kramer Fund 11. Philadelphia: University Museum, 1989.
Bellinger, W. H., Jr. "Psalms of the Falsely Accused: A Reassessment." *Society of Biblical Literature Seminar Papers* 25 (1986): 463–69.
Bentzen, A. *Introduction to the Old Testament.* 2 vols. 2nd ed. Copenhagen: Gad, 1952.
Bergren, R. V. *Prophets and the Law.* Monographs of the Hebrew Union College 4. Cincinnati: Hebrew Union College Press, 1974.
Berlin, A. *Poetics and Interpretation of Biblical Narrative.* Winona Lake, Ind.: Eisenbrauns, 1994.

———. "A Search for a New Biblical Hermeneutics: Preliminary Observations." Pages 195–207 in *The Study of the Ancient Near East in the Twenty-First Century: The William Foxwell Albright Centennial Conference*. Edited by J. S. Cooper and G. M. Schwartz. Winona Lake, Ind.: Eisenbrauns, 1996.

Berquist, J. L. *Judaism in Persia's Shadow: A Social and Historical Approach*. Minneapolis: Fortress, 1995.

Beuken, W. A. M., ed. *The Book of Job*. Bibliotheca ephemeridum theologicarum lovaniensium 104. Leuven: Leuven University Press, 1994.

Birch, B. *Let Justice Roll Down: The Old Testament, Ethics, and Christian Life*. Louisville: Westminster John Knox, 1991.

Birkeland, H. *Die Feinde des Individuums in der israelitischen Psalmenliteratur*. Oslo: Grøndahl & Sons, 1933.

Black, H. C., J. R. Nolan, J. M. Nolan-Haley, M. J. Connolly, S. C. Hicks, and M. N. Alibrandi. *Black's Law Dictionary*. 6th ed. St. Paul: West, 1990.

Blank, S. H. "The Confessions of Jeremiah and the Meaning of Prayer." *Hebrew Union College Annual* 21 (1948): 331–54.

———. "The Curse, the Blasphemy, the Spell, the Oath." *Hebrew Union College Annual* 23 (1950–1951): 73–95.

Blenkinsopp, J. *Ezra-Nehemiah*. Old Testament Library. Philadelphia: Westminster, 1988.

———. "The Mission of Udjahorresnet and Those of Ezra and Nehemiah." *Journal of Biblical Literature* 106 (1987): 409–21.

———. "Was the Pentateuch the Civic and Religious Constitution of the Jewish Ethnos in the Persian Period?" Pages 41–62 in *Persia and Torah: The Theory of Imperial Authorization of the Pentateuch*. Edited by J. W. Watts. Society of Biblical Literature Symposium Series 17. Atlanta: Society of Biblical Literature, 2001.

———. *Wisdom and Law in the Old Testament: The Ordering of Life in Israel and Early Judaism*. Oxford Bible Series. Oxford: Oxford University Press, 1983.

Bloch, M. *The Historian's Craft*. With an Introduction by J. R. Strayer. Translated by P. Putnam. New York: Vintage Books, 1953.

———. "Two Strategies of Comparison." Pages 39–41 in *Comparative Perspectives: Theories and Methods*. Edited by A. Etzioni and F. L. Dubow. Boston: Little, Brown, 1970.

Blois, K. F. de. "How to Deal with Satan?" *The Bible Translator* 37 (1986): 301–9.

Bloom, J. "Ancient Near Eastern Temple Assemblies." Ph.D. diss., Annenberg Research Institute, 1992.

Blum, E. *Die Komposition der Vätergeschichte*. Wissenschaftliche Monographien zum Alten und Neuen Testament 57. Neukirchen-Vluyn: Neukirchener Verlag, 1984.

Bobbio, N. "Law and Force." *Monist* 49 (1965): 321–41.

Bock, D. L. *Blasphemy and Exultation in Judaism: The Charge against Jesus in Mark 14:53–65*. Grand Rapids: Baker, 1998.

Boecker, H. J. "Erwägungen zum Amt des Mazkir." *Theologische Zeitschrift* 17 (1961): 212–16.

———. *Law and the Administration of Justice in the Old Testament and Ancient East*. Translated by J. Moiser. Minneapolis: Augsburg, 1980.

———. *Redeformen des Rechtsleben im Alten Testament*. Wissenschaftliche Monographien zum Alten und Neuen Testament 14. Neukirchen-Vluyn: Neukirchener Verlag, 1963.

Bolla, S. von. *Untersuchungen zur Tiermiete und Viehpacht im altertum*. 2nd ed. Münchener Beiträge zur Papyrusforschung und antiken Rechtsgeschichte 30. Munich: Beck, 1969.

Bongenaar, A. C. V. M. *The Neo-Babylonian Ebabbar Temple at Sippar: Its Administration and its Prosopography*. Uitgaven van Het Nederlands Historisch-Archaeologisch Instituut te Istanbul 80. Istanbul: Nederlands Historisch-Archaeologisch Instituut te Istanbul, 1997.

Boorer, S. "A Matter of Life and Death: A Comparison of Proverbs 1–9 and Job." Pages 187–204 in *Prophets and Paradigms: Essays in Honor of Gene M. Tucker*. Edited by S. B. Reid. Journal for the Study of the Old Testament: Supplement Series 229. Sheffield: Sheffield Academic, 1996.

Bordreuil, P., F. Israel, and D. Pardee. "Deux ostraca Paléo-Hébreux de la collection Sh. Moussaïeff." *Semitica* 46 (1996): 48–76.

———. "King's Command and Widow's Plea: Two New Ostraca of the Biblical Period." *Near Eastern Archaeology* 61 (1998): 2–13.

Borger, R. *Handbuch der Keilschriftliteratur*. 3 vols. Berlin: de Gruyter, 1967–75.

———. *Assyrisch-babylonische Zeichenliste*. 2nd ed. Alter Orient und Altes Testament 33/33A. Neukirchen-Vluyn: Neukirchener Verlag, 1981.

Bottéro, J. "The 'Code' of Ḫammurabi." Pages 156–84 in *Mesopotamia: Writing, Reasoning, and the Gods*. Translated by Z. Bahrani and M. Van de Mieroop. Chicago: University of Chicago Press, 1992. Translation of "Le 'Code' de Hammurabi." *Annali della Scuola Normale Superiore di Pisa* 12 (1982): 409–44.

———. "Divination and the Scientific Spirit." Pages 125–37 in *Mesopotamia: Writing, Reasoning, and the Gods*. Translated by Z. Bahrani and M. Van de Mieroop. Chicago: University of Chicago Press, 1992.

———. *Mesopotamia: Writing, Reasoning, and the Gods*. Translated by Z. Bahrani and M. Van de Mieroop. Chicago: University of Chicago Press, 1992.

———. "L'ordalie en Mésopotamie ancienne." *Annali della Scuola Normale Superiore di Pisa* 11 (1981): 1005–67.

Botterweck, G. J., H. Ringgren, and H. J. Fabry, eds. *Theological Dictionary of the Old Testament*. Translated by J. T. Willis, G. W. Bromiley, and D. E. Green. Grand Rapids: Eerdmans, 1974– .

Bovati, P. *Re-Establishing Justice: Legal Terms, Concepts and Procedures in the Hebrew Bible*. Translated by M. J. Smith. Journal for the Study of the Old Testament: Supplement Series 105. Sheffield: Sheffield Academic, 1994.

Boyle, M. O'R. "The Covenant Lawsuit of the Prophet Amos: III 1–IV 13." *Vetus Testamentum* 21 (1971): 338–62.

Brenner, A. "God's Answer to Job." *Vetus Testamentum* 31 (1981): 129–37.

———. "Some Observations on the Figurations of Women in Wisdom Literature." Pages 50–66 in *A Feminist Companion to Wisdom Literature*. Edited by A. Brenner. Feminist Companion to the Bible 9. Sheffield: Sheffield Academic, 1995.

———, ed. *A Feminist Companion to Exodus to Deuteronomy*. Feminist Companion to the Bible 6. Sheffield: Sheffield Academic, 1995.

―――, ed. *A Feminist Companion to the Latter Prophets*. Feminist Companion to the Bible 8. Sheffield: Sheffield Academic, 1995.

―――, ed. *A Feminist Companion to Wisdom Literature*. Feminist Companion to the Bible 9. Sheffield: Sheffield Academic, 1995.

Brichto, H. C. *The Problem of "Curse" in the Hebrew Bible*. Journal of Biblical Literature Monograph Series 8. Philadelphia: Society of Biblical Literature and Exegesis, 1963.

Bright, J. *History of Israel*. 3rd ed. Old Testament Library. Philadelphia: Westminster, 1981.

Brinkman, J. A. "A Legal Text from the Reign of Erība-Marduk (c. 775 B.C.)." Pages 37–47 in *DUMU-E$_2$-DUB-BA-A: Studies in Honor of Åke W. Sjöberg*. Edited by H. Behrens, D. Loding, and M. T. Roth. Occasional Publications of the Samuel Noah Kramer Fund 11. Philadelphia: University Museum, 1989.

Brock-Utne, A. "Der Feind: Die alttestamentliche Satansgestalt im Lichte der sozialen Verhältnisse des nahen Orients." *Klio* 28 (1935): 219–37.

Brooks, P., and P. Gewirtz, eds. *Law's Stories: Narrative and Rhetoric in the Law*. New Haven: Yale University Press, 1996.

Brown, F., S. R. Driver, and C. A. Briggs, *A Hebrew and English Lexicon of the Old Testament*. 1907. Reprint, Lafayette, Ind.: Book Publisher's, 1981.

Bryce, G. E. "Omen-Wisdom in Ancient Israel," *Journal of Biblical Literature* 94 (1975): 19–37.

Budde, K. F. R., ed. *Vom Alten Testament*. Beihefte zur Zeitschrift für die alttestamentliche Wissenschaft 41. Giessen: Alfred Töpelmann, 1925.

Burns, J. B. "Cursing the Day of Birth." *Proceedings of the Eastern Great Lakes and Midwest Biblical Societies* 8 (1993): 11–29.

Buss, M. J. "The Distinction Between Civil and Criminal Law in Ancient Israel." Pages 51–62 in *Proceedings of the 6th World Congress of Jewish Studies*. Edited by A. Shinan. Vol. 1. Jerusalem: World Union of Jewish Studies, 1977.

―――. "Legal Science and Legislation." Pages 88–90 in *Theory and Method in Biblical and Cuneiform Law: Revision, Interpolation, and Development*. Edited by B. M. Levinson. Journal for the Study of the Old Testament: Supplement Series 181. Sheffield: Sheffield Academic, 1994.

Buttenwieser, M. *The Book of Job*. Chicago: University of Chicago Press, 1922.

Buttrick, G. A., ed. *The Interpreter's Dictionary of the Bible*. 4 vols. Nashville: Abingdon, 1962.

Buttrick, G. A., T. S. Kepler, H. G. May, J. Knox, S. Terrien, and E. S. Bucke. *The Interpreter's Bible*. 12 vols. New York: Abingdon, 1951–57.

Cagni, L. *The Poem of Erra*. Sources from the Ancient Near East 1. Malibu: Undena, 1977.

Camp, C. *Wisdom and the Feminine in the Book of Proverbs*. Sheffield: Almond, 1985.

Cantor, P. "Friedrich Nietzsche: The Use and Abuse of Metaphor." Pages 89–105 in *Metaphor: Problems and Perspectives*. Edited by D. S. Miall. Sussex: Harvester, 1982.

Caquot, A. "Israelite Perceptions of Wisdom and Strength in the Light of the Ras Shamra Texts." Pages 25–33 in *Israelite Wisdom: Theological and Literary Essays in Honor of Samuel Terrien*. Edited by J. C. Gammie et al. Missoula, Mont.: Scholars Press, 1978.

Carbasse, J.-M., and L. Depambour-Tarride, eds. *La Conscience du juge dans la tradition juridique européenne*. Paris: PUF, 1999.
Cardascia, G. *Les Archives des Murašû: Une famille d'hommes d'affaires Babyloniens à l'époque perse (455–403 av. J.-C.)*. Paris: Imprimerie Nationale, 1951.
———. "Le caractère volontaire ou involontaire des atteintes corporelles dans les droits cunéiformes." Pages 163–207 in vol. 4 of *Studi in Onore di Cesare Sanfilippo*. Edited by D. A. Giuffrè. 8 vols. Milan: Università di Catania Facoltà di Giurisprudenza, 1985.
———. "Droits cunéiformes et droit biblique." Pages 63–70 in vol. 1 of *Proceedings of the 6th World Congress of Jewish Studies*. Edited by A. Shinan. Jerusalem: World Union of Jewish Studies, 1977.
Carr, D. M. *Reading the Fractures of Genesis*. Louisville: Westminster, 1996.
Carradice, I., ed. *Coinage and Administration in the Athenian and Persian Empires: The Ninth Oxford Symposium on Coinage and Monetary History*. BAR International Series 343. Oxford: B.A.R., 1987.
Carson, D. A. "Mystery and Faith in Job 38:1–42:16." Pages 373–79 in *Sitting with Job: Selected Studies on the Book of Job*. Edited by R. B. Zuck. Grand Rapids: Baker, 1992. Reprinted from pages 171–78 of *How Long, O Lord? Reflections on Suffering and Evil*. Grand Rapids: Baker, 1990.
Cathcart, K. J. "Micah 5, 4–5 and Semitic Incantations." *Biblica* 59 (1978): 38–48.
Chapman, S. *Story and Discourse*. Ithaca, N.Y.: Cornell University Press, 1978.
Charpin, D. "Lettres et procès paléo-babyloniens." Pages 67–111 in *Rendre la justice en Mésopotamie: Archives judiciaires du Proche-Orient ancien (III$^e$–I$^{er}$ millénaires avant J.-C.)*. Edited by F. Joannès. Saint-Denis: Presses Universitaires de Vincennes, 2000.
Charpin, D., and F. Joannès. *Marchands, diplomates et empereurs: Études sur la civilisation mésopotamienne offertes à Paul Garelli*. Paris: Éditions Recherche sur les Civilisations, 1991.
Chazan, R., W. W. Hallo, and L. H. Schiffman, eds. *Ki Baruch Hu: Ancient Near Eastern, Biblical, and Judaic Studies in Honor of Baruch A. Levine*. Winona Lake, Ind.: Eisenbrauns, 1999.
Cheney, M. *Dust, Wind, and Agony: Character, Speech and Genre in Job*. Coniectanea biblica: Old Testament Series 36. Stockholm: Almqvist & Wiksell, 1994.
Cheyne, T. K. *Job and Solomon*. New York: Thomas Wittaker, 1893.
Chin, C. "Job and the Injustice of God: Implicit Arguments in Job 13.17–14.2." *Journal for the Study of the Old Testament* 64 (1994): 91–101.
Chisholm, R. B., Jr. "Does God Deceive?" *Bibliotheca Sacra* 155 (1998): 11–28.
Chung, T. W. (D.) "The Development of the Concept of Satan in Old Testament and Intertestamental Literature." Ph.D. diss., Southwestern Baptist Theological Seminary, 2000.
Civil, M. Appendix to Erica Reiner, "The Babylonian Fürstenspiegel in Practice." Pages 324–26 in *Societies and Languages of the Ancient Near East: Studies in Honour of I. M. Diakonoff*. Edited by M. A. Dandamayev et al. Warminster: Aris & Phillips, 1982.
Claassen, W. *Texts and Context: Old Testament and Semitic Studies for F. C. Fensham*. Journal for the Study of the Old Testament: Supplement Series 48. Sheffield: Sheffield Academic, 1988.

Clay, A. T. *Babylonian Business Transaction of the First Millennium B.C.* Babylonian Records in the Library of J. Pierpont Morgan 1. New York: privately printed, 1912.

———. *Business Documents of Murashû Sons of Nippur Dated in the Reign of Darius II*. Publications of the Babylonian Section 2/1. Philadelphia: University of Pennsylvania, 1912.

———. *Business Documents of Murashû Sons of Nippur Dated in the Reign of Darius II (424–404 B.C.)*. The Babylonian Expedition of the University of Pennsylvania. Series A: Cuneiform Texts 10. Philadelphia: University of Pennsylvania, 1904.

———. *Legal and Commercial Transactions Dated in the Assyrian, Neo-Babylonian, and Persian Periods, Chiefly from Nippur*. The Babylonian Expedition of the University of Pennsylvania. Series A: Cuneiform Texts 8/1. Philadelphia: University of Pennsylvania, 1908.

———. *Neo-Babylonian Letters from Erech*. Yale Oriental Series, Texts 3. New Haven: Yale University Press, 1919.

Clements, R. E. "Achan's Sin: Warfare and Holiness." Pages 113–26 in *Shall Not the Judge of All the Earth Do What Is Right? Studies on the Nature of God in Tribute to James L. Crenshaw*. Edited by D. Penchansky and P. L. Redditt. Winona Lake, Ind.: Eisenbrauns, 2000.

Clercq, Louis de, and J. Ménant. *Collection de Clercq, catalogue méthodique et raisonné, antiquités assyriennes, cylindres orientaux, cachets, briques, bronzes, bas-reliefs etc.* Part II: *Cachets, Briques, Bronzes, Bas-reliefs*. Paris: Leroux, 1903 (1888–1990).

Clines, D. J. A. "Deconstructing the Book of Job." Pages 65–80 in *The Bible as Rhetoric: Studies in Biblical Persuasion and Credibility*. Edited by M. Warner. London: Routledge, 1990.

———. *Ezra, Nehemiah, Esther*. New Century Bible. Grand Rapids: Eerdmans, 1984.

———. "False Naiveté in the Prologue to Job." *Hebrew Annual Review* 9 (1985): 127–36.

———. *Job 1–20*. Word Biblical Commentary 17. Dallas: Word, 1989.

Cocquerillat, D. *Palmeraies et Cultures de l'Eanna d'Uruk*. Ausgrabungen der Deutschen Forschungsgemeinschaft in Uruk-Warka 8. Berlin: Gebr. Mann, 1968.

Cogan, M., B. L. Eichler, and J. H. Tigay, eds. *Tehillah le-Moshe: Biblical and Judaic Studies in Honor of Moshe Greenberg*. Winona Lake, Ind.: Eisenbrauns, 1997.

Cohen, H. R. *Biblical Hapax Legomenon in the Light of Akkadian and Ugaritic*. Society of Biblical Literature Dissertation Series 37. Missoula, Mont.: Scholars Press, 1978.

Cole, S. W. *Nippur IV: Early Neo-Babylonian Governor's Archive from Nippur*. Oriental Institute Publications 114. Chicago: University of Chicago Press, 1996.

Coleson, J., and V. H. Matthews, eds. *Go to the Land I Will Show You: Studies in Honor of Dwight W. Young*. Winona Lake, Ind.: Eisenbrauns, 1996.

Collins T. J. "Natural Illness in Babylonian Medical Incantations." 2 vols. Ph.D. diss., University of Chicago, 1999.

Conklin, B. "The Means of Marking Oath Content in Hebrew and Akkadian." Paper presented at the annual meeting of the Society of Biblical Literature, San Antonio, Texas, November 23, 2004.

Contenau, G. *Contrats et letters d'Assyrie et de Babylonie*. Textes cunéiformes. Musée du Louvre 9. Paris: Geuthner, 1926.
———. *Contrats néo-babyloniens I: Téglath-phalasar III á Nabonide*. Textes cunéiformes. Musée du Louvre 12. Paris: Geuthner, 1927.
———. *Contrats néo-babyloniens II: Achémén et Séleucides*. Textes cunéiformes. Musée du Louvre 13. Paris: Geuthner, 1929.
Cook, J. M. *The Persian Empire*. London: Dent, 1983.
Cooper, A. "Reading and Misreading the Prologue to Job." *Journal for the Study of the Old Testament* 46 (1990): 67–79.
Cooper, J. S. *Reconstructing History from Ancient Inscriptions: The Lagash-Umma Border Conflict*. Sources from the Ancient Near East 2. Malibu: Undena, 1983.
Cooper, J. S., and G. M. Schwartz, eds. *The Study of the Ancient Near East in the Twenty-First Century: The William Foxwell Albright Centennial Conference*. Winona Lake, Ind.: Eisenbrauns, 1996.
Cotter, D. W. *A Study of Job 4–5 in Light of Contemporary Literary Theory*. Society of Bibilical Literature Dissertation Series 124. Atlanta: Scholars Press, 1992.
Cover, R. "The Bonds of Constitutional Interpretation: Of the Word, the Deed, and the Role." *Georgia Law Review* 20 (1986): 815–33.
———. "The Folktales of Justice: Tales of Jurisdiction." Pages 173–201 in *Narrative, Violence, and the Law: Essays of Robert Cover*. Edited by M. Minow, M. Ryan, and A. Sarat. Ann Arbor: University of Michigan Press, 1992.
———. "The Supreme Court, 1982 Term—Forward: Nomos and Narrative." *Harvard Law Review* 97 (1983): 1–63.
———. "Violence and Word." *Yale Law Journal* 95 (1986): 1601–29.
Cowley, A. E. *Aramaic Papyri of the Fifth Century B.C.* Innsbruck: Zeller, 1967 (1923).
———. "The Aramaic Proverbs of Ahiqar." Pp. 427–30 in *Ancient Near Eastern Texts Relating to the Old Testament*. Edited by J. B. Prichard. 3rd ed. Princeton: Princeton University Press, 1969.
Cox, D. "The Book of Job as Bi-Polar Mašal: Structure and Interpretation." *Antonianum* 62 (1987): 12–25.
———. *The Triumph of Impotence*. Rome: Università Gregoriana, 1978.
Crenshaw, J. L. "Job, Book of." Pages 858–68 in vol. 3 of *The Anchor Bible Dictionary*. Edited by D. N. Freedman. 6 vols. New York: Doubleday, 1992.
———. "The Wisdom Literature." Pages 369–407 in *The Hebrew Bible and Its Modern Interpreters*. Edited by D. A. Knight and G. M. Tucker. Philadelphia: Fortress, 1985.
———, ed. *Studies in Ancient Israelite Wisdom*. New York: Ktav, 1976.
———, ed. *Theodicy in the Old Testament*. Philadelphia: Fortress, 1983.
Crenshaw, J. L., and J. T. Willis, eds. *Essays in Old Testament Ethics*. New York: Ktav, 1974.
Crook, M. D. *The Cruel God: Job's Search for the Meaning of Suffering*. Boston: Beacon, 1959.
Cross, F. M. *Canaanite Myth and Hebrew Epic: Essays in the History of the Religion of Israel*. Cambridge, Mass.: Harvard University Press, 1973.
———. "The Council of Yahweh in Second Isaiah." *Journal of Near Eastern Studies* 12 (1953): 274–77.
———. "Epigraphic Notes on Hebrew Documents of the Eighth–Sixth Centuries

B.C.; II, The Muraba'at Papyrus and the Letter Found Near Yabneh-Yam." *Bulletin of American Schools of Oriental Research* 165 (1962): 34–46.

———. *From Epic to Canon: History and Literature in Ancient Israel*. Baltimore: Johns Hopkins University Press, 1998.

———. "A Papyrus Recording a Divine Legal Decision and the Root $rḥq$ in Biblical and Near Eastern Legal Usage." Pages 311–20 in *Texts, Temples, and Traditions: A Tribute to Menahem Haran*. Edited by M. V. Fox, V. A. Hurowitz, A. Hurvitz, et al. Winona Lake, Ind.: Eisenbrauns, 1996.

Cryer, F. H. *Divination in Ancient Israel and Its Near Eastern Environment: A Socio-Historical Investigation*. Journal for the Study of the Old Testament: Supplement Series 142. Sheffield: JSOT Press, 1994.

Cunningham, G. *"Deliver Me from Evil": Mesopotamian Incantations 2500–1500 BC*. Studia Pohl Series Maior 17. Rome: Pontifical Biblical Institute, 1997.

Cuq, E. "Le droit de gage en Chaldée à l'époque Néo-Babylonienne." *Revue d'assyriologie et d'archéologie orientale* 12 (1915): 85–113.

———. "Essai sur l'organisation judiciaire de la Chaldée à l'époque de la première dynastie babylonienne." *Revue d'assyriologie et d'archéologie orientale* 7 (1910): 65–101.

Curtis, J. B. "On Job's Response to Yahweh." *Journal of Biblical Literature* 98 (1979): 497–511.

———. "On Job's Witness in Heaven." *Journal of Biblical Literature* 102 (1983): 549–62.

Dahood, M. "Congruity of Metaphors." Pages 40–49 in *Hebräische Wortforschung: Festschrift zum 80. Geburtstag von Walter Baumgartner*. Edited by B. Hartmann et al. Vetus Testamentum Supplements 16. Leiden: Brill, 1967.

———. "Northwest Semitic Philology and Job." Pages 55–74 in *The Bible in Current Catholic Thought*. Edited by J. L. McKenzie. New York: Herder & Herder, 1962.

Daiches, S. *The Jews in Babylonia in the Time of Ezra and Nehemiah according to Babylonian Inscriptions*. London: Publication of Jews' College of London, 1910.

Dalley, S. *A Catalogue of the Akkadian Cuneiform Tablets in the Collections of the Royal Scottish Museum, Edinburgh, with Copies of the Texts*. Royal Scottish Museum Art and Archaeology 2. Edinburgh: Royal Scottish Museum, 1979.

Dandamaev, M. A. "A Babylonian Document Concerning the Illegal Sale of a Temple Slave-Girl" (in Russian). *Palestinskiæi sbornik* 19 (1982): 1–6.

———. "The Condition of Slaves in Later Babylonia" (in Russian). *VDI* (1969): 3–17.

———. "Economy of Ṭābiya, a Babylonian in the Sixth Century B.C." *Oikumeme* 5 (1986): 51–53.

———. "Egyptian Settlers in Babylonia" (in Russian). *Palestinskiæi sbornik* 17 (1980): 41–46.

———. "The Neo-Babylonian Citizens." *Klio* 63 (1981): 45–49.

———. "The Neo-Babylonian Elders." Pages 38–41 in *Societies and Languages of the Ancient Near East: Studies in Honour of I. M. Diakonoff*. Edited by M. A. Dandamaev et al. Warminster: Aris & Phillips, 1982.

———. "The Neo-Babylonian Popular Assembly." Pages 63–71 in *Šulmu: Papers on the Ancient Near East Presented at International Conference of Socialist Coun-

*tries. Prague 30 September to 3 October, 1986.* Edited by P. Vabroušek and V. Souček. Prague: Univerzita Karlova, 1988.

———. "Politische und wirtschaftliche Geschichte." Pages 15–58 in *Beiträge zur Achämenidengeschichte.* Edited by G. Walser. Historia 18. Wiesbaden: Franz Steiner, 1972.

———. *Slavery in Babylonia: From Nabopolassar to Alexander the Great (626–331 B.C.).* 1974. Edited by M. A. Powell and D. B. Weisberg. Translated by V. A. Powell. DeKalb, Ill.: Northern Illinois University Press, 1984.

———. "Witness Testimonies of Slaves in the Courts in Babylonia in the 6th Century B.C." (in Russian). *VDI* (1968): 1–12.

Dandamaev, M. A., and V. G. Lukonin. *The Culture and Social Institutions of Ancient Iran.* 1980. Edited and translated by P. L. Kohl. Cambridge: Cambridge University Press, 1989.

Dandamaev, M. A., et al., eds. *Societies and Languages of the Ancient Near East: Studies in Honour of I. M. Diakonoff.* Warminster: Aris & Phillips, 1982.

Daniels, D. R. "Is There a 'Prophetic Lawsuit' Genre?" *Zeitschrift für die alttestamentliche Wissenschaft* 99 (1987): 339–60.

Dassow, E. von. "Introducing the Witnesses in the Neo-Babylonian Documents." Pages 3–22 in *Ki Baruch Hu: Ancient Near Eastern, Biblical, and Judaic Studies in Honor of Baruch A. Levine.* Edited by R. Chazan, W. W. Hallo, and L. H. Schiffman. Winona Lake, Ind.: Eisenbrauns, 1999.

Davidson, A. B. *The Book of Job.* Cambridge Bible for Schools and Colleges 15. Cambridge: Cambridge University Press, 1891.

Davies, P. R. "Whose History? Whose Israel? Whose Bible? Biblical Histories, Ancient and Modern." Pages 104–22 in *Can a "History of Israel" be Written?* Edited by L. L. Grabbe. European Seminar in Historical Methodology 1. Journal for the Study of the Old Testament: Supplement Series 245. Sheffield: Sheffield Academic, 1997.

———, ed. *Second Temple Studies I. Persian Period.* Journal for the Study of the Old Testament: Supplement Series 117. Sheffield: Sheffield Academic, 1991.

Day, P. L. *An Adversary in Heaven: śāṭān in the Hebrew Bible.* Harvard Semitic Monographs 43. Atlanta: Scholars Press, 1988.

———, ed. *Gender and Difference in Ancient Israel.* Minneapolis: Fortress, 1989.

Deist, F. E. Review of B. M. Levinson, *Theory and Method in Biblical and Cuneiform Law: Revision, Interpolation, and Development. Journal of Northwest Semitic Languages* 21 (1995): 128–31.

Dell, K. J. *The Book of Job as Skeptical Literature.* Beihefte zur Zeitschrift für die alttestamentliche Wissenschaft 197. Berlin: de Grutyer, 1991.

Deller, K. "Rolle des Richters im neuassyrischen Prozessrechts." Pages 639–53 in vol. 6 of *Studi in Onore di Edoardo Volterra.* 6 vols. Università di Roma Facoltà di giurisprudenza 45. Rome: A. Giuffrè, 1971.

Demuth, L. "Fünfzig Rechts- und Verwaltungsurkunden aus der Zeit des Königs Kyros (538–529 v. Chr.)." *Beiträge zur Assyriologie* 3 (1898): 393–444.

Denning-Bolle, S. *Wisdom in Akkadian Literature: Expression, Instruction, Dialogue.* Leiden: Ex Oriente Lux, 1992.

Derrida, J. "Force of Law: 'The Mystical Foundation of Authority.' " *Cardozo Law Review* 11 (1990): 920–1045.

———. "The Retrait of Metaphor." *Enclitic* 2 (Fall 1978): 5–33.
Dhorme, E. *A Commentary on the Book of Job*. Translated by H. Knight. London: Thomas Nelson & Sons, 1967.
Diakonoff, I. M. "A Babylonian Political Pamphlet from about 700 B.C." Pages 343–49 in *Studies in Honour of Benno Landsberger on His Seventy-Fifth Birthday*. Edited by H. G. Güterbock and T. Jacobsen. Assyriological Studies 16. Chicago: University of Chicago Press, 1965.
Dick, M. "Job 31: A Form-critical Study." Ph.D. diss., The Johns Hopkins University, 1977.
———. "Job 31, The Oath of Innocence, and the Sage." *Zeitschrift für die alttestamentliche Wissenschaft* 95 (1983): 31–53.
———. "The Legal Metaphor in Job 31." *Catholic Biblical Quarterly* 41 (1979): 37–50.
Dietrich, M. *Cuneiform Texts from Babylonian Tablets in the British Museum: Neo-Babylonian Letters from the Kuyunjik Collections*. Cuneiform Texts from the Babylonian Tablets in the British Museum 54. London: British Museum Publications, 1978.
Dijk, J. J. A. van. *La sagesse Suméro-Accadienne: Recherches sur les genres littéraires des textes sapientiaux*. Leiden: Brill, 1953.
Dillmann, A. *Hiob*. 3rd ed. Leipzig: Hirzel, 1891.
Dion, P.-E. "Formulaic Language in the Book of Job: International Background and Ironical Distortions." *Studies in Religion* 16 (1987): 187–93.
———. "Un nouvel éclairage sur le contexte culturel des malheurs de Job." *Vetus Testamentum* 34 (1984): 213–25.
Dobbs-Allsopp, F. W. "The Genre of the Meṣad Ḥashavyahu Ostracon." *Bulletin of the American Schools of Oriental Research* 295 (1994): 49–55.
Dombradi, E. *Die Darstellung des Rechtsaustrags in den Altbabylonischen Prozessurkunden*. 2 vols. Freiburger Altorientalische Studien 20. Stuttgart: Franz Steiner, 1996.
Donbaz, V., and M. W. Stolper. *Istanbul Murašu Texts*. Uitgaven van het Nederlands Historisch-Archaeologisch Instituut te Istanbul 79. Istanbul: Nederlands Historisch-Archaeologisch Instituut te Istanbul, 1997.
Donner, H., et al., eds. *Beiträge zur altestamentlichen Theologie*. Göttingen: Vandenhoeck & Ruprecht, 1977.
Doty, L. T. "Cuneiform Archives from Hellenistic Uruk." Ph.D. diss., Yale University, 1977.
Dougherty, R. P. *Archives from Erech: Neo-Babylonian and Persian Periods*. Goucher College Cuneiform Inscriptions 2. New Haven: Yale University Press, 1933.
———. *Archives from Erech: Time of Nebuchadrezzar and Nabonidus*. Goucher College Cuneiform Inscriptions 1. New Haven: Yale University Press, 1923.
———. "The Babylonian Principle of Suretyship as Administered by Temple Law." *American Journal of Semitic Languages and Literature* 46 (1930): 73–103.
———. *Nabonidus and Belshazzar: A Study in the Closing Events of the Neo-Babylonian Empire*. Yale Oriental Series, Researches 15. New Haven: Yale University Press, 1929.
———. *Records from Erech: Time of Nabonidus (555–538 B.C.)*. Yale Oriental Series, Texts 6. New Haven: Yale University Press, 1920.

———. *The Shirkûtu of Babylonian Deities*. Yale Oriental Series, Researches 5/2. New Haven: Yale University Press, 1923.
Driver, G. R. "On Job 5:5." *Theologische Zeitschrift* 12 (1956): 485–86.
———, eds. *The Babylonian Laws*. 2 vols. Oxford: Clarendon, 1956, 1960.
Driver, G. R., and J. C. Miles. "Ordeal by Oath at Nuzi." *Iraq* 7 (1940): 132–38.
Driver, S. R. *The Book of Job in the Revised Version*. Oxford: Clarendon, 1908.
———. "Problems in Job." *American Journal of Semitic Languages and Literature* 52 (1935–36): 160–69.
———. "Some Problems in the Hebrew Text of Job." Pages 72–93 in *Wisdom in Israel and in the Ancient Near East*. Edited by M. Noth and D. W. Thomas. Vetus Testamentus Supplements 3. Leiden: Brill, 1955.
Driver, S. R., and G. B. Gray. *A Critical and Exegetical Commentary on the Book of Job*. International Critical Commentary. Edinburgh: T&T Clark, 1921.
Droge, A. J. "*MORI LUCRUM*: Paul and Ancient Theories of Suicide." *Novum Testamentum* 30 (1988): 261–86.
Droge, A. J., and J. D. Tabor. *A Noble Death: Suicide and Martyrdom Among Greeks and Romans, Jews and Christians in the Ancient World*. San Francisco: HarperSanFrancisco, 1992.
Duhm, D. B. *Das Buch Hiob*. Kurner Hand-Commentar zum Alten Testament 16. Tübingen: Mohr, 1897.
Duhn, H. *Die bösen Geister im Alten Testament*. Tübingen: Mohr, 1904.
Duquoc, C., and C. Foristan, eds. *Job and the Silence of God*. New York: Seabury, 1983.
Durand, J.-M. *Documents Cunéiformes de la IV$^e$ Section de L'Ecole pratique des Hautes Etudes*. Vol 1. Hautes Études Orientales 18. Geneva: Librairie Droz, 1982.
———. *Textes babyloniens d'époque récente*. Recherche sur les grandes civilisations 6. Paris: Éditions A.D.P.F., 1981.
Dworkin, R. M. "How Is Law like Literature?" Pages 146–66 in *A Matter of Principle*. Cambridge, Mass.: Harvard University Press, 1985.
Ebeling, E. *Die Akkadische Gebetsserie "Handerhebung."* Deutsche Akademie der Wissenschaften zu Berlin Institut für Orientforschung 20. Berlin: Akademie-Verlag, 1953.
———. *Aus dem Leben der jüdischen Exulanten in Babylonien*. Jahresbericht des Humboldt-Gymnasiums Ostern 39. Berlin: Weidmann, 1914.
———. *Glossar zu den neubabylonischen Briefen*. Sitzungsberichte der bayerischen Akademie der Wissenschaften Philosophisch-historische Klasse 1953. Vol. 1. Munich: Bayerische Akademie der Wissenschaften, 1953.
———. *Keilschrifttexte aus Assur religiösen Inhalts*. Wissenschaftliche Veröffentlichungen der deutschen Orientgesellschaft 28. Leipzig: Hinrichs, 1919.
———. "Kriminalfälle aus Uruk." *Archiv für Orientforschung* 16 (1952–1953): 67–69.
———. *Literarische Keilschrifttexte aus Assur*. Berlin: Akademie-Verlag, 1953.
———. *Neubabylonische Briefe*. Abhandlungen der Bayerischen Akademie der Wissenschaften Philosophisch-Historische Klasse Neue Folge 30. Munich: Bayerischen Akademie der Wissenschaften, 1949.
———. *Neubabylonische Briefe aus Uruk*. 4 vols. Beiträge zur Keilschriftforschung und Religionsgeschichte des Vorderen Orients. Berlin: By the author, Gutshof-Str. 6, 1930–34.

Eichler, B. L. "Literary Structure in the Laws of Eshnunna." Pages 71–84 in *Language, Literature and History: Philological and Historical Studies Presented to Erica Reiner*. Edited by F. Rochberg-Halton. American Oriental Series 67. New Haven: American Oriental Society, 1987.

Eissfeldt, O. *The Old Testament: An Introduction*. Translated by P. R. Ackroyd. New York: Harper & Row, 1965.

Eliade, M., ed. *The Encyclopedia of Religion*. 16 vols. New York: Macmillan, 1987.

Embler, W. *Metaphor and Meaning*. Deland, Fl.: Everett/Edwards, 1966.

Eph'al, I. "The Western Minorities in Babylonia in the 6th–5th Centuries B.C.: Maintenance and Cohesion." *Orientalia* n.s. 47 (1978): 74–90.

Eph'al, I., and M. Cogan, eds. *A Highway from Egypt to Assyria: Studies in Ancient Near Eastern History and Historiography Presented to Hayim Tadmor*. Jerusalem: Magnes, 1990.

Eph'al, I., and J. Naveh. "Remarks on the Recently Published Moussaieff Ostraca." *Israel Exploration Journal* 48 (1998): 269–73.

Epsztein, L. *Social Justice in the Ancient Near East and the People of the Bible*. Translated by J. Bowen. London: SCM, 1986.

Eskenazi, T. C., and K. H. Richards, eds. *Second Temple Studies 2. Temple Community in the Persian Period*. Journal for the Study of the Old Testament: Supplement Series 175. Sheffield: Sheffield Academic, 1994.

Eslinger, L., and G. Taylor. *Ascribe to the Lord: Biblical and Other Studies in Memory of Peter C. Craigie*. Journal for the Study of the Old Testament: Supplement Series 67. Sheffield: Sheffield Academic, 1988.

Etzioni, A., and F. L. Dubow. *Comparative Perspectives: Theories and Methods*. Boston: Little, Brown, 1970.

Evans, C. D., W. W. Hallo, and J. B. White, eds. *Scripture in Context: Essays on the Comparative Method*. Pittsburgh: Pickwick, 1980.

Evans, L. "Early Mesopotamian Assemblies." *Journal of the American Oriental Society* 78 (1958): 1–11.

Evans, M. J. "'A Plague on Both Your Houses': Cursing and Blessing Reviewed." *Vox evangelica* 24 (1994): 79–89.

Evetts, B. T. A. *Inscriptions of the Reigns of Evil-Merodach (B.C. 562–559), Neriglissar (B.C. 559–555) and Laborosoarchod (B.C. 555)*. Babylonische Texte 6B. Leipzig: Eduard Pfeiffer, 1892.

Fales, F. M. "Un dieu comme 'jude' dans un texte néo-assyrien." *Revue d'assyriologie et d'archéologie orientale* 71 (1977): 177–79.

―――. "The Impact of Oracular Material on the Political Utterances and Political Action of the Sargonic Dynasty." Pages 99–114 in *Oracles et prophéties dans l'antiquité: Actes du Colloque de Strasbourg, 15–17 Juin 1995*. Edited by J.-G. Heintz. Paris: Boccard, 1997.

Falk, Z. W. "Forms of Testimony." *Vetus Testamentum* 11 (1961): 88–91.

―――. *Hebrew Law in Biblical Times*. Jerusalem: Wahrmann Books, 1964.

―――. "Hebrew Legal Terms I." *Journal of Semitic Studies* 5 (1960): 350–54.

―――. "Hebrew Legal Terms II." *Journal of Semitic Studies* 12 (1967): 241–44.

―――. "Hebrew Legal Terms III." *Journal of Semitic Studies* 14 (1969): 39–44.

―――. "Oral and Written Testimony." *Rivista internazionale di diritto romano e antico* 19 (1968): 113–19.

Falkenstein, A. *Die neusumerischen Gerichtsurkunden.* 3 vols. ABAW Philosophisch-Historische Klasse n.F. 39, 40, 44. Munich: Bayerische Akademie der Wissenschaften, 1956–1957.
Falkenstein, A., and W. Von Soden. *Sumerische und akkadische Hymnen und Gebete.* Zurich: Artemis, 1953.
Feigin, S. I. *Legal and Administrative Texts of the Reign of Šamšu-Iluna.* Yale Oriental Series, Texts 12. New Haven: Yale University Press, 1979.
Fensham, F. C. "Malediction and Benediction in Ancient Near Eastern Vassal-Treaties and the Old Testament." *Zeitschrift für die alttestamentliche Wissenschaft* 33 (1962): 1–9.
———. "Widow, Orphan, and the Poor in Ancient Near Eastern Legal and Wisdom Tradition." *Journal of Near Eastern Studies* 21 (1962): 129–39.
Ferguson, R. A. "Untold Stories in the Law." Pages 84–98 in *Law's Stories: Narrative and Rhetoric in the Law.* Edited by P. Brooks and P. Gewirtz. New Haven: Yale University Press, 1996.
Fichtner, J. "Hiob in der Verkündigung unserer Zeit." *Wort und Dienst* 2 (1950): 71–89.
Figulla, H. H. *Business Documents of the Neo-Babylonian Period.* Ur Excavations, Texts 4. London: Trustees of the British Museum and of the University of Pennsylvania, 1949.
———. "Lawsuit Concerning a Sacrilegious Theft at Erech." *Iraq* 13 (1951): 95–101.
———, ed. *Cuneiform Texts from Babylonian Tablets in the British Museum: Old-Babylonian Naditu Records.* Cuneiform Texts from the Babylonian Tablets in the British Museum 47. London: Trustees of the British Museum, 1967.
Fingarette, H. "The Meaning of Law in the Book of Job." *Hastings Law Journal* 29 (1978): 1581–1617. Reprinted at pages 249–86 in *Revisions: Changing Perspectives in Moral Philosophy.* Edited by S. Hauerwas and A. MacIntrye. Notre Dame: University of Notre Dame Press, 1983.
Finkel, I. L. "A Study in Scarlet: Incantations against Samana." Pages 71–106 in *Festschrift für Rykle Borger zu seinem 65. Geburtstag am 24. Mai 1994.* Edited by S. M. Maul. Cuneiform Monographs 10. Groningen: Styx, 1998.
Finkelstein, J. J. "Ammiṣaduqa's Edict and the Babylonian 'Law Codes.'" *Journal of Cuneiform Studies* 15 (1961): 91–104.
———. "Bible and Babel: A Comparative Study of the Hebrew and Babylonian Religious Spirit." *Commentary* 26 (1958): 431–44. Reprinted at pages 355–80 in *Essential Papers on Israel and the Ancient Near East.* Edited by F. E. Greenspahn. Essential Papers on Jewish Studies. New York: New York University Press, 1991.
———. "An Old Babylonian Herding Contract and Genesis 31:38f." Pages 30–36 in *Essays in Memory of E. A. Speiser.* Edited by W. W. Hallo. American Oriental Series 53. New Haven: American Oriental Society, 1968.
———. *The Ox that Gored.* Transactions of the American Philosophical Society 71.2. Philadelphia: American Philosophical Society, 1981.
———. "Some New *Misharum* Material and its Implications." Pages 233–51 in *Studies in Honour of Benno Landsberger on His Seventy-Fifth Birthday.* Edited by H. G. Güterbock and T. Jacobsen. Assyriological Studies 16. Chicago: University of Chicago Press, 1965.

———, ed. *Cuneiform Texts from Babylonian Tablets in the British Museum: Old-Babylonian Legal Documents.* Cuneiform Texts from the Babylonian Tablets in the British Museum 48. London: Trustees of the British Museum, 1968.
Fishbane, M. *Biblical Interpretation in Ancient Israel.* Oxford: Clarendon, 1985.
———. "The Book of Job and Inner-Biblical Discourse." Pages 86–98, 240 in *The Voice from the Whirlwind: Interpreting the Book of Job.* Edited by L. G. Perdue and W. C. Gilpin. Nashville: Abingdon, 1992.
———. "Jeremiah 4:23–26 and Job 3:3–13: A Recovered Use of the Creation Pattern." *Vetus Testamentum* 21 (1971): 151–67.
Fishbane, M., and M. Tov. *"Sha'arei Talmon": Studies in the Bible, Qumran, and the Ancient Near East Presented to Shemaryahu Talmon.* Winona Lake, Ind.: Eisenbrauns, 1992.
Fisher, L. R. "An Amarna Age Prodigal." *Journal of Semitic Studies* 3 (1958): 113–22.
Fisher, W. B., et al. *The Cambridge History of Iran.* 7 vols. Cambridge: Cambridge University Press, 1968–91.
Fiss, O. "Objectivity and Interpretation." *Stanford Law Review* 34 (1982): 739–63.
Fitzpatrick-McKinley, A. *The Transformation of Torah from Scribal Advice to Law.* Journal for the Study of the Old Testament: Supplement Series 287. Sheffield: Sheffield Academic, 1999.
Flanagan, J. W., and A. W. Robinson, eds. *No Famine in the Land: Studies in Honor of John L. McKenzie.* Missoula, Mont.: Scholars Press, 1975.
Fohrer, G. *Das Buch Hiob.* Kommentar zum Alten Testament 16. Gütersloh: Gerd Mohn, 1963.
———. *Introduction to the Old Testament.* Nashville: Abingdon, 1968.
———. "The Righteous Man in Job 31." Pages 3–22 in *Essays in Old Testament Ethics.* Edited by J. L. Crenshaw and J. T. Willis. New York: Ktav, 1974.
———. *Studien zum Buch Hiob.* Gütersloh: Gerd Mohn, 1963.
———. *Studiem zum Buch Hiob (1956–79).* Beihefte zur Zeitschrift für die alttestamentliche Wissenschaft 159. Berlin: de Gruyter, 1983.
Folkers, T., et al., eds. *Symbolae ad Iura Orientis Antiqui Pertinentes Paulo Koschaker Dedicatae.* Leiden: Brill, 1939.
Follis, E., ed. *Directions in Hebrew Poetry.* Journal for the Study of the Old Testament: Supplement Series 40. Sheffield: Sheffield Academic, 1987.
Fontaine, C. R. "The Social Roles of Women in the World of Wisdom." Pages 24–49 in *A Feminist Companion to Wisdom Literature.* Edited by A. Brenner. Feminist Companion to the Bible 9. Sheffield: Sheffield Academic, 1995.
Forrest, R. W. E. "The Two Faces of Job: Imagery and Integrity in the Prologue." Pages 387–98 in *Ascribe to the Lord: Biblical and Other Studies in Memory of Peter C. Craigie.* Edited by L. Eslinger and G. Taylor. Journal for the Study of the Old Testament: Supplement Series 67. Sheffield: Sheffield Academic, 1988.
Forsyth, N. *The Old Enemy: Satan and the Combat Myth.* Princeton: Princeton University Press, 1987.
Fortner, J. D. "Adjudicating Entities and Levels of Legal Authority in Lawsuit Records of the Old Babylonian Era." Ph.D. diss., Hebrew Union College–Jewish Institute of Religion, 1996.
Foster, B. F. *Before the Muses: An Anthology of Akkadian Literature.* 2 vols. 2nd ed. Bethesda, Md.: CDL, 1996.

———. "Social Reform in Ancient Mesopotamia." Pages 165–75 in *Social Justice in the Ancient World*. Edited by K. Irani and M. Silver. Westport, Conn.: Greenwood, 1995.
Foucault, M. *Language, Counter-Memory, Practice: Selected Essays and Interviews*. Translated and edited by D. F. Bouchard. Ithaca, N.Y.: Cornell University Press, 1977.
———. *Power/Knowledge: Selected Interviews and Other Writings 1972–77*. Edited by C. Gordon. New York: Random House, 1980.
Fox, M. V. "Egyptian Onomastica and Biblical Wisdom." *Vetus Testamentum* 36 (1986): 302–10.
Fox, M. V., V. A. Hurowitz, A. Hurvitz et al., eds. *Texts, Temples, and Traditions: A Tribute to Menahem Haran*. Winona Lake, Ind.: Eisenbrauns, 1996.
Freedman, D. N., ed. *The Anchor Bible Dictionary*. 6 vols. New York: Doubleday, 1992.
Freedman, D. N., A. C. Meyer, and A. B. Beck, eds., *Eerdmans Dictionary of the Bible*. Grand Rapids: Eerdmans, 2000.
Freedman, L. R. "Biblical Hebrew 'rb, 'To Go Surety,' and Its Nominal Forms." *Journal of the Ancient Near Eastern Society of Columbia University* 19 (1989): 25–29
Frei, P. "Persian Imperial Authorization." Translated by J. W. Watts. Pages 5–40 in *Persia and Torah: The Theory of Imperial Authorization of the Pentateuch*. Edited by J. W. Watts. Society of Biblical Literature Symposium Series 17. Atlanta: Society of Biblical Literature, 2001.
———. "Zentralgewalt und Lokalautonomie im Achämenidenreich." Pages 8–131 in *Reichsidee und Reichsorganisation im Perserreich*. Edited by P. Frei and K. Koch. Orbis biblicus et orientalis 55. Freiburg: Universitätsverlag; Göttingen: Vandenhoeck & Ruprecht, 1984; 2nd ed., 1996.
Frei, P., and K. Koch, eds. *Reichsidee und Reichsorganisation im Perserreich*. 2nd ed. Orbis biblicus et orientalis 55. Göttingen: Vandenhoeck & Ruprecht, 1996.
Frick, F. S. "Widows in the Hebrew Bible: A Transactional Approach." Pages 139–51 in *A Feminist Companion to Exodus to Deuteronomy*. Edited by A. Brenner. Feminist Companion to the Bible 6. Sheffield: Sheffield Academic, 1995.
Fried, L. S. "'You Shall Appoint Judges': Ezra's Mission and the Rescript of Artaxerxes." Pages 63–90 in *Persia and Torah: The Theory of Imperial Authorization of the Pentateuch*. Edited by J. W. Watts. Society of Biblical Literature Symposium Series 17. Atlanta: Society of Biblical Literature, 2001.
Friedlaender, S., ed. *Probing the Limits of Representation: Nazism and the Final Solution*. Cambridge, Mass.: Harvard University Press, 1992.
Friedman, R. E., and H. G. M. Williamson, eds. *The Future of Biblical Studies*. Atlanta: Scholars Press, 1987.
Friedrich, J., J. G. Lautner, and J. Miles, eds. *Symbolae ad Iura Orientis Antiqui Pertinentes Paulo Koschaker Dedicatae*. Studia et Documenta 2. Leiden: Brill, 1939.
Frye, J. B. "Legal Language in the Book of Job." Ph.D. diss., University of London, 1973.
———. "The Use of Māŝāl in the Book of Job." *Semitics* 5 (1977): 59–66.
Frye, R. N. "Institutions." Pages 83–93 in *Beiträge zur Achämenidengeschichte*. Edited by G. Walser. Wiesbaden: Franz Steiner, 1972.

Frymer-Kensky, T. S. "The Judicial Ordeal in the Ancient Near East." 2 vols. Ph.D. diss., Yale University, 1977.
———. "The Nungal-hymn and the Ekur-prison." Pages 78–89 in *The Treatment of Criminals in the Ancient Near East*. Edited by J. Sasson. *Journal of the Economic and Social History of the Orient* 20. Leiden: Brill, 1977.
———. "Suprarational Legal Procedures in Elam and Nuzi." Pages 115–31 in *Studies on the Civilization and Culture of Nuzi and the Hurrians in Honor of Ernest R. Lacheman on his Seventy-Fifth Birthday, April 29, 1981*. Edited by M. A. Morrison and D. I. Owen. Winona Lake, Ind.: Eisenbrauns, 1981.
Fuchs, A., and S. Parpola. *The Correspondence of Sargon II. Part III: Letters from Babylonia and the Eastern Provinces*. State Archives of Assyria 15. Helsinki: Helsinki University Press, 2001.
Fuchs, G. *Mythos und Hiobdichtung: Aufnahme und Umdeutung altorientalischer Vorstellungen*. Stuttgart: Kohlhammer, 1993.
Fuller, R. T. "Cuneiform Texts XLVIII: A Transliteration and Translation with Philological Notes, Commentary, and Indices." Ph.D. diss., Hebrew Union College-Jewish Institute of Religion, 1992.
Fullerton, K. "The Original Conclusion to the Book of Job." *Zeitschrift für die alttestamentliche Wissenschaft* 42 (1924): 116–36.
Fyall, R. S. *Now My Eyes Have Seen You: Images of Creation and Evil in the Book of Job*. New Studies in Biblical Theology 12. Downers Grove, Ill.: InterVarsity, 2002.
Gammie, J. G. "The Angelology and Demonology in the Septuagint of the Book of Job." *Hebrew Union College Annual* 56 (1985): 1–19.
———. "Behemoth and Leviathan: On the Didactic and Theological Significance of Job 40:15–41:26." Pages 217–31 in *Israelite Wisdom: Theological and Literary Essays in Honor of Samuel Terrien*. Edited by J. G. Gammie et al. Missoula, Mont.: Scholars Press, 1978.
Gammie, J. G., and L. G. Perdue. *The Sage in Israel and the Ancient Near East*. Winona Lake, Ind.: Eisenbrauns, 1990.
Gammie, J. G., et al., eds. *Israelite Wisdom: Theological and Literary Essays in Honor of Samuel Terrien*. Missoula, Mont.: Scholars Press, 1978.
Garbini, G. *History and Ideology in Ancient Israel*. Translated by J. Bowden. New York: Crossroad, 1988.
Garelli, P., ed. *Le palais et la royauté et civilisation: Compte rendu*. Compte Rendu Rencontre Assyriologique 19. Paris: Geuthner, 1974.
Gaster, T. H. "Satan." Pages 224–25 of vol. 4 of *The Interpreter's Dictionary of the Bible*. Edited by G. A. Buttrick. 4 vols. Nashville: Abingdon, 1962.
Gelb, I. J., A. L. Oppenheim, E. Reiner, M. T. Roth, and R. D. Biggs, eds. *The Assyrian Dictionary of the Oriental Institute of the University of Chicago*. Chicago: University of Chicago Press, 1956– .
Geller, M. J. *Forerunners to Udug-Hul: Sumerian Exorcistic Incantations*. Stuttgart: Franz Steiner, 1983.
———. "An Incantation against Curses." Pages 127–40 in *Festschrift für Rykle Borger zu seinem 65. Geburtstag am 24. Mai 1994*. Edited by S. M. Maul. Cuneiform Monographs 10. Groningen: Styx, 1998.
———. "A New Piece of Witchcraft." Pages 193–205 in *DUMU-E$_2$-DUB-BA-A: Stud-

*ies in Honor of Åke W. Sjöberg*. Edited by H. Behrens, D. Loding, and M. T. Roth. Occasional Publications of the Samuel Noah Kramer Fund 11. Philadelphia: University Museum, 1989.

———. "The Šurpu Incantations and Lev. V.1–5." *Journal of Semitic Studies* 25 (1980): 181–92.

Gemser, B. "The *rîb*—or Controversy-Pattern in Hebrew Mentality." Pages 120–37 in *Wisdom in Israel and in the Ancient Near East Presented to Professor Harold Henry Rowley*. Edited by M. Noth and D. W. Thomas. Vetus Testamentum Supplements 3. Leiden: Brill, 1955.

George, A. R. "Cuneiform Texts in the Birmingham City Museum." *Iraq* 41 (1979): 121–40.

Gerstenberger, E. S. *Leviticus: A Commentary*. Translated by D. W. Stott. Old Testament Library. Louisville: Westminster John Knox, 1996.

Gese, H. *Lehre und Wirklichkeit in der alten Weisheit*. Tübingen: Mohr Siebeck, 1958.

Gevirtz, S. "West-Semitic Curses and the Problem of the Origins of Hebrew Law." *Vetus Testamentum* 11 (1961): 137–58.

Gewirtz, P. "Narrative and Rhetoric in the Law." Pages 2–22 in *Law's Stories: Narrative and Rhetoric in the Law*. Edited by P. Brooks and P. Gewirtz. New Haven: Yale University Press, 1996.

Gibson, E. C. S. *The Book of Job with Introduction and Notes*. 3rd ed. London: Methuen, 1919.

Gilkey, L. "Power, Order, Justice, and Redemption." Pages 159–70 in *The Voice from the Whirlwind: Interpreting the Book of Job*. Edited by L. G. Perdue and W. C. Gilpin. Nashville: Abingdon, 1992.

Ginsberg, H. L. "Job, The Book of." Pages 111–22 in vol. 10 of *The Encyclopaedia Judaica*. Edited by C. Roth. 16 vols. Jerusalem: Encyclopaedia Judaica, 1972.

———. "Job the Patient and Job the Impatient." Pages 88–111 in *Congress Volume: Rome, 1968*. Edited by G. W. Anderson et al. Vetus Testamentum Supplements 17. Leiden: Brill, 1969.

Glatzer, N. N., ed. *The Dimensions of Job: A Study and Selected Readings*. New York: Schocken Books, 1969.

Good, E. M. *In Turns of Tempest: A Reading of Job*. Stanford: Stanford University Press, 1990.

———. *Irony in the Old Testament*. 2nd ed. Bible and Literature Series 3. Philadelphia: Westminster, 1982.

———. "Job and the Literary Task: A Response [to David Robertson]." *Soundings* 56 (1973): 470–84.

Goodrich, P. *Legal Discourse: Studies in Linguistics, Rhetoric, and Legal Analysis*. New York: St. Martin's, 1987.

Gordis, R. *The Book of God and Man: A Study of Job*. Chicago: University of Chicago Press, 1965.

———. *The Book of Job: Commentary, New Translation, and Special Notes*. Moreshet Series 2. New York: Jewish Theological Seminary of America, 1978.

———. "Na'alam and Other Observances on the Ain Fashka Scrolls." *Journal of Near Eastern Studies* 9 (1950): 44–47.

Gordon, C. H. "The Legal Background of Hebrew Thought and Literature." M.A. thesis, University of Pennsylvania, 1928.

———. *Smith College Tablets: 110 Cuneiform Texts Selected from the College Collection.* Smith College Studies in History 38. Northampton, Mass.: Department of History of Smith College, 1952.

Gordon, E. I. "A New Look at the Wisdom of Sumer and Akkad." *Bibliotheca orientalis* 17 (1960): 122–52.

Grabbe, L. L. *Comparative Philology and the Text of Job: A Study in Methodology.* Society of Biblical Literature Dissertation Series 34. Missoula, Mont.: Scholars Press, 1977.

———. "The Law of Moses in the Ezra Tradition: More Virtual Than Real." Pages 91–114 in *Persia and Torah: The Theory of Imperial Authorization of the Pentateuch.* Edited by J. W. Watts. Society of Biblical Literature Symposium Series 17. Atlanta: Society of Biblical Literature, 2001.

———. *Leviticus.* Old Testament Guides. Sheffield: Sheffield Academic, 1993.

———. "Reconstructing History from the Book of Ezra." Pages 98–106 in *Second Temple Studies I. Persian Period.* Edited by P. R. Davies. Journal for the Study of the Old Testament: Supplement Series 117. Sheffield: Sheffield Academic, 1991.

———. "What was Ezra's Mission?" Pages 286–99 in *Second Temple Studies 2: Temple Community in the Persian Period.* Edited by T. C. Eskenazi and K. H. Richards. Journal for the Study of the Old Testament: Supplement Series 175. Sheffield: Sheffield Academic, 1994.

———, ed. *Can a "History of Israel" Be Written?* European Seminar in Historical Methodology 1. Journal for the Study of the Old Testament: Supplement Series 245. Sheffield: Sheffield Academic, 1997.

Grafton, A. *Forgers and Critics: Creativity and Duplicity in Western Scholarship.* Princeton: Princeton University Press, 1990.

Graham, J. N. "'Vinedressers and Plowmen': 2 Kings 25:12 and Jeremiah 52:16." *Biblical Archaeologist* 47 (1984): 55–58.

Gray, G. B. *A Critical and Exegetical Commentary on Numbers.* International Critical Commentary. New York: Charles Scribner's Sons, 1903.

Gray, J. "The Book of Job in the Context of Near Eastern Literature." *Zeitschrift für die alttestamentliche Wissenschaft* 82 (1970): 251–69.

Gray, J., J. C. Greenfield, and N. H. Sarna. *The Book of Job, a New Translation According to the Traditional Hebrew Text.* Philadelphia: Jewish Publication Society of America, 1980.

Greenberg, M. "Crimes and Punishments." Pages 733–44 in vol. 1 of *The Interpreter's Dictionary of the Bible.* Edited by G. A. Buttrick. 4 vols. Nashville: Abingdon, 1962.

———. "More Reflections on Biblical Criminal Law." Pages 1–17 in *Studies in Bible.* Edited by S. Japhet. Scripta hierosolymitana 31. Jerusalem: Magnes, 1986.

———. "Some Postulates of Biblical Criminal Law." Pages 5–28 in *Studies in Bible and Jewish Religion: Yehezkel Kaufmann Jubilee Volume.* Edited by M. Haran. Jerusalem: Magnes, 1960.

Greengus, S. "Israelite Law: Criminal Law." Pages 475–78 in vol. 7 of *The Encyclopedia of Religion.* Edited by M. Eliade. 16 vols. New York: Macmillan, 1987.

———. "Legal and Social Institutions of Ancient Mesopotamia." Pages 469–84 in vol. 1 of *Civilizations of the Ancient Near East.* Edited by J. Sasson. 4 vols. New York: Scribner, 1995.

———. "The Old Babylonian Marriage Contract." *Journal of the American Oriental Society* 89 (1969): 505–32.

———. *Old Babylonian Tablets from Ishchali and Vicinity*. Uitgaven van het Nederlands Historisch-Archaeologisch Instituut te Istanbul 44. Istanbul: Dutch Historical-Archaeological Institute, 1979.

———. "Some Issues Relating to the Comparability of Laws and the Coherence of the Legal Tradition." Pages 60–87 in *Theory and Method in Biblical and Cuneiform Law: Revision, Interpolation, and Development*. Edited by B. M. Levinson. Journal for the Study of the Old Testament: Supplement Series 181. Sheffield: Sheffield Academic, 1994.

———. "A Textbook Case of Adultery in Ancient Mesopotamia." *Hebrew Union College Annual* 40–41 (1969–1970): 33–44.

Greenhouse, C. J. "Reading Violence." Pages 105–39 in *Law's Violence*. Edited by A. Sarat and T. R. Kearns. Ann Arbor: University of Michigan Press, 1992.

Greenspahn, F. E. *Hapax Legomena in Biblical Hebrew: A Study of Their Phenomenon and Its Treatment Since Antiquity with Special Reference to Verbal Forms*. Society of Biblical Literature Dissertation Series 74. Chico, Calif.: Scholars Press, 1984.

———, ed. *Essential Papers on Israel and the Ancient Near East*. Essential Papers on Jewish Studies. New York: New York University Press, 1991.

Greenstein, E. L. "A Forensic Understanding of the Speech from the Whirlwind." Pages 241–58 in *Texts, Temples, and Traditions: A Tribute to Menahem Haran*. Edited by M. V. Fox, V. A. Hurowitz, A. Hurvitz, et al. Winona Lake, Ind.: Eisenbrauns, 1996.

———. "In Job's Face/Facing Job." Pp. 301–17 in *The Labour of Reading: Desire, Alienation, and Biblical Interpretation*. Edited by Fiona C. Black, Roland Boer, and Erin Runions. Semeia Studies 36. Atlanta: Society of Biblical Literature, 1999.

Gustafson, J. M. "A Response to the Book of Job." Pages 172–84, 251 in *The Voice from the Whirlwind: Interpreting the Book of Job*. Edited by L. G. Perdue and W. C. Gilpin. Nashville: Abingdon, 1992.

Guillaume, A. *Studies in the Book of Job*. Edited by J. Macdonald. Annual of Leeds University Oriental Society Annual Supplement 2. Leiden: Brill, 1968.

Gurney, O. R. *Middle Babylonian Legal and Economic Texts from Ur*. London: British School of Archaeology in Iraq, 1983.

Güterbock, H. G., and T. Jacobsen, eds. *Studies in Honour of Benno Landsberger on His Seventy-Fifth Birthday*. Assyriological Studies 16. Chicago: University of Chicago Press, 1965.

Gutiérrez, G. *On Job: God-Talk and the Suffering of the Innocent*. Translated by M. J. O'Connell. Maryknoll, N.Y.: Orbis, 1987.

Haag, H. *Teufelsglaube*. Tübingen: Katzman, 1971.

Habel, N. C. *The Book of Job*. Cambridge: Cambridge University Press, 1975.

———. *The Book of Job: A Commentary*. Old Testament Library. Philadelphia: Westminster, 1985.

———. "In Defense of God the Sage." Pages 21–38, 232–33 in *The Voice from the Whirlwind: Interpreting the Book of Job*. Edited by L. G. Perdue and W. C. Gilpin. Nashville: Abingdon, 1992.

———. "'Only the Jackal Is My Friend': On Friends and Redeemers in Job," *Interpretation* 31 (1977): 227–36.

Hackett, J. A., and J. Huehnergard. "On Breaking Teeth." *Harvard Theological Review* 77 (1984): 259–75.

Hallo, W. W. "Biblical History in its Near Eastern Setting: The Contextual Approach." Pages 1–26 in *Scripture in Context: Essays on the Comparative Method*. Edited by C. D. Evans, W. W. Hallo, and J. B. White. Pittsburgh: Pickwick, 1980.

———. "Compare and Contrast: The Contextual Approach to Biblical Literature." Pages 1–26 in *The Bible in the Light of Cuneiform Literature: Scripture in Context III*. Edited by W. W. Hallo, B. W. Jones, and G. L. Mattingly. Ancient Near Eastern Texts and Studies 8. Lewiston, N.Y.: Edwin Mellen, 1990.

———. "New Moons and Sabbaths: A Case-Study in the Contrastive Approach." *Hebrew Union College Annual* 43 (1977): 1–13.

———, ed. *Canonical Compositions from the Biblical World*. Vol. 1 of *The Context of Scripture*. Leiden: Brill, 1997.

———, ed. *Essays in Memory of E. A. Speiser*. American Oriental Series 53. New Haven: American Oriental Society, 1968.

Hallo, W. W., and H. Tadmor. "A Lawsuit from Hazor." *Israel Exploration Journal* 27 (1977): 1–11.

Hallo, W. W., B. W. Jones, and G. L. Mattingly, eds. *The Bible in the Light of Cuneiform Literature: Scripture in Context III*. Ancient Near Eastern Texts and Studies 8. Lewiston, N.Y.: Edwin Mellen, 1990.

Hallo, W. W., J. C. Moyer, and L. G. Perdue, eds. *Scripture in Context II: More Essays on the Comparative Method*. Winona Lake, Ind.: Eisenbrauns, 1983.

Halpern, B. *The First Historians: The Hebrew Bible and History*. San Franscisco: Harper & Row, 1988.

———. "YHWH's Summary Justice in Job XIV 20." *Vetus Testamentum* 28 (1978): 472–74.

Halpern, B., and J. Huehnergard. "El Armara Letter 252." *Orientalia* n.s. 51 (1982): 228–29.

Hamilton, V. P. "Satan." Pages 985–89 in vol. 5 of *The Anchor Bible Dictionary*. Edited by D. N. Freedman. 6 vols. New York: Doubleday, 1992.

Hanson, P. D. "Jewish Apocalyptic Against Its Near Eastern Environment." *Revue biblique* 78 (1971): 31–58.

Haran, M., ed. *Studies in Bible and Jewish Religion: Yehezkel Kaufmann Jubilee Volume*. Jerusalem: Magnes, 1960.

Harper, R. F. *Assyrian and Babylonian Letters Belonging to the K(ouyunjik) Collection(s) of the British Museum*. 14 vols. Chicago: University of Chicago Press, 1892–1914.

Harris, R. *Ancient Sippar: A Demographic Study of an Old-Babylonian City 1894–1595 B. C.* Istanbul: Nederlands Historisch-Archaeologisch Instituut te Istanbul, 1975.

Hart, H. L. A. *The Concept of Law*. 1961. 2nd ed. Oxford: Clarendon, 1994.

Hartley, J. E. *The Book of Job*. New International Commentary on the Old Testament. Grand Rapids: Eerdmans, 1988.

———. *Leviticus*. Word Biblical Commentary 4. Dallas: Word, 1992.

Hartmann, B., et al., eds. *Hebräische Wortforschung: Festschrift zum 80. Geburtstag von Walter Baumgartner*. Vetus Testamentum Supplements 16. Leiden: Brill, 1967.

Harvey, J. "Le 'rib–Pattern': Requisitoire Prophetique sur la Rupture de L'Alliance." *Biblica* 43 (1962): 172–96.
Hasel, G. F. "Health and Healing in the Old Testament," *Andrews University Seminary Studies* 21 (1983): 191–202.
Hauerwas, S., and A. MacIntrye, eds. *Revisions: Changing Perspectives in Moral Philosophy*. Notre Dame: University of Notre Dame Press, 1983.
Havice, H. "The Concern for the Widow and Fatherless in the Ancient Near East." Ph.D. diss., Yale University, 1979.
Hay, D. "Time, Inequality, and Law's Violence." Pages 141–73 in *Law's Violence*. Edited by A. Sarat and T. R. Kearns. Ann Arbor: University of Michigan Press, 1992.
Hayden, R. E. "Court Procedure at Nuzu." Ph.D. diss., Brandeis University, 1962.
Hecht, N. S., et al., eds. *An Introduction to the History and Sources of Jewish Law*. Oxford: Clarendon, 1996.
Heeßel, N. P. "Diagnosis, Divination and Disease: Towards an Understanding of the Rationale Behind the Babylonian *Diagnostic Handbook*." Pp. 97–116 in *Magic and Rationality in Ancient Near Eastern and Graeco-Roman Medicine*. Edited by H. F. J. Hortmanshoff and M. Stol. Studies in Ancient Medicine 27. Leiden: Brill, 2004.
———, ed. *Babylonisch-assyrische Diagnostik*. AlterOrient and Altes Testament 43. Münster: Ugarit, 2000.
Heltzer, M. "Neh. 11,24 and the Provincial Representative at the Persian Royal Court." *Transeuphratène* 8 (1994): 109–19.
Hermisson, H.-J. "Observations on Creation Theology in Wisdom." Translated by B. Howard. Pages 43–57 in *Israelite Wisdom: Theological and Literary Essays in Honor of Samuel Terrien*. Edited by J. G. Gammie et al. Missoula, Mont.: Scholars Press, 1978.
Hiebert, P. S. "'Whence Shall Help Come to Me?': The Biblical Widow." Pages 125–41 in *Gender and Difference in Ancient Israel*. Edited by P. L. Day. Minneapolis: Fortress, 1989.
Hillers, D. R. *Covenant: The History of a Biblical Idea*. Baltimore: Johns Hopkins University Press, 1969.
———. "Delocative Verbs in Biblical Hebrew." *Journal of Biblical Literature* 86 (1967): 320–34.
Hilprecht, H. V., and A. T. Clay. *Business Documents of Murashû Sons of Nippur Dated in the Reign of Artaxerxes I (464–424 B.C.)*. The Babylonian Expedition of the University of Pennsylvania. Series A: Cuneiform Texts 9. Philadelphia: University of Pennsylvania, 1898.
Hobbs, T. *Leviathan*. Edited by C. B. MacPherson. New York: Penguin Books, 1986.
Hoffman, Y. *A Blemished Perfection: The Book of Job in Context*. Journal for the Study of the Old Testament: Supplement Series 213. Sheffield: Sheffield Academic, 1996.
———. "The Root *qrb* as a Legal Term." *Journal of Northwest Semitic Languages* 10 (1982): 67–73.
Hoffner, H. A. "Some Contributions of Hittology to Old Testament Study." *Tyndale Bulletin* 20 (1969): 27–55.
Hoglund, K. G. *Achaemenid Imperial Administration in Syria-Palestine and the Mission*

of Ezra and Nehemiah. Society of Biblical Literature Dissertation Series 125. Atlanta: Scholars Press, 1992.
Holladay, W. L. *Jeremiah 1.* Hermeneia. Philadelphia: Fortress, 1986.
———. "Jeremiah's Lawsuit with God." *Interpretation* 17 (1963): 280–87.
Hölscher, G. *Das Buch Hiob.* Handbuch zum Alten Testament 17. Tübingen: J. C. B. Mohr (Paul Siebeck), 1937.
Honderich, T., ed. *Oxford Companion to Philosophy.* Oxford: Oxford University Press, 1995.
Horowitz, W., T. Oshima, and S. Sanders. "A Bibliographical List of Cuneiform Inscriptions from Canaan, Palestine/Philistia, and the Land of Israel." *Journal of the American Oriental Society* 122 (2002): 753–66.
Horst, F. "Der Eid im Alten Testament." Pages 292–314 in *Gottes Recht: Gesammelte Studien zum Recht im Alten Testament.* Edited by H. W. Wolff. Theologische Bücherei 12. Munich: Kaiser, 1961.
———. *Hiob.* 4th ed. Biblischer Kommentar, Altes Testament 16. Edited by M. Noth and H. W. Wolff. Neukirchen-Vluyn: Neukirchener Verlag, 1983.
Hostetler, M. J. "The Rhetoric of Christian Martyrdom: An Exploration of the Homiletical Uses of Ultimate Terms." Ph.D. diss., Northwestern University, 1993.
Huffmon, H. B. "The Covenant Lawsuit in the Prophets. *Journal of Biblical Literature* 78 (1959): 285–95.
Hunger, H. "Das Archiv des Nabû-Ušallim." *Baghdader Mitteilungen* 5 (1970): 193–304.
Hurowitz, V. A. "Alliterative Allusions, Nebus Writing, and Paronomastic Punishment: Some Aspects of Word Play in Akkadian Literature," in *Puns and Pundits: Word Play in the Hebrew Bible and Ancient Near Eastern Literature.* Edited by S. B. Noegel. Bethesda, Md.: CDC Press, 2000), 83–87.
———. Inu Anum ṣīrum: *Literary Structures in Non-Juridical Sections of Codex Hammurabi.* Occasional Publications of the Samuel Noah Kramer Fund 15. Philadelphia: University Museum, 1994.
Hurvitz, A. "The Date of the Prose Tale of Job Linguistically Reconsidered." *Harvard Theological Review* 67 (1974): 17–34.
Irani, K., and M. Silver, eds. *Social Justice in the Ancient World.* Westport, Conn.: Greenwood, 1995.
Iser, W. *The Act of Reading: A Theory of Aesthetic Response.* Baltimore: Johns Hopkins University Press, 1978.
———. *The Implied Reader: Patterns of Communication in Prose Fiction from Bunyan to Beckett.* Baltimore: Johns Hopkins University Press, 1974.
———. "Talk Like Whales: A Reply to Stanley Fish." *Diacritics* 11 (1981): 82–87.
Ishida, T. *Studies in the Period of David and Solomon and Other Essays: Papers read at the International Symposium for Biblical Studies, Tokyo, 5–7 December, 1979.* Winona Lake, Ind.: Eisenbrauns, 1982.
Jackson, B. S. "Modelling Biblical Law: The Covenant Code." *Chicago-Kent Law Review* 70 (1995): 1745–1827.
———. "Narrative Models in Legal Proof." Pages 158–78, 333–35 in *Narrative and the Legal Discourse: A Reader in Storytelling and the Law.* Edited by D. R. Papke. Liverpool: Deborah Charles, 1991.

———. "Practical Wisdom and Literary Artifice in the Covenant Code." Pages 1745–1827 in *The Jerusalem 1990 Conference Volume*. Edited by B. S. Jackson and S. M. Passamaneck. Atlanta: Scholars Press, 1992.
———. *Theft in Early Jewish Law*. Oxford: Clarendon, 1972.
———. "'Two or Three Witnesses.'" Pages 153–71 in *Essays in Jewish and Comparative Legal History*. Studies in Judaism in Late Antiquity 10. Leiden: Brill, 1975.
———., ed. *Jewish Law Association Studies*. Vol. 1. Chico, Calif.: Scholars Press, 1982.
Jackson, B. S., and S. M. Passamaneck, eds. *The Jerusalem 1990 Conference Volume*. Atlanta: Scholars Press, 1992.
Jacobsen, T. "An Ancient Mesopotamian Trial for Homicide." Pp. 130–50 in *Studia Biblica et Orientalia*, vol. 3, *Oriens Antiquus*. Analecta biblica 12. Rome: Biblical Institute Press, 1959. Reprinted at pages 193–214 in *Toward the Image of Tammuz and Other Essays on Mesopotamian History and Culture*. Edited by W. L. Moran. Harvard Semitic Studies 21. Cambridge, Mass.: Harvard University Press, 1970.
———. "Early Political Development in Mesopotamia." *Zeitschrift für Assyriologie* 52 (1957): 91–140. Reprinted at pages 132–56 in *Toward the Image of Tammuz and Other Essays on Mesopotamian History and Culture*. Edited by W. L. Moran. Harvard Semitic Studies 21. Cambridge, Mass.: Harvard University Press, 1970.
———. "Primitive Democracy in Ancient Mesopotamia." *Journal of Near Eastern Studies* 2 (1943): 159–72. Reprinted at pages 157–70 in *Toward the Image of Tammuz and Other Essays on Mesopotamian History and Culture*. Edited by W. L. Moran. Harvard Semitic Studies 21. Cambridge, Mass.: Harvard University Press, 1970.
———. *Toward the Image of Tammuz and Other Essays on Mesopotamian History and Culture*. Edited by William L. Moran. Harvard Semitic Studies 21. Cambridge, Mass.: Harvard University Press, 1970.
Jacobson, R. "Satanic Semiotics: Jobian Jurisprudence." *Semeia* 19 (1981): 63–71.
Janzen, D. "The 'Mission' of Ezra and the Persian-Period Temple Community." *Journal of Biblical Literature* 119 (2000): 619–43.
Janzen, J. G. *Job*. Interpretation: A Biblical Commentary for Teaching and Preaching. Atlanta: John Knox, 1985.
Japhet, S., ed. *Studies in Bible*. Scripta Hierosolymitana 31. Jerusalem: Magnes, 1986.
Jas, R. M. *Neo-Assyrian Judicial Procedures*. State Archives of Assyria Studies 5. Helsinki: Neo-Assyrian Text Corpus Project-University of Helsinki, 1996.
Jastrow, M. *The Book of Job: Its Origin, Growth, and Interpretation*. Philadelphia: Lippincott, 1920.
Joannès, F. *Archives de Borsippa: La famille Ea-ilūta-bani*. Hautes Études Orientales 25. Geneva: Droz, 1989.
———. "Une chronique judiciaire d'époque hellénistique et le châtiment des sacrileges à Babylone." Pages 193–212 in *Assyriologica et Semitica: Festschrift für Joachim Oelsner anläßlich seines 65. Geburtstages am 18. Februar 1997*. Edited by J. Marzahn and H. Neumann. Alter Orient und Altes Testament 252. Münster: Ugarit, 2000.
———. "La pratique du serment à l'époque néo-babylonienne." Pages 163–74 in

*Jurer et maudire: pratiques politiques et usages juridiques du serment dans le Proche-Orient ancien.* Edited by S. Lafont. Paris: L'Harmattan, 1997.

———. "Les textes judiciaires néo-babylioniens." Pages in 201–39 in *Rendre la justice en Mésopotamie: Archives judiciaires du Proche-Orient ancien (III<sup>e</sup>–I<sup>er</sup> millénaires avant J.-C. ).* Edited by F. Joannès. Saint-Denis: Presses Universitaires de Vincennes, 2000.

———, ed. *Rendre la justice en Mésopotamie: Archives judiciaires du Proche-Orient ancien (III<sup>e</sup>–I<sup>er</sup> millénaires avant J.-C.).* Saint-Denis: Presses Universitaires de Vincennes, 2000.

Jobling, D., P. L. Day, and G. T. Sheppard, eds. *The Bible and the Politics of Exegesis: Essays in Honor of Norman K. Gottwald on His Sixty-Fifth Birthday.* Cleveland: Pilgrim, 1991.

Johns, C. H. W. *Assyrian Deeds and Documents.* 4 vols. Cambridge: Deighton, Bell, 1898–1924.

———. *Babylonian and Assyrian Law, Contracts and Letters.* New York: Charles Scribner's Sons, 1904.

Jung, C. G. *Answer to Job.* New York: Pastoral Psychology Book Club, 1955.

Jursa, M. "Akkad, das Eulmaš und Gubāru." *Wiener Zeitschrift für die Kunde des Morgenlands* 86 (1996): 197–211.

———. "Neu- und Spätbabylonische Texte aus den Sammlungen der Birmingham Museums and Art Gallery." *Iraq* 59 (1997): 97–174.

Kallen, H. M. *The Book of Job as Greek Tragedy Restored.* New York: Moffat, 1981.

Kataja, L. "A Neo-Assyrian Document on Two Cases of River Ordeal." *State Archives of Assyria Bulletin* 1 (1987): 66–68.

Katz, R., and N. Ben-Dor, "Widowhood in Israel." Pages 317–27 in *Widows.* Vol 1: *The Middle East, Asia, and the Pacific.* Edited by H. Z. Lopata. 2 vols. Durham, N.C.: Duke University Press, 1987.

Kaufman, S. "The Job Targum from Qumran." *Journal of the American Oriental Society* 93 (1973): 317–27.

Kaupel, H. *Die Dämonen im Alten Testament.* Augsburg: Benno Filser, 1930.

Kautzsch, E., ed. *Gesenuis' Hebrew Grammar.* Translated by A. E. Cowley. Oxford: Claredon, 1960.

Keck, L. E., ed. *New Interpreter's Bible.* 12 vols. Nashville: Abingdon, 1994– .

Keel, O. *Jahwes Entgegnung an Ijob.* Forschungen zur Religion und Literatur des Alten und Neuen Testaments 121. Göttingen: Vandenhoeck & Ruprecht, 1978.

Keiser, C. E. *Letters and Contracts from Erech Written in the Neo-Babylonian Period.* Babylonian Inscriptions in the Collection of James B. Nies 1. New Haven: Yale University Press, 1917.

Keller, S. R. "Written Communications Between the Human and Divine Spheres in Mesopotamia and Israel." Pages 299–313 in *The Biblical Canon in Comparative Perspective: Scripture in Context IV.* Edited by K. L. Younger, W. W. Hallo, and B. F. Batto. Ancient Near Eastern Texts and Studies 11. Lewiston, N.Y.: Edwin Mellen, 1991.

Kelsen, H. *General Theory of Law and the State.* 1945. Translated by A. Wedberg. New York: Russell & Russell, 1961.

———. *Pure Theory of Law.* Berkeley: University of California Press, 1967.

Kennedy, G. A. *New Testament Interpretation Through Rhetorical Criticism*. Chapel Hill: University of North Carolina Press, 1984.
Kessler, R. "Ich weiß, daß mein Erlöser lebet: Sozialgeschichtlicher Hintergrund und theologische Bedeutung der Löser-vorstellung in Hiob 19:25." *Zeitschrift für katholische Theologie* 89 (1992): 139–58.
Kinet, D. "The Ambiguity of the Concepts of God and Satan in the Book of Job." Pages 30–35 in *Job and the Silence of God*. Edited by C. Duquoc and C. Foristan. New York: Seabury, 1983.
King, L. W. *Babylonian Boundary-Stones and Memorial Tablets in the British Museum*. London: British Museum, 1912.
———. *Babylonian Magic and Sorcery, Being "Prayers of the Lifting of the Hand."* New York: Georg Olms, 1975.
———. *Cuneiform Texts from Babylonian Tablets in the British Museum*. Cuneiform Texts from Babylonian Tablets in the British Museum 29. London: Trustees of the British Museum, 1910.
Kinnier Wilson, J. V. "Medicine in the Land and Times of the Old Testament," Pages 337–75 in *Studies in the Period of David and Solomon*. Edited by T. Ishida. Winona Lake, Ind.: Eisenbrauns, 1982.
Kissane, E. J. *The Book of Job*. Dublin: Browne & Nolan, 1939.
Kittel, G., and G. Friedrich, eds. *Theological Dictionary of the New Testament*. Translated by G. W. Bromiley. 10 vols. Grand Rapids: Eerdmans, 1964–76.
Kiuchi, N. *The Purification Offering in the Priestly Literature: Its Meaning and Function*. Journal for the Study of the Old Testament: Supplement Series 56. Sheffield: Sheffield Academic, 1987.
Klein, L. R. "Job and the Womb: Text about Men, Subtext about Women." Pages 186–200 in *A Feminist Companion to Wisdom Literature*. Edited by A. Brenner. Feminist Companion to the Bible 9. Sheffield: Sheffield Academic, 1995.
Kluger, R. S. *Satan in the Old Testament*. Translated by H. Nagel. Evanston, Northwestern University Press, 1967.
Knauf, E. A. "Tema." Pages 346–47 in vol. 6 of *The Anchor Bible Dictionary*. Edited by D. N. Freedman. 6 vols. New York: Doubleday, 1992.
Knight, D. A., and P. J. Paris, eds. *Justice and the Holy: Essays in Honor of Walter Harrelson*. Atlanta: Scholars Press, 1989.
Knight, D. A., and G. M. Tucker, eds. *The Hebrew Bible and Its Modern Interpreters*. Philadelphia: Fortress, 1985.
Knoppers, G. N. "An Achaemenid Imperial Authorization of Torah in Yehud." Pages 115–34 in *Persia and Torah: The Theory of Imperial Authorization of the Pentateuch*. Edited by J. W. Watts. Society of Biblical Literature Symposium Series 17. Atlanta: Society of Biblical Literature, 2001.
Knudtzon, J. A. *Die el-Amarna Tafeln*. Leipzig: Hinrichs, 1908–15.
Koch, K. "Ezra and the Origins of Judaism." *Journal of Semitic Studies* 19 (1974): 173–97.
Kocourek, A. *An Introduction to the Science of Law*. Boston: Little, Brown, 1930.
Koehler, L., W. Baumgartner, and J. J. Stamm. *The Hebrew and Aramaic Lexicon of the Old Testament*. Translated and edited under the supervision of M. E. J. Richardson. 4 vols. Leiden: Brill, 1994–99.

Kohler, J., and F. E. Peiser. *Aus dem babylonischen Rechtsleben*. 4 vols. Leipzig: Pfeiffer, 1890–98.
Kohler, J., and A. Ungnad. *Hammurabi's Gesetz*, vol. 4. Leipzig: Eduard Pfeiffer, 1909.
———. *Hundert ausgewählte Rechtsurkunden aus der Spätzeit des babylonischen Schrifttums von Xerxes bis Mithridates II (485–93 v. Chr.)*. Leipzig: Pfeiffer, 1911.
Köhler, L. H. "Justice in the Gate." Pages 149–75 in *Hebrew Man: Lectures Delivered at the Invitation of the University of Tübingen, December 1–16, 1952*. Translated by P. R. Ackroyd. London: SCM, 1956.
Kort, A., and S. Morschauser. *Biblical and Related Studies Presented to Samuel Iwry*. Winona Lake, Ind.: Eisenbrauns, 1985.
Koschaker, P. *Babylonisch-assyrisches Bürgschaftsrecht: Ein Beitrag zur Lehre von Schuld und Haftung*. Leipzig: Teubner, 1911.
———. *Rechtsvergleichende Studien zur Gesetzgebung Hammurapis Königs von Babylon*. Leipzig: Veit, 1917.
Kraeling, E. G. *The Brooklyn Museum Aramaic Papyri: New Documents of the Fifth Century B.C. from the Jewish Colony at Elephantine*. New Haven: Yale University Press, 1953.
Kraus, F. R. "Ein zentrales Problem des altmesopotamischen Rechts: Was ist der Codex Hammu-rabi?" *Geneva* 8 (1960): 283–96.
Krause, G., and G. Müller, eds. *Theologische Realenzyklopädie*. New York: de Gruyter, 1977– .
Krüchmann, O. *Neubabylonische Rechts- und Verwaltungs-Texte*. Texte und Materialien der Frau Professor Hilprecht Collection 2–3. Leipzig: Hinrichs, 1933.
Kruse, H. "Das Reich Satans." *Biblica* 58 (1977): 29–62.
Kübben, A. J. F. "Comparativists and Non-Comparativists in Anthropology." Pages 581–96 in *A Handbook of Method in Cultural Anthropology*. Edited by R. Naroll and R. Cohen. New York: Columbia University Press, 1970.
Kugel, J. L. "The Case Against Joseph." Pages 271–87 in *Lingering Over Words: Studies in Ancient Near Eastern Literature in Honor of William L. Moran*. Edited by T. Abusch, J. Huehnergard, and P. Steinkkeller. Harvard Semitic Studies 37. Atlanta: Scholars Press, 1990.
Kuhrt, A. *The Ancient Near East c. 3000–330 BC*. 2 vols. London: Routledge, 1995.
———. "Non Royal Women in the Late Babylonian Period." Pages 215–43 in *Women's Earliest Records from Ancient Egypt and Western Asia*. Edited by B. Lesko. Brown Judaic Studies 116. Atlanta: Scholars Press, 1989.
Kuklin, B., and J. W. Stempel. *Foundations of the Law: An Interdisciplinary and Jurisprudential Primer*. St. Paul: West, 1994.
Kümmel, H. M. *Familie, Beruf und Amt im spätbabylonischen Uruk*. Berlin: Gebr. Mann, 1979.
Kwasman, T. *Neo-Assyrian Legal Documents in the Kouyunjik Collection of the British Museum*. Studia Pohl, Series Maior 14. Rome: Pontifical Biblical Institute, 1988.
Kwasman, T., and S. Parpola. *Legal Transactions of the Royal Court of Nineveh, Part I: Tiglath-Pileser III through Esarhaddon*. State Archives of Assyria 6. Helsinki: Helsinki University Press, 1991.

Labat, R. *Manuel d'épigraphie akkadienne.* 6th ed. Paris: Geuthner, 1988.
———. *Traité akkadien de diagnostics et pronostics médicaux.* Leiden: Brill, 1951.
Labuschagne, C. J. *The Incomparability of Yahweh in the Old Testament.* Leiden: Brill, 1966.
Lafont, S. "Ancient Near Eastern Laws: Continuity and Pluralism." Pages 91–118 in *Theory and Method in Biblical and Cuneiform Law: Revision, Interpolation, and Development.* Edited by B. M. Levinson. Journal for the Study of the Old Testament: Supplement Series 181. Sheffield: Sheffield Academic, 1994.
———. "Considérations sur la pratique judiciaire en Mésopotamie." Pages 15–34 in *Rendre la justice en Mésopotamie: Archives judiciaires du Proche-Orient ancien (III$^e$–I$^{er}$ millénaires avant J.-C.).* Edited by F. Joannès. Saint-Denis: Presses Universitaires de Vincennes, 2000.
———. *Femmes, droit et justice dans l'antiquité orientale.* Orbis biblicus et orientalis 165. Göttingen: Vandenhoeck & Ruprecht, 1999.
———. "Le juge biblique." Pages 541–56 in *La Conscience du juge dans la tradition juridique européenne.* Edited by J.-M. Carbasse and L. Depambour-Tarride. Paris: PUF, 1999.
———. "La procédure par serment au Proche-Orient ancien." Pages 185–98 in *Jurer et maudire: pratiques politiques et usages juridiques du serment dans le Proche-Orient ancien.* Edited by S. Lafont. Paris: L'Harmattan, 1997.
———, ed. *Jurer et maudire: pratiques politiques et usages juridiques du serment dans le Proche-Orient ancien.* Paris: L'Harmattan, 1997.
Lambdin, T. O. *Introduction to Biblical Hebrew.* New York: Charles Scribner's Sons, 1971.
Lambert, M. "Les 'reformes' d'Urukagina." *Revue d'assyriologie et d'archéologie orientale* 50 (1956): 182–233.
Lambert, W. G. "A Babylonian Prayer to Anūna." Pages 321–29 in *DUMU-E$_2$-DUB-BA-A: Studies in Honor of Åke W. Sjöberg.* Edited by H. Behrens, D. Loding, and M. T. Roth. Occasional Publications of the Samuel Noah Kramer Fund 11. Philadelphia: University Museum, 1989.
———. *Babylonian Wisdom Literature.* Oxford: Clarendon, 1960.
———. "DINGIR.ŠÀ.DIB.BA Incantations." *Journal of Near Eastern Studies* 33 (1974): 267–322.
———. "A Further Attempt at the Babylonian 'Man and His God.'" Pages 187–202 in *Language, Literature and History: Philological and Historical Studies Presented to Erica Reiner.* Edited by F. Rochberg-Halton. American Oriental Series 67. New Haven: American Oriental Society, 1987.
———. "The Laws of Hammurabi in the First Millennium." Pages 95–98 in *Reflets des Deux Fleuves: Volume de Mélanges Offerts à André Finet.* Edited by M. Lebeau and P. Talon. Akkadica Supp 6. Leuven: Peeters, 1989.
———. "Nebuchadnezzar King of Justice." *Iraq* 27 (1965): 1–11.
———. "The Qualifications of Babylonian Diviners." Pages 141–58 in S. M. Maul, ed. *Festschrift für Rykle Borger zu seinem 65. Geburtstag am 24. Mai 1994.* Edited by S. M. Maul. Cuneiform Monographs 10. Groningen: Styx, 1998.
———. "Questions Addressed to the Babylonian Oracle: The Tamītu Texts." Pages 85–98 in *Oracles et prophéties dans l'antiquité: Actes du Colloque de Strasbourg, 15–17 Juin 1995.* Edited by J.-G. Heintz. Paris: Boccard, 1997.

Lambert, W. G., and A. R. Millard, eds. *Cuneiform Texts from Babylonian Tablets in the British Museum: Babylonian Literary Texts*. Cuneiform Texts from the Babylonian Tablets in the British Museum 46. London: Trustees of the British Museum, 1965.

Landsberger, B. "Die babylonischen Termini für Gesetz und Recht." Pages 219–34 in *Symbolae ad Iura Orientis Antiqui Pertinentes Paulo Koschaker Dedicatae*. Edited by T. Folkers et al. Leiden: Brill, 1939.

———. "The Conceptual Autonomy of the Babylonian World." *Monographs on the Ancient Near East* 1 (1979): 57–71.

———. *The Date Palm and its By-Products according to the Cuneiform Sources*. Archiv für Orientforschung Beiheft 17. Graz: Ernst F. Weidner, 1967.

———. "Remarks on the Archive of the Soldier Ubarum." *Journal of Cuneiform Studies* 9 (1955): 123–24.

Laney, J. C. "The Role of the Prophets in God's Case against Israel." *Bibliotheca sacra* 138 (1981): 313–25.

Lanfranchi, G. B., and S. Parpola. *The Correspondence of Sargon II. Part II: Letters from the Northern and Northeastern Provinces*. State Archives of Assyria 5. Helsinki: Helsinki University Press, 1990.

Langdon, S. *Babylonian Penitential Psalms*. Oxford Editions of Cuneiform Texts 6. Paris: Librairie Orientaliste Paul Geuthner, 1927.

Laserson, M. "Power and Justice." *Judaism* 2 (1953): 52–60.

Lasine, S. "Job and His Friends in the Modern World: Kafka's *The Trial*." Pages 144–55, 247–52 in *The Voice from the Whirlwind: Interpreting the Book of Job*. Edited by L. G. Perdue and W. C. Gilpin. Nashville: Abingdon, 1992.

Lautner, J. G. *Die richterliche Entscheidung und die Streitbeendigung im altbabylonischen Prozessrechte*. Leipziger rechtswissenschaftliche Studien 3. Leipzig: Theodor Weicher, 1922.

Lawson, J. N. "The Concept of Fate in Ancient Mesopotamia of the First Millennium: Toward an Understanding of 'Simtu' (First Millennium B.C.E., Namburi Ritual)." Ph.D. diss., Hebrew Union College-Jewish Institute of Religion, 1992.

Laytner, A. *Arguing with God: A Jewish Tradition*. Northvale, N.J.: Jason Aronson, 1990.

Lebeau, M., and P. Talon, eds. *Reflets des Deux Fleuves: Volume de Mélanges Offerts à André Finet*. Akkadica Supp 6. Leuven: Peeters, 1989.

Lebram, J. C. H. "Die Traditionsgeschichte der Esragestalt und die Frage nach dem historischen Esra." Pages 103–38 in *Sources, Structures, and Synthesis: Proceedings of the Groningen 1983 Achaemenid History Workshop*. Edited by H. Sancisi-Weerdenburg. Achaemenid History 1. Leiden: Nederlands Instituut voor het Nabije Oosten, 1987.

Lehmann, P. *The Transfiguration of Politics*. New York: Harper & Row, 1975.

Leichty, E. "A Legal Text from the Reign of Tiglath-Pileser III." Pages 227–29 in *Language, Literature, and History: Philological and Historical Studies Presented to Erica Reiner*. Edited by F. Rochberg-Halton. American Oriental Series 67. New Haven: American Oriental Society, 1987.

Lemche, N. P. "Justice in Western Asia in Antiquity, or: Why No Laws Were Needed!" *Chicago-Kent Law Review* 70 (1995): 1695–1716.

Lesko, B., ed. *Women's Earliest Records from Ancient Egypt and Western Asia.* Brown Judaic Studies Series 116. Atlanta: Scholars Press, 1989.
Levenson, J. D. "The Hebrew Bible, the Old Testament, and Historical Criticism." Pages 19–59 in *The Future of Biblical Studies.* Edited by R. E. Friedman and H. G. M. Williamson. Atlanta: Scholars Press, 1987.
Lévêque, J. *Job et son Dieu: Essai d'Exégèse et de Théologie Bibique.* 2 vols. Etudes Bibliques. Paris: Gabalda, 1970.
Levinas, E. Postscript to *Job and the Excess of Evil,* by P. Nemo. Translated by M. Kigel. Pittsburgh: Duquesne University Press, 1998.
Levine, B. A. *Numbers.* 2 vols. Anchor Bible 4–4A. New York: Doubleday, 1993, 2000.
Levinson, B. M. "The Case for Revision and Interpolation within the Biblical Legal Corpora." Pages 37–59 in *Theory and Method in Biblical and Cuneiform Law: Revision, Interpolation, and Development.* Edited by B. M. Levinson. Journal for the Study of the Old Testament: Supplement Series 181. Sheffield: Sheffield Academic, 1994.
———. *Deuteronomy and the Hermeneutics of Legal Innovation.* New York: Oxford University Press, 1997.
———, ed. *Theory and Method in Biblical and Cuneiform Law: Revision, Interpolation, and Development.* Journal for the Study of the Old Testament: Supplement Series 181. Sheffield: Sheffield Academic, 1994.
Levitats, I. "Punishment." Pages 1386–90 in vol. 8 of *The Encyclopaedia Judaica.* Edited by C. Roth. 16 vols. Jerusalem: Encyclopaedia Judaica, 1972.
Lévy, E., ed. *La codification des lois dans l'antiquité: Actes du Colloque de Strasbourg 27–29 Novembre 1997.* Travaux du Centre de Recherche sur le Proche-Orient et la Grèce antiques 16. Paris: Boccard, 2000.
Lewis, T. J. "Belial." Pages 654–56 in vol. 1 of *The Anchor Bible Dictionary.* Edited by D. N. Freedman. 6 vols. New York: Doubleday, 1992.
Libson, G. "The Use of the Sacred Object in the Administration of a Judicial Oath." Pages 53–60 in *Jewish Law Association Studies I.* Edited by B. S. Jackson. Chico, Calif.: Scholars Press, 1982.
Lieberman, A. I. "Studies in the Trial by River Ordeal in the Ancient Near East during the Second Millennium B.C.E." Ph.D. diss., Brandeis University, 1969.
Liebesny, H. "Evidence in Nuzi Legal Procedure." *Journal of the American Oriental Society* 61 (1941): 130–42.
———. "The Oath of the King in the Legal Procedure of Nuzi." *Journal of the American Oriental Society* 61 (1941): 62–63.
Limburg, J. "The Lawsuit of God in the Eighth Century Prophets." Th.D. diss., Union Theological Seminary (Virginia), 1969.
———. "The Root ריב and the Prophetic Lawsuit Speeches." *Journal of Biblical Literature* 88 (1969): 291–304.
Linafelt, T. "The Undecidability of ברך in the Prologue to Job and Beyond." *Biblical Interpretation* 4 (1996): 154–72.
Lindblom, H. *La composition du livre de Job.* Kungl. Humanistiska Vetenskapssamfundet I lund Årserättelse 1944–45. Lund: Gleerup, 1945.
Lindenberger, J. M. *Ancient Aramaic and Hebrew Letters.* Edited by K. H. Richards. Society of Biblical Literature Writings from the Ancient World 4. Atlanta: Scholars Press, 1994.

Lipiński, E. "Textes juridiques et economiques araméens." *Acta Antiqua Academiae Scientiarum Hungaricae* 22 (1974): 373–84.
Lipschits, O., and J. Blenkinsopp, eds. *Judah and the Judeans in the Neo-Babylonian Period*. Winona Lake, Ind.: Eisenbrauns, 2003.
Locher, C. "Deuteronomium 22, 13–21: Vom Prozeßprotokoll zum kasuistischen Gesetz." Pages 298–303 in *Das Deuteronomium*. Edited by N. Lohfink. Leuven: University Press, 1985.

———. *Die Ehre Einer Frau in Israel: Exegetische und rechtsvergleichende Studien zu Deuteronomium 22,13–21*. Orbis biblicus et orientalis 70. Göttingen: Vandenhoeck & Ruprecht, 1986.
Lods, A. "Les origins de la figure de satan, ses functions à la cour céleste." Pages 649–60 in vol. 2 of *Mélanges Syriens offerts à Monsieur René Dussaud*. 2 vols. Paris: Geuthner, 1939.
Loewenstamm, S. "The Cumulative Oath of Witnesses and Parties in Mesopotamian Law." Pages 341–45 in *Comparative Studies in Biblical and Ancient Oriental Literatures*. Alter Orient und Altes Testament 204. Neukirchen-Vluyn: Neukirchener Verlag, 1980.

———. "The Laws of Adultery and Murder in Biblical and Mesopotamian Law." Pages 146–53 in *Comparative Studies in Biblical and Ancient Oriental Literatures*. Alter Orient und Altes Testament 204. Neukirchen-Vluyn: Neukirchener Verlag, 1980.

———. "The Phrase X (or) X plus one in Biblical and Old Oriental Laws." Pages 443–44 in *Comparative Studies in Biblical and Ancient Oriental Literatures*. Alter Orient und Altes Testament 204. Neukirchen-Vluyn: Neukirchener Verlag, 1980.
Lohfink, N., ed. *Das Deuteronomium*. Leuven: University Press, 1985.
Lopata, H. Z., ed. *Widows*. Vol 1: *The Middle East, Asia, and the Pacific*. 2 vols. Durham, N.C.: Duke University Press, 1987.
Lorton, D. "The Treatment of Criminals in Ancient Egypt through the New Kingdom." Pages 2–64 in *The Treatment of Criminals in the Ancient Near East*. Edited by J. Sasson. *Journal of the Economic and Social History of the Orient* 20. Leiden: Brill, 1977.
Losier, M. A. "Witness in Israel of the Hebrew Scriptures in the Context of the Ancient Near East." Ph.D. diss., University of Notre Dame, 1973.
Lotman, J. M. "Point of View in a Text." *New Literary History* 6 (1975): 339–52.
Lutz, H. F. *Neo-Babylonian Administrative Documents from Erech: Parts I and II*. University of California Publications 9/1. Berkeley: University of California Press, 1927.
Lyons, J. *Semantics 2*. Cambridge: Cambridge University Press, 1977.
Mabee, C. "Jacob and Laban: The Structure of Judicial Proceedings (Genesis XXXI 25–42)." *Vetus Testamentum* 30 (1980): 192–207.

———. "The Problem of Setting in Hebrew Royal Judicial Narratives." Ph.D. diss., Claremont Graduate School, 1977.
Machinist, P. "Palestine, Administration of (Assyrio-Babylonian)." Pages 69–81 in vol. 5 of *The Anchor Bible Dictionary*. Edited by D. N. Freedman. New York: Doubleday, 1992.

———. "The Question of Distinctiveness in Ancient Israel." Pages 196–212 in *A*

*Highway from Egypt to Assyria: Studies in Ancient Near Eastern History and Historiography Presented to Hayim Tadmor*. Edited by I. Ephʿal and M. Cogan. Jerusalem: Magnes, 1990. Reprinted at pages 420–42 in *Essential Papers on Israel and the Ancient Near East*. Edited by F. E. Greenspahn. Essential Papers on Jewish Studies. New York: New York University Press, 1991.

Macholz, G. C. "Zur Geschichte der Justizorganisation in Juda." *Zeitschrift für die alttestamentliche Wissenschaft* 84 (1972): 318–40.

Mafico, T. "Just, Justice." Pages 1127–29 in vol. 3 of *The Anchor Bible Dictionary*. Edited by D. N. Freedman. 6 vols. New York: Doubleday, 1992.

Magdalene, F. R. "Ancient Near Eastern Treaty Curses and the Ultimate Texts of Terror: A Study of the Language of Divine Sexual Abuse in the Prophetic Corpus." Pages 326–52 in *A Feminist Companion to the Latter Prophets*. Edited by A. Brenner. Feminist Companion to the Bible 8. Sheffield: Sheffield Academic, 1995.

———. "Bless, Blessing." Page 192 in *Eerdmans Dictionary of the Bible*. Edited by D. N. Freedman, A. C. Meyer, and A. B. Beck. Grand Rapids: Eerdmans, 2000.

———. "Curse." Page 301 in *Eerdmans Dictionary of the Bible*. Edited by D. N. Freedman, A. C. Meyer, and A. B. Beck. Grand Rapids: Eerdmans, 2000.

———. "Job's Wife as Hero: A Feminist-Forensic Reading of the Book of Job," *Biblical Interpretation* 14 (2006): 374–423.

———. "On the Scales of Righteousness: Law and Story in the Book of Job." Ph.D. diss., Iliff School of Theology and University of Denver (Colorado Seminary), 2003.

———. "Sexual Euphemisms in Hebrew and Omissions in English: A Eu-feministic Analysis of Sexual Imagery in the NRSV." Paper presented at the annual meeting of the Society of Biblical Literature. Orlando, Fla., November 21, 1998.

———. "Who Is Job's Redeemer? Job 19:25 in Light of Neo-Babylonian Law," *Zeitschrift für altorientalische und biblische Rechtgeschichte* 10 (2004): 292–316.

Maine, H. 1861. Reprint, *Ancient Law*. Tucson: University of Arizona Press, 1986.

Malamat, A. "Kingship and Council in Israel and Sumer." *Journal of Near Eastern Studies* 22 (1963): 247–53.

Malchow, B. V. *Social Justice in the Hebrew Bible: What Is New and What Is Old*. Collegeville, Minn.: Liturgical Press, 1996.

Malina, B. "Interpretation: Reading, Abduction, Metaphor." Pages 253–66 in *The Bible and the Politics of Exegesis: Essays in Honor of Norman K. Gottwald on His Sixty-Fifth Birthday*. Edited by D. Jobling, P. L. Day, and G. T. Sheppard. Cleveland: Pilgrim, 1991.

Malinine, M. "Deux documents égyptiens relatifs au depot." *Mitteilungen des Deutschen Archäologischen Instituts Abteilung Kairo* 16 (1958): 219–29.

Malul, M. *The Comparative Method in Ancient Near Eastern and Biblical Legal Studies*. Alter Orient und Altes Testament 227. Neukirchen-Vluyn: Neukirchener Verlag, 1990.

———. *Studies in Mesopotamian Legal Symbolism*. Alter Orient und Altes Testament 221. Neukirchen-Vluyn: Neukirchener Verlag, 1988.

Mangan, C. "The Targum of Job." Pages 5–98 in *The Targums of Job, Proverbs, Qohelet*.

Edited by M. McNamara et al. Aramaic Bible 15. Collegeville, Minn.: Liturgical Press, 1991.
Many, G. "Der Rechtsstreit mit Gott (rîb) im Hiobbuch." Ph.D. diss., Katholisch-theologische Fakultät der Ludwig-Maximilian Universität, 1970.
Marx, V. "Die Stellung der Frauen in Babylonien gemäss den Kontrakten aus der Zeit von Nebukadnezar bis Darius (604–485)." *Beiträge zur Assyriologie* 4 (1902): 1–77.
Marzahn, J., and H. Neumann, eds. *Assyriologica et Semitica: Festschrift für Joachim Oelsner anläßlich seines 65. Geburtstages am 18. Februar 1997*. Alter Orient und Altes Testament 252. Münster: Ugarit, 2000.
Matthews, V. H. "The Anthropology of Slavery in the Covenant Code." Pages 119–35 in *Theory and Method in Biblical and Cuneiform Law: Revision, Interpolation, and Development*. Edited by B. M. Levinson. Journal for the Study of the Old Testament: Supplement Series 181. Sheffield: Sheffield Academic, 1994.
———. "Entrance Ways and Threshing Floors: Legally Significant Sites in the Ancient Near East." *Fides et Historia* 19 (1987): 25–40.
Matthews, V. H., B. M. Levinson, and T. Frymer-Kensky, eds. *Gender and Law in the Hebrew Bible and the Ancient Near East*. Journal for the Study of the Old Testament: Supplement Series 262. Sheffield: Sheffield Academic, 1998.
Mattingly, G. L. "The Pious Sufferer: Mesopotamia's Traditional Theodicy." Pages 305–48 in *The Bible in the Light of Cuneiform Literature: Scripture in Context III*. Edited by W. W. Hallo, B. W. Jones, and G. L. Mattingly. Ancient Near Eastern Texts and Studies 8. Lewiston, N.Y.: Edwin Mellen, 1990.
Maul, S. M. "How the Babylonians Protected Themselves against Calamities Announced by Omens. Pages 123–29 in *Mesopotamian Magic: Textual, Historical, and Interpretive Perspectives*. Edited by T. Abusch and K. van der Toorn. Groningen: Styx, 1999.
Mays, J. L., D. L. Petersen, and K. H. Richards, eds. *Old Testament Interpretation: Past, Present, and Future: Essays in Honor of Gene M. Tucker*. Nashville: Abingdon, 1995.
McCarter, P. K. *Ancient Inscriptions: Voices from the Biblical World*. Washington, D.C.: Biblical Archaeology Society, 1996.
———. *1 Samuel: A New Translation with Introduction, Notes, and Commentary*. Anchor Bible 8. Garden City, N.Y.: Doubleday, 1980.
———. "The Religious Reforms of Hezekiah and Josiah." Pages 57–80 in *Aspects of Monotheism: How God Is One*. Edited by H. Shanks and J. Meinhardt. Washington, D.C.: Biblical Archaeological Society, 1997.
———. "Rib-Adda's Appeal to Aziru (EA 162, 1–21)." *Oriens antiquus* 12 (1973): 15–18.
———. "The River Ordeal in Israelite Literature." *Harvard Theological Review* 66 (1973): 403–412.
———. *Textual Criticism: Recovering the Text of the Hebrew Bible*. Guides to Biblical Scholarship. Philadelphia: Fortress, 1986.
McCarthy, D. J. "The Wrath of Yahweh and the Structural Unity of the Deuteronomistic History." Pages 97–110 in *Essays in Old Testament Ethics*. Edited by J. L. Crenshaw and J. T. Willis. New York, Ktav, 1974.

McDowell, A. G. *Jurisdiction in the Workmen's Community of Deir-el-Medina*. Leiden: Nederlands Instituut voor het Nabije Oosten, 1990.

McEwan, G. J. P. *The Late Babylonian Tablets in the Ashmolean Museum*. Oxford Edition of Cuneiform Texts 10. Oxford: Clarendon, 1984.

———. *The Late Babylonian Tablets in the Royal Ontario Museum*. Royal Ontario Museum Cuneiform Texts 2. Toronto: Royal Ontario Museum, 1982.

McFague, S. *Models of God: Theology for an Ecological, Nuclear Age*. Philadelphia: Fortress, 1987.

McKay, H., and D. J. A. Clines, eds. *Of Prophets' Visions and the Wisdom of Sages: Essays in Honour of R. Norman Whybray on His Seventieth Birthday*. Journal for the Study of the Old Testament: Supplement Series 162. Sheffield: Sheffield Academic, 1993.

McKeating, H. "The Development of Law on Homicide in Ancient Israel." *Vetus Testamentum* 25 (1975): 46–48.

McKenna, D. *Job*. The Communicator's Commentary. Waco: Word, 1986.

McKenzie, D. A. "Judicial Procedure at the Town Gate." *Vetus Testamentum* 14 (1964): 100–104.

McKenzie, J. L. *Second Isaiah: Introduction, Translation, and Notes*. Anchor Bible 20. Garden City, N.Y.: Doubleday, 1968.

———, ed. *The Bible in Current Catholic Thought*. New York: Herder & Herder, 1962.

McKenzie, S. L., and S. R. Hayes, eds. *To Each Its Own Meaning: An Introduction to Biblical Criticisms and Their Application*. Louisville: Westminster John Knox, 1993.

McKnight, E. V. "Reader Response Criticism." Pages 197–219 in *To Each Its Own Meaning: An Introduction to Biblical Criticisms and Their Application*. Edited by S. L. McKenzie and S. R. Hayes. Louisville: Westminster John Knox, 1993.

McNamara, M., et al., eds. *The Targums of Job, Proverbs, Qohelet*. Aramaic Bible 15. Collegeville, Minn.: Liturgical Press, 1991.

Mendelsohn, I. *Slavery in the Ancient Near East*. New York: Oxford University Press, 1949.

Mendenhall, G. E. "Samuel's 'Broken Rîb': Deuteronomy 32." Pages 63–74 in *No Famine in the Land: Studies in Honor of John L. McKenzie*. Edited by J. W. Flanagan and A. W. Robinson. Missoula, Mont.: Scholars Press, 1975.

Messerschmidt, L., and A. Ungnad. *Die bildlichen Darstellungen auf vorderasiatischen Denkmälern der königlichen Museen zu Berlin*. Vorderasiatische Schriftdenkmäler der Königlichen Museen zu Berlin 1. Leipzig: Hinrichs, 1907.

Mettinger, T. N. D. "The God of Job: Avenger, Tyrant, or Victor?" Pages 39–49, 233–36 in *The Voice from the Whirlwind: Interpreting the Book of Job*. Edited by L. G. Perdue and W. C. Gilpin. Nashville: Abingdon, 1992.

———. "Intertextuality: Allusion and Vertical Context Systems in Some Job Passages." Pages 257–80 in *Of Prophets' Visions and the Wisdom of Sages: Essays in Honour of R. Norman Whybray on His Seventieth Birthday*. Edited by H. McKay and D. J. A. Clines. Journal for the Study of the Old Testament: Supplement Series 162. Sheffield: Sheffield Academic, 1993.

Miall, D. S., ed. *Metaphor: Problems and Perspectives*. Sussex: Harvester, 1982.

Miles, J. *God: A Biography.* New York: Knopf, 1995.
Milgrom, J. *Cult and Conscience: The "Asham" and the Priestly Doctrine of Repentance.* Leiden: Brill, 1976.
———. "The Cultic שגגה and Its Influence in Psalms and Job." *Jewish Quarterly Review* 58 (1967): 115–25.
———. *Leviticus: A New Translation with Introduction and Commentary.* 3 vols. Anchor Bible 3, 3A, 3B. New York: Doubleday, 1991–2001.
———. *Studies in Cultic Theology and Terminology.* Leiden: Brill, 1983.
Millard, A. "The Last Tablets of Ugarit." Pages 119–24 in *Actes du colloque: Le pays d'Ougarit autour de 1200 av. J.-C. Ras Shamra-Ougarit 11.* Paris: ERC, 1995.
Miller, G. P. "Contracts of Genesis," *Journal of Legal Studies* 22 (1993): 15–45.
———. "Forward: The Development of Ancient Near Eastern Law." *Chicago-Kent Law Review* 70 (1995): 1623–30.
Miller, J. M. "Approaches to the Bible Through History and Archaeology: Biblical History as a Discipline." *Biblical Archaeologist* 45 (1982): 211–23.
———. "Israelite History." Pages 1–30 in *The Hebrew Bible and Its Modern Interpreters.* Edited by D. A. Knight and G. M. Tucker. Philadelphia: Fortress, 1985.
———. *The Old Testament and the Historian.* Guides to Biblical Scholarship. Philadelphia: Fortress, 1976.
Miller, J. M., and J. H. Hayes. *A History of Ancient Israel and Judah.* Philadelphia: Westminster, 1985.
Miller, P. D., Jr. "Cosmology and the World Order in the Old Testament: The Divine Council as Cosmic-Political Symbol." *Horizons in Biblical Theology* 9 (1987): 58–78.
———. "Divine Council and the Prophetic Call to War." *Vetus Testamentum* 18 (1968): 100–107.
Minow, M. "Introduction: Robert Cover and Law, Judging, and Violence." Pages 1–11 in *Narrative, Violence, and the Law: Essays of Robert Cover.* Edited by M. Minow, M. Ryan, and A. Sarat. Ann Arbor: University of Michigan Press, 1992.
Minow, M., M. Ryan, and A. Sarat, eds. *Narrative, Violence, and the Law: Essays of Robert Cover.* Ann Arbor: University of Michigan Press, 1992.
Mitchell, S., *The Book of Job.* 2nd ed. New York: Harper Collins, 1987.
Mitchell, W. J. T., ed. *On Narrative.* Chicago: University of Chicago Press, 1981.
Moore, E. W. *Neo-Babylonian Business and Administrative Documents.* Ann Arbor: University of Michigan Press, 1935.
———. *Neo-Babylonian Documents in the University of Michigan Collection.* Ann Arbor: University of Michigan Press, 1939.
Moore, F. C. T. "On Taking Metaphor Literally." Pages 1–13 in *Metaphor: Problems and Perspectives.* Edited by D. S. Miall. Sussex: Harvester, 1982.
Moore, R. D. "The Integrity of Job." *Catholic Biblical Quarterly* 45 (1983): 17–31.
Moran, W. L. *The Amarna Letters.* Baltimore: Johns Hopkins University Press, 1992.
———. "Notes on the Hymn to Marduk in *Ludlul Bēl Nēmequi.*" Pages 255–60 in *Studies in Literature from the Ancient Near East Dedicated to Samuel Noah Kramer.* Edited by J. M. Sasson. American Oriental Series 65. New Haven: American Oriental Society, 1984.
———. "Rib-Hadda: Job at Byblos?" Pages 173–81 in *Biblical and Related Studies Pre-*

*sented to Samuel Iwry.* Edited by A. Kort and S. Morschauser. Winona Lake, Ind.: Eisenbrauns, 1985.
Morrison, M. A., and D. I. Owen, eds. *Studies on the Civilization and Culture of Nuzi and the Hurrians in Honor of Ernest R. Lacheman on His Seventy-Fifth Birthday, April 29, 1981.* Winona Lake, Ind.: Eisenbrauns, 1981.
Morrison, M. A., and G. Wilhelm, eds. *Studies on the Civilization and Culture of Nuzi and the Hurrians.* 14 vols. Winona Lake, Ind.: Eisenbrauns; Bethesda, Md.: CDL, 1981– .
Morrow, W. S. "Consolation, Rejection, and Repentance in Job 42:6." *Journal of Biblical Literature* 105 (1986): 576–78.
———. "A Generic Discrepancy in the Covenant Code." Pages 136–51 in *Theory and Method in Biblical and Cuneiform Law: Revision, Interpolation, and Development.* Edited by B. M. Levinson. Journal for the Study of the Old Testament: Supplement Series 181. Sheffield: Sheffield Academic, 1994.
———. "Toxic Religion and the Daughters of Job" *Studies in Religion* 27 (1998): 263–76.
Mowinckel, S. "Hiobs *go'el* und Zeuge im Himmel." Pages 207–22 in *Vom Alten Testament.* Edited by K. Budde. Beihefte zur Zeitschrift für die alttestamentliche Wissenschaft 41. Giessen: Alfred Töpelmann, 1925.
Muff, J. *Studies in Aramaic Legal Papyri from Elephantine.* Studia et Documenta ad Iura Orientalis Antiqui Pertinentia 8; Leiden: Brill, 1969.
Mullen, E. T. *The Divine Council in Canaanite and Early Hebrew Literature.* Harvard Semitic Monographs 24. Chico, Calif.: Scholars Press, 1980.
Müller, H.-P. *Das Hiobproblem: Seine Stellung und Entstehung in Alten Orient und im Alten Testament.* Darmstadt: Wissenschaftliche Buchgesellschaft, 1978.
———. "Keilschriftliche Parallelen zum Biblischen Hiobbuch: Möglichkeit und Grenze des Vergleichs." *Orientalia* n.s. 47 (1978): 360–75.
Murphy, R. E. "The Concept of Wisdom Literature." Pages 46–54 in *The Bible in Current Catholic Thought.* Edited by J. L. McKenzie. New York: Herder & Herder, 1962.
———. *Wisdom Literature: Job, Proverbs, Ruth, Canticles, Ecclesiastes, and Esther.* Forms of the Old Testament Literature 13. Grand Rapids: Eerdmans, 1981.
Myer, T. M. *Ezra, Nehemiah.* Anchor Bible 14. Garden City, N.Y.: Doubleday, 1965.
Naroll, R., and R. Cohen, eds. *A Handbook of Method in Cultural Anthropology.* New York: Columbia University Press, 1970.
Naveh, J. "A Hebrew Letter from the Seventh Century B.C." *Israel Eexploration Journal* 10 (1960): 129–39.
Nel, P. J. "The Conception of Evil and Satan in Jewish Traditions in the Pre-Christian Period." Pages 1–21 in *Like a Roaring Lion: Essays on the Bible, Church, and Demonic Powers.* Edited by P. G. R. de Villiers. Pretoria: University of South Africa, 1987.
Nemo, P. *Job and the Excess of Evil.* With a postscript by E. Levinas. Translated by M. Kiegel. Pittsburgh: Duquesne University Press, 1998.
Neusner, J., E. S. Frerichs, and N. M. Sarna, eds. *From Ancient Israel to Modern Judaism: Essays in Honor of Marvin Fox.* Brown Judaic Studies 159. Atlanta: Scholars Press, 1989.
Newell, B. L. "Job: Repentant or Rebellious?" Pages 441–56 in *Sitting with Job: Selected*

*Studies on the Book of Job.* Edited by R. B. Zuck. Grand Rapids: Baker, 1992. Reprinted from *Westminster Theological Journal* 46 (1984): 298–316.

Newsom, C. "The Book of Job." Pages 319–637 in vol. 4 of the *New Interpreter's Bible.* Edited by L. E. Keck. 12 vols. Nashville: Abingdon, 1994– .

———. "The Character of Pain: Job in Light of Elaine Scarry's *The Body in Pain.*" Paper presented at the annual meeting of the Society of Biblical Literature. Orlando, Fla., November 23, 1998.

———. "Cultural Politics in the Book of Job." *Biblical Interpretation* 1 (1993): 119–34.

———. "Job." Pages 138–44 in *The Women's Bible Commentary*. Edited by C. Newsom and S. H. Ringe. 1992. 2nd ed. Louisville: Westminster John Knox, 1998.

———. "Job and Ecclesiastes." Pages 177–94 in *Old Testament Interpretation: Past, Present, and Future: Essays in Honor of Gene M. Tucker*. Edited by J. L. Mays, D. L. Petersen, and K. H. Richards. Nashville: Abingdon, 1995.

Newsom, C., and S. H. Ringe, eds. *The Women's Bible Commentary.* 1992. 2nd ed. Louisville: Westminster John Knox, 1998.

Niebuhr, R. *The Nature and Destiny of Man: A Christian Interpretation.* New York: Charles Scribner's Sons, 1943.

Niehr, H. "Religio-Historical Aspects of the 'Early Post-Exilic' Period." Pages 228–44 in *The Crisis of Israelite Religion: Transformation of Religious Tradition in Exilic and Post-Exilic Times*. Edited by B. Becking and M. C. A. Korpel. Old Testament Studies 42. Leiden: Brill, 1999.

Nielsen, K. "'Whatever Became of You, Satan' Or A Literary-Critical Analysis of the Rôle of Satan in the Book of Job." Pages 129–34 in *Goldene Äpfel in silbernen Schalen: 13th Congress of the International Organization for the Study of the Old Testament*. Beiträge zur Erforschung des Alten Testaments und des antiken Judentum 20. Frankfurt: Lang, 1992.

———. *Yahweh as Prosecutor and Judge: An Investigation of the Prophetic Lawsuit (Rib-Pattern).* Journal for the Study of the Old Testament: Supplement Series 9. Sheffield: JSOT Press, 1978.

Nies, J. B., and C. E. Keiser. *Historical, Religious, and Economic Texts and Antiquities.* Babylonian Inscriptions in the Collection of J. B. Nies 2.. New Haven: Yale University Press, 1920.

Nissen, H.-J., and J. Renger, eds. *Mesopotamien und seine Nachbarn: Politische und kulturelle Wechselbeziehungen im Alten Vorderasien vom 4. bis 1. Jahrtausend v. Chr.* 2 vols. XXV Rencontre Assyriologique Internationale Berlin. Berlin: Dietrich Reimer, 1982.

Nissinen, Martti, with contributions by C. L. Seow and Robert K. Ritner. *Prophets and Prophecy in the Ancient Near East*. Edited by P. Machinist. Society of Biblical Literature Writings from the Ancient World 12. Atlanta: Society of Biblical Literature, 2003.

Nörr, D., and D. Simon. *Gedächtnisschrift für Wolfgang Kunkel.* Frankfurt: Vittorio Klostermann, 1984.

Norris, K. *The Cloister Walk.* New York: Riverhead Books, 1996.

North, R. "Civil Authority in Ezra." Pages 377–404 in vol. 6 of *Studi in onore di Edoardo Volterra*. Università di Roma Facoltà di giurisprudenza 45. Milan: Giuffrè, 1971.

Noth, M. *Exodus: A Commentary*. Translated by J. S. Bowden. Old Testament Library. Philadelphia: Westminster, 1962.
———. *Leviticus: A Commentary*. Old Testament Library. Translated by J. E. Anderson. London: SCM, 1965.
———. *Numbers: A Commentary*. Translated by J. D. Martin. Old Testament Library. Philadelphia: Westminster, 1968.
Noth, M., and D. W. Thomas, eds. *Wisdom in Israel and in the Ancient Near East Presented to Professor Harold Henry Rowley*. Vetus Testamentum Supplements 3. Leiden: Brill, 1955.
Nougayrol, J. "(Juste) souffrant (R.S. 25.460)." *Ugaritica* 5 (1968): 265–83.
———. "Une version ancienne du 'juste souffrant,'" *Revue biblique* 59 (1952): 237–50.
O'Connor, K. M. *The Confessions of Jeremiah: Their Interpretation and Role in Chapters 1–25*. Society of Biblical Literature Dissertation Series 94. Atlanta: Scholars Press, 1988.
Oden, R. A. "Hermeneutics and Historiography: Germany and America." *Society of Biblical Literature Seminar Papers* 19 (1980): 135–57.
Oelsner, J., B. Wells, and C. Wunsch. "Neo-Babylonian Period." Pages 911–74 in vol. 2 of *A History of Ancient Near Eastern Law*. Edited by R. Westbrook. 2 vols. Handbook of Oriental Studies 72. Leiden: Brill, 2003.
Olmstead, A. T. "Darius as Lawgiver." *American Journal of Semitic Languages and Literature* 51 (1934/1935): 247–49.
Olsen, S. H. "Understanding Literary Metaphors." Pages 36–54 in *Metaphor: Problems and Perspectives*. Edited by D. S. Miall. Sussex: Harvester, 1982.
Oppenheim, A. L. *Ancient Mesopotamia: Portrait of a Dead Civilization*. 2nd ed. Chicago: University of Chicago Press, 1977.
———. "Assyriological Gleanings." *Bulletin of the American Schools of Oriental Research* 93 (1944): 14–17.
———. "Deux notes de lexicographie accadienne." *Orientalia* n.s. 9 (1940): 219–22.
———. "The Eyes of the Lord." *Journal of the American Oriental Society* 88 (1968): 173–80.
———. *Letters from Mesopotamia*. Chicago: University of Chicago Press, 1967.
———. "The Neo-Babylonian Preposition *la*." *Journal of Near Eastern Studies* 1 (1942): 369–72.
Oppert, Mm. J., and J. Ménant. *Documents Juridiques de l'Assyrie de la Chaldée*. Paris: Maisonneuve, 1877.
Orlinsky, H. M. "The Forensic Character of the Hebrew Bible." Pages 89–97 in *Justice and the Holy: Essays in Honor of Walter Harrelson*. Edited by D. A. Knight and P. J. Paris. Atlanta: Scholars Press, 1989.
Otto, E. "Aspects of Legal Reforms and Reformulations in Ancient Cuneiform and Israelite Law." Pages 160–98 in *Theory and Method in Biblical and Cuneiform Law: Revision, Interpolation, and Development*. Edited by B. M. Levinson. Journal for the Study of the Old Testament: Supplement Series 181. Sheffield: Sheffield Academic, 1994.
———. *Das Deuteronomium: Politische Theologie und Rechtsreform in Juda und Assyrien*. Beihefte zur Zeitschrift für die alttestamentliche Wissenschaft 284. New York: de Gruyter, 1999.

───. "Kodifizierung und Kanonisierung von Rechtssätzen in keilschriftlichen und biblischen Rechtssammlungen." Pages 77–124 in *La Codification des lois dans l'antiquité: Actes du Colloque de Strasbourg, 27–29 Novembre 1997*. Edited by E. Lévy. Travaux du Centre de Recherche sur le Proche-Orient et la Grèce antiques 16. Paris: Boccard, 2000.

───. "Neue Aspekte zum keilschriftlichen Prozeßrecht in Babylonien und Assyrien." *Zeitschrift für altorientalische und biblische Rechtsgeschichte* 4 (1998): 263–83.

───. "Recht/Rechtstheologie/Rightsphilosophie I. Alter Orient und Altes Testament." Pages 197–209 of vol. 28 in *Theologische Realenzyklopädie*. Edited by G. Krause and G. Müller. New York: de Gruyter, 1977– (vol. 28, 1997).

───. Review of P. Bovati, *Re-Establishing Justice: Legal Terms, Concepts and Procedures in the Hebrew Bible*. *Zeitschrift für altorientalische und biblische Rechtgeschichte* 1 (1995): 159–66.

───. Review of W. W. Hallo, *Origins: The Ancient Near Eastern Background of Some Modern Western Institutions*. *Zeitschrift für altorientalische und biblische Rechtgeschichte* 3 (1997): 250–58.

Papke, D. R., ed. *Narrative and the Legal Discourse: A Reader in Storytelling and the Law*. Liverpool: Deborah Charles, 1991.

Pardes, I. *Countertraditions in the Bible: A Feminist Approach*. Cambridge, Mass.: Harvard University Press, 1992.

Parker, B. "The Nimrud Tablets, 1952—Business Documents." *Iraq* 16 (1954): 29–58.

Parker, P. "The Metaphorical Plot." Pages 133–58 in *Metaphor: Problems and Perspectives*. Edited by D. S. Miall. Sussex: Harvester, 1982.

Parpola, S. *The Correspondence of Sargon II. Part I: Letters from Assyria and the West*. State Archives of Assyria 1. Helsinki: Helsinki University Press, 1987.

───. *Cuneiform Texts from Babylonian Tablets in the British Museum: Neo-Assyrian Letters from the Kuyunjik Collection*. Cuneiform Texts from the Babylonian Tablets in the British Museum 53. Edited by S. Parpola. London: British Museum Publications, 1979.

───. *Letters from Assyrian and Babylonian Scholars*. State Archives of Assyria 10. Helsinki: Helsinki University Press, 1993.

Patrick, D. *Arguing with God: The Angry Prayers of Job*. St. Louis: Bethany. 1977.

───. *Old Testament Law*. Atlanta: John Knox, 1985.

───. "The Translation of Job XLII 6." *Vetus Testamentum* 26 (1976): 369–71.

───. "Who is the Evolutionist?" Pages 152–59 in *Theory and Method in Biblical and Cuneiform Law: Revision, Interpolation, and Development*. Edited by B. M. Levinson. Journal for the Study of the Old Testament: Supplement Series 181. Sheffield: Sheffield Academic, 1994.

Paul, S. M. "Daniel 3:29—A Case of 'Neglected' Blasphemy." *Journal of Near Eastern Studies* 42 (1983): 291–94.

───. *Studies in the Book of the Covenant in the Light of Cuneiform and Biblical Law*. Vetus Testamentum Supplements 18. Leiden: Brill, 1970.

───. "Unrecognized Biblical Legal Idioms in Light of Comparative Akkadian Expressions." *Revue biblique* 86 (1976): 231–39.

Peake, A. S. *Job*. New Century Bible. London: T. C. & E. C. Jack, 1904.
Peiser, F. E. *Babylonische Verträge des Berliner Museums im Autographie, Transcription und Übersetzung*. Berlin: Wolf Peiser, 1890.
———. *Jurisprudentiae Babylonicae quae supersunt; commentatio Assyriologica de nonnullis quae in museis et Britannico et Berolinensi exstant tabulis*. Cöthen: Druck von P. Schettler's Erben, 1890.
———. "Studien zum Babylonischen Rechtswesen." *Zeitschrift für Assyriologie* 3 (1888): 62–92.
———. *Texte juristischen und geschäftlichen Inhalts*. Berlin: Reuther & Reichard, 1896.
Penchansky, D. *The Betrayal of God: Ideological Conflict in Job*. Louisville: Westminster John Knox, 1990.
Penchansky, D., and P. L. Redditt, eds. *Shall Not the Judge of All the Earth Do What Is Right? Studies on the Nature of God in Tribute to James L. Crenshaw*. Winona Lake, Ind.: Eisenbrauns, 2000.
Perdue, L. G. "Metaphorical Theology in the Book of Job: Theological Anthropology in the First Cycle of Job's Speeches (Job 3; 6–7; 9–10)." Pages 129–56 in *The Book of Job*. Edited by W. A. M. Beuken. Bibliotheca ephemeridum theologicarum lovaniensium 104. Leuven: Leuven University Press, 1994.
———. *Wisdom in Revolt: Metaphorical Theology in the Book of Job*. Journal for the Study of the Old Testament: Supplement Series 112. Sheffield: Sheffield Academic, 1991.
Perdue, L. G., and W. C. Gilpin, eds. *The Voice from the Whirlwind: Interpreting the Book of Job*. Nashville: Abingdon, 1992.
Petschow, H. "Die §§ 45 and 46 des Codex Ḫammurapi—Ein Beitrag zum altbabylonischen Bodenpachtrecht und zum Problem: Was ist der Codex Ḫammurapi." *Zeitschrift für Assyriologie* 74 (1984): 181–212.
———. *Neubabylonisches Pfandrecht*. Abhandlungen der Sächsischen Akademie der Wissenschaften zu Leipzig, Philologisch-historische Klasse 48/1. Berlin: Akademie Verlag, 1956.
Pfeiffer, C. F. "Neo-Babylonian Documents in the John Fredick Lewis Collection of the Free Library of Philadelphia." Ph.D. diss., Dropsie College for Hebrew and Cognate Learning, 1953.
Pfeiffer, R. H. "Edomite Wisdom." *Zeitschrift für die alttestamentliche Wissenschaft* 44 (1926): 13–25.
———. *Introduction to the Old Testament*. New York: Harper & Brothers, 1948.
———. *State Letters of Assyria: A Transliteration and Translation of 355 Official Assyrian Letters dating from the Sargonid Period (722–625)*. American Oriental Series 6. New Haven: Yale University Press, 1935.
Pfeiffer, R. H., and E. A. Speiser. *One Hundred Selected Nuzi Texts*. Annual of the American Schools of Oriental Research 16. New Haven: American Schools of Oriental Research, 1936.
Phillips, A. *Ancient Israel's Criminal Law: A New Approach to the Decalogue*. Oxford: Blackwell, 1970.
Pinches, T. G. "Two Late Tablets of Historical Interest." *Proceedings of the Society of Biblical Archaeology* 38 (1916): 27–34.
———, ed. *The Cuneiform Inscriptions of Western Asia*. Vol. 5: *A Selection from the Miscellaneous Inscriptions of Assyria and Babylonia*. London: Nachdruck, 1909.

———, ed. *Cuneiform Texts from the Babylonian Tablets in the British Museum*. Cuneiform Texts from the Babylonian Tablets in the British Museum 2, 4, 6, 12. London: British Museum, 1896, 1898, 1898, 1901.

———, ed. *Cuneiform Texts from Babylonian Tablets in the British Museum: Neo-Babylonian and Achaemenid Economic Texts*. 3 vols. Cuneiform Texts from the Babylonian Tablets in the British Museum 55–57. London: British Museum, Publications, 1982.

———, ed. *Cuneiform Texts from Babylonian Tablets in the British Museum: Old-Babylonian Business Documents*. Cuneiform Texts from the Babylonian Tablets in the British Museum 45. London: British Museum, 1964.

Pinker, A. "Satanic Verses: Satan in the Hebrew Bible." *Jewish Bible Quarterly* 25 (1997): 90–100.

Ploeg, J. P. M. van der. "Studies in Hebrew Law, I: The Terms." *Catholic Biblical Quarterly* 12 (1950): 248–59.

Pohl, A. *Neubabylonische Rechtsurkunden aus den Berliner Staatlichen Museen*. 2 vols. Analecta orientalia 8–9. Rome: Pontificio Istituto Biblico, 1933–1934.

Polley, M. E. "Hebrew Prophecy Within the Council of Yahweh, Examined in Its Ancient Near Eastern Setting: The Contextual Approach." Pages 141–56 in *Scripture in Context: Essays on the Comparative Method*. Edited by C. D. Evans, W. W. Hallo, and J. B. White. Pittsburgh: Pickwick, 1980.

Pope, M. H. *Job*. 3rd ed. Anchor Bible 15. Garden City, N.Y.: Doubleday, 1979.

Porten, B. *Archives from Elephantine: The Life of an Ancient Jewish Military Colony*. Berkeley: University of California Press, 1968.

———. "Cowley 7 Reconsidered." *Orientalia* n.s. 56 (1987): 89–92.

———. *The Elephantine Papyri in English: Three Millennia of Cross-Cultural Continuity and Change*. Documenta et Monumenta Orientis Antiqui Studies in Near Eastern Archaeology and Civilization 22. Leiden: Brill, 1996.

Porten, B., and A. Yardini. *Textbook of Aramaic Documents from Ancient Egypt*. 2 vols. Winona Lake, Ind.: Eisenbrauns, 1989.

Porteous, N. "Old Testament and History." *Annual of the Swedish Theological Institute* 8 (1970–71): 21–77.

Postgate, J. N. *Early Mesopotamia: Society and Economy at the Dawn of History*. London: Routledge, 1992.

———. *Fifty Neo-Assyrian Legal Documents*. Warminster: Aris & Phillips, 1976.

———. "Royal Exercise of Justice under the Assyrian Empire." Pages 417–26 in *Le palais et la royauté et civilisation: Compte rendu*. Edited by P. Garelli. Compte Rendu Rencontre Assyriologique 19. Paris: Geuthner, 1974.

Powell, M. A., and R. H. Sack. *Studies in Honor of Tom B. Jones*. Alter Orient und Altes Testament 203. Neukirchen-Vluyn: Neukirchener Verlag, 1979.

Preuss, H. D. "Jahwes Antwort an Hiob und die sogenannte Hiobliteratur des alten Vorderen Orients." Pages 304–43 in *Beiträge zur altestamentlichen Theologie*. Edited by H. Donner et al. Göttingen: Vandenhoeck & Ruprecht, 1977.

Price, I. M. "The Oath in Court Procedure in Early Babylonia and the Old Testament." *Journal of the American Oriental Society* 49 (1929): 22–39.

Pritchard, J. B., ed. *Ancient Near Eastern Texts Relating to the Old Testament*. 3rd ed. Princeton: Princeton University Press, 1969.

Rad, G. von. "διάβολος." Pages 72–81 in vol. 2 of *Theological Dictionary of the New*

*Testament*. Edited by G. Kittel and G. Friedrich. Translated by G. W. Bromiley. 10 vols. Grand Rapids: Eerdmans, 1964–76.

———. "Hiob xxxviii und die altägyptische Weisheit." Pages 293–301 in *Wisdom in Israel and in the Ancient Near East: Presented to Professor Harold Henry Rowley in Celebration of His Sixty-Fifth Birthday*. Edited by M. Noth and D. W. Thomas. Vetus Testamentum Supplements 3. Leiden: Brill, 1955. Translated as "Job XXXVIII and Ancient Egyptian Wisdom." Pages 281–91 in *The Problem of the Hexateuch and Other Essays*. New York: McGraw Hill, 1966. Reprinted at pages 267–77 in *Studies in Ancient Israelite Wisdom*. Edited by J. L. Crenshaw: New York: Ktav, 1976.

Radner, K. "Die Goldschmiede von Assur im 7. Jhd. v. C. Die Texte des neuassyrischen Privatarchivs N33 im Voderasiatischen Museum." M.A. thesis, Universität Wien, 1994.

———. *Die neuassyrischen Privatrechtsurkunden als Quelle für Mensch und Umwelt*. State Archives of Assyria Studies 6. Helsinki: Neo-Assyrian Text Corpus Project, 1997.

Rainey, A. F. "The Satrapy 'Beyond the River,'" *Australian Journal of Biblical Archaeology* 1 (1969): 51–78.

Raphael, R. "Things Too Wonderful: A Disabled Reading of Job." *Perspectives in Religious Studies* 31 (2004): 399–424.

Rawlinson, H. C. *The Cuneiform Inscriptions of Western Asia*. 2nd ed. London: British Museum, 1891.

Redford, B. D. "The So-Called 'Codification' of Egyptian Law under Darius I." Pages 135–59 in *Persia and Torah: The Theory of Imperial Authorization of the Pentateuch*. Edited by J. W. Watts. Society of Biblical Literature Symposium Series 17. Atlanta: Society of Biblical Literature, 2001.

Redford, S. *The Harem Conspiracy: The Murder of Ramesses III*. DeKalb: Northern Illinois University Press, 2002.

Reid, S. B., ed. *Prophets and Paradigms: Essays in Honor of Gene M. Tucker*. Journal for the Study of the Old Testament: Supplement Series 229. Sheffield: Sheffield Academic, 1996.

Reiner, E. "Lipšur Litanies," *Journal of Near Eastern Studies* 15 (1956): 129–49.

———. *Šurpu—A Collection of Sumerian and Akkadian Incantations*. AfO Beiheft 11. Graz: Ernest F. Weidner, 1958.

Reiner, E., with M. Civil. "The Babylonian Fürstenspeigel in Practice." Pages 320–36 in *Societies and Languages of the Ancient Near East: Studies in Honour of I. M. Diakonoff*. Edited by M. A. Dandamaev et al. Warminster: Aris & Phillips, 1982.

Renger, J. "Notes on the Goldsmiths, Jewelers and Carpenters of Neobabylonian Eanna." *Journal of the American Oriental Society* 91 (1971): 494–503.

———. "Wrongdoing and Its Sanctions: On 'Criminal' and 'Civil' Law in the Old Babylonian Period." Pages 65–77 in *The Treatment of Criminals in the Ancient Near East*. Edited by J. Sasson. *Journal of the Economic and Social History of the Orient* 20. Leiden: Brill, 1977.

Reventlow, H. G. "Das Amt des Mazkir: Zur Rechtsstruktur des öffentlichen Lebens in Israel." *Theologische Zeitschrift* 15 (1959): 161–75.

———. "Participial Formulations: Lawsuit, Not Wisdom—A Study in Prophetic

Language." Pages 375–82 in *Texts, Temples, and Traditions: A Tribute to Menahem Haran.* Edited by M. V. Fox, V. A. Hurowitz, A. Hurvitz, et al. Winona Lake, Ind.: Eisenbrauns, 1996.

Reviv, H. *The Elders in Ancient Israel: A Study of a Biblical Institution.* Translated by L. Plitmann. Jerusalem: Magnes, 1989.

———. "The Traditions Concerning the Inception of the Legal System in Israel." *Zeitschrift für die alttestamentliche Wissenschaft* 94 (1982): 566–75.

Richards, K. H. "Bless/Blessing." Pages 753–55 in vol. 1 of *The Anchor Bible Dictionary.* Edited by D. N. Freedman. 6 vols. New York: Doubleday, 1992.

———. "Death." Pages 108–10 in vol. 2 of *The Anchor Bible Dictionary.* Edited by D. N. Freedman. 6 vols. New York: Doubleday, 1992.

Richter, H. "Erwägungen zum Hiobproblem." *Evangelische Theologie* 18 (1958): 302–11.

———. *Studien zu Hiob: Der Aufbau des Hiobbuches dargestellt an den Gattungen des Rechtslebens.* Theologische Arbeiten 11. Berlin: Evangelische Verlagsanstalt, 1959.

Ricoeur, P. *The Rule of Metaphor: Multidisciplinary Studies of the Creation of Meaning in Language.* Translated by R. Xzerny with K. McLaughlin and J. Costello. Toronto: University of Toronto Press, 1981.

Riddle, D. W. *The Martyrs: A Study in Social Control.* Chicago: University of Chicago Press, 1931.

Ries, G. "Altbabylonische Beweisurteile." *Zeitschrift der Savigny-Stiftung für Rechtsgeschichte* 106 (1989): 56–80.

———. "Ein Neubabylonischer Mitgiftprozess (559 v. Chr.): Gleichzeitig ein Eintrag zur Frage der Geltung keilschriftlicher Gesetze." Pages 345–63 in *Gedächtnisschrift für Wolfgang Kunkel.* Edited by D. Nörr and D. Simon. Frankfurt: Vittorio Klostermann, 1984.

———. "Zur Strafbarkeit des Meineids im Recht des Alten Orients." Pages 457–68 in *Festschrift für Dieter Medicus zum 70. Geburtstag.* Edited by V. Beuthien et al. Cologne: Heymanns, 1999.

Ries, J. "Blessing." Translated by J C. Haight and A. S. Mahler. Pages 247–53 in vol. 2 of *The Encyclopedia of Religion.* Edited by M. Eliade. 16 vols. New York: Macmillan, 1987.

Ritner, R. K. *The Mechanics of Ancient Egyptian Magical Practice.* Studies in Ancient Oriental Civilizations 54. Chicago: University of Chicago Press, 1993.

Roberts, J. J. M. "Job and the Israelite Religious Tradition." *Zeitschrift für die alttestamentliche Wissenschaft* 89 (1977): 107–14.

———. "Job's Summons to Yahweh: The Exploitation of a Legal Metaphor." *Restoration Quarterly* 16 (1973): 159–65.

———. "Myth versus History: Relaying the Comparative Foundations." *Catholic Biblical Quarterly* 38 (1976): 1–13.

Robertson, D. "The Book of Job: A Literary Study." *Soundings* 56 (1973): 446–69.

———. *The Old Testament and the Literary Critic.* Guides to Biblical Scholarship. Philadelphia: Fortress, 1977.

Robinson, H. W. "The Council of Yahweh." *Journal of Theological Studies* 45 (1944): 151–57.

Rochberg-Halton, F., ed. *Language, Literature and History: Philological and Historical*

Studies Presented to Erica Reiner. American Oriental Series 67. New Haven: American Oriental Society, 1987.

Roche, Michael de. "Yahweh's rîb Against Israel: A Reassessment of the So-Called 'Prophetic Lawsuit' in the Preexilic Prophets." *Journal of Biblical Literature* 102 (1983): 563–74.

Rollston, C. A. "Non-Provenanced Epigraphs I: Pillaged Antiquities, Northwest Semitic Forgeries, and Protocols for Laboratory Tests." *Maarav* 10 (2003): 135–93.

Roth, C., ed. *The Encyclopaedia Judaica*. 16 vols. Jerusalem: Encyclopaedia Judaica, 1972.

Roth, M. T. "A Case of Contested Status." Pages 481–89 in *DUMU-E$_2$-DUB-BA-A: Studies in Honor of Åke W. Sjöberg*. Edited by H. Behrens, D. Loding, and M. T. Roth. Occasional Publications of the Samuel Noah Kramer Fund 11. Philadelphia: University Museum, 1989.

———. "Gender and Law: A Case Study from Ancient Mesopotamia." Pages 173–84 in *Gender and Law in the Hebrew Bible and the Ancient Near East*. Edited by V. H. Matthews, B. M. Levinson, and T. Frymer-Kensky. Journal for the Study of the Old Testament: Supplement Series 262. Sheffield: Sheffield Academic, 1998.

———. "Homicide in the Neo-Assyrian Period." Pages 351–65 in *Language, Literature and History: Philological and Historical Studies Presented to Erica Reiner*. Edited by F. Rochberg-Halton. American Oriental Series 67. New Haven: American Oriental Society, 1987.

———. "The Law Collection of King Hammurabi: Toward an Understanding of Codification and Text." Pages 9–31 in *La Codification des lois dans l'antiquité: Actes du Colloque de Strasbourg, 27–29 Novembre 1997*. Edited by E. Lévy. Travaux du Centre de Recherche sur le Proche-Orient et la Grèce antiques 16. Paris: Boccard, 2000.

———. *Law Collections from Mesopotamia and Asia Minor*. 1995. 2nd ed. Society of Biblical Literature Writings from the Ancient World 6. Atlanta: Scholars Press, 1997.

———. "Mesopotamian Legal Traditions and the Laws of Hammurabi." *Chicago-Kent Law Review* 71 (1995): 13–39.

———. Review of B. M. Levinson, *Theory and Method in Biblical and Cuneiform Law: Revision, Interpolation, and Development*. *Shofar* 14 (1996): 177–80.

———. "fTašamētu-damqat and Daughters." Pages 387–400 in *Assyriologica et Semitica: Festschrift für Joachim Oelsner anläßlich seines 65. Geburtstages am 18. Februar 1997*. Edited by J. Marzahn and H. Neumann. Alter Orient und Altes Testament 252. Münster: Ugarit, 2000.

———. "Women in Transition and the Bīt Mār Banî." *Revue d'assyriologie et d'archéologie orientale* 82 (1988): 131–38.

Roth, W. M. W. "The Numerical Sequence x/x+1 in the Old Testament." *Vetus Testamentum* 12 (1962): 300–11.

Roux, G. *Ancient Iraq*. 3rd ed. New York: Penguin, 1992.

Rowley, H. H. "The Book of Job and Its Meaning." Pages 141–83 in *From Moses to Qumran: Studies in the Old Testament*. London: Lutterworth, 1963.

———. *Job*. Century Bible. London: Thomas Nelson and Sons, 1970.

Rudolph, W. *Esra und Nehemia samt 3. Esra.* Handbuch zum Alten Testament 20. Tübingen: Mohr Siebeck, 1949.
Sack, R. H. *Amel-Marduk 562–560 B.C.: A Study Based on Cuneiform, Old Testament, Greek, Latin, and Rabbinical Sources.* Alter Orient und Altes Testament 4. Neukirchen-Vluyn: Neukirchener Verlag, 1972.
———. *Cuneiform Documents form the Chaldean and Persian Periods.* London: Associated University Press, 1993.
———. *Neriglissar—King of Babylon.* Alter Orient und Altes Testament 236. Neukirchen-Vluyn: Neukirchener Verlag, 1994.
Salmon, J. M. "Judicial Authority in Early Israel: An Historical Investigation of Old Testament Institutions." Ph.D. diss., Princeton Theological Seminary, 1968.
Sancisi-Weerdenburg, H., ed. *Sources, Structures, and Synthesis: Proceedings of the Groningen 1983 Achaemenid History Workshop.* Achaemenid History 1. Leiden: Nederlands Instituut voor het Nabije Oosten, 1987.
Sancisi-Weerdenburg, H., and A. Kuhrt, eds. *Centre and Periphery: Proceedings of the Groningen 1986 Achaemenid History Workshop.* Achaemenid History 4. Leiden: Nederlands Insituut voor het Nabije Oosten, 1990.
Sandmel, S. "Parallelomania." *Journal of Biblical Literature* 81 (1962): 1–13.
San Nicolò, M. *Babylonische Rechtsurkunden des ausgehenden 8. und des 7. Jahrhunderts v. Chr.* 2 vols. Abhandlungen der Bayerischen Akademie der Wissenschaften 34. Munich: Beck, 1951.
———. *Beiträge zu einer Prosopographie neubabylonischer Beamten der Zivil- und Tempelverwaltung.* Sitzangsberichte der Bayerischen Akademie der Wissenschaften, Philosophisch-historische Abteilung 2.2. Munich: Bayerischen Akademie der Wissenschaften, 1941.
———. *Beiträge zur Rechtsgeschichte im Bereiche der keilschriftlichen Rechtsquellen.* Cambridge, Mass.: Harvard University Press, 1931.
———. "Eine Kleine Gefängnismeuterei in Eanna zur Zeit des Kambyses." Pages 1–10 in vol. 2 of *Festschrift für Leopold Wenger: Zu seinem 70. Geburtstag dargebracht von Freunden, Fachgenossen und Schülern.* 2 vols. Münchener Beiträge zur Papyrusforschung und antiken Rechtsgeschichte 34–35. Munich: Beck, 1945.
———. "Materialien zur Viehwirtschaft in den neubabylonischen Tempeln: Part II." *Orientalia* n.s. 18 (1949): 288–306.
———. "Materialien zur Viehwirtschaft in den neubabylonischen Tempeln: Part V." *Orientalia* n.s. 25 (1956): 24–38.
———. "Parerga Babylonica VII: Der §8 des Gesetzbuches Ḫammurapis in den neubabylonische Urkunden." *Archiv Orientální* 4 (1932): 327–48.
———. "Parerga Babylonica IX: Der Monstreprozeß des Gimillu, eines širku von Eanna." *Archiv Orientální* 5 (1933): 61–77.
———. "Parerga Babylonica XI: Die *maš'altu*-Urkunden im neubabylonische Strafverfahren." *Archiv Orientální* 5 (1933): 287–302.
———. Review of G. Cardascia, *Les Archives des Murašû, une famille d'hommes d'affaires Babyloniens à l'époque perse (455–403 av. J. C.). Orientalia* n.s. 23 (1954): 227–83.
———. "Ein Urteil des königlichen Gerichtes in Babylon aus der Zeit des Nabonid." Pages 219–34 in *Symbolae ad Iura Orientis Antiqui Pertinentes*

*Paulo Koschaker Dedicatae*. Edited by J. Friedrich, J. G. Lautner, and J. Miles. Studia et Documenta 2. Leiden: Brill, 1939.

———. *Zur Nachbürgschaft in den Keilschrifturkunden und in dem gräko-ägyptischen Papyri*. Sitzungsberichte der Bayerischen Akademie der Wissenschaften 6. Munich: Bayerischen Akademie der Wissenschaften, 1937.

San Nicolò, M., and H. Petschow. *Babylonische Rechtsurkunden aus dem 6. Jahrhundert v. Chr*. Abhandlungen der Bayerischen Akademie der Wissenschaften, Philosophisch-Historische Abteilung, Neue Folge 51. Munich: Bayerische Akadmie der Wissenschaften, 1960.

San Nicolò, M., and A. Ungnad. *Neu-babylonische Rechts- und Verwaltungsurkunden: Übersetzt und Erläutert*. Vol. 1. *Rechts- und Wirtschaftsurkunden der Berliner Museen aus Vorhellenistischer Zeit*. Leipzig: Hinrichs, 1935.

Sarat, A., and T. R. Kearns, "Making Peace with Violence: Robert Cover on Law and Legal Theory." Pages 211–50 in *Law's Violence*. Edited by A. Sarat and T. R. Kearns. Ann Arbor: University of Michigan Press, 1992.

———, eds. *Law's Violence*. Ann Arbor: University of Michigan Press, 1992.

Sarna, N. M. "Epic Substratum in the Prose of Job." *Journal of Biblical Literature* 76 (1957): 13–25.

———. "Legal Terminology in Psalms 3:8." Pages 175–81 in *"Sha'arei Talmon": Studies in the Bible, Qumran, and the Ancient Near East Presented to Shemaryahu Talmon*. Edited by M. Fishbane and M. Tov. Winona Lake, Ind.: Eisenbrauns, 1992.

———. "Naboth's Vineyard Revisited (1 Kings 21)." Pages 119–26 in *Tehillah le-Moshe: Biblical and Judaic Studies in Honor of Moshe Greenberg*. Edited by M. Cogan, B. L. Eichler, and J. H. Tigay. Winona Lake, Ind.: Eisenbrauns, 1997.

Sasson, J. M. "Treatment of Criminals at Mari: A Survey." Pages 90–113 in *The Treatment of Criminals in the Ancient Near East*. Edited by J. Sasson. *Journal of the Economic and Social History of the Orient* 20. Leiden: Brill, 1977.

———, ed. *Civilizations of the Ancient Near East*. 4 vols. New York: Charles Scribner's Sons, 1995.

———, ed. *Studies in Literature from the Ancient Near East Dedicated to Samuel Noah Kramer*. American Oriental Series 65. New Haven: American Oriental Society, 1984.

———, ed. *The Treatment of Criminals in the Ancient Near East*. *Journal of the Economic and Social History of the Orient* 20. Leiden: Brill, 1977.

Scafa, P. N. "'*ana pani abulli šaṭir*': Gates in the Texts of the City of Nuzi." Pages 139–62 in vol. 9 of *Studies on the Civilization and Culture of Nuzi and the Hurrians*. Edited by M. A. Morrison, D. I. Owen, et al. Winona Lake, Ind.: Eisenbrauns; Bethesda, Md.: CDL, 1981–.

Scarry, E. *The Body in Pain: The Making and Unmaking of the World*. New York: Oxford University Press, 1985.

———. "The Declaration of War: Constitutional and Unconstitutional Violence." Pages 23–76 in *Law's Violence*. Edited by A. Sarat and T. R. Kearns. Ann Arbor: University of Michigan Press, 1992.

Scharbert, J. "brk." Pages 279–308 in vol. 2 of the *Theological Dictionary of the Old Testament*. Edited by G. J. Botterweck, H. Ringgren, and H. J. Fabry. Translated by J. T. Willis, G. W. Bromiley, and D. E. Green. Grand Rapids: Eerdmans, 1974–

Scheil, V. *Actes juridiques Susiens*. Mémoires de la Mission archéologique en Iran 23. Paris: Librarie Ernest Leroux, 1930.

———. "La libération judiciaire d'un fils: donné en gage sous Neriglissar en 558 Av. J.-C." *Revue d'assyriologie et d'archéologie orientale* 12 (1915): 1–13.

———. "Notules." *Revue d'assyriologie et d'archéologie orientale* 14 (1917): 139–63.

Schenker, A. "Der Unterschied zwischen Sündopfer ḥṭ't und Schuldopfer ʾšm im Licht von Lv 5,17–19 und 5,1–6." Pages 104–12 in *Recht und Kult im Alten Testament: Achtzehn Studien*. Orbis biblicus et orientalis 172. Göttingen: Vandenhoeck & Ruprecht, 2000.

———. "Zeuge, Bürge, Garant des Rechts: Die drei Funktionen des 'Zeugen' im Alten Testament." Pages 3–6 in *Recht und Kult im Alten Testament: Achtzehn Studien*. Orbis biblicus et orientalis 172. Göttingen: Vandenhoeck & Ruprecht, 2000.

Scholes, R. *Textual Power*. New Haven: Yale University Press, 1985.

Scholnick, S. H. "Lawsuit Drama in the Book of Job." Ph.D. diss., Brandeis University, 1975.

———. "The Meaning of *Mišpāṭ* in the Book of Job." Pages 349–58 in *Sitting with Job: Selected Studies on the Book of Job*. Edited by R. B. Zuck. Grand Rapids: Baker, 1992. Reprinted from *Journal of Biblical Literature* 101 (1982): 521–29.

———. "Poetry in the Courtroom: Job 38–41." Pages 185–204 in *Directions in Hebrew Poetry*. Edited by E. Follis. Journal for the Study of the Old Testament: Supplement Series 40. Sheffield: Sheffield Academic, 1987.

Schorr, M. *Urkunde des altbabylonischen Zivil- und Prozessrechts*. Vorderasiatische Bibliothek 5. Leipzig: Hinrichs, 1913.

Schroer, S. "Wise and Counselling Women in Ancient Israel: Literary and Historical Ideals of the Personified *ḥokmâ*." Pages 67–84 in *A Feminist Companion to Wisdom Literature*. Edited by A. Brenner. Feminist Companion to the Bible 9. Sheffield: Sheffield Academic, 1995.

Schultz, C. "The Cohesive Issue of *mišpāṭ* in Job." Pages 159–76 in *Go to the Land I Will Show You: Studies in Honor of Dwight W. Young*. Edited by J. Coleson and V. H. Matthews. Winona Lake, Ind.: Eisenbrauns, 1996.

Schwartz, B. J. "The Bearing of Sin in the Priestly Literature." Pages 3–21 in *Pomegranates and Golden Bells: Studies in Biblical, Jewish, and Near Eastern Ritual, Law, and Literature in Honor of Jacob Milgrom*. Edited by D. P. Wright, D. N. Freedman, and A. Hurvitz. Winona Lake, Ind.: Eisenbrauns, 1995.

Scurlock, J., and B. R. Andersen. *Diagnoses in Assyrian and Babylonian Medicine: Ancient Sources, Translations, and Modern Medical Analyses*. Urbana: University of Illinois Press, 2005.

Seeligmann, I. L. "Zur Terminologie für das Gerichtsverfahren im Wortschatz des biblischen Hebräisch." Pages 251–87 in *Hebräische Wortforschung: Festschrift zum 80. Geburtstag von Walter Baumgartner*. Edited by B. Hartmann et al. Vetus Testamentum Supplements 16. Leiden: Brill, 1967.

Seidl, E. *Einführung in die ägyptische Rechtsgeschichte bis zum Ende des Neuen Reiches*. Ägyptologische Forschungen 10. Glückstadt: Augustin, 1951.

Seitz, C. R. "The Divine Council: Temporal Transition and New Prophecy in the Book of Isaiah." *Journal of Biblical Literature* 109 (1990): 229–47.

Shaffer, S., ed. *Comparative Criticism*. 3 vols. Cambridge: Cambridge University Press, 1981.
Shanks, H., and J. Meinhardt, eds. *Aspects of Monotheism: How God Is One*. Washington, D.C.: Biblical Archaeology Society, 1997.
Sheldon, L. J. "The Book of Job as Hebrew Theodicy: An Ancient Near Eastern Intertextual Dispute Between Cosmology and Law." Ph.D. diss., University of California Berkeley and Graduate Theological Union Joint Degree Program in Near Eastern Religion, 2002.
Shinan, A., ed. *Proceedings of the 6th World Congress of Jewish Studies*. 2 vols. Jerusalem: World Union of Jewish Studies, 1977.
Shupak, N. "A New Source for the Study of the Judiciary and Law of Ancient Egypt: 'The Tale of the Eloquent Peasant.'" *Journal of Near Eastern Studies* 51 (1992): 1–18.
Sinha, S. P. *What Is Law? The Differing Theories of Jurisprudence*. New York: Paragon, 1989.
Ska, J. L. *Introduction à la lecture du Pentateuque: Clés pour l'interprétation des cinq premiers livres de la Bible*. Le livre et le rouleau. Paris: Cerf, 2000.
———. "'Persian Imperial Authorization': Some Question Marks." Pages 161–82 in *Persia and Torah: The Theory of Imperial Authorization of the Pentateuch*. Edited by J. W. Watts. Society of Biblical Literature Symposium Series 17. Atlanta: Society of Biblical Literature, 2001.
Smick, E. M. "Another Look at the Mythological Elements in the Book of Job." *Westminster Theological Journal* 40 (1978): 213–28.
———. "Architectonics, Structural Poems, and Rhetorical Devices in the Book of Job." Pages 87–104 in *A Tribute to Gleason Archer*. Edited by W. C. Kaiser and R. F. Youngblood. Chicago: Moody Press, 1986.
Smith, M. "The Common Theology of the Ancient Near East." *Journal of Biblical Literature* 71 (1952): 135–47. Reprinted at pages 49–65 in *Essential Papers on Israel and the Ancient Near East*. Edited by F. E. Greenspahn. Essential Papers on Jewish Studies. New York: New York University Press, 1991.
———. *Palestinian Parties and Politics that Shaped the Old Testament*. 1971. 2nd ed. London: SCM, 1987.
———. "The Present State of Old Testament Studies." *Journal of Biblical Literature* 88 (1969): 19–35.
Smith, M. S. *The Laments of Jeremiah and Their Contexts: A Literary and Redactional Study of Jeremiah 11–20*. Society of Biblical Literature Monograph Series 42. Atlanta: Scholars Press, 1990.
Smith, W. K. *The Literature of Ancient Egypt*. 2nd ed. New Haven: Yale University Press, 1973.
Snaith, N. H. *The Book of Job: Its Origin and Purpose*. Studies in Biblical Theology. Second Series 11. London: SCM, 1968.
Snyder, J. W. "Babylonian Suretyship Litigation: A Case History." *Journal of Cuneiform Studies* 9 (1955): 25–28.
Soden, W. von. *Akkadisches Handwörterbuch*. 3 vols. Wiesbaden: Otto Harrassowitz, 1965, 1972, 1981.
———. "Das Fragen nach der Gerechtigkeit Gottes im Alten Orient." *Mitteilungen der Deutschen Orient-Gesellschaft* 96 (1965): 41–59.

———. Review of H. H. Figulla, *Ur Excavations, Texts IV: Business Documents of the New Babylonian Period*, *Journal of the American Oriental Society* 71 (1951): 267–68.

Soggin, J. A. *A History of Israel: From the Beginnings to the Bar Kochba Revolt, A.D. 135*. London: SCM, 1984.

Sokoloff, M. *Targum to Job from Qumran Cave XI*. Ramat-Gan: Bar-Ilan University Press, 1974.

Spar, I. "Studies in Neo-Babylonian Economic and Legal Texts." Ph.D. diss., University of Minnesota, 1972.

———. "Three Neo-Babylonian Trial Depositions from Uruk." Pages 157–72 in *Studies in Honor of Tom B. Jones*. Edited by M. A. Powell and R. H. Sack. Alter Orient und Altes Testament 203. Neukirchen-Vluyn: Neukirchener Verlag, 1979.

Speiser, E. A. "An Angelic 'Curse'" Exodus 14:20." Pages 106–12 in *Oriental and Biblical Studies: Collected Writings of E. A. Speiser*. Edited by J. J. Finkelstein and M. Greenberg. Philadelphia: University of Pennsylvania Press, 1967.

———. "Authority and Law in Mesopotamia." Pages 313–23 in *Oriental and Biblical Studies: Collected Writings of E. A. Speiser*. Edited by J. J. Finkelstein and M. Greenberg. Philadelphia: University of Pennsylvania Press, 1967.

———. "The Root *pll* in Hebrew." *Journal of Biblical Literature* 82 (1963): 301–6.

Stambovsky, P. *The Depictive Image: Metaphor and Literary Experience*. Amherst: University of Massachusetts Press, 1988.

Stamm, J. J. "Die Theodizee in Babylon und Israel." *Jaarbericht van het Vooraziatisch-Egyptisch Gezelschap (Genootschap) Ex oriente lux* 9 (1944): 99–107.

Steiner, R. C. "The *mbqr* at Qumran, the *episkopos* in the Athenian Empire, and the Meaning of *lbqr'* in Ezra 7:14: On the Relation of Ezra's Mission to the Persian Legal Project." *Journal of Biblical Literature* 120 (2001): 623–46.

Steinmann, A. E. "The Graded Numerical Sayings in Job." Pages 288–97 in *Fortunate the Eyes That See: Essays in Honor of David Noel Freedman in Celebration of his Seventieth Birthday*. Edited by A. B. Beck, A. H. Bartelt, P. R. Raabe, and C. A. Franke. Grand Rapids: Eerdmans, 1995.

Sperling, D. "The Akkadian Legal Term *dinu u dababu*." *Journal of the Ancient Near Eastern Society of Columbia University* 1 (1968): 35–40.

Stevenson, W. B. *Critical Notes on the Hebrew Text of the Poem of Job*. Glasgow University Oriental Society. Aberdeen: Aberdeen University Press, 1951.

———. *The Poem of Job: A Literary Study with a New Translation*. Schweich Lectures of the British Academy 1943. London: British Academy (Oxford University Press), 1947.

Stewart, D. T. "A Comparison of the Legal Tradition of Job's Oath of Clearance and Ancient Near Eastern Legal Codes." Paper presented at the annual meeting of the Society of Biblical Literature. Washington, D.C., November 22, 1992.

Stier, F. *Das Buch Ijjob, hebräisch und deutsch*. Munich: Kösel, 1954.

Stigers, H. G. "Neo- and Late Babylonian Business Documents from the John Frederick Lewis Collection." *Journal of Cuneiform Studies* 28 (1978): 3–59.

Stol, M. *Epilepsy in Babylonia*. Cuneiform Monographs 2. Groningen: Styx, 1993.

———. "Eine Prozeßurkunde über 'falsches Zeugnis.'" Pages 333–39 in *Marchands, diplomates et empereurs: Etudes sur la civilisation mésopotamienne offertes à Paul Garelli*. Edited by D. Charpin and F. Joannès. Paris: Éditions Recherche sur les Civilisations, 1991.

———. "Psychosomatic Suffering in Ancient Mesopotamia." Pages 57–68 in *Mesopotamian Magic: Textual, Historical, and Interpretive Perspectives*. Edited by T. Abusch and K. van der Toorn. Groningen: Styx, 1999.

Stol, M., and S. P. Vleeming, eds. *The Care of the Elderly in the Ancient Near East*. Studies in the History and Culture of the Ancient Near East 14. Leiden: Brill, 1998.

Stolper, M. W. *Entrepreneurs and Empire: The Murašû Archive, The Murašû Firm, and Persian Rule in Babylonia*. Uitgaven van het Nederlands Historisch-Archaeologisch Instituut te Istanbul 54. Leiden: Nederlands Instituut voor het Nabije Oosten, 1985.

———. "The Genealogy of the Murašu Family." *Journal of Cuneiform Studies* 28 (1976): 189–200.

———. "The Governor of Babylon and Across-the-River in 486 B.C." *Journal of Near Eastern Studies* 4 (1989): 283–305.

———. "Late Achaemenid Texts from Dilbat." *Iraq* 54 (1992): 122–25.

———. "Management and Politics in Later Achaemenid Babylonia: New Texts from the Murašû Archive." Ph.D. diss., University of Michigan, 1974.

———. "No Harm Done: on Late Achaemenid *pirku* Guarantees." Pages 467–78 in *Assyriologica et Semitica: Festschrift für Joachim Oelsner anläßlich seines 65. Geburtstages am 18. Februar 1997*. Edited by J. Marzahn and H. Neumann. Alter Orient und Altes Testament 252. Münster: Ugarit, 2000.

Stover, E., and E. Nightingale. *The Breaking of Minds and Bodies*. New York: Freeman, 1985.

Strassmaier, J. N. *Inschriften von Cambyses, König von Babylon (529–521 v. Chr.)*. Leipzig: Eduard Pfeiffer, 1890.

———. *Inschriften von Cyrus, König von Babylon (538–529 v. Chr.)*. Leipzig: Eduard Pfeiffer, 1890.

———. *Inschriften von Darius, König von Babylon (521–485 v. Chr.)*. Leipzig: Eduard Pfeiffer, 1897.

———. *Inschriften von Nabonidus, König von Babylon (555–538 v. Chr.)*. Leipzig: Eduard Pfeiffer, 1889.

———. *Inschriften von Nabuchodonosor, König von Babylon (604–561 v. Chr.)*. Leipzig: Eduard Pfeiffer, 1889.

Sukenik, E. L. *The Dead Sea Scrolls of the Hebrew University*. Jerusalem: Magnes, 1955.

Sutherland, R. *Putting God on Trial: The Biblical Book of Job*. Victoria, B.C.: Trafford, 2004.

Szubin, H. Z., and B. Porten. "Litigation Concerning Abandoned Property at Elephantine." *Journal of Near Eastern Studies* 42 (1983): 279–84.

Tabor, J. D. "Martyr, Martyrdom." Pages 574–79 in vol. 4 of *The Anchor Bible Dictionary*. Edited by D. N. Freedman. 6 vols. New York: Doubleday, 1992.

Tadmor, H. "'The People' and the Kingship in Ancient Israel: The Role of Political Institutions in the Biblical Period." *Cahiers d'Historie Mondiale* 11 (1968): 3–23.

———. "Treaty and Oath in the Ancient Near East: A Historian's Approach." Pages 127–52 in *Humanizing America's Iconic Book*. Society of Biblical Literature

Biblical Scholarship in North America 6. Edited by G. Tucker and D. A. Knight. Chico, Calif.: Scholars Press, 1982.

Talmon, S. "The 'Comparative Method' in Biblical Interpretation—Principles and Problems." Pages 320–56 in *Congress Volume: Göttingen, 1977*. Vetus Testamentum Supplements 29. Leiden: Brill, 1977. Reprinted at pages 381–419 in *Essential Papers on Israel and the Ancient Near East*. Edited by F. E. Greenspahn. Essential Papers on Jewish Studies. New York: New York University Press, 1991.

Terrien, S. *Job*. Commentaire de l'Ancien Testament 13. Neuchâtel: Delachaux et Niestlé, 1963.

———. "Job as a Sage." Pages 243–62 in *The Sage in Israel and the Ancient Near East*. Edited by J. G. Gammie and L. G. Perdue. Winona Lake, Ind.: Eisenbrauns, 1990.

———. *Job: Poet of Existence*. Indianapolis: Bobbs-Merrill, 1957.

———. "Le poème de Job: Drame para-rituel du Nouvel-an?" Pages 220–35 in *Congress Volume: Rome, 1968*. Edited by G. W. Anderson et al. Vetus Testamentus Supplements 17. Leiden: Brill, 1969.

———. "Quelques remarques sur les affinities de Job avec law Deutero-Esaie." Pages 295–310 in *Volume du Congrès: Genève, 1965*. Vetus Testamentum Supplements 15. Leiden: Brill, 1965.

Terrien, S., and P. Scherer. "The Book of Job: Introduction and Exegesis." Pages 877–1198 in vol. 3 of *The Interpreter's Bible*. Edited by G. A. Buttrick et al. 12 vols. New York: Abingdon, 1951–57.

Thompson, R. C., ed. *Cuneiform Texts from Babylonian Tablets in the British Museum*. Cuneiform Texts from Babylonian Tablets in the British Museum 22. London: Trustees of the British Museum, 1906.

———, ed. *The Devils and Evil Spirits of Babylonia*. 2 vols. London: Luzac, 1903.

———, ed. *Late Babylonian Letters*. London: Luzac, 1906.

Thompson, T. A. "Historiography (Israelite)." Page 312 in vol. 3 of *The Anchor Bible Dictionary*. Edited by D. N. Freedman. 6 vols. New York: Doubleday, 1992.

Thrupp, S. C. "Editorial." *Comparative Studies in Society and History* 1 (1958/1959): 3.

Thureau-Dangin, F. *Rituels accadiens*. 1921. Innsbruck: Zeller, 1975.

Tillie, M. M. "Ascetic Body and the (Un)Making of the World of the Martyr." *Journal of the American Academy of Religion* 59 (1991): 467–79.

Toorn, K. van der. *Sin and Sanction in Israel and Mesopotamia*. Assen/Maastricht: Van Gorcum, 1985.

Tov, E. *Textual Criticism of the Hebrew Bible*. Minneapolis: Fortress, 1992.

Tremayne, A. *Records from Erech: Time of Cyrus and Cambyses (538–521 B.C.)*. Yale Oriental Series, Texts 7. New Haven: Yale University Press, 1925.

Trible, P. *God and the Rhetoric of Sexuality*. Philadelphia: Fortress, 1978.

———. *Rhetorical Criticism: Context, Method, and the Book of Jonah*. Guides to Biblical Scholarship. Minneapolis: Fortress, 1994.

Tsevat, M. "The Meaning of the Book of Job." *Hebrew Union College Annual* 37 (1966): 73–106.

Tucker, G., and D. A. Knight, eds. *Humanizing America's Iconic Book*. Society of Biblical Literature Biblical Scholarship in North America 6. Chico, Calif.: Scholars Press, 1982.

Tuplin, C. "The Administration of the Achaemenid Empire." Pages 109–58 in *Coinage and Administration in the Athenian and Persian Empires: The Ninth Oxford Symposium on Coinage and Monetary History*. Edited by I. Carradice. Biblical Archaeology Review International Series 343. Oxford: B.A.R., 1987.
Tur-Sinai (Torczyner), N. H. *The Book of Job: A New Commentary*. 2d ed. Jerusalem: Kiryath-Sepher, 1967.
———. "How Satan Came into the World." *Expository Times* 48 (1936–37): 563–65.
Ungnad, A. *Babylonian Letters of the Ḫammurapi Period*. Publications of the Babylonian Section, University Museum, University of Pennsylvania 7. Philadelphia: University of Pennsylvania, 1915.
———. *Neubabylonische Rechts- und Verwaltungsurkunden*. Vol. 1: *Glossar*. Leipzig: Hinrichs, 1937.
———. *Neubabylonische Urkunden*. 2 vols. Vorderasiatische Schriftdenkmäler der Königlichen Museen zu Berlin 4 (reprinted as 20) and 6. Leipzig: Hinrichs, 1907–8.
———. *Selected Business Documents of the Neo-Babylonian Period*. Semitic Study Series 10. Leiden: Brill, 1908.
United States Supreme Court. *Federal Rules of Evidence*. Washington, D.C.: U.S. Government Printing Office, 1991
Unterman, J. "The Socio-Legal Origin for the Image of God as Redeemer גואל of Israel." Pages 399–406 in *Pomegranates and Golden Bells: Studies in Biblical, Jewish, and Near Eastern Ritual, Law, and Literature in Honor of Jacob Milgrom*. Edited by D. P. Wright, D. N. Freedman, and A. Hurvitz. Winona Lake, Ind.: Eisenbrauns, 1995.
Vabroušek, P., and V. Souček, eds. *Šulmu: Papers on the Ancient Near East Presented at International Conference of Socialist Countries. Prague 30 September to 3 October, 1986*. Prague: Univerzita Karlova, 1988.
Vanderhooft, D. S. *The Neo-Babylonian Empire and Babylon in the Latter Prophets*. Harvard Semitic Monographs 59. Atlanta: Scholars Press, 1999.
Van Driel, G. "Care of the Elderly: The Neo-Babylonian Period." Pages 161–97 in *The Care of the Elderly in the Ancient Near East*. Edited by M. Stol and S. P. Vleeming. Studies in the History and Culture of the Ancient Near East 14. Leiden: Brill, 1998.
Van Seters, J. *In Search of History: Historiography in the Ancient World and the Origins of Biblical History*. New Haven: Yale University Press, 1983.
Vaux, R. de. *Ancient Israel: Its Life and Institutions*. Translated by J. McHugh. London: Darton, Longman, & Todd, 1961. Reprinted in Biblical Resource Series. Grand Rapids: Eerdmans, 1997.
Vawter, B. *Job and Jonah: Questioning the Hidden God*. New York: Paulist, 1983.
Veenhof, K. R. "'In Accordance with the Words of the Stele': Evidence for Old Assyrian Legislation." *Chicago-Kent Law Review* 70 (1995): 1717–44.
Veenker, R. A. "The Old Babylonian Judiciary and Legal Procedure." Ph.D. diss., Hebrew Union College–Jewish Institute of Religion, 1967.
———. "An Old Babylonian Legal Procedure for Appeal: Evidence from the *ṭuppi lā ragāmim*." *Hebrew Union College Annual* 45 (1974): 1–15.
Vermes, G. *The Complete Dead Sea Scrolls in English*. New York: Penguin, 1997.
Vermeylen, J. *Job, Ses Amis et Son Dieu*. Leiden: Brill, 1986.

Viberg, Å. *Symbols of Law: A Contextual Analysis of Legal Symbolic Acts in the Old Testament*. Coniectanea biblica: Old Testament Series 34. Stockholm: Almqvist & Wiksell, 1992.
Villiers, P. G. R. de, ed. *Like a Roaring Lion: Essays on the Bible, Church, and Demonic Powers*. Pretoria: University of South Africa, 1987.
Vorländer, H. *Mein Gott: Die Vorstellungen vom persönlichen Gott im Alten Orient und im Alten Testament*. Alter Orient und Altes Testament 23. Neukirchen-Vluyn: Neukirchener Verlag, 1975.
Wald, P. E. "Violence under the Law: A Judge's Perspective." Pages 77–103 in *Law's Violence*. Edited by A. Sarat and T. R. Kearns. Ann Arbor: University of Michigan Press, 1992.
Waldman, M. R. "'The Otherwise Unnoteworthy Year 711': A Reply to Hayden White." Pages 40–54 in *On Narrative*. Edited by W. J. T. Mitchell. Chicago: University of Chicago Press, 1981.
Waldow, H. E. von. "Social Responsibility and Social Structure in Early Israel." *Catholic Biblical Quarterly* 32 (1970): 182–204.
———. *Der Traditionsgeschichtliche Hintergrund der prophetischen Gerichtsreden*. Beihefte zur Zeitschrift für die alttestamentliche Wissenschaft 85. Berlin: de Gruyter, 1983.
Walser, G. *Beiträge zur Achämenidengeschichte*. Historia 18. Wiesbaden: Franz Steiner, 1972.
Walther, A. *Das altbabylonischen Gerichtswesen*. Leipziger semitische Studien 6/4–6. Leipzig: Hinrichs, 1917.
Waltke, B. K., and M. O'Connor, *An Introduction to Biblical Hebrew Syntax*. Winona Lake, Ind.: Eisenbrauns, 1990.
Warner, M., ed. *The Bible as Rhetoric: Studies in Biblical Persuasion and Credibility*. London: Routledge, 1990.
Warton, J. A. *Job*. Louisville: Westminster John Knox, 1999.
Waskow, A. I. *Godwrestling*. New York: Schocken Books, 1978.
Waterman, L. *Royal Correspondence of the Assyrian Empire*. University of Michigan Studies Humanistic Series 17–20. Ann Arbor: Univeristy of Michigan Press, 1930–36.
Watson, W. G. E. "Reflexes of Akkadian Incantations in Hosea." *Vetus Testamentum* 34 (1984): 242–47.
Watts, J. W., ed. *Persia and Torah: The Theory of Imperial Authorization of the Pentateuch*. Society of Biblical Literature Symposium Series 17. Atlanta: Society of Biblical Literature, 2001.
Weidner, E. "Assyrische Beschreibungen der Kriegs-Reliefs Aššurbanipals." *Archiv für Orientforschung* 8 (1932–1934): 175–203.
———. "Hochverat gegen Nebukadnezar II. Ein Grosswürdenträger vor dem Königsgericht." *Archiv für Orientforschung* 17 (1954–1956): 1–9.
Weiher, E. Von, ed. *Spätbabylonische Texte aus Uruk*. 3 vols. Ausgrabungen der Deutschen Forschungsgemeinschaft in Uruk-Warka 9–10, 12; Berlin: Mann, 1976–88.
Weinfeld, M. "Job and Its Mesopotamian Parallels—A Typological Analysis." Pages 217–26 in *Texts and Context: Old Testament and Semitic Studies for F. C. Fensham*. Edited by W. Claassen. Journal for the Study of the Old Testament: Supplement Series 48. Sheffield: Sheffield Academic, 1988.

———. "Judge and Officer in Ancient Israel and in the Ancient Near East." *Israel Oriental Studies* 7 (1977): 65–88.

———. "'Justice and Righteousness' in Israel against the Background of 'Social Reforms' in the Ancient Near East." Pages 491–519 in vol. 2 of *Mesopotamien und seine Nachbarn: Politische und kulturelle Wechselbeziehungen im Alten Vorderasien vom 4. bis 1. Jahrtausend v. Chr.* Edited by H.-J. Nissen and J. Renger. 2 vols. 25th Rencontre Assyriologique Internationale Berlin. Berlin: Dietrich Reimer, 1982.

———. *Justice and Righteousness in Israel and the Nations: Equality and Freedom in Ancient Israel in Light of Social Justice in the Ancient Near East.* Jerusalem: Magnes, 1985 (in Hebrew).

———. *Social Justice in Ancient Israel and in the Ancient Near East.* Minneapolis: Fortress, 1995.

Weisberg, D. B. *Guild Structure and Political Allegiance in Early Achaemenid Mesopotamia.* Yale Near Eastern Researches 1. New Haven: Yale University Press, 1967.

———. "Royal Women of the Neo-Babylonian Period." Pages 447–54 in *Le palais et la royauté et civilisation: Compte rendu.* Edited by P. Garelli. Compte Rendu Rencontre Assyriologique 19. Paris: Geuthner, 1974.

———. *Texts from the Time of Nebuchadnezzar.* Yale Oriental Series, Texts 17. New Haven: Yale University Press, 1980.

Weisberg, R. H. *Poethics, and Other Strategies of Law and Literature.* New York: Columbia University Press, 1992.

———. "Private Violence as Moral Action: The Law as Inspiration and Example." Pages 175–210 in *Law's Violence.* Edited by A. Sarat and T. R. Kearns. Ann Arbor: University of Michigan Press, 1992.

Weiser, A. *Das Buch Hiob.* 4th ed. Das Alte Testament Deutsch 13. Göttingen: Vandenhoeck & Ruprecht, 1963.

Weisman, Z. "The Place of the People in the Making of Law and Judgment." Pages 407–20 in *Pomegranates and Golden Bells: Studies in Biblical, Jewish, and Near Eastern Ritual, Law, and Literature in Honor of Jacob Milgrom.* Edited by D. P. Wright, D. N. Freedman, and A. Hurvitz. Winona Lake, Ind.: Eisenbrauns, 1995.

Weiss, M. *The Story of Job's Beginning: Job 1–2, A Literary Analysis.* Jerusalem: Magnes, 1983.

Wellhausen, J. Review of A. Dillmann, ed., *Kurzgefaßtes exegetisches Handbuch zum Alten Testament. Zweite Lieferung: Hiob. Jahrbuch für deutsche Theologie* 16 (1871): 552–57.

Wenham, G. J. *The Book of Leviticus.* New International Commentary on the Old Testament. Grand Rapids: Eerdmans, 1979.

Wells, B. "The Law of Testimony in the Pentateuchal Codes." Ph.D. diss., The Johns Hopkins University, 2002. Published as *The Law of Testimony in the Pentateuchal Codes.* Beihefte zur Zeitschrift für Altorientalische und Biblische Rechtsgeschichte 4. Wiesbaden: Harrassowitz, 2004.

West, R. L. "Adjudication Is Not Interpretation: Some Reservations about the Law-As-Literature Movement." *Tennessee Law Review* 54 (1987): 203–78.

Westbrook, R. "Biblical and Cuneiform Law Codes." *Revue biblique* 92 (1985): 247–65.

———. "Biblical Law." Pages 1–17 in *An Introduction to the History and Sources of Jewish Law*. Edited by N. S. Hecht et al. Oxford: Clarendon, 1996.

———. "The Character of Ancient Near Eastern Law." Pages 1–90 in vol. 1 of *A History of Ancient Near Eastern Law*. Edited by R. Westbrook. 2 vols. Handbook of Oriental Studies 72. Leiden: Brill 2003.

———. "Codification and Canonization." Pages 33–46 in *La codification des lois dans l'antiquité: Actes du Colloque de Strasbourg 27–29 Novembre 1997*. Edited by E. Lévy. Travaux du Centre de Recherche sur le Proche-Orient et la Grèce antiques 16. Paris: Boccard, 2000.

———. "Cuneiform Law Codes and the Origins of Legislation." *Zeitschrift für Assyriologie* 79 (1990): 201–22.

———. "The Deposit Law of Exodus 22,6–12." *Zeitschrift für die alttestamentliche Wissenschaft* 106 (1994): 390–403.

———. "The Enforcement of Morals in Mesopotamian Law." *Journal of the American Oriental Society* 104 (1984): 753–56.

———. "Legalistic 'Glosses' in Biblical Narratives." *Israel Law Review* 33 (1999): 787–97.

———. "Lex Talionis and Exodus 21, 22–25." *Revue biblique* 93 (1986): 54–69.

———. "A Matter of Life and Death." *Journal of the Ancient Near Eastern Society of Columbia University* 27 (1997): 61–69.

———. *Old Babylonian Marriage Law*. Archiv für Orientforschung 123. Horn: Berger, 1988.

———. "The Prohibition on Restoration of Marriage in Deuteronomy 24:1–4." Pages 387–405 in *Studies in Bible*. Edited by S. Japhet. Scripta hierosolymitana 31. Jerusalem: Magnes, 1986.

———. *Property and the Family in Biblical Law*. Journal of the Study of the Old Testament: Supplement Series 113. Sheffield: JSOT Press, 1991.

———. "Punishments and Crimes." Pages 546–56 in vol. 5 of *The Anchor Bible Dictionary*. Edited by D. N. Freedman. 6 vols. New York: Doubleday, 1992.

———. "Recensiones: Eva Dombradi, *Darstellung des Rechtsaustrags in den Altbabylonischen Prozessurkunden*." *Orientalia* n.s. 68 (1999): 122–27.

———. "Slave and Master in Ancient Near Eastern Law." *Chicago-Kent Law Review* 70 (1995): 1631–76.

———. "Social Justice in the Ancient Near East." Pages 149–63 in *Social Justice in the Ancient World*. Edited by K. Irani and M. Silver. Westport, Conn.: Greenwood, 1995.

———. *Studies in Biblical and Cuneiform Law*. Paris: Gabalda, 1988.

———. "The Trial Scene in the Iliad." *Harvard Studies in Classical Philology* 94 (1991): 53–76.

———. "What is the Covenant Code?" Pages 15–36 in *Theory and Method in Biblical and Cuneiform Law: Revision, Interpolation, and Development*. Edited by B. M. Levinson. Journal for the Study of the Old Testament: Supplement Series 181. Sheffield: Sheffield Academic, 1994.

———, ed. *A History of Ancient Near Eastern Law*. 2 vols. Handbook of Oriental Studies 72. Leiden: Brill 2003.

Westermann, C. *Basic Forms of Prophetic Speech*. Translated by H. C. White. Philadelphia: Westminster, 1967
———. "Die Begriffe für Fragen und Suchen im Alten Testament." *Kerygma und Dogma* 6 (1961): 2–30.
———. *The Structure of the Book of Job: A Form-Critical Analysis*. Translated by C. A. Muenchow. Philadelphia: Fortress, 1981.
Wharton, J. A. *Job*. Westminster Bible Companion. Louisville: Westminster/John Knox, 1999.
Whedbee, W. "The Comedy of Job." *Semeia* 7 (1977): 1–40.
White, H. "Historical Emplotment and the Problem of Historical Truth." Pages 37–53 in *Probing the Limits of Representation: Nazism and the Final Solution*. Edited by S. Friedlaender. Cambridge, Mass.: Harvard University Press, 1992.
———. *Metahistory: The Historical Imagination in Nineteenth-Century Europe*. Baltimore: Johns Hopkins University Press, 1973.
———. "The Historical Text as Literary Artifact." Pages 41–62 in *The Writing of History: Literary Form and Historical Understanding*. Edited by R. H. Canary and H. Kozicki. Madison: University of Wisconsin Press, 1978.
———. "The Question of Narrative in Contemporary Historical Theory." *History and Theory* 23 (1984): 2–42.
———. "The Value of Narrativity in the Representation of Reality." Pages 1–23 in *On Narrative*. Edited by W. J. T. Mitchell. Chicago: University of Chicago Press, 1981.
Whitelam, K. W. *The Just King: Monarchical Judicial Authority in Ancient Israel*. Journal for the Study of the Old Testament: Supplement Series 12. Sheffield: Sheffield Academic, 1979.
———. "Recreating the History of Israel." *Journal for the Study of the Old Testament* 35 (1986): 45–70.
Whybray, R. N. *The Heavenly Counsellor in Isaiah XL 13–14: A Study of the Sources of Theology of Deutero-Isaiah*. Society for Old Testament Studies Monograph Series 1. Cambridge: Cambridge University Press, 1971.
———. *The Intellectual Tradition in the Old Testament*. Beihefte zur Zeitschrift für die alttestamentliche Wissenschaft 135. Berlin: de Gruyter, 1974.
———. *Job*. Sheffield: Sheffield Academic, 1998.
Wiesehöfer, J. "'Reichsgesetz' oder 'Einzelfallgerechtigkeit'? Bemerkungen zu P. Freis These von der Achämenidischen 'Reichs-autorisation.'" *Zeitschrift für altorientalische und biblische Rechtsgeschicte* 1 (1995): 36–46.
Wilcox, J. T. *The Bitterness of Job: A Philosophical Reading*. Ann Arbor: University of Michigan Press, 1989.
Wilkinson, J. *The Bible and Healing: A Medical and Theological Commentary*. Grand Rapids: Eerdmans, 1998.
Williams, J. G. "Deciphering the Unspoken: The Theophany of Job." Pages 359–72 in *Sitting with Job: Selected Studies on the Book of Job*. Edited by R. B. Zuck. Grand Rapids: Baker, 1992. Reprinted from *Hebrew Union College Annual* 49 (1978): 59–72.
Williams, R. J. "Theodicy in the Ancient Near East." Pages 42–56 in *Theodicy in the Old Testament*. Edited by J. L. Crenshaw. Philadelphia: Fortress, 1983.

Williamson, H. G. M. *Ezra, Nehemiah*. Word Biblical Commentary 16. Waco: Word, 1985.

———. "Palestine, Administration of (Persian)." Pages 81–86 in vol. 5 of *The Anchor Bible Dictionary*. Edited by D. N. Freedman. 6 vols. New York: Doubleday, 1992.

Willis, T. M. *The Elders of the City: A Study of the Elders-Laws in Deuteronomy*. Society of Biblical Literature Monograph Series 55. Atlanta: Society of Biblical Literature, 2001.

———. *Job Translation Segments*. Waco, Tex.: World Bible Translation Center, 1995.

Wilson, E. B. "*Rîb* in Israel's Historical and Legal Traditions: A Study of the Israelite Setting of *Rîb*-Form." Ph.D. diss., Drew University, 1970.

Wiseman, D. J. *The Alalakh Tablets*. British Institute of Archaeology in Ankara Occasional Publications 2. London: British Institute of Archaeology in Ankara, 1953.

———. "A New Text of the Babylonian Poem of the Righteous Sufferer." *Anatolian Studies* 30 (1980): 101–07.

Wolde, E. van. "The Development of Job: Mrs. Job as Catalyst." Pages 201–21 in *A Feminist Companion to Wisdom Literature*. Edited by A. Brenner. Feminist Companion to the Bible 9. Sheffield: Sheffield Academic, 1995.

———. "Job 42, 1–9: The Reversal of Job." Pages 223–50 in *The Book of Job*. Edited by W. A. M. Beuken. Bibliotheca ephemeridum theologicarum lovaniensium 104. Leuven: Leuven University Press, 1994.

Wolff, H. W. *Anthropology of the Old Testament*. Translated by M. Kohl. Philadelphia: Fortress, 1974.

———, ed. *Gottes Recht: Gesammelte Studien zum Recht im Alten Testament*. Theologische Bücherei 12. Munich: Kaiser, 1961.

Wright, D. P., D. N. Freedman, and A. Hurvitz, eds. *Pomegranates and Golden Bells: Studies in Biblical, Jewish, and Near Eastern Ritual, Law, and Literature in Honor of Jacob Milgrom*. Winona Lake, Ind.: Eisenbrauns, 1995.

Wright, G. E. "The Lawsuit of God: A Form-Critical Study of Deuteronomy 32." Pages 26–67 in *Israel's Prophetic Heritage: Essays in Honor of James Muilenburg*. Edited by B. W. Anderson and W. Harrelson. New York: Harper & Brothers, 1962.

———. *The Old Testament Against its Environment*. Studies in Biblical Theology 2. London: SCM, 1950.

Wunsch, C. *Das Egibi-Archive I: Die Felder und Gärten*. 2 vols. Cuneiform Monographs 20A–B. Groningen: Styx, 2000.

———. "Neubabylonische Geschäftsleute und ihre Beziehungen zu Palast- und Tempelverwaltungen: Das Beispiel der Familie Egibi." Pp. 95–118 in *Interdependency of Institutions and Private Entrepreneurs: Proceedings of the Second MOS Symposium (Leiden 1998)*. Edited by A. C. V. M. Bongenaar. Istanbul: Netherlands Historisch-Archaeologisch Instituut, 2000.

———. "Die Richter des Nabonid." Pages 557–98 in *Assyriologica et Semitica: Festschrift für Joachim Oelsner anläßlich seines 65. Geburtstages am 18. Februar 1997*. Edited by J. Marzahn and H. Neumann. Alter Orient und Altes Testament 252. Münster: Ugarit, 2000.

———. "Eine Richterurkunde aus der Zeit Neriglissars." Pp. 241–54 in *Arbor*

*Scientiae: Estudios del Proximo Oriente Antiguo dedicados a Gregorio del Olmo Lete con ocasión de su 65 aniversario.* Edited by J. Sanmartín et al. *Aula Orientalis* 17–18 (1999–2000).

———. "Und die Richter Berieten . . . : Streitfälle in Babylon aus der Zeit Neriglissars und Nabonids." *Archiv für Orientforschung* 44–45 (1997–98): 59–100.

———, ed. *Mining the Archives: Festschrift for Christopher Walker on the Occasion of his 60th Birthday, 4 October 2002.* Babylonische Archive 1. Dresden: ISLET, 2002.

Yamauchi, E. M. *Persia and the Bible.* Grand Rapids: Baker, 1990.

Yaron, R. *Introduction to the Law of the Aramaic Papyri.* Oxford: Clarendon, 1961.

Younger, K. L. *Ancient Conquest Accounts: A Study in Ancient Near Eastern and Biblical History Writing.* Journal for the Study of the Old Testament: Supplement Series 98. Sheffield: Sheffield Academic, 1990.

Younger, K. L., W. W. Hallo, and B. F. Batto, eds. *The Biblical Canon in Comparative Perspective: Scripture in Context IV.* Ancient Near Eastern Texts and Studies 11. Lewiston, N.Y.: Edwin Mellen, 1991.

Zadok, R. *The Jews in Babylonia during the Chaldean and Achaemenian Periods according to the Babylonian Sources.* Haifa: Haifa University, 1979.

———. *On West Semites in Babylonia during the Chaldean and Achaemenian Periods: An Onomastic Study.* Jerusalem: Wanaarta, 1977.

———. "The Representation of Foreigners in Neo- and Late-Babylonian Legal Documents (Eighth through Second Centuries B.C.E.)," Pages 471–589 in *Judah and the Judeans in the Neo-Babylonian Period.* Edited by O. Lipschits and J. Blenkinsopp. Winona Lake, Ind.: Eisenbrauns, 2003.

Zaharopoulos, D. *Theodore of Mospuestia on the Bible: A Study of His Old Testament Exegesis.* New York: Paulist, 1989.

Zakovitch, Y. "Psalm 82 and Biblical Exegesis," Pages 213–228 in *Sefer Moshe: The Moshe Weinfeld Jubilee Volume.* Edited by C. Cohen, A. Hurvitz, and S. M. Paul. Winona Lake, Ind.: Eisenbrauns, 2004.

Zawadzki, S. "A Contribution to the Understanding of *širkūtu* in the Light of a Text from the Ebabbar Archive." *Archiv für Orientforschung* 24 (1997): 226–30.

Zimmerli, W. "Zur Struktur der altestamentlichen Weisheit." *Zeitschrift für die alttestamentliche Wissenschaft* 51 (1933): 177–204.

Zimmern, H. *Die Keilinschriften und das Alte Testament.* 3rd ed. Berlin: Ruether & Reichard, 1903.

Zuck, R. B. *Sitting with Job: Selected Studies on the Book of Job.* Grand Rapids: Baker, 1992.

Zuckerman, B. "Job, Targum of." Pages 868–71 in vol. 3 of *The Anchor Bible Dictionary.* Edited by D. N. Freedman. 6 vols. New York: Doubleday, 1992.

———. *Job the Silent: A Study in Historical Counterpoint.* New York: Oxford University Press, 1991.

# Index of Citations

*Hebrew Bible*

**Genesis**
| | |
|---|---:|
| 1:2 | 173-74 |
| 1:4 | 174 |
| 1:5 | 174 |
| 1:18 | 174 |
| 1:31 | 174 |
| 2:2 | 174 |
| 3:19 | 173 |
| 4:24 | 261 |
| 6:2 | 103 |
| 6:4 | 103 |
| 11:6 | 210, 259 |
| 18:19 | 149, 214 |
| 18:23-25 | 168 |
| 19:29 | 175 |
| 21:25-27 | 191-92 |
| 22:1 | 107 |
| 25:22 | 108 |
| 26:21 | 163 |
| 26:23 | 98 |
| 27:41 | 163 |
| 29:25-28 | 4 |
| 31:22 | 159 |
| 31:25-55 | 138, 196 |
| 31:27 | 138 |
| 31:30 | 138 |
| 31:31 | 149 |
| 31:31-32 | 138 |
| 31:32-35 | 124 |
| 31:33-35 | 138 |
| 31:36-37 | 158 |
| 31:36-42 | 138, 146 |
| 31:37 | 166 |
| 31:42 | 166 |
| 31:43-44 | 138 |
| 31:44 | 158 |
| 31:45-54 | 138 |
| 32:26 | 193 |
| 32:26-27 | 193 |
| 32:27 | 193 |
| 32:28-30 | 193 |
| 37:26 | 153 |
| 38:24 | 159 |
| 39:14 | 107, 171 |
| 39:17 | 113, 123 |
| 39:17-19 | 4 |
| 39:20 | 123 |
| 41:1 | 123, 257 |
| 42:6-17 | 128 |
| 42:7 | 128 |
| 42:7-17 | 4 |
| 42:9 | 260 |
| 42:12 | 128 |
| 42:14 | 108 |
| 42:15 | 128 |
| 42:15-16 | 108 |
| 42:15-20 | 123 |
| 42:21 | 209 |
| 43:12 | 186 |
| 43:15 | 261 |
| 44:8-13 | 124 |
| 44:16 | 141 |
| 44:18-34 | 209 |
| 49:23 | 163 |
| 50:13 | 163 |

**Exodus**
| | |
|---|---:|
| 15:25 | 107 |
| 15:26 | 24 |
| 16:4 | 107 |
| 18:15 | 108, 203 |
| 18:21 | 153 |
| 20:5 | 201 |
| 20:13 | 194 |
| 20:16 | 158 |
| 20:20 | 107 |
| 21:18-19 | 106 |
| 22:1 | 105 |
| 22:2 | 105 |
| 22:3 | 10, 212 |
| 22:6 | 261 |
| 22:6-12 | 139 |
| 22:8 | 261 |
| 22:27 | 104 |
| 23:1-2 | 194 |
| 23:7 | 158 |
| 23:8 | 151 |
| 23:20-26 | 24 |
| 28:43 | 236 |
| 32:13 | 98, 244 |

**Leviticus**
| | |
|---|---:|
| 4:1-35 | 133 |
| 4:22 | 186 |
| 4:27 | 186 |
| 5:1 | 116, 159, 194, 236 |
| 5:1-4 | 133, 149 |
| 5:2-4 | 210 |
| 5:2-6 | 210 |

340  Index of Citations

**Leviticus** (*cont.*)
| | |
|---|---:|
| 5:5-6 | 210 |
| 5:14-15 | 133 |
| 5:15 | 186 |
| 5:17 | 236 |
| 5:18 | 186 |
| 5:21 | 149 |
| 5:21-26 | 149 |
| 10:2 | 119 |
| 17:16 | 236 |
| 19:13 | 149 |
| 19:17-18 | 110 |
| 20:2-5 | 116 |
| 20:9 | 105 |
| 20:11 | 105 |
| 20:12 | 105 |
| 20:13 | 105 |
| 20:14 | 113 |
| 20:16 | 105 |
| 20:17 | 105 |
| 22:6 | 230 |
| 24:10-23 | 4, 105 |
| 24:11 | 104 |
| 24:12 | 123 |
| 24:14 | 104 |
| 24:15 | 236 |
| 24:15-16 | 236, 244 |
| 24:16 | 104 |
| 24:23 | 104 |
| 26:14-16 | 24 |
| 26:14-42 | 133 |
| 26:18 | 261 |
| 26:24 | 261 |
| 26:28 | 261 |

**Numbers**
| | |
|---|---:|
| 5:6-7 | 133, 149, 202 |
| 5:11-31 | 4 |
| 5:31 | 236 |
| 12:6 | 121 |
| 12:7-8 | 98 |
| 14:23 | 104 |
| 14:24 | 98 |
| 14:34 | 236 |
| 15:22-29 | 133 |
| 15:24-29 | 186 |
| 15:30 | 105, 133 |
| 15:32-34 | 123 |
| 15:32-36 | 4 |
| 16:30 | 104 |
| 16:35 | 119 |
| 18:22 | 236 |
| 22:32 | 163 |
| 30:16 | 236 |
| 35:9-35 | 106 |
| 35:11 | 186 |
| 35:15 | 186 |
| 35:27 | 105 |
| 35:30 | 194, 219 |

**Deuteronomy**
| | |
|---|---:|
| 1:16 | 166 |
| 4:42 | 186 |
| 5:9 | 201 |
| 8:2 | 107-8, 216 |
| 8:2-3 | 124 |
| 8:16 | 107, 124 |
| 9:1-13 | 106 |
| 9:27 | 98 |
| 10:17-18 | 155 |
| 13:4 | 107, 217 |
| 13:7-12 | 219 |
| 13:8 | 205 |
| 13:9 | 116 |
| 13:14 | 107 |
| 13:15 | 108 |
| 16:19 | 153 |
| 17:2-4 | 101 |
| 17:2-7 | 61, 219 |
| 18:11 | 108 |
| 19:10 | 105 |
| 19:11 | 103 |
| 19:15 | 219 |
| 19:15-19 | 135 |
| 19:16-21 | 158 |
| 19:18 | 108, 194 |
| 21:8 | 105 |
| 21:18-21 | 141 |
| 21:19 | 97, 123 |
| 22:8 | 105, 200 |
| 22:13-21 | 158 |
| 22:14 | 197 |
| 22:15 | 97 |
| 22:21 | 105 |
| 22:24 | 97 |
| 22:28 | 106 |
| 24:16 | 208 |
| 25:8 | 141 |
| 27:18 | 186 |
| 28:22 | 23 |
| 28:29 | 149 |
| 28:33 | 153 |
| 29:17-19 | 110 |
| 31:20 | 104 |
| 31:21 | 194 |
| 32:21 | 105, 230 |
| 32:39 | 204 |
| 33:8 | 108, 226 |

**Joshua**
| | |
|---|---:|
| 1:2 | 98 |
| 1:7 | 98 |
| 2:14 | 186 |
| 2:20 | 159 |
| 7:15 | 105 |
| 7:19-20 | 132 |
| 7:19-26 | 4, 133 |
| 7:20 | 141, 209 |
| 7:24-25 | 130 |
| 8:23 | 130 |
| 8:29 | 97 |
| 20:3 | 186 |
| 20:4 | 97, 211 |
| 20:9 | 186 |

**Judges**
| | |
|---|---:|
| 1:6 | 130 |
| 2:22 | 107, 124 |
| 2:22-3:4 | 124 |
| 3:1 | 124 |
| 6:29 | 108, 135 |
| 12:6 | 130 |
| 16:21 | 130 |
| 16:26-31 | 99 |
| 20:6 | 105 |
| 20:22 | 191 |
| 21:20-23 | 193 |
| 21:23 | 193 |

**1 Samuel**
| | |
|---|---:|
| 2:7 | 252 |
| 3:1-4:22 | 105 |
| 3:14 | 105, 111 |
| 8:3 | 154 |

Index of Citations  341

| | | | | | | |
|---|---|---|---|---|---|---|
| 8:13 | 153, 213 | 11:23 | 163 | **Isaiah** | | |
| 9:9 | 108 | 11:25 | 163 | 1:17 | | 154 |
| 10:24 | 99 | 14:5 | 108 | 2:4 | | 166 |
| 12:3 | 107-8, 149, | 14:6 | 192, 208 | 2:17 | | 252 |
| | 151-53, | 14:8 | 98 | 3:13-14 | | 151 |
| | 195, 216 | 15:29 | 98 | 3:13-15 | | 165 |
| 12:3-4 | 153 | 20:7 | 141 | 3:14 | | 149 |
| 12:4 | 142, 151 | 20:39-40 | 150 | 3:14-15 | | 152-53 |
| 12:17 | 206 | 21:1-16 | 4 | 5:24 | 104, 135, 206 | |
| 14:33 | 159 | 21:1-29 | 105, 158 | 6:1 | | 100 |
| 15:12-35 | 133 | 21:13 | 104, 153, 219 | 8:19 | | 108 |
| 22:6 | 121 | 21:19 | 158 | 8:19-22 | | 105 |
| 22:6-23 | 4 | 21:19-24 | 158 | 8:21 | | 104, 213 |
| 22:11-16 | 165 | 21:23-24 | 158 | 9:3-20 | | 105 |
| 22:12 | 121, 212, 232 | 21:27-29 | 133, 158 | 9:16 | | 104-5 |
| 22:13 | 121, 232 | 22:5 | 203, 207, 228 | 10:2 | | 154 |
| 22:14 | 141 | 22:7 | 108 | 14:13 | | 100 |
| 22:15 | 197 | 22:8 | 108 | 14:21 | | 201 |
| 23:26 | 130 | 22:20-23 | 119 | 16:5 | | 149 |
| 26:17-24 | 121 | 22:22 | 119 | 20:3 | | 98 |
| 26:18-19 | 120 | 22:26-27 | 123 | 22:20 | | 98, 119 |
| 26:21 | 186 | | | 28:7 | | 186 |
| 29:4 | 163 | **2 Kings** | | 28:16 | | 107 |
| | | 1:2 | 108 | 29:13-14 | | 110 |
| **2 Samuel** | | 1:3 | 108 | 29:21 | | 97 |
| 4:10 | 130 | 1:6 | 108 | 32:6 | | 104 |
| 7:5 | 98 | 1:16 | 108, 203 | 37:17 | | 104 |
| 12:1-6 | 149 | 3:11 | 108 | 37:23 | | 104 |
| 12:4 | 151 | 3:16-28 | 4 | 37:24 | | 104 |
| 12:1-14 | 150 | 6:26 | 132, 150, | 40:2 | | 261 |
| 12:1-24 | 155 | | 215-16 | 41:8-9 | | 98 |
| 13:12 | 105 | 8:8 | 217 | 44:1-2 | | 98 |
| 13:13 | 105 | 9:1-10:17 | 158 | 44:24 | | 175 |
| 14:2-22 | 150 | 9:25-26 | 105, 158 | 45:4 | | 98 |
| 14:4-11 | 4 | 9:26 | 158 | 48:10 | | 107, 124 |
| 14:12 | 150 | 9:36 | 98 | 49:3 | | 98 |
| 15:2 | 97 | 9:36-37 | 158 | 51:14 | | 162 |
| 15:3 | 166 | 10:8 | 97 | 52:13 | | 98 |
| 15:4 | 136 | 10:9 | 139, 161 | 53:7 | | 141 |
| 21:1-10 | 201 | 10:10 | 98 | 56:11 | | 153 |
| 24:1-25 | 133 | 14:25 | 98 | 57:17 | | 153 |
| | | 18:5 | 99, 214 | 58:9 | | 161, 201 |
| **1 Kings** | | 19:4-38 | 105 | 59:4 | | 141 |
| 2:9-13 | 101 | 19:16 | 104 | 61:8 | | 149 |
| 2:41 | 159 | 19:22 | 104 | 65:7 | | 105 |
| 5:18 | 163 | 22:18 | 108 | | | |
| 8:47 | 209 | 25:12 | 33 | **Jeremiah** | | |
| 11:14 | 163 | 26:5 | 130 | 2:4 | | 121 |

## Index of Citations

**Jeremiah** (*cont.*)
2:23 — 206
2:29 — 138
3:2 — 206
4:23-26 — 171
5:1 — 101
6:13 — 153
6:15 — 216, 237
6:22-30 — 124
6:27 — 107-8, 216
7:6 — 132, 134, 149, 151, 163, 173, 239
8:10 — 153
9:1-11 — 124
9:6 — 108, 175, 220
10:21 — 203
11:20 — 107-8, 215
12:1 — 139, 156, 169
12:2-3 — 110
12:3 — 107-8
17:10 — 107-8, 217, 220
17:18 — 261
20:7 — 159
20:7-10 — 159
20:12 — 107-8, 159, 211
21:2 — 108
21:12 — 149, 151
22:17 — 149, 153-54
23:14-15 — 116
23:17 — 104
23:18 — 100
23:22 — 99
25:9 — 98
26:1-24 — 4
26:10-11 — 75
26:18 — 229
27:6 — 98, 183
29:21-23 — 105
29:23 — 105
31:29 — 189, 201
31:30 — 208
32:2-3 — 123
37:7 — 108
37:13 — 121, 239
37:14 — 130
37:14-16 — 123
37:20 — 121, 243
38:7 — 97
39:5 — 130, 139
43:3 — 121
49:8 — 237
49:19 — 166
50:20 — 135
50:31 — 237
50:31-34 — 135
50:44 — 166
52:9 — 130

**Ezekiel**
14:3 — 108
14:7 — 108
14:10 — 236
14:20 — 5
18:1-32 — 208
18:18 — 149
18:29 — 208
20:1-2 — 203
20:1-4 — 203
20:3 — 108
20:27 — 105
20:31 — 108
21:18 — 106-7, 141
22:7 — 151
22:12 — 149, 153-54
22:13 — 153
22:27 — 153
22:29 — 149, 212
28:8 — 162
33:31 — 153
34:6 — 186
44:12 — 236
45:20 — 186

**Hosea**
2:12 — 105
4:1-2 — 151
4:4 — 99, 141
5:11 — 149, 153
6:1 — 204
6:9 — 113
9:8 — 163
12:3 — 193
12:5 — 193, 217

**Amos**
4:1 — 149, 151, 153
4:13 — 175
5:6 — 203
5:8 — 175
5:10 — 212
5:12 — 97
5:15 — 97
7:4 — 105, 141

**Jonah**
1:4 — 119
2:7 — 162

**Micah**
1:2 — 121
2:2 — 149, 151
3:2-3 — 149, 151
4:3 — 166
6:1 — 121
6:1-5 — 229
6:2 — 141
7:19 — 205

**Habakkuk**
2:1 — 141
2:9 — 153

**Haggai**
2:23 — 98

**Zechariah**
3:1-2 — 163
3:1-5 — 100
4:7 — 253
4:10 — 101
7:10 — 110, 149
8:16 — 97
8:17 — 110, 158
12:4 — 178
13:9 — 107

**Malachi**
3:5 — 149

**Psalms**
1:21 — 181
4:2 — 141, 201
5:2 — 121
7:6-11 — 151

| | | | | | | |
|---|---|---|---|---|---|---|
| 7:8 | 134, 201 | 71:13 | 163 | 1:1 | 96, 117, 261 |
| 7:9-12 | 108 | 72:4 | 149, 152 | 1:2-3 | 97 |
| 7:16 | 162 | 72:14 | 221 | 1:3 | 125 |
| 8:5 | 205 | 73:8 | 149 | 1:5 | 98, 104, 111, 128 |
| 9:11 | 165, 175 | 74:10 | 104 | | |
| 10:3 | 104, 153 | 74:18 | 104 | 1:6 | 103, 127 |
| 10:12 | 105 | 74:22 | 104 | 1:7-12 | 127 |
| 11:4 | 178 | 76:9 | 151 | 1:8 | 98-99, 103 |
| 11:5 | 107 | 77:3 | 203 | 1:9 | 98, 100, 120, 162 |
| 14:1 | 104 | 79:8 | 205 | | |
| 16:10 | 162 | 81:8 | 107 | 1:11 | 104 |
| 17:1 | 121 | 82 | 167 | 1:12 | 103, 118-20, 125 |
| 17:2 | 151 | 82:1 | 100, 175 | | |
| 17:2-3 | 135 | 82:1-5 | 175 | 1:13 | 127-28 |
| 17:11 | 105 | 82:2 | 153 | 1:16 | 119 |
| 17:22 | 105 | 82:5 | 175 | 1:19 | 119 |
| 18 | 155 | 89:6 | 100 | 1:20 | 96, 98, 131 |
| 19:10 | 97 | 89:8 | 100 | 1:21 | 98 |
| 27:12 | 135, 216 | 89:15 | 151 | 1:22 | 130 |
| 28:3-4 | 151 | 91:8 | 178 | 2 | 99 |
| 30:9 | 209 | 94:1-3 | 160 | 2:1 | 102-3 |
| 32:3-5 | 133 | 94:2-4 | 151 | 2:3 | 98-99, 119-20, 122, 162, 183-84, 248 |
| 34:11 | 203 | 94:5 | 152 | | |
| 35:7 | 162 | 94:10 | 166 | | |
| 35:10 | 149 | 94:12-13 | 204 | | |
| 35:11 | 135 | 94:13 | 162 | 2:5 | 104, 120 |
| 35:23 | 136 | 94:16 | 103 | 2:6 | 118-19 |
| 38:3-8 | 24 | 96:10 | 175 | 2:7 | 103, 120, 125, 173 |
| 38:14-15 | 141 | 97:2 | 151 | | |
| 38:15 | 141 | 99:1-4 | 151 | 2:8 | 131 |
| 38:21 | 163 | 101 | 155 | 2:9 | 98, 155, 187 |
| 44:10 | 139 | 103:6 | 149 | 2:10 | 97-98, 104, 187 |
| 44:22 | 107-8, 110 | 105:4 | 203 | 3 | 96, 99, 126, 132, 158, 171 |
| 49:10 | 162 | 109:4 | 163 | | |
| 50:4 | 141 | 109:6 | 163 | 3–29 | 188 |
| 50:7 | 142, 194 | 109:20 | 163 | 3–31 | 196 |
| 51:16 | 105 | 109:29 | 163 | 3:1 | 132, 158, 196 |
| 53:2 | 104 | 119:36 | 153 | 3:2 | 194 |
| 55:3 | 163 | 119:137 | 151 | 3:3-13 | 171 |
| 55:18 | 140 | 119:153-59 | 151 | 3:4 | 124 |
| 55:24 | 162 | 119:155 | 203 | 3:8 | 132 |
| 56:1 | 130, 153 | 143:1 | 121 | 3:9 | 174 |
| 59:6 | 237 | 143:2 | 152, 201 | 3:11-19 | 170 |
| 62:11 | 149 | 146:7 | 149, 151 | 3:19-30 | 189 |
| 64:2 | 140 | | | 3:20 | 174 |
| 66:10 | 107 | **Job** | | 3:20-26 | 171 |
| 69:5 | 149 | 1 | 7, 120 | 4–27 | 96 |
| 69:33 | 203 | 1-2 | 96, 122 | 4:8 | 200 |

## 344  Index of Citations

**Job** (*cont.*)

| Reference | Page(s) |
|---|---|
| 4:8-9 | 200 |
| 4:10-11 | 164 |
| 4:12-21 | 142 |
| 4:17-19 | 10, 212 |
| 4:17-21 | 200-201 |
| 4:18 | 197 |
| 5:1 | 10, 142, 165, 201, 213, 242 |
| 5:2 | 201 |
| 5:2-3 | 201 |
| 5:3 | 200 |
| 5:4 | 201, 208 |
| 5:6 | 202 |
| 5:7 | 202 |
| 5:8 | 35, 141, 175, 202-3 |
| 5:12-14 | 212 |
| 5:15 | 164 |
| 5:17 | 204-5, 213, 216 |
| 5:17-18 | 205 |
| 5:18 | 163 |
| 5:19-26 | 206 |
| 5:27 | 195, 216 |
| 6 | 216-17 |
| 6:2-3 | 131 |
| 6:4 | 103, 131 |
| 6:6-7 | 133 |
| 6:8-9 | 156, 184 |
| 6:10 | 184 |
| 6:11 | 173 |
| 6:13 | 103 |
| 6:18-19 | 216 |
| 6:24 | 186, 230 |
| 6:28-30 | 187 |
| 6:29 | 219 |
| 7:3-4 | 131, 134, 174 |
| 7:5 | 131, 133 |
| 7:7 | 132, 215 |
| 7:8 | 173 |
| 7:11 | 140 |
| 7:12 | 161, 173, 175 |
| 7:15-16 | 132, 191 |
| 7:16 | 173, 208 |
| 7:17 | 134, 160 |
| 7:18 | 108, 237 |
| 7:20 | 131, 137 |
| 7:20-21 | 178 |
| 7:21 | 173 |
| 8:1 | 194 |
| 8:2 | 218 |
| 8:11-12 | 214 |
| 9 | 190 |
| 9:1 | 194 |
| 9:2-4 | 142 |
| 9:3-35 | 233 |
| 9:5-13 | 175 |
| 9:8 | 175 |
| 9:9 | 175 |
| 9:12 | 130, 160 |
| 9:12-15 | 130 |
| 9:14-15 | 167, 178 |
| 9:14-32 | 177 |
| 9:15 | 183, 192, 194 |
| 9:17 | 131, 163, 175 |
| 9:19 | 165, 182 |
| 9:20 | 162, 183 |
| 9:21 | 132, 183 |
| 9:23 | 169 |
| 9:25 | 132 |
| 9:27-29 | 140, 178, 182 |
| 9:30-31 | 162 |
| 9:32 | 234 |
| 9:32-35 | 242, 245 |
| 9:33 | 166, 228, 234 |
| 9:35 | 131, 134 |
| 10:1 | 132, 140, 176 |
| 10:2 | 155, 172, 179 |
| 10:3 | 156 |
| 10:4-5 | 165 |
| 10:4-8 | 135 |
| 10:7 | 166, 182, 234, 242 |
| 10:8 | 162, 175 |
| 10:16 | 164, 176 |
| 10:16-17 | 164 |
| 10:17 | 164 |
| 10:20 | 172-73, 208 |
| 10:20-22 | 173, 191 |
| 10:21 | 173 |
| 11 | 10 |
| 11:3 | 104 |
| 11:4 | 10, 212 |
| 11:10 | 143, 160 |
| 11:15 | 10, 131, 212 |
| 11:16 | 131 |
| 11:17 | 132, 134 |
| 11:18 | 132 |
| 11:18-19 | 131, 134 |
| 11:19 | 99 |
| 12 | 216 |
| 12:3 | 216 |
| 12:4 | 183 |
| 12:6 | 169 |
| 12:7-15 | 174 |
| 12:9-10 | 162 |
| 12:10 | 173 |
| 12:12 | 217-18 |
| 12:13-15 | 174 |
| 12:13-25 | 175 |
| 12:14 | 160 |
| 12:15 | 175 |
| 12:16 | 186 |
| 12:16-13:13 | 144 |
| 12:24 | 171, 174 |
| 13 | 7, 190 |
| 13:2 | 216 |
| 13:3 | 140 |
| 13:6 | 140-41, 195 |
| 13:7-9 | 218 |
| 13:7-11 | 217 |
| 13:8 | 231 |
| 13:10 | 217 |
| 13:11 | 218 |
| 13:13 | 217-18 |
| 13:15 | 6, 143 |
| 13:17 | 195 |
| 13:18 | 103, 181, 242 |
| 13:22 | 142, 144, 179, 182 |
| 13:23 | 179 |
| 13:24 | 162, 165, 180, 226 |
| 13:26 | 161-62, 180, 181 |
| 13:27 | 130, 134, 160, 227 |
| 14 | 172-73 |
| 14:1-3 | 136 |
| 14:3 | 136 |
| 14:5-6 | 172 |
| 14:7-12 | 173 |

Index of Citations 345

| | | | | | | | |
|---|---|---|---|---|---|---|---|
| 15:1 | 194 | 19:4 | 186 | 22 | 9 |
| 15:2-3 | 215-16 | 19:5 | 216-17 | 22:1-20 | 9 |
| 15:4 | 206 | 19:6 | 180 | 22:9-11 | 141 |
| 15:5-6 | 206 | 19:9 | 132, 163 | 22:16 | 212 |
| 15:8 | 99, 206 | 19:10 | 132 | 22:20 | 212 |
| 15:12 | 207 | 19:10-12 | 131 | 22:21-30 | 10, 212 |
| 15:13 | 200 | 19:12 | 130 | 22:23 | 10, 212 |
| 15:14-16 | 200-201 | 19:13-18 | 134 | 22:26 | 212, 222 |
| 15:17 | 195 | 19:13-19 | 163 | 23:1 | 194 |
| 15:20-35 | 207 | 19:15 | 192 | 23:2 | 131, 140 |
| 15:30 | 214 | 19:16-20 | 180 | 23:3-7 | 196 |
| 16:1 | 194 | 19:18 | 132 | 23:3-9 | 165 |
| 16:2 | 217 | 19:20 | 131, 133, 164 | 23:4 | 103, 141, 197, 242 |
| 16:4-5 | 217 | | | | |
| 16:6 | 131 | 19:21-22 | 180 | 23:5 | 144 |
| 16:7 | 164 | 19:23 | 180 | 23:6 | 197 |
| 16:7-8 | 164 | 19:23-24 | 180 | 23:6-7 | 197 |
| 16:8 | 131, 133, 164, 194 | 19:25 | 165, 221, 223, 240 | 23:7 | 184 |
| | | | | 23:10 | 108, 186 |
| 16:9 | 131, 163 | 19:26 | 143 | 23:11-12 | 184 |
| 16:10-11 | 134, 163 | 20 | 10, 156, 211 | 23:15-16 | 131, 165 |
| 16:12 | 175, 203 | 20:1 | 194 | 24:1-12 | 156 |
| 16:15-16 | 131 | 20:3 | 195 | 24:4-5 | 200 |
| 16:16 | 132 | 20:5 | 211 | 24:9 | 156 |
| 16:17 | 132, 163, 186 | 20:10 | 211 | 24:12 | 170 |
| | | 20:11-13 | 159 | 24:13-17 | 170, 174 |
| 16:18-22 | 221 | 20:14 | 160, 211 | 24:13-25 | 9, 157, 214 |
| 16:20 | 131 | 20:14-15 | 211 | 24:18-20 | 170 |
| 16:22 | 173 | 20:16-23 | 211 | 24:25 | 218 |
| 17 | 220 | 20:18 | 160 | 25:1 | 9, 194 |
| 17:1 | 132, 134 | 20:20-21 | 211 | 25:2-6 | 9, 10, 201, 212 |
| 17:2 | 217 | 20:22-25 | 211 | | |
| 17:2-3 | 222 | 20:24-28 | 211 | 25:4-6 | 200 |
| 17:3 | 222 | 20:26 | 211 | 26:1-4 | 9 |
| 17:5 | 195 | 20:28 | 211 | 26:5-14 | 9, 214 |
| 17:7 | 131, 133 | 21 | 9 | 27:1-7 | 9 |
| 17:8-9 | 220 | 21-28 | 9 | 27:2 | 132, 134, 164 |
| 17:12 | 132, 134, 174 | 21:1-30 | 163 | 27:3 | 173 |
| 17:15 | 173 | 21:1-34 | 9 | 27:3-4 | 187 |
| 17:15-16 | 132 | 21:2 | 195 | 27:6 | 186 |
| 18:3 | 218 | 21:4 | 140 | 27:8-12 | 9-10, 213 |
| 18:11-20 | 214 | 21:6 | 131, 133 | 27:10 | 10, 213 |
| 18:16 | 214 | 21:7 | 169 | 27:11 | 230 |
| 18:18 | 214 | 21:17 | 165 | 27:13-23 | 9 |
| 19 | 156, 181 | 21:26 | 173 | 28 | 10, 96 |
| 19:1 | 194 | 21:27 | 103 | 28:4 | 103 |
| 19:2 | 217 | 21:28-30 | 220 | 28:28 | 96 |
| 19:3 | 217 | 21:30-33 | 169 | 29 | 185 |

346    *Index of Citations*

| Job (cont.) | | | | | |
|---|---|---|---|---|---|
| 29:1 | 194 | 31:30 | 138 | 34:1 | 239, 244 |
| 29:11 | 194 | 31:32 | 189 | 34:2-10 | 243 |
| 29:12-16 | 97 | 31:34 | 189 | 34:5-6 | 233 |
| 29:14 | 183, 185 | 31:35 | 144, 166, | 34:7 | 104, 235 |
| 29:16-17 | 97 | | 180-82, 190, | 34:7-9 | 235 |
| 29:17 | 164 | | 230, 234, | 34:13 | 239 |
| 29:21-25 | 99 | | 242, 245 | 34:14-15 | 239 |
| 30:1-14 | 132, 134, 163 | 31:35-37 | 9, 190 | 34:20 | 239 |
| 30:12 | 103 | 31:36 | 190 | 34:21-30 | 240 |
| 30:15 | 131-32, | 31:37 | 190, 197-98 | 34:29-30 | 244 |
| | 134, 245 | 31:38-40 | 9, 189-90 | 34:30 | 235 |
| 30:16 | 132 | 31:40 | 188, 190, | 34:31 | 6, 236 |
| 30:17 | 131, 134, | | 197, 225 | 34:31-32 | 236 |
| | 174 | 32:3 | 226 | 34:34-35 | 244 |
| 30:18 | 131 | 32:5 | 195, 226 | 34:35 | 195, 241 |
| 30:19 | 162, 173 | 32:6 | 194 | 34:36-37 | 236 |
| 30:20 | 143, 164 | 32:6-16 | 226 | 35:1 | 194 |
| 30:21 | 164 | 32:6-7 | 234 | 35:2-8 | 237 |
| 30:22 | 132, 134 | 32:10 | 195, 229-30 | 35:13-14 | 227 |
| 30:23 | 173 | 32:12 | 195, 228 | 35:14 | 144 |
| 30:24-25 | 185 | 32:14 | 230 | 36:2 | 145, 227, |
| 30:28 | 132, 134 | 32:17 | 230 | | 229, 234, |
| 30:31 | 131 | 32:17-20 | 229 | | 239, 240 |
| 31 | 7, 112, 181, | 32:20 | 195, 230 | 36:2-3 | 234 |
| | 188, 198 | 32:22 | 230 | 36:17 | 233 |
| 31:2-4 | 188 | 33:1 | 143-44, 149, | 36:17-21 | 235 |
| 31:4 | 134 | | 153-54, 195, | 36:18 | 104, 235 |
| 31:5-6 | 188 | | 226-27, 229, | 36:21 | 227, 239 |
| 31:5-40 | 189 | | 230, 233-34, | 36:22 | 239 |
| 31:6 | 183, 188 | | 238-39, 258 | 36:26-30 | 239 |
| 31:7 | 189 | 33:2 | 230 | 36:33 | 165, 195 |
| 31:7-8 | 188 | 33:3-4 | 231 | 37:2 | 195 |
| 31:9 | 189 | 33:6-7 | 232 | 37:6-13 | 239 |
| 31:9-10 | 188 | 33:8-11 | 226 | 37:14 | 123, 195, |
| 31:9-11 | 112 | 33:9 | 227, 234, | | 229-30, 241 |
| 31:11 | 112, 189 | | 238, 241 | 37:16 | 6 |
| 31:13-15 | 189 | 33:9-11 | 234 | 37:18 | 6, 241 |
| 31:14 | 135-36, | 33:10 | 226 | 37:19-20 | 241 |
| | 237 | 33:11 | 227 | 37:23 | 205, 239 |
| 31:15 | 162, 189 | 33:12 | 195, 234, | 38-39 | 251 |
| 31:19-21 | 189 | | 238-39 | 38-41 | 96, 248 |
| 31:23 | 164, 189 | 33:13 | 233 | 38:3 | 197 |
| 31:24-27 | 189 | 33:14 | 195, 238, 258 | 38:4 | 206, 250, |
| 31:26-27 | 112 | 33:23-30 | 241 | | 252-53 |
| 31:26-28 | 113 | 33:31 | 153, 231, 243 | 38:4-11 | 252 |
| 31:27 | 189 | 33:31-33 | 231 | 38:10 | 253 |
| 31:28 | 112 | 33:32 | 229, 232 | 38:12-14 | 256 |
| | | 33:33 | 230, 243 | 38:12-15 | 252 |

Index of Citations    347

| | | | | | |
|---|---|---|---|---|---|
| 38:16-23 | 250, 256 | 5:19-20 | 186 | **Lamentations** | |
| 38:17 | 255 | 5:23 | 186 | 2:10-11 | 131 |
| 38:24-30 | 253 | 6:24-25 | 110 | 3:12 | 131 |
| 38:24-34 | 250 | 9:10 | 96 | 3:31-32 | 204 |
| 38:27 | 254 | 10:4 | 203 | 3:33 | 205 |
| 38:31-32 | 253, 256 | 11:15 | 222 | 3:33-36 | 205 |
| 38:33 | 250, 253 | 12:16 | 201 | 3:34 | 152 |
| 38:37-41 | 256 | 12:17 | 158, 194 | 3:34-36 | 152 |
| 38:39-41 | 254 | 14:31 | 149, 185 | | |
| 39:1-3 | 250 | 15:3 | 178, 204 | **Ecclesiastes** | |
| 39:1-4 | 255 | 15:12 | 204 | 4:1 | 149 |
| 39:5-8 | 255-56 | 15:23 | 201 | 5:5 | 186 |
| 39:13-18 | 251 | 15:27 | 153-54 | 5:7 | 149 |
| 39:19-25 | 254 | 15:33 | 96 | 10:5 | 186 |
| 39:26-30 | 250 | 16:6 | 96 | | |
| 40:2 | 145, 248, 255-56, 261 | 17:3 | 107-8 | **Esther** | |
| | | 19:5 | 158, 216-17 | 2:21-23 | 107 |
| | | 19:27 | 186 | 2:22 | 159 |
| 40:3-5 | 96, 257 | 19:28 | 153, 218 | 2:23 | 135 |
| 40:4-5 | 197 | 20:1 | 186 | | |
| 40:5 | 6, 198 | 20:16 | 222 | **Daniel** | |
| 40:6 | 194, 247 | 21:3 | 149 | 2:5 | 105 |
| 40:7 | 197, 249, 252, 259 | 21:5 | 149 | 3:17-18 | 99 |
| | | 21:12-13 | 162, 201 | 3:29 | 99, 104-5 |
| | | 21:28 | 142, 158, 194 | 7:9-10 | 100, 102 |
| 40:7-14 | 252 | | | | |
| 40:8 | 145 | | | | |
| 40:10-14 | 252, 256 | 22:8 | 200 | **Ezra** | |
| 40:27-28 | 256 | 22:12 | 178 | 4:6 | 98, 163 |
| 40:27-41:26 | 256 | 22:22 | 149, 201 | 6:11 | 105 |
| 41:21 | 103 | 22:22-23 | 151, 152 | 7:11-26 | 36 |
| 41:22 | 103 | 23:28 | 130 | 10:8 | 105 |
| 42:1 | 194 | 24:3 | 253 | | |
| 42:1-6 | 96 | 24:12 | 108 | **Nehemiah** | |
| 42:3 | 6, 259 | 24:23-24 | 153 | 5:1-13 | 4 |
| 42:3-4 | 259 | 24:24 | 260 | 5:8 | 141 |
| 42:6 | 128, 196 | 25:18 | 158, 194 | 9:18 | 131 |
| 42:7-17 | 4, 96 | 26:27 | 162 | 9:26 | 104 |
| 42:8 | 104, 259-60 | 27:13 | 222 | | |
| 42:9 | 260 | 27:21 | 107 | **1 Chronicles** | |
| 42:11 | 6, 260 | 28:3 | 149 | 10:13 | 108 |
| | | 28:10 | 186 | 10:14 | 108 |
| **Proverbs** | | 28:13 | 133 | 16:11 | 203 |
| 1:7 | 96 | 28:17 | 105 | 21:30 | 108 |
| 1:19 | 153 | 29:24 | 116, 159, 204 | 28:9 | 108, 110, 203, 205 |
| 1:30-31 | 261 | 31:23 | 97 | | |
| 2:5-8 | 96 | | | | |
| 3:7 | 96 | **Ruth** | | **2 Chronicles** | |
| 3:7-8 | 24 | 4:1 | 97 | 6:37 | 209 |

# 348  Index of Citations

| 2 Chronicles (cont.) | |
|---|---|
| 11:13 | 103, 211 |
| 15:2 | 203 |
| 16:9 | 101 |
| 16:12 | 203 |
| 18:4 | 203, 213 |
| 18:6 | 108 |
| 18:7 | 108 |
| 19:8-9 | 97 |
| 25:4 | 208 |
| 26:5 | 203 |
| 32:16 | 98 |
| 32:17 | 104 |
| 32:17-23 | 105 |
| 32:31 | 107-8 |
| 34:26 | 108 |

*Apocrypha*

**Ben Sira**

| 46:19 | 151 |
|---|---|

**2 Maccabees**

| 7:1-42 | 99 |
|---|---|

*Hebrew and Aramaic Inscriptions*

**Qumran**

| 4QtgJob | 6 |
|---|---|
| 11QtgJob | 6, 11 |

**Kraeling**

| 1 | 71 |
|---|---|

**Lindenberger**

| 14 | 40 |
|---|---|
| 31 | 40 |
| 32 | 40 |
| 40 | 40 |
| 47 | 40 |

**Proverbs of Ahiqar**

| | 10, 11 |
|---|---|

**Samaria**

| 2 | 4 |
|---|---|

**TAD**

| B2.8 | 71 |
|---|---|
| B7.1 | 75, 81 |
| B7.2 | 75 |
| B7.3 | 81 |
| B7.4 | 81 |

*Egyptian Texts*

**Admonitions of Ipuwer**

| | 2 |
|---|---|

**Dispute between a Man and His Ba**

| | 2 |
|---|---|

**Harem Conspiracy Trial**

| | 107 |
|---|---|

**Protest of an Eloquent Peasant**

| | 2, 10, 23 |
|---|---|

*Cuneiform Texts*

**A Dialogue of Pessimism**

| | 2 |
|---|---|

**A Man and His God**

| | 22, 133 |
|---|---|

**AASOR**

| 16, 73 | 70 |
|---|---|

**ABL**

| 307 | 73 |
|---|---|
| 314 | 73 |
| 326 | 72 |
| 500 | 146 |
| 928 | 58 |
| 965 | 83 |

**ADD**

| 101 | 84 |
|---|---|
| 780 | 102 |

**Advice to a Prince** 147

**AfO**

| 17, 2 | 40, 57-58, 62, 77, 89-90 |
|---|---|
| 44, 76 no. 5 | 70, 74-75, 88 |
| 44, 78 no. 6 | 19, 39, 60, 70, 74-75, 88 |
| 44, 81 no. 9 | 19 |
| 44, 83 no. 13 | 60, 72, 79, 87, 92 |
| 44, 88 no. 19 | 19, 39 |

**Alalakh**

| 7 | 70 |
|---|---|
| 17 | 77 |

**AnOr**

| 8, 21 | 43, 45, 56, 69 |
|---|---|
| 8, 27 | 55, 60-61, 76-77 |
| 8, 38 | 60, 62, 67, 77, 87 |
| 8, 39 | 55, 61, 86-87 |
| 8, 45 | 64, 91 |
| 8, 46 | 64, 91 |
| 8, 50 | 91 |
| 8, 56 | 19, 39, 44, 55, 75, 88 |
| 8, 61 | 57 |
| 8, 74 | 43, 60, 63-64, 89 |
| 8, 79 | 43 |

**Appu and His Two Sons (Hittite)** 2

**Babylonian Theodicy**

| | 2, 104 |
|---|---|

**BaghM**

| 5, 1 | 90 |
|---|---|
| 5, 15 | 44, 71, 90 |

**BE**

| 8/1, 42 | 43, 89 |
|---|---|

*Index of Citations* 349

| | | | | | |
|---|---|---|---|---|---|
| 9, 24 | 72, 79, 86-87, 89-90 | 2, 43 | 70 | DINGIR.ŠÀ.DIB.BA | |
| | | 6, 34b | 67 | Incantations | 16, 20, 21, 109, 183, 264 |
| 9, 69 | 62, 67, 69, 92 | 22, 105 | 19, 40, 56, 72 | | |
| 10, 9 | 66, 79, 92-93, 196, 261 | 22, 160 | 58, 60, 148 | | |
| | | 22, 174 | 76 | **Durand Textes** | |
| | | 22, 202 | 68 | **babyloniens** | |
| **BIN** | | 22, 210 | 44, 88 | 6 | 60-61, 77, 81 |
| 1, 28 | 68 | 22, 228 | 44 | | |
| 1, 49 | 40 | 22, 229 | 44, 75 | | |
| 1, 106 | 49 | 22, 230 | 76-77 | **EE** | |
| 1, 113 | 56, 60, 62, 66, 77-78, 89 | 22, 231 | 58, 72 | 91 | 89 |
| | | 22, 234 | 44, 56, 60, 72 | 109 | 44, 62, 66, 79, 92-93 |
| 1, 141 | 93 | 22, 235 | 44 | | |
| 1, 142 | 43, 78 | 22, 247 | 58 | **Fs. Walker** | |
| 1, 169 | 89 | 46, 45 | 40, 56, 59, 83, 148 | 356 | 62, 66, 77-78, 89 |
| 2, 108 | 57 | | 58 | | |
| 2, 132 | 83 | 54, 170 | | | |
| | | 54, 212 | 147 | | |
| **BM** | | 54, 463 | 58, 146 | **GCCI** | |
| 40717 | 71 | 54, 510 | 58 | 1, 15 | 49 |
| 77425 | 81 | 55, 110 | 76 | 1, 380 | 86-87 |
| 78156 | 71 | | | 2, 65 | 56 |
| | | **CTMMA** | | 2, 103 | 89 |
| **BMS** | | 3, 83 | 76 | 2, 350 | 43, 45 |
| 1 | 16 | | | | |
| 2 | 19 | **Cyr** | | **Gezer** | |
| 4 | 19 | 281 | 60, 62, 76 | 3 | 4 |
| 6 | 14, 19 | 307 | 74, 89 | 4 | 4 |
| 12 | 19 | 311 | 45, 78 | | |
| 19 | 14 | 312 | 37, 45, 60, 62, 74, 78, 89 | **HSS** | |
| 30 | 19 | | | 19, 89 | 222 |
| | | 332 | 34, 60, 62, 70, 87, 89-90 | **IMT** | |
| **Camb** | | | | 105 | 44, 62, 66, 79, 92-93 |
| 85 | 37, 56, 62 | | | | |
| 321 | 43, 62, 90 | | | | |
| 329 | 56, 62, 68 | | | | |
| 412 | 60 | **Dalley Edinburgh** | | | |
| | | 69 | 18, 39, 43, 56, 62, 66, 70, 74, 78, 87-88, 90 | **Instructions to the Border Guard Commander (Hittite)** | |
| **CM** | | | | | |
| 20, 166 | 81 | | | | 147 |
| **CT** | | | | | |
| 2, 2 | 43, 61-62, 66-67, 70, 75-77, 87-88, 180 | **Dar** | | **Jas** | |
| | | 53 | 67-68, 82, 88 | 11 | 102 |
| | | | | 31 | 73 |
| | | 128 | 57, 72 | 53 | 84 |

## JCS
| | |
|---|---|
| 9, 26 | 44, 87 |
| 28, 45 no. 39 | 45, 87 |
| 28, 198-99 | 92 |

## KAR
| | |
|---|---|
| 184 | 19, 182 |

## Kirta
| | |
|---|---|
| | 2 |

## LE
| | |
|---|---|
| §§36-37 | 87 |

## LH
| | |
|---|---|
| §5 | 231 |
| §34 | 147 |
| §109 | 73 |
| §163 | 146 |

## LKA
| | |
|---|---|
| 139 | 21 |

## *Ludlul bēl nēmeqi*
| | |
|---|---|
| | 2, 22-23 |

## MAL
| | |
|---|---|
| A §2 | 104 |

## NBDM
| | |
|---|---|
| 28 | 90 |
| 49 | 68, 92 |

## Nbk
| | |
|---|---|
| 52 | 77, 86 |
| 104 | 60, 62, 86-87 |
| 183 | 56, 60, 77, 87 |
| 359 | 92 |
| 361 | 86 |
| 363 | 86 |
| 365 | 93 |
| 366 | 86 |
| 419 | 89-90 |

## NBL
| | |
|---|---|
| §1 | 81 |
| §7 | 89-90 |

## Nbn
| | |
|---|---|
| 13 | 60, 70, 74-75, 77, 87-90 |
| 52 | 203 |
| 314 | 72, 87, 92 |
| 343 | 43, 74 |
| 495 | 74 |
| 626 | 92 |
| 665 | 92 |
| 668 | 70, 92-93 |
| 679 | 92 |
| 720 | 39, 44, 60, 66, 75, 79, 107 |
| 1113 | 70, 79, 87-88 |
| 1128 | 55, 56, 60, 66, 70, 75, 87-89 |

## Ner
| | |
|---|---|
| 23 | 87 |

## OIP (Nippur 4)
| | |
|---|---|
| 114, 5 | 40 |
| 114, 19 | 40 |
| 114, 20 | 58, 72, 76 |
| 114, 21 | 40 |
| 114, 38 | 83 |
| 114, 65 | 68 |
| 114, 109 | 40, 68 |
| 114, 110 | 44, 83 |
| 114, 128 | 147 |

## PBS
| | |
|---|---|
| 1/1, 2 | 15 |
| 2/1, 140 | 61-62, 68-69, 82, 92 |

## Prayer to Anūna
| | |
|---|---|
| | 15, 109, 113 |

## Prayers of the Lifting of the Hand
| | |
|---|---|
| | 16 |

## RA
| | |
|---|---|
| 12, 6-7 | 18-19, 39, 43, 60, 66, 70, 74-75, 77-78 |
| 14, 158 no. 152 | 74, 86-87, 116 |
| 24, 112 | 73 |
| 67, 148-49 | 66, 74-75, 77-78, 85, 87 |

## RawlCu
| | |
|---|---|
| 4 | 15 |
| 5, 5 | 57 |

## ROM
| | |
|---|---|
| 2, 36 | 75 |
| 2, 38 | 44, 71, 90 |

## RS
| | |
|---|---|
| 25.460 ("The Just Sufferer" from Ugarit) | 2, 22 |

## SAA
| | |
|---|---|
| 15, 73 | 73 |

## SAAB
| | |
|---|---|
| 1, 66-68 | 105 |

## Sack
| | |
|---|---|
| 78 | 43 |
| 79 | 74, 89-90 |
| 80 | 61 |

## Spar
| | |
|---|---|
| 1 | 82 |
| 2 | 62, 66 |
| 3 | 60-62, 75 |

## Stolper
| | |
|---|---|
| 399-400 | 62, 79, 92-93 |

## Šurpu Incantations
| | |
|---|---|
| | 16-18, 20, 22, 24, 109, 116, 134, 179, 182-83, 187, 199, 208 |

Index of Citations  351

| TCL | | | | | |
|---|---|---|---|---|---|
| 12, 24 | 71, 90 | 4, 191 | 40 | 6, 208 | 62, 66, 68, 78 |
| 12, 26 | 43, 92 | 4, 201 | 56, 62 | | 77 |
| 12, 50 | 86-87 | **VAS** | | 6, 214 | 68, 75-76 |
| 12, 60 | 86 | 1, 36 | 72 | 6, 223 | 56, 60, 62, |
| 12, 70 | 82, 86 | 4, 66 | 57 | 6, 224 | 64, 67, 78, |
| 12, 77 | 71, 78, 86-87 | 4, 87 | 56, 60 | | 82, 85, 91 |
| | | 4, 192 | 57 | 6, 225 | 66, 70, 74, |
| 12, 86 | 43, 66, 88-89 | 4, 252 | 57 | | 77-78, 82 |
| | | 6, 38 | 43, 79 | 6, 230 | 78 |
| 12, 96 | 44, 87 | 6, 82 | 43, 56, 62, | 6, 231 | 62, 78-79, |
| 12, 106 | 86-87 | | 67, 73 | | 82, 84-85, |
| 12, 115 | 43, 90, 92 | | 45, 56, 60 | | 87 |
| 12, 117 | 56, 62, 107 | 6, 99 | 74 | 6, 235 | 45, 67, |
| 12, 119 | 87 | 6, 127 | 56 | | 78-79, 107 |
| 12, 120 | 74 | 6, 128 | 43 | 7, 10 | 62 |
| 12, 122 | 60, 70, 74, 79, 87, 89-90 | 16, 181 | | 7, 15 | 61, 77-78 |
| | | **YNER** | | 7, 24 | 86 |
| | | 1, 2 | 55, 82, 84, 86-87 | 7, 25 | 49, 89 |
| 13, 124 | 43 | | | 7, 26 | 86 |
| 13, 125 | 67 | | | 7, 28 | 88 |
| 13, 132 | 77 | **YOS** | | 7, 31 | 19, 56, 64, 91 |
| 13, 134 | 43, 67 | 3, 35 | 19, 56 | | |
| 13, 137 | 89 | 3, 145 | 57 | 7, 42 | 62, 67, 72, 75-79, 88 |
| 13, 147 | 43 | 3, 182 | 40 | | |
| 13, 151 | 76-77 | 6, 57 | 43, 56, 62 | 7, 50 | 89 |
| 13, 154 | 76-77 | 6, 60 | 43, 60 | 7, 56 | 43, 63-64 |
| 13, 170 | 62, 67-68, 74-76, 79, 82, 115 | 6, 71 | 61 | 7, 66 | 60, 89 |
| | | 6, 72 | 61 | 7, 69 | 89 |
| | | 6, 77 | 62, 76 | 7, 77 | 76 |
| 13, 179 | 68-69, 82 | 6, 79 | 43 | 7, 78 | 77 |
| 13, 181 | 55, 62, 66, 68, 71, 79, 82, 116 | 6, 80 | 43 | 7, 88 | 85 |
| | | 6, 108 | 89 | 7, 91 | 34, 87 |
| | | 6, 116 | 87 | 7, 96 | 44, 57, 66, 68, 71, 75, 79 |
| 13, 212 | 43 | 6, 119 | 44, 87 | | |
| 13, 215 | 76 | 6, 122 | 86 | | |
| 13, 219 | 39, 44, 60, 66, 75, 79, 89, 90, 107 | 6, 131 | 49 | 7, 97 | 62, 66, 69, 74, 85, 107 |
| | | 6, 134 | 87 | | |
| | | 6, 137 | 76-77, 87 | 7, 102 | 43, 62 |
| 13, 222 | 19, 39, 45, 56 | 6, 144 | 44, 68-69, 75-76, 78 | 7, 115 | 64, 91 |
| | | | | 7, 137 | 37, 72, 76, 85, 89, 105 |
| | | 6, 152 | 49, 71 | | |
| | | 6, 153 | 44, 86-87 | 7, 144 | 76-77 |
| **UCP** | | 6, 156 | 70, 82 | 7, 146 | 60, 62 |
| 9/1, 2 37 | 86 | 6, 165 | 49, 78 | 7, 152 | 57, 67, 78, 82, 85-86 |
| | | 6, 169 | 82 | | |
| **UrET** | | 6, 175 | 71, 87 | 7, 159 | 56, 60 |
| 4, 171 | 81 | 6, 191 | 45, 78 | 7, 177 | 45 |
| 4, 186 | 19, 56, 81 | | | | |

## Index of Citations

| YOS (cont.) | | | | ZA | |
|---|---|---|---|---|---|
| 7, 187 | 89 | 12, 325 | 67 | 3, 224 no. 2 | 89 |
| 7, 189 | 45, 63, 66, 77-78 | 17, 32 | 86-87 | 43, 92 | 73 |
| | | 17, 320 | 43, 55 | | |
| | | 19, 97 | 86-87 | | |
| 7, 192 | 60 | 19, 98 | 74, 86-87, 115 | | |
| 7, 196 | 62 | | | | |
| 7, 198 | 56, 60, 62 | | | | |

# Index of Authors

Abusch, I. Tzvi, 14, 20-22, 102
Ackerman, J., 100, 102-3, 117
Ackroyd, P. R., 1
Ahlström, G. W., 36-37
Albertson, R. G., 2, 13, 234, 246
Allam, S., 81
Alonso Schöckel, L., 6
Andersen, B. R., 14, 17, 103
Andersen, F. I., 6, 98, 103, 106, 119
Anderson, B. W., 151
Anderson, G. W., 143
Ap-Thomas, D. R., 163
Avalos, H., 14, 21, 23-24
Aytoun, R. A., 188

Bakon, S., 6-7
Barstad, H. M., 33
Bartelt, A. H., 257
Beach, E. F., 6, 131, 171, 260-61
Beaulieu, P.-A., 40, 89
Beck, A. B., 257
Becking, B., 36
Bentzen, A., 10
Bergren, R. V., 150, 167
Berlin, A., 11, 50
Berquist, J. L., 33
Beuken, W. A. M., 173
Birch, B., 154
Blank, S. H., 79, 98, 163, 209
Blenkinsopp, J., 35-37, 101
Bloch, M., 29-30
Bloom, J., 61
Bobbio, N., 94
Bock, D. L., 104

Boecker, H. J., 29, 45, 61, 69, 93, 97, 143, 150, 181
Boer, P. A. H. de, 259
Bongenaar, A. C. V. M., 39, 58, 60
Boorer, S., 171
Bordreuil, P., 4
Borger, R., 14, 16
Bottéro, J., 17, 40, 67
Bovati, P., 4, 8, 24, 99, 108, 131, 135, 137-41, 143, 145-46, 151-52, 154, 158-59, 162, 164-66, 178, 186, 193, 202-3, 206, 209, 236
Brenner, A., 99, 251
Brooks, P., 47-48
Brown, F., 29
Bryce, G. E., 147
Budde, K. F. R., 223
Burns, J. B., 8
Buttenwieser, M., 98

Cagni, L., 104
Cardascia, G., 29, 72, 106
Carradice, I., 35
Cathcart, K. J., 24
Chapman, S., 50
Cheney, M., 98
Chin, C., 3, 6-7, 137
Chisholm, R. B., 119
Civil, M., 147
Claassen, W., 3
Clements, R. E., 132
Clines, D. J. A., 5, 10, 36, 96, 103, 106, 130, 143-44, 160, 164, 166, 169, 184, 191-92, 200, 202, 216, 218, 222-23

Cohen, H. R., 30, 102
Cole, S., 58, 147
Collins, T. J., 14
Conklin, B., 69, 106
Cook, J. M., 34
Cotter, D. W., 11
Cover, R., 48, 94, 99
Cowley, A. E., 11
Cox, D., 7, 51, 245
Crenshaw, J. L., 6, 11, 132, 188
Crook, M. D., 142, 201
Cross, F. M., 100, 115
Cryer, F. H., 147
Cunningham, G., 14, 16
Cuq, E., 38
Curtis, J. B., 259

Daiches, S., 37
Dalley, S., 18, 39, 43, 55, 56, 62, 66, 70, 74, 78, 87-88, 90
Dandamaev, M. A., 34-35, 37, 40-41, 43, 56, 60-63, 67-68, 76-77, 85, 93, 101, 130, 147
Daniels, D. R., 151
Davies, P. R., 36
Day, P. L., 7, 10, 72, 97, 101-2, 115
Derrida, J., 94
Dhorme, E., 5, 98, 227, 238
Diakonoff, I. M., 37, 147
Dick, M., 2, 7-8, 15, 21, 23-24, 113, 137, 143, 165, 181, 188, 197
Dietrich, M., 57
Dillmann, A., 10
Dion, P.-E., 11
Dobbs-Allsopp, 4, 69, 106, 143, 150
Dombradi, E., 38-39, 61, 67, 70, 80-81, 90
Doty, L. T., 32
Dougherty, R. P., 61, 63, 67, 76-77, 85, 89
Driver, G. R., 80
Driver, S. R., 2, 5, 192
Droge, A. J., 99
Dubow, F. L., 29
Duquoc, C., 97
Durand, J.-M., 44, 60-61, 77, 81
Dworkin, R. M., 49

Ebeling, E., 21, 58, 81, 83
Eliade, M., 260

Eph'al, I., 4
Epsztein, L., 154
Eskenazi, T. C., 36
Etzioni, A., 29
Evans, C. D., 30, 100
Evans, L., 61

Fales, F. M., 18
Falk, Z. W., 163, 209
Falkenstein, A., 19, 38
Fensham, F. C., 2, 154
Ferguson, R. A., 48
Figulla, H. H., 62, 81, 87
Finkel, I. L., 14
Finkelstein, J. J., 31, 35, 58, 138, 148
Fishbane, M., 5, 108, 134, 171
Fisher, L. R., 200, 207, 222
Fiss, O., 49
Flanagan, J. W., 150
Fohrer, G., 5, 188
Follis, E., 1
Foristan, C., 97
Forsyth, N., 97
Fortner, J. D., 32
Foster, B. F., 40, 148, 154
Fox, M. V., 4, 11
Franke, C. A., 257
Freedman, D. N., 236
Freedman, L. R., 222-23
Frei, P., 34
Fried, L. S., 35-37
Frye, J. B., 7, 137, 195-96
Frymer-Kensky, T. S., 40, 73, 80
Fuller, R. T., 32
Fullerton, K., 259

Gammie, J. G., 97, 173
Garelli, P., 58
Gaster, T. H., 103
Geller, M. J., 14, 16-17, 23-24, 109, 116
Gemser, B., 1, 6-7, 14, 18-19, 23-24, 134-35, 137, 141, 144, 150, 163, 180-81, 196, 209
Gevirtz, S., 107
Gewirtz, P., 47-49, 218, 231
Gilpin, W. C., 5, 8, 174
Ginsberg, H. L., 142

Good, E. M., 7-8, 10, 106, 112-13, 115, 119, 166, 192, 218, 225, 228, 248, 253, 258
Gordis, R., 2, 10-11, 98, 143, 151, 192, 216, 218, 222, 230, 238, 240, 252, 257
Gordon, C. H., 1, 6, 137
Grabbe, L. L., 36
Graham, J. N., 33
Gray, G. B., 2, 5, 192
Gray, J., 2
Greenberg, M., 4, 105, 201
Greengus, S., 40, 52, 72
Greenspahn, F. E., 30
Greenstein, E. L., 4, 6-7, 137, 143, 217, 248, 251, 258, 259
Gurney, O. R., 32
Güterbock, H. G., 58, 147
Gutiérrez, G., 6

Haag, H., 101
Habel, N. C., 2, 4, 7-8, 10, 97-99, 112-13, 119-20, 137-38, 142-44, 164, 166, 170-71, 174-75, 180, 184, 188, 192, 200, 216-18, 220, 229-30, 233, 252-53, 255, 257-58
Hallo, W. W., 2, 4, 30, 100, 138
Halpern, B, 72, 180
Hamilton, V. P., 97
Hanson, P. D., 30
Haran, M., 4
Harper, R. F., 9, 151
Harrelson, W., 151
Harris, R., 235
Hartley, J. E., 9, 10, 104, 135, 200, 207
Hartmann, B., 144
Harvey, J., 150
Hasel, G. F., 23
Havice, H., 154
Hayden, R. E., 38
Hecht, N. S., 97
Hermisson, H.-J., 173, 175
Hillers, D. R., 135, 145, 150
Hoffner, H. A., 11
Holladay, W. L., 7-8, 106, 136-37, 139, 160
Horowitz, W., 4
Huehnergard, J., 72

Huffmon, H. B., 150
Hunger, H., 44, 90
Hurowitz, V. A., 10, 147-48
Hurvitz, A., 6, 102, 236

Irani, K., 56, 148
Iser, W., 51
Ishida, T., 14
Israel, F., 4

Jackson, B. S., 31, 48, 202, 258
Jacobsen, T., 58, 73, 147
Janzen, D., 36
Janzen, J. G., 10
Jas, R. M., 38-39, 58, 72-73, 80, 84, 90, 93, 102
Jastrow, M., 192
Joannès, F., 5, 38, 45, 55, 68, 76, 79, 82-84, 89
Jones, B. W., 30
Jung, C. G., 259
Jursa, M., 76

Kataja, L., 72, 83
Kearns, T. R., 93-94
Keel, O., 176
Keller, S. R., 97
Kinet, D., 97
Kinnier Wilson, J. V., 14
Kissane, E. J., 5-6, 169
Kluger, R. S., 101
Knight, D. A., 5
Knoppers, G. N., 36
Knox, J., 6, 10, 154
Koch, K., 34, 37
Kohler, J., 61, 68, 93
Köhler, L. H., 1, 97
Korpel, M. C. A., 36
Koschaker, P., 34
Kraeling, E. G., 71, 81
Kraus, F. R., 17, 67
Kruse, H., 97
Kübben, A. J. F., 30
Kuhrt, A., 5
Kümmel, H. M., 60

Labat, R., 14, 17

## Index of Authors

Labuschagne, C. J., 251
Lafont, S., 39, 55-57, 59, 61, 72-73, 80, 82
Lambert, W. G., 13-16, 18, 20, 22, 40, 104, 109, 133
Landsberger, B., 58, 72, 147
Langdon, S., 15
Laserson, M., 6-7
Lasine, S., 7, 51, 245
Lautner, J. G., 8, 38, 61, 93
Lawson, J. N., 14, 18
Laytner, A., 163, 209
Leichty, E., 71
Lesko, B., 5
Lévêque, J., 117
Levinson, B. M., 18, 29, 31, 61, 73, 219
Lewis, T. J., 153
Lieberman, A. I., 80
Limburg, J., 150
Linafelt, T., 98
Lindenberger, J. M., 40
Lipiński, E., 43
Lipschits, O., 37
Locher, C., 70
Lods, A., 101-2
Loewenstamm, S., 80
Lohfink, N., 70
Losier, M. A., 86
Lotman, J. M., 50
Lukonin, V. G., 34-35, 41, 101
Lyons, J., 69

Mabee, C., 138, 158
Machinist, P., 22, 33
Mafico, T., 151, 154, 159-60, 167
Magdalene, F. R., 3, 13, 89, 132, 165, 260
Malamat, A., 61, 93
Malchow, B. V., 154
Malinine, M., 81
Malul, M., 29, 30, 222
Many, G., 4, 6-7, 137
Matthews, V. H., 56, 73, 97
Mattingly, G. L., 30
Maul, S. M., 22
McCarter, P. K., 4, 72
McDowell, A. G., 32
McEwan, G. J. P., 75
McKay, H., 5

McKenzie, D. A., 97, 150
Mendenhall, G. E., 150
Mettinger, T. N. D., 5, 174-75, 252, 255-56
Miles, J., 3
Milgrom, J., 98, 133, 162, 236
Millard, A. R., 83
Miller, G. P., 46
Miller, P. D., Jr., 100
Moore, E. W., 74, 79
Moore, R. D., 99
Moran, W. L., 73
Morrison, M. A., 70
Mowinckel, S., 223
Moyer, J. C., 2
Mullen, E. T., 100, 103, 118-19
Müller, H.-P., 2
Murphy, R. E., 6, 52

Naveh, J., 4
Nel, P. J., 97
Newell, B. L., 254, 256-57
Newsom, C., 2, 10, 130-31, 135, 184, 225
Niehr, H., 36
Nielsen, K., 150
Nightingale, E., 132
Nissen, H.-J., 57
Nissinen, Martti, 22
North, R., 36-37
Noth, M., 1, 11

Oelsner, J., 27, 39, 45, 56-57, 66, 76, 81-82, 88, 89
Ojeda, J. L., 6
Olmstead, A. T., 35
Oppenheim, A. L., 72-73, 101
Oshima, T., 4
Otto, E., 57, 84, 93
Owen, D. I., 56, 70

Papke, D. R., 48
Pardee, D., 4
Pardes, I., 99
Parpola, S., 58, 146
Patrick, D., 6-7, 11-12, 137
Paul, S. M., 31, 99, 102, 104, 202
Peake, A. S., 11, 106

Peiser, F. E., 68
Penchansky, D., 132
Perdue, L. G., 2, 5, 8, 173-75
Petschow, H., 89
Pfeiffer, R. H., 9-10, 230
Phillips, A., 37, 42, 147
Pinches, T. G., 89
Pinker, A., 97
Pohl, A., 14
Polley, M. E., 100, 118
Pope, M. H., 1, 10, 103, 169, 192, 200, 202, 207, 221-23, 227, 238
Porten, B., 69, 71
Postgate, J. N., 58, 80
Powell, M. A., 34, 44

Raabe, P. R., 257
Rad, G. von., 11
Radner, K., 39
Raphael, R., 161, 256
Redford, S., 107
Reid, S. B., 171
Reiner, E., 16-18, 22, 71, 147
Renger, J., 42, 57, 60, 89
Richards, K. H., 36, 202, 260
Richter, H., 2, 7, 137
Ries, G., 69, 80, 89
Ries, J., 260
Ritner, R. K., 22
Roberts, J. J. M., 1, 5
Robertson, D., 1, 7-8, 137, 259
Robinson, A. W., 150
Robinson, H. W., 100
Rochberg-Halton, F., 22, 71
Roche, Michael de., 151
Rollston, C. A., 4
Roth, M. T., 10, 31, 35, 37, 45, 55, 57, 73, 75, 77, 87
Rowley, H. H., 1, 5-6, 9, 11, 96, 169, 192

Sack, R. H., 44
Sanders, S., 4
San Nicolò, M., 34, 38, 42-44, 61-62, 73, 76, 89, 91
Sarat, A., 93-94
Sarna, N. M., 10
Sasson, J. M., 42, 58

Scafa, P. N., 56
Scarry, E., 130, 132
Scharbert, J., 260
Scherer, P., 103
Scholnick, S. H., 1-2, 4, 6-8, 136-37, 143, 249, 258
Schorr, M., 32, 61, 93
Schwartz, B. J., 236
Scurlock, J., 14, 17
Seeligmann, I. L., 144
Seidl, E., 81
Seitz, C. R., 100
Seow, C. L., 22
Sheldon, L. J., 2-3, 23, 24
Shinan, A., 29
Silver, M., 56, 148
Smick, E. M., 96
Snaith, N. H., 5, 10
Snyder, J. W., 44
Soden, W. von., 19, 72, 81
Souček, V., 61
Spar, I., 34, 44, 60, 68, 82
Speiser, E. A., 138, 163
Stamm, J. J., 1-2, 7, 137
Steiner, R. C., 14, 34, 36, 38
Steinmann, A. E., 257
Stevenson, W. B., 10
Stewart, D. T., 188-89
Stier, F., 7, 137, 155
Stol, M., 14, 17, 20-21, 133-34
Stolper, M. W., 35, 62, 79, 81, 92-93
Stover, E., 132
Sukenik, E. L., 151
Sutherland, R., 6-7
Szubin, H. Z., 71

Tabor, J. D., 99
Tadmor, H., 4
Talmon, S., 30
Terrien, S., 103, 131, 171, 173
Thomas, D. W., 1, 5-6, 11
Thompson, R. C., 14
Thrupp, S. C., 30
Thureau-Dangin, F., 102
Tillie, M. M., 99
Toorn, K. van der., 14, 20, 22-23
Tov, E., 6, 11

Tsevat, M., 262
Tucker, G. M., 171
Tuplin, C., 35, 101
Tur-Sinai (Torczyner), N. H., 101, 143

Ungnad, A., 61, 93

Vabroušek, P., 61
Vanderhooft, D. S., 5, 33, 41
Vawter, B., 248, 257, 259
Veenker, R. A., 38-39, 61, 80, 93
Villiers, P. G. R. de, 97
Vorländer, H., 23

Waldow, H. E. von., 150, 154
Walser, G., 34
Walther, A., 32, 61, 93
Watson, W. G. E., 24
Watts, J. W., 35-36
Weidner, E., 16, 40, 58, 77, 105
Weinfeld, M., 2, 57, 102, 148-49, 151, 154
Weisberg, D. B., 34, 89
Weiser, A., 216
Weiss, M., 96-98, 101, 112, 127, 128
Wellhausen, J., 10
Wells, B., 17, 24, 27, 29, 31, 44, 59, 81, 84-86, 89, 91, 116, 142, 158, 168, 194-95, 219, 236, 258
West, R. L., 49
Westbrook, R., 4, 10, 17-18, 27, 31-32, 39-40, 42, 46, 56-57, 67-68, 70, 76, 81, 83-84, 87, 90, 97, 105-6, 111-12, 116-17, 124, 133, 138-39, 141, 146-54, 156, 165, 167, 181, 189, 202, 219, 245, 249, 260
Westermann, C., 2, 108, 135, 150
Wharton, J. A., 6-7, 98-99, 130-32, 137, 158
White, J. B., 30, 100, 150
Whybray, R. N., 5-6, 99, 170-71, 201-2
Wiesehöfer, J., 35
Wilcox, J. T., 8
Wilhelm, G., 56
Wilkinson, J., 23-24
Williams, J. G., 251
Williamson, H. G. M., 35
Willis, J. T., 188
Willis, T. M., 61, 93
Wilson, E. B., 150
Wolde, E. van., 99, 130
Wright, D. P., 236
Wright, G. E., 151
Wunsch, C., 27, 39, 42, 81, 92-93

Yaron, R., 81

Zadok, R., 37
Zakovitch, Y., 102
Zuck, R. B., 1, 251, 254
Zuckerman, B., 7, 137, 202

# Index of Subjects

Abimelech, 191
Abraham, 98, 168, 169, 191
abuse of authority, 9, 58, 138, 145-58,
    162, 164-65, 168, 176, 182, 184,
    198, 205, 211, 237, 243, 264
accusations, 9, 43, 47, 57, 66-79, 85-87,
    95, 101, 106, 112-14, 117-23, 126,
    129, 131, 137-46, 156-59, 162, 190-
    91, 194, 215, 219, 221, 227, 232-33,
    245, 262, 265
Achan, 132
*actus reus*, 106, 109-15
adjudication, 48-49, 53, 58-62, 64-65,
    141, 166, 228, 265
adultery, 70, 113
adversarial legal system, 48, 65-66, 75,
    93, 103, 231, 249
affliction, 4, 23, 227, 235, 238
Ahab
    murder of Naboth, 105, 119, 133,
        158, 164
Ahijah, 98
Ahimelech: trial of, 121, 141, 232
aiding and abetting, 74, 85, 116, 121,
    157, 204
ambiguity, 11, 103
angel, 193-94, 197, 200, 201, 241
anger
    divine, 15, 16, 18, 19, 20-21, 23, 110,
        129, 134, 161, 164-65, 175, 213,
        240, 252, 256, 259
    Job's, 128, 207, 220, 226, 237
    kings's, 123
    *See also* rage, wrath

anguish, 104, 131, 140
Anūna, 15-16, 109, 113
apostasy, 104, 105, 108, 110, 219, 236
appeal, 6, 7, 8, 23, 43, 45, 49, 57 64-66,
    91-92, 123, 129, 182, 193, 209
arbiter, 93, 166, 228, 230, 242, 248
    Elihu as, 230
    of the text, 51
arbitration, 8
archaeology, 42, 56
Artaxerxes, 36
assembly, 37, 49, 56-57, 60-63, 65-66, 68,
    71, 75, 77, 82, 88, 91-93, 100, 138,
    148, 158, 160, 170, 189, 207, 219,
    225, 244, 247
    of the wise, 242-43, 245, 262, 265
Assur, 59, 104, 105
Assurbanipal, 59, 104

Babylon, 1, 5, 19, 33, 35, 37, 39, 41, 56,
    58, 60, 65, 85, 88-89, 91, 98, 147,
    263
*bēl dabābi*, 72, 102, 180
*bēl dini*, 72, 102
Benjamin, 124, 128, 209
Benjaminites, 193
bet, 118. *See also* dare, wager
Bîl, 19
Bildad, 9-10, 157, 191, 194, 199, 201,
    208-10, 212-18, 223, 226, 231-32,
    260
bill: of particulars, 155, 179-80, 190-91,
    198. *See also* writ

blasphemy, 9, 17, 58, 98, 100, 104-7, 111-18, 122-25, 132-33, 139, 153, 155, 158, 175, 187, 190, 203, 208, 213, 219, 228, 234-38, 242-47, 259, 262-65. *See also* curse

calamity, 22, 168, 169, 186, 187, 214, 263. *See also* disaster
Caleb, 98
Cambyses, 89
Civil Law legal systems, 31, 45, 65. *See also* Continental legal systems, inquisitorial systems
civil lawsuits, 8, 39, 42, 57
collateral action/attack, 6-7, 8, 137
collateral matters, 45, 74
colonial powers, 28, 33-38
Common Law legal systems, 31, 32, 45, 48, 75, 111, 116. *See also* adversarial legal systems
contempt
    divine, 171, 176, 260
    human, 109-10
    *See also* despise, hate
Continental legal systems, 31, 45, 65. *See also* Civil legal systems
contract(s), 32, 34, 42, 44-45, 71, 84, 139, 148
countersuit, 9, 69-71, 99, 127, 129, 137-46, 157-58, 167, 176, 179, 182, 190-92, 195, 225-29, 233-36, 240, 247, 259, 262, 264. *See also* Job's countersuit
courage, 179, 198
courts, 12, 19, 34, 42-43, 55-56, 59-61, 64-65, 81, 84, 86-88, 91-95, 97, 132, 152, 219, 222, 265
    divine, 11, 13, 15, 20, 22-23, 25, 27, 108-9, 123, 129-30, 132, 134, 136, 177, 189-90, 263
    royal, 61, 65. *See also* judges, royal
    secular, 42, 56, 65, 84, 91
    system of, 27, 41, 55-57, 65
    temple, 42, 56, 61, 63-65, 83, 86, 88, 91
courthouse, 19, 56. *See also* house of decision, house of judges, house of judgment

covenant
    divine, 23
    Job's, 188
    Leviathan's, 256
    not-to-sue, 92
    of settlement, 138, 158, 191
crime, criminal, 9, 16-22, 25, 34, 42-45, 51, 61, 67, 69, 72-79, 85-88, 95, 101-26, 132-33, 136, 143, 153, 186, 188-90, 203-4, 208-9, 215, 228, 236, 238, 244
cross-examine, 48, 217, 249, 257
culpability, 78, 80, 82, 84, 115, 204
    level of, 89, 111-12, 124, 133, 238, 237, 238, 245
curse, 7-8, 17, 67, 98, 99, 104, 106, 111-12, 116, 118, 119, 120, 122, 132, 190, 201, 214, 232. *See also* blasphemy
Cyrus, 34, 57, 89

Damkina, 19
dare, 118, 152, 230. *See also* bet, wager
Darius, 34-36
David, 98, 121, 122, 203
defendants
    testimony of, 66-67, 78, 85, 118
    *See also* God, as defendant; Job's defense
demand (legal), 40, 66, 68, 75, 94, 191-92
demon(s), 13, 15, 16, 20, 129, 202
depositions, 88, 92. *See also* testimony
despising, human, 104, 109, 132. *See also* contempt, hate
Deuteronomic Code, 190, 219
disability, 2, 23-24, 117, 136, 148, 227
disaster, 2, 15, 23, 25, 117, 120, 136, 169, 185, 227. *See also* calamity
disease, 2, 15, 19, 21, 23, 24, 105, 117, 124, 136, 227. *See also* illness, sickness
divination, 17, 21-22, 147
Divine Council, 9, 27, 96, 99-103, 110-22, 125-29, 132, 157, 163, 167, 175, 183, 194, 201, 232, 242-48, 261, 264
divine justice, 13, 17, 105, 118, 184-85, 201, 262, 265. *See also* social justice

## Index of Subjects    361

Eanna temple, 38, 41, 45, 56, 60, 68, 76
Ebabbar temple, 41, 58, 60
elders, 37, 60-61, 152, 171, 219, 226, 245
Eli, 105, 116
Eliakim, 98
Elihu, 7, 9-10, 96, 143-45, 191, 194-96, 199, 223, 225-48, 258, 262, 265
Elijah, 98, 158
Eliphaz, 9-10, 98, 142-44, 156, 165, 186, 191, 194-209, 212-18, 223, 226, 228, 230-32, 239, 242, 259, 265
Eli's sons, 105, 116
entrapment, 107, 113-17
Esarhaddon, 83, 147
evidence
   circumstantial, 66, 87
   documentary, 62, 65-66, 75, 87
   physical, 87
examine (as in investigate), 135, 160, 218, 227, 228. *See also* cross-examine, test, investigation(s)
execution documents, 90
execution of judgment, verdict, or court order 40, 43, 66, 71, 77, 88-90, 93, 97, 106, 123
execution of pledge, 79
expiation, 16, 18, 98, 105-6, 111-12, 133, 149, 203, 208, 212. *See also* sacrifice
extispicy, 20
Eye of the King, 101-2, 125
Ezra, 36-37

false accusation, 9, 70, 74, 90, 122 128, 133, 138, 145-47, 157-58, 162, 167, 175, 218, 234, 248, 259, 262, 264
fate, 14, 117, 201-02, 203, 206, 207 211, 215
fool, foolishness, 156, 162, 201-5, 242, 257, 265
fragmentary nature of text, 48, 81, 95-96, 122, 196

gate
   judicial role of, 1, 56, 68, 97, 152, 245
ghost, 21

God
   as accuser, 155, 177, 179, 181, 198, 206, 238, 241. *See also* accusations
   as defendant, 129, 145, 199, 206, 212, 222-28, 233-34, 241, 245, 248-52, 256, 264-65
   settling case with Job, 261-62, 265. *See also* settlement

habeas corpus, 6-7, 8, 137. *See also* writ
hate
   divine, 163
   human, 109-10, 116, 154, 204, 260
   Job's 132, 243
   *See also* contempt, despise
hedge, 9, 100, 104, 115, 116, 172
Hezekiah, 98, 99
Holiness Code, 190
homicide, 106. *See also* murder
house
   of decision, 19
   of judges, 19, 56
   of judgment, 19, 56
   *See also* courthouse

Íkur, 19
illness, 14, 15, 16, 17, 18, 19, 20, 21, 22, 23-24, 128. *See also* disease, sickness
impleader, 68, 71-72, 157
incantations, 14, 16, 22, 24, 109, 125, 133-34, 171, 179, 182, 187, 208, 210, 263-64. *See also* ritual incantation texts
incest, 105
Inninna, 16, 109
inquisitorial
   legal system, 48, 65-66, 75, 78, 93, 130-31, 231, 246, 247, 249
   torture, 130-31
   trials, 65-66
intent (legal), 21-22, 106-18, 122, 124-25, 133, 139, 159, 183, 186-87, 189, 190, 194, 199-201, 210, 238. *See also mens rea*
intention
   Elihu's, 230-31, 234
   God's, 134, 161, 205

362  *Index of Subjects*

investigation(s), 25, 28, 43-47, 51-52, 61-62, 67-68, 73-79, 82, 85, 88, 95, 102, 108-11, 115-38, 159-60, 169, 178, 180-82, 187, 191, 198-99, 203, 206, 227, 232, 235, 237-38, 240, 263-64. *See also* examine, test
Isaiah, 98

Jacob
    as God's servant, 98
    Laban's accusation against, 128, 138, 145-46, 158, 193-94, 196, 236
Jeremiah, 5, 7, 24, 33, 106, 110, 121-24, 137, 139, 156, 159, 160, 163, 169, 171, 209, 243-44
Jezebel: false suit against Naboth, 158, 164
Job
    as elder, 1
    as judge, 1, 7
    as potential martyr, 98, 143, 192
Job, book of
    dating, 5, 160
    epilogue, 10, 225
    prologue, 10, 96, 129, 225, 230, 232
    rearrangement of third cycle, 9
    textual unity, 9-11, 246
Job's children, 119, 208-9, 260-61, 265
Job's concession at trial, 9, 195, 197, 258-59, 261-62, 265
Job's countersuit, 155, 164-65, 167, 177, 187, 201, 205-6, 212, 227-28, 233, 235, 238, 241-42, 265. *See also* countersuit
Job's defense, 8, 137, 164, 177, 181-85, 190, 198, 226, 236, 264
Job's demand, 197-98, 208, 264
Job's friends, 7, 24, 127-31, 156, 180-87, 191, 195-96, 199, 212, 215-32, 238, 242, 245, 259-61, 264-65. *See also* Bildad; Eliphaz; Zophar
Job's oath, 113, 180, 188-90, 196, 226, 257-58, 264. *See also* oaths
Job's wife, 98-99, 183, 192
Jonah, 98, 119
Joseph
    accusation against brothers, 107-8, 113, 123, 128, 203, 209

Joshua, 132
Judah (person), 209
Judah (place), 33-38, 41, 99, 124, 138 193, 194, 244
judges, 15, 19, 23, 37-40, 55-57, 66-71, 74, 85, 89, 93, 103, 110, 136, 147-48, 153, 165, 167, 171, 231, 240-43, 248
    parties as, 65, 146-47, 165
    royal, 58-64, 77, 88, 91-92, 141, 244
judicial authority, 57, 61, 127, 159, 242
jurisdiction, 59-65, 125, 162, 242
    *in personam*, 59, 63-65, 260
    *in rem*, 59, 63-65
    subject matter, 59, 74

king, 35, 37, 56-60, 72-73, 77, 89, 91, 99, 102, 105, 120-23, 143, 147-50, 155, 165, 170, 254

Laban, 138, 145-46, 158, 193-94, 196, 236
Lady of Uruk, 91
law
    divine, 23-27, 36-37, 105, 113, 160, 167, 184, 194, 199, 226, 228, 233, 264
    Israelite, 29, 219, 245
    of Moses, 36
    Neo-Babylonian, 9, 37-38, 78, 81, 115, 119, 145, 157, 165, 219
    *See also* trial procedure, Neo-Babylonian
law and literature, 28, 52, 263
law codes, 34-35
Laws of Eshnunna, 87
Laws of Hammurabi, 10, 57, 61, 93, 146-47, 231
Laws of Lipit-Ishtar, 10, 57
Laws of Ur-Nammu, 10, 57
lawsuit, 4, 6, 40, 47, 70-71, 77, 88, 92, 135-39, 141, 146-47, 151-53, 163, 166, 185, 193, 197, 201-9, 233, 235, 241
    divine, 27, 226. *See also* God, as accuser
legal practice: documents of, 4, 27, 49, 53, 148, 264

Index of Subjects 363

Marduk, 14, 147
Masoretic Text, 151, 166, 170, 192, 202
*mens rea*, 9, 106-16, 125, 128, 133, 187, 190, 242, 245, 247, 262, 264. *See also* intent
Meṣad Ḥashavyahu (Yavneh Yam) ostracon, 4, 149, 151
messenger, 119
metaphor, 13, 93, 162, 176, 222
    legal metaphor, 1-3, 6, 8, 12-13, 16, 18, 24-28, 46, 50, 53, 263
method, methodology, 12-13, 27-53
    comparative-historical, 2-4, 28-29, 31-32, 38-39, 45, 52, 219, 264
Middle Assyrian Laws, 104
Miriam, 121
misappropriation, 105, 249
Moses, 36, 98, 121, 124
Murašu family, 93, 261
murder, 20, 69, 158, 219. *See also* homicide

Nabonidus, 34, 45, 57, 61
Nabopolassar, 56, 57
Naboth, 105, 153, 158, 219
*namburi* rituals, 22
narrative(s), 2, 10, 11, 28, 46-52 95-96, 104, 122, 263
    legal, 46-51, 95. *See also* trial procedure, narratives of
Nebuchadnezzar, 40, 58, 148, 154
negotiations: related to settlement of trial, 9, 191-92, 194, 196-99, 209, 223, 232, 248, 257, 264
Neo-Assyrian, 4, 33, 38-39, 58, 71-74, 80-81, 83-84, 90, 93, 102, 146-47, 219
Neo-Babylonian Laws, 81, 89-90
Neo-Babylonian trial records, 4-5, 8-11, 25-29, 32, 40, 44, 51-52, 55, 58, 60, 78, 83, 89-90, 94, 123, 125, 180, 191, 209, 232-33, 263-64

oaths, 47, 62, 68-69, 78-84, 188, 226
    assertory, 79
    court-ordered, 79-82, 84, 86, 90, 188, 219

    promissory, 79, 84
    sacred, 105
    weakened form of, 80-82, 106, 188
    *See also* Job's oath
oracle, 21, 208, 212
ordeal, 40, 44, 79, 82, 83

particulars, 137, 155, 179-80, 190-91, 198. *See also* bill, writ
Persia(n), 5-6, 28, 34-37, 41-42, 56, 58, 101, 246
point of view, 11, 50, 127, 128
Potiphar's wife, 123
priest(s), 60, 97, 136, 171, 183
priestly source, 5
prison, 40, 76, 85, 105, 130, 174
profane actions, 105
prohibition of suits, 90
prophecy, false, 105
prosecution, prosecutor, 8-9, 72-75, 86, 101-2, 125, 164, 210, 221, 225, 232, 238, 244-48, 265
prostitute, 65
punishment
    capital, 89, 105, 147, 149, 158, 241
    corporal, 89, 123
    monetary, 90, 147, 149, 260, 261
    for sin, 15

Qumran, 6

rage
    divine, 15, 165
    Job's, 214, 252
    wicked's, 170
    *See also* wrath
redeemer, 221, 223, 241
release
    from liability, 43, 90, 92
    from prison, 76
religion, 36, 98, 99, 102, 148
righteousness: of the legally innocent, 160, 163, 183, 188, 239, 252
ritual incantation texts, 13-25, 51, 104, 109, 123, 125, 129, 133-36, 146, 148, 177, 179, 182-83, 198, 209-10, 223, 227-28, 238, 263-64
royal edicts, 148

## Index of Subjects

sabbath, violation of, 105
sacred
   oath, 202
   property, 105
sacrifice, 97, 106, 111, 261. *See also* expiation
Šamaš, 14, 17, 19, 21, 60
Samuel, 13, 151, 153, 154
*sartennu*, 37, 56, 60, 63
Saul, 99, 120-21, 141, 201-02, 232
Satan, the, 6-8, 10, 27, 97-104, 106-7, 111-32, 135, 157, 162-63, 172, 184, 187-88, 199, 206, 232-33, 238, 242, 245-48, 261-65
second accusers, 9, 66, 73-74, 84-87, 120, 219, 221-25, 231-33, 240-41, 245, 247, 258, 264-65. *See also* accusations
self-rule, Judah's, 36-37
Septuagint, 6, 151, 166
settlement, 9, 62, 68, 71, 79, 93-95, 99, 138, 173, 177, 191-99, 223, 232, 248, 256-61, 264-65
   mid-trial, 77, 88, 209, 262
   negotiations, 9, 191-98, 199, 209, 232, 233, 248, 257, 264
   post-trial, 71, 92, 209, 265
   pre-trial, 76-77, 93, 193, 197
sexual offenses, 105, 112-13
Sheol, 157, 161-62, 173, 214
sickness, 15, 18, 19, 22, 186. *See also* disease, illness
sin, sinful, 14-25, 58, 89, 96, 109-10, 112, 124-25, 129, 135, 137, 161, 179-80, 186-87, 190, 200, 203, 206, 209-10, 219, 235-37, 244, 265
   unintentional, 22, 109, 185-86, 260
Sippar, 41, 58, 60, 70, 88
Simeon, 123
slaves, 63-64, 73, 76-77, 85, 88-93, 130, 172, 256
social justice, 57, 97, 103, 117, 149, 151-57, 167-68, 175-76, 185, 207, 213-17, 223, 240, 248, 252, 255-56, 262, 264
Solomon, 203
Songs of Isaiah, 98

sons of God, 99, 102-4, 117, 122
sorcery, 15, 20, 21, 105
Suffering Servant, 98
*sukkallu*, 60
summary judgment, 17, 22, 123, 129, 142, 177, 182, 193, 227, 240
summons, 43, 66-67, 77-78, 91, 121, 123, 141, 160, 164, 166, 171, 177, 179, 232
suprarational evidence, 33, 79, 83-84, 86, 94. *See also* oaths; oracle; ordeal
surety, 76, 78, 88, 222-23
swear/swearing, 68, 80-82
   Elihu's, 230
   false, 105
   Job's, 112, 187-90, 197-98
Syria-Palestine, 4

taboos, 15, 105
temple officials, 56-63, 68, 77, 85, 91, 171. *See also* courts, temple
test
   divine, 6, 7, 8, 23, 107-8, 118, 125, 160, 167, 189, 227, 237
   legal human investigation as, 243
   river ordeal as, 44, 49
   the Satan's, 113-15
   scenarios by reader, 50
   *See also* examine, investigation(s)
testimony, 9, 22, 44, 47, 60, 63, 66-67, 71, 74-88, 91, 95, 98, 110, 120-23, 142, 164, 174, 183, 187, 192-96, 199, 206, 208, 212, 217-20, 229-32, 235, 239, 241-44, 247-48, 264-65. *See also* witnesses
textual disruptions, 9, 50-51
theft, 43, 45, 67-69, 71, 74, 76-77, 115-16, 150, 189
theodicy, 13, 22-25, 51
theology, 1-2, 6, 11, 20, 27, 51-53, 97, 118, 175, 184, 203, 236, 263
torture, 76, 98, 123, 130-32
treason, 58, 67, 77, 105, 121
trial procedure, 4, 27, 40, 52, 58, 65, 79, 95, 135, 160, 264
   Israelite, 4-5, 27, 29, 124

Index of Subjects    365

narratives of, 28, 46-51, 53, 263
Neo-Babylonian, 25, 55-94, 123, 125.
    See also Neo-Babylonian trial
    records
    See also courts

Uruk, 32, 41, 44-45, 56, 60-61, 63, 77, 89, 91

verdicts, 6, 8, 14-15, 20, 43-44, 49, 66-67, 77, 79-80, 84, 86-90, 93, 168, 177-81, 197, 228, 260
    conditional, 44, 57, 62, 73, 77-78, 84-88, 115, 123

wager, 6, 8, 100, 103, 105, 125. See also bet, dare
wisdom literature, 10-11, 22, 24-25, 122-23, 129, 133
Wise woman of Tekoa, 150
witchcraft, 13, 15, 16, 19, 20, 21, 129. See also sorcery
witnesses, 43, 47-48, 55-57, 61-62, 66, 75, 78, 80, 84-88, 91, 115, 135-36, 153, 164, 168, 194, 196, 212, 218-22, 230-31, 248-52

need for two witnesses, 61, 86, 135, 219
third-party, 66, 73, 78, 81, 85, 87-88, 199, 208, 218
woman, women, 63, 75, 85, 89, 104, 107, 110, 112, 113, 115, 136, 172, 189, 193, 200
worship, 33, 110, 163, 209
    error in, 105
    of false gods, 113
    Job's, 96
    of Molech, 116
wrath
    divine, 20, 22, 134, 202, 221, 244
    Job's, 235, 237
    See also anger, rage
writ
    of appeal, 45, 91
    of habeas corpus, 6-7, 8, 137
    of particulars, 137

Xerxes, 35

Zerubbabel, 98
Zophar, 9-10, 143, 156-57, 160, 191, 194-95, 199, 210-12, 215, 218, 223, 226, 231-32, 235, 238, 240

www.ingramcontent.com/pod-product-compliance
Lightning Source LLC
Chambersburg PA
CBHW030104010526
44116CB00005B/97